Downtown
N
DUPONT CIRCLE
DUPONT CIRCLE
Heurich Mansion (Historical Society of Washington, D.C.)
New Hampshire Ave.
21st St.
20th St.
19th St.
18th St.
17th St.
16th St.
15th St.
14th St.
13th St.
12th St.
11th St.
10th St.
9th St.
8th St.
7th St.
6th St.
5th St.
4th St.
3rd St.
2nd St.
1st St.
R St.
Q St.
P St.
O St.
N St.
M St.
L St.
K St.
I St.
H St.
G St.
F St.
E St.
D St.
C St.
Church St.
Corcoran St.
Jefferson Pl.
B'nai B'rith Museum
National Geographic Society (Explorers Hall)
DeSales St.
Connecticut Ave.
SCOTT CIRCLE
THOMAS CIRCLE
LOGAN CIRCLE
Vermont Ave.
Massachusetts Ave.
Rhode Island Ave.
SHAW
Warner St.
Franklin St.
Neal Pl.
Florida Ave.
Bates St.
Lincoln Rd.
Quincy Pl.
Eckington Pl.
NW
NE
MT. VERNON SQ-UDC
MT. VERNON SQUARE
Washington International Hostel (AYH/IH)
The Washington Post
FARRAGUT NORTH
FARRAGUT WEST
FARRAGUT SQUARE
McPHERSON SQUARE
McPHERSON SQ
FRANKLIN PARK
Ansel Adams Collection
Natl. Museum of Women in the Arts
Convention Center
CHINATOWN
New Jersey Ave.
Capital Children's Museum
Parker St.
Union Station
COLUMBUS CIRCLE
Delaware Ave.
Capitol Plaza
Louisiana Ave.
Senate Office Buildings
Maryland Ave.
Stanton Park
0 300 yards
0 300 meters
395
JUDICIARY SQ
Natl. Building Museum
Dept. of Labor
Federal Courthouse
D.C. Courthouse
John Marshall Park
ARCHIVES-NAVY MEMORIAL
National Archives
Indiana Ave.
Market Pl.
Shakespeare Theatre
Natl. Museum of American Art & Natl. Portrait Gallery
GALLERY PLACE
Martin Luther King Jr. Library
9:30 club
Ford's Theatre
Petersen House
FBI
Dept. of Justice
Internal Revenue Service
Pennsylvania Ave.
Penn. Ave. N.
METRO CENTER
Warner Theatre
Natl. Theatre
New York Ave. Presbyterian Church
Visitor Information Center
FEDERAL TRIANGLE
District Building
Dept. of Commerce & National Aquarium
Dept. of the Treasury
Treasury Pl.
Penn. Ave. S.
White House
The Ellipse
Ellipse Rd.
E. Executive Pl.
S. Executive Pl.
U.S. Chamber of Commerce
St. John's Church
LAFAYETTE SQUARE
Decatur House
Renwick Gallery
Blair House
Old Executive Office Building
State Pl.
Octagon
Corcoran Gallery
American Red Cross
D.A.R. Museum & Constitution Hall
Organization of American States
Dept. of the Interior
World Bank
General Services Administration
George Washington University
Virginia Ave.
Constitution Ave.

Central Washington, D.C.

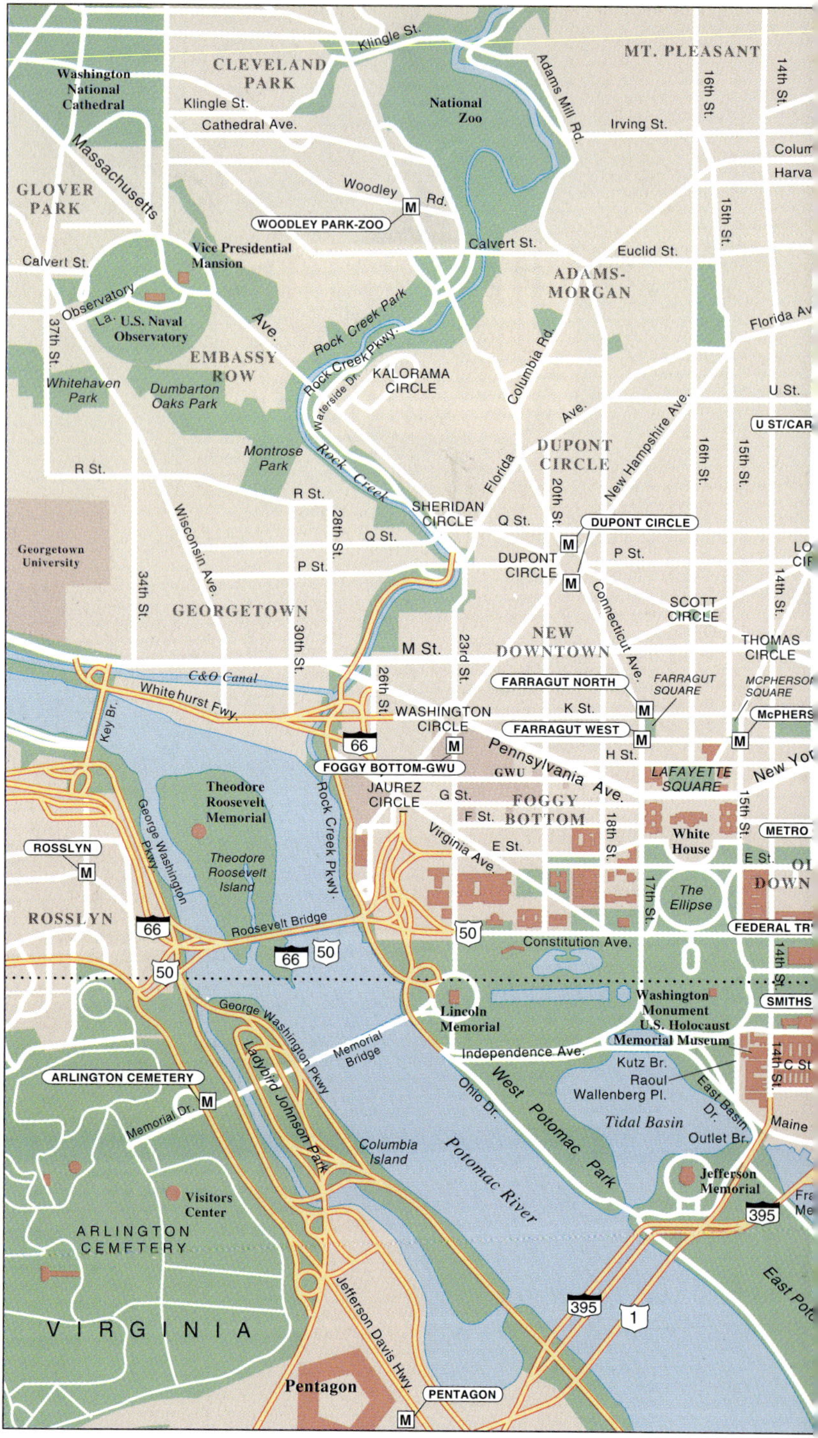

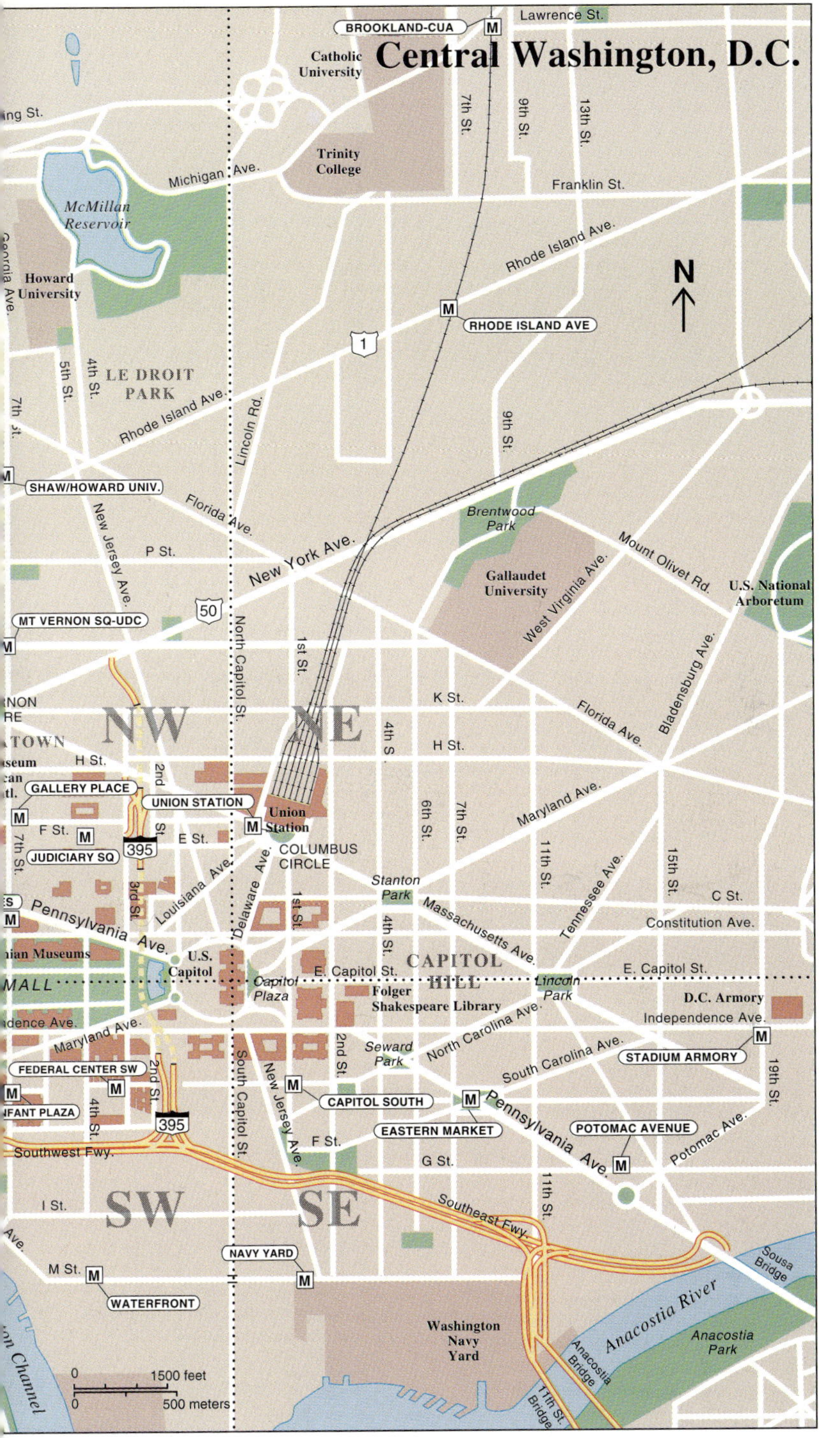
Central Washington, D.C.
N
BROOKLAND-CUA
Lawrence St.
Catholic University
7th St.
9th St.
13th St.
Trinity College
Michigan Ave.
Franklin St.
McMillan Reservoir
Howard University
Rhode Island Ave.
RHODE ISLAND AVE
1
LE DROIT PARK
5th St.
4th St.
Rhode Island Ave.
Lincoln Rd.
9th St.
SHAW/HOWARD UNIV.
Florida Ave.
Brentwood Park
Mount Olivet Rd.
New Jersey Ave.
P St.
New York Ave.
Gallaudet University
West Virginia Ave.
U.S. National Arboretum
MT VERNON SQ-UDC
50
North Capitol St.
1st St.
Bladensburg Ave.
K St.
Florida Ave.
NW
NE
4th St.
H St.
H St.
GALLERY PLACE
2nd St.
UNION STATION
Union Station
6th St.
7th St.
Maryland Ave.
F St.
E St.
395
JUDICIARY SQ
COLUMBUS CIRCLE
11th St.
15th St.
Tennessee Ave.
Stanton Park
C St.
Louisiana Ave.
Delaware Ave.
3rd St.
1st St.
Pennsylvania Ave.
4th St.
Massachusetts Ave.
Constitution Ave.
CAPITOL HILL
U.S. Capitol
E. Capitol St.
E. Capitol St.
MALL
Capitol Plaza
Lincoln Park
Folger Shakespeare Library
D.C. Armory
Independence Ave.
Maryland Ave.
North Carolina Ave.
2nd St.
Seward Park
South Carolina Ave.
STADIUM ARMORY
19th St.
FEDERAL CENTER SW
2nd St.
South Capitol St.
New Jersey Ave.
CAPITOL SOUTH
Pennsylvania Ave.
4th St.
395
EASTERN MARKET
POTOMAC AVENUE
Potomac Ave.
Southwest Fwy.
F St.
G St.
I St.
SW
SE
Southeast Fwy.
11th St.
NAVY YARD
M St.
WATERFRONT
Sousa Bridge
Anacostia River
Washington Navy Yard
Anacostia Bridge
Anacostia Park
11th St. Bridge
0
1500 feet
0
500 meters

The Mall Area, Washington, D.C.

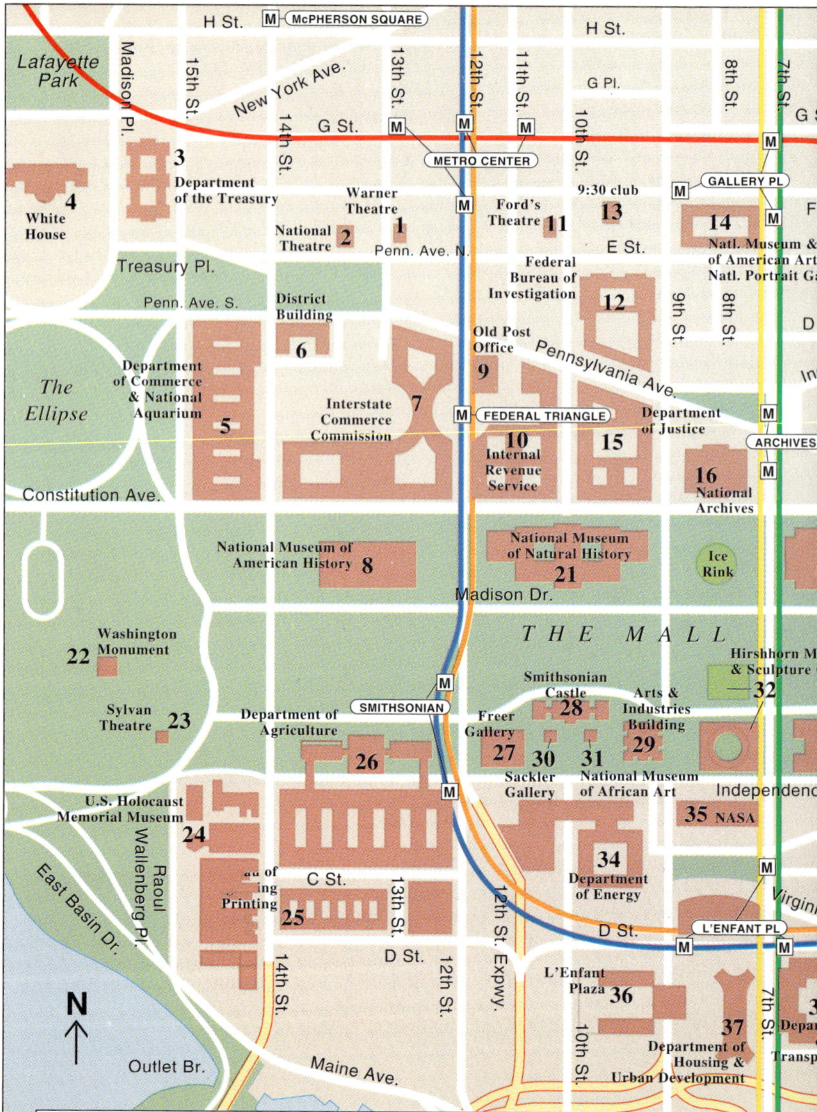

Mall Area

9:30 club, 13
Arts & Industries Building, 29
Bureau of Engraving & Printing, 25
Cannon House Office Building, 50
D.C. Courthouse, 17
Department of Agriculture, 26
Department of Commerce, 5
Department of Energy, 34
Department of Health & Human Services, 40
Department of Housing & Urban Development, 37
Department of Justice, 15
Department of Labor, 19
Department of Transportation, 38
Department of the Treasury, 3
Dirksen Senate Office Building, 46
District Building, 6
Federal Bureau of Investigation, 12
Federal Courthouse, 20
Folger Shakespeare Library, 48
Ford's Theatre, 11
Freer Gallery, 27
Hirshhorn Museum & Sculpture Garden, 32
Internal Revenue Service, 10
Interstate Commerce Commission, 7
L'Enfant Plaza, 36
Library of Congress, 49
Longwoth House Office Building, 51
National Aquarium, 5

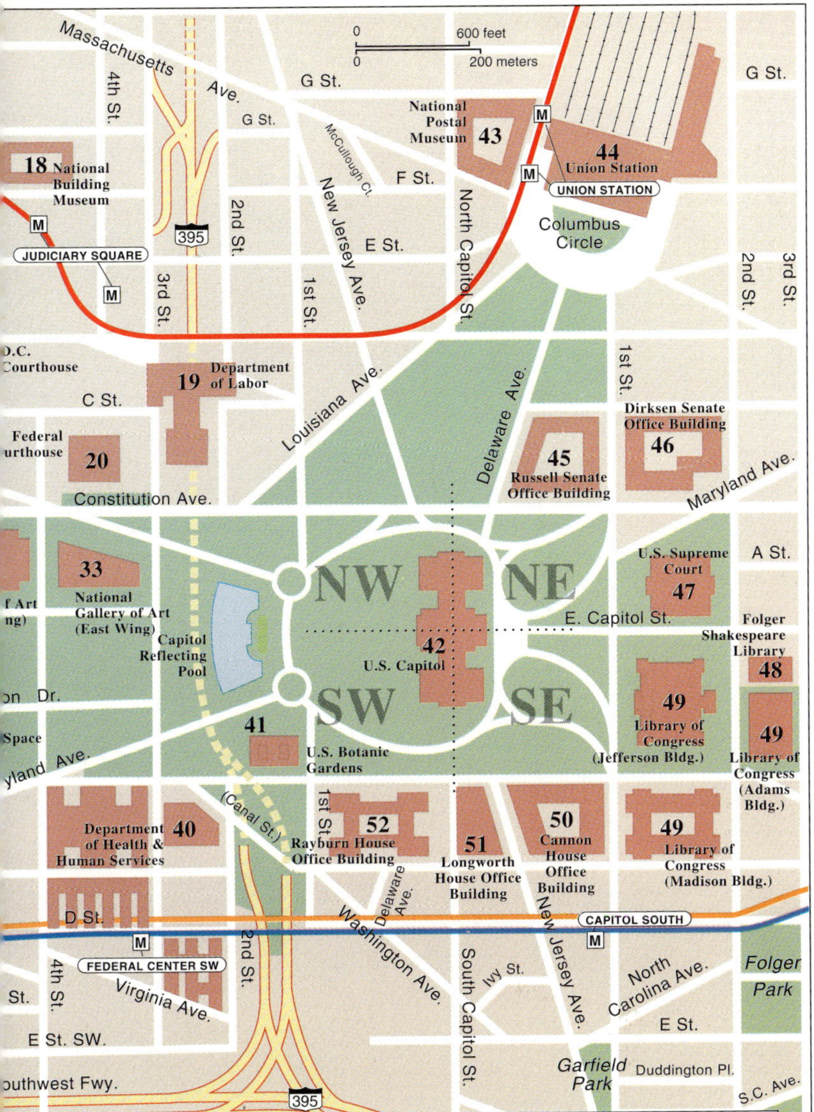

NASA, 35
National Air & Space Museum, 39
National Archives, 16
National Building Museum, 18
National Gallery of Art, 33
National Museum of African Art, 31
National Museum of American Art, 14
National Museum of American History, 8
National Museum of Natural History, 21
National Portrait Gallery, 14
National Postal Museum, 43
National Theatre, 2
Old Post Office, 9
Rayburn House Office Building, 52
Russell Senate Office Building, 45
Sackler Gallery, 30
Smithsonian Castle, 28
Sylvan Theatre, 23
Union Station, 44
U.S. Botanic Gardens, 41
U.S. Capitol, 42
U.S. Holocaust Memorial Museum, 24
U.S. Supreme Court, 47
Warner Theatre, 1
Washington Monument, 22
White House, 4

White House Area, Foggy Bottom, and Nearby Arlington

White House Area, Foggy Bottom, and Nearby Arlington
THOMAS CIRCLE
M St.
L St.
K St.
I St.
H St.
G Pl.
G St.
F St.
E St.
D St.
C St.
Jefferson Pl.
DeSales St.
Connecticut Ave.
20th St.
19th St.
18th St.
17th St.
16th St.
15th St.
14th St.
13th St.
12th St.
11th St.
10th St.
9th St.
8th St.
Vermont Ave.
Massachusetts Ave.
New York Ave.
Pennsylvania Ave.
Constitution Ave.
Independence Ave.
Madison Dr.
Market Pl.
Jackson Pl.
Madison Pl.
State Pl.
Treasury Pl.
Executive Ave.
Ellipse Rd.
S. Executive Pl.
National Geographic Society
The Washington Post
FARRAGUT NORTH
FARRAGUT WEST
FARRAGUT SQUARE
McPHERSON SQUARE
McPHERSON SQ
Franklin Park
MT. VERNON SQUARE
U.S. Chamber of Commerce
St. John's Church
National Museum of Women in the Arts
Convention Center
Decatur House
LAFAYETTE SQUARE
Renwick Gallery
Blair House
World Bank
U.S. Treasury
New York Ave. Presbyterian Church
Martin Luther King Jr. Library
METRO CENTER
Old Executive Office Building
White House
Visitor Information Center
Natl. Theatre
Warner Theatre
9:30 club
Ford's Theatre
General Services Administration
Octagon
Corcoran Gallery
District Building
Federal Bureau of Investigation
FEDERAL TRIANGLE
Old Post Office
Interior Department
D.A.R. Constitution Hall
THE ELLIPSE
Department of Commerce
Department of Justice
Organization of American States
Internal Revenue Service
National Archives
Constitution Gardens
Memorial to the Signers of the Declaration of Independence
Natl. Museum of American History
Natl. Museum of Natural History
THE MALL
Arts & Industries Building
Reflecting Pool
Washington Monument
Freer Gallery of Art
Smithsonian Castle
SMITHSONIAN
Sylvan Theatre
D.C. War Memorial
U.S. Holocaust Memorial Museum
Natl. Museum of African Art
Department of Agriculture
Department of Energy
Kutz Br.
Japanese Lantern
East Basin Dr.
Bureau of Engraving & Printing
12th St. Expwy.
L'Enfant Promenade
L'Enfant Plaza
Paddleboats
Tidal Basin
W. Basin Dr.
Cherry Trees
Outlet Br.
Maine Ave.
West Potomac Park
Ohio Dr.
Jefferson Memorial
Francis Case Memorial Br.
Maine Ave.
Water St.
395
Washington Channel
George Mason Bridge
Williams Memorial Bridge
Natl. Park Service Visitors Welcome Center & Park Police Headquarters
East Potomac Park
1

Metrorail System, Washington, D.C.

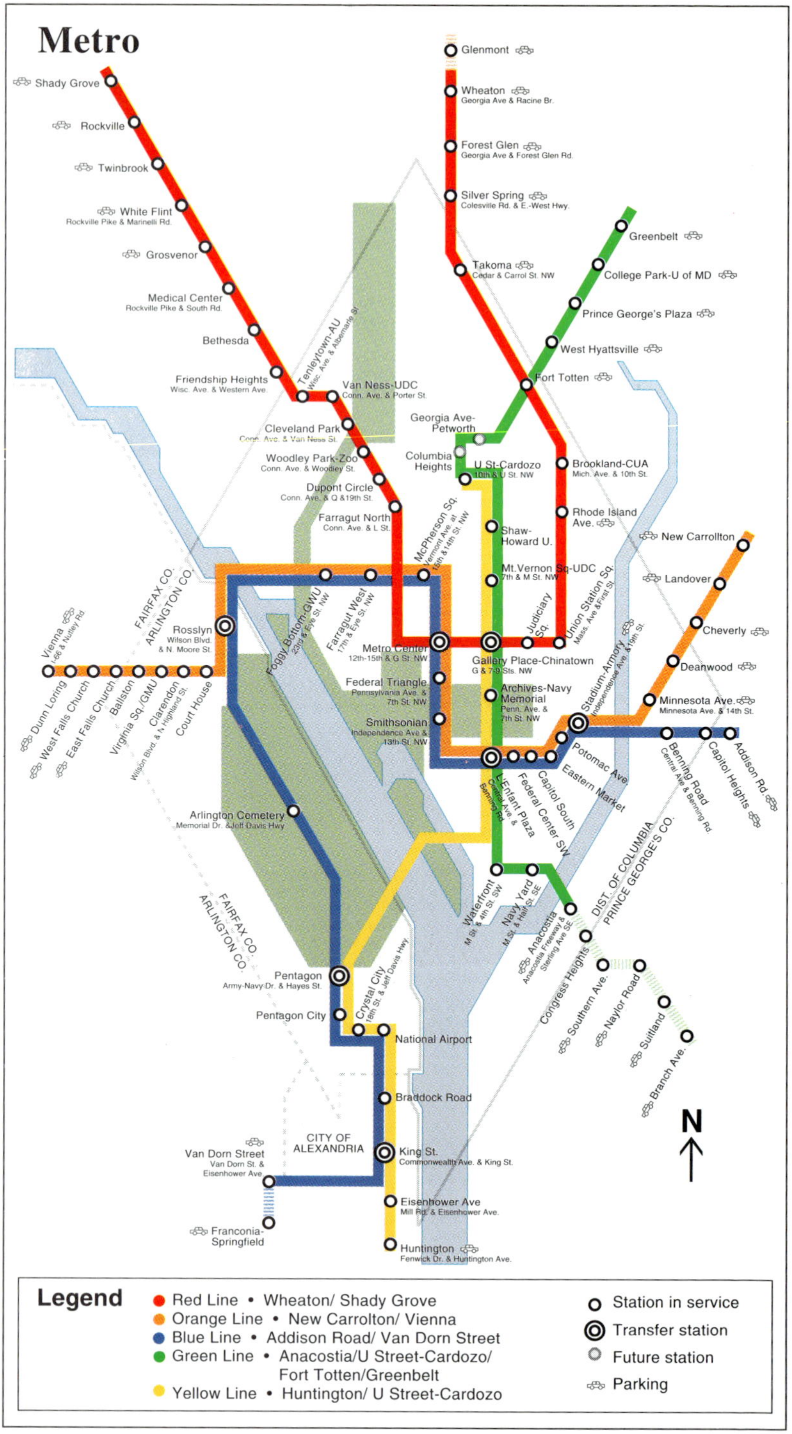

LET'S GO:

Washington, D.C.

"Its yearly revision by a new crop of Harvard students makes it as valuable as ever."
—*The New York Times*

"Value-packed, unbeatable, accurate, and comprehensive."
—*The Los Angeles Times*

"A world-wise traveling companion—always ready with friendly advice and helpful hints, all sprinkled with a bit of wit." **—*The Philadelphia Inquirer***

"Lighthearted and sophisticated, informative and fun to read. [Let's Go] helps the novice traveler navigate like a knowledgeable old hand."
—*Atlanta Journal-Constitution*

"All the essential information you need, from making a phone call to exchanging money to contacting your embassy. [Let's Go] provides maps to help you find your way from every train station to a full range of youth hostels and hotels." **—*Minneapolis Star Tribune***

"Unbeatable: good sight-seeing advice; up-to-date-info on restaurants, hotels, and inns; a commitment to money-saving travel; and a wry style that brightens nearly every page." **—*The Washington Post***

Let's Go researchers have to make it on their own.

"The writers seem to have experienced every rooster-packed bus and lunar-surfaced mattress about which they write." **—*The New York Times***

"Retains the spirit of the student-written publication it is: candid, opinionated, resourceful, amusing info for the traveler of limited means but broad curiosity." **—*Mademoiselle***

No other guidebook is as comprehensive.

"Whether you're touring the United States, Europe, Southeast Asia, or Central America, a Let's Go guide will clue you in to the cheapest, yet safe, hotels and hostels, food and transportation. Going beyond the call of duty, the guides reveal a country's latest news, cultural hints, and off-beat information that any tourist is likely to miss." **—*Tulsa World***

Let's Go is completely revised each year.

"Up-to-date travel tips for touring four continents on skimpy budgets."
—*Time*

"Inimitable.... Let's Go's 24 guides are updated yearly (as opposed to the general guidebook standard of every two to three years), and in a marvelously spunky way." **—*The New York Times***

Let's Go Publications

Let's Go: Alaska & The Pacific Northwest
Let's Go: Britain & Ireland
Let's Go: California
Let's Go: Central America
Let's Go: Eastern Europe
Let's Go: Ecuador & The Galápagos Islands
Let's Go: Europe
Let's Go: France
Let's Go: Germany
Let's Go: Greece & Turkey
Let's Go: India & Nepal
Let's Go: Ireland
Let's Go: Israel & Egypt
Let's Go: Italy
Let's Go: London
Let's Go: Mexico
Let's Go: New York City
Let's Go: Paris
Let's Go: Rome
Let's Go: Southeast Asia
Let's Go: Spain & Portugal
Let's Go: Switzerland & Austria
Let's Go: USA
Let's Go: Washington, D.C.

*Let's Go **Map Guide:** Boston*
*Let's Go **Map Guide:** London*
*Let's Go **Map Guide:** New York City*
*Let's Go **Map Guide:** Paris*
*Let's Go **Map Guide:** San Francisco*
*Let's Go **Map Guide:** Washington, D.C.*

LET'S GO

The Budget Guide to

Washington, D.C.

1997

Lisa Ann Halliday
Editor

St. Martin's Press New York

HELPING LET'S GO

If you want to share your discoveries, suggestions, or corrections, please drop us a line. We read every piece of correspondence, whether a postcard, a 10-page e-mail, or a coconut. All suggestions are passed along to our researcher-writers. Please note that mail received after May 1997 may be too late for the 1998 book, but will be retained for the following edition. **Address mail to:**

Let's Go: Washington, D.C.
67 Mt. Auburn Street
Cambridge, MA 02138
USA

Visit Let's Go at **http://www.letsgo.com,** or send e-mail to:

Fanmail@letsgo.com
Subject: "Washington, D.C."

In addition to the invaluable travel advice our readers share with us, many are kind enough to offer their services as researchers or editors. Unfortunately, the charter of Let's Go, Inc. enables us to employ only currently enrolled Harvard-Radcliffe students.

Map revisions pp. 20-21, 53, 115, 144-145, 150, 153, 158, 171, 181, 240-241, 248-249, by Let's Go, Inc.

Distributed outside the USA and Canada by Macmillan.

ISBN: 0-312-14669-8

First edition
10 9 8 7 6 5 4 3 2 1

Let's Go: Washington, D.C. is written by Let's Go Publications, 67 Mt. Auburn Street, Cambridge, MA 02138, USA.

Printed in the USA on recycled paper with biodegradable soy ink.

Contents

Maps

Color Maps

Researcher-Writers

Ethan Drogin *Maryland, Virginia, West Virginia, Washington, D.C.*
Ethan befriended the entire East Coast. He played pick-up hoops with Annapolites, drank Virginian microbrew with bartenders in Williamsburg, offered tidings to "Ryan" outside a 7-Eleven at 3am, and chivalrously escorted an Argentinian girl to her first Orioles game. When not procuring his posse, Ethan conquered an itinerary that, at times—at *best*—was merciless. But he endured it all (the travails of driving, nights in less-than-accommodating accommodations, and a backbreaking budget) to indulge in the capital's nightlife, sport, and recreation, as well as to discover amid ubiquitous crabcakes some of Maryland's finest Greek food. Via magnificent marginalia, pristine prose, and grayboxes galore, Ethan brought a little Southern sun to a dreary Cambridge desk. Thank you, Ethan; the check's in the mail.

Neil Lawande *Alexandria, Arlington, and Fairfax, VA; Washington, D.C.*
Neil did all but don a gray suit and a briefcase in order to disclose Washington's businessfolk-revered establishments to the naive budgeteer. Braving the early morning stampede for coffee and a croissant ($1), Neil unearthed Farragut's haven of corporate-catering cafés, Dupont Circle's bohemian *vivres,* and Alexandria's out-of-the-way urbane gems. And he had more fun at Mount Vernon than you can shake your wooden teeth at. Neil spent hours on the road so that you can spend hours at the airport—waiting for your plane to take off rather than chasing it down the runway—and he immortalized in prose our postcard-perfect national backyard, the Mall. With a fervent curiosity concerning credit cards and cocktails, Neil brought D.C. natives' prime hotspots to your provincial hands.

Eunice Park *Arlington, VA; Bethesda, MD; Washington, D.C.*
We at the office would like to think that Eunice, a *Let's Go* veteran, hasn't forgotten us to become a worldly cosmopolite. However, though we miss Eunice since she left the production room's nest to embrace D.C. in all of its citified splendor, I will be eternally grateful for the vicarious experience. Eunice has enlightened me with a D.C. that I never knew, and, in turn, has graced the pages of *Let's Go* with the most invaluable of hindsight, insight, and forethought—all imbued with her ineffable humor. I now have a collection of approx. 12,000 incredible postcards, as well as marginalia (detailing the Smithsonian experience of Eunice-as-hand-holding-kindergartner versus that of Eunice-as-seasoned-Researcher-Writer) that sends me into fits of laughter still. If only I could buy you that dog, Eunice—it's the least I could do.

Acknowledgements

Thanks to my fellow *Let's Go* staff: Kevin C. Murphy for investing my book with his wit and illustrative inclinations, for teaching me about our fair nation's *other* capital, and for genuinely believing that there is life on Mars; the authentic Liz Mayer for being a city-guide-savvy and just plain fantastic ME; the Domestic Room for making me laugh, Allison Crapo for making me cry, and Nick Corman for making me tremble. Celeste Young: I owe you my *Let's Go* debut—*grazie.*

Thank you Stacey (our coffee breaks were too few and far between), Mallory, and Kat for getting me through the spring. Thank you 411 (and Lacey, Bridger, Liz, Josh, and Lucy) for sheltering me from the cold, dark, collegiate world and introducing me to the warm, fuzzy world of German toasts and dominoes. Thank you everyone who blessed my summer with incredible vacations: Susan and Marshall for the week of sun and sailing, the Kelcourses for sponsoring a reunion of sorts, and S&M again for the NYC jaunt. Thank you Kristen, Steph, and Nicole for not forgetting about me. Thank you Mimi and Peepa for everything from balloon Rudolphs to pancake breakfasts to *Side by Side*; Daddy and Donna for being unconditionally wonderful and for never giving up on camping in Maine; Andrea for being my quirky, beautiful sister and friend; and Ralph for perpetuating the teasing well beyond my formative years (see below).

Thanks also to my roommates: Clete, whose smile (and sincere appreciation for John Lincoln Wright & the Sour Mash Boys) I adore; Pinsky, whose dancin' feet and acrid yet terrific sense of humor have made yet another summer memorable; and Jed, my best friend, who has made the past few months incessantly wonderful.

This book is for my mother (*"mom?"*), who is one of the few reasons that I am able to dedicate anything to anyone. She is an incredible person to whom I owe more than I could ever give, and I love her very much. —*LAH*

Editor	Lisa Ann Halliday
Managing Editor	Elisabeth Mayer
Publishing Director	Michelle C. Sullivan
Production Manager	Daniel O. Williams
Associate Production Manager	Michael S. Campbell
Cartography Manager	Amanda K. Bean
Editorial Manager	John R. Brooks
Editorial Manager	Allison Crapo
Financial Manager	Stephen P. Janiak
Personnel Manager	Alexander H. Travelli
Publicity Manager	SoRelle B. Braun
Associate Publicity Manager	David Fagundes
Associate Publicity Manager	Elisabeth Mayer
Assistant Cartographer	Jonathan D. Kibera
Assistant Cartographer	Mark C. Staloff
Office Coordinator	Jennifer L. Schuberth
Director of Advertising and Sales	Amit Tiwari
Senior Sales Executives	Andrew T. Rourke
	Nicholas A. Valtz, Charles E. Varner
General Manager	Richard Olken
Assistant General Manager	Anne E. Chisholm

About Let's Go

THIRTY-SIX YEARS OF WISDOM

Back in 1960, a few students at Harvard University banded together to produce a 20-page pamphlet offering a collection of tips on budget travel in Europe. This modest, mimeographed packet, offered as an extra to passengers on student charter flights to Europe, met with instant popularity. The following year, students traveling to Europe researched the first, full-fledged edition of *Let's Go: Europe*, a pocket-sized book featuring honest, irreverent writing and a decidedly youthful outlook on the world. Throughout the 60s, our guides reflected the times; the 1969 guide to America led off by inviting travelers to "dig the scene" at San Francisco's Haight-Ashbury. During the 70s and 80s, we gradually added regional guides and expanded coverage into the Middle East and Central America. With the addition of our in-depth city guides, handy map guides, and extensive coverage of Asia, the 90s are also proving to be a time of explosive growth for Let's Go, and there's certainly no end in sight. The first editions of *Let's Go: India & Nepal* and *Let's Go: Ecuador & The Galapagos Islands* hit the shelves this year, and work toward next year's series has already begun.

We've seen a lot in 37 years. *Let's Go: Europe* is now the world's bestselling international guide, translated into seven languages. And our new guides bring Let's Go's total number of titles, with their spirit of adventure and their reputation for honesty, accuracy, and editorial integrity, to 30. But some things never change: our guides are still researched, written, and produced entirely by students who know first-hand how to see the world on the cheap.

HOW WE DO IT

Each guide is completely revised and thoroughly updated every year by a well-traveled set of 200 students. Every winter, we recruit over 120 researchers and 60 editors to write the books anew. After several months of training, Researcher-Writers hit the road for seven weeks of exploration, from Anchorage to Ankara, Estonia to El Salvador, Iceland to Indonesia. Hired for their rare combination of budget travel sense, writing ability, stamina, and courage, these adventurous travelers know that train strikes, stolen luggage, food poisoning, and marriage proposals are all part of a day's work. Back at our offices, editors work from spring to fall, massaging copy written on Himalayan bus rides into witty yet informative prose. A student staff of typesetters, cartographers, publicists, and managers keeps our lively team together. In September, the collected efforts of the summer are delivered to our printer, who turns them into books in record time, so that you have the most up-to-date information available for *your* vacation. And even as you read this, work on next year's editions is well underway.

WHY WE DO IT

At Let's Go, our goal is to give you a great vacation. We don't think of budget travel as the last recourse of the destitute; we believe that it's the only way to travel. Living cheaply and simply brings you closer to the people and places you've been saving up to visit. Our books will ease your anxieties and answer your questions about the basics—so you can get off the beaten track and explore. Once you learn the ropes, we encourage you to put Let's Go away now and then to strike out on your own. As any seasoned traveler will tell you, the best discoveries are often those you make yourself. When you find something worth sharing, drop us a line. We're Let's Go Publications, 67 Mt. Auburn St., Cambridge, MA 02138, USA (e-mail: fanmail@letsgo.com).

HAPPY TRAVELS!

How To Use This Book

I conceive that it is the knowledge of books on which the basis of all other knowledge rests.

-George Washington

Hence *Let's Go: Washington, D.C., 1997.* Any metropolis can be menacing to even the most seasoned of travelers. Yet with this little yellow book guiding you through the burnished halls of bureaucracy, the cool atriums of world-renowned art, and the lush hillsides of Virginia, you'll have a leg up on the ins and outs of the nation's capital. Expensive cuisine and four-star suites are easy to find in D.C., but hard on the wallet; for each pricey and exorbitant urban pleasure there exist five affordable indulgences available for the tourist's taking. *Let's Go* knows those five, and we'll share them with you.

Washington, D.C.: An Introduction highlights not only the District's arts, culture, and media, but also that for which the city is most famous—an historically rich national tradition of government and politics. **Essentials** provides the information necessary for **Planning Your Trip, Getting There,** and **Getting Around,** in addition to a comprehensive section for the intern-to-be. **Accommodations** are listed in order of value, based on price, location, safety and comfort. The **Food** chapter is organized alphabetically, but with a star denoting Let's Go Picks: the best values according to quality and price. **Sights** offers highlights of the District's neighborhoods, while **Museums & Galleries** frames D.C.'s artful, archival realm on and around the National Mall as well as in Washington's peripheries. **Nightlife & Entertainment** lists the best bars, clubs, theaters, dance troupes, cinemas, and concerts in the city so that the nights are ne'er spent in the dark, while **Sports & Recreation** provides information on various ways to while away the days. **Shops & Services** offers malls and specialty establishments that, if nothing else, offer hours of browsing pleasure. **Daytripping from D.C.** lures you away from the District to Annapolis, Baltimore, Virginia, and other regions (and beaches!) worth your time and effort to explore. The **Appendix** addresses Washington's infamous climate and perpetual special events, and includes Metrorail, mileage, and telephone code charts.

Most chapters' listings are in order of preference; those that are not are listed alphabetically, with **Let's Go Picks** highlighting the best of the best. Geographical subdivisions begin with Capitol Hill, Washington's physical and symbolic hub, and rotate clockwise.

Use *Let's Go* as your instinct's mere companion. You don't need this book to tell you that a walk along the Reflecting Pool at 5am is a potentially breathtaking and serene experience. *Let's Go* is merely a supplement to your own tastes and intuition amid the Washington metropolis. D.C. is a fantastic city, filled with historical significance, gorgeous sights, and archival collections that draw thousands of visitors every year.

A NOTE TO OUR READERS

The information for this book is gathered by *Let's Go*'s researchers during the late spring and summer months. Each listing is derived from the assigned researcher's opinion based upon his or her visit at a particular time. The opinions are expressed in a candid and forthright manner. Other travelers might disagree. Those traveling at a different time may have different experiences since prices, dates, hours, and conditions are always subject to change. You are urged to check beforehand to avoid inconvenience and surprises. Travel always involves a certain degree of risk, especially in low-cost areas. When traveling, especially on a budget, always take particular care to ensure your safety.

Washington, D.C.: An Introduction

I went to Washington the other day...and I felt that the sun in all its course could not look down upon a better sight than that majestic home of the Republic that had taught the world its best lessons in liberty.
—Henry W. Grady, journalist and author

While elaborate monuments, museums, and monolithic edifices inspire awe among those to whom the District plays host, those who never venture beyond the pomp and gleam of Federal Washington merely scratch the city's surface. D.C.'s street plan employs two networks of roads; beneath the broad avenues radiating from the white-domed Capitol and the White House, the grid of local streets indicates the presence of a sovereign dimension, a thriving commercial and residential metropolis with its own sights, treasures, and protocol.

The two discrete cities of Federal Washington and local D.C. coexist in the diamond-shaped District without much conflict or contradiction. Only blocks away in every direction from the National Mall's haven of tourism, D.C. communities—yuppie, gay, Latino, black—dwell and prosper, separate from the government grind. From the bars and businesses around Dupont Circle and the ethnic delights of Adams-Morgan to the collegiates in Georgetown and Foggy Bottom, Washington's second city has more to offer than downtown can possibly put on display, and more to see than any tour guide could ever expound upon.

But there is a dark side to the city's duality. D.C. runs a budget deficit which rivals that of the federal government, and local officials have neither the funds nor the prestige to keep the city afloat. The recent loss of home rule in the District increased the irony of the juxtaposition of the two bureaucracies: one powerful, the other powerless. Meanwhile, the city's impoverished population braces itself against a barrage of crime, drugs, and broken families. The squalor endures, largely because the transient policy bigwigs—who return after work to the suburban plushness of Maryland and Virginia—have little interest in cleaning it all up.

Despite difficult urban problems, the ambitious and strange experiment of Washington—an infant nation building a capital from scratch—has matured into one of America's most intriguing, and consequently most visited, urban centers. A conglomerate of political powerhouse, sleepy Southern town, decaying metropolis, and vigorous urban center yields D.C.'s impressive, intimidating, but entertaining and ultimately distinctive character.

History

FOUNDING AND EARLY YEARS

No nation had ever before the opportunity offered them of deliberately deciding on the spot where their Capital City should be fixed.
—Pierre L'Enfant, letter to George Washington (1789)

Like many a young adult fresh out of college, the post-Revolution Continental Congress realized that independence meant little without a place to stay. While the weak, decentralizing Articles of Confederation governed the new United States, the Congress convened in Philadelphia in 1783 and tried to decide where to park itself for good. Kingston, NY, Nottingham, NJ, and Williamsburg, then the capital of Virginia, were all candidates for the honor. Before the Congress could make a decision, a mob of Continental Army veterans converged on Philadelphia demanding back pay, and the scared legislators hightailed it to Princeton, NJ, Annapolis, MD, Trenton, NJ, and finally to New York City, where George Washington's inauguration (socialists take note) took place on Wall Street. By this point, the Congress had two pressing questions: where to put the permanent capital and whether the U.S. should fund the states' leftover war debt. Politicians from the mercantile northern states, led by the wily Alexander Hamilton, wanted the capital for themselves, but also yearned for debt relief. The prosperous, agrarian South didn't want to subsidize the North, but also sought the capital. As a compromise, the Congress assumed the states' obligations but decided on a southern capital, instructing George Washington to pick a spot "no more than ten miles square" along the Potomac River. George chose the Potomac's intersection with the Anacostia River, since the point was close to Mount Vernon, his home, and also ideal (in theory) for a port. Maryland and Virginia together agreed to donate a diamond-shaped parcel of 100 sq. mi. ("ten miles square"), French engineer Pierre L'Enfant was hired to design Washington City, and the real fun began.

L'Enfant was enchanted by stately Paris and wanted to make Washington the French capital's more rational cousin. The "L'Enfant Plan" laid out central Washington in a grid pattern with an overlay of diagonal avenues, named for states and radiating (mostly) from the Capitol and White House to an effusion of monumental squares. The plan covered only what was then called "Washington City," not Georgetown, Alexandria, or the miles of farmland around their edges. L'Enfant planned a central canal and port facilities, but his real love seemed to be the public spaces and wide avenues of his design. The plan had already offended the area's landed gentry by seizing more land for roads than they expected, and L'Enfant's "artistic temperament" hardly endeared him to political superiors. When L'Enfant tore down an aristocrat's porch (it stood in the way of New Jersey Ave. SE), not even his friend George W. could save him from the wrath of the rich. L'Enfant was fired; his deputies Benjamin Banneker and Andrew Ellicott replaced him. (Banneker, an accomplished astronomer, may have been the first African-American recognized within the "intellectual" community. He supervised the city's construction for three months before poor health forced him to quit.) The ousted Pierre refused to take the conciliatory sum offered by Congress, then spent the early 19th century wandering around Washington trying to get paid.

The "city of magnificent distances" (D.C.'s 19th-century nickname) was far from magnificent and far from a city. In 1800 the capital village held scattered wooden buildings, dirt roads, and only 3244 residents, with 123 free African-Americans and over 500 slaves. (The nickname really meant there was very little between the public buildings.) Early "improvements" didn't help matters: Tiber Creek was diverted and dammed to form the Washington Canal, whose stagnant water proved a boon to mosquitoes and bred the enduring but false legend that Washington was built on a swamp. The paint was barely dry on the original Capitol before the War of 1812 brought British troops here in August 1814 to burn the city down (in a civilized way, of course). The government buildings bit the dust, and Dolly Madison (the fourth President's wife) made a name for herself by carrying from the flaming White House one of Gilbert Stuart's many portraits of George Washington. Washingtonians have fled in August ever since.

Though rain put out the British blaze, Congress was almost ready to throw in the towel; a postwar vote on a proposal to move the capital lost by only eight votes. The capital stayed, but so did the problems. As a port city between two plantation states, the District made a logical first stop for slave traders, whose shackled cargo awaited sale in crowded pens on the Mall and near the White House. Foreign diplomats were properly disgusted, deeming D.C. "Southern." Between the slave trade and the swamp air, elected officials understandably decided D.C. was no place for families: America's elected elite lived in all-male boarding houses, chewed tobacco, and fought frequent duels in a famous valley near Bladensburg, MD. National politics became an affair of personalities: after one debate on the Senate floor, South Carolina representative Preston Brooks clobbered anti-slavery Massachusetts senator Charles Sumner with a cane. Another senator's marriage to Peggy Eaton, the beautiful daughter of a tavern-keeper, began a chain of social snubs and reactions that caused the resignation of Andrew Jackson's Vice President John Calhoun, who would articulate the doctrine that later justified secession.

Though subject to severe racial prejudice, a town-within-the-town of free African-Americans was growing faster than the rest of the city. By 1850 Washington held 2000 slaves, 8000 free blacks, and 30,000 whites. White fear of uprisings had already given rise to discriminatory laws and social unrest (like the Snow Riots of 1835), but the thriving community close to the "upper South" plantations continued to draw African-American migrants. Black residents established 15 schools in Georgetown and Washington City before the Civil War.

During the 1830s and '40s British travelers felt compelled to publish their Washington journals—a long record of unpaved streets, testy officials, half-erected buildings, broad vistas, and horrifying slave traffic. Charles Dickens, who dropped by in 1842, called D.C. "the City of Magnificent Intentions":

> *Spacious avenues, that begin in nothing, and lead nowhere; streets, mile-long, that only want houses, roads and inhabitants; public buildings that need but a public...One might fancy the season over, and most of the houses gone out of town forever with their masters.*

CIVIL WAR TO WORLD WAR I

"Such as it is, it is likely to remain," began Dickens's next paragraph. He hadn't counted on the War Between the States, whose outbreak in 1861 turned all military eyes on Washington and turned the capital from the Union's appendix to its jugular vein. The city's social elite brought picnic baskets to the First Battle of Bull Run, but an unexpected Confederate victory forced the Union military to harden up the capital. Soon forts encircled the city, and soldiers slept in government offices and overran the Mall. (Military Rd. NW still links some of these forts.) While Abraham Lincoln sent troops to keep Maryland loyal, D.C. society turned out to help the Union, and the President himself attended a skirmish in his trademark stovepipe hat. (When he stood for a better view of the battle, a Union officer shouted "Get down, you fool!") Though every other building seemed full of troops, Lincoln directed that work continue on the Capitol dome: "It is a sign," he reasoned, "that the Union shall go on." An 1862 *Harper's* magazine cover showed "Convalescent Troops Passing Through Washington," an everyday sight in the overcrowded wartime capital.

The Civil War sent tens of thousands of former slaves north for a better life; for a time, they instead were worse off in spontaneous shanty towns such as Murder Bay, a few blocks from the White House. The postwar period spelled better times for black people. The five years after 1868 were called the "Golden Age of Black Washington," with new, enforced civil-rights laws, black senators and congressmen, a black public-school system, an African-American at the helm of Georgetown University, and the founding of Dunbar High School and Howard University, for 50 years a two-step path into D.C.'s black elite. President Grant appointed former slave turned abolitionist Frederick Douglass the District's recorder of deeds. With Sella Martin, Douglass edited the aptly named *New Era;* his 1877 "Lecture on the Nation's Capital" angered Congressmen and still makes good reading.

In May 1870, Congress gave Washington the right to choose a mayor. Deputy Mayor Alexander "Boss" Shepherd took *de facto* charge in 1871; protected by his friendship with President Grant, Boss Shepherd resurfaced the streets, planted trees, and employed thousands of laborers in his super-efficient city improvement plan, just as L'Enfant would have wished. He tore down decrepit buildings, built sewers, parks, and new roads, and installed streetlights. Of course, all this cost money; the controversial, fast-acting Shepherd sent the city into record-breaking debt, and the federal bailout that followed reattached control of the city to Congress and robbed D.C. of self-government for over 100 years.

As D.C. temporarily prospered, federal Washington floundered. The political patronage system plus the corruption of the Grant years led a torrent of office-seekers to Washington, grinding down congressmen with persistent requests for favors and jobs. Charles J. Guiteau, universally described as a "disgruntled office seeker," shot President James A. Garfield in 1881. Not long afterward, in 1885, new President Grover Cleveland (by most accounts the first honest Chief since Lincoln) stayed up all night reading job applications patronage-seekers had hand-delivered; it was time for a change, and Cleveland made one by enforcing the 1882 Civil Service Act, setting in place the not-entirely-partisan federal bureaucracy we know and love today. Cleveland struggled through his early-1890s second term, as national depression brought strikes to Chicago and Coxey's Army of 300 unemployed workers to Washington. It was D.C.'s first big protest march, and Cleveland dithered while federal police crushed encampments.

Washington had more or less become modern, with apartment houses, telephones, and electric streetcars. But the capital was hardly a place of beauty. Vigorous President Theodore Roosevelt, who charged into office in 1901, appointed the McMillan Commission to give the adolescent city a shave and a haircut. The commission—architects Daniel Burnham and Charles McKim, sculptor Augustus Saint-Gaudens, and landscape bigshot Frederick Law Olmsted—was the principal planner of D.C.'s current public spaces and monuments, and it shares responsibility for the "feel" of the city with L'Enfant. The commission decided to make the muddy Mall a permanent lawn, build a memorial to Lincoln at one end, designate land elsewhere for parks, erect Memorial Bridge, and build Union Station (among other things).

Meanwhile D.C.'s African-Americans were losing economic power, even as their numbers (and artistic achievements) increased. As employment segregation tightened, most became obliged to work in service industries (driving taxis, catering); the gains of Reconstruction had disappeared. Roosevelt himself listened to the black community, but Georgia-born Woodrow Wilson supported a segregation so thorough that black leader "Lady Mollie" Mary Church Terrell couldn't get young poet Langston Hughes considered for a job at the Library of Congress—not even as a page. Newspapers fanned white "Negrophobia" into the race riots of 1919. Cafeterias and even public parks became segregated facilities; at the 1922 dedication of the Lincoln Memorial, world-famous educator Booker T. Washington was made to sit in a "colored" section. Though activists tried to increase hiring, "more federal jobs meant more messengers and janitors," in the words of historian David Lewis. Black Washington in these years was almost an autonomous city, with its own movie houses, theaters, shops, social clubs, political leaders, and demographic patterns. The city-within-a-city was hardly unified, though; middle-class black people in LeDroit Park had little to do with the impoverished "alley dwellings" in SW and SE.

FDR and WWII

After the stock market crash of 1929, President Hoover responded to the Great Depression with platitudes instead of money. The "Bonus Army" of unemployed veterans marched to the Mall to demand new benefits but was dispersed by the National Guard instead. The election of Franklin Delano Roosevelt in 1932 gave the country a New Deal: to D.C., it brought a herd of idealistic liberals anxious to make the "Alphabet Soup" of new agencies and relief programs work. NRA, WPA, AAA, YCC, FHA, and SEC were just a few of the novel acronyms FDR's "try-anything" philosophy spawned; his liberal ideas enraged Washington's old-money "cave dwellers," who snubbed the government from 16th St. and Dupont Circle while newcomers with Ph.D.s moved into Georgetown. The influx began to transform the city from a "sleepy Southern town" into an expanding young metropolis eternally envious of New York's sophistication.

As professionals continued to move into Washington, Nazi Germany began invading its neighbors, and D.C. had to prepare for war. In 1940 and '41, the President tried discreetly to persuade a country still clinging to isolationism to help Great Britain save Europe. With the national government swollen to its post-Depression size and international conflict taking center stage, Washington became the hub of patriotism and the focus of protest. Isolationist pickets surrounded the White House, Nazi puppet ambassadors showed up along Massachusetts Ave., and Congress, as late as 1941, decided to renew the military draft by only one vote. After Japan attacked Pearl Harbor on December 7, 1941 and the U.S. entered the war, Washington's bureaucracy ballooned. Soldiers on leave filled Washington's ballrooms, FDR's handpicked coordinators (like Leon Henderson and Donald Nelson) tried to straighten out the wartime economy, the War Department seized hotels for office space, and civilians of both sexes poured into D.C. as war-related clerical jobs opened up daily. A 1943 guidebook called the District "the Cinderella City."

Black Washington was changing too, but more slowly, and persistent prejudice sparked protest in many forms. The city's segregation came to national attention when the Daughters of the American Revolution barred African-American opera star Marian Anderson from singing at Constitution Hall. Anderson sang instead, on Easter Sunday, 1939, on the steps of the Lincoln Memorial to an audience of 75,000. It had, unfortunately, only a symbolic effect on segregation in Washington. In 1940, Phillip Randolph threatened to organize a march on Washington unless Roosevelt demanded fair federal hiring; he got what he asked for, but the decree did little good. The "alley dwelling" problem was worse than ever; a federal agency "cleared" the slums by kicking out the poor and creating (as a brochure actually announced) "Low-Income Housing for White Families." The tradition of the sit-in began in the '40s when Howard University students entered Thompson's Restaurant and refused to leave until they were served. (Mary Church Terrell led a more successful sit-in there years later.)

FDR's successor, Harry S. Truman, dropped a bomb on Washington's racism when his appointed commission released its 1947 report and President Truman desegregated the military. The Supreme Court's 1953 "Lost Laws" ruling (that civil rights laws from 1872 could still be enforced) essentially desegregated most of the city. Paradoxically, the integration of movie theaters, stores, and eating establishments destroyed many black-owned businesses, and the African-American commercial districts north of Massachusetts Ave. began to deteriorate. In a similar vein, Dunbar High School—reputable such that black families had come from the Deep South just to educate their children there—became nothing special after 1954's *Brown v. Board of Education* Supreme Court decision integrated America's formerly all-white schools.

Sen. Joseph McCarthy's witch hunts for Communists terrorized the bureaucracy in the early 1950s, but the government and its city kept getting bigger. (McCarthy finally disgraced himself in the famous, televised Army-McCarthy hearings of 1954.) A crew of Cold Warriors conducted affairs of state throughout the '50s and '60s; John F. Kennedy's narrow victory in 1960 enchanted the press and brought a new cultural savvy to the still-provincial capital. His Texan successor, Lyndon Johnson, once the Senate's shrewd Majority Leader, stampeded the Congress into civil rights action and anti-poverty legislation, then steered the nation deep into the Vietnam War. The District had meanwhile grown beyond its borders—the area's population doubled from 1950 to 1970, but much of the increase came in suburbs, where the '50's bourgeoisie loved to live.

RECENT DECADES

During the turbulent, politicized 1960s, Washington hosted one demonstration after the next. Martin Luther King, Jr. led two of the most important. The 1963 March on Washington, site of his famous "I Have a Dream" speech, gathered 250,000 people of all races on the Mall. The '63 marchers, black and white, middle-class and poor, demanded an end to legal segregation, while those who came to D.C. in the 1968 Poor Peoples' Campaign demanded economic empowerment. When news of King's assassination (April 4, 1968) reached Washington, days of riots destroyed historic parts of the city.

Goings-on around Washington held the nation rapt during the Watergate years of 1972-4, when the authorized break-ins and the recorded White House audiotapes of President Richard Nixon effected his disgrace and resignation. The U.S. bicentennial in 1976 drew tourists in record numbers to the capital. The Carter administration

(1977-81) brought in Democratic outsiders from Georgia, while the Reagan administration (1981-89) imported conservative outsiders and smooth operators, many from his native California. The two Reagan inaugurals were the most expensive ever. Not surprisingly, the federal deficit tripled in the first three years of the Reagan era. During these years, conservative appointees clashed with more moderate federal workers, pro-business attitudes paralyzed regulators, and the Pentagon's $1000 toilet seats became the stuff of legend. While the "Teflon President's" popularity cowed Congress for several years, the Iran-Contra scandals of 1986-88 demonstrated either astounding disregard for the law or incredible ignorance at the top. President Bush's administration bore witness to the passing of communism in Eastern Europe and the Soviet Union, and fought a high-profile war in the Middle East. Amid the pomp and circumstance of the victory parade, scandals—ranging from the very small (the House banking scandal) to the very large (the B.C.C.I. scandal)—sent voter confidence plummeting.

With Fleetwood Mac's "Don't Stop Thinkin' About Tomorrow" playing in the background, Democrat Bill Clinton headed to the White House in early 1993 with a mandate to cut the U.S. deficit and improve the nation's health care system. Since then, the President has fought an uphill battle; the administration's plan for health-care reform was scuttled by a Congress too timid to ask employers to pay for universal health care coverage. Minor foreign policy victories buoyed Clinton's sinking reputation; he supervised (but did not really catalyze) the Israeli-Arab peace agreements and spontaneously normalized U.S. relations with Vietnam. Since the 1994 Congressional election turned both houses overwhelmingly Republican, Clinton has vacillated between cooperation with the demanding Congress and insistence on a stricter breed of "responsibility" liberalism. Attempts at compromise on a balanced budget plan are evidence of the former; the Chief's hard line in favor of affirmative action (following the '95 Court ruling) move him staunchly into the liberal camp.

Downtown developers kept the economy moving from the late '70s to the late '80s, though often at the expense of residential areas. While the city's population dropped to 617,000 in 1988, the suburbs ballooned, producing pseudo-urban areas like Rockville, Maryland—the state's second largest city. Much of the burgeoning black middle class fled to the suburbs, where anti-discrimination laws unlocked homeowning opportunities and lower taxes increased the appeal. D.C.'s population in 1988 was 70% black, today it's 75%. The white population in the District itself tends to live west of Rock Creek Park; some white residents are moneyed, many are not. While the '70s produced flight to suburban outposts, the '80s lured many back to the townhouses of formerly run-down or blue-collar neighborhoods in the midst of controversial gentrification. Hopeful immigrants keep arriving in city and suburbs, especially in Mount Pleasant, Adams-Morgan, Arlington, and Montgomery County. All these groups together fuel the metropolitan area with plenty of cultural and commercial vitality. But a large (and more publicized) segment of Washington sees fewer reasons for optimism: the mid-'80s advent of crack, a cheap, condensed, smokeable form of cocaine, incapacitated thousands of addicts ("pipeheads"). Teens without functional families or schools saw crack as their only career opportunity; dealers' turf wars, often fought with machine guns, made the body count higher than ever. Crack (now replaced, to some degree, by heroin) brought the despair and easy access to guns that effect dangerous and bleak areas.

A century of Congressional-committee rule came largely to an end in 1973, when Congress passed the Home Rule Act, giving D.C. an elected mayor, a city council, and a non-voting delegate in Congress. The first mayor, Walter Washington, represented the native, middle-class black establishment; the second one, Marion Barry, grew up in rural North Carolina. Elected in 1978 by a multi-racial coalition, Barry was known as a '60s civil-rights leader. Though he promised liberal reforms, his first term was noted mostly for attracting business to the city. In the '80s, however, the shine wore off. Barry hadn't reformed the city, and some members of his administration were accused of misusing city funds and other forms of corruption. The mayor himself was caught smoking crack by undercover federal agents in January 1990. Political outsider Sharon Pratt Kelly, who campaigned with a broom in her hand, was elected mayor in November 1990. She was subsequently voted out of office in 1994, to be replaced by Marion Barry himself.

THE TIMES, THEY ARE A CHANGIN'

In response to what many a Democrat as well as most Republicans have considered a mediocre President, Republicans swept elections across the country in 1994, sending masses of fresh faces to D.C. and erasing the majority that Democrats had enjoyed in both the House and Senate for over 50 years. The once little-known **Newt Gingrich** became one of America's most popular magazine cover stories, as the Republicans were propelled into power by their **"Contract with America,"** a document outlining that which Republicans would change if elected. The new Congress has held firm to its promises, slashing social programs to trim the deficit. However, many Americans deem the "contract" a failure, and immaturity (Newt's complaints about his Air Force seating on the return from Israel's Prime Minister Yitzak Rabin's funeral) and the re-emergence of the Religious Right have splintered the G.O.P and inaugurated the counter-revolution. Clinton, once again the Comeback Kid, led Republican candidate Bob Dole by 17 points in the polls, a seemingly insurmountable lead—Perot or no. The Presidential Election in November '96 promises (as *Let's Go: Washington, D.C. 1997* goes to press) to be a heated battle.

On the local level, former crack-smoker **Marion Barry,** claiming a need for redemption, was re-elected Mayor of D.C. in 1994. He inherited a deficit of around $700 million, but he won't have to worry about it too much: after a 12-year failed trial period of autonomy, the **Washington Home Rule Charter** was revoked. Today, Barry and his bureaucracy have to answer to a Congressionally-appointed (and GOP-allied) financial control board. The control board tells the City Council how much money needs to be cut, and the Council gets to figure out where to cut. This arrangement will be in place until the city is out of the red.

U.S. Government and Politics

The structure of the U.S. government is mostly dictated by the **Constitution,** a document penned by 18th-century aristocrats (mostly by James Madison) and designed to prevent the twin horrors of executive tyranny and mob rule. The Constitution divides power between the U.S. government and the 50 states; there's a list of powers delegated to Congress and to the President, an "elastic clause" letting Congress do other things, and an Amendment (the 10th) giving all the leftover powers to the states. The federal government has three branches: **legislative, executive,** and **judicial,** each of which limits the power of the others (the "checks and balances" system). **Congress** drafts and votes on **bills;** the **President** (the Chief Executive) can sign them (making them **laws**) or veto them. A vetoed bill returns to Congress, which has to vote for it by a two-thirds majority the second time around to override the Prez and make the bill law. (If Congress is soon to adjourn, the President can ignore a bill and make it go away—a "pocket veto.") The **federal court system,** topped by the **Supreme Court,** interprets federal laws; the Supremes interpret the Constitution and throw out laws that violate it (even state laws).

Congress, the legislative branch, is bicameral, consisting of the 435-member **House of Representatives** and the 100-member **Senate.** House Members are popularly elected and serve two-year terms, representing numbered **districts** of about 575,000 people within a state (which are redrawn every 10 years after the Census). 1992 saw new seats created in growing states like California, and incumbents running against other incumbents in declining states like Michigan and Pennsylvania. Senators serve six-year terms; each state has two. Until the Seventeenth Amendment was added to the Constitution in 1913, most senators were chosen by state legislatures; now state voters elect them. As the original "representative" chamber, only the House may initiate bills that change taxes. Originally the elite chamber, the Senate gives "advice and consent" to Presidential appointments like federal judges, Supreme Court justices, Cabinet secretaries, and ambassadors. In practice this means the Senate must **confirm** them before they can officially assume their jobs; lower-level nominees are often taken "hostage" by senators who block their confirmations pending some favor from the executive branch.

Though the whole House or Senate can meet to debate and vote on a bill, almost all their work gets done in **standing committees;** the House has 22, the Senate 16. These committees consider facts and write and edit bills; each one has separate staffers whose job is to be more informed than the members on whatever issues the committee deals with. **Select** or **special** committees are convened to hold investigations (as for the Iran-Contra scandal), administer Congressional affairs (like the House gym), and make members look good (e.g., the Select Committee on Aging). Especially powerful standing committees are the **House Ways and Means Committee** and the **Senate Rules Committee,** which decide when and how a bill will be debated when it gets "reported" from the committee to the House or Senate floor. Most Members have urgent desires to sit on committees related to their state or district (forestry for Oregon, transportation for Michigan). Most also yearn to be on powerful committees, especially House Appropriations or Senate Finance, which get to mark up and vote on all budgets. Low-status committees, especially Ethics, are nearly powerless.

The **party leadership,** the top Democrats and Republicans in each chamber, decides who gets to sit on what committee; all the committees are led by chairpersons from the majority party and ranking minority members from the other side. Both houses have **majority** and **minority leaders** and **whips** (deputy leaders). While the **Speaker of the House,** chosen from the majority party, presides *de jure* and *de facto* over that chamber, the official head of the Senate is the Vice President, who has little real power and only votes to break ties. Speaker of the House (now Newt Gingrich, R-Georgia) and Senate Majority Leader (currently Trent Lott, R-Miss.) are therefore roughly equivalent jobs. Both men argue that their influence is equivalent to that of the Prez himself. (The House Majority Leader is Richard Armey, R-Texas; the Minority Leader is Richard Gephardt, D-Missouri. The Senate Minority Leader is Thomas Daschle, D-South Dakota.) These guys also coordinate and orchestrate each party's legislative agenda. The whole setup depends on the **two-party system,** and America's split into Democrats and Republicans prevents splinter groups and one-issue parties from holding the influence they sometimes wield in parliamentary systems like Italy's or Israel's.

President Bill Clinton, besides signing off on laws, is Commander-in-Chief of the armed forces and head of the Executive Branch. Al Gore, his **Vice President,** presides over the Senate (but only votes in case of a tie) and serves as the President's emissary (unless the President dies or gets too sick to do his job, in which case the Veep takes the office of the President). Presidents are elected for four-year terms; the 22nd Amendment, a reaction to Franklin Roosevelt's death during his fourth term, has banned presidents since from serving more than two. The President is the summit of the complex pyramid of federal bureaucracy, where those near the top are political appointees, those lower down career civil servants. Fourteen **departments** together do most of the government's work; their Secretaries together make up the **Cabinet.** The State Department, now run by Warren Christopher, conducts foreign policy; the Treasury Department, run by former Goldman-Sachs exec. Robert Rubin, formulates economic policy and collects taxes and fees (through the IRS). The Defense Department, headed by William Perry, presides over military matters. The Attorney General (currently Janet Reno) steers the Justice Department, which acts as the government's law firm, representing the executive branch in civil and criminal cases. Independent **regulatory agencies,** like the Environmental Protection Agency and the Food and Drug Administration, enforce their designated laws outside the purview of government departments. The White House also has its own **executive staff** (which Clinton shrank by 25%), which writes the President's speeches, draws up his schedules, and digs up information for him; the supposedly advisory National Security Council was a favorite tool for illegal covert action.

In what was largely interpreted by the national press as an attempt to restore (or at least create the image of) order and direction to a floundering administration, Bill Clinton chose July of 1994 to announce the most dramatic reshuffling of his White House staff to date. His long-time friend and kindergarten classmate Thomas "Mack" McLarty was removed as Chief of Staff and replaced by Clinton's former budget director Leon Panetta. Erstwhile Republican spin-meister David Gergen, who had been earlier hired by Clinton as a special presidential advisor in the area of "communications," moved from the White House to new office space in the State Department to assume a more prominent role in the formulation and mass-marketing of the administration's foreign policy initiatives. Political consultant Dick Morris, regarded suspiciously by many Democrats for his work with their Republican rivals, has now filled Gergen's shoes as Clinton's unofficial advisor.

The real wheels of the government are oiled by more than just elected officials. Thousands of **staffers** grind away each day researching for Congressfolk, communicating with constituents, and running campaigns. And millions of civil-service bureaucrats spread funds and forms around the nation.

The **Supreme Court's** nine justices are appointed for life by the President, but must be confirmed by the Senate. The current Chief Justice is the conservative William Rehnquist. The justices hear and vote on cases involving Constitutional issues; because they interpret the law rather than decide facts, no jury is involved in their deliberations. The court is the ultimate guarantor of civil liberties and civil rights, the protections from government intrusion contained in or implied chiefly by the Bill of Rights (the first ten Constitutional amendments) and the Fourteenth Amendment. The Supreme Court accepts cases for review from federal appellate courts or state supreme courts; only about 5% of those presented are heard. Presidents understandably try to appoint justices who share their philosophies, but they've often been unpleasantly surprised; Eisenhower maintained that the worst mistake he made as President was appointing the groundbreakingly liberal Chief Justice Earl Warren. (Even the Reaganauts have had surprises, such as David Souter and Anthony Kennedy's reluctance to go all-out for the conservative agenda.)

Throughout the Bush administration, the Court became increasingly conservative as Reagan and Bush nominees replaced justices from the '60s and '70s who died or retired in ill health; the court slowly rolled back the broad civil liberties recently created and guaranteed, issued muddy rulings on civil rights and racial issues, took the government's side against criminal defendants, curtailed the right to privacy, made the death penalty easier to impose, and edged toward overturning the watershed 1973 *Roe v. Wade* abortion-rights decision. Most recently, centrists Ruth Bader Ginsburg and Stephen G. Breyer were appointed to the nation's top judicial body by striving-to-be-centrist President Clinton. Bader Ginsburg, a noted feminist appellate judge, brings to the court her vigorous support for women's rights and strong committment to preserving a woman's constitutional right to an abortion. Breyer, a Harvard law professor confirmed in August of 1994, is an articulate consensus-builder often criticized by liberals for his allegedly pro-business leanings. Since these appointments the Court has kept up its trend toward centrism with several close and controversial rulings: in 1994, it upheld *Roe* by a narrow 5-4 margin, but in 1995, by the same margin, it called for stricter scrutiny of affirmative action laws.

Elected officials want to be reelected. Swarms of **interest groups** are happy to help them, for a price: "lobbies" for specific corporations, industries (like tobacco or steel), and constituencies (like small businesses, gun owners, or teachers) contribute to the campaigns of Congresspeople and other elected officials, generally as a reward or an incentive for certain votes or positions. These organizations, especially the non-corporate ones who can't compete in the contribution race, can pull their members together and swamp Congressional offices with calls, letters, and reasons to favor their cause. In the mid-'70s, concern over the power of rich people and corporations led to a law limiting individual giving; the law, in turn, led to **Political Action Com-**

mittees (PACs), organizations that collect and disperse contributions. Congressional incumbents (especially in the House) are more likely than not to get reelected, so PACs like to give to them rather than to their challengers; this in turn widens incumbents' financial edge, making their re-election even more likely.

Arts and Culture

ARCHITECTURE

Pierre L'Enfant's design for central Washington was meant to be a holistic work of art—this unified vision is most evident on a map. The L'Enfant plan designates the Capitol building as D.C.'s architectural focus; low government buildings with similar façades were supposed to flank the broad avenues, making most of Washington's vistas converge on the Congress and the dome above it. L'Enfant also expected—and got—a plethora of trees all over the city (not to mention those in Rock Creek Park). The National Mall was to be a central promenade, leading from the Capitol to some sort of Washington Monument, with trees on either side.

The international metropolis that is now D.C. is a modern testament to the Neoclassical notions sweeping the late 18th-century Western world. In 1755, Johann Joachim Wincklemann's *Thoughts on the Imitation of Greek Works* was published; Wincklemann advocated the Greek aesthetic not only as a way of emulating the beauty of Greek art, but also as a way to appropriate Greek "noble simplicity and calm grandeur" in all aspects of life. What words better epitomize that which a nation's capital strives to be?

Evidently, D.C.'s early architects felt similarly. They self-consciously designed a republic—in their eyes, the most important one since the Romans'—whose Federal style unapologetically echoed Athens and Rome with columns, pediments, friezes, and a quarry's worth of marble. Many of these designs—William Thornton's original Capitol and James Hoban's White House, for example—were selected in anonymous competitions that, for the most part, involved amateur planners. The mid-1800s saw the advent of the professional architect; the new breed was more interested in modern European than in ancient Greek models, and many of their works were private homes or churches. Among these progressives was Benjamin Latrobe, whose St. John's Church and Decatur House (near the White House) were models of sophistication and outstanding design.

Boss Shepherd (in charge 1871-74) sunk megabucks into new sewers, paved roads, and trees. He also paved the road to Victorian excess by authorizing A.B. Mullet's State, War, and Navy Building (now the Old Executive Office Building); the gingerbread windows delight tourists now, but the severe Neoclassicists of the early 1900s were understandably underwhelmed, and attempted to have the building demolished. While the O.E.O. building goes overboard on ornamentation, the Smithsonian's Arts and Industries Building is a garish flood of contrasting colors. The Library of Congress's Jefferson Building, the magnificent Pension building (now the National Building Museum), and the Old Post Office are more traditional examples of the dignified Victorian style.

The budget-inspired freeze on building that followed Boss Shepherd's fall from power thawed around the turn of the century, when Daniel Burnham brought the Beaux Arts style to Washington. The McMillan Commission revamped Washington's public spaces and commissioned Burnham's Union Station. The Commission also proposed the Lincoln Memorial, which heralded a neo-Neoclassicism: the Greek aesthetic was amplified and made somewhat more sparse. John Russell Pope, the undisputed emperor of '30s and '40s pseudo-Greco-Roman building, made his masterpiece the domed West Building of the National Gallery of Art on the Mall.

When the dust of World War II cleared, European avant-garde architects had settled in America and brought with them the International-style office building, unaffectionately nicknamed the "glass box." As perpetually was the case, Washington was about a decade behind New York City in the celebration of new architectural trends.

D.C. firms strived to blend international modernism's clean lines and brutal simplicity with the monumental marbleness of already-extant buildings; the Kennedy Center and the National Geographic building are two fairly successful examples. I.M. Pei's popular 1978 East Wing (of the National Gallery of Art) obeys the letter of modernist dictates (big planes, no ornaments, no paint, exposed structural elements) but certainly violates its spirit—the quite beautiful array of glass and white triangles was emphatically not designed for efficiency. In this it heralded the postmodern architecture that earnestly migrated from New York in the late '80s. Postmodern buildings rewrite old styles in modernism's plainer, planar vocabulary, with unusually shaped windows (for example) set into two-color blocks of sheer granite; the Canadian embassy, which puts Greek elements where the Greeks would never think to put them, is certainly the best "postmodern" example now standing in D.C. A few especially nice postmodern offices stand among mediocre older buildings at 20th and M St. NW (at the northwest corner) and along K St.

A few considerations make Washington's urban plan unusual. The most obvious is the height limit—roughly the elevation of the Capitol dome and the Washington monument: approximately 13 stories. On one hand, this results in office buildings that, in order to be of sufficient size, are horizontally sprawling and ugly; on the other hand, downtown always affords a view of the sky and the Capitol dome. A number of 20th-century buildings have had to occupy awkward acute angles where avenues and circles or numbered or lettered streets intersect; there are as many solutions to this dilemma as there are angles (though the East Wing and an otherwise boring office building—at the corner of Dupont Circle, Connecticut, and P St. NW—provide rather interesting solutions). Architects of new embassies have had to decide to what extent the building should fit into Washington, or instead, to what extent it should reflect the style and culture of its respective nation; the Canadian Embassy succeeds at the former, the British and Japanese at the latter. However, the omnipresent Classical vocabulary of domes, columns, long steps, and such, poses to every architect the choice of aesthetic conformity versus deviation; the city's inevitable monumental air and the overriding Roman grid plan will forever dictate architectural endeavors to some extent.

VISUAL ARTS

The body politic's craze to commemorate has burdened D.C. with a profusion of public art. Eagles squint from cornices, workers labor heroically from the neo-Hellenic friezes above public buildings, and generals and statesmen gesture from horseback in almost every traffic circle. Most public statues date from between the 1870s, when public art remembered Civil War figures, and World War II, when the government found more urgent financial demands. Though few of these statues are worthy of a Phidias, many still merit interest: some bear curious anecdotes (like Gen. Scott in Scott Circle or Benito Juarez on Virginia Ave. NW), others have curious inscriptions (like the modern memorial on Roosevelt Island), and still others may even impart a little historical knowledge. Aesthetic delights are found in Lafayette Park and at the Grant Memorial near the Capitol, the statue of Robert Emmet near Dupont Circle, and the Adams Memorial in Rock Creek Cemetery.

The public memorial as a hybrid art form, half sculpture and half architecture, may have reached its quintessence in Washington. In actuality just an outgrowth of the often-employed outdoor statue idea, memorials give designers more room to innovate and viewers more space to contemplate. (Though he ordered trees removed so that he could watch the Jefferson Memorial being built, FDR said he wanted his own monument to be no bigger than his desk.) D.C.'s monuments are concentrated west of the Mall, where the Washington Monument and the Lincoln and Jefferson memorials lurk; designs range from neoclassical to the spare self-reflection of the Vietnam Veterans Memorial, the simplest and most affecting piece of outdoor art in D.C. Since 1986, the government has laid down the law on future monuments: the honoree must have been dead for at least 25 years, three commissions must approve the project, and the construction must not use federal funds.

Collector Duncan Phillips's museum was showing off modern art while New York's MoMA was still just a building fund, but D.C. had no indigenous painters of note until a generation later, when Kenneth Noland's clean-lined abstractions, Gene Davis's parallel stripes, and the experimental canvases of critics' darling Morris Louis were said to form the Washington Color School.

Though it's not a hotbed of visual innovation (blame it on the Republicans), Washington nevertheless boasts world-renowned museum collections. The West Wing of the National Gallery of Art presents the work of masters from Giotto to Raphael to Vermeer. Twentieth-century and touring exhibitions go up in the Gallery's Pei-faced East Wing. The Hirshhorn's cylindrical form is powered by two engines: contemporary art and 20th-century sculpture, one indoors, the other outside in the adjacent Sculpture Garden. Beyond the Mall are the Phillips Collection (the U.S.'s first modern art museum), the Corcoran Gallery (housing 19th- and 20th-century American art), the Renwick (American crafts), and the National Museum of American Art (see **Museums and Galleries,** page 184).

MUSIC

Washington tunes began inauspiciously with John Philip Sousa, who led the Marine Corps Marching Band from the 1880s to the 1900s. Peppy Sousa taught the band to play, then initiated the bevy of military brass concerts and parades that toot, stomp, and honk near the Mall to this day. Things later began to swing: the Howard Theater and other jazz venues cultivated a string of Washington artists, most notably the immortal Duke Ellington. Jazz songstresses from D.C. include Roberta Flack and Shirley Horne; the latter still performs in District clubs. Classical music performances began to thrive with the building of the Kennedy Center, which gave the National Symphony Orchestra, the Washington Ballet, as well as many lesser musical groups a home as shiny and multi-chambered as a nautilus shell.

D.C. didn't go far in rock-and-roll until punk touched down in the early '80s; then, inspired by charismatic (and short-lived) bands like Minor Threat, "straightedge" punks shaved their heads and drew Xs on their hands to declare their abstinence from drugs and alcohol. Where rock elsewhere affected combativeness with leather, studs, and long-winded guitar fuzz, D.C. punks, some as young as 13, packaged honest teen angst in two-minute songs. As the decade wore on, they combined their no-nonsense attitude with real political activism: all-ages shows in rented halls to benefit the likes of the Washington Free Clinic and the American Civil Liberties Union are the best venues for what's left of "hard core," as the music is and was called. The winnowing of the punk moment has made space for a profusion of new sounds: bratty feminist girl-rockers and unrepentant old-time punks have taken to heavy percussion (performed at outdoor festivals at monuments or on the Supreme Court steps), while a new generation of bands is quietly reinventing the New Wave, running record labels out of their basements (most notably Tsunami and the Simple Machines label), and sparring with Olympia, Washington, and Providence, Rhode Island, for the title of capital of the International Pop Underground. The city recoiled when d.c. space, a punk-friendly fixture of the D.C. scene, retired on New Year's Day, 1992. The 9:30 Club and The Black Cat pick up some of the slack; after a show there, you can join the performers during their 3am snacks at Dante's on 14th St. The 200-seat Capitol Ballroom promises to expand the size and scale of the D.C. scene. Record-hunters may seek out Dischord Records vinyl by Scream, Gray Matter, or Rites of Spring, or LPs by Government Issue; important bands still around include Wingtip Sloat, Circus Lupus, Unrest, and nationally known Fugazi.

Though rap music is as strong here as in most urban centers (Basehead lives in SE), the indigenous dance sound of D.C. is go-go. Repeated efforts to turn go-go music from a D.C. thing into a national craze have failed; some say producers and promoters have failed to do it justice, while others maintain that the experience of live go-go just can't be copied on vinyl. The best go-go bands blend African percussion and instrumental virtuosity with the trimmings of rap; some have over ten performers. One premier act, E.U. (once known as Experience Unlimited), went national with their dance hit "Da Butt." Other perennials include Rare Essence and Chuck Brown and the Soul Searchers. Hear live go-go outdoors at festivals like Malcolm X Day, Marvin Gaye Day, or Adams-Morgan Day, or call CJ the TJ (telephone jockey), at 543-GOGO for chill recorded listings of the week's performances. For more information on clubs' music scene, see **Nightlife & Entertainment** (p. 207).

THEATER AND FILM

Washington has had professional theater for a long time, and that's not counting Congress or the President. The "Washington Theatre" in 1821 and the National Theatre in 1835 started a trend that flowered over a hundred years later, when Zelda Fichandler's Arena Stage gave birth to the American regional-theater movement. The movement in turn spawned venues such as Ford's Theater, which was running a spectacular *Our American Cousin* when John Wilkes Booth shot President Lincoln in April of 1865. Mounting new productions with its own repertory company, Arena succeeded hundreds of miles from Broadway, launching (among other shows) Lorraine Hansberry's *Raisin in the Sun*. The elegant Warner Theater has gone from vaudeville to rap to Sondheim-type stage productions (after renovations and under new management) over the past century. While the multi-performing-art Kennedy Center allures, the cup of small-stage innovation has passed to the theater district of 14th St. NW, where several young groups experiment their hearts out.

The **movies** haven't passed D.C. by either: Jimmy Stewart (*Mr. Smith Goes to Washington*) tried to make it honest, Klaatu (*The Day the Earth Stood Still*) landed a spaceship in it, the journalists of *Broadcast News* seemed to ooze right through the city, and *Dave* took over for the look-alike President. Robert Redford and Dustin Hoffman played out the events of 1972-73 in *All the President's Men.* Clint Eastwood enacted what should have happened on November 22, 1963, in a classic of Monday-morning filmmaking (*In the Line of Fire*). Other recent flicks include John Grisham's *The Pelican Brief,* starring Denzel Washington and Julia Roberts, and *No Way Out,* starring Kevin Costner (see No Way Down, p. 146). Most recently, Michael Douglas braved widowerhood in the White House and the controversy due to his being smitten with political adversary Annette Bening in *The American President;* while aliens descended upon D.C. in an immense, city-sized spacecraft and proceeded to blow up 1600 Pennsylvania Ave. and its vicinity in the 1996 summer blockbuster *Independence Day.*

Haunted Hangout

The Exorcist, starring Linda Blair as a teenage possessed by Satan, was filmed in Georgetown, and the stairway site of the movie's most gruesome scenes (a few priests were thrown from the ledge) remain haunted—by local college students.

LITERATURE

> *The White House of future poems, of dreams, of dramas, there in the soft and copious moon—*
>
> —Walt Whitman, Specimen Days

More than a pit stop but less than Parnassus, D.C. has briefly inspired and housed many of America's famous writers. Though British novelists like Dickens and Trollope have left vitriolic records of their visits to Washington, the first 1st-class scribbler to settle in the capital was poet Walt Whitman, whose years of volunteer work as a Union Army nurse are recorded in his memoir *Specimen Days.* Whitman's Lincoln elegies and his Civil War poems (collectively titled *Drum-Taps*) were surely influenced by his D.C. days, when cattle milled about the Washington Monument and Union encampments filled the avenues. (Contemporaries recall the poet as skilled and tender in his care of the wounded.) Frederick Douglass lived in Anacostia when he finished his last autobiography in the 1870s and '80s. Initially ignored by the masses, the book has been studied as fine literature in recent years. It records the trials and experiences of the former slave, abolitionist, orator, and diplomat. The historian and grumpy belletrist Henry Adams "took it for granted" (in his own words) that he would someday live in the White House, just like his grandpa John Quincy Adams; he didn't get the White House, but he did get a well-appointed house nearby where he and his wife gathered diplomats and historians such as Henry Cabot Lodge and George Bancroft in a turn-of-the-century literary salon.

More poetry, and perhaps better writing, emanated from the African-American community in the early 20th century, when the famous Harlem Renaissance established a D.C. outpost around U St., through Shaw and in LeDroit Park. Ballad-poet Paul Dunbar's move to D.C. was emulated by Langston Hughes and Jean (*Cane*) Toomer. The MuSoLit club gave black intelligentsia a gathering place. Later poems of black Washington emanated from residents Sterling Brown, E. Ethelbert Miller and native daughter Elizabeth Alexander. Other poets made strange pilgrimages to see *Cantos* verse-maker Ezra Pound, who was confined in St. Elizabeth's for criminal insanity. Literary lions and doves converged on the city for the 1968 March on the Pentagon, led by novelist Norman Mailer and by Robert Lowell, whose poem "July in Washington" may be the best ever written about the city. Since World War II, the Library of Congress has attracted important poets for the two-year job of Poetry Consultant; in the mid-'80s the title changed to Poet Laureate (held now by Pulitzer Prize winner Rita Dove). The post has made the LoC the only place for consistently high-class literary events in Washington. More demotic art forms have found Washington more congenial: popular interest in the machinations of government spawned its very own genre, the "Washington novel."

If, like the ancient Greeks and Romans, English-speaking peoples counted persuasive writing as literature, Washington has produced a whole genre of American writing. The memorable line (now known as the soundbite) has flourished here at least since Daniel Webster's toast "Liberty and Union, now and forever, one and inseparable." Today's equivalents sound more folksy than sonorous, but Presidents and their speechwriters still specialize in the ringing aphorism. FDR said "We have nothing to fear but fear itself" when he promised Americans a New Deal. Truman convinced Congress to send millions in postwar aid to Europe partly by invoking the name of its planner, General George Marshall. Martin Luther King, Jr., came to D.C. to tell the world he had a dream. The past two decades of political follies have brought a new irony to political talk; though more dough than ever goes to media gurus, the most memorable lines are those that ring false, from Nixon's laughable "I am not a crook" to Reagan's summary of Iran-contra: "Mistakes were made." Two more recent entries, Bush's "Read my lips...no new taxes" and President Clinton's "The era of big government is over" prove that words and deeds rarely go hand in hand. Nevertheless, no matter for what you think the U.S. stands, Washington has always been *the* place in which to scribble a speech, stand up, and be heard.

The Statehood Debate

> *It is not easy to ever estimate the influence of the people of the District of Columbia. Aside from American women, they are now the only people in the Republic denied the elective franchise.*
>
> —Frederick Douglass, "Lecture on the Nation's Capital" (1877)

Although District residents have been able to vote for Presidential electors since 1961 and have enjoyed limited home rule from 1973 to 1995, many Washingtonians feel that they are being denied the rights due to them as American citizens. Although they must pay an income tax imposed by Congress, District residents have no representation in the Senate and only a non-voting delegate, Eleanor Holmes Norton (D), in the House. Congress is still able, and frequently willing, to meddle in Washington's local affairs, blocking, for example, changes in D.C.'s sex laws and preventing the District from imposing a tax on commuters from Virginia and Maryland. That Congress is

Financial Woes

Since the beginning of Home Rule in 1973, running Washington has been a financial matter. The city has had a budget deficit since the first years under the Home Rule Charter, when a ban on taxing commuters made two-thirds of the salaries paid within the District untaxable. During the mid-1970s, Mayor Marion Barry used deep cuts and later extravagant spending to balance the city budget and create surpluses. Barry's expansionary fiscal policy of increasing the number of workers and contractors on the government payroll would have worked if those beneficiaries had remained within the city limits and paid income tax on their salaries. Taking advantage of the commuter tax ban, most made the move across the District line to the cheaper real estate of Maryland and Virginia, taking any hopes of a broader tax base with them.

Barry's successor, Sharon Pratt Kelly, took office with the promise that she would undo the financial damage Barry had done. Her spending record, however, was no better. In 1994, the city deficit hovered around an unprecedented $700 million. With the loss of Home Rule and D.C.'s apparent incapability to support itself financially, the District's statehood vision is looking even dimmer.

mostly white and the District population mostly black casts additional doubt on the justice of the arrangement.

Some Washingtonians feel that the only sure path to equality is for most of the current District to become the 51st state, leaving a small enclave of federal buildings as the Constitutionally mandated federal district. Some say it's too small, yet more people live in the District than in the full-fledged states of Alaska or Wyoming. Thinking along these lines, members of the small Statehood Party have advocated statehood since 1969. Their efforts peaked in the early 1980s when D.C. voters called for a convention to write a constitution for the proposed state and later approved the resulting document. Since then, however, scandals in the D.C. government, a declining population, the recent loss of home rule, and dwindling interest among Washingtonians have lessened the chances that a 51st star will be added to the flag anytime soon.

The Media

As a rule, the newspaper correspondents in Washington were unfriendly, and the lobby sceptical.

—Henry Adams, The Education of Henry Adams (1902)

Where industrial cities might depend on oil or ore, Washington depends on information. Politicians prepare proposals, release reactions, and seek soundbites for newspapers and TV before scouring the evening's news to find out if the photographer managed to get their good side. Ambitious bureaucrats and White House insiders conduct their in-fighting through press statements, unattributed quotations, "leaks," and surreptitious traffic with journalists ("Sources close to the President said today..."). And the government needs hard facts on everything from rutabagas to rent rates just to make its regulations and mete out funds. All this makes D.C. a veritable ant farm of journalists.

READ ALL ABOUT IT

Washington papers began as political organs for individual politicians. President Woodrow Wilson got hip to the power of the press in the 1910s and began to take reporters' questions at semi-regular conferences. FDR wowed reporters with weekly conferences and regular access, though he also bypassed them and addressed America directly in his radio "fireside chats." JFK coddled reporters (and consequently improved his press), but journalism became more adversarial as race riots, youth movements, and the Vietnam War began to fracture America. Nixon spewed venom at the liberal press via Vice President Spiro Agnew and appointed inquisitional White

House "plumbers" to stop the leaks. Perhaps driven by indignation, investigative reporting reached new heights. In 1970, Daniel Ellsberg and the *New York Times* published the famous "Pentagon Papers," which exposed government duplicity about Vietnam. A few years later, *Washington Post* reporters Bob Woodward and Carl Bernstein forced President Nixon out of office with their revelation of the Watergate scandal. The White House's latest inhabitant, Bill Clinton, had a reputation for wowing reporters until he took office, at which point the media relations that had once soared began to sour. Nowadays, like rabid watchdogs, scores of fame/scandal-seeking journalists dredge up political sludge.

Today's Washington journalists often stay close to the government even as they try to dig up its dirt. Reporters must cultivate well-placed sources to hear the latest inside news; some say this makes the press inevitably partial. Op-ed pundits are as much a part of the sprawling permanent government as Congressional staffers or Pentagon bureaucrats. Televised press conferences let the President reward friendly journalists by calling on them for questions, though the Chief is sometimes tripped up by a sharp, unknown reporter. During and after the Reagan years, pundits worried that video charisma and sophisticated advertising would make political journalism irrelevant. And reporters complained of Pentagon "manipulation" during the bloody-on-one-side Persian Gulf war. Yet alongside the designer media firms, the made-for-TV statements, and non-events, the old-time religion of investigative journalism holds on to a mission and no small following.

In this town of news junkies, the **Washington Post** is the ubiquitous opiate, a newspaper of record with comprehensive, if not always incisive, political, national, and international coverage. Though the liberal *Post* hopes someday to repeat its Watergate glory days, its most obvious influence of late has been local. Disgraced mayor Marion Barry rode to power on the white votes the *Post's* endorsement brought him in 1978; as if to make up for it, a *Post* endorsement spurred the 1991 election of relative underdog Sharon Pratt Kelly as the new mayor of D.C. In the most recent Mayoral election, the *Post* backed Kelly in the primary and she lost; they then committed the liberal sin of backing Republican candidate Carol Schwartz in the election–all to avoid showing support for guess who? Alas, Barry is back in power. The Metro section covers local news, festivals, and shootings. Style is a Washington institution all by itself, a definitive fluffy gossip sheet that is read religiously by all in the know. Sunday's *Outlook* bursts with political opinion, while Friday's Weekend section helps readers (especially families) decide what to do with the next two days.

The Washington **City Paper** (Baltimore has one too) is a thick, free, "alternative" weekly distributed (on Fri.) to vending machines and stores around town. *City Paper* provides excellent local investigative reporting, features, and more comprehensive listings of the arts in D.C. (especially theater and popular music) than the staid *Post* seems able to provide. (Use the *Post's* movie listings, but rely on *City Paper's* reviews and club listings.) The paper occasionally offers special coupons for clubs. *City Paper* also has a Classifieds section—including the city's best personals (if you're into that) and a large number of apartment and roommate listings.

The **Washington Times,** a conservative daily left over from the early '80s "Reagan Revolution," has since lost momentum due to staff shake-ups, hard-right columnists, and widespread awareness that Rev. Sun Myung Moon's Unification Church funds the paper (hence its nickname, *The Moonie Times*). But once in a blue moon, the *Times* does find local stories that the *Post* has missed.

Some national news-and-views magazines base themselves in Washington. The best known is the highly respected weekly **The New Republic,** which once carried the standard for American liberalism and now devotes a fair share of its pages to mounting a passive-aggressive campaign against the President and favorite son Al Gore. *TNR* prints news analysis and arts pieces from all over, including a roving "Diarist" column and a by-line by Andrew Sullivan.

The smaller, more wonkish **Washington Monthly** likes to boast that it broke famous stories, like Mayor Barry's corruption, National Security Council misdeeds, and design flaws in the space shuttle, years before better-known pages got hold of them. The scrappy *Monthly* is a favorite of aspiring policymakers; the magazine keeps tabs on the bureaucracy, but not always on the city as a whole.

Away from the bright lights of national news, Washington's communities run their own papers. The daily **Washington Afro-American** covers black D.C. in a friendly, interested way, with attention to individual citizens' achievements. The well-written, free weekly **Washington Blade,** stacked in various stores (especially around Dupont Circle), is the strong gay and lesbian community's paper, with articles, listings, an events calendar, and a directory of gay professionals.

If it's Congress you're interested in, read **Roll Call,** which prints gossip, news, and an events calendar for members of the House, the Senate, and their lucky staffers twice a week. Free **Intermission** serves Washington's smaller theaters. Monthly **Washingtonian** is almost the neighborhood magazine of the affluent suburbs; plenty of articles on celebrities and real estate mix with interesting D.C. trivia, surprising, money-saving tidbits, and lots of lists ("top 10 delis," etc.). **Regardie's** magazine mixes business news with gossip and satire.

The Capitol Hill neighborhood cleans up weekly with **Hill Rag,** an area paper distributed all over downtown. The **In Towner** covers local issues (zoning and crime, for example) for Dupont Circle, Adams-Morgan, and points east (Scott and Logan Circles) and west (Cleveland Park). The **Georgetowner** does the same for its namesake. The monthly **Old Town Crier** runs news and restaurant and gallery listings for Old Town Alexandria. A hip, bold, funny, informative, and opinionated new paper, **Generation Next** is nothing short of a brilliant representation of 20-something interests and concerns. Search for a free copy at establishments all over Dupont Circle. Events listings of interest to the tourist community congregate in **Go** and **Where,** slick, free magazines distributed at downtown hotels, where even a scruffy budget traveler can pick one up. Or stop by one of the friendly neighborhood D.C. libraries:

Martin Luther King, Jr. Public Library, 901 G St. NW (727-1111, book info. 727-0321). Metro: Metro Center. The main branch of D.C.'s public-library system. Open Mon., Wed.-Thurs. 10am-7pm, Tues. 10am-9pm, Fri.-Sat. 10am-5:30pm.

Library of Congress, 1st St. SE (707-5000, recorded events schedule 707-8000), between East Capitol and Independence Ave. Metro: Capitol South. The vast collection, including rare items, is open to anyone of college age or older with a legitimate research purpose. It's a closed-stack library, so they'll bring the books to you. It's also a non-circulating library, so you must do your reading there. Most reading rooms open Mon.-Fri. 8:30am-9:30pm, Sat. 8:30am-6pm.

Garfield, Schmarfield

No one can deny that there exists an inherent hilarity in the goings-on of government. Political silliness (purported to be serious) is the fodder for many a comic strip set in the District, and the supposed "intellectually witty" humor of **political cartoons** has given rise to a modern art form. Caricature and satire pack a commentative wallop via a "Doonesbury" punchline: Gary Trudeau's overtly political "Mr. Butts" mocks the legislation surrounding the tobacco industry, while more personal jabs include an "invisible" President Bush and spelunkers braving the netherworld of President Reagan's brain.

Washingtonian magazine recently named Peter Steiner (featured in the *Washington Times* and regularly in *The New Yorker*), "Best Cartoonist"; Steiner's one-panel sketches exploit the humor in everything from marriage relations to generation gaps to the corporate realm. Patrick M. Reynolds adheres more to District-specific laughs—his "Flashbacks" (*Washingtonian*'s "Best Comic-Strip Idea" award-winner) in the *Washington Post*'s Sunday comics, is a strip of historical vignettes about Washington that both tickles *and* teaches. Nevertheless, even Washingtonians must admit that Garfield the Cat will always be funnier than Garfield the President.

Folger Shakespeare Library, 201 East Capitol St. SE (544-4600). Houses the world's largest collection of Shakespeareana, and hosts exhibits related to Shakespeare and his culture. Only those working on a Ph.D. thesis may access the books. Exhibits open Mon.-Sat. 10am-4pm; library open Mon.-Fri. 8:45am-4:45pm.

ON THE RADIO (AND TV)

Not all points can be made in print, and in a city where image is everything, visual media matter as much or more than the written word. Due to their proximity to government activity, local television networks and radio stations sometimes beat national ones to newsworthy stories.

National TV shows filmed in Washington are not usually the studio audience type. Political programs like MacNeil/Lehrer's hour of interviews and the McLaughlin Group's heated discussions aren't exactly the spectator sort, and regardless, if you really want to know what's going on in Congress, you can tune in to the nonstop CNN and C-SPAN coverage (accompanied by free commentary) for play-by-play at most Capitol Hill area bars and restaurants. Or, sit in on Congress yourself; see **Congressional Chambers,** (p. 113).

After five years of going AWOL, **Top 40 returns** to Washington, D.C. **WXTR-FM** (104.1) has dropped its 15-month-old '70s agenda o' disco and taken on "straight-ahead, pop CHR [contemporary hit radio]." If you prefer news or more genre-inclined tunes, try these Washington favorites: **AM:** 630, **WMAL** (news/talk/sports); 730, **WBZS** (financial news); 1260, **WWDC** (big band/original hits); 1300, **WJFK** (talk/jazz; FM 106.7); 1500, **WTOP** (news); 1580, **WPGC** (hip hop; FM 95.5). **FM:** 88.5, **WAMU** (NPR; news/talk/music); 97.1, **WASH** (adult contemporary); 98.7, **WMZQ** (country); 99.1, **WHFS** (modern rock); 99.5 **WGAY** (soft adult contemporary); 100.3 **WBIG** (oldies); 103.5, **WGMS** (classical); 107.3, **WRQX** ('70s, '80s, and '90s mix).

Washington's TV stations and affiliations are: Channel 4, **WRC/NBC;** Channel 5, **WTTG/Fox;** Channel 7, **WJLA/ABC;** Channel 9, **WUSA/CBS;** Channel 20, **WDCA/Ind.;** Channel 26, **WETA/PBS.**

Essentials

An elegant urban space with an impeccable public transit system, D.C. is hardly a mysterious city. With the exception of government, Washington's primary business is tourism; visitors are barraged with an overwhelming amount of free information from travel offices, tourist information centers, and special-interest organizations. The following, however, is information you will most likely want to have in hand prior to your District jaunt.

PLANNING YOUR TRIP

When To Go

With blue skies, soft winds, and rich landscapes, only an ingrate would complain of the few admittedly difficult months.
—Federal Writers Project, District of Columbia

Being in the right place at the right time can make all the difference to a traveler. D.C., as well as the rest of the U.S., is rife with tourists from **Memorial Day** to **Labor Day** (May 26 to Sept. 1 in 1997); expect things to be in full, photo-op swing. However, D.C.'s off-season is appealing; hotels might be cheaper, sights might be less crowded, and the weather will most definitely be more comfortable.

Washington weather tends to be pleasantly mild, with the exception of those few unbearably hot and humid summer months. The opposite extreme—sub-zero temperatures—is a novelty. (See the **Appendix: Climate,** on p. 291.)

If you are nonetheless unfazed by the summertime broil, and more inclined to organize your itinerary according to D.C.'s ubiquitous seasonal festivals and annual celebrations, see the **Appendix: Special Events,** on p. 292.

On the Rocks

D.C.'s summer humidity is legendarily repellent; a French foreign minister blamed the heat when he killed himself here in the 1890s (the suicide note explained his aversion to iced drinks, one he shared with President Zachary Taylor, who died of a massive brain embolism upon drinking a mint julep one fateful day in 1850).

Useful Information

GOVERNMENT INFORMATION OFFICES

General information for foreigners planning to travel to the U.S. is provided by the **United States Travel & Tourism Administration,** Department of Commerce, 14th St. and Constitution Ave. NW, Washington, D.C., 20230 (202-482-4003 or 202-482-3811). The USTTA has branches in Australia, Canada, and the United Kingdom; contact the Washington office for details on the branch in your country.

TRAVEL ORGANIZATIONS

American Automobile Association (AAA) Travel Related Services, 1000 AAA Dr. (mail stop 100), Heathrow, FL 32746-5080 (407-444-8411). Provides road maps and travel guides, emergency road services, travel services, and auto insurance (free for members, small fee for nonmembers). For emergency road services, call 800-222-4357; to become a member, call 800-926-4222 for the nearest office.

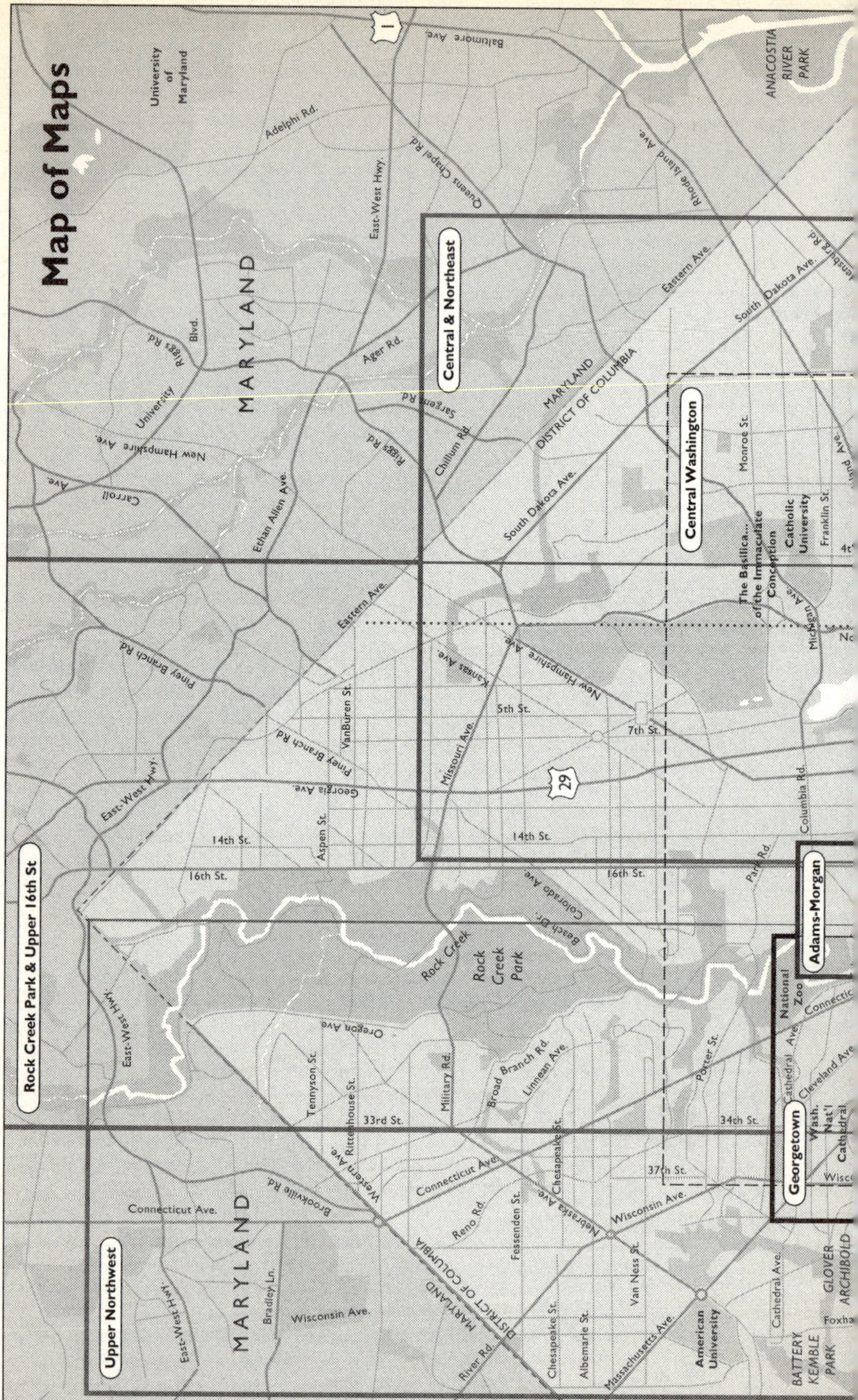
Map of Maps
Upper Northwest
Rock Creek Park & Upper 16th St
Central & Northeast
Central Washington
Adams-Morgan
Georgetown
MARYLAND
DISTRICT OF COLUMBIA
University of Maryland
Rock Creek Park
American University
Catholic University
The Basilica of the Immaculate Conception
National Zoo
Wash. Nat'l Cathedral
ANACOSTIA RIVER PARK
BATTERY KEMBLE PARK
GLOVER ARCHIBOLD

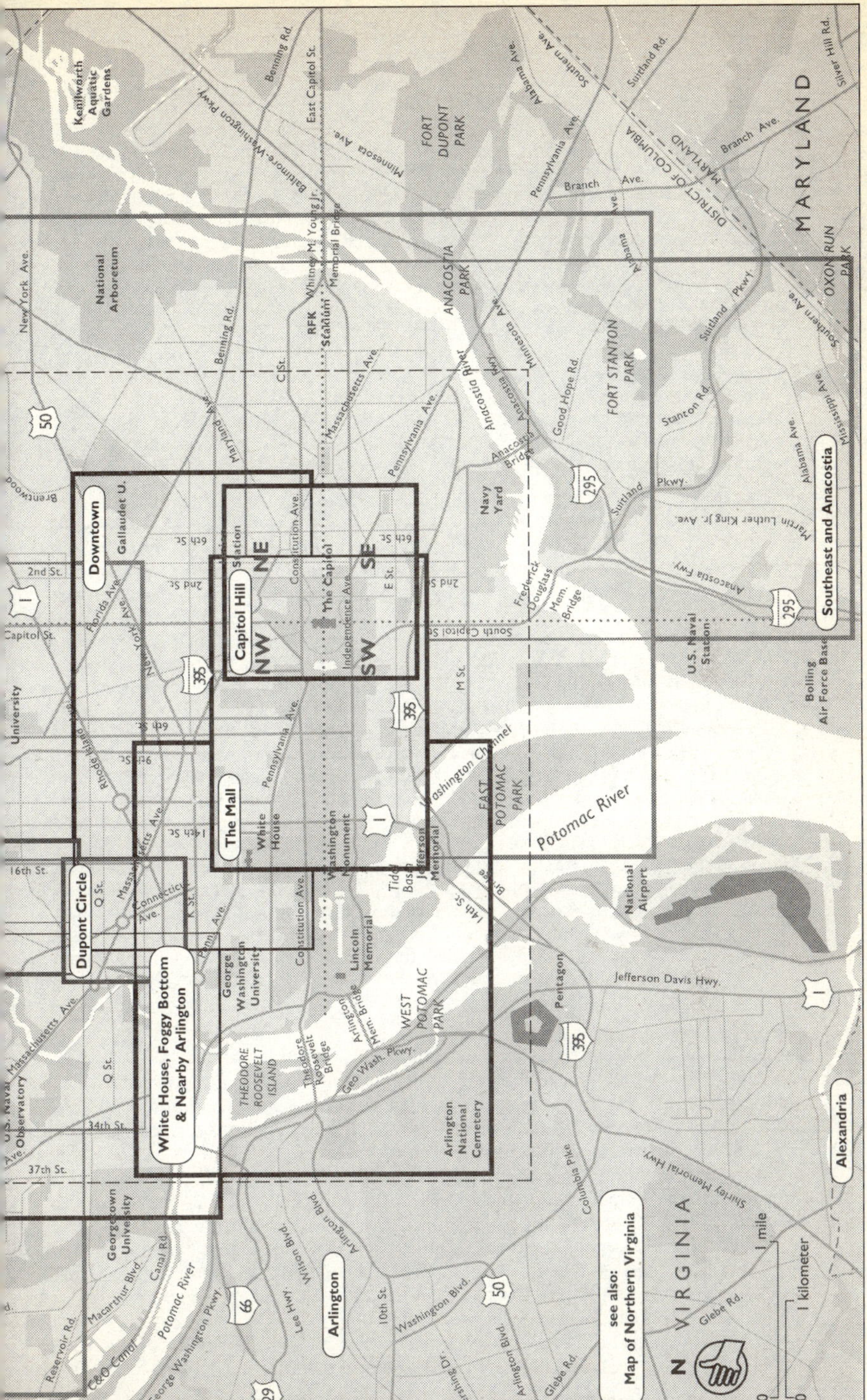
Downtown
Capitol Hill
The Mall
Dupont Circle
White House, Foggy Bottom & Nearby Arlington
Southeast and Anacostia
Arlington
Alexandria
see also:
Map of Northern Virginia
MARYLAND
VIRGINIA
DISTRICT OF COLUMBIA
MARYLAND
Kenilworth Aquatic Gardens
National Arboretum
FORT DUPONT PARK
ANACOSTIA PARK
FORT STANTON PARK
OXON RUN PARK
RFK Stadium
Navy Yard
U.S. Naval Station
Bolling Air Force Base
National Airport
Pentagon
Arlington National Cemetery
THEODORE ROOSEVELT ISLAND
WEST POTOMAC PARK
EAST POTOMAC PARK
Potomac River
Anacostia River
Washington Channel
Tidal Basin
Jefferson Memorial
Lincoln Memorial
Washington Monument
White House
The Capitol
George Washington University
Georgetown University
Gallaudet U.
U.S. Naval Observatory
C&O Canal
NW
NE
SW
SE
Pennsylvania Ave.
Constitution Ave.
Independence Ave.
Massachusetts Ave.
New York Ave.
Rhode Island Ave.
Florida Ave.
Connecticut Ave.
Jefferson Davis Hwy.
George Washington Pkwy.
Baltimore-Washington Pkwy.
Martin Luther King Jr. Ave.
Anacostia Fwy.
Suitland Pkwy.
Benning Rd.
Minnesota Ave.
Alabama Ave.
Good Hope Rd.
Branch Ave.
Southern Ave.
Wilson Blvd.
Washington Blvd.
Arlington Blvd.
Columbia Pike
Shirley Memorial Hwy.
Glebe Rd.
Lee Hwy.
1 mile
1 kilometer
N

Council on International Educational Exchange (Council), 205 East 42nd St., New York, NY 10017-5706 (888-COUNCIL (268-6245); fax 212-822-2699; e-mail info@ciee.org; http://www.ciee.org). A private, nonprofit organization, Council administers work, volunteer, and academic programs around the world. They also offer identity cards, including the ISIC and the GO25, and a range of publications, including the magazine *Student Travels* (free). Call or write for more information.

Federation of International Youth Travel Organizations (FIYTO), Bredgade 25H, DK-1260 Copenhagen K, Denmark (tel. (45) 33 33 96 00; fax 33 93 96 76; e-mail mailbox@fiyto.org), is an international organization promoting educational, cultural, and social travel for young people. Members include language schools, educational travel companies, national tourist boards, accommodation centers, and others who serve students and young travelers. FIYTO sponsors the GO25 Card.

International Student Travel Confederation, Herengracht 479, 1017 BS Amsterdam, The Netherlands (tel. (31) 204 21 28 00; fax 204 21 28 10; http://www.istc.org; e-mail istcinfo@istc.org). The ISTC is a nonprofit confederation of student travel organizations whose focus is to develop, promote, and facilitate travel among young people and students. Member organizations include International Student Rail Association (ISRA), Student Air Travel Association (SATA), ISIS Travel Insurance, and the International Association for Educational and Work Exchange Programs (IAEWEP).

USEFUL PUBLICATIONS

In addition to this guide, Let's Go offers travelers the detailed, fold-out maps and handy, pocket-sized coverage of *Let's Go Map Guide: Washington, D.C.* ($7.95). Many mail-order shops offer books and supplies catering to special travel interests:

Adventurous Traveler Bookstore, P.O. Box 1468, Williston, VT 05495 (801-860-6776; fax 802-860-6607, or both at 800-282-3963; e-mail books@atbook.com; http://www.gorp.com/atbook.htm). Free 40-page catalogue upon request. Specializes in outdoor adventure travel books and maps for the U.S. and abroad.

Bon Voyage!, 2069 W. Bullard Ave., Fresno, CA 93711-1200 (800-995-9716, from abroad 209-447-8441, e-mail 70754.3511@compuserve.com). Annual mail-order catalog offers a range of products: books, travel accessories, luggage, electrical converters, maps, videos, and more. All merchandise may be returned for exchange or refund within 30 days of purchase, and prices are guaranteed (lower advertised prices will be matched and merchandise shipped free).

Rand McNally, 150 S. Wacker Dr., Chicago, IL 60606 (800-333-0136), publishes one of the most comprehensive road atlases of the U.S. and Canada. Available in their stores throughout the country, as well as most other bookstores, for $9.

Travel Books & Language Center, Inc., 4931 Cordell Ave., Bethesda, MD 20814 (800-220-2665; fax 301-951-8546; e-mail travelbks@aol.com). Sells over 75,000 items, including books, cassettes, atlases, dictionaries, and a wide range of specialty travel maps, Michelin maps, and beer maps of the U.S. Free catalogue upon request.

GETTIN' IT ONLINE :)

Along with everything else in the '90s, budget travel is moving rapidly into the information age. And with the growing user-friendliness of personal computers and internet technology, much of this information—including cyber-fodder geared toward your D.C. visit—can be yours with the click of a mouse.

There are a number of ways to access the **Internet.** Most popular are commercial internet providers, such as **America Online** (800-827-6394) and **Compuserve** (800-433-0389); in addition to offering an abundance of information, they offer services such as online airline reservations. Unlike the corporate gateways above, many employers and schools also offer free access to the Internet. The Internet itself can be used in many different forms, but the most useful to 'net-surfing budget travelers are the World Wide Web and Usenet newsgroups.

While navigating the 'net is not extraordinarily difficult, the system's overwhelming size can make trying to find useful information troublesome. If you have **World**

Wide Web (WWW) access, try one of the Web's search engines, such as **Webcrawler** (http://webcrawler.com) or **Yahoo** (http://www.yahoo.com/Entertainment/Travel); type in one or more keywords (e.g., "Baltimore travel") and the engine will generate a list of information headings. The **Student and Budget Travel Resource Guide** (http://asa.ugl.lib.umich.edu/chdocs/travel/travel-guide.html, or send e-mail to travel-guide@umich.edu) is among the most helpful Web pages; it has links to the CIA world factbook, consular information sheets, state travel advisories, Amtrak train schedules, the Internet Guide to Hostelling, a subway navigator, a jet lag diet, and more. **City.Net** (http://www.city.net) is a very impressive collection of regional- or city-specific web pages, providing links to web pages related to a specified geographic area. **USA CityLink** (http://www.usacitylink.com/citylink) has a similar service specifically for the United States.

Try **newsgroups** and **mailing lists** if you're really in the mood to browse; unfortunately, their "signal-to-noise ratio" (the percentage of useful information) is often depressingly low. **IRC** (Internet Relay Chat) allows real-time typed conversation with users around the world; from most UNIX systems, type "irc" and then "/help newuser." The following are some potentially informative web pages:

Dr. Memory's Favorite Travel Pages (http://www.access.digex.net/~drmemory/cyber_travel.html) is a great place to start surfing. Dr. Memory has links to hundreds of different web pages of interest to travelers of all kinds.

Rent-A-Wreck's Travel Links (http://www.rent-a-wreck.com/raw/travlist.html). For more information, see **Car Rental** (p. 63).

Big World Magazine (http://boss.cpcnet.com/personal/bigworld/bigworld.html), a budget travel 'zine with a web page and great travel page links.

The CIA World Factbook (http://www.odci.gov/cia/publications/95fact) offers the vital statistics of your destined country as well as an overview of a country's economy or an explanation of their system of government.

Shoestring Travel (http://www.stratpub.com) is a budget travel 'zine, with feature articles, links, user exchange, and accommodations information.

The Interactive Travel Guide (http://www.developnet.com/travel).

In addition to the web sites above, *Let's Go* also lists web sites whenever relevant, throughout the guide. Web sites come and go very rapidly; a promising web site may disappear within a week, and a new one may take its place. Thus, transcend the realm of worldly travel, and independently explore via cyber-travel as well.

Documents and Formalities

Foreign visitors who wish to travel to the United States should plan early in order to complete all the necessary paperwork in time. All foreign visitors are required to have a **passport, visitor's visa,** and **proof of intent to leave** (i.e., a round-trip airline ticket). Be sure to file all applications several months in advance of your planned departure dates. Remember, you are relying on government agencies to complete these transactions: a backlog in processing can spoil your plans.

EMBASSIES AND CONSULATES

Contact your nearest embassy or consulate to obtain information regarding visas and passports to the United States and Canada.

Embassies: Canada, 100 Wellington St., Ottawa, Ontario K1P 5T1 (613-238-5335).
United Kingdom, 24 Grosvenor Sq., London W1A 1AE (17 14 99 90 00).
Ireland, 42 Elgin Rd., Ballsbridge, Dublin 4 (353 16 68 71 22).
Australia, Moonah Place, Canberra, ACT 2600 (61 62 70 50 00).
New Zealand, 29 Fitzherbert Terr., Thorndon, Wellington (64 44 72 20 68).
South Africa, 225 Pretorius St., P.O. Box 9536, Pretoria (271 23 42 10 48).

Consulates: Canada, 1155 Saint Alexandre St., Montreal, Quebec, P.O. Box 65 Station Desjardins, H5Z 1Z1 (514-398-9695).
United Kingdom, Queen's House, 14 Queen St., BT1 6EQ, Belfast, N. Ireland (232 32 82 39).
Australia, MLC Centre, 19-29 Martin Place, 59th Fl., Sydney NSW 2000 (61 23 73 92 00).
New Zealand, 4th Fl., Yorkshire General Bldg., corner of Shortland and O'Connell St., P.O. Box 42022, Auckland 1 (64 93 03 27 24).
South Africa, P.O. Box 6773, Roggebaai 8012 (27 21 25 41 51).

PASSPORTS

Before you leave, be sure to photocopy the page of your passport that contains your photograph and identification, especially your passport number; this will help prove your citizenship and facilitate the issuing of a new passport if your old one is **lost** or **stolen**. Carry one copy in a safe place apart from your passport, and leave another copy at home. Consulates recommend that you also carry an expired passport or an official copy of your birth certificate. If you do lose your passport, notify the local police and the nearest embassy or consulate of your home government *immediately*. If you have your passport information, identification, and proof of citizenship, some consulates can issue a new passport within two days; of course, it may take weeks. In an emergency, ask for immediate temporary traveling papers which will permit you to return to your home country. Remember: your passport is a public document that belongs to your nation's government; you may have to surrender it to a foreign government official. If you don't get it back in a reasonable amount of time, inform the nearest embassy or consulate of your home country.

Canadian citizens may cross the U.S.-Canada border with only proof of citizenship (e.g. a birth certificate or a voter's registration card along with a photo ID; a driver's license alone will not be enough). Canadian citizens under 16 need notarized permission from both parents.

British citizens can apply in person or by mail to a passport office for a full passport, valid for 10 years (five years if under 16). The fee is UK£18. Children under 16 may be included on a parent's passport. Processing by mail takes four to six weeks. The London office offers same-day, walk-in rush service; arrive early.

Irish citizens can apply for a passport by mail to either the Department of Foreign Affairs, Passport Office, Setanta Centre, Molesworth St., Dublin 2 (01 671 16 33), or the Passport Office, 1A South Mall, Cork (021 627 25 25). Obtain an application at a local Garda station or request one from a passport office. The new Passport Express Service offers a two-week turnaround and is available for an extra IR£3. Passports cost IR£45 and are valid for 10 years. Citizens under 18 or over 65 can request a three-year passport that costs IR£10.

Australian citizens must apply for a passport in person at either a post office, a passport office, or an Australian diplomatic mission. An appointment may be necessary. A parent may file an application for a child under 18. Application fees are frequently adjusted. For more info, call toll-free (in Australia) 13 12 32.

New Zealand citizens can obtain passport application forms from travel agents or the Department of Internal Affairs Link Centre. Completed applications may be lodged at Link Centres and at overseas posts, or forwarded to the Passport Office, P.O. Box 10-526, Wellington, New Zealand. Processing time is 10 working days from receipt of a correctly completed application. The application fee for an adult is NZ$80 in New Zealand, and NZ$130 overseas. An urgent service is also available.

South African citizens can apply for a passport at any Home Affairs Office. Two photos, either a birth certificate or an identity book, and a SAR80 fee must accompany a completed application. Passports are valid for 10 years.

U.S. ENTRANCE REQUIREMENTS AND VISAS

Foreign visitors to the United States must have a **passport** and **visa/proof of intent to leave** (see below). A visa, stamped into a traveler's passport by the government of a host country, allows the bearer to stay in that country for a specified purpose and period of time. To obtain a U.S. visa, contact the nearest U.S. embassy or consulate.

Travelers from certain nations may enter the U.S. without a visa through the **Visa Waiver Pilot Program.** Visitors qualify as long as they are traveling for business or pleasure, are staying for 90 days or less, have proof of intent to leave (e.g., a returning plane ticket), a completed I-94W, and enter via particular air or sea carriers. Participating countries are Andorra, Austria, Belgium, Brunei, Denmark, Finland, France, Germany, Iceland, Italy, Japan, Lichtenstein, Luxembourg, Monaco, the Netherlands, New Zealand, Norway, San Marino, Spain, Sweden, Switzerland, and the UK. The U.S. consulate can provide the most recent list.

Most visitors obtain a **B-2,** or **"pleasure tourist," visa,** usually valid for six months. Don't lose your visa. If you do lose your I-94 form (arrival/departure certificate attached to your visa upon arrival), you can replace it at the nearest **U.S. Immigration and Naturalization Service** office, though it's very unlikely that the form will be replaced within your stay's duration. There are many different visa classifications; for specific, personal information, concerning **visa extensions,** for example, call your local INS; the number can be found in a local phone directory under Federal Government: Dept. of Justice: INS Dept. For a list of offices or other general information, write the INS Central Office, 425 I St. NW #5044, Washington, D.C. 20536 (recorded information: 202-514-4316). To obtain a visa request form, call 800-870-FORM (870-3676). The **Center for International Business and Travel (CIBT),** 25 W. 43rd St., Ste. 1420, New York, NY 10036 (800-925-2428 or 212-575-2811 from NYC), secures travel visas to and from all possible countries (service charge varies).

U.S. CUSTOMS: COMING...

Passing customs should be routine, but also taken seriously; don't joke around with customs officials or airport security personnel. It is illegal to transport perishable food like fruit and nuts, which may carry pests. Officials may seize articles made from certain protected species, such as your illegally purchased cowboy boots or furs. For information on carrying prescription drugs, see Alcohol and Drugs (p. 32).

You may bring the following into the U.S.: $200 in gifts; 200 cigarettes (1 carton) or 100 cigars; and personal belongings such as clothes and jewelry. Travelers ages 21 and over may also bring up to one liter of alcohol, although state laws may further restrict the amount of alcohol you can carry. Money (cash or traveler's checks) can be transported, but amounts over $10,000 must be reported. Customs officers may ask how much money you're carrying and your planned departure date in order to ensure that you'll be able to support yourself while in the U.S.

The **U.S. Customs Service,** 1301 Constitution Ave., Washington, D.C. 20229 (202-927-6724), publishes a helpful brochure entitled, *Know Before You Go*. It details the essentials regarding international travelers' customs requirements.

...AND GOING

Upon returning home, you must declare all articles you acquired abroad and pay a duty on the value of those articles that exceed the allowance established by your country's customs service. Goods and gifts purchased at duty-free shops abroad are not exempt from duty or sales tax at your point of return; you must declare these items, as well. "Duty-free" merely means that you need not pay a tax in the country of purchase. Each country allows the importation of specific amounts of alcohol, tobacco, gifts, and cash, but the quantities vary per country. Call or write to your customs service for specific information.

British citizens contact Her Majesty's Customs and Excise, Custom House, Nettleton Road, Heathrow Airport, Hounslow, Middlesex TW6 2LA (tel. (181) 910 37 44; fax (181) 910 37 65).

Irish citizens contact The Revenue Commissioners, Dublin Castle (tel. 679 27 77; fax 671 20 21; e-mail taxes@ior.ie; http:\\www.revenue.ie) or The Collector of Customs and Excise, The Custom House, Dublin 1.

Australian citizens contact Australian Customs Service, G.P.O. Box 8, Sydney NSW 2001 (tel. 02 213 20 00; fax 213 40 00).

New Zealand citizens consult the *New Zealand Customs Guide for Travelers,* available from customs offices, or contact New Zealand Customs, 50 Anzac Ave., Box 29, Auckland (09 377 35 20; fax 309 29 78).

South African citizens contact the Commissioner for Customs and Excise, Private Bag X47, Pretoria 0001, which distributes the pamphlet *South African Customs Information,* for visitors and residents who travel abroad. South Africans residing in the U.S. should contact the Embassy of South Africa, 3051 Massachusetts Ave. NW, Washington, D.C. 20008 (202-232-4400; fax 202-244-9417).

YOUTH, STUDENT, AND TEACHER IDENTIFICATION

Many U.S. establishments will honor an ordinary university ID for student discounts. Still, two main forms of student and youth identification are extremely useful, especially for the insurance packages that accompany them.

International Student Identity Card (ISIC) The 1997 card is valid from Sept. 1996-Dec. 1997 and costs $18. Flashing this card can procure you discounts for sights, theaters, museums, accommodations, train, ferry, and airplane travel, and more. Present the card wherever you go, and ask about discounts even when none are advertised. Applicants must be at least 12 years old and degree-seeking students of a secondary or post-secondary school. Because of the proliferation of phony ISICs, many airlines and some other services require other proof of student identity: a signed letter from the registrar attesting to your student status and stamped with the school seal and/or your school ID card. The card provides accident insurance of up to $3000 with no daily limit, as well as $100 per day of in-hospital care for up to 60 days. In addition, cardholders have access to a toll-free **Traveler's Assistance hotline** (800-626-2427 in U.S. and Canada, elsewhere call collect 713-267-2525) whose multilingual staff can provide help in medical, legal, and financial emergencies overseas. When you apply for the card, ask for a copy of the *International Student Identity Card Handbook,* which lists some available discounts. Most of the Budget Travel Agencies listed in *Let's Go* (see p. 43) issue the ISIC. The **International Teacher Identity Card (ITIC)** is $19 and offers similar but limited discounts, as well as medical insurance coverage. For more info. on these handy cards consult the organization's new web site (http:\\www.istc.org).

International Youth Discount Travel Card or **GO25 Card** is issued by the **Federation of International Youth Travel Organizations (FIYTO),** Bredgade 25H, 1260, Copenhagen K, Denmark, (tel. 45 33 33 96 00; fax 45 33 93 96 76). Issues a discount card to travelers who are under 26 but not students. This one-year card offers many of the same benefits as the ISIC, and most organizations that sell the ISIC also sell the GO25 Card. A brochure that lists discounts is free when you purchase the card. $10, CDN$15, UK£5 (without travel insurance), $16 (with insurance); prices subject to change.

INTERNATIONAL DRIVER'S PERMIT

Although not required in the U.S., the International Driving Permit (IDP) can smooth out difficulties with American police officers and serves as an additional piece of identification. A valid driver's license from your home country must always accompany the IDP. Your IDP must be issued in your own country before you depart; check with your national automobile association. Also make sure you have proper insurance (required by law). Some foreign driver's licenses are valid in the U.S. for up to one year; check before you leave.

Money Matters

CURRENCY AND EXCHANGE

The Greenback (the U.S. dollar)

CDN$1 = US$.73	**US$1= CDN$1.37**
UK£1 = US$1.54	**US$1 = UK£0.65**
IR£1 = US$1.58	**US$1 = IR£0.63**
AUS$1 = US$0.79	**US$1 = AUS$1.26**
NZ$1 = US$0.67	**US$1 = NZ$1.48**

The main unit of currency in the U.S. is the **dollar;** the dollar is divided into 100 cents. The color of paper money is green in the U.S.; bills come in denominations of $1, $2 (though rare), $5, $10, $20, $50, and $100. The U.S. has 1¢ (penny), 5¢ (nickel), 10¢ (dime), and 25¢ (quarter) coins.

No matter how tight your budget or how short your trip, you won't be able to carry all your cash with you. Even if you think you can, don't; non-cash reserves are wise. Personal checks aren't readily accepted from abroad or out of state.

Banks in Washington, D.C. are usually open from Monday to Friday 9am to 3pm; some extend their hours on Friday; some are open Saturdays from 9am to noon or 1pm. All banks are closed on legal holidays.

TRAVELER'S CHECKS

Traveler's checks are one of the safest and least troublesome means of carrying funds. Several agencies and many banks sell them, usually for face value plus a 1% commission. (Members of the American Automobile Association can get American Express checks commission-free through AAA.) American Express and Visa are the most widely recognized, though other major checks are sold, exchanged, cashed, and refunded with comparable ease. Keep in mind that in small towns, traveler's checks are less readily accepted than in cities with large tourist industries. Nonetheless, there will probably be at least one place in every town where you can exchange them for local currency. If you're ordering your checks, do so well in advance, especially if large sums are being requested.

Each agency provides refunds if your checks are lost or stolen, and many provide additional services. (You may need a police report verifying the loss or theft.) Inquire about your destinations' toll-free refund hotlines, emergency message relay services, and stolen credit card assistance when you purchase your checks.

You should expect a fair amount of red tape and delay in the event of theft or loss of traveler's checks. To expedite the refund process, keep your check receipts separate from your checks and store them in a safe place or with a traveling companion; record check numbers when you cash them and leave a list of check numbers with someone at home; and ask for a list of refund centers when you buy your checks. American Express and Bank of America have over 40,000 centers worldwide. Keep a separate supply of cash or traveler's checks for emergencies. Be sure never to countersign your checks until you're prepared to cash them. And always be sure to bring your passport when you plan to use the checks.

American Express: Call 800-221-7282 in the U.S. and Canada; in the U.K. 800 52 13 13; in New Zealand 011 0800 44 10 68; in Australia 008 25 19 02. Elsewhere, call U.S. collect (801-964-6665). American Express traveler's checks are now available in 11 currencies including Australian, British, Canadian, and U.S. They are the most widely recognized worldwide and the easiest to replace if lost or stolen. Checks can be purchased for a small fee at American Express Travel Service Offices, banks, and American Automobile Association offices. Cardmembers can also purchase checks at American Express Dispensers at Travel Service Offices in airports, by ordering them via phone (800-ORDER-TC (673-3782)), or through America OnLine. AmEx offices cash their checks commission-free, although their rates are often slightly worse than those at banks. You can also buy *Cheques for Two* which can be signed by either of two people traveling together.

Citicorp: Call 800-645-6556 in the U.S. and Canada; in the U.K. 181 297 4781; from elsewhere call U.S. collect 813-623-1709. Sells both Citicorp and Citicorp Visa traveler's checks in U.S., Australian, Canadian, and U.S. dollars, and British pounds. Commission is 1-2% on check purchases. Checkholders are automatically enrolled for 45 days in the Travel Assist Program (hotline 800-250-4377 or collect 202-296-8728) which provides travelers with English-speaking doctor, lawyer, and interpreter referrals as well as check refund assistance and general travel information. Citicorp's World Courier Service guarantees hand-delivery of traveler's checks when a refund location is not convenient. Call 24 hrs a day, seven days a week.

Thomas Cook MasterCard: Call 800-223-9920 in the U.S. and Canada; elsewhere call U.S. collect 609-987-7300; from the U.K. call (011) 08 00 62 21 01 free or (011) 17 33 50 29 95 collect or (011) 44 17 33 31 89 50 collect. Offers checks in U.S., Canadian, and Australian dollars, British pounds, and ECUs. Commission 1-2% for purchases. Try buying the checks at a Thomas Cook office for potentially lower commissions; checks are cashed at Thomas Cook offices commission-free.

Visa: Call 800-227-6811 in the U.S.; in the U.K. (011) 08 00 89 54 92; from anywhere else in the world call (011) 017 33 31 89 49 and reverse the charges. If provided with your zip code, an operator at any of the numbers will tell you where their closest office is. All Visa traveler's checks can be reported as lost at the above numbers.

CREDIT CARDS

Credit cards are not accepted at many small, cheap locations where traveler's checks are welcomed, and pricey establishments which cheerfully accept them can quickly deplete your account. Still, credit cards can be invaluable in the U.S., and are sometimes expected or required (for example, at many car rental agencies). Credit cards are also useful when an emergency, such as necessary car repairs, leaves you temporarily without other resources. In addition, some cards carry services for users; these services range from personal or car rental insurance to emergency assistance. Major credit cards can be used to instantly extract cash advances from associated banks and ATMs; this can be a great bargain for foreign travelers; credit card companies get the wholesale exchange rate, which is generally 5% better than the retail rate used by banks. However, you will be charged ruinous interest rates if you don't pay off the bill quickly, so be careful when using this service.

MasterCard (outside North America, "EuroCard" or "Access") and **Visa** ("Carte Bleue" or "Barclaycard") are the most accepted; both sell cards through banks. In the event of a lost or stolen card: Visa (800-336-8472); Mastercard (800-999-0454).

American Express cards also work in some ATMs, as well as at AmEx offices and major airports. This card has a hefty annual fee ($55); however, students have the option of obtaining the free Optima card. Both of these American Express cards offer extensive travel-related services. In the event of a lost or stolen card: (800-CASH-NOW/528-4800).

ATM CARDS

Before you arrive in the District, you may want to find out if your bank is networked with any D.C. banks; two major ATM networks in the U.S. are **Mastercard/Cirrus** (800-4-CIRRUS/424-7787) and **PLUS** (800-843-7587). Inquire at your bank about fees charged for ATM transactions. If you plan to stay for a while, open a savings account at one of the local banks and acquire a local ATM card, which you can use 24 hours a day citywide. Credit card holders should also ask their banks or credit card companies for a four-digit **PIN** (Personal Identification Number); PINs (in conjunction with a credit card) allow cash withdrawal at participating ATMs.

MONEY FROM HOME

If you run out of money on the road, you can have more mailed to you in the form of traveler's checks bought in your name, a certified check, or through postal money orders, available at post offices (85¢ fee; $600 limit per order; cash only). Certified checks are redeemable at any bank, while postal money orders can be cashed at post offices upon display of two IDs (1 of which must be a photo ID). Keep receipts; money orders are refundable if lost. **Personal checks** from home will probably not be acceptable no matter how many forms of identification you have.

Wiring money can cost from around $15 (for domestic service) to $35 (international), depending on the bank, in addition to a fee ($7-15) for receiving the money. Once you've found a bank that will accept a wire, write or telegram your home bank with your account number, the name and address of the bank to receive the wire, and a routing number. Also notify the bank of the form of ID that the second bank should accept before paying the money. As a very last resort, consulates will wire home for you and deduct the cost from the money you receive.

Western Union (800-CALL-CASH) is a well-known and expensive service that can be used to cable money with your Visa or MasterCard within the domestic United States. You or someone else can phone in a credit card number or bring cash to a Western Union office for pick-up at another Western Union location. The rates for sending cash are generally $10 cheaper than with a credit card. Rates to send cash from a local office are $29 to send $250, $40 to send $500, and $50 to send $1000. You will need an ID to pick up the money.

American Express is one of the easiest ways to get money from home. AmEx allows green-card holders to draw cash from their checking accounts at any of its major offices and many of its representatives' offices, up to $1000 every 21 days (no service charge, no interest). AmEx also offers **Express Cash,** with over 100,000 ATMs in airports, hotels, banks, office complexes, and shopping areas around the world. Express Cash withdrawals are automatically debited from the Cardmember's specified bank account or line of credit. Green card holders may withdraw up to $1000 in a seven-day period. There is a 2% transaction fee for each cash withdrawal with a $2.50 minimum. To enroll in Express Cash, Cardmembers may call 1-800-CASH-NOW. Outside the U.S. call collect (904) 565-7875. Unless using the AmEx service, avoid cashing checks in foreign currencies; they usually take weeks and a $30 fee to clear.

TAXES AND TIPPING

The prices quoted throughout *Let's Go: Washington, D.C.* are the amounts before sales tax has been added. Sales tax in D.C. is 6%. Hotel tax is 13%, with an additional $1.50 occupancy tax per room per night.

Remember that service is never included on a D.C. tab. Tip cab drivers and waiters about 15%; exceptionally good waiters—or those who work at exceptionally good restaurants—are often tipped 20% of the tab. Tip hairdressers 10% and bellhops around $1 per bag. Bartenders usually expect between 50¢ and $1 per drink.

Safety and Security

Emergency (police, fire, ambulance): 911, TDD 727-3323. **Police:** 727-1010. Use this for inquiries that are not urgent. 24hr.

SAFETY

In 1942, D.C. doubled New York City's murder rate, and, according to *Newsweek*,.became the "Murder Capital of the U.S." Exactly 50 years later, the title was resurrected, thanks to widespread crack addiction and the increasing availability of assault weapons. The nation's capital is no longer its leading supplier of corpses, but Washington is still no city with which to trifle. The murder epidemic, while mostly an affair of drug dealers shooting one another, sometimes catches innocents in its crossfire. Most slaughters occur in places unfrequented by visitors, such as NE, SE, and east of 14th St. NW (although hold-ups and shootings, often in daylight, do take place in other, more touristed areas). Try only to enter these regions in a car, and exercise extreme caution.

Use common sense. Protect yourself first, then your money. Avoid public parks after dark. Walk on busy, well-lit streets whenever possible. When you're walking alone, walk fast and look impatient to get where you're going—even if you don't know where you're going. Avoid dark alleys and doorways. Don't walk through parking lots at night. Whenever possible, *Let's Go* warns of seemingly unsafe neighborhoods, but only your eyes can tell you for sure if you've wandered into one; buildings in disrepair, vacant lots, and general desertedness are often indicative.

Peripheral areas such as Logan Circle and Chinatown host community patrols consisting of civic-minded civilians in **orange hats;** these volunteers pound the pavement to scare away drug dealers and reassure neighbors that the streets belong to everyone. Count on the orange hats for directions or other friendly assistance.

Both men and women may want to carry a small whistle to scare off attackers or to attract attention. To call 911 for police or for an ambulance is cost-free on any public phone. The Metro system itself is almost crime-free, but some areas in which it stops are not. When choosing accommodations, consider the relative location of the places you plan to visit late at night, and how you plan to return—especially in Adams-Morgan, a wonderful neighborhood with lousy Metro connections. After the Metro shuts down, around midnight, D.C.'s cheap zone-fare system makes taxis a good choice for returning home.

There are no sure-fire precautions that will protect you from all of the situations you might encounter when you travel. A good self-defense course will give you more concrete ways to react to different types of aggression, but it might cost more money than your trip will. **Model Mugging**, a national organization with offices in several major cities, teaches a very effective, comprehensive course on self-defense. Contact Lynn S. Auerbach on the East Coast (617-232-7900); Alice Tibits in the Midwest (612-645-6189); and Cori Couture on the West Coast (415-592-7300). Course prices vary from $400-500. Both women's and men's courses are offered. Community colleges frequently offer self-defense courses at more affordable prices.

SECURITY

Thieves prey on tourists for one good reason: they carry more money than the rest of the world. Your best bet is not to look like one, especially away from the Mall. The farther you go from the Smithsonian, the less you should stand out. Dress modestly. Leave the three cameras at home, and don't hang the one you did bring around your neck. Don't gawk at buildings or people, don't unfold maps on the sidewalk, and use discretion when asking for directions (when in doubt, try a storekeeper). Keep a sharp eye out for fast-fingered pickpockets and slick con artists. Also, be alert in public telephone booths. If you must say your calling-card number, do so very quietly. And if somebody really insists on using the booth, give the phone up pronto—drug dealers often make transactions on public phones.

As for your property—don't carry your money in your back pocket; don't count it on the street; and don't leave it dangling from a bag or pouch that can be easily grabbed off your shoulder. Women should sling **purses** diagonally, from one shoulder to the opposite hip. Keep your important documents—ID, passport, traveler's check numbers and receipts—separate from the bulk of your belongings, along with a credit card. **Necklace pouches** that stay under your shirt are the best money carriers; however, they are not easily accessible, and large ones can be quite uncomfortable. **Money belts** can be worn around your waist and buried under one or all your layers of clothing—these are more convenient and nearly theft-proof. Try to memorize as many of your important numbers as possible in case your documentation disappears: passport, ID, driver's license, health-insurance policy, traveler's checks, and credit cards. Making **photocopies** of important documents will allow you to replace them with greater ease in case they are lost or stolen.

Regardless of where you stow your belongings, during the day or night, keep your valuables on your person. In the dorm-style rooms of some hostels, consider this rule ironclad. *Even a trip to the shower can cost you a wallet or camera.* At night, sleep with your valuables under your pillow, and put the straps of your bag around the leg of your bed. **Lockers** at bus and train stations are generally safe. **Safes** are fine in higher-quality hotels of international repute, but in guest houses, you may want to think twice before leaving your prized possessions with the owner.

Travel Assistance International by Worldwide Assistance Services, Inc. provides its members with a 24-hr. hotline for emergencies and referrals. Their year-long frequent traveler package ($226) includes medical and travel insurance, financial assistance, and aid in the reissuing of lost documents. Call 800-821-2828 or 202-828-5894; fax 202-828-5896; or write them at 1133 15th St. NW, Suite 400, Washington, D.C. 20005-2710.

ALCOHOL AND DRUGS

You must be 21 years old to purchase **alcoholic beverages** legally in D.C. Many bars and stores will want to see a photo ID (a driver's license or other valid government-issued document) before selling you alcohol. Popular drinking spots, as well as upscale liquor stores, are likely to card—and ruthlessly, at that. Bars and clubs are allowed to serve alcohol until 3am. If you want to drink hard alcohol on Sundays, stock up on Saturday night—only beer and wine can be sold in D.C. on Sunday.

Possession of marijuana, cocaine, and most opiate derivatives (among many other chemicals) is punishable by stiff fines and imprisonment. Driving under the influence of alcohol or drugs is stupid. It is also punishable by law.

If you carry **prescription drugs,** have a copy of the prescriptions ready for U.S. Customs to inspect.

HELP LINES

Traveler's Aid Society: Main office at 512 C St. NE (546-3120). Helpful in emergencies. Open Mon.-Fri. 9am-5pm. Other desks at Union Station (546-3120, TDD 371-1937; open Mon.-Sat. 9:30am-5:30pm, Sun. 12:30-5:30pm), National Airport (703-419-3972, TDD 703-419-3977; open Mon.-Fri. 9am-9pm, Sat.-Sun. 9am-6pm), and Dulles International Airport (703-661-8636, TDD 703-260-0175; open Mon.-Fri. 10am-9pm, Sat.-Sun. 10am-6pm).
AIDS Information Line: 332-2437, Mon.-Fri. 10am-9pm, Sat.-Sun. 10am-6pm.
Alcohol and Drug Hotline: 783-1300. Mon.-Fri. 9am-5pm.
Dept. of Human Services Crisis Line: 561-7000. 24hr.
Rape Crisis Center: 333-7273. 24hr.
National Organization for Victim Assistance: 232-6682. 24hr.
Gay and Lesbian Hotline: 833-3234. 7-11pm.
Medical Referral: George Washington University Hospital: 994-4112. 24hr.
Poison Center: 625-3333. 24hr.
Park Police: 619-7300. Emergencies in Rock Creek Park or on federal parklands.

ESSENTIALS

Health

BEFORE YOU GO

A compact **first-aid kit** should suffice for minor problems on the road. The following items are useful in many situations: multi-sized bandages, aspirin or other pain killer, antibiotic cream, a thermometer, a Swiss Army knife with tweezers, moleskin, a decongestant for colds, motion sickness remedy, medicine for diarrhea or stomach problems, sunscreen, insect repellent, and burn ointment.

In your **passport** or other document, write the names of any people you wish to be contacted in case of a medical emergency and list any allergies or medical conditions of which doctors should be aware. Bring any **medication** you regularly take and may need while traveling, as well as a copy of the **prescription** and a statement of any pre-existing medical conditions, especially if you will be bringing insulin, syringes, or any narcotics into the U.S. It is always a good idea to get a **check-up** before traveling, especially if you will be abroad for more than a month or two or if you will be hiking, camping, or visiting rural or unindustrialized regions. Allergy sufferers should find out if their conditions are likely to be aggravated in the regions they plan to visit, and obtain a supply of any necessary medication before the trip, since matching a prescription to a foreign equivalent is not always easy, safe, or possible. If you wear **glasses** or **contact lenses,** carry an extra prescription and pair. The following organizations have helpful medical information:

American Diabetes Association, 1600 Duke St., Alexandria, VA 22314 (800-232-3472). Call or write for a copy of *Travel and Diabetes* and a diabetic ID card.

American Red Cross, 285 Columbus Ave., Boston, MA 02116-5114 (800-564-1234). Call to purchase the Red Cross's invaluable *First-Aid and Safety Handbook* ($15), or for info. on well-taught and inexpensive first-aid and CPR courses.

Global Emergency Medical Services (GEMS), 2001 Westside Dr., Suite 120, Alpharetta, GA 30201 (800-860-1111; fax 770-475-0058). Subscribers have immediate 24-hr. access to an emergency room registered nurse with online access to your personal medical history, your primary physician, and a worldwide network of English-speaking medical providers.

International Association for Medical Assistance to Travelers (IAMAT) offers a membership ID card and a directory of doctors who treat members for a set fee schedule. Membership is free, though donations are appreciated and used for further research. In the **U.S.,** 417 Center St., Lewiston, NY 14092 (716-754-4883; fax 519-836-3412; e-mail iamat@sentex.net; http://www.sentex.net/iamat). In **Canada,** 40 Regal Road, Guelph, Ontario, N1K 1B5 (519-836-0102) or 1287 St. Clair Avenue West, Toronto, M6E 1B8 (416-652-0137; fax 519-836-3412).

Medic Alert Foundation, 2323 Colorado Ave., Turlock, CA, 95382 (24-hr. hotline 800-432-5378). For travelers with medical conditions that cannot be easily recognized (diabetes, epilepsy, heart conditions, allergies to antibiotics, etc.). Membership includes the internationally recognized Medic Alert Identification Tag and an annually updated wallet card. Lifetime membership is $35 the first year, and $15 annually thereafter.

ON-THE-ROAD AILMENTS

Common sense is the simplest prescription for good health on the road. **Always eat well, drink lots of fluids, and get enough sleep.** *About 95% of headaches are caused by dehydration*—drink even if you're not thirsty, especially while subjected to D.C.'s sweltering heat. Pure water is best. Many travelers experience fatigue, discomfort, or mild diarrhea upon arriving in a new area; allow time for your body to adjust before becoming worried. If you suffer from any ailments in a severe form for a significant period of time, seek medical help as soon as possible:

Children's National Medical Center, 111 Michigan Ave. NW (884-5000).
Georgetown University Medical Center, 3800 Reservoir Rd. NW (687-2000).
Howard University Hospital, 2041 Georgia Ave. NW (865-6100).
Sibley Memorial Hospital, 5255 Loughboro Rd. NW (537-4000).
George Washington Univ. Medical Center, 901 23rd St. NW (994-1000).

AIDS, HIV, AND STDS

Acquired Immune Deficiency Syndrome (AIDS) is a growing problem around the world. The World Health Organization estimates that there are around 13 million people infected with HIV, the virus that leads to AIDS. Well over 90% of adults newly infected with HIV acquired the virus through heterosexual sex; women now represent 50% of all new HIV infections. In the U.S. it is estimated that more than 1 million people are infected with HIV, and that 80% of those people do not realize that they are infected. The easiest mode of HIV transmission is through direct blood to blood contact with an HIV+ person; never share intravenous drug, tattooing, or other needles. The most common mode of transmission is sexual intercourse. In order to lessen your chances of contracting HIV or any other **sexually transmitted disease** (STD), such as gonorrhea, chlamydia, genital warts, syphilis, and herpes (which are a lot easier to catch than HIV, and can be just as deadly), use a latex condom every time you have sex. **Contraception** is easily obtainable in the U.S.; condoms can be found in any pharmacy, usually right on the shelves (though it doesn't hurt to stock up before you set out). Opt for water-based lubricants over oil-based formulas which render latex useless in preventing viral transfer. The **U.S. Center for Disease Control** (800-342-2437) can provide more information.

Insurance

Beware of buying unnecessary travel coverage—regular policies may well extend to many travel-related accidents. **Medical insurance** (especially university policies) often cover costs incurred abroad—check with your provider. **Medicare's** foreign travel coverage is valid only in Canada and Mexico. Canadians are protected by their home province's health insurance plan for 90 days after leaving the country; check with the provincial Ministry of Health or Health Plan Headquarters for details. Australia has Reciprocal Health Care Agreements (RHCAs) with several countries; when traveling in these nations Australians are entitled to many of the services that they would receive at home. The Commonwealth Department of Human Services and Health can provide more information. Your **homeowners' insurance** (or your family's coverage) often covers theft during travel. Homeowners are generally covered against loss of travel documents (passport, plane ticket, railpass, etc.) up to $500.

ISIC and **ITIC** provide travel insurance to members (see Youth, Student, & Teacher ID, p. 26). Call for more information. To supplement ISIC's insurance, **Council** (see Travel Organizations, p. 19) offers the inexpensive **Trip-Safe plan** with options covering medical treatment and hospitalization, accidents, baggage loss, and charter flights missed due to illness; they and **STA** also offer more comprehensive and expensive policies. **American Express** cardholders receive automatic car rental (required to decline collision insurance) and travel accident insurance on flight purchases made with the card. (Customer Service 800-528-4800.)

Remember that insurance companies usually require a copy of the police report for thefts, or evidence of having paid medical expenses (doctor's statements, receipts) before they will honor a claim and may have time limits on filing for reimbursement. Always carry policy numbers and proof of insurance. Check with each insurance carrier for specific restrictions and policies. The carriers listed below have 24-hr. hotlines.

Access America, 6600 West Broad St., P.O. Box 11188, Richmond, VA 23230 (800-284-8300; fax 804-673-1491). Covers trip cancellation/interruption, on-the-spot hospital admittance, emergency evacuation, sickness, and baggage loss.

The Berkley Group/Carefree Travel Insurance, 100 Garden City Plaza, P.O. Box 9366, Garden City, NY 11530-9366 (800-323-3149 or 516-294-0220; fax 516-294-1096). Offers two comprehensive packages including coverage for trip cancellation/interruption/delay, accident and sickness, medical, baggage loss, bag delay, accidental death and dismemberment, and travel supplier insolvency. Trip cancellation/interruption may be purchased separately at a rate of $5.50 per $100 of coverage. 24-hr. worldwide emergency assistance hotline.

Travel Guard International, 1145 Clark St., Stevens Point, WI 54481 (800-826-1300 or 715-345-0505; fax 715-345-0525). Comprehensive insurance programs starting at $44. Programs cover trip cancellation and interruption, bankruptcy and financial default, lost luggage, medical coverage abroad, emergency assistance, and accidental death.

Wallach and Company, Inc., 107 West Federal St., P.O. Box 480, Middleburg, VA 20118-0480 (800-237-6615; fax 540-687-3172; e-mail wallach.r@mediasoft.net). Comprehensive medical insurance including evacuation and repatriation of remains and direct payment of claims to providers of services. Other optional coverages available.

Alternatives to Tourism

INTERNSHIPS

Sensible year-round Washington politicos escape in the summer from their sweltering city. Their ranks are replenished by an influx of collegiate go-getters from all over the country. To some, the pilgrimage to D.C. is the requisite first step toward the Power and Glory of politics on a national scale. They are the **summer interns,** and for them, a summertime spent working in Washington represents an opportunity to work for—or, more importantly, to become—the "best and the brightest."

However, these dreams of glamour soon dissipate into a more monotonous reality. The projects pursued by most interns are so far removed from the heartbeat of American politics that they might as well be working as caddies. Interns are generally **glorified secretaries/gofers** who may, if they're lucky, get thrown a minor project to work on at the behest of a low-level staffer. Still, proximity to power is a decent substitute for the real thing; even if interns have little to do with the day's debates and scandals, they may at least converse about them perpetually.

Congress is the main employer of summer interns; senators might hire anywhere from five to 15 interns, and the typical representative's office has two or three. House interns usually hail from their boss's own district, whereas Senate internships are less geographically inclined. Many interns work for a committee or a subcommittee, meaning that they work for the committee chair (since the 1994 elections, invariably a Republican). Other prime intern-havens are think tanks, lobbying groups, and executive-branch departments or agencies such as the State Department. If you're interested, start early; January is not too soon to be making inquiries. Connections help, of course—this *is* politics.

To begin the process, send many, many, many cover letters/resumes to congressional offices, the White House, government departments, the Smithsonian, and any other agency that interests you. The following is a list of potentially useful publications that may facilitate your search; many are out of print but available in libraries.

Peterson's Internships 1997, (Princeton NJ, Peterson's (800-338-3282; fax 609-243-9150; http://www.petersons.com).

The Complete Guide to Washington Internships, edited by Jeffrey Marc Parness (Brooklyn, NY; Washington Intern Services, 1988).

Student Access Guide to America's Top 100 Internships, by Mark Oldman (NY, NY; Villard Books, 1993).

Internships and Careers in International Affairs, by James P. Muldoon (NY, NY; United Nations, 1992).

The Technology and Society Internships Directory: A Comprehensive Guide to Washington, D.C. Internships 1985-86 (Student Pugwash Internship Clearinghouse, 1985). Still provides useful information; check it out at a library.

Directory of Washington Internships: A Guide to Current Internship Programs and Placements in the Nation's Capitol, by Debra L. Mann (National Society for Internships and Experiential Education).

Many prospective interns limit themselves solely to positions within the federal government, jobs generally carrying little responsibility and minimal stimulation. As a rule, the smaller departments or firms offer more exciting and rewarding positions.

The above guides not only list internship opportunities within the political spectrum, but also provide information about smaller, private businesses.

The vast majority of the summer opportunities for college students are non-paying, and life in Washington is rarely cheap. Fortunately, there are ways to finagle some cash out of the deal. Some universities and foundations award **grants** to students to cover the summer expenses of working at an unpaid public-sector job. Here and there, a government branch might have some intern funds at its disposal; the House of Representatives, for instance, retains an endowment (the Lyndon Baines Johnson, or LBJ, fund) that gives each Member $2000 to split among any number of interns from his or her home district. In any case, interning in D.C. is rarely a profitable endeavor and may require either a supplementary night job waiting tables or a magical source of disposable funds (or a well-placed extended family). Interning for half the summer is a viable and common option that allows time for some gainful employment; the wiliest get themselves out of Washington before the real dog days of August hit.

The intern social scene can be remarkably homogeneous; as a group, these upstart men and women are probably less diverse than the people that run our country (if that's possible). Most collegiate interns live in the dorms of George Washington, American, or Georgetown Universities (all of which are usually booked by April), in Georgetown townhouse sublets, or in apartments near Capitol Hill. Most of them also go to happy hours after work (to load up on free buffets for dinner), hobnob in Georgetown or Hill bars at night, and play softball on weekends on the Mall for their college's D.C. summer squad. At all these locales—bus, bar, dorm—the unspoken main business of an ambitious Washington summer intern is going on: the schmoozing and smiling, the handshaking and remembering—the social interaction with similarly minded peers may someday pay off.

But for all the cynicism that a D.C. internship might inspire, it has the potential to be an unqualified winner. While many interns do spend their summer pushing paper, some are given truly important work. Interning in Washington is the most basic way of getting a foot in the door of national politics and the best way to start learning how the nation's capital really works. For every internship that's reserved for someone's kid as a political favor, there are four that aren't. You could end up on the Advance Team. And despite the swelter, summertime Washington has a mysterious ability to perpetually convince young people that it is *the* place to be.

STUDY

If you are interested in studying in the U.S., there are a number of different paths you can take. One possibility is to enroll in a language education program, particularly if you are interested in a short-term stay. Almost all U.S. institutions accept applications from foreign students directly. If English is not your native language, you will likely be required to take the Test of English as a Foreign Language (TOEFL), which is administered in many countries. Requirements are set by each school. Contact the **TOEFL/TSE Publications,** P.O. Box 6154, Princeton, NJ 08541-6154 (609-771-7100; http://www.toefl.org.). **Council** sponsors over 40 study abroad programs throughout the world. Contact them for more information (see Travel Organizations, p. 19).

World Learning, Inc., P.O. Box 676, Brattleboro, VT 05302 (800-345-2929 or 802-257-7751; http://www.worldlearning.org), runs the International Students of English program, which offers intensive language courses at select U.S. campuses. The price of a four-week program averages $1800.

Institute of International Education (IIE), 809 United Nations Plaza, New York, NY 10017-3580 (212-984-5413 for recorded information; fax 212-984-5358). For book orders: IIE Books, Institute of International Education, P.O. Box 371, Annapolis Junction, MD 20701 (800-445-0443; fax 301-953-2838; e-mail iiebooks@iie.org). A nonprofit international and cultural exchange agency, the IIE is an excellent source of information on studying in the U.S., Canada, and abroad. Publishes *Academic Year Abroad* ($43 plus $4 shipping) detailing over 2300 semester-/year-long programs worldwide and *Vacation Study Abroad* ($37 plus $4 shipping) which lists over 1800 short-term, summer, and language programs.

Eurocentres, 101 N. Union St. #300, Alexandria, VA 22314 (800-648-4809; fax 703-684-1495; http://www.clark.net/pub/eurocent/home.htn) or Eurocentres, Head Office, Seestrasse 247, CH-8038 Zurich, Switzerland (tel. 01 485 50 40; fax 481 61 24). Coordinates language programs and homestays for college students and adults in Alexandria, VA, Washington, D.C., and New York City. Programs cost $500-5000 and last from 2 weeks to 3 months. Some financial aid is available.

U.S. STUDENT VISAS

Foreign students who wish to study in the United States must apply for either a J-1 visa (for exchange students) or an F-1 visa (for full-time students enrolled in an academic or language program). To obtain a J-1, you must fill out an IAP-66 eligibility form, issued by the program in which you will enroll. Both are valid for the duration of stay, which includes the length of your particular program and a brief grace period thereafter. In order to extend a student visa, submit an I-538 form 15-60 days before your original departure date.

If you are studying in the U.S., you can take any on-campus job once you have applied for a social security number and have completed an Employment Eligibility Form (I-9). If you are studying full-time in the U.S. on an F-1 visa, you may take any on-campus job provided you do not displace a U.S. resident. On-campus employment is limited to 20 hours per week while school is in session, but you may work full-time during vacation if you plan to return to school. For more information, contact the international students office at the institution you plan to attend.

Specific Concerns

WOMEN TRAVELERS

Women exploring any area on their own inevitably face additional safety concerns. Forego cheap accommodations in seemingly unsafe peripheries and take to heart our recommended youth hostels, university accommodations, bed and breakfasts, and organizations offering rooms to women only. A woman should *never* hitchhike alone; even in groups it can be dangerous.

If you find yourself the object of catcalls or unwelcome propositions, your best answer is no answer. Always look as if you know where you're going (even when you don't), and maintain an assertive, confident posture wherever you go. If you feel uncomfortable asking strangers for information or directions, it may be easier to approach other women or couples. Always carry enough change for a bus, taxi, or phone call. And in emergencies, don't hesitate to yell for help.

For general information, contact the **National Organization for Women (NOW),** which boasts branches across the country that can refer women travelers to rape crisis centers and counseling services. NOW also provides lists of feminist events. Main offices include 22 W. 21st St., 7th Fl., **New York,** NY 10010 (212-260-4422); 1000 16th St. NW, 7th Fl., **Washington, D.C.** 20004 (202-331-0066); and 3543 18th St., **San Francisco,** CA 94110 (415-861-8960).

Know the emergency numbers for the area you're visiting; see **Safety and Security,** p. 32 and **Help Lines,** p. 34. More information and safety tips can be found in Maggie and Gemma Moss's *Handbook for Women Travelers* (UK£9), available from Piatkus Books, 5 Windmill St., London W1P 1HF, England (tel. (171) 631 07 10). The folks who produced *Gaia's Guide* (no longer available) are now publishing *Women Going Places* ($14), a women's travel and resource guide emphasizing women-owned and -operated enterprises. The guide is aimed at lesbians but useful to all women, and is available from Inland Book Company, 1436 W. Randolph St., Chicago, IL 60607 (800-243-0138) or from a local bookstore. The latest book on women's travel to hit the market, *A Journey of One's Own* by Thalia Zepatos, provides lots of good advice as well as a specific and manageable bibliography of books and resources. The book is published by Eighth Mountain Press and retails for $17.

OLDER TRAVELERS

Discounts abound in D.C. for travelers 60 and over. All you need is identification proving your age. Pick up the free *Golden Washingtonian Club Gold Mine* directory—which lists establishments offering 10-20% discounts to seniors on goods and services—at local hotel desks or at the **D.C. Office on Aging** at 441 4th St. NW (724-5626). The D.C. Office on Aging also offers an information and referral service to residents and visitors 60 and over, and distributes a Senior Network booklet which lists caregivers and professionals of interest to senior citizens. You can obtain information over the phone on a range of topics affecting seniors, including nutrition, housing, transportation, Medicare, legal aid, and recreation (open Mon.-Fri. 8:15am-4:45pm). The following are other organizations of interest to older travelers:

AARP (American Association of Retired Persons), 601 E St., NW, Washington, D.C. 20049 (202-434-2277). Members 50 and over receive benefits and services including the AARP Motoring Plan from AMOCO (800-334-3300), and discounts on lodging, car rental, and sight-seeing. Annual fee $8 per couple; lifetime membership $75.

Elderhostel, 75 Federal St., 3rd Fl., Boston, MA 02110-1941 (617-426-7788; fax 617-426-8351; http://www.elderhostel.org). For those 55 or over (spouse of any age). Programs at colleges, universities, and other learning centers in over 50 countries on varied subjects lasting one to four weeks.

National Council of Senior Citizens, 1331 F St. NW, Washington, D.C. 20004 (202-347-8800). Memberships are $12 a year, $30 for three years, or $150 for a lifetime. Individuals or couples can receive hotel and auto rental discounts, a senior citizen newspaper, use of a discount travel agency, supplemental Medicare insurance (if you're over 65), and a mail-order prescription drug service.

Pilot Books, 103 Cooper St., Babylon, NY 11702 (516-212-2225). Publishes a large number of helpful guides including *The International Health Guide for Senior Citizens* ($5, postage $2). Call or write for a complete list of titles.

Unbelievably Good Deals and Great Adventures That You Absolutely Can't Get Unless You're Over 50, by Joan Rattner Heilman. After you finish reading the title page, check inside for some great tips on senior discounts and the like. Contemporary Books, $10

BISEXUAL, GAY, AND LESBIAN TRAVELERS

Washington's bisexual, gay, and lesbian communities are exceptional for their diversity, visibility, and the comfortable geographic and legal positions they occupy within the city. D.C. law boasts a strong civil rights tradition which includes sexual orientation legal rights; the June 1995 ruling by the Court of Appeals in favor of adoption by gay couples is only one of the most recent examples of the openness of the city. Aided by this positive reinforcement, a number of gay neighborhoods have developed throughout the Washington area.

Dupont Circle is the hub of gay activity in D.C. Easily accessible by Metro, the neighborhood offers whole blocks of gay and gay-friendly establishments from bars to bookstores. **P St.** is especially fruitful, where most bars and restaurants cluster around **17th** and P St. between **21st** and **22nd.** In Baltimore, the *Baltimore Alternative* and the *Fun Map* cover bars, restaurants, and hotels for gays and lesbians. **Southeast** Washington contains upwards of 10 bars and clubs. Despite this area's commercial and social appeal, it is traditionally one of the city's most dangerous. Exercise caution and common sense if you choose to explore Southeast. Don't go alone at night and try to drive or take a cab home. Most clubs have free cab phones on the premises as well as parking lots, so use them.

There are a handful of **gay publications** in D.C. Most are free and widely circulated. The **Washington Blade** is an indispensable source of news, reviews, and club list-

ESSENTIALS

ings; published every Friday, it's available in virtually every storefront and many restaurants in Dupont Circle. **MW,** a newer arts and entertainment weekly, contains brief public interest items, short fiction, extensive nightlife coverage, and is almost as easy to find as the *Blade*. **Woman's Monthly,** a lesbian periodical, may be somewhat more difficult to find. *The Gay and Lesbian Services Guide* ($4) lists businesses and organizations in the metro area that serve the gay community; you can pick it up at the **Lambda Rising** bookstore, 1625 Connecticut Ave. NW (462-6969), near R St. (open daily 10am-midnight).

Let's Go: Washington, D.C. 1997 includes gay, lesbian, and bisexual establishments throughout its listings. The following are some gay/lesbian **information and advice lines** for the D.C. area, as well as potentially useful **travel publications:**

Gay and Lesbian Switchboard: 628-4667. Separate lesbian number: 628-4666. Daily 7:30-10:30pm. Counseling, general information, and referrals.
Gay Deaf Assistance: TDD 628-4669.
Gay and Lesbian Hotline: 833-3234. Counseling and referral daily 7-11pm.
Gay Information and Assistance: 363-3881. 24hr. Counseling and information.
Gay Men's VD Clinic: 745-6129, general information 745-6125. Provides free routine testing for sexually transmitted diseases; men only. Walk-in hours Tues. and Thurs. 6-7:30pm at 1701 14th St. NW.
Gay and Lesbian Alliance Against Defamation: 2001 O St. NW, 429-9500.
Gay Men and Lesbians Opposing Violence: 2000 L St. NW, 452-7448. Call to report hate crimes; all calls are confidential and can be anonymous.
Sexual Minority Youth Assistance League: 333½ Pennsylvannia Ave. SE, 546-5940. Metro: Eastern Market or Capitol South. Counseling and social programs for bisexuals, gays, and lesbians ages 14-21. Hotline staffed Mon.-Fri. 7-10pm; drop-in hours 2nd and 4th Fri. of the month 6-8pm; Sat. youth groups meet noon-3pm.

Damron Travel Guides, P.O. Box 422458, San Francisco, CA 94142 (415-255-0404 or 800-462-6654). Publishers of the *Damron Address Book* ($15), which lists bars, restaurants, guest houses, and services in the United States, Canada, and Mexico catering to gay men. The *Damron Road Atlas* ($15) contains color maps of 56 major U.S. and Canadian cities and gay and lesbian resorts and listings of bars and accommodations. *The Women's Traveller* ($12) includes maps of 50 major U.S. cities and lists establishments catering to lesbians. Forthcoming in 1997 is *Damron's Accommodations*, listing gay and lesbian hotels around the world ($19). Mail order available; add $5 shipping.

Ferrari Guides, P.O. Box 37887, Phoenix, AZ 85069 (602-863-2408; fax 439-3952; e-mail ferrari@q-net.com). Gay and lesbian travel guides: *Ferrari Guides' Gay Travel A to Z* (US $16), *Ferrari Guides' Men's Travel in Your Pocket* (US $14), *Ferrari Guides' Women's Travel in Your Pocket* (US $14), *Ferrari Guides' Inn Places* (US $16). Available in bookstores or by mail. (Postage/handling $4.50 for the first item, US $1 per additional item mailed within the US. Overseas, call or write for shipping cost.)

Gayellow Pages, P.O. Box 533, Village Station, New York, NY 10014. (212-674-0120; fax 420-1126). An annually updated listing of accommodations, resorts, hotlines, and other items of interest to the gay traveler. USA/Canada edition $16.

Spartacus International Gay Guides ($32.95), published by Bruno Gmunder, Postfach 110729, D-10837 Berlin, Germany (tel. (30) 615 00 30; fax (30) 615-9134). Lists bars, restaurants, hotels, and bookstores around the world catering to gays. Also lists hotlines for gays and homosexuality laws for each country. Available in bookstores and in the U.S. by mail from Giovanni's Room (listed above).

ESSENTIALS

TRAVELERS WITH DISABILITIES

With a little research and planning ahead, the disabled traveler can gain access to all but the most awkwardly built establishments. Parts of Washington, especially the federally owned parts, do their best to accommodate those with disabilities. Call ahead to inquire about restrictions on motorized wheelchairs.

Visually impaired persons should write to **Washington Ear, Inc.,** 35 University Blvd. E., Silver Spring, MD 20901 (301-681-6636), which sells, and will mail, large-print and tactile atlases of the Washington area. **Columbia Lighthouse for the Blind,** 1421 P Street NW, Washington, D.C. 20005 (462-2900) distributes free tactile maps of the Metro system, as well as two free pamphlets: *Guide to Washington, D.C. for Visually Impaired People* and *Washington Highlights: Tour Information for People with Disabilities.*

Arrange transportation well in advance to ensure a smooth trip. Given sufficient notice, some major **car rental agencies** (Hertz, Avis, and National) offer hand-controlled vehicles at select locations. In the U.S. both **Amtrak** and the airlines will accommodate disabled passengers if notified at least 72 hours in advance. Hearing-impaired travelers may contact Amtrak (800-872-7245, in PA 800-322-9537) using teletype printers. **Greyhound** buses will also provide free travel for a companion; if you are without a fellow traveler, call Greyhound (800-752-4841) at least 48 hours, but no more than one week, before you plan to leave and they will make arrangements to assist you. For information on transportation availability in individual U.S. cities, contact the local chapter of the Easter Seals Society.

If you are planning to visit a national park or attraction in the United States run by the National Park Service, you should obtain a free **Golden Access Passport,** which is available at all park entrances and from federal offices whose functions relate to land, forests, or wildlife. The Golden Access Passport entitles disabled travelers and their families to enter parks for free and provides a 50% reduction on all campsite and parking fees.

A number of more general books are also helpful to travelers with disabilities. The following organizations provide potentially useful information or publications:

American Foundation for the Blind, 11 Penn Plaza, New York, NY 10011 (212-502-7600), open Mon.-Fri. 8:30am-4:30pm. Provides information and services for the visually impaired. For a catalogue of products, contact Lighthouse Y, 10011 (800-829-0500).

Facts on File, 11 Penn Plaza, 15th Floor, New York, NY 10001 (212-967-8800). Publishers of *Disability Resource*, a reference guide for travelers with disabilities ($45 plus shipping). Retail bookstores or by mail order.

Moss Rehab Hospital Travel Information Service, (215-456-9600, TDD 215-456-9602). A telephone information resource center on international travel accessibility and other travel-related concerns for those with disabilities.

Society for the Advancement of Travel for the Handicapped (SATH), 347 Fifth Ave., #610, New York, NY 10016 (212-447-7284; fax 212-725-8253). Publishes quarterly travel newsletter *SATH News* and information booklets (free for members, $13 each for nonmembers) with advice on trip planning for people with disabilities. Annual membership $45, students and seniors $25.

Twin Peaks Press, P.O. Box 129, Vancouver, WA 98666-0129 (360-694-2462, orders only MC and Visa 800-637-2256; fax 360-696-3210). Publishers of *Travel for the Disabled,* which provides travel tips, lists of accessible tourist attractions, and advice on other resources for disabled travelers ($20). Also publishes *Directory for Travel Agencies of the Disabled* ($20), *Wheelchair Vagabond* ($15), and *Directory of Accessible Van Rentals* ($10). Postage $3 for first book, $1.50 for each additional book.

The following organizations arrange tours or trips for disabled travelers:

Directions Unlimited, 720 N. Bedford Rd., Bedford Hills, NY 10507 (800-533-5343; in NY 914-241-1700; fax 241-0243). Specializes in arranging individual and group vacations, tours, and cruises for the physically disabled.

Flying Wheels Travel Service, 143 W. Bridge St., Owatonne, MN 55060 (800-535-6790; fax 451-1685). Arranges trips in the USA and abroad for groups and individuals in wheelchairs or with other sorts of limited mobility.

The Guided Tour Inc., Elkins Park House, Suite 114B, 7900 Old York Road, Elkins Park, PA 19027-2339 (800-783-5841 or 215-782-1370; fax 635-2637). Organizes travel programs for persons with developmental and physical challenges and those requiring renal dialysis. Call, fax, or write for a free brochure.

KOSHER AND VEGETARIAN TRAVELERS

Vegetarians won't have any problem eating well and cheap in D.C. *Let's Go* lists the best vegetarian places we could find. Contact the **North American Vegetarian Society,** P.O. Box 72, Dolgeville, NY 13329 (518-568-7970) for the *Vegetarian Journal's Guide to Natural Food Restaurants in the U.S. and Canada* ($11.95). Membership to the Society is $20; family membership is $26 and members receive a ten percent discount on all publications. Travelers who keep **kosher** should call the **Jewish Information Line** at 301-770-4848 for information about kosher restaurants. *The Jewish Travel Guide* ($12 plus $1.75 shipping), from Ballantine-Mitchell Press, is available in the U.S. from Sepher-Hermon Press, 1265 46th St., Brooklyn, NY 11219 (718-972-9010; $13.95 plus $2.50 shipping).

TRAVELERS WITH TOTS

Family vacations are recipes for disaster—unless you slow your pace and plan ahead a bit. Washington overflows with great opportunities for kids; some are obvious (the National Zoo), others are less so (the Folklife Festival). When deciding where to stay, remember the special needs of young children; if you pick a B&B, call and make sure it's child-friendly. If you rent a car, make sure the rental company provides a car seat for younger children. Restaurants often have children's menus and discounts. Virtually all museums and tourist attractions also have a children's rate. Be sure that your child carries some sort of ID in case of an emergency or he or she gets lost. And arrange a reunion spot in case of separation when sight-seeing (e.g., Dorothy's ruby shoes at the Smithsonian).

Let's Go lists many sights of particular interest to children. The most comprehensive lists of kid-friendly events, however, appear every Friday in the *Washington Post's* Weekend section. Smithsonian Kite Day in April and the Navy Band Lollipop Concert in August are always popular (see **Appendix: Special Events,** on p. 292). The following books can help you avoid the constant complaints of boredom: *Going Places with Children in Washington, D.C.* ($11.95), published by the staff of Green Acres School, 11701 Danville Drive, Rockville, MD 20852 (301-881-4100), and *Washington! Adventure for Kids,* published by Vandamere.

Some of the following publications offer tips for adults traveling with children or distractions for the kids themselves. You can also contact the publishers to see if they have other related publications that you might find useful.

The **Kidding Around** series ($10-13, postage under $5). Illustrated books for children about Spain, Paris, London, Boston, New York, L.A., Chicago, Hawaii. Educational (and distracting) books that could prove invaluable for keeping little ones happy on long trips. Published by John Muir Publications, P.O. Box 613, Santa Fe, NM 87504 (800-285-4078; fax 505-988-1680).

Travel with Children by Maureen Wheeler ($11.95, postage $1.50). Published by Lonely Planet Publications, Embarcadero West, 155 Filbert St., #251, Oakland, CA 94607 (800-275-8555 or 510-893-8555; fax 893-8563; e-mail info@lonelyplanet.com; http://www.lonelyplanet.com). Also P.O. Box 617, Hawthorn, Victoria 3122, Australia.

GETTING THERE

Budget Travel Agencies

HI-AYH Travel Center, 1108 K St. NW (783-4943), below Asian Kabab House. Metro: Metro Center or Mt. Vernon Sq. Travel guides, backpacks, and other equipment to go with your new *Let's Go* books. Discounts on airfares, Eurail passes, and binders full of information on different countries. HI-AYH cards and discounts on merchandise. Open Mon.-Fri. 10am-6pm, Sat. 10am-5pm.

Campus Travel, 52 Grosvenor Gardens, London SW1W 0AG (http://www.campus-travel.co.uk). 41 branches in the U.K. Student and youth fares on plane, train, boat, and bus travel. Flexible airline tickets. Discount and ID cards for youths, travel insurance for students and those under 35, and maps and guides. Puts out travel suggestion booklets. Telephone booking service: in Europe call (0171) 730 3402; in North America call (0171) 730 2101; worldwide call (0171) 730 8111; in Manchester call (0161) 273 1721; in Scotland (0131) 668 3303.

Council Travel (http://www.ciee.org/cts/ctshome.htm), the travel division of Council, is a full-service travel agency specializing in youth and budget travel. They offer railpasses, discount airfares, hosteling cards, guidebooks, budget tours, travel gear, and student (ISIC), youth (GO25), and teacher (ITIC) identity cards. U.S. offices include: Emory Village, 1561 N. Decatur Rd., **Atlanta,** GA 30307 (404-377-9997); 2000 Guadalupe, **Austin,** TX 78705 (512-472-4931); 273 Newbury St., **Boston,** MA 02116 (617-266-1926); 1138 13th St., **Boulder,** CO 80302 (303-447-8101); 1153 N. Dearborn, **Chicago,** IL 60610 (312-951-0585); 10904 Lindbrook Dr., **Los Angeles,** CA 90024 (310-208-3551); 1501 University Ave. SE, **Minneapolis,** MN 55414 (612-379-2323); 205 E. 42nd St., **New York,** NY 10017 (212-822-2700); 953 Garnet Ave., **San Diego,** CA 92109 (619-270-6401); 530 Bush St., **San Francisco,** CA 94108 (415-421-3473); 4311½ University Way, **Seattle,** WA 98105 (206-632-2448); 3300 M St. NW, **Washington, D.C.** 20007 (202-337-6464). **For U.S. cities not listed,** call 800-2-COUNCIL (226-8624). Also 28A Poland St. (Oxford Circus), **London,** W1V 3DB (0171 437 77 67).

Educational Travel Centre (ETC), 438 North Frances St., Madison, WI 53703 (800-747-5551; fax 608-256-2042; e-mail: edtrav@execpc.com). Flight information, HI-AYH cards, Eurail, and regional rail passes. Write for their free pamphlet *Taking Off.*

Let's Go Travel, Harvard Student Agencies, 67 Mt. Auburn St., Cambridge, MA 02138 (800-5-LETS GO/553-8746 or 617-495-9649). Railpasses, HI-AYH memberships, ISICs, ITICs, FIYTO cards, guidebooks (including all of the *Let's Go* guides and Map Guides), maps, bargain flights, and a complete line of budget travel gear. All items available by mail; call or write for a catalog.

STA Travel, 6560 Scottsdale Rd. #F100, Scottsdale, AZ 85253 (800-777-0112 nationwide; fax 602-922-0793). A student and youth travel organization with over 100 offices worldwide offering discount airfares for young travelers, railpasses, accommodations, tours, insurance, and ISICs. 16 offices in the U.S. including: 297 Newbury Street, **Boston,** MA 02115 (617-266-6014); 429 S. Dearborn St., **Chicago,** IL 60605 (312-786-9050); 7202 Melrose Ave., **Los Angeles,** CA 90046 (213-934-8722); 10 Downing St., Ste. G, **New York,** NY 10003 (212-627-3111); 4341 University Way NE, **Seattle,** WA 98105 (206-633-5000); 2401 Pennsylvania Ave., **Washington, D.C.** 20037 (202-887-0912); 51 Grant Ave., **San Francisco,** CA 94108 (415-391-8407); **Miami,** FL 33133 (305-461-3444). In the U.K., 6 Wrights Ln., **London** W8 6TA (tel. (171) 938 47 11 for North American travel). In New Zealand, 10 High St., **Auckland** (tel. (09) 309 97 23). In Australia, 222 Faraday St., **Melbourne** VIC 3050 (tel. (03) 349 69 11).

Travel CUTS (Canadian Universities Travel Services Limited): 187 College St., Toronto, Ont. M5T 1P7 (416-979-2406; fax 979-8167; e-mail mail@travelcuts). Canada's national student travel bureau and equivalent of Council, with 40 offices across Canada. Also in the U.K., 295-A Regent St., **London** W1R 7YA (tel. (171) 637 31 61). Discounted domestic and international airfares open to all; special student fares to all destinations with valid ISIC. Issues ISIC, FIYTO, GO25, and HI hostel cards, as well as railpasses. Offers free *Student Traveller* magazine, as well as information on the Student Work Abroad Program (SWAP).

Winging It

When dealing with any commercial airline, buying in advance is almost always the best bet. The commercial carriers' lowest regular offer is the **APEX** (Advanced Purchase Excursion Fare); specials advertised in newspapers may be cheaper, but have correspondingly more restrictions and fewer available seats. APEX fares provide you with confirmed reservations and often allow **"open-jaw"** tickets (landing and returning from different cities). APEX tickets must usually be purchased two to three weeks ahead of the departure date. Since it's impossible to predict exactly how far in advance a given ticket will need to be purchased, it's best to call for information as soon as you have even a rough idea of when you'll be traveling. Be sure to inquire about any restrictions on length of stay.

To obtain the **cheapest fare,** buy a round-trip ticket, stay over at least one Saturday, and limit your trip to less than 30 days if possible; traveling on off-peak days (Mon.-Thurs. morning) is usually $30-40 cheaper than traveling on the weekends. You will need to pay for the ticket within 24 hours of booking the flight, and tickets are entirely non-refundable. Any change in plans incurs a fee of between $25 (for some domestic flights) and $150 (for many international flights), even if only to change the date of departure or return. Since travel peaks between June and August and around holidays, reserve a seat several months in advance for these times. When inquiring about fares, get advance purchase as well as length of stay requirements, or else you may not be able to buy your ticket in time, or be forced to return home sooner than expected. Be aware that in the last few years, the major U.S. carriers have taken to waging **price wars** (sometimes including two-for-one specials) in the spring and early summer months. Because there is no way to tell when (if at all) such sales will occur, advance purchase may not always guarantee the lowest fare. It will guarantee a seat, though, which has its advantages.

The chances of receiving discount fares increase on **competitive routes;** flying smaller airlines instead of the national giants can also save money. Most airlines allow children under two to fly for free on the lap of an adult, but discounts for older children and seniors are more rare. Consider the **discount travel agencies** and **student-oriented agencies** listed on p. 40. Almost without exception, 21-day advance fares are cheaper than all other fares. Last-minute travelers should also ask about **"red-eye"** (all-night) flights, which are common on popular business routes.

Whenever and however you fly, call the airline the day before your departure to **reconfirm** your flight reservation. Get to the airport early to ensure that you have a seat; airlines often overbook. (On the other hand, being **"bumped"** from a flight does not spell doom if your travel plans are flexible—you will probably leave on the next flight and receive either a free ticket or a cash bonus. You might even want to bump yourself when the airline asks for volunteers.)

COMMERCIAL AIRLINES

Southwest Airlines (800-435-9792) offers quite a few outrageously low fares, but only flies to BWI. The slight inconvenience is probably worth it for the tremendous discounts. Southwest also offers occasional dirt-cheap **24-hour advance** fares, and always offers student and senior discounts. **"Friends Fly Free"** allows you to take along someone for free when you purchase a regular round-trip fare.

From New York's **La Guardia Airport,** the **Delta Shuttle** (800-221-1212) and the **USAir Shuttle** (800-428-4322) provide competing hourly flights to National Airport seven days a week (flights depart between approx. 7am and 9pm on weekdays, and approx. 8:30am-9pm weekends). While the shuttles were designed for businessfolk—with prices to match ($160 each flight on weekdays)—student and senior fares, available for anyone under 24 or over 65 (10:30am-2:30pm and 7:30-9:30pm weekdays), are $75 at all times. And on weekends (all day Sat. and until 3pm on Sun.), fares drop to $75 for all. Buy shuttle tickets at the gate in New York or D.C.

If you qualify for student or senior fares, expect to traverse the New York-D.C. route frequently, and have the cash on hand, you might consider buying the Delta or USAir **Flight Pack** (4 tickets $229, 8 tickets $419). Discount tickets can be used only on weekends and 10am-2pm and 7-9:30pm weekdays. Purchase Flight Packs at the airport; ID required. Both airlines also offer discounts (available to all travelers) to those who reserve early; call seven days in advance for round-trip flights around $160, or 14 days in advance for rates around $140.

Major Airlines

American, (800-433-7300).
Continental, 2929 Allen Parkway, Houston, TX 77210 (800-525-0280; fax 713-590-2150).
Delta, Hartsfield International Airport, Atlanta, GA 30320 (800-241-4141).
Southwest, P.O. Box 36611, Dallas, TX 75235-1611 (800-435-9792).
TWA, 1 City Center, 515 N. 6th St., St. Louis, MO 63101 (800-221-2000).
United, P.O. Box 66100, Chicago, IL 60666 (800-241-6522).
USAir, (800-428-4322).

Travelers arriving from elsewhere in the U.S. may find it cheaper to fly into New York and catch a commuter shuttle than to fly directly to Washington. Call to see if this applies to your route.

CHARTER, COURIER, CONSOLIDATOR, AND STANDBY FLIGHTS

Charters save you a lot of money on peak-season flights if you can be flexible. Companies reserve the right to change the dates of your flight or even cancel the flight a mere 48 hours in advance. Delays are not uncommon. Restrictions on the length of your trip and the time frame for reservations may also apply. To be safe, get your ticket as early as possible, and arrive at the airport several hours before departure time. Think carefully when you book your departure and return dates; you will lose all or most of your money if you cancel your ticket. Prices and destinations can change markedly from season to season, so be sure to contact as many organizations as possible in order to get the best deal. Contact **Council Travel** or **Travel CUTS** for more information (see **Budget Travel Organizations,** p. 40).

Courier travel works like this: you are a traveler seeking an inexpensive ticket to a particular location; the courier service is a company seeking to transport merchandise to a particular location. If your destinations and schedules coincide, the courier service will sell you a cheap ticket in exchange for use of the luggage space which accompanies it. Courier services offer some great prices, but with restrictions: their schedules may be confining, luggage is limited to carry-on bags only, etc. For a practical guide to the air courier scene, check out Kelly Monaghan's *Insider's Guide to Air Courier Bargains* ($15 plus $3 shipping), available from Upper Access Publishing (UAP), P.O. Box 457, Hinesburg, VT 05461 (800-356-9315), or consult the *Courier Air Travel Handbook* ($10 plus $3.50 shipping), published by Bookmasters, Inc., P.O. Box 2039, Mansfield, OH 44905 (800-507-2665; fax 419-281-6883).

Consolidators come in three varieties: wholesale only, who sell only to travel agencies; specialty agencies (both wholesale and retail); and "bucket shops" or discount retail agencies. You, as a private consumer, can deal directly only with the latter, but you have access to a larger market if you use a travel agent, who can also get tickets from wholesale consolidators. Look for "bucket shops'" tiny ads in weekend papers—the *Sunday New York Times* is best. Before committing, contact the local Better Business Bureau to find out your company's track record. If possible, deal with consolidators close to home so you can visit in person, if necessary. Get the company's policy in writing: insist on a receipt that gives full details about the tickets, refunds, and restrictions, and record who you talked to and when. For more information and a list of consolidators, consult Kelly Monaghan's *Consolidators: Air Travel's Bargain Basement* ($7 plus $2 shipping) from the Intrepid Traveler, P.O. Box 438, New York, NY 10034 (e-mail intreptrav@aol.com).

Standby brokers sell not tickets but the promise that you will get to a destination near where you're intending to go, within a window of time (usually 5 days), from a location in a region you've specified. You call in before your date-range to hear all of your flight options for the next seven days and your probability of boarding. You then decide which flights you want to try to make and present a voucher at the airport which grants you the right to board a flight on a space-available basis. This procedure must be followed again for the return trip. Flexibility of schedule and destination is often necessary, but all companies guarantee you a flight or a refund if all available flights that fit your date and destination range were full.

The following companies offer all three services:

Airhitch, 100 North Sepulveda Blvd. 903, El Segundo, CA 90245 (800-326-2009 or 212-864-2000 on the East Coast; 800-397-1098 or 310-726-5000 on the West Coast), works to and from a greater number of cities than most courier companies. In exchange, you must often list 3 cities within a given region to which you are willing to fly; Airhitch guarantees that you will get to one of them. You must also give a 5-day travel window for domestic flights. The "USAhitch" program connects the northeastern United States with the West (NYC to Seattle or Baltimore to L.A. $129), and California to Hawaii ($129). "Sunhitch" program offers round-trip tickets from the East coast to the Caribbean or Mexico for $189. Be sure to read *all* the fine print. Programs change frequently; call for the latest information. Consumers should make careful inquiries and understand that travel with Airhitch requires a certain level of flexibility.

Air Tech, 584 Broadway #1007, New York, NY 10012 (212-219-7000). Space available flights and last-minute confirmed flights at discounts. Domestic travelers must give a travel window of two days. International flights D.C. to Europe $169 each way. Flights depart primarily from NYC, but Boston departures are also possible. Travelers should always make sure to get all the details, and understand that travel with Air Tech may require flexible travel plans..

A final caveat for the budget conscious: don't get caught up in a seemingly great deal. Always read the fine print; check for restrictions and hidden fees. There are amazingly cheap fares waiting to be found, but **you can't get something for nothing.**

FROM EUROPE

Travelers from Europe will experience the least competition for inexpensive seats during the off-season. Peak-season rates generally take effect between mid-May and early June and run until mid-September. Don't count on getting a seat right away during these months. The worst crunch leaving Europe takes place from mid-June to early July; August is uniformly tight for returning flights. Take advantage of cheap off-season flights within Europe to reach an advantageous point of departure for North America. (London is a major connecting point for budget flights to the U.S.; New York City is often the destination.) To make your way out West, catch a coast-to-coast flight once you're in the U.S.

Major airlines that tend to offer relatively inexpensive fares for a round-trip ticket from Europe include: **British Airways** (800-247-9297), **Continental** (800-525-0280), **Northwest** (800-225-2525), **TWA** (800-221-2000), and **United** (800-538-2929). Smaller, budget airlines often undercut major carriers by offering bargain fares on regularly scheduled flights. Competition for seats on smaller carriers can be fierce—book early. Other trans-Atlantic airlines include **Virgin Atlantic Airways** (800-862-8621) and **IcelandAir** (800-223-5500).

FROM ASIA, AFRICA, AND AUSTRALIA

Whereas European travelers may choose from a variety of regular reduced fares, travelers from Asia, Australia, and Africa must rely on APEX (see p. 45). One good place to start searching for tickets is the local branch of an international budget travel agency (see **Budget Travel Agencies,** p. 43). **STA Travel,** with offices in Sydney, Melbourne, and Auckland, is probably the largest, and thus most accessible, international agency.

Qantas (800-227-4500), **United,** and **Northwest** fly between Australia or New Zealand and the United States. Advance purchase fares from Australia have extremely tough restrictions. If you are uncertain about your plans, pay extra for an advance purchase ticket that has only a 50% penalty for cancellation. Many travelers from Australia and New Zealand take **Singapore Air** (800-742-3333) or other Far East-based carriers for the initial leg of their trip.

Delta Airlines (800-241-4141), **Japan Airlines** (800-525-3663), **Northwest** (800-225-2525), and **United Airlines** (800-538-2929) offer service from Japan. A round-trip ticket from Tokyo to L.A. usually ranges $1250-2500. Round-trip fares from Hong Kong generally run $300-400 less than from Tokyo.

South African Airways (800-722-9675), **American** (800-433-7300), and **Northwest** connect South Africa with North America.

By Train

Locomotion is still one of the cheapest ways to tour the U.S. and Canada, but keep in mind that discounted air travel, particularly on longer trips, may be cheaper than train travel. *As with airlines, you can save lots of money by purchasing your tickets as far in advance as possible, so plan ahead and make reservations early.* It is essential to travel light on trains; not all stations will check your baggage.

Amtrak (800-872-7245, or 800-USA-RAIL) is the only provider of intercity passenger train service in the U.S. Most cities have Amtrak offices which directly sell tickets, but tickets must be bought through an agent in some small towns. **Discounts on full rail fares:** senior citizens (15% off); travelers with disabilities (15% off); children under 15 accompanied by a parent (50% off); children under age two (free); current members of the U.S. armed forces, active-duty veterans, and their dependents (25% off). Circle trips and holiday packages can also save money. Call for up-to-date info. and reservations. Amtrak also offers some **special packages:**

All-Aboard America: This fare divides the Continental U.S. into three regions—Eastern, Central, and Western. During the summer (June 14-Aug. 18), rates are $228 for travel within one region, $318 within and between two regions, and $378 among all three (rates for the remainder of the year, excepting late Dec., are $198, $258, and $318). The price includes travel with up to three stopovers within a 45-day period. The route may not be changed once travel has begun, though the times may be changed at no cost. Fares are subject to availability; make reservations for summer travel well in advance.

Air-Rail Travel Plan: Amtrak and United Airlines allow you to travel in one direction by train and return by plane, or to fly to a distant point and return home by train. The train portion of the journey can last up to 30 days and include up to 3 stopovers. The transcontinental plan, which allows coast-to-coast travel originating on either coast, sells for $492 during peak season (May 24-Sept. 14) and $431 off-season. The East Coast plan, which allows travel roughly as far west as Atlanta including destinations in Florida, Ohio, and Ontario, Canada, costs $353/$309. The West Coast plan, which allows travel roughly as far east as Tucson, AZ, including cities from Las Vegas to Seattle, sells for $248/$214. A multitude of variations are available; contact **Great American Vacations** (see below) for details.

USA Rail Pass: a discount option available only to those who aren't citizens of North America; allows unlimited travel and unlimited stops over a period of either 15 or 30 days. A 30-day nationwide travel pass sells for $440 during peak season (June 17-Aug. 21) and $350 during the off-season (except late Dec.); a 15-day nationwide pass is $355/$245. A 30-day pass limited to travel in the western region (as far east as Denver) is $330/290; the 15-day pass for the west is $265/$215; a 30-day pass to the eastern region (as far west as Chicago) is $265/$240; and the 15-day version is $205/$185.

Great American Vacations, 1220 Kensington, Oakbrook, IL 60521 (800-437-3441). An Amtrak-affiliated travel agency which offers packages in conjunction with airlines and hotel chains and, occasionally, discounts not to be found anywhere else. Programs vary throughout the year; call for details.

Amtrak's trains connect Washington to most other parts of the country through **Union Station,** 50 Massachusetts Ave. NE (484-7540). For most routes you can choose to take either a Metroliner or a regular train; Metroliners (800-523-8720) are speedier, more expensive, and usually not worth the money. Regular trains are efficient and quite pleasant.

Amtrak may be the speediest route to D.C. from **New York City,** although the USAir and Delta shuttles give it a run for its money. On weekdays, Metroliners (3hr.) leave approximately hourly between 6am and 7pm from Manhattan's Penn Station for Union Station; fares are $106 each way. Regular trains (3½hr.) leave at 3:45am, and about once an hour between 6am and 9:40pm; unreserved fares are $60-75. Amtrak also leaves for D.C. from **Baltimore** (Metroliner: $20-22, 30min.; regular: 45min., $15-17), **Philadelphia** (Metroliner: 1hr. 38min., $55-76; regular: 120min., $33), and **Boston** (9hr., $61; no Metroliner, but Northeast direct trains available $66). Additional routes to Washington start in Richmond ($18-23); Williamsburg ($29-34); and Virginia Beach ($40-49).

Maryland's commuter trains, **MARC** (410-859-7400), also depart from Union Station. These offer weekday commuter service to **Baltimore** ($5.75, round-trip $10.25) and **Harpers Ferry, WV** ($7.25, round-trip $13.25). Call for schedule.

By Bus

Getting in and out of D.C. can be done less expensively and more scenically by bus or train than by plane. Especially if you're coming from rural America or have a seriously tight budget, buses may be your best bet. **Greyhound** (800-231-2222) operates the largest number of lines, departing for D.C. daily from **Philadelphia** ($15, round-trip $27), **New York City** ($26, round-trip $49), **Baltimore** ($6, round-trip $10), and **Richmond** ($16, round-trip $30). Washington's modern **Greyhound** station, 1005 1st St. NE at L St., rises over a rather decrepit neighborhood.

A number of **discounts** are available on Greyhound's standard-fare tickets (restrictions apply): senior citizens ride for 10-15% off, children under 11 ride for 50-60% off, and children under two ride for free in the lap of an adult. Travelers with disabilities receive a 25% discount. Greyhound also offers **Ameripass,** deals for **unlimited travel** for 7 ($179) to 60 ($559) days. Call for details.

East Coast Explorer, an alternative bus service connecting the cities of Boston, New York, and Washington, travels on back roads, stopping at sites of historic interest—a good bargain for those trying to tour the East Coast for cheap. Trips from New York to Washington leave Thursday mornings and visit the Amish countryside of Lancaster, PA. Trips from Washington to New York leave Friday mornings, stop at Newcastle, DE, Independence National Park in Philadelphia, Princeton University, and arrive in NYC on a Staten Island ferry. Passenger vans (with A/C) make pick-ups and drop-offs at most hostels and budget hotels; call between one month and one day in advance for reservations (718-694-9667 or 800-610-2680, Sun.-Fri. 8am and 11pm). New York-Washington $32. Vans traveling between New York and Boston leave on Mondays (northbound) and Tuesdays (southbound); $29 each way. Costs for all trips include tolls and tour guide.

By Car

The **speed limit** in and around D.C. is 55 miles per hour. D.C. is ringed by the **Capital Beltway,** or **I-495** (except where it's part of I-95); the Beltway is bisected by **U.S. 1,** which incorporates several local thoroughfares, and is intruded upon via Virginia by **I-395. I-95** shares the eastern half of the Beltway, jets up from Florida, links Richmond, VA to Washington and Baltimore, then rockets up the East Coast past Boston (parallel to U.S.1). The high-speed **Baltimore-Washington Parkway** (part of U.S.1) also connects D.C. and Baltimore. **I-270** runs northwest through Montgomery County to link up with the east-west freeway **I-70** in western Maryland. **I-595** trickles off the Capital Beltway and runs scenically east to Annapolis. **I-66** heads west through Virginia.

Most drivers arrive from the north or south, on or parallel to I-95. **To go downtown from the Baltimore-Washington Pkwy.,** follow signs for **New York Ave**. From I-95, get onto the **Capital Beltway** and get off the merry-go-round at whichever exit you choose. Three of the easiest and most useful exits are Wisconsin Ave. (to upper NW and Georgetown), Connecticut Ave. (Chevy Chase, Upper NW, Adams-Morgan, Dupont Circle, and downtown), and New Hampshire Ave. (through Takoma to downtown). From the south, take I-95 to I-395 directly to the 14th St. Bridge or Memorial Bridge (both lead downtown). From the west, take I-66 east over the Roosevelt Bridge and follow signs for Constitution Ave. I-66 is simpler and faster than I-495. Due to outrageously congested rush hours (Mon.-Fri. 5:30-9:30am on I-66 east and 3-7pm on I-66 west), the extreme left lane is reserved to those vehicles with at least two passengers ("High Occupancy Vehicles," or HOV-2; the HOV-2 law incurs a hefty ticket to violators). An extra lane is open to rush-hour traffic; nevertheless, try to steer clear of I-66, I-495, I-270, and I-95 during these hours.

ONCE THERE

Washington, D.C.'s Airports

From within the U.S., it's most convienent (and scenic) to fly into **National Airport** (703-419-8000), located in Arlington County, VA. Doing so will save you money and headaches, since National is on the Metro and close to Washington by car. Driving from downtown is straightforward (take I-395 south to the George Washington Pkwy. southbound; follow signs for the airport). In theory the ride from downtown to the terminal should take about 15 minutes; in traffic, it can take much longer.

Metrorail's Blue and Yellow Lines serve National Airport; the terminals are a short walk (and a shorter shuttle ride) away from the Metro. Cabs are obviously the most convenient way to get to and from the airport, but convenience carries a price ($10-15 from downtown); for all but the most luggage-laden, there's little reason not to take the Metro. **From National to downtown,** the **Washington Flyer Express** (703-685-1400) bus runs between National and the city every 30 minutes on weekdays 6:25am to 9:25pm; on weekends they leave hourly from 6:25am to 12:25pm and every 30 minutes from 12:55pm to 9:25pm ($8, round-trip $14, children under 6 free). Allow about 20 to 30 minutes travel time between downtown and National. $2-4 discount on all Flyer buses for International Student ID Card holders.

Though National is more convenient, **Dulles International Airport** (703-419-8000), in rural Chantilly, VA, is Washington's major international airport; a number of domestic flights also touch down here. Driving from downtown Washington will take you about 40 minutes—but more during rush hour. (To reach the airport, take the Capital Beltway (I-495) or I-66 through Arlington to the Dulles Access Rd.) Taxis to Dulles from downtown cost over $40. **From Dulles to downtown D.C.,** the **Washington Flyer Dulles Express Bus** hits the West Falls Church Metro every 20-30 minutes. (Mon.-Fri. 6am-10pm, Sat.-Sun. 7:30am-10pm; last bus from Metro 11pm. One-way trip $8.) Non-express buses to the city center leave every 30 minutes from 5:20am to 10:20pm on weekdays; on weekends they leave hourly from 5:20am to 12:20pm and every 30 minutes from 12:50pm to 10:20pm. (45-60min., $16, round-trip $26, children under 6 free.)

Less convenient but generally cheaper flights jet into **Baltimore-Washington International (BWI) Airport** (301-261-1000), which lies 10 miles south of Baltimore's center. From D.C., take I-95 north to exit 47A; then follow airport signs. From Baltimore, take I-695 to exit 22A (the Baltimore-Washington Pkwy.) and then follow signs for the airport. Driving time is about 50 minutes from Washington and 20 minutes from Baltimore; but as always, allow for mega-traffic. **From BWI to downtown D.C.,** the **MARC** offers the least expensive option ($5 to or from Union Station). **Amtrak** also provides train service (40min., $10-11) and the **SuperShuttle** (301-369-0009) runs buses every hour at 10 past the hour, daily 6:10am to 11:10pm (50min., $19, $29 round-trip, children under 6 free).

Tourist Information

TOURISM BUREAUS

Don't hesitate to contact the tourism bureaus in Washington no matter how long your stay. They're useful; some will even make reservations for you.

Washington, D.C. Convention and Visitors Association (WCVA), 1212 New York Ave., Ste. 600 NW (789-7000). Does not expect walk-ins. Write or call for copies of *The D.C. Visitor's Guide and Visitor Map* and a calendar of events.

White House Visitor Information Center, 1450 Pennsylvannia Ave. NW (208-1631). Metro: Metro Center. Opened in spring of 1995. Distributes maps to all sights run by the National Parks Service as well as other major D.C. sights.

D.C. Committee to Promote Washington, 1212 New York Ave. NW, Ste. 200 (347-2873). Affiliated with the WCVA. Call or write for a tourist package containing information on events, festivals, and lots of other free materials.

Meridian International Center, 1630 Crescent Pl. NW (667-6800). Metro: Dupont Circle. Call or write for brochures in a variety of languages. Office open Mon.-Fri. 9am-5pm.

The following offices may also be helpful: **Conference and Visitors Bureau of Montgomery,** 12900 Middlebrook Rd., Ste. 1400, Germantown, MD 20874 (800-925-0880, 301-428-9702; fax 301-428-9705); **Prince Georges County Maryland Conference and Visitors Bureau,** 9200 Basil Ct., Ste. 101, Largo, MD 20774 (301-925-8300; fax 301-925-2053); **Delaware Tourism Office,** 99 King's Highway, Dover, DE 19903

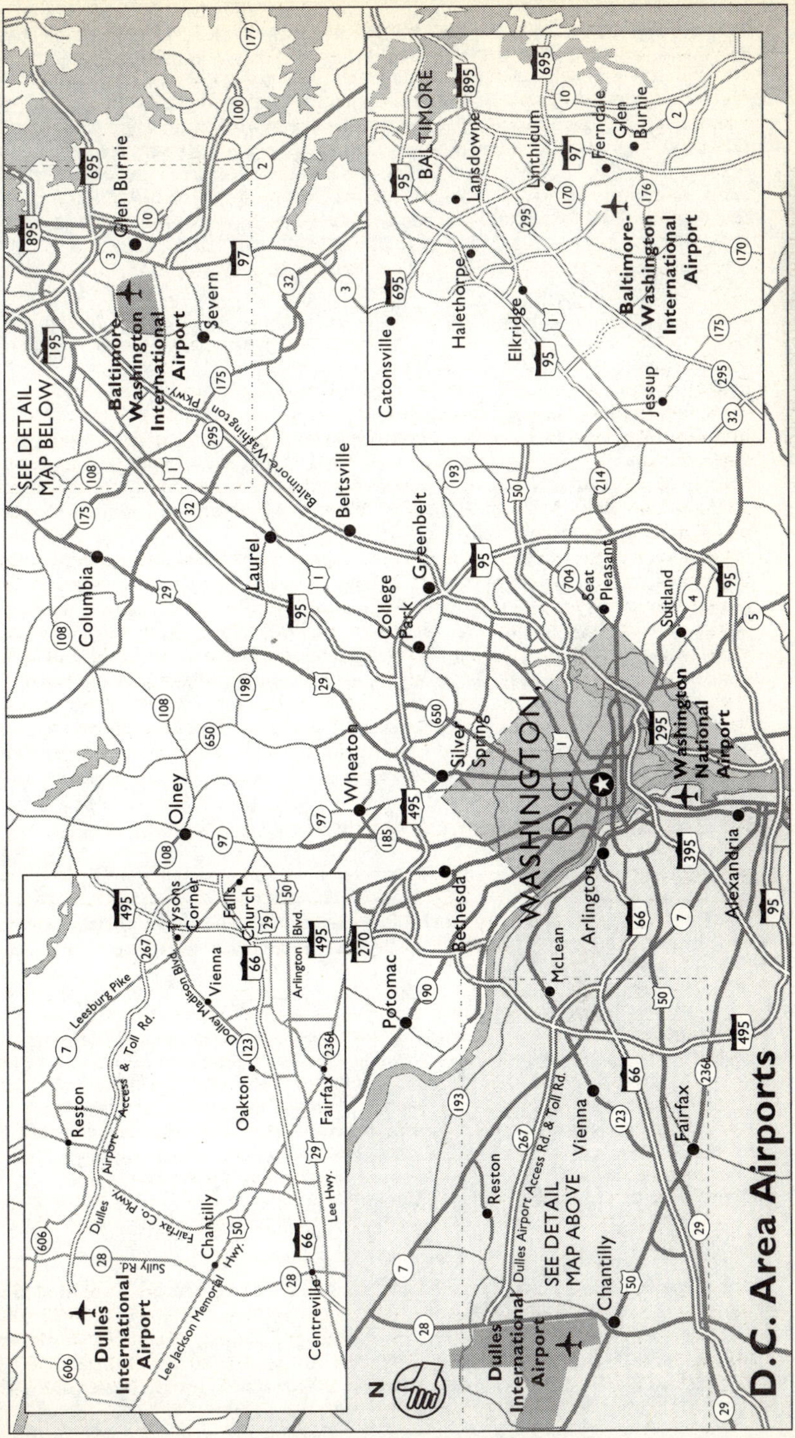
D.C. Area Airports
WASHINGTON, D.C.
Washington National Airport
Baltimore-Washington International Airport
Dulles International Airport
SEE DETAIL MAP BELOW
SEE DETAIL MAP ABOVE
BALTIMORE
Glen Burnie
Severn
Columbia
Laurel
Beltsville
Greenbelt
College Park
Olney
Wheaton
Silver Spring
Bethesda
Potomac
McLean
Arlington
Alexandria
Seat Pleasant
Suitland
Vienna
Fairfax
Reston
Chantilly
Baltimore-Washington Pkwy.
Dulles Airport Access Rd. & Toll Rd.
Catonsville
Halethorpe
Lansdowne
Linthicum
Ferndale
Elkridge
Jessup
Tysons Corner
Falls Church
Oakton
Centreville
Leesburg Pike
Airport Access & Toll Rd.
Dolley Madison Blvd.
Arlington Blvd.
Fairfax Co. Pkwy.
Lee Jackson Memorial Hwy.
Lee Hwy.
Sully Rd.
N

(800-441-8846, **Delaware Economics Development Office,** 302-739-4271); **Maryland Division of Tourism,** 217 E. Redwood St., 9th Floor, Baltimore, MD 21202 (410-767-3400, for info. packet: 800-543-1036); **Virginia Department of Tourism,** 901 E. Byrd St., Richmond, VA 23219 (804-786-4484; fax 804-786-1919); D.C. Branch, 1629 K St. NW 20006 (202-659-5523); and the **West Virginia Travel Office,** 2101 Washington St. East, Charleston, WV 25305-0312 (304-558-2766, 800-225-5982; fax 304-558-2777).

INFORMATION LINES

Time: 844-1212.
Weather: 936-1212.
News (*Post-Haste* a free service of the *Washington Post*): 334-9000. Ext. 5000 for AP news, 5100 for abridged news, 3000 for financial news, 2000 for stock market information, 4000 for sports. Anything else you could possibly want to know (dining info. 3463, recreational sites 9200) is accessible via other extensions.
Dial-a-Hike: 547-2326. Sierra Club outings; updated weekly.
Dial-a-Museum: 357-2020. Smithsonian events; updated daily.
Dial-a-Park: 619-PARK (7275). Information on parks/monuments; updated daily.

Foreign Embassies

Australia, 1601 Massachusetts Ave. NW, Washington, D.C. 20036 (202-797-3000); **Canada,** 501 Pennsylvania Ave. NW, Washington, D.C. 20001 (202-682-1740); **Ireland,** 2234 Massachusetts Ave. NW, Washington, D.C. 20008 (202-462-3939); **New Zealand,** 37 Observatory Circle NW, Washington, D.C. 20008 (202-328-4800); **South Africa,** 3051 Massachusetts Ave. NW, Washington, D.C. 20008 (202-232-4400); **United Kingdom,** 3100 Massachusetts Ave. NW, Washington, D.C. 20008 (202-462-1340). For a full listing, consult the local Yellow Pages under Embassies & Legations.

Orientation

Make no little plans, for they have no power to stir men's minds.
—Daniel Burnham (designer of Union Station), 1899

When Pierre L'Enfant laid out D.C.'s streets, he had two things in mind: magnificent vistas and simple logic. Downtown Washington achieves both. The city is roughly diamond-shaped, with the four tips of the diamond pointed in the four cardinal directions. The irregular southwestern border is the Potomac River, flowing between D.C. and runaway Arlington, VA, which split off from the District in 1846. The other three borders are straight lines separating D.C. from Maryland. Washington's street names and addresses split up into four quadrants: NW, NE, SE, and SW, defined by their relation to the U.S. Capitol. NW is the largest; SW is tiny. The names of the four quadrants distinguish otherwise identical addresses: there are four intersections of 7th St. and G St., and consequently four addresses marked 700 G St., one falling in each of the four quadrants.

The basic street plan is a rectilinear grid. Streets that run from east to west run north and south from the Capitol alphabetically, from two A Streets two blocks apart (nearest the Capitol) out to two W Streets dozens of blocks apart. There is no A or B St. in NW and SW. Since the street plan was devised from the Roman alphabet, in which "I" and "J" are the same letter, there is also no J St. anywhere. After W St., east-west streets take on two-syllable names, then three-syllable names, then (at the north end of NW) names of trees and flowers. These names run in alphabetical order, but sometimes repeat or skip a letter and the number and frequency of discrepancies increase as you get farther away from downtown. The Mt. Pleasant neighborhood, for example, contains the following streets, in order: Belmont, Clifton, Chapin, Euclid. Streets running north-south are numbered (1st St., 2nd St., etc.) all the way out to 52nd St. NW and 63rd St. NE (both one block long). Numbered and lettered streets sometimes stop existing for a block, then keep going as if nothing happened. Addresses on lettered streets indicate the numbered cross street (1100 D St. SE is on the corner of D and 11th). The same trick works with addresses on some avenues (Pennsylvania but not Massachusetts or Wisconsin). The farther you get from the central city, the more these streets get interrupted or replaced by others not part of the alphanumeric system.

Downtown, the interruptions have a logic of their own. L'Enfant's plan included a sheaf of state avenues radiating outward from the U.S. Capitol (Pennsylvania, New Jersey, Delaware, Maryland) and the White House (New York, Connecticut, Vermont) and otherwise crossing downtown (Massachusetts, New Hampshire, Virginia). Massachusetts Ave. runs NW-SE parallel to, but north of, Pennsylvania Ave. Rhode Island Ave. does the same for New York Ave., both running SW-NE. This network of avenues is superimposed over the grid pattern, and the business traffic on these major thoroughfares overwhelms otherwise quiet areas with its constant motion. As the nation added states, the city added streets, and the Last Colony thus contains avenues named for all fifty. (Well, almost. California *Street* is an anomaly.) Besides the Capitol and the White House, downtown avenues meet at circles and squares: some important ones are Dupont Circle (Connecticut, Massachusetts, and New Hampshire Ave.); Washington Circle (New Hampshire and Pennsylvania); Scott Circle (Massachusetts Ave., Rhode Island Ave., and 16th St.); and Mt. Vernon Square (Massachusetts and New York Ave.).

A separate group of streets runs in compass directions from the Capitol: North Capitol St., East Capitol St., and South Capitol St. separate the quadrants. There is no "West Capitol St."; instead, the Mall (a huge green lawn flanked on either side by the Smithsonian buildings) extends west of the Capitol. An imaginary line down the middle of the Mall, from the Capitol to the Potomac River, divides NW from SW. Independence Ave. runs east-west south of the Mall (where B St. SW should be); Constitution Ave. runs east-west north of the Mall (where B St. NW should be).

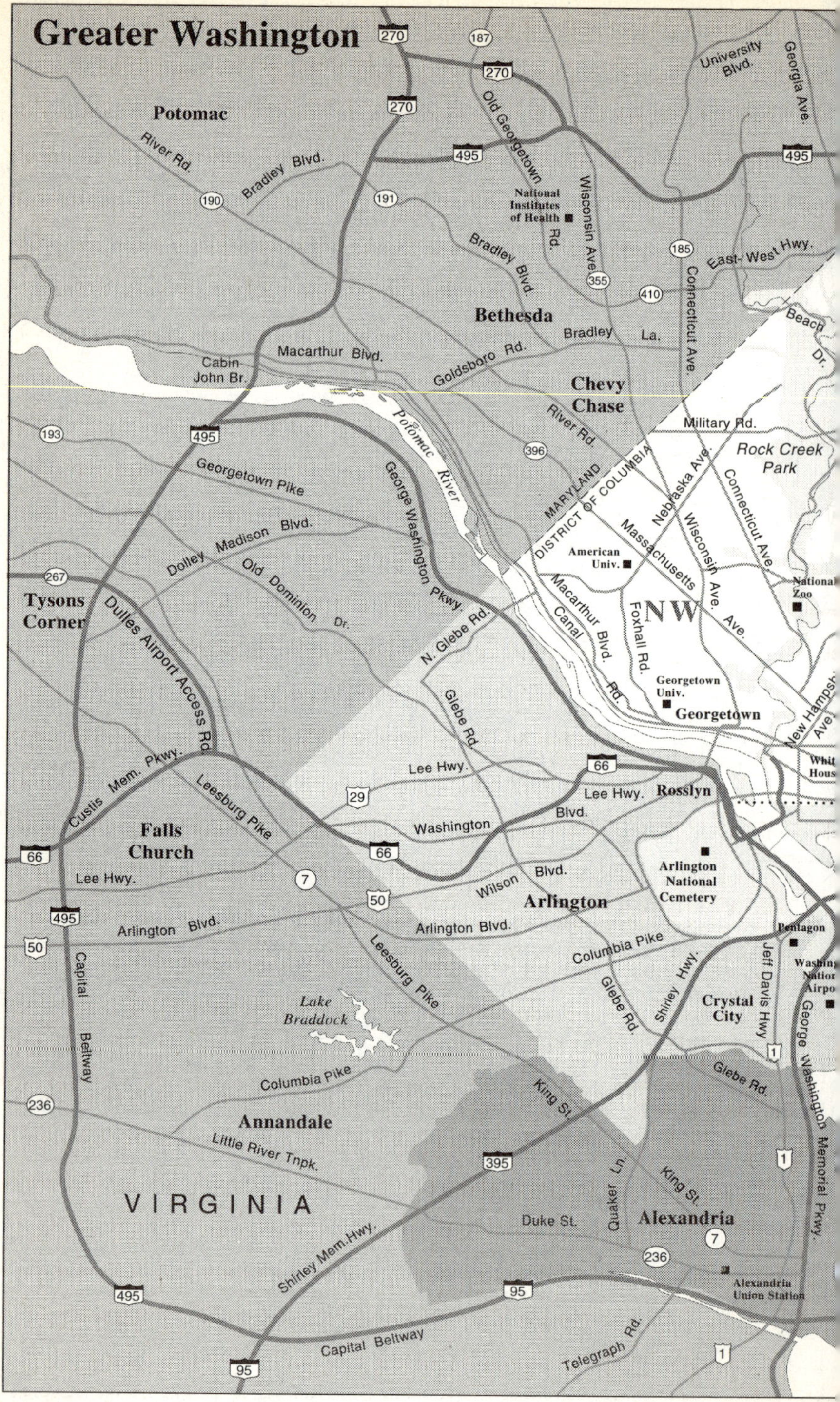
Greater Washington
Potomac
River Rd.
Bradley Blvd.
National Institutes of Health
Old Georgetown Rd.
Wisconsin Ave.
University Blvd.
Georgia Ave.
East-West Hwy.
Connecticut Ave.
Bethesda
Bradley La.
Beach Dr.
Macarthur Blvd.
Cabin John Br.
Goldsboro Rd.
Chevy Chase
River Rd.
Military Rd.
Rock Creek Park
Potomac River
Georgetown Pike
George Washington Pkwy.
MARYLAND
DISTRICT OF COLUMBIA
Nebraska Ave.
Massachusetts Ave.
Connecticut Ave.
American Univ.
National Zoo
Dolley Madison Blvd.
Old Dominion Dr.
Tysons Corner
Dulles Airport Access Rd.
N. Glebe Rd.
Macarthur Blvd.
Canal Rd.
Foxhall Rd.
NW
Georgetown Univ.
Georgetown
New Hampshire Ave.
Glebe Rd.
Lee Hwy.
Rosslyn
Custis Mem. Pkwy.
Leesburg Pike
Washington Blvd.
Falls Church
Lee Hwy.
Wilson Blvd.
Arlington
Arlington National Cemetery
Arlington Blvd.
Pentagon
Columbia Pike
Capital Beltway
Glebe Rd.
Shirley Hwy.
Crystal City
Jeff Davis Hwy
Lake Braddock
Columbia Pike
Glebe Rd.
King St.
Annandale
Little River Tnpk.
George Washington Memorial Pkwy.
VIRGINIA
King St.
Quaker Ln.
Duke St.
Alexandria
Shirley Mem. Hwy.
Alexandria Union Station
Capital Beltway
Telegraph Rd.

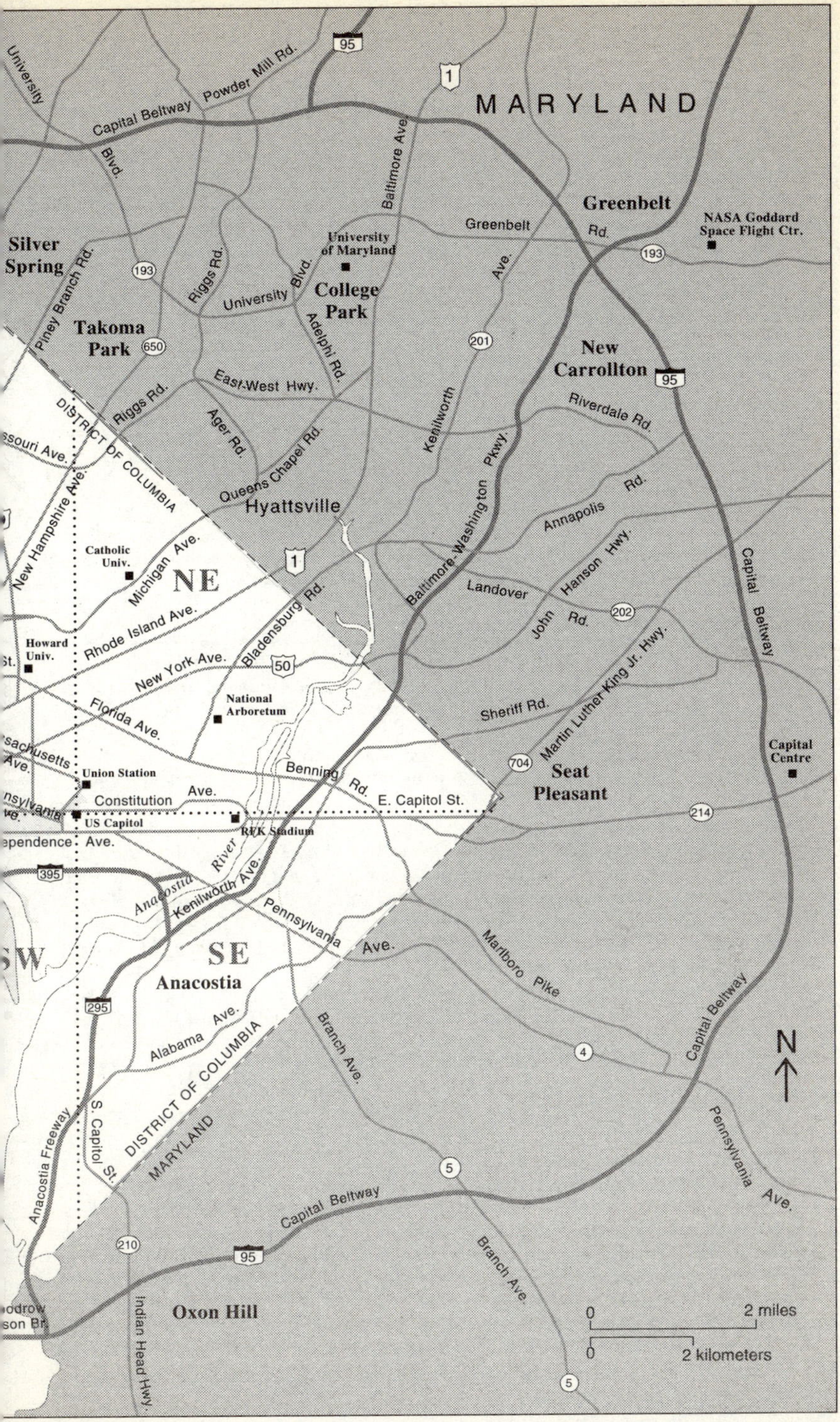
MARYLAND
Greenbelt
NASA Goddard Space Flight Ctr.
Silver Spring
Takoma Park
University of Maryland
College Park
New Carrollton
Hyattsville
Catholic Univ.
NE
Howard Univ.
National Arboretum
Union Station
US Capitol
RFK Stadium
Seat Pleasant
Capital Centre
SW
SE
Anacostia
Oxon Hill
DISTRICT OF COLUMBIA
DISTRICT OF COLUMBIA
MARYLAND
Capital Beltway
Capital Beltway
Capital Beltway
Capital Beltway
Powder Mill Rd.
University Blvd.
Baltimore Ave.
Greenbelt Rd.
Piney Branch Rd.
Riggs Rd.
University Blvd.
Adelphi Rd
East-West Hwy.
Riggs Rd.
Ager Rd
Queens Chapel Rd.
Kenilworth Ave.
Riverdale Rd.
Baltimore-Washington Pkwy.
Annapolis Rd.
Landover Rd.
John Hanson Hwy.
Martin Luther King Jr. Hwy.
Sheriff Rd.
Michigan Ave.
New Hampshire Ave.
Rhode Island Ave.
New York Ave.
Bladensburg Rd.
Florida Ave.
Constitution Ave.
Benning Rd.
E. Capitol St.
Independence Ave.
Anacostia River
Kenilworth Ave.
Pennsylvania Ave.
Marlboro Pike
Branch Ave.
Alabama Ave.
S. Capitol St.
Anacostia Freeway
Pennsylvania Ave.
Branch Ave.
Indian Head Hwy.
95
1
193
193
650
201
95
1
50
202
704
214
395
295
4
5
210
95
5
N
0
2 miles
0
2 kilometers

Some areas of the city have their own ideas of logic. Crowded, eternally fashionable Georgetown runs west of 28th St. between K and (approximately) R St. NW. (Many visitors wrongly think it's far from downtown.) Though Georgetown's streets predate L'Enfant's plan, the older grid harmonized with his, and many of Georgetown's streets have numbers and letters; many, however, retain older names (Thomas Jefferson St., Potomac St.). Wisconsin Ave. NW is Georgetown's north-south artery and main drag. Rock Creek Park beckons from below to drivers hightailing it along Pennsylvania Ave. between Georgetown and downtown (Penn becomes M as it hits 28th). Along the Creek, Rock Creek Parkway offers sheltered, scenic backdoor access to the Mall. And blighted Anacostia must have been slighted by D.C.'s original planners as well: its street plan is the most confusing in the city.

Some **major roads** in the city are **Pennsylvania Ave.,** which runs SE-NE from Anacostia to Capitol Hill to the Capitol, through downtown, past the White House, and ends finally in Georgetown; **Connecticut Ave.,** which runs north-northwest from the White House through Dupont Circle, past the Zoo, and out into the suburbs of Chevy Chase, MD; **Wisconsin Ave.,** north from Georgetown past the Cathedral to Bethesda; **16th St. NW,** which zooms from the White House north through hotels, offices, townhouses, Adams-Morgan, and Mt. Pleasant (in that order) and then forms Rock Creek Park's eastern border until it continues into Maryland; **K St. NW,** a major artery downtown; **Constitution and Independence Ave.,** just north and south of the Mall; **Massachusetts Ave.,** from American University past the Cathedral, then through Dupont and Old Downtown to Capitol Hill; **New York Ave.,** whose principal arm runs from the White House through NE; **Rock Creek Pkwy.,** north-south through Rock Creek Park; and high-speed **North Capitol St.**

NEIGHBORHOODS

Tourists who see the Smithsonian and the government halls, but don't escape the Mall and see the neighborhoods, have only scratched Washington's surface. Nearly 600,000 residents inhabit the federal city; rich and poor, black, white, Asian, and Latino are all well-represented.

Capitol Hill extends east from the Capitol; its townhouses and bars mix white- and blue-collar locals with legislation-minded pols. **The Mall** is not a neighborhood but a long grassy stretch west of the Capitol, flanked by Smithsonian buildings. West of the Mall proper, lawns are peppered with famous monuments such as the Lincoln Memorial. The **Southwest** quadrant of the city, south of the Mall, begins as federal offices, then passes under I-395 and becomes a low-income neighborhood (to the east) and the waterfront area (to the west). North of the Mall, **Old Downtown** plays host to private business and government bureaucracy accompanied by **Foggy Bottom** (sometimes called the "West End") on the other side of the White House and **Farragut,** the area around K St. west of 15th St. NW.

Georgetown draws crowds and sucks away bucks from its center at Wisconsin Ave. and M St. NW. This townhouse neighborhood harbors students and a few millionaires. Business and pleasure, embassies and streetlife, straight and gay converge around **Dupont Circle;** east of 16th St. the Dupont Circle character changes to struggling **Logan Circle,** to rundown **Shaw,** and finally to Howard University and **LeDroit Park,** an early residence for Washington's African-American elite. A strong Hispanic community rather peacefully coexists with black, white, and hip in **Adams-Morgan,** north of Dupont and east of Rock Creek Park; farther north in the equally multi-racial **Mount Pleasant** area, residents lead a more uneasy coexistence.

West of the park and north of Georgetown, spacious **upper Northwest** plays host to several smaller, mostly white neighborhoods, the National Zoo, and the Cathedral. American University and the affluent, landscaped Foxhall Road hover around the city's northwestern edges. 16th Street zooms due north past the Walter Reed Army Medical Center to Silver Spring, MD. Nearby suburb **Takoma Park** hangs out its batiks along the District's northeast edge. The NE quadrant itself, east of North Capitol St., includes the middle-class **Brookland** area, home of Catholic University, along with poorer neighborhoods and the expansive Arboretum. Across the Anacostia

River, the rest of **Southeast** (including **Anacostia**), has been seriously damaged and further isolated by poverty, drugs, and guns.

Getting Around

METRO

Metrorail

Metrorail, the Washington subway system, is a sight in its own right. (Its friends call it the "**Metro.**") In 1996, Metro celebrated its 20th birthday as an operating bus-rail system; it includes 74 stations and 89 miles of line, with 764 rail cars and 1,322 buses. The Wheaton station has the world's longest escalator—230 ft. from street to mezzanine level. The sterile, monumental stations, with their high, curved ceilings and relentlessly brown-and-beige color scheme, awe first-time riders with their uniformity and efficiency; even the rows of parallel ceiling lozenges, meant to depress echoes, suggest the honeycomb decor of a beehive. (Please don't interfere with the busy routine of the Washington drones; stand only on the right side of the escalators, leaving the left side open for commuters on the move.) While designer Harry Weese's futuristic plan may seem lifeless and official to some visitors; others will find its space-age sleekness aesthetically appealing. The **main office,** 600 5th St. NW, is open Mon.-Fri. 8:30am-4pm. (Metro: Judiciary Square.) Metro system route maps, rail and bus passes are sold at the sales office (636-3425; at Metro Center, open Mon.-Fri. 8am-1pm and 2-4pm. Metrorail phone information (637-7000, TDD 638-3780) is available Mon.-Fri. 6am-10:30pm, Sat.-Sun. 8am-10:30pm.)

Metro **trains** run Mon.-Fri. 5:30am to midnight, Sat.-Sun. 8am-midnight, and are clean, quiet, carpeted, and air-conditioned. Between the profusion of brown-capped Metro cops and the stations themselves, which leave hoods no place to hide, the system has remained **nearly crime-free.** Stations in troubled Anacostia opened in 1991; other stations in progress will open between 1997 and 2001.

The Metro operates on a computerized **fare-card** system. Metro fares rose slightly in June 1995. Peak-hour (5:30am-9:30am and 3pm-8pm) **fares** now range from $1.10 to $3.25, depending on the distance traveled. At all other times, fares range from $1.10 to $2.10. Before you pass through the turnstiles, purchase a card from the machines in the station—you may choose to put any amount from $1.10 to $45 on it. You must pass it through an electronic reader in a turnstile when you enter *and* when you leave the subway. The system calculates how far you've traveled and charges you appropriately. If there's still money on the card, you get it back; otherwise, the turnstile gobbles it up. If you don't have enough money on the card to cover the trip, insert the card into an exit fare machine and deposit whatever amount you're short. The fares for all destinations (from your current location) are posted in each station. Be sure to note the appropriate rate: rush hour or regular. If you plan to connect with a bus after your ride, get a transfer pass from machines on the platform before boarding the train (transfers are not valid within four blocks of the station where they are issued). Certain bus routes have reduced rates with a valid transfer; consult the "All About Metro Fares" pamphlet (available at stations or by sending a self-addressed, stamped envelope to: Washington Metropolitan Area Transit Authority, 600 Fifth St. NW, Washington, D.C., 20001) for useful general fare information. Bus schedules also include details about fares. If you plan to ride the subway several times, buy a $5 **One Day Pass.** This is undoubtedly the most economical choice for a day's sightseeing. The pass offers unlimited Metro usage from 9:30am to closing. **Flash Passes** (with unlimited usage of Metrobus and/or Metrorail for two weeks or a month) are also available. Passes are available at the main office, Metro Center station, other Metro sales offices, some Giant, Safeway, and SuperFresh grocery stores; as well as through TicketMaster (432-7328). Call 962-1326 for information about *advance* fare purchases for groups. You will get a 10% bonus on farecards of $20 or more (max. farecard value is $45). Senior citizens and disabled persons are entitled to discount fares but need a special Metro ID. For more information, senior citizens can call 637-7000; persons with disabilities can call 962-1245 (TDD 628-8973). Elevators facilitate the use of wheelchairs and strollers.

See the **Appendix: Quick-Glance Metro Rail Chart** (p. 296) for D.C.'s Metro stops, lines, and corresponding major sights.

Metrobus

The extensive, complicated Metrobus (same address, phone, and hours as Metrorail) system reliably serves Georgetown, downtown, and the suburbs. Downtown, the bus stops every few blocks. Regular fare in the District is $1.10 (exact change required); fares may vary in Maryland. Seniors and disabled persons are entitled to discounts. Special lower fares and school fares apply to certain routes; up to two children four years old or younger ride free when accompanied by a paying passenger. Schedules and route maps for buses operating near Metrorail stations are available in those stations. A comprehensive **bus map** is available from the main Metro office; call or write (ZIP code 20001) for availability and price. Alexandria (**DASH**) and Montgomery County (**Ride-On**) also have their own, smaller bus systems; these routes are included in the Metro maps. Metro information (637-7000) can describe the alchemical mix of buses and trains needed to reach any destination.

Bus routes with a letter followed by a number (e.g., D4, S2) or with a two-digit number make stops in D.C. and Maryland, sometimes (like the "J" buses) only in Maryland. Some routes (like the 30-something buses) run only in D.C. If the number precedes the letter (18L, 5D), the route runs in Virginia. (Most Virginia routes connect to the Pentagon Metro stop.) 30-something buses run from downtown to some stretch of Wisconsin Ave. NW; #30, 32, 34 and 36 buses take Pennsylvania Ave. NW to Georgetown, then drive up Wisconsin. The immensely useful D2, D4, and D8 lines zip from far NW to Glover Park, Q St. in Georgetown, Dupont Circle, Farragut, and Metro Center before ending up in far NE. Metro L2 buses run from downtown up Connecticut Ave. NW.

The Museum Bus, the first citywide transportation among museums on the Mall and throughout D.C., is a service available to individual members of the Cultural Alliance of Greater Washington, the Smithsonian Associates, and members of all participating museums. Visitors who are not members of one of these organizations may purchase a one-week Visitor Membership ($5 per person, $12 per family) at participating museum shops and at TICKETplace (202-TICKETS). The membership includes unlimited boarding of the bus, free admission to participating museums, and discounts at museum gift shops and restaurants.

TAXIS

Washington cab fares are lower but more idiosyncratic than in other American cities; fares are based not on a meter but on a map that splits the city into 8 zones and a dizzying number of sub-zones. Roundabout routes—designed to push up fares by crossing as many zones as possible—should be a thing of the past as fares are now based only on the zones where rides begin and end. Zone prices are fixed, so your driver can—but probably won't—ask you for the fare at the beginning of your trip. Prices between the confusing subzones within the zones vary only slightly. It's the major zone prices that really matter. A zone map and corresponding fare chart are posted in every legal cab. Be sure your destination is in the District before you hail a cab, though; cab trips to, from, and within Maryland and Virginia are priced by distance rather than zones and are exorbitant rather than affordable.

Within the sub-zones that surround the Capitol building, your fare will be around $3. **Fares** between other zones run $3.20 to $10.80 (the maximum fare for any ride within D.C.). During rush hours (Mon.-Fri. 4-6:30pm), there is a $1 surcharge. Fares are doubled during official snow emergencies. Groups riding to the same destination may be charged $1.25 for each extra person. (Due to recent increases in the cost of gasoline, a fuel surcharge of 70¢ went into effect on June 1, 1996. The D.C. Taxicab Commission implemented the fee as a 120-day emergency measure; its duration will likely be contingent on future fuel costs.) Travel into Maryland or Virginia will cost you $4 for the first mile and $1.40 for each additional mile or part thereof—a surcharge which quickly gets ridiculous. The Metro system obviates daytime taxi-riding; but cabs are quite useful after dark in subwayless Georgetown or Adams-Morgan, to get home from bars and clubs, or wherever you feel unsafe walking around. A cab ride from the heart of the club district in Adams-Morgan or Dupont Circle to the accommodations-saturated Metro Center area runs about $4-5.

Hail a cab downtown, but in peripheral areas, call **Yellow Cab** (544-1212). Be ready to give some directions or you might need to send the first few cabs away. Dispatched taxis cost $1.50 extra. Zone maps are available from the **D.C. Taxicab Commission,** Rm. 200, 2041 Martin Luther King, Jr. Ave. SE, Washington, D.C. 20020 (645-6005). Metro: Anacostia. The Commission is far from centrally located and is very busy conducting daily business. Any necessary information should be obtained by writing or by contacting the public information officer (645-6018; fax 889-3604). And remember, if you feel you're being ripped off, get the receipt, write down the cab number, and call either the D.C. Commission or the very helpful **Mayor's Office** (727-2980). The Mayor's Office is open Mon.-Fri. 8:30am-5:30pm; the Mayor also has a 24-hr. emergency assistance number (727-6161).

DRIVING

Drivers from rabid, cabbie-infested cities such as New York City or Boston often think Washington drivers are wimps. They're right. D.C. drivers are fairly polite, but that doesn't mean you can sleep all the way down North Capitol Street. **Rush-hour commuter traffic** can leave you in gridlock for hours. Traveling downtown (especially from Virginia) from 7am to 9:30am and leaving the city from 4pm to 6:30pm, your car will idle for so long you could probably get where you're going faster by walking. Lunchtime can also pose traffic problems, and Friday afternoons bring the worst nightmares. Most of the sights downtown are more easily accessible by Metro or by bus. In upper NW and in NE, a car couldn't hurt; in attempting to travel to some outlying attractions, you'd be nowhere without one.

Expect to pay $10 or more for **garage parking.** Finding **on-street parking** during the day is almost impossible, especially near the Smithsonian. During afternoon rush hours (Mon.-Fri. 4-6:30pm) most downtown spaces are temporarily illegal. Read the signs; cops tow. Nighttime parking is tough only in Georgetown and Adams-Morgan, the places to which you're most likely to drive (the Metro doesn't serve them).

All those numbers and letters are meant to make D.C. streets comprehensible. While the city makes sense to pedestrians, its alleged order can seem chaotic from behind the steering wheel. Some streets, like Connecticut Ave., have "reversible lanes" whose directions depend on the time of day; a few turn one-way during rush hour. Watch for street signs indicating this. Certain intersections on the edge of Washington tend to plunge drivers into Maryland or Virginia unawares. These are K St. NW west of 24th St., where the Whitehurst Freeway splits off above it; 8th St. SW south of D St., which sends drivers to Arlington or Anacostia, and the one-way spaghetti around the Lincoln Memorial. D.C. roads are infamously confusing; be prepared to encounter construction work that may warrant an alternative route.

Some parts of Washington have their very own logic, incomprehensible to outsiders. Congress is one. **Rock Creek Park** is another. Over the creek and through the woods is often the quickest way from one part of the city to another, since there are almost no traffic lights in the Park. But the park follows neither the grid nor the radial-avenue plan; instead, a few roads traverse the wooded areas and the major artery—the Rock Creek Parkway—follows the Creek itself from Maryland through D.C. to the Potomac. Check a map before you race through the environs. Most of Rock Creek Parkway turns one-way in rush hour (south in the morning, north in the afternoon). Beach Drive is closed to cars from Saturday at 7am until Sunday at 7pm. After a snow-

Speed-Demon Diplomats

Dangerous are the diplomats, foreign functionaries, and anyone else with a red-white-and-blue license plate beginning with "D" or "S." These drivers have diplomatic immunity, which means 13-year-old Sven may be racing down Wisconsin Ave. in the ambassadorial family car. Give them a wide berth.

storm, Rock Creek Park is probably your best bet; the Park Service promptly plows its roads.

Into, out of, or around the suburbs, you're bound to encounter the behemoth **Capital Beltway,** whose signs leave tourists panicked while cars race past exits at over 60 mph. A few hints: **I-495** and **I-95** both refer to the Beltway, which makes a huge circle around the city; **I-95** continues north and south to other states, though it also completes the loop of the beltway. For local traffic, the two numbers are interchangeable. The inner loop of the Beltway travels clockwise and the outer loop travels counterclockwise. Signs at entrance ramps often ask you to choose between Richmond or Baltimore when you want no part of either; read "south" for Richmond and "north" for Baltimore. Exits labeled with a number followed by an "A" lead to locations outside of the beltway loop (away from the city); exits labeled "B" lead inside the Beltway. If you screw up, just take the next exit and then reverse course; local signs usually give good return-to-Beltway directions.

The 14th St. Bridge, which downed an Air Florida plane in 1983, serves the more helpful and prosaic function of linking downtown D.C. and the Mall to Arlington, the George Washington Pkwy., and, through the parkway, Alexandria and the Beltway. (The 14th St. Bridge is technically two bridges, the George Mason and the Arland Williams, running north and south respectively.) Arlington Memorial Bridge, universally called "Memorial Bridge," zips from Arlington Cemetery to the Lincoln Memorial at the Mall's western end. The Theodore Roosevelt Bridge, a.k.a. I-66, runs from the George Washington Pkwy. to Constitution Ave. NW. Key Bridge, also on the G.W. Pkwy., links austere Rosslyn, VA, to happening Georgetown.

To pay a **D.C. traffic ticket,** go to the Bureau of (Traffic) Adjudication at 65 K St. NE (727-5000; open Mon.-Fri. 8am-7pm; Metro: Union Station). Hearings close at 2pm each day. Pay with cash or credit card (MasterCard or Visa). Otherwise, make a check or money order payable to the D.C. Treasurer and send it to the Bureau of Adjudication, Washington, D.C. 20002. If your car is **towed,** go to the Bureau of Adjudication to pay for your towing fee and request directions to the Brentwood Impoundment lot in far-off NE. Towing will cost you $75 plus a $10 daily storage fee which takes effect 24 hours after the car has been towed.

CAR RENTAL

Although the cost of renting a car for days at a time can be prohibitively expensive, renting for local trips is often reasonable, especially if several people share the cost. When dealing with any car-rental company, make certain the price includes insurance against theft and collision. American Express automatically insures any car rented with the card. Although rental charges run $25-55 per day for an economy car, plus 30-40¢ per mile, most companies have special deals (especially on weekends). If you have a major credit card, you might avoid having to leave a large cash deposit, and you'll have a better chance of not being spurned by minimum-age requirements. Rental regulations vary with dates and location; call around to see if you can make arrangements for your particular plan. Companies may also rent to individuals under 25 if they are a corporate contractor for your employer. Some major companies are:

Alamo (800-327-9633). Ages 21-24 with a major credit card can rent for a $20-per-day additional fee, $50-per-day or $200-per-week deposit, and proof of employment or phone bill in own name.

Avis (800-331-1212). Min. age 25, unless the renter has a corporate account.

Budget (800-527-0700). Most branches rent to 25 and over only. Some branches rent to ages 21-24 for a $5-15-per-day surcharge.

Dollar (800-800-4000). At most branches, ages 21-24 may rent with a credit card (with $250 credit available and an additional daily fee of $15 per day). Rental may be driven anywhere within the continental U.S.

Enterprise Rent-a-Car, 927 N. Kansas St. (703-243-5404, 800-325-8007), in Arlington. $32 per day, $180 per week for a compact car (but expect rates to differ from branch to branch). Unlimited mileage. Min. age 21, with major credit card or cash deposit. Ages 21-24 pay $8-per-day surcharge. Open Mon.-Fri. 7:30am-6pm, Sat. 8am-noon.

Hertz (800-654-3131). Min. age 25, or 21-24 with a corporate account.

National (800-227-7368). Min. age 25 (with credit card), or 21-24 with a corporate account.

Rent-A-Wreck (800-421-7253); local branch: 5455 Butler Road (800-664-2526), in Bethesda. All branches are independently owned and specialize in supplying vehicles that are past their prime. Cars may have dents and purely decorative radios, but they run and they're cheap. Min. age 25, or 21-24 (with a credit card) for $5-per-day surcharge. For more information, see **Gettin' it Online** (p. 22).

Thrifty (800-367-2277). Ages 21-24 *may* be able to rent at some locations for an additional fee of $15 per day.

Local companies often charge less than major companies, although you'll generally have to return the car to your point of origin. Rentals are cheapest in Arlington, VA.

Bargain Buggies Rent-a-Car, 912 N. Lincoln St. (703-841-0000), in Arlington. $24.95 per day plus 15¢ per mile, with 100 free miles. $125.95 per week (local rental), with 500 free miles. $69.95 per weekend, with 200 free miles. Rates may differ from branch to branch. Min. age 18, with major credit card or cash deposit of $250. Those under 21 need full insurance coverage of their own. Rates may be contingent on rental length and make of car. Open Mon.-Fri. 8am-7pm, Sat. 9am-3pm, Sun. 9am-noon.

BICYCLING

When cars leave the District each night, the emptied avenues are a cyclist's dream. Biking during the day can be more harried, as you dodge crazed, spandex-clad bike messengers, frenzied taxis, and mammoth tourmobiles. You must obtain a **Bike-on-Rail permit** to bring your bicycle aboard Metro trains. To obtain a permit, you must pass a 30-minute written test on *Bike-on-Rail* rules and regulations; the test is given at Metro's main office. Permits cost $15 and are good for three years; permit holders can bring bicycles on Metro trains Mon.-Fri. 10am-2pm and after 7pm, as well as all day Sat.-Sun. and federal holidays except July 4th. Call 962-1116 for more information. Helmetlessness is illegal in Maryland, though not in D.C. and VA. If you must leave your bike unattended, use a strong "U" lock. Thieves laugh at (and then cut through) weaker chain locks. For information on bike rental companies and prices, as well as cycling in and around D.C., see **Sports and Recreation,** p. 225.

Keeping In Touch

MAIL

Individual offices of the U.S. Postal Service are usually open Monday to Friday from 9am to 5pm and sometimes on Saturday. All are closed on national holidays. **Post-cards** mailed within the U.S. cost 20¢ and **letters** cost 32¢ for the first ounce and 23¢ for each additional ounce. Within the U.S., up to two pounds of material can be sent **Priority Mail** (2-3 days to domestic locations) for $3. To Canada and Mexico, it costs 30¢ to mail a postcard. Postcards mailed overseas cost 40¢, and letters are 50¢ for a half-ounce, 95¢ for an ounce, and 39¢ for each additional half-ounce up to 64 ounces. **Aerogrammes,** printed sheets that fold into envelopes ready to be airmailed, are sold at post offices for 45¢. Most U.S. post offices offer an **International Express Mail** service, which is the fastest way to send an item overseas. For information on **Federal Express** services, call 800-463-3339.

The U.S. is divided into postal zones, each with a five- or nine-digit **ZIP code** particular to a region, city, or part of a city. Writing this code on letters is essential for timely delivery. Dial 202-526-3920 for the 24-hr. automated **Postal Answer Line (PAL),** which provides information on a variety of postal services and rates.

Receiving Mail

If you want to receive mail while on the road, it can be sent to you c/o **General Delivery.** Picking up mail sent to General Delivery in D.C. is more difficult than catching a moonbeam in your hands; rather than going to a post office downtown, it goes to the main national sorting facility on Brentwood Rd. NE, miles from everywhere and not served by Metrorail (the closest is Rhode Island Ave.). Worse still, you can't send General Delivery mail to another D.C. post office, even if you know the ZIP—it all ends up at Brentwood. The envelope should also say "Please hold until (...)," the blank filled in with a date a couple of weeks after your correspondent expects you to pick up the letter (letters are normally held for around 30 days). When you claim your mail, you'll have to present an ID; if you don't claim a letter within two to four weeks, it will be returned to its sender. Almost any morsel of D.C.-related postal information can be retrieved through the computer that answers the phone at the Postal Answer Line (see above).

American Express offices throughout the U.S. will act as a mail service for cardholders if you contact them in advance. Under this free "Client Letter Service," they will hold mail for 30 days, forward upon request, and accept telegrams. The last name of the person to whom the mail is addressed should be capitalized and underlined, and "Client Letter Service" should be written on the front of the envelope. For *Traveler's Companion,* which includes a complete list of offices and instructions on how to use the service, call 800-528-4800.

Post Office Branches

Call 635-5300 to find the post office nearest you. Individual listings can be found in **Daytripping from D.C.** Some D.C. branches are:

Main office: indescribably inconvenient at 900 Brentwood Rd. NE (635-5300). ZIP code: 20090. Mail sent "General Delivery" always comes here—a good reason not to have anything sent General Delivery. Open Mon.-Fri. 8am-8pm, Sat. 10am-6pm. Sun. noon-6pm.

North Capital Station: 2 Massachusetts Ave. NE (523-2628), at Union Station Metro. Open Mon.-Fri. 7am-midnight, Sat.-Sun. 7am-8pm.

Farragut Station: 1145 19th St. NW (523-2506). Open Mon.-Fri. 8am-6pm.

Temple Heights Station: 1921 Florida Ave. NW (232-7613), near Connecticut Ave. between Dupont Circle and Adams-Morgan. Open Mon.-Fri. 8:30am-5:30pm.

Martin Luther King Jr. Station: 1400 L St. NW (523-2000). Open Mon.-Fri. 8am-7pm and Sat. 10am-2pm.

Columbia Heights Station: 1423 Irving St. NW (523-2397). Open Mon.-Fri. 8am-5:30pm, Sat. 8:30am-3pm.

Georgetown: 1215 31st St. NW (523-2405). Open Mon.-Fri. 8am-5:30pm, Sat. 8:30am-2pm.

TELEPHONES

Most of the information you will need about telephone usage—including area codes for the U.S., foreign country codes, and rates—is in the front of the local **white pages** telephone directory. Use the **yellow pages,** published at the end of the white pages or in a separate book, to look up the phone numbers of businesses and other services. Federal, state, and local **government listings** are provided in the blue pages at the back of the directory. To obtain local phone numbers or area codes of other cities, call **directory assistance** at 411. Calling "0" will get you the **operator,** who can assist you in reaching a phone number and provide you with general information. For long-distance directory assistance, dial 1-(area code)-555-1212. The operator will help you with rates or other information and give assistance in an emergency. Directory assistance or the operator is free from any pay phone.

Telephone numbers in the U.S. consist of a three-digit area code, a three-digit exchange, and a four-digit number, written as 123-456-7890. Only the last seven digits are used in a **local call. Non-local calls within the area code** from which you are dialing require a "1" before the last seven digits, while **long-distance calls outside the area code** from which you are dialing require a "1" and the area code. For example, to call **Booeymonger** Restaurant in Georgetown from outside D.C., you'd dial 1-202-333-4810. Generally, discount rates apply after 5pm on weekdays and Sunday and economy rates every day between 11pm and 8am; on Saturday and on Sunday until 5pm, economy rates are also in effect. Numbers beginning with area code 800 are **toll-free calls** requiring no coin deposit. Numbers beginning with 900 are **toll calls** and charge you (often exorbitantly) for the provided "service."

The **country code** is 1 for the U.S. and Canada; 44 for the U.K.; 353 for the Republic of Ireland; 61 for Australia; 64 for New Zealand; and 972 for Israel.

You can place **international calls** from most telephones. To call direct from the U.S., dial the universal international access code (011) followed by the country code, the city code, and the local number. Country codes and city codes may sometimes be listed with a zero in front (e.g., 033), but when using 011 (or whatever your international access code happens to be), drop successive zeros (e.g., 011 33). In some countries, especially in small villages, you may have to go through the operator. In others, you must wait for a tone after the international access code.

English-speaking operators are often available for both local and international assistance. Operators in most countries will place **collect calls** for you. It's cheaper to find a pay phone and deposit just enough money to be able to say "Call me" and give your number (though some pay phones cannot receive calls).

Some companies, seizing upon this "call-me-back" concept, have created callback phone services. Under these plans, you call a specified number, ring once, and hang up. The company's computer calls back and gives you a dial tone. You can then make as many calls as you want, at rates about 20-60% lower than you'd pay using credit cards or pay phones. This option is most economical for loquacious travellers, as services may include a $10-25 minimum billing per month. For information, call America Tele-Fone (800-321-5817), Globaltel (770-449-1295), International Telephone (800-638-5558), and Telegroup (800-338-0225).

A **calling card** is another, cheaper alternative; your local long-distance phone company will have a number for you to dial while travelling (either toll-free or charged as a local call) to connect instantly to an operator in your home country. The calls (plus a small surcharge) are then billed either collect or to a calling card. For more information, call **AT&T** about its **USADirect** and **World Connect** services (800-331-1140, from abroad (412-553-7458)), **Sprint** (800-877-4646), or **MCI WorldPhone** and **World Reach** (800-996-7535). MCI's WorldPhone also provides access to MCI's Traveler's Assist, which gives legal and medical advice, exchange rate information, and translation services. For similar services for countries outside the U.S., contact your local phone company. In Canada, contact Bell Canada **Canada Direct** (800-565-4708); in the U.K., British Telecom **BT Direct** (tel. (800) 34 51 44); in Ireland, Telecom Éireann **Ireland Direct** (tel. (800) 25 02 50); in Australia, Telstra **Australia Direct** (tel. 13 22 00); in New Zealand, **Telecom New Zealand** (tel. 123); and in South Africa, **Telkom South Africa** (tel. 09 03).

Phone rates tend to be highest in the morning, lower in the evening, and lowest on Sunday and late at night. Also, remember **time differences** when you call. Britain, Ireland, Portugal, and Iceland are on Greenwich Mean Time (GMT)—five hours ahead of Eastern Standard Time. Finland, Estonia, Latvia, Lithuania, western Russia, Romania, Bulgaria, Greece, and Turkey are two hours ahead of GMT. Moscow is three hours ahead. Some countries ignore daylight savings time, and fall and spring switchover times often vary among those countries that do use it.

OTHER COMMUNICATION

Domestic and international **telegrams** offer an option slower than phone but faster than post. Fill out a form at any post or telephone office; cables to North America arrive in one or two days. Telegrams can be quite expensive, so you may wish to consider **faxes,** for more immediate, personal, and cheaper communication. Major cities across Europe have bureaus where you can pay to send and receive faxes.

Between May 2 and Oktoberfest, **EurAide,** P.O. Box 2375, Naperville, IL 60567 (708-420-2343; fax 420-2369), offers **Overseas Access,** a service useful to travelers without a set itinerary. The cost is $15 per week or $40 per month plus a $15 registration fee. To reach you, people call, fax, or e-mail to leave a message; you receive it by calling Munich whenever you wish, which is cheaper than calling overseas. You may also leave messages for callers to pick up by phone. For an additional $20 per month, EurAide will forward mail sent to Munich to any addresses you specify.

Electronic mail (e-mail) is an increasingly popular means of communication. With a minimum of computer knowledge and a little planning, you can beam messages anywhere for no per-message charges. Befriend college students as you go and ask if you can use their e-mail accounts. If you're not the finagling type, look for bureaus that offer access to e-mail for sending individual messages. Search through http://www.easynet.co.uk/pages/cafe/ccafe.html to find a list of cybercafes around the world from which you can drink a cup of joe and e-mail him, too. Another possibility is **America Online,** 8615 Westwood Center Drive, Vienna, VA 22070 (800-827-6364). The interactive computer service now offers "GLOBALnet," making it possible for American net-junkies to access the internet, sexy chat rooms, and of course e-mail through their home accounts while traveling in 70 countries. The only hurdles for budget travelers are the $6-12 per hour surcharge and the fact that GLOBALnet only works on computers with AOL software already installed; in other words, to use the service you must travel with your own portable computer or install the software on computers as you go and log on as a guest.

Let's Go Picks

Every high school yearbook employs the time-honored tradition of superlatives; *Let's Go* follows suit with some D.C.-oriented slam-bang "bests" of its own. Ever wonder how a Researcher-Writer spends his day (or night) off? Perhaps an occasion will arise that neccessitates one of our mood-catering pleasures; though some of the following are indeed on the Tourmobile route, they can also satisfy a less-than generic tourist desire. If a quirk in your trip to the District or surrounding areas and cities turned out for the "best," please do not hesitate to send a postcard *Let's Go*'s way—there certainly exist more than the miscellany of "bests" below.

Best natural harbor of romance (read "cheap date"): Dumbarton Oaks (see **Museums & Galleries,** p. 204) offers 10 acres of otherwordly terraced gardens that afford a breathtaking walk year-round. Insulated from the metropolis by the rest of the estate, Dumbarton Oaks Park, and the Danish Embassy, the gardens are a gorgeously landscaped haven of serenity; if your botanical inclinations are such (and your date doesn't mind), you may check out the gardens' library as well.

Best place at which to be when the sun sets: Washington Harbor/Marina (see **Sights: The Waterfront,** p. 123). The Waterfront doubles as the place affording the **best view of the Watergate complex and Roosevelt Island,** most spectacular as the day wanes. Beauty and bureacracy all at once—not to mention an even less expensive romantic endeavor than Dumbarton Oaks.

Best museum in which to experience the collective impassioned patriotism of 20,000 tourists: National Air and Space Museum (see **Museums & Galleries,** p. 190). Especially in the wake of 1996's blockbuster *Independence Day* and the timely discovery of supposed evidence of Martian life, the museum incites and inspires an incomparable sense of bonding among earthlings—as well as the patriotic giddiness that accompanies every exhibit displaying an American flag.

Best museums in which to experience a serene aesthetic free from tourist throngs: the Arthur M. Sackler and Freer Galleries (see **Museums & Galleries,** p. 193-194). When honking taxis, wailing sirens, and the inane heat (or the Air and Space Museum) become too much, these unassuming Smithsonian understatements can be the ideal remedies. Quiet, cool, and exquisite, they showcase an Asian aesthetic that tempers D.C.'s overtaxing patriotic tendencies. You don't even have to brave the outside world in order to get from one to the other.

Best new culture 'zine: Link: A Critical Journal on the Arts in Baltimore and the World. While D.C. has a number of papers and literary magazines reviewing all that proffers to be artistic and/or entertaining, backwater Baltimore has previously been out of the cultural-discourse loop. *Link,* a "mosaic of voices and visions," aims to bring Baltimore's arts scene to the surface and to get people talking about it. The debut issue addresses everything from 19th-century Parisian cabaret to contemporary controversial photographer Sally Mann. The next issue is due out in the spring of 1997, and will be devoted to a discussion of the new American Visionary Art Museum. (Available at many Baltimore bookstores for $7.)

Accommodations

D.C.'s B&Bs, hotels, and temporary lodgings have been hard to come by since the Jackson administration (1829), when 15,000 Americans deluged the Capitol for Old Hickory's inauguration. One witness to the democratic exuberance wrote of the tumult, "lodgings could not be obtained, and the newcomers had to go to Georgetown, which soon overflowed, and others had to go to Alexandria." The situation hasn't improved much in the last 168 years. Business travelers desert D.C. during the summer months, leaving business hotels to discount deeply and swell with tourists on summer weekends; discounts from June to August can run anywhere from $10 to 50% off the usual weekday rates (which hover around $100-120 in the summer). No less busy during the summer touring season are the hostels, guest houses, and university dormitories that round out the selection of D.C.'s temporary residences. For longer stays, the transiency of the D.C. population means that apartments for sublet or rent abound at all times of the year (though the supply is greatest at the beginning and end of the summer and when a new administration arrives in Washington). Unfortunately, the demand for housing at these times equals the supply; you'll have to be both aggressive and early to secure the place you want.

■ For a Visit

If you plan to stay in D.C. for less than a month, you might consider the time-honored institution of budget travel: the **hostel.** Students, Australians, and other downmarket *Let's Go* types fill up D.C.'s amiable HI-AYH hostel. Some hostels favor international travelers over Americans; most offer low weekly rates and a chance to meet other visitors; and almost all want advance notification. **Guest houses** (many are around Dupont Circle and Adams-Morgan), though costlier than hostels, are generally smaller, more personable, and better-looking than budget hotels.

Downtown **hotels** range from moderately to crazily expensive but, if you stay on a weekend in the off-season (read: "sweltering summer"), you can live like a corporate executive for half the regular price or less. The *New York Times* Sunday Travel section lists the latest deals, though a little bargaining can conjure a room for even less. D.C. adds an automatic **13% occupancy tax** and another **$1.50 surcharge per room per night** to your bill. Hotels around D.C. usually charge per room, not per guest; even a $100 room becomes reasonable when you split it four ways and many places will give your third or fifth occupant a cot at no extra charge. Suite hotels offer an especially good deal for groups of three or more (free breakfast and unlimited afternoon cocktails are often included).

The annually updated *National Directory of Budget Motels* ($6, plus $2 shipping), from **Pilot Books,** 103 Copper St., Babylon, NY 11702 (516-422-2225 or 422-2227; fax 422-2227), provides the price, phone, location, etc. on over 2200 American chain budget-motels. Pilot Books also puts out *The Hotel/Motel Special Program and Discount Guide* ($6, plus $2.00 shipping), which lists those hotels and motels in the U.S. offering special discounts. Also try *State by State Guide to Budget Motels* ($13) from Marlor Press, Inc., 4304 Brigadoon Dr., St. Paul, MN 55126 (800-669-4908 or 612-484-4600; fax 490-1182; e-mail marlor@ix.netcom.com).

Many hotels offer parking, though usually for a fee. With garage parking in the District a whopping $10 per day, the automobile-encumbered might find it easier to stay in a hotel in Arlington, VA, or Bethesda, MD, where there's no central-city real estate crunch to preclude parking lots (and many hotels offer free parking). Alexandria, VA, 20 minutes by car from D.C., offers more **motel** options. Unless you know someone in the area, obtaining a parking permit (which allows on-street parking in one of the District's "zones") will be difficult.

The following organizations offer potentially helpful services regarding your accommodations search:

Bed & Breakfast Accommodations, Ltd., P.O. Box 12011 (328-3510; fax 332-3885), Washington, D.C. 20005. Reserves a wide range of accommodations, from budget to luxury, as well as apartments for families or guests requiring longer stays. Rates in private home B&Bs start at $45 for singles, $55 for doubles in summer; rates are higher in-season. $15 extra per additional person. Some historic properties and an interesting array of hosts and hostesses. Open Mon.-Fri. 10am-5pm, Sat. 10am-1pm.

The Bed & Breakfast League, P.O. Box 9490 (363-7767), Washington, D.C. 20016. Reserves rooms in private homes, from Capitol Hill townhouses to Cleveland Park inn-style mansions. All are accessible by public transportation. Room prices vary. Singles $40-110, with private bath $50-115. Doubles $55-95, with private bath $65-135. Booking fee $10; non-refundable room deposit $25. Call for reservations Mon.-Thurs. 9am-5pm, Fri. 9am-1pm.

■ For the Summer

Interns and similar summer guests tend to stay in **university dorms,** where rates are cheap and students abound. Most university housing programs don't want, or even permit, non-student tourists. And even collegians who crave university summer housing should come up with a job or an official excuse to visit D.C. and then write or call several months in advance. Some colleges, at least in the United States, sponsor "summer in Washington" programs, which can put students in touch with D.C.-based alums who need **housesitting** or desire guests; if you're in school, see if yours has one before you visit the city.

Subletting an apartment or townhouse for the summer from local students provides a more homey and potentially cheaper alternative to dorms. **Newspaper listings** often include apartments for rent and for sublet, as well as requests for roommates and housesitters. Check *The Washington Post* (especially Fri.-Sun.) and *City Paper*. Also try the roommate assistance companies listed below.

■ For a Year

Bulletin boards and **newsletters** can help you find rentals and sublets; some are for everybody, others are special-interest. **Georgetown University's** off-campus housing office at Leavey Center 308 (687-8467) publishes listings for D.C., MD, and VA, with a separate listing for summer sublets. Office open Mon.-Wed. 10am-1pm, Thurs.-Fri. 1-4pm. (Other university housing offices might provide similar help.) The **Food for Thought** restaurant in Dupont Circle (see **Food,** p. 96) fills its bulletin board with all sorts of neighborhood requests, including those for apartments, tenants, and roommates. Gay and lesbian travelers especially should check the resource centers at **Lammas** and **Lambda Rising** bookstores, also in Dupont Circle. Apartments for rent are listed in **local newspapers,** including the *Post* and *City Paper*.

Roommates Preferred, 2262 Hall Pl. NW, Suite 202 (965-4004). Metro: Tenleytown. Matches people who want roommates with those seeking rooms. The personable director will meet and talk with you, then suggest people with whom you might want to live. If you decide to use the service after the conversation, the fee is $50. Open Mon.-Fri. 10am-7pm, Sat. 11am-3pm.

Capital Reservations, 1730 Rhode Island Ave. NW, Suite. 1114 (800-847-4832; fax 452-0537). An efficient telephone service that offers discounted rates on hotels around Washington. They claim to screen all hotels for security. Room rates vary with the season but usually start at about $59. Credit card required. Open Mon.-Fri. 8:30am-6:30pm, Sat. 9am-1pm.

Home Exchange, P.O. Box 567, Northhampton, MA 01061, offers a registry service, linking homeowners all over the U.S. and U.K. Subscribers (US $50 fee) list their homes in a directory that is sent to all subscribers for the purpose of free exchange or rental.

University Housing

Georgetown University Summer Housing is available only for summer educational (i.e., non-profit) pursuits; they gladly take college-aged interns and members of summer programs, but cannot house self-declared tourists. Housing is single-sex. 3-week min. stay for residence hall rooms, 8-week min. stay for apartments. Nearly all rooms are double occupancy and all have A/C. Residence hall rooms with a community bath $17 per night, with carpet $19; carpeted rooms with four people sharing a bath $20. All apartments are carpeted, with kitchens and bathrooms. Apartments accommodate 4,5, or 6 people. Rooms available early June to early Aug. Apartments with kitchens also available, but must be rented for 5 weeks ($532) or 10 weeks ($1197). Bring your own linens and pillows. Requires mail application (or fax at 687-4590) and 20% non-refundable deposit. Balance must be paid in full by the time of occupancy. Checks, Visa, and Mastercard payments only; Georgetown student interns may have their student accounts billed. Call or write G.U. Office of Housing and Conferences Services, Washington, D.C. 20057 (687-4560) or visit them on campus at 100 Harbin Hall (open Mon.-Fri. 9am-5pm during the academic year; summer hours Mon.-Thurs. 9am-9pm, Fri.-Sat. 9am-5pm, Sun. 1-9pm). The on-campus housing office at 530 Leavey Center, G.U. (687-8467; open Mon.-Wed. 10am-1pm, Thurs.-Fri. 1-4pm) lists on-campus sublets in a weekly listings; separate listings for the District, Maryland, Virginia, and summer sublets are printed. Drop by and pick one up for $1 when on campus (they won't mail them to non-Georgetown affiliates).

American University Summer Housing: Write to: Summer Housing Office, Rockwood Building, 4400 Massachusetts Ave. NW, Washington, D.C. 20016-8142 (885-2669) for info. and an application. Metro: Tenleytown-AU. Provides simple dorm rooms with A/C for students and interns from mid-May to mid-Aug. Double rooms ($119 per week per person) and triple rooms ($98 per week per person) available with hall bathrooms; come with a friend or they will find one for you. Required 4-week min. stay. A valid university ID (from any university) and full payment for stay must be presented at check-in. Reserve early for check-in dates in June; after mid-July first-come, first-served. Most interns stay on the Tenley campus, which is just steps from the Metro. $300 deposit required.

George Washington University Housing: Write to: 2121 I St. NW, Suite 402, Washington, D.C. 20052 (994-6688). Metro: Foggy Bottom. For interns or students in academic programs only. Average dorm rooms with hardwood floors and clean bathrooms. Apartments available. Suites may consist of one large room or two smaller ones. Laundry in dorms; restaurants close by. All rooms have A/C. Singles with kitchen $30 per night. Doubles with kitchen $44-50 per night. Suites with microwave $22-25 per person per night. A 30-night minimum stay is required and a $600 deposit must be submitted with the application. Rooms are available from late May to mid-Aug.

Catholic University Housing: Write to: Office of Conferences and Summer Programs, 106 St. Bonaventure Hall, Catholic U., Washington, D.C. 20064 (319-5277). Metro: Brookland-CUA. Close to the Metro but far from almost everything else; try other college housing first. Available from early May to early Aug., the rooms in the new Centennial Village complex are spacious with huge bay windows, large closets, and private baths. Non-CU student rates: without A/C, singles $19, doubles $17 per person. With A/C, singles $21, doubles $19 per person. Stays of 30-74 days discounted 5%; stays over 75 days are discounted 10%. 20% deposit required in advance. Call ahead for an application, which must be received at least three business days before expected arrival.

Howard University Housing: Requests for applications should be directed to Rev. James Coleman at the Office of Student Development: Residential Life (806-5661 or 806-9539). Metro: Shaw-Howard U. Housing is available for interns and students in the D.C. area for the summer. Not a great neighborhood. Affordable hostel-like rates in your choice of singles, doubles, and suites (with or without A/C) in the university dorms. Single rooms $14, with A/C $18. Payment required in full upon arrival. Variable meal plans are available through university dining services (806-7400). Linen service $5 per week. Rooms available June 1-July 31.

Hostels

Washington International Hostel (HI-AYH), 1009 11 St. NW 20001 (737-2333). Metro: Metro Center; take the 11th St. exit, then walk 3 blocks north (away from the Mall). Located in a relatively safe area (northwest of here becomes a little suspect), the HI-AYH is not your average under-$20 place to stay. The front-porch awning welcomes you to this well-kept, bright and spacious hostel, run by a friendly and helpful college-aged staff that caters to travelers' needs. Clean, air-conditioned rooms hold 8-18 beds, and are accessible by elevator. Shared bathrooms are well-maintained. Staff organizes free activities every day, including movies, picnics, walking tours, and theater outings. Other facilities include a common room, kitchen, game room, smoking lounge, laundry, and luggage and bicycle storage. Alcohol and drugs prohibited. Open 24hr. $18 per night for HI-AYH members ($3 surcharge per night for non-HI-AYH-members). (After 6 nights' stay, foreigners automatically become HI-AYH members.) Wheelchair access. Telephone reservations recommended and accepted up to 24 hours prior to arrival, written reservations must be received 2 weeks in advance (include self-addressed, stamped envelope for confirmation).

Washington International Student Center, 2451 18th St. NW (800-567-4150 or 667-7681). Metro: Woodley Park-Zoo (15-min. walk). This clean hostel is located amidst some of Adams-Morgan's best restaurants and clubs and maintains a very relaxed and enjoyable community atmosphere. The young guests and friendly staff congregate in a large common room with cable TV and share the two kitchens and three bathrooms. Each of the four bedrooms has A/C and 6-8 beds. Bicycle rental $7 per day. No lock-out; keys are issued. Bed $15 per night. Breakfast included (an ideal time to chat with other visitors and hear accents from around the world). Lockers available. Free parking two nights. Call for free pick-up from the Greyhound Bus or Union Stations.

Guest Houses and Hotels

Kalorama Guest House at Kalorama Park, 1854 Mintwood Place NW (667-6369; fax 319-1262), off Columbia Rd. in Adams-Morgan. Metro: Woodley Park-Zoo (a long walk). In the upscale western slice of Adams-Morgan near Rock Creek Park, Kalorama offers well-run, impeccably decorated and immaculate rooms in four Victorian townhouses. Visitors enjoy evening sherry or lemonade among oriental rugs by the fire in winter or on the patio in summer. All rooms have A/C and a clock radio. Refrigerator space, washing machines, and a guest phone available for local calls. Office open Mon.-Fri. 9am-5pm. Singles with shared bath $40-65, doubles $45-75. Rooms with private baths $55-85 per person, $60-95 per two. Two-room suite with private bath (3-6 people) $80-$115. Free continental breakfast. Reservations with full prepayment or credit card required (try to call 1 to 2 weeks in advance). Limited parking by reservation only $7 per night.

Kalorama Guest House at Woodley Park, 2700 Cathedral Ave. NW (328-0860). Metro: Woodley Park-Zoo. By the people who brought you the Kalorama Guest House at Kalorama Park. This place meets the same high standards of quality, cleanliness, value, and Victorian charm as its older sibling—complete with the complimentary sherry. Desk open Mon.-Fri. 9am-5pm. Rooms with shared bath $40-65 for one, $45-75 for two. Rooms with private baths $55-85 for one, $60-95 for two. $5 per additional person. Free continental breakfast. Laundry facilities. Reservations with full prepayment or credit card required; reserve by phone 1-2 weeks in advance, and cancel by mail at least 2 weeks in advance for a full refund. Limited parking (by reservation only) $7.

Adams Inn, 1744 Lanier Place NW (745-3600 or 800-578-6807), near Ontario Rd. behind the Columbia Rd. Safeway supermarket, 2 blocks from the center of Adams-Morgan. Metro: Woodley Park-Zoo, then a 12 min. walk; or #42 bus to Columbia Rd. from Dupont Circle. Adams Inn's elaborate, elegant Victorian townhouses (smothered in Persian rugs) are run by a super-nice and helpful staff. All rooms have A/C; all shared-bath rooms have private sinks. Outdoor patio, coin laundry facilities, pay phones, and eating facilities. TV in lounge. Office open Mon.-Sat.

8am-9pm, Sun. 1-9pm. Singles with shared bath $45, with private bath $60. Doubles with shared bath $55, with private bath $70. 10% ISIC discount. Breakfast included. Reservations require deposit. Limited parking $7 per night.

The Oakwood Guest House, 20005 Columbia Rd. NW (265-4006); centrally located, ½ block from the Washington Hilton and Embassy Row—also close to the Washington Cathedral and the Mall. Recently renovated, this historic patrician townhouse is architecturally intriguing and aesthetically pleasing with its dark wood paneling, polished hardwood floors, and ornate fireplaces. Pretty and neatly furnished rooms: singles $23-29, doubles $35-45, triples $45-55; $10 per additional occupant. Students and hostel members 10-15% discount; group rates also available. All prices are negotiable.

Capitol Hill Guest House, 101 5th St. NE (547-1050 or 800-261-2768). Metro: Capitol South. This converted townhouse features three floors and ten rooms, including singles and doubles, some with private bathrooms. Desk-drawer graffiti of past inhabitants lends a sense of friendly conversational interaction; furniture is otherwise well-maintained. No smoking. Singles with shared bath $40-65, doubles $55-75. Single with private bath $80-100, double $90-120. Continental breakfast (8-11am) and maid service included.

Hereford House, 604 South Carolina Ave. SE (543-0102). Metro: Eastern Market. If you're facing the Metro escalator, South Carolina Ave. is at 10 o'clock; Hereford House is less than a block down. A British-style bed and breakfast in a Capitol Hill townhouse, this enchanting accommodation reconciles downtown convenience with quiet B&B charm. Friendly English hostess rents four rooms, each named for a county in the U.K. Singles $40-50, doubles $55-60. Two shared baths, laundry facilities, A/C, refrigerator, living room, garden patio, and dog ("Jip") make this place feel like home. No smoking. Continental breakfast served 7:30-9:30am; cold breakfast 8 and 8:30am. Senior discount 10% for stays longer than a week, $5 per day. Credit cards not accepted. Reservations advised.

Lincoln Suites, 1823 L St. NW (223-4320, 800-424-2970; fax 223-8546), near 18th St. Metro: Farragut North or Farragut West. Recent renovations by a new management gave all 99 classically decorated studio suites a wet bar or kitchen facilities, refrigerator, microwave, and a coffee/tea maker. Other features include electronic key locks, complimentary passes to nearby Bally's Holiday Spa, and a dry cleaning/laundry service. Rates range from $89-139 for all suites; special extended-stay rates also offered. Reservations recommended.

Tabard Inn, 1739 N St. NW (785-1277; fax 785-6173), at 17th St. Metro: Dupont Circle. Romantic inn offers complimentary breakfast in a maze of darkened lounges, narrow stairwells, and big, heavy chairs. A lovely flowered carpet and a contemplative Buddha are among the curios in the lobby. The wood-floored rooms vary tremendously in size—some lilliputian, some gargantuan—but all are well-kept and stocked with antique furnishings. Dining outdoors in the courtyard. Singles $59-79, with private bath $99-135. $12 per additional person.

Savoy Hotel, 2505 Wisconsin Ave. NW (337-9700, 800-964-5377; fax 337-3644), near Calvert St. north of Georgetown. Metro: Tenleytown, Foggy Bottom, or Friendship Heights—#30, 32, 34, 35, or 36 bus from those stops, or from Georgetown. Savoy also provides free shuttle service to and from Woodley Park-Zoo Metro stop. Shuttle runs every half-hour Mon.-Fri. 6:30-10am and 4-8pm, Sat. 8am-noon and 4-8pm, Sun. 10am-2pm and 4-8pm. Well-maintained, spacious rooms, excellent for families on a budget. Some rooms have kitchenettes and jacuzzis, and all have either one king- or two queen-size beds. For rooms without kitchenettes, a microwave and refrigerator are available by request, free of charge. (Don't hesitate to ask for a room with a jacuzzi and a view; these beauties go at no extra cost.) Call as far in advance as possible— for weekends of big events such as Georgetown's graduation or major holidays, all rooms are reserved months in advance. Singles $79-129, depending on hotel's occupancy. Doubles $89-139. Students affiliated with local universities will receive the lowest rate. Those under 18 stay free with parents. Parking is free for hotel guests.

Quality Hotel Downtown, 1315 16th St. NW (232-8000, 800-228-5151; fax 667-9827). Metro: Farragut North, at Scott Circle. Huge, amenity-filled rooms, most with 2 double beds, some with a sofabed and kitchenette as well. No pool, but free passes to the National Health Club (at 17th St. NW and Rhode Island Ave.) are available. Summer weekend room rates (per 1-2 people; $15 per additional adult) start at $105, fall $69, winter $85. Ask for promotional weekday rates (subject to availability, of course). Kids under 18 stay free; senior discount 30%, AAA discount 10%. Parking incurs a small charge.

Days Inn Downtown, 1201 K St. NW (371-1473 or 800-562-3350; fax 289-0336). Metro: Metro Center. In addition to a great view of the Capitol, the Days Inn offers newly renovated rooms that are comfortable, sizable, and include TV, A/C, and coffeemaker; some have kitchenettes. Bar/lounge and rooftop pool (open seasonally). Facilities include underground parking ($9 per day), laundry, and free use of hotel fitness room. Rates $80-90, but are subject to availability. Courtesy bus tours of the city leave at 7:55am, 1:30pm, 7:20pm.

Holiday Inn Central, 1501 Rhode Island Ave. NW (483-2000, 800-248-0016; fax 797-1078). Metro: McPherson Square, one block from Scott Circle. Comfortable, inviting rooms are equipped with hairdryers and cable TV. Underground parking available, as well as a fitness room, game room, and seasonal rooftop swimming pool. Electronic key system and safe deposit boxes. Rates $89-139; subject to availability. Rates for seniors and AARP/AAA members start at $79.

Connecticut Woodley Guest House, 2647 Woodley Rd. NW (667-0218). Metro: Woodley Park-Zoo; one block away, across the street from the Sheraton Washington. The tidy rooms are modestly furnished. Office open daily 7:30am-midnight. Singles with shared bath $42-46, with private bath $53-60. Doubles with shared bath $48-51, with private bath $58-66. Group, family, and long-term rates available. Max. stay 4 weeks. No wheelchair access. A/C and free parking.

Holiday Inn, 1155 14th St. NW (737-1200, reservations 800-465-4329; fax 783-5733), at Thomas Circle. Metro: McPherson Square. A little bit older, but every bit as pleasant as its sister up the street at Rhode Island Ave. Rooms afford a great view of Farragut and Thomas Circle, and offer cable TV and modem hookups. Other perks include a rooftop pool. Pleasant singles and doubles range from $89-139; subject to availability. Rates for seniors and AARP/AAA members start at $79. Underground parking $10 per day.

Davis House, 1822 R St. NW (232-3196; fax 232-3197), near 19th St. Metro: Dupont Circle. Charming and spacious wood-floored building equipped with common living room, sun room, patio, refrigerator, and microwave. Accepts international visitors, staff of Quaker organizations, and "representatives of other organizations working on peace and justice concerns." Other visitors occasionally accepted on a same-day, space-available basis. No smoking or alcohol. Max. stay 2 weeks. Open daily 8am-10pm. Singles in a shared room $30, private singles $35, doubles $60 (with hall bath). One night's deposit required. Reserve as early as possible. No credit cards accepted; not wheelchair accessible.

Brickskeller Inn, 1523 22nd St. NW (293-1885), between P and Q St. Metro: Dupont Circle. Small, clean, recently renovated rooms, usually with private sinks and shared bathrooms; some rooms have private bath, A/C, and TV. Singles $45-60, doubles $65-75. Weekly rates: singles from $150, doubles from $225.

HoJo Inn, 600 New York Ave. NE (546-9200; fax 546-6348). Metro: Union Station. A long (½-hr.) walk from the Metro; take N. Capitol St., then turn right on New York Ave. A cab or car is safer than walking. Clean, carpeted rooms with A/C and TV. Electronic key card system. Outdoor pool and free continental breakfast. Shuttle buses to the Mall, monuments, and Metro at 7:30, 8:30, and 9:30am daily ($4 per person, $2 per each additional party member). Singles $56, doubles $60. Seniors and military 10% discount.

The Governor's House, 1615 Rhode Island Ave. NW (296-2100, 800-821-4367; fax 331-0227), at 17th St. Metro: Farragut North at Scott Circle. Oversized rooms have all the amenities, including cable TV and a complimentary *Washington Post;* some have kitchenettes and sofa beds as well. Swimmers can hit the pool or use the free pass to the YMCA next door. July-Aug., $89 on weekdays, $69 on weekends; subject to availability. $110 the rest of the year. 10% discount for seniors.

Swiss Inn, 1204 Massachusetts Ave. NW (371-1816, 800-955-7947). Metro: Metro Center. Four blocks from Metro Center; close to downtown. Seeming more like a B&B or guest house, the Swiss Inn offers 7 clean, quiet studio apartments with refrigerators, private baths, high ceilings, kitchenettes, and air-conditioning. Free local phone calls and laundry. International crowd welcomed by French- and German-speaking managers. Singles and doubles $98 ($78 in summer), with 20% discount for travel-club members (including HI-AYH), *Let's Go* readers, and seniors 60 and over. Weekly rates: singles and doubles $78 per night. Parking $5 per day weekdays (free weekends); managers will pick up patrons from the bus stop, Metro station, or downtown airport terminal.

Windsor Park Hotel, 2116 Kalorama Rd. NW (483-7700, fax 332-4547). Metro: Woodley Park-Zoo, followed by a 5-min. walk across the Calvert St. Bridge and a right on Kalorama. Small, cozy rooms at reasonable rates include cable TV, phone, refrigerator, private bath, and A/C. Singles $88, doubles $98. Weekends $64. Rates vary with hotel occupancy. 10% discount for International Student ID Card holders. Complimentary continental breakfast.

Allen Lee Hotel, 2224 F St. NW (331-1224, 800-462-0186), near 23rd St. and George Washington University. Metro: Foggy Bottom-GWU. Large, aging, and blue. Rooms vary widely in size, furnishings, and state of repair; look at several before accepting one. Rooms do have A/C. Singles $35, with private bath $45. Doubles $45, with private bath $56. Twins $45, with private bath $56.

Harrington Hotel, 11th and E St. NW (628-8140 or 800-424-8532; fax 347-3924). Metro: Metro Center. The Harrington Hotel resides in the business-like center of Old Downtown, 3 blocks from the Smithsonian and closer to other major sights. International visitors abound. Elevators and hallways are old-fashioned yet aging gracefully; the 264 rooms are generally large and clean with TV, A/C, and great views. June-Aug. singles and doubles $79, weekends $69, student singles $49, student doubles $54. Sept.-May singles $75, weekends $69, students $49, doubles $54. Weekend rate all week for seniors. 10% off with International Student ID.

Super 8 Motel, 501 New York Ave. NE (543-7400), on the New York Ave. motel strip. Metro: Union Station. A 25-min. walk from the station on N. Capitol St., then a right on New York Ave.; a car/cab is safer than walking at night. Standard, clean motel rooms with TV, A/C, and private bath. Outdoor pool. Shuttle bus to Metro and Mall at 7:35, 8:35, and 9:35am daily ($4 per person, $2 each additional party-member). Singles $55. Doubles $65. Seniors and military 10% discount.

Travelodge Center City Hotel, 1201 13th St. NW (682-5300; fax 371-9624). Metro: McPherson Square. Two blocks from Thomas Circle. Clean, tastefully furnished rooms with TV, A/C, and coffeemakers. Laundry service available. Complimentary continental breakfast and free use of hotel fitness center. Lockout 10pm-6am. Singles $79, doubles $89. $10 each additional person. Parking $10 per day. Seniors, students, and AAA members 10% discount. International Student ID Card rates: singles $50, doubles $59. Wheelchair accessible.

Holiday Inn, 2101 Wisconsin Ave. NW (338-4600; fax 333-4458), in northern Georgetown. Metro: Foggy Bottom, Tenleytown, or Friendship Heights—take the #30, 32, 34, 35, or 36 bus from those stops or from Georgetown to the front of the hotel. Attractive, newly renovated rooms. Singles $124, doubles $134; students $92; seniors 10% discount. "Great Rates," can be as low as $69 in the summer; rates are dependent on hotel's occupancy. Rollaway beds $10. Free use of hotel fitness center. Outdoor swimming pool; nearby Safeway and Bread and Circus. Wheelchair accessible. Those 19 or under traveling with parents sleep for free, those 12 and under eat for free. Guest parking $8.50 per day.

Best Western Downtown-Capitol Hill, 724 3rd Street, NW (842-4466, 800-242-4831; fax 842-4831). A small (58 rooms), elegant hotel in a convenient location. Singles $95, doubles $105. All rooms with TV and A/C. Complimentary continental breakfast (7-9am in basement cafeteria). Lower rates subject to availability. Weekend rate all rooms $91. AAA/AARP members 10% discount. Take a cab at night.

Holiday Inn on the Hill, 415 New Jersey Ave. NW (638-1616, 800-638-1116; fax 346-1813), across from the Hyatt Regency. Metro: Union Station. Walk 3 blocks northwest on New Jersey Ave. from the Capitol. Standard, clean rooms, 24-hr. reception, and friendly front desk. Swimming pool. Singles and doubles $99-$159, depending on season and availability.

WEEKEND RATES AND SPECIALS

One Washington Circle Hotel, One Washington Circle NW, between 23rd and New Hampshire (872-1680, reservations 800-424-9671; fax 887-4989). Metro: Foggy Bottom-GWU—sensational location. The promise of the beautifully designed and decorated circular lobby is amply fulfilled in this gracious hotel— dark blue hallways and plush carpets lead to well-appointed suites, each with a full kitchen and abundant closet space. First-class service; complimentary *Post* (delivered each morning except Sun.) and pass to nearby health club. Laundry and dry cleaning available. Variable summer weekend rates go as low as $89 for a double. Underground parking $10 per day.

The Windsor Inn, 1842 16th St. NW (667-0300, 800-423-9111; fax 234-3309), between Swann and T St. Metro: Dupont Circle. Clean guest rooms (with private baths) in a 1920s Art Deco townhouse. Atmosphere somewhere between quaint B&B and large hotel. 24-hr. reception desk. Complimentary continental breakfast, evening sherry, and daily newspaper. Singles $69-110, doubles $79-130, suites $99-150. Summer weekends non-suites $55, subject to availability. Rates negotiable during the off-season (July-Aug., Nov.-Jan.). Seniors and AAA 10% discount.

Embassy Inn, 1627 16th St. NW (234-7800, 800-423-9111; fax 234-3309), near R St. Metro: Dupont Circle. The same management as Windsor Inn rents small, pastel rooms with complimentary sherry, daily newspaper, and continental breakfast. Library in living room. All with private bath and A/C. Singles $69-99, doubles $79-105. Summer weekends $55, subject to availability. Seniors 10% discount.

St. James Hotel, 950 24th St. NW (457-0500, 800-852-8512; fax 659-4492), near K St. Metro: Foggy Bottom-GWU. Euro-chic hotel just off Pennsylvania Ave. Small but sleek lobby belies almost 200 spacious rooms that come complete with kitchens. Fitness facilities and compact swimming pool with Roman mural. Coin laundry. Wheelchair access. Complimentary breakfast Mon.-Fri. 7-9am, Sat.-Sun. 8-10am. $135-195, $79-109 on weekends. Special off-season rates of $69 and $79.

Carlyle Suites Hotel, 1731 New Hampshire Ave. NW (234-3200, 800-964-5377; fax 387-0085), between R and S St. Metro: Dupont Circle. Sparkles in renovated Art Deco charm; the "Official Art Deco Hotel" in D.C. Efficiency suites with kitchenettes. Singles $129, doubles $139. Children under 18 with parents stay free. Weekend rate $69 (Fri.-Sun. or Sat.-Mon.) on availability. Rates are negotiable for large groups, especially during slow summer months. Laundry facilities and same-day dry cleaning available. Seniors and AAA 10% discount.

New Hampshire Suites Hotel, 1121 New Hampshire Ave. NW (457-0565, 800-762-3777; fax 331-9421). Metro: Foggy Bottom (10-min. walk along 22nd St. and through Washington Circle). Fair-sized rooms with TVs, small refrigerators, small coffeemakers, and even smaller microwaves; irons, ironing boards, and hairdryers. Singles with queen-sized bed $125, doubles with pull-out sofa $135. Breakfast included. Ask about special packages. Health club passes $5. Valet parking $16.50, regular $11. Reserve in advance.

Normandy Inn, 2118 Wyoming Ave. NW (483-1350, 800-424-3729; fax 387-8241), near Connecticut Ave. Metro: Dupont Circle or Woodley Park-Zoo (a hike from either). Quiet, old-world-style inn renting charming, comfortable rooms equipped with private baths, refrigerators, and coffee-makers. Singles $103. Doubles $113. $10 each additional person. Weekends all rooms $69, subject to availability.

Comfort Inn, 500 H St. NW (289-5959; fax 682-9152). Metro: Gallery Place-Chinatown. 2 blocks to Metro. This upper mid-range hotel serenely presides over Chinatown, with a red brick exterior and peaceful natural-toned interior. Friendly service and comfortable rooms. Prices vary by season and availability. 24-hr. check-in. Jun.-Aug. singles $109, doubles $119, weekend rates $79 and $89. Inquire about the "Summer Sizzler" deal (800-234-6423): singles $69 (includes breakfast and one-day Metro pass), doubles $79 (includes breakfast and 2 passes).

Hotel Lombardy, 2019 Pennsylvania Ave. NW (828-2600, 800-424-5486; fax 872-0503), near 21st St. Metro: Farragut West, three blocks from the Metro. Add a little European feel to your D.C. trip. This elegant, charming, old-fashioned hotel harbors enormous rooms (they were once apartments), most of which have kitchenettes; all have wet bars, refrigerators, and coffeemakers. Fancy time-warp feature:

ACCOMMODATIONS

an open-the-door-yourself elevator. Singles $115-145, doubles $140-170; $20 per additional guest.

GAY AND LESBIAN ACCOMMODATIONS

Several D.C. hotels in the Dupont Circle area and in nearby Upper Northwest advertise as being especially gay-friendly. Among these are the Carlyle Suites Hotel, the Embassy and Windsor Inns, and the Kalorama Guest Houses (see listings above).

The Brenton, 1708 16th St. NW (332-5550, 800-673-9042). Eight spacious rooms and B&B treatment in the Victorian splendor of a 16th St. townhouse. Gay men preferred. Singles $69, doubles $79. $10 per each additional person. Includes continental breakfast and evening happy hour. Reservations recommended.

Long-Term Lodgings

International Student House, 1825 R St. NW (387-6445; fax 387-4115), near 18th St. Metro: Dupont Circle. Welcomes primarily long-term international and some domestic students grandly and warmly in a romantic Tudor townhouse with a mammoth dining hall, important-looking library, large patio, and garden. The modern, dormitory-like rooms are fully furnished, single-sex, and have A/C. Doubles, triples, and quads $600-760 per person per month; singles $805-850 per month. Additional fee for stays under 4 months. First month's fee due upon arrival. Daily breakfast and dinner included (except Sat. dinner). Parking $50 per month when available. Must be at least 20 years old. Write to them (ZIP 20009) for an application or more information. Open Mon.-Tues. and Thurs.-Fri. 9am-5pm, Wed. 9am-8pm, Sat. 11am-1pm. Reserve early.

Thompson-Markward Hall, 235 2nd St. NE (546-3255), just four blocks from Union Station near C St., across from the Hart Senate office building. Metro: Union Station. For women ages 18-34 only. 112 dorm-like single rooms and three double rooms line the upper floors' old but clean hallways. Small bedrooms (about 15x10 ft.) have A/C and phones; communal baths are large and clean. Laundry room. Maid service provided. Bring your own sheets. Two cafeteria-style meals per day in a pleasant dining hall. Piano, library, common rooms, and garden. Men aren't allowed beyond the first floor, but may visit in the lavish lobby, adjoining lounge, and library. Two-week min. stay, two-year max. stay. $120 per week, $595 per month. Nonrefundable $50 deposit (credited to rent) required with reservation. Summer reservations should be made by early March.

Bethesda, MD

Manor Inn Bethesda, 7740 Wisconsin Ave. (301-656-2100, reservations 800-874-0050; fax 986-0375). Metro: Bethesda; walk 2 blocks north. Comfortable clone motel. Big, carpeted rooms with TVs and A/C. Free continental breakfast. Coin-operated laundry. Free shuttle to NIH—great for conventions. Check-out noon. Singles $75, doubles $85 (lower off-season rates). Parking $5 per night.

American Inn of Bethesda, 8130 Wisconsin Ave. (301-656-9300, 800-323-7081; fax 656-2907). Clean, generic inn with A/C, free cable TV, complimentary continental breakfast, microwave use, and outdoor pool. All rooms have been recently renovated. Children under 18 stay free with parents. Singles $100, doubles $110. Substantially discounted weekend rates: singles $60, doubles $70.

The Bethesda Ramada, 8400 Wisconsin Ave. (301-654-1000, 800-228-2828; fax 654-0751). Metro: Medical Center, then walk 3 blocks along Wisconsin toward Bethesda (if Wisconsin suddenly turns into Rockville Pike, you're going in the wrong direction). Clean rooms with A/C, TVs, 2 doubles or 1 king-size bed, and decor a bit nicer than the usual. Courtyard pool. Guests are charged by room; four may stay for the price of two. Singles or doubles $110. Great weekend rates: Fri.-Sat. singles and doubles $69-89. Parking $3 per night.

Arlington, VA

Quality Hotel, 1200 North Courthouse Rd. (703-524-4000; fax 522-6814). Steep 10-min. walk from Courthouse Metro. A complex of buildings; each building has rooms of a specific type and price range. Rooms begin at $85 weeknights, $75 weekends. Ask about extended stay rates. Amenities like kitchenettes come with the pricier rooms; all rooms are ample and tidy. Pool and fitness facilities. AAA/AARP 10% discount. Wheelchair access.

Quality Inn Iwo Jima, 1501 Arlington Blvd. (703-524-5000, reservations 800-221-2222; fax 522-5484), on Rte. 50. Metro: Rosslyn. 10-min. walk from Metro stop. Dependable hotel with small, modern rooms, swimming pool, laundry facilities, hairdryers, HBO, and free parking. Convenient to Georgetown, though the walk is long. Summer singles $83, doubles $88. Fall and winter singles $87, doubles $92. Weekend rates: summer $65, fall/winter $60. Children under 18 free with parent. AAA/AARP 10% discount. Wheelchair access.

Holiday Inn Westpark Hotel, 1900 North Fort Myer Dr. (703-807-2000). Metro: Rosslyn. Just across the street from the Metro. All rooms have balconies; some have a view. Pool, sauna, and weight room. Weekday rates $109; special weekend rates: double $77(with 2 double beds). Wheelchair access. Free parking.

Highlander Motor Inn, 3336 Wilson Blvd. (703-524-4300, 800-786-4301). Metro: Clarendon. Two double beds in each room. Clean, spacious, aging motel rooms. Refrigerators upon request. Free coffee and donuts around 6am. Singles $55, in winter $50. Doubles $60, in winter $55. Flash a copy of *Let's Go* for a $5 discount.

Rosslyn Key Bridge Hotel, 1850 North Fort Myer Dr. (703-522-0400; fax 524-5275). Across from Rosslyn Metro. Friendlier than most, with a helpful staff. Ideal for large families, since kids under 19 stay for free and kids under 12 eat for free in summer. Comfortable bedrooms. Pool, game room, and free parking. Depending on availability and season, rooms from $69. AAA/AARP weekday rate $95.

Alexandria, VA

The **Alexandria Hotel Association** (800-296-1000) provides information and assists in reservations for all Alexandria hotels. The area from the Metro stop to Washington St. is not particularly safe; at night, take a cab to your hotel. **Metro: Braddock,** for all of the following:

Best Western Old Colony Inn, 625 1st St. (703-739-2222, 800-528-1234; fax 549-2568), near N. Washington St. Lobby at St. Asaph St. The area is generally considered safe, though a walk from King St. and Old Town Alexandria. The courtyard offers reasonably priced, clean rooms; the main lobby leads to more upscale lodgings. Near a convenience store; boasts indoor and outdoor pools, sauna, fitness center, and cable TV. Complimentary shuttle to National Airport and Metro. Standard rate of $89. Weekend rate $80. AAA rate $69.

EconoLodge, 702 N. Washington St. (703-836-5100; fax 519-7015), at Wythe St. Neat, standard motel rooms with cable TV, A/C, and no-frills service. Convenient to bus stop and Metro; close to restaurants and other hotels. Complimentary shuttle to National Airport. Singles $45 (weekends $55), seniors $45. Doubles $60 (weekends $70). $5 per extra person. $10 key deposit required.

Holiday Inn Hotel and Suites, 625 First St. (703-548-6300; fax 348-8032); a 10-15-min. walk to central Old Town. Elegant and spacious rooms, some overlooking a beautiful courtyard. Indoor and outdoor pools, saunas, and fitness center. Free shuttle to National Airport. Reg. rate $129. AAA rate $99.

Ramada Hotel, 901 N. Fairfax St. (703-683-6000; fax 683-7597), at Montgomery St. A 15-min. walk from the Metro station. Pool and restaurant on the premises; tennis courts across the street. Nice rooms, some with a view of the river, some specifically for women. Free shuttle to National Airport and Old Town Alexandria. Rooms $98-130. Seniors 20% discount. $10 each additional person over 3. 4-5 people max. per room. Kids under 18 with a parent stay for free.

Suburban Maryland

Comfort Inn, 16216 Frederick Rd. (301-330-0023, reservations 800-228-5150; fax 258-1950), at Shady Grove Rd. in Gaithersburg. Metro: Shady Grove. By car: take I-270 to exit 8 onto Shady Grove Rd., turn right onto Frederick Rd. (Rte. 355). Comfortable rooms and large baths decorated in pastels; some rooms offer desks and couches. Free shuttle service to the Metro, ½mi. away. Complimentary continental breakfast. Singles from $65, doubles from $72; off-season weekend rates: singles $49, doubles $55. $6 per additional person. Wheelchair access.

Colonial Manor Inn, 11410 Rockville Pike (301-881-5200, 800-752-3800; fax 231-7668), across from White Flint Mall. Metro: White Flint. The Colonial Manor offers an outdoor pool, fitness room, and video game room. 10-min. walk to hotel from Metro or take the free shuttle to White Flint Mall, across from the hotel. Coin-op laundry. Rooms $69-$89, depending on the number of room occupants (with kitchenette, $99). AARP members 10% discount.

Quality Hotel, 8727 Colesville Rd. (301-589-5200 or 800-221-2222; fax 301-588-1841), at Spring St. in Silver Spring. Metro: Silver Spring. Some aesthetic elements show signs of aging, but the rooms are generally clean and comfy. Access to an indoor pool, fitness center, sauna, game room, cable TV, and breakfast included. Suites $59-100. Special $70 double weekend rate. All rates vary seasonally. Children 18 and under stay free; AAA and (significant) senior citizen discounts.

Camping

Cherry Hill Park, 9800 Cherry Hill Rd. (301-937-7116; fax 595-7181). By car: (½-hour) from D.C. take route I-95 towards Baltimore, then take exit 29B onto Rte. 212. Follow 212 for a mile, then turn onto Cherry Hill Rd. From Baltimore and elsewhere take exit 25B off I-95 or I-495; make the first right onto Cherry Hill Rd. Once on Cherry Hill Rd.; signs direct to park. The closest campground to Washington has 400 sites (most for RVs) and modern amenities. Metrobus stop located right on the grounds accesses the Greenbelt Metro stop (every 15min. during rush hour, otherwise every 30min.). Cable hookup available; coin-operated laundry; heated swimming pool with whirlpool and sauna, and playground. Pets allowed. 2-person tent site $25; RV site with electricity, water, and sewer $34. Extra person $3. $25 deposit required. Reservations recommended. Seniors, AAA, military, and KOA members 10% discount.

Capitol KOA, 768 Cecil Ave. (410-923-2771, 987-7477; fax 923-3709), near Millersville. Full facilities for tents, RVs, and cabins include a free pool and films. From D.C., take John Hanson Hwy. (Rte. 50) to Robert Crain Hwy. (Rte. 3 North), and bear right after 10mi. onto Veterans Hwy. (Rte. 197). After a short distance and a left turn under the highway, blue signs direct to the campground. 18mi. from Baltimore Beltway, 25mi. from D.C., 10mi. from Annapolis. Free weekday shuttle to D.C./Baltimore trains; commuter train (MARC) $6.75 round-trip to Union Station, ½-price for children. Weekend shuttle to New Carroll Metro. Tent site for two $24, with electricity $28. RV site $29.75 with complete hookup. Each additional adult $4. Off-season prices: tent site $19, with electricity $24, with full hookup $26.75. Open April-Nov.

Greenbelt Park, 6565 Greenbelt Rd. (301-344-3948). By car: take I-95 South to exit 23 onto Kenilworth Ave. (Rte. 201), then head south toward Bladensburg and follow the signs. You can also take the Baltimore-Washington Pkwy. (I-295), exit onto Greenbelt Rd. (Rte. 193 East), and follow the signs. 174 sites available for tents, trailers, and campers at this park, 12mi. from D.C. Showers are down Greenbelt Rd. at the Greenbelt Recreation Center and Pool (free). Camping limited to 7 days from Memorial Day to Labor Day and to 14 days the remainder of the year. Long drive to the tenting area. Admission $10 (flat fee; cash preferred), 50% discount for seniors with Golden Eagle Pass. If no ranger is present, the campground operates under a self-registration system. No reservations.

Food

D.C. makes up for its days as a "sleepy Southern town" with a kaleidoscope of international restaurants. Haughty European dining rooms strive to impress the expense-account crowd, while bargains from Africa, Southeast Asia, and the Americas feed a melange of immigrants (and wise locals) from all over. Smithsonian-visitors should plan to lunch far away from the triceratops and the biplanes: tourists on the Mall are lured into mediocre cafeterias, when the respectable food on Capitol Hill is just blocks away.

It's an open secret among interns that **happy hours** provide the cheapest sustenance in Washington. Bars desperate to attract early-evening drinkers present plates, platters, and tables of free appetizers; the trick is to munch a lot but drink little. The best provisions seem to concentrate, along with the interns, on Capitol Hill or south of Dupont. The occasional public reception in a small museum or office lobby can also offer the courageous a free snack (especially those dressed for success). Nonstop nachos, batter-fried onions, and stuffed mushrooms could make anyone (except an intern) sick; still, a dinner of happy-hour appetizers has salvaged many a knowing student from virtual starvation. (See **Bars,** p. 207.)

If you feel like getting away from eating elbow-to-elbow with the crowd (and saving a few pennies in the process), try picnicking with supplies from a local supermarket or specialty store. Prime picnic spots include Rock Creek Park, the Tidal Basin, and the Mall. Most large supermarkets have an excellent selection of prepared foods (including lasagne, salads, and even roasted chicken) and fresh breads, cheeses, and fruits. Smaller ethnic markets offer more unusual fare.

If you prefer to dine in, many D.C. and suburban restaurants deliver— for free or for a small surcharge; there is often a minimum order as well. **Takeout Taxi**'s D.C.-area service includes upper NW Washington and Bethesda (986-0111), and lower NW Washington and Arlington (703-578-3663). **À La Carte Express** (546-8646) delivers to Dupont Circle and Capitol Hill.

We have prefaced the restaurant listings, which are organized by neighborhood, with a full list of D.C.-area restaurants, cross-referenced by type of food and by features. **Let's Go Picks** (denoted by a star) reconcile exceptional cuisine with prices that are either reasonable or, in light of quality and taste, easily overlooked. Every restaurant listed in these sections is followed by an abbreviated neighborhood label, which directs you to the section within the *By Neighborhood* section where you'll find the restaurant's complete listing. The abbreviations are as follows:

CH	Capitol Hill	*AR*	Arlington, VA
WF	Waterfront	*OD*	Old Downtown
CHT	Chinatown	*FB*	White House Area and Foggy Bottom
G	Georgetown		
F	Farragut	*DP*	Dupont Circle
SH	Shaw	*AM*	Adams-Morgan
UN	Upper Northwest	*NE*	Northeast
B	Bethesda, MD	*TP*	Takoma Park, MD
AL	Alexandria, VA	★	*Let's Go* pick

BY TYPE OF FOOD

African

Café Bukom *AM*
Dahlak *AM*
★ Meskerem *AM*
★ Red Sea *AM*
★Zed's Ethiopian Cuisine *G*

Standard American

American Café *CH, OD, G*
The Art Gallery Grill *F*
Lite 'n' Fair *AL*
★Ben's Chili Bowl *SH*
★Booeymonger *G, UN*
Chadwick's *UN*
Cone E. Island *FB*
Dupont Down Under *DP*
El Pollo Primo *AM*
★Florida Ave. Grill *SH*
The Gangplank *WF*
Hard Times Café *AR, AL*
Hawk 'n' Dove *CH*
Houston's *G*
Jan Drake's Garden Café *OD*
Jonathan's Gourmet Deli/Market *FB*
Lindy's Bon Apétit *FB*
★The Market Lunch *CH*
Mr. Henry's Victorian Pub *CH*
Outlaw's Kitchen *SH*
Philadelphia Mike's *B*
Polly's Café *SH*
Recessions *F*
Royal Restaurant *AL*
Scoop Grill and Homemade Ice Cream *AL*
Sholl's Colonial Cafeteria *F*
Tiffany's Deli *OD*
2 Quail *CH*

Bagels

Chesapeake Bagel Bakery *F*
Georgetown Bagelry *G*
Whatsa Bagel *F*

Bakery

Le Madeleine *AL*
Palais du Chocolat F, *UN, TP*

Bar and Grill

Colonel Brooks Tavern *NE*
Hawk 'n' Dove *CH*
Takoma Station Tavern *TP*

Barbecue and Ribs

Kenny's Smoke House *CH*
King Street Blues *AL*
Red Hot and Blue *AR*
★Rocklands *UN*
Wingmaster's Grill Chicken and Ribs *UN*

Café

Afterwords Café *DP*
a.k.a. Frisco's *UN*
Bread and Chocolate *CH*
Café Amadeus, *OD*
Caffè Northwest *G*
Cup'A Cup'A *F*
Everyday Gourmet *TP*
Food & Co. Gourmet Café *FB*
Jolt 'N' Bolt *DP*
★Le Bon Café *CH*
Le Madeleine *AL*
New World Café *OD*
Old Town Sandwich Shop *AL*
Peacock Café and Market *G*
★The Pop Stop *DP*
Reeve's *OD*
Roasters on the Hill *CH*
★Soho Tea & Coffee *DP*

Cambodian, Thai, Burmese, and Vietnamese

Burma Restaurant *CHT*
Busara *G*
Café Dalat *AR*
★Café Saigon *AR*
The Cambodian Restaurant *AR*
Little Viet Garden *AR*
Pad Thai *G*
★Queen Bee *AR*
Saigon Gourmet Restaurant *UN*
Saigon Inn *G, UN*
Saigonnais *AM*
Sala Thai *DP*
★Star of Siam *F, AM*
Thai Kingdom *F*
Thai Taste *UN*
Vietnam-Georgetown Restaurant *G*

Central and Eastern European

★Misha's Deli *CH*

Chinese & Mongolian

Chinatown Express *CHT*
★City Lights of China *DP*
Go Lo's *CHT*
Ho Wah Restaurant *CHT*
Hunan Chinatown *CHT*

Hunan Dynasty *CH*
Mr. Yung's *CHT*
New Big Wong *CHT*
Szechuan Gallery *CHT*
Tai Shan *CHT*
Tony Cheng's Mongolian Restaurant *CHT*
Yenching Palace *UN*

Cookies

Holly's Cookie Company *FB*
Bread and Chocolate *CH*

Creole, Cajun, and Caribbean

Hibiscus Café *G*
★Heart & Soul Café *CH*
★The Islander *AM*
Louisiana Express *B*
Montego Café *AM*
Negril's Jamaican Bakery *WF*
Tom Sarris' Orleans House *AR*

Deli

Bob Rubin's New York Deli *AL*
Ebbitt Express *F*
German Deli *OD*
GW Deli *FB*
Irene's Deli *WF*
La Prima Market Café *F*
Krupin's *UN*
★Misha's Deli *CH*
Neil's Outrageous Deli *CH*
New York Gourmet Deli *F*
★The Parkway Deli *UN*
Prego's *CH*
Provisions *CH*
So's Your Mom *AM*
World Gourmet *FB*

Diner

The Georgetown Dinette *G*
Jimmy T's *CH*
Murry and Paul's Restaurant *NE*
Tastee Diner *B*
Trio Restaurant *DP*

Fast Food

Vie de France *F*

French

Café La Ruche *G*
Le Madeleine *AL*
Vie de France *F*

German

German Deli *OD*

Greek and Middle Eastern

Bacchus Restaurant *DP*
Eye St. Café *F*
Fettoosh *G*
Food Factory *AR*
Lebanese Castle *F*
Kabul Caravan *AR*
The Lebanese Taverna *UN*
★Moby Dick House of Kabob *G*
Mediterranean Deli *UN*
Olympic Carry-Out *G*
Paradise Restaurant *B*
Persepolis Restaurant *B*
Quick Pita *G*
★Skewers *DP*
Taverna the Greek Islands *CH*
Tom Tom *AM*
Yanni's *UN*
★Zorba's Café *DP*

Health Food/Organic

★Food for Thought *DP*
Health Zone *OD*
Health's A-Poppin! *CH*

Ice Cream

Bob's Famous Homemade Ice Cream *B*
Ice in Paradise *CH*
Max's Best Ice Cream *UN*
Scoop Grill and Homemade Ice Cream *AL*
Thomas Sweet *G*

Indian and Nepalese

★Aditi *G*
Deli Dhaba *AR*
Paru's Indian Vegetarian Restaurant *DP*
Rajaji *UN*
Tandoor *G*
A Taste of India *UN*

Italian

Café Luna *DP*
Café Parma *DP*
Caffè Sorrento *G*
Dupont Italian Kitchen *DP*
Ecco Café *AL*
Eye St. Café *F*
★Faccia Luna *UN, AR*
Julio's *AM*
Mama Marie and Enzio's *G*
Milo's *FB*
★Paolo's *G*
Pasta Mia Trattoria *AM*
Piccolo *G*
Positano and Aldo Café *B*

Stromboli Family Restaurant *B*
Taliano's *TP*
Treviso *FB*
Tuscana West *F*

Japanese and Korean

Atami *AR*
★Sushi-Ko *G*
★Tako Grill *B*
★Tokyo Terrace *F*
Yosaku *UN*

Kitsch

Gadsby's Tavern *AL*

Latin American and Spanish

The Argentine Grill *AM*
Casa Blanca *F*
El Caribe *G*
El Pollo Rico *AR*
El Tamarindo *AM, UN*
Jaleo *OD*
Julia's Empanadas *AM*
Las Pampas *G*
Terramar *B*

Mexican/Tex-Mex

★Austin Grill *UN*
Burrito Brothers *G*
Cactus Cantina *UN*
Casa Juanita's *OD*
Enriqueta's *G*
Lauriol Plaza *DP*
★Mixtec *AM*
★Rio Grande Café *B*
South Austin Grille *AL*

Microbrew

Capitol City Brewing Company *OD*
★Faccia Luna *UN*
★Hard Times Café *AR*

Multi-Ethnic

Atami *AR*
DJ's *FB*
Ivy's Place *UN*
Mark's Kitchen *TP*
Pan-Asian *F*
Pan Asian Noodles and Grill *DP*
Perry's *AM*

Pizza

Armand's Chicago Pizzeria *CH, UN, AL*
DC Café *DP*
Ecco Café *AL*
★Faccia Luna *UN, AR*
Geppeto's *G*
★Pizzeria Paradiso *DP*
Taliano's *TP*
Trio Pizza *DP*

Seafood

Lite 'n' Fair AL
★Bethesda Crab House *B*
Chesapeake Seafood Crab House *AR*
The Dancing Crab *UN*
The Fish Market *AL*
Hogate's *WF*
Steamer's *B*

Soul Food

Dixie Grill *OD*
★Florida Avenue Grill *SH*
★Heart & Soul Café *CH*
★Rocklands *UN*

South Asian

★Sarinah *G*

BY FEATURES

Delivery

Armand's Chicago Pizzeria *AL*
Burrito Brothers *G*
DC Café *DP*
Dupont Italian Kitchen *DP*
Gepetto's *G*
Hard Times Café *AL*
Hunan Dynasty *CH*
Louisiana Express *B*
Milo's *FB*
New Big Wong *CHT*
Pad Thai *G*
Peacock Café and Market *G*
Persepolis Restaurant *B*
Quick Pita *G*
Saigonnais *AM*
Star of Siam *AM*
Stromboli Family Restaurant *B*
Trio Pizza *DP*
Trio Restaurant *DP*

Open Late

Afterwords Café *DP*

The Art Gallery Grille *FB*
★Ben's Chili Bowl *SH*
★ Booeymonger *UN*
Café Bukom *AM*
Chadwick's *G, UN*
Colonel Brooks Tavern *NE*
DC Café *DP*
Dahlak *AM*
El Tamarindo *UN*
Fettoosh *G*
The Fish Market *AL*
★Food for Thought *DP*
Go-Lo *CHT*
Hawk 'n' Dove *CH*
Ho Wah Restaurant *CHT*
Julio's *AM*
Montego Café *AM*
★Paolo's *G*
Perry's *AM*
Polly's Café *SH*
★The Pop Stop *DP*
Quick Pita *G*
Steamers *B*
Takoma Station Tavern *TP*
Tastee Diner *B*
Trio Pizza *DP*

Let's Go Picks

★Aditi *G*
★Austin Grill *UN*
★Ben's Chili Bowl *SH*
★Bethesda Crab House *B*
★Booeymonger *G, UN*
★Cactus Cantina *UN*
★Café Saigon *AR*
★City Lights of China *DP*
★Faccia Luna *UN*
★Florida Avenue Grill *SH*
★Food for Thought *DP*
★Heart & Soul Café *CH*
★The Islander *AM*
★Le Bon Café *CH*
★Market Lunch *CH*
★Meskerem *AM*
★Misha's *CH*
★Mixtec *AM*
★Moby Dick House of Kabob *G*
★Paolo's *G*
★Pizzeria Paradiso *DP*
★The Pop Stop *DP*
★Queen Bee *AR*
★Rio Grande Café *B*
★Rocklands *UN*
★Sarinah *G*
★Skewers *DP*
★Soho Tea & Coffee *DP*
★Sushi-Ko *G*
★Star of Siam *F*
★Tako Grill *B*
★Tokyo Terrace *F*
★Zed's Ethiopian Cuisine *G*
★Zorba's *DP*

BY NEIGHBORHOOD

Capitol Hill

The secret to fine dining on "the Hill" is to venture away from all the white marble; peripheral areas harbor reasonably priced establishments free from congressional bigwigs and government flunkies. Pennsylvania Ave. dominates the restaurant scene, but Mass. Ave. NE offers some more attractive (and expensive) alternatives. At night, the areas northeast of Union Station or southeast of Lincoln Park warrant wariness. Over 50 eateries inhabit **Union Station** (Metro: Union Station); the station's interior is glitzy suburban-mall-esque; in the **food court** on the lower level, cheap take-out counters ring the walls, offering sustenance for under $5.

Government workers tend to lunch in **government cafeterias,** whose cheap, acceptable sandwiches and salads are served up in many a building's basement along North Capitol St. One such place is the **Capitol Forum Bar and Grill** (Metro: Union Station) in the sunken plaza of the building at 941 North Capitol St. (682-0060)—a relatively upscale cafeteria serving mighty affordable burgers ($2) and fries ($1). (Open Mon.-Fri. 6am-5pm.)

Do-it-yourselfers should brave the bustle of block-long **Eastern Market** (546-2698), on 7th St. SE between Pennsylvania and Independence. Inside, butchers, bakers, and even the occasional candlestick-makers hawk their wares all week long. On weekends, they are joined by local farmers and growers who line the walk outside with fresh flowers and produce—even in December. Saturday is the best day for produce; Sunday tends to be more of a flea market. From the Eastern Market Metro, walk less than half a block northwest along Pennsylvania Ave., then turn right on 7th St. (open Tues.-Sat. 7am-6pm, Sun. 9am-4pm).

American Café, 227 Massachusetts Ave. NE (547-8500). Metro: Union Station. A modern, upscale spot with substantial outdoor seating, this café boasts a healthy selection of non-fried American basics with Italian and Thai accents. American is a great place for a quick and light sit-down lunch. Signature Sandwiches run $5.25-8 and entrees range from $7 to $14 (tender baby back ribs). Take-out available from market entrance. Sun. brunch served 10:30am-2:30pm (all entrees $7). Happy hour Mon.-Fri. 4-8pm. Live music nightly. Open Mon.-Thurs. 11am-11pm, Fri.-Sat. 11am-midnight, Sun. 10:30am-10pm.

Bread and Chocolate, 666 Pennsylvania Ave. SE (547-2875). Metro: Eastern Market. The offerings are much, much more than the name suggests: an upscale café, bakery, and gourmet food-mart all in one, with a friendly staff who will guide you through everything on the board. Patrons may choose an omelette ($6), a sandwich ($6-7), a generous entree salad ($6-9), or from a selection from the enticing display of cakes and pastries; or they can swing by to pick up fresh strawberries ($4). Open Mon.-Sat. 7am-7:30pm, Sun. 8am-6:30pm.

Hawk 'n' Dove, 329 Pennsylvania Ave. SE (543-3300). Metro: Capitol South. With the feel of an old English pub, Hawk 'n' Dove is a popular neighborhood meeting place and watering hole with serviceable bar food, which interns, regulars, and powerful politicos eagerly consume. Restored to re-create its historic turn-of-the-century atmosphere, the Hawk 'n' Dove cheerfully serves up sandwiches $4-6.50. 14 kinds of bottled beer, and 11 drafts ($1.75 and up). Breakfast served Mon.-Thurs. 11pm-1am, Fri.-Sat. 11pm-2am ($7, with steak $9). Open Sun.-Thurs. 10am-2am, Fri.-Sat. 10am-3am.

Health's A' Poppin', 209½ Pennsylvania Ave. SE (544-3049). Metro: Capitol South. This deli-style establishment, with an appetizing salad bar and a wide array of munchable delights ($4 per lb), hosts a health-conscious lunch throng. Also served up are ready-made salads ($3-5), made-to-order sandwiches ($3-4.25), and fusions of the two. Open Mon.-Fri. 7am-6:30pm, Sat. 11am-5:30pm.

★ **Heart & Soul Café,** 424 8th Street SE (547-1892), off Pennsylvania Ave. Metro: Eastern Market. The spacious, unpretentiously elegant surroundings preface "an experience in fine Southern cuisine." Sandwiches $4.50-5, entrees $9-13. Specialties of the South include the Heart & Soul Gumbo (cup $4) and the country fried chicken ($9). Enjoy a buffet brunch Sat. 10am-2pm and Sun. 11:30am-4pm for $9. 10% discount for *Let's Go*ers. Open Mon.-Thurs. 11:30am-10pm, Fri. 11:30am-11pm, Sat. 10am-11pm, Sun. 11:30am-10pm. Plans are in the works to extend weekend hours in order to accommodate late-night revelers.

Hunan Dynasty, 215 Pennsylvania Ave. SE (546-6161, 546-6262). Metro: Capitol South. Located upstairs; ultra-modern pale pink surroundings include an aquarium of goldfish, a huge mural of the Great Wall, and Hill staff at power-lunches. Weekday lunch specials ($6, until 3pm). Entrees range from $5 to $12. Generous portions and reasonably good fare; a sushi bar complements the Chinese cuisine. Take-out available. Open Mon.-Thurs. 11:30am-2:30pm and 5:30-10pm, Fri. 11:30am-2:30pm and 5:30-11pm, Sat. 5:30-11pm, Sun. 5:30-10pm.

Ice in Paradise, 615 Pennsylvania Ave. SE (547-1554). Metro: Eastern Market. Named for the Middle Eastern dessert *yakh-dar-behesht* ("ice in paradise"). Counters take up most of the space, but 5 small tables seat 2 people apiece. Large selection of Hershey's ice cream (single scoop $1.35) as well as vegetarian and meat-filled sandwiches ($3-4). The Dolmeh Moe Platter provides a variety of items ($4). Outdoor seating available on the back patio. Open Mon.-Sat. 9am-7pm.

Jimmy T's, 501 East Capitol St. (546-3646). Metro: Eastern Market. At the corner of East Capitol and 5th St. under the brick octagonal turret. A throwback to the 1950s (including the telephone booth): the paint is chipped, the red vinyl benches look old, and there are more bar stools than tables, just as a diner should be—it's all part of the old-time charm. Capitol Hill workers, political big-wigs, and neighborhood regulars alike come for the friendly service and the fresh fare. Nothing over $6. Sandwiches $1.50-3.55, dinner entrees $5. Open Tues.-Fri. 6:30am-9pm, Sat. 8am-9pm, Sun. 8am-3pm. (Hours may vary; call ahead.)

Kenny's Smoke House, 732 Maryland Ave. NE (547-4561). Metro: Union Station. A bit of a hike from the Capitol, but those in the know make the pilgrimage regularly for Kenny's delicious barbecued ribs and chicken. Wafting odors of smoked fare compel anyone within 40 yards. Pigs decorate the pleasant polished wood and brick interior, and there's abundant outdoor seating. Lunchtime platters of ribs ($6.50) or chicken ($6) come with cornbread and a side order. Dinner sandwiches $6-8, entrees $8-16. Larger parties can order ribs by the slab ($15). Take-out available around the corner on 8th St. Open daily 11am-10pm.

★ **Le Bon Café,** 210 2nd St. SE (547-7200). Metro: Capitol South. Catching up on the news is the thing to do here; bring your own paper or borrow one from Le Bon's supply. A stone's throw from the Capitol (a brick's throw from the Supreme Court), this café makes exquisite food from scratch with all-natural ingredients. Espresso $1; café au lait $1.45. Buy 10 espressos, get 1 free (and shake like a leaf on a tree). Breakfast pastries 95¢-$1.35 (until 11am). Sandwiches (after 11am) $4-6. Elegant salads $3-6. Open Mon.-Fri. 7:30am-6:30pm, Sat.-Sun. 8:30am-3:30pm.

★ **The Market Lunch,** 225 7th St. SE (547-8444), in the Eastern Market complex. Metro: Eastern Market. Newspapers around D.C. hail The Market Lunch as one of the best deals in town. Strong smells of fresh fish and meat waft over a dozen stools. Crab cakes ($6-9) are the local specialty, but the Blue Bucks (buckwheat blueberry pancakes $3), have people lined up around the corner on Sat. mornings. Open Tues.-Sat. 7:30am-3pm.

★ **Misha's Deli,** 210 7th St. SE (547-5858), north of Pennsylvania Ave. on 7th St., across from the Eastern Market building. Metro: Eastern Market. Inexpensive Russian and Eastern European food. The friendly immigrant owner will help you practice your Russian amid posters of past and present Soviet leaders (the scorecard: Gorbachev 2, Yeltsin 1, Lenin 1). Tasty knishes $2, blintzes $1.75. Plenty of meats, cheeses, and breads to buy for your very own sandwich. Borscht $2-2.50; wide array of sweets and desserts. Some outdoor seating available. Open Mon.-Fri. 8am-7:30pm, Sat. 7am-6pm, Sun. 9am-5pm.

Mr. Henry's Victorian Pub, 601 Pennsylvania Ave. SE (546-8412). Metro: Eastern Market. Hardwood paneling and checkered tablecloths provide the backdrop for cheap, substantial burgers and sandwiches ($3.25-7), and entrees ($6-8), listed on an enormous menu board offering a hearty variety. Its proximity to the Capitol attracts tourists; the tavern draws a mostly gay and lesbian crowd. A patio provides outdoor seating on the pub's 6th-St. side. Open daily 11:30am-1:30am.

Neil's Outrageous Deli, 208 Massachusetts Ave. NE (546-6970). Metro: Union Station. The purple sign is *very* visible. Neil's deli/liquor store offers creative sandwiches to go (such as the "Crazy Louie," sour-dough rye topped with Dijon mustard, pastrami, turkey, and Thousand Island dressing for $4.30) and wines stacked to the ceiling. Lunchers have to find someplace else to eat their "killer subs"; all of Neil's wine, cheese, and meat leaves little room for a sit-down feast. An appealing array of sandwiches (24) ranges in price from $3 to $4.30. Open Mon.-Tues. 9am-7:30pm, Wed.-Sat. 9am-9pm.

Prego, 210 7th St. SE (547-8686). Metro: Eastern Market, next to Misha's Deli. Prego's deli boasts Italian take-out and delicious bread shipped fresh daily ($1-2 per loaf). Also sells olives, olive oil, and Italian wines. Outdoor seating only. Sandwiches $3.25-4.25. The "Prego Special," bursts at the seams with Italian cold cuts, tomatoes, lettuce, and cheese ($3.25). Open Mon.-Fri. 9am-6:30pm, Sat. 9am-7pm, Sun. noon-5pm.

Provisions, 218 7th St. SE (543-0694), across from the Eastern Market. Metro: Eastern Market. Provisions provides everything from teapots and jam to salads and sandwiches to chocolate. A handful of tables crouch in a 2-story red brick alcove with a wall-to-wall skylight. Gourmet sandwiches ($3.50-6) keep 'em lined up at lunchtime. Ever-popular is the "218" sandwich, a sumptuous concoction of smoked ham and lingonberry jam ($5.50). Daily coffee specials. Open Mon.-Fri. 10am-7pm, Sat. 7am-6pm, Sun. 8:30am-4:30pm.

Roasters on the Hill, 666 Pennsylvania Ave. SE (543-8355). Metro: Eastern Market. Hides around the corner on the 7th-St. side of the building. Exhausted workers roast and grind coffee while you relax on a cushioned stool at the counter or sip the end product at a table outside. Can't take a shot of espresso on an empty stomach? There's a plethora of biscotti ($1), scones ($1.50), and muffins ($1-1.50) to buffer the caffeine. Friendly, energetic service amid a colorful decor. Iced coffee 95¢. A variety of quirky espresso drinks ($1-2). Open Mon.-Fri. 7am-6:30pm, Sat. 7am-6pm, Sun. 8am-5:30pm.

Taverna the Greek Islands, 307 Pennsylvania Ave. SE (547-8360). Metro: Capitol South. White stucco walls carry the requisite Greek Tourist Bureau posters and harbor the site of frequent Kennedy sightings. Offerings include *moussaka alla* Greek islands ($7), as well as other Greek sandwiches and entrees ($5.50-11). The *Saganaki alla Paros* (melted cheese, $5) conjures shooting 8-ft. flames from your plate. A downstairs deli has provisions as well. Open Mon.-Sat. 11am-midnight.

2 Quail, 320 Massachusetts Ave. NE (543-8030). Metro: Union Station. Three restored Victorian townhouses get cutely sumptuous with flowered curtains, flowered wallpaper, and wicker room dividers; tables set with cozy armchairs and plush, fluffy pillows—romance is in the air. Uncategorizable and consistently excellent cuisine changes every season; entrees vary in taste from the teriyaki ribeye steak to pan-seared flounder. Early-bird *prix fixe* (seated by 6:30pm) includes soup or salad, choice of entree, glass of wine or dessert, and coffee or tea ($18). Open Mon.-Thurs. 11:30am-2:30pm and 5-10:30pm, Fri. 11:30am-2:30pm and 5:30-11:15pm, Sat. 5:30-11:15pm, Sun. 5-10pm.

Waterfront

Next door to the wharf markets on Water St. lie the Waterfront restaurants, mammoth seafood restaurant/monuments with the grand air of an Atlantic City boardwalk. Most, if not all, are exclusively for high rollers.

The Gangplank, 600 Water St. SW (554-5000). Metro: Waterfront. Even here, the most reasonable of the Waterfront restaurants, entrees hover in the $17 range; perhaps eschew the Upper Deck restaurant in favor of the less expensive **Gangplank Patio Café** (burgers and sandwiches $3-9, entrees $9-13). Karaoke Thurs., with a DJ and live shows Wed. and Fri.-Sat.; all entertainment 7-11pm. Upper deck open Mon.-Thurs. 11:30am-1:30pm and 5:30-9:30pm; café open daily 4-11pm.

Hogate's, 800 Water St. (484-6300), at Maine Ave. and 9th St. Metro: L'Enfant Plaza. If nothing else will do but a true waterfront meal, the fried seafood ($8-11) and seafood sandwiches ($7.25-9.25) are the most affordable. It may be worth it just to see Hogate's endless (and endlessly tacky—read: lobster-shaped door-handles) interior. Open Mon.-Fri. 11am-10pm, Sat. noon-11pm, Sun. 10:30am-10pm.

Irene's Deli, 300 7th St. SW (488-5555), between C and D St. in the Reporter's Building. Metro: L'Enfant Plaza. Irene's relaxed outdoor lunch spot offers a needed respite from the overly businesslike L'Enfant Plaza. Standard breakfast items 50¢-$2, lunch sandwiches $2-3.50 or $2.75-4 if served as a sub. Lunch served after 10:30am. No indoor seating. Open Mon.-Fri. 6:30am-4pm.

Negril the Jamaican Bakery, 401 M St. SW (488-3636), in the Waterside Mall. Metro: Waterfront. Take-out only. Regulars line up for chicken loaves—a cross between a calzone and a pot pie ($1.75)—and vegetable patties (same principle, $1.60). Open Mon.-Fri. 6:30am-7pm, Sat. 9am-5pm.

Old Downtown

Except for Chinatown (below), D.C.'s Old Downtown offers few quality restaurants. The hype-heavy **Pavilion** at the **Old Post Office,** at Pennsylvania Ave. and 12th St. NW (289-4224), stuffs its concourse with ethnic food stalls and their many out-of-town patrons (open Mon.-Sat. 10am-9pm, Sun. noon-8pm; Metro: Federal Triangle). Somewhat less tourist-infested are the **Shops at National Place & Press,** 1331 Pennsylvania Ave. NW (783-9090), a three-level mall with the usual endless array of eateries (open Mon.-Sat. 10am-7pm, Sun. noon-5pm; Metro: Metro Center). Many delis and cafés provide a surprisingly interesting selection, offering diverse cuisines or specialty foods in addition to the standard fare of sandwiches, salads and burgers. Ubiquitous hot-dog stands dot downtown streets, posing to hungry pedestrians an age-old dilemma: half-smoke or Super-Dog?

Metro: Metro Center, unless otherwise noted, for all of the following:

American Café, 1331 Pennsylvania Ave. NW (626-0770) in the Shops at National Place; enter at the corner of 13th and F St. NW. A take-out market and sit-down bar supplement the restaurant, which features all-American fare from burgers ($5.45-6.45) and pastas ($8-14) to chicken Caesar salad pizza ($8.25) and 100-mph chili (cup $3, bowl $4). Restaurant open Tues.-Sat. 11am-11pm, Sun.-Mon. 11:30am-10pm. Café/market open Mon.-Fri. 7:30am-8pm, Sat.-Sun. 10am-8pm.

Capitol City Brewing Company, 1100 New York Ave. NW (628-CCBC (2222)), entrance on the corner of 11th and H. St. CCBC was the first brewery in the District of Columbia after Prohibition, which means poor Washingtonians are sadly late on the microbrew scene. This stylized version of an industrial warehouse is known for its home-brewed beer, but also offers hearty grub, such as the Vienna country sausage sandwich ($9) and the grilled sausage salad ($8.75). Open Sun.-Thurs. 11am-11pm, Fri.-Sat. 11am-midnight. For brewery hours, see **Entertainment & Nightlife,** p. 208.

Restaurante Casa Juanita's, 908 11th St. NW (737-2520), near I St. Authentic Mexican and Salvadoran cuisine comes in huge portions heaping with beans and rice. Free chips and salsa are served up by a friendly staff. Entrees include *La Libertad* (shrimp smothered in onions, peppers, and tomatoes, $12.75) and the *Santa Ana* (3 chicken enchiladas with cheese and tangy Spanish sauce, $7.75). Decor consists of piñatas hanging from the ceiling and sombreros on the walls. Free delivery ($10 min.). Open Sun.-Thurs. 11am-10:30pm, Fri.-Sat. 11am-11pm.

Dixie Grill, 518 10th St. NW (628-4800), next to the Petersen House, "the house that Lincoln died in." Dixie's Southern roots shine through in its menu and its down-home atmosphere. First-floor restaurant operates off a chalkboard menu, with dishes and prices changing every meal. However, the house specialty is the chicken fried steak ($11), and red beans and rice are available at any meal ($4). Upstairs is a "roadhouse" bar complete with pool tables, barrels of peanuts, and race-car memorabilia. Wed. features local rockabilly bands, reminiscent of the sleepy Southern town that was once D.C. Bar and restaurant open Mon. and Sat. 11:30am-9pm, Tues.-Wed. 11:30am-11pm (kitchen closes at 10pm), Thurs.-Fri. 11:30am-1am (kitchen closes 11pm, bar menu until midnight).

Ebbitt Express, 675 15th St. NW (347-8881), in the Metropolitan Square plaza. Across 15th St. from the Treasury Building. The **Old Ebbitt Grill,** father of Ebbitt Express, lounges next door, reminiscing about the days when its clientele included presidents McKinley, Cleveland, Harding, Grant, Johnson (A.), and Roosevelt (T.). Prices reflect the undeniable snob appeal, but next door, in the air-conditioned Metropolitan Square, Ebbitt Express offers affordable items including the daily pasta special (always $6), a stuffed baked potato ($2), or a yogurt fruit shake ($2.75), as well as a free view of the Grill's stuffy patrons eating their steaks and lobsters. You can tell your friends that you lunched at Ebbitt's. Open Mon.-Thurs. 7:30am-8pm, Fri. 7:30am-6pm.

German Deli, 1331 H St. NW (347-5732), The front of a space that also contains the pricey Café Mozart, near the National Museum for Women in the Arts. Gourmet deli proffers specialty crackers, coffees, hors-d'oeuvres, and tricky-to-pronounce delicacies like chicken *schnitzel* ($6), *sauerbrauten* ($6) and *spaetzle*. Cramped storefront conceals a roomy interior. Sandwiches ($5-7) and pastries ($3-4) are superb. Free downtown delivery until 4pm ($20 min.). Open Mon.-Fri. 7:30am-10pm, Sat. 9am-10pm, Sun. 11am-10pm.

Jaleo, 480 7th St. NW (628-7949). Metro: Gallery Place-Chinatown. Two blocks down 7th St. from the Metro to the corner of 7th and E St. Jaleo reconciles yuppie dining with Spanish authenticity, and offers over 40 different kinds of tapas. Larger-than-life murals of flamenco dancers adorn the walls and supervise your meal. The entrees are pricey at dinnertime ($10.50-15), but you can make a meal out of gazpacho ($4.50), a tapas ($3-7.50) and unlimited bread. Open for lunch Mon.-Sat. 11:30am-2:30pm. For dinner, Mon. 5:30-10pm, Tues.-Thurs. 5:30-10:30pm, Fri.-Sat. 5:30-11pm, Sun. 5:30-10pm. For late-night tapas, Tues.-Thurs. 10:30-11:30pm, Fri.-Sat. 11pm-midnight, Sun. brunch 11:30am-3pm. Tapas and dessert menu available 2:30-5:30pm and one hour prior to closing.

Jan Drake's Garden Café, 401 7th St. NW (393-1150), located on Gallery Row. Metro: Gallery Place-Chinatown. The homey atmosphere is a relief from intimidating downtown office buildings. Deli sandwiches madc to order $3.30-5.25, regular-sized salads (vegetable, tuna, and chicken) $4-5. $3 breakfast special includes scrambled eggs, meat, home fries or grits, and toast, English muffin, or bagel (available Mon.-Fri. 7-10:30am, Sat. 8-10:30am). Open Mon.-Fri. 6:30am-7pm, Sat. 8am-5pm, Sun. 11am-5pm.

New World Café, 720 I St. NW (842-0045, fax 842-0667), across the street from the Greater New Hope Baptist Church. Metro: Gallery Place-Chinatown, one block up and one to the left of the 7th and H St. exit. This café offers a grill, gourmet deli provisions, a salad bar with Chinese fare, and a namesake sandwich: the New World Café Club (Virginia baked ham, turkey, bacon, lettuce, tomato, mayonnaise, and provolone on whole wheat ($4.59)). Espresso and cappuccino $1.15-1.80, salad bar $4.19 per lb., sandwiches $4-5. Open Mon.-Fri. 6:30am-4pm.

Reeves, 1306 G St. NW (628-6350, fax 628-6340). This bakery/café is an Old Downtown institution; it's been around in some shape or form since 1886. Today it's best known for its breakfasts. Pancakes or french toast (made with cinnamon or raisin bread) $3-4.35; all-you-can-eat fruit and breakfast bar $5-6 for adults, $3.50-4 for children (prices vary depending on day of the week). Slices of their "world-famous" pies about $2. Open Mon.-Sat. 7am-6pm.

Tiffany's Deli, 415 12th St. NW (628-5751). This friendly, heavily patronized restaurant features a huge Chinese buffet/salad and fresh fruit bar ($3.89 per lb.). Hot subs & sandwiches $4-5.35. Large drink selection. Open Mon.-Fri. 6am-5pm.

CHINATOWN

You don't have to dig a hole to China (or Burma or Mongolia) to find authentic Asian food and groceries; Some of D.C.'s best Chinese, Burmese, and Mongolian restaurants cling to tiny H St. NW. Don't be turned off by a decrepit-seeming exterior (or interior, even). A restaurant's appearance has little relation to its quality; apparent dives often serve wonderful food. **Metro: Gallery Place-Chinatown** (parking is limited to garages), for all of the following.

Burma Restaurant, upstairs at 740 6th St. NW (638-1280). Burma is a deviation from Chinatown's somewhat repetitive menus. The owner, a retired Burmese diplomat and former U.N. delegate, loves to talk about Burma's rare cuisine, which replaces soy sauce with pickles, mild curries, and unique spices. The *Kauswe Thoke,* rice noodles with ground shrimp, fried onion, cilantro, hot pepper, garlic, and fresh lemon juice ($7.50), or anything served in the *Kotang* sauce, made from sesame, soya, cilantro, ginger, garlic, onions, and lemon juice, demand a try. Most entrees $8, noodle dishes $7.50. Open Mon.-Fri. 11am-3pm, Fri.-Sat. 6pm-10:30pm, Sun.-Thurs. 6-10pm.

Chinatown Express, 744-746 6th St. NW (638-0424/5, fax 787-2941). Choose your lunch special ($4) from 26 dishes offered; order an additional dish for just $1 extra (includes rice; served daily 10am-5pm). Dinner can range from $4.25 to $12, or find 3 friends and pay $30 for a "family dinner." Open daily 10am-11pm.

Go-Lo's, 604 H St. NW (347-4656, fax 783-2941). Two large dragons greet you from above as you enter the restaurant—go low. Go-Lo's Home-Style Cooking entrees, such as little neck clams in black bean sauce ($9.25), are worth a try. Lunch specials ($5-6) vary according to the day of the week. Kids' meals: lunch $3, dinner $5. What the menu doesn't tell you—although a plaque outside does—is that Go-Lo's used to be the Surrat Boardinghouse, where conspirators plotted the abduction of President Lincoln. Go low indeed. Open Sun.-Thurs. 11am-10:30pm, Fri.-Sat. 11am-2:30am.

Ho Wah Restaurant, 611 H. St. NW (408-8115). For the bargain-hunter—$4 for lunch (Mon.-Fri. 10:30am-3:30pm) and dinner's not much more (dinner specials $4.50). Enormous selection of beef, pork, chicken, seafood, and noodle dishes (9 types of soup!). Free delivery 10:30am-10pm (898-0823; $10 min.). Six tables in a small downstairs room. Open Sun.-Thurs. 10:30am-3am, Fri.-Sat. 10:30am-4am.

Hunan Chinatown, 624 H St. NW (783-5858). A haven for lovers of spicy food. Dinner can be pricey, so fire-eaters might want to munch on the Hot Spicy Eggplant ($8.50), the Kung Pao chicken ($10), or the hot and sour soup ($2) from the "Light Menu," the restaurant's new nutritional venture (it's also cheaper than the regular menu) Open Sun.-Thurs. 11am-10pm, Fri.-Sat. 11am-11pm.

Szechuan Gallery, 617 H St. NW (898-1180/1). Recognize this place? Schwarzenegger extravaganza *True Lies* was filmed here—the scene where Jamie Lee Curtis meets with her would-be lover—and they've got an autographed picture of Arnold himsel and one of Jamie Lee with staff members to prove it. Stunning Taiwanese (mostly sea food) dishes, once hidden from English-speaking diners, have surfaced on the menu as Chef's Recommendations. Menu supplement features favorites of Chinese-fare con noisseurs. Fragrant Crab (whole crabs in spicy egg batter) $10. Open Sun.-Thurs 11am-10pm, Fri.-Sat. 11am-11pm.

Tony Cheng's Mongolian Restaurant, 619 H St. NW (842-8669). Patrons can fill their bowls with beef, leeks, mushrooms, sprouts, and such, then watch the cooks make it sizzle and shrink to a manageable portion (1 serving $8.50, all-you-can-eat $14) at lunch. Originating (supposedly) with the armies of Genghis Khan, this style of sizzling meats on metal over glowing coal is known as "Mongolian barbecue." It's both dining and entertainment, as the cooks perform the ritual in the center of the room. Two or more can stir up their own feast in charcoal hotpots provided by the restaurant for $5 per person; more meat extra. Open Sun.-Thurs. 11am-11pm, Fri.-Sat. 11am-midnight.

Tai Shan Restaurant, 622 H St. NW (639-0266, fax 639-0978). Offers a good selection of standard meat and vegetable dishes, dim sum, noodle soups (under $5), and special dishes including pig knuckle and duck ($6-7). Lunch special $5. Open Sun.-Thurs. 11am-11pm, Fri.-Sat. 11am-3am.

New Big Wong Restaurant, 610 H St. NW (628-0491). Friendly, airy downstairs restaurant specializes in Cantonese cuisine. Pint- (about $5) and quart- (about $7) sized take-out entrees. Free delivery ($10 min.). Open Mon.-Sat. 11am-10pm.

Mr. Yung's Restaurant, 740 6th St. NW (628-1098, fax 628-1128). The pleasant and attentive waitstaff serves patrons in a large, comfortable dining room. Most dinner entrees $7-12, specials $5-7. 10% discount on take-out orders over $30. Open daily 11am-11pm.

FOOD

White House Area and Foggy Bottom

Cheap, friendly restaurants congregate around the hungry youth of George Washington University. Prime budget dining lies north of F St., especially along Pennsylvania Ave.—the fare close to the White House is varied but more expensive. **Metro: Foggy Bottom-GWU,** unless otherwise noted, for all of the following:

Cone E. Island, in the mall at 2000 Pennsylvania Ave. (822-8460). No old-fashioned soda fountain here—this small, decidedly modern parlor features arcade game tables and Ionic columns ringed in neon lights. Tasty nonfat frozen yogurt vies with the many, many flavors of rich ice cream. Cone $1.60-2.60, plus 40¢ for homemade cones. Open daily noon-midnight.

DJ's, 2145 G St. NW (429-0230), near 22nd St. A smorgasbord of ethnic foods. Korean chef speedily serves up tasty Italian, Chinese, American, and Middle Eastern fare. A cluttered, unsophisticated cafeteria-style diner, packed with collegians throughout the year—beware the lunchtime crowd. Most entrees (including good vegetarian options) are under $5. Open Mon.-Thurs. 7:15am-8:30pm, Fri. 7:15am-5:30pm, Sat. 10am-2:30pm.

Food & Co. Gourmet Café, 1200 New Hampshire Ave. NW (223-8070), at M St. Brown paper packages of biscotti tied up with strings, gourmet cheeses, pasta salads, ice cream, and anything else the gustatory snob might need. Goat cheese and sun-dried tomato on crusty bread, $4. Twenty different salads and sandwiches ($3-6.25), entrees $6-8.50. Open Mon.-Fri. 8am-9pm, Sat. 9am-7pm, Sun. 10am-5pm.

Holly's Cookie Company, 1800 G St. NW (289-6899), at 18th St. Metro: Farragut West. Around the corner from the Old Executive Office, this small shop offers huge cookies ($6 per lb.) in seven flavors, in addition to a relaxed preface to the workday: classical music, coffee, and a muffin ($1). Open Mon.-Fri. 6am-4pm.

Jonathan's Gourmet Deli/Market, 2142 L St. NW (331-8458). Don't be intimidated by the gold-plated exterior. Inside, Jonathan's boasts a salad bar and a hot Chinese food bar which conspire to attract middle-aged corporate types. Business suits are *not* the dress code. Deli sandwiches $2.50-4.60. Gyro $4, burger $3.60. Open Mon.-Fri. 7am-8pm, Sat. 8am-3:30pm.

Leo's GW Deli, 2133 G St. NW (331-9391), near 22nd St. Sandwiches ($1.50-4) and fresh salads make this deli popular with students. Sandwiches are deli-variety—ham, turkey, roast beef, etc. Breakfast sandwiches ($1-3), pre-packaged snacks, drinks, and grocery items, too. No seating; perfect if you're on-the-run. Open Mon.-Fri. 6:30am-8:30pm, Sat. 8am-4pm.

Lindy's Bon Apétit, 2040 I St. NW (452-0055), near Pennsylvania Ave. and Tower Records. Ronald Reagan once said that life at George Washington University was not complete without a bone burger from this take-out deli. Pepper-loaded "Capitol Punishment" burger ($3.05, double $5.25). Bacon cheeseburger ($3.35, double $5.30). Monterey sandwich with refried beans, raw onions, and American cheese ($3, double $5.05). Six-in. sub ($3-4). Breakfast sandwiches under $2. Open Mon.-Fri. 8am-8pm, Sat.-Sun. 11am-4pm.

Milo's, 2142 Pennsylvania Ave. NW (338-3000). GWU students and locals enjoy Italian food amid Euro-chic scene of Mediterranean pictures and Italian pop music. All-you-can-eat lunch (pasta, pizza, and salad; $7) and dinner (soup, salad, pasta, pizza, and *stromboli;* $8). *Gelati.* Free delivery ($10 min.). Open Mon.-Fri. 11:30am-2:30pm and 5-9pm, Sat. 5-10pm, Sun. 4-9pm.

Treviso, 2138½ Pennsylvania Ave. NW (338-5760). Affordable, quality Italian food, white leather chairs, red tablecloths, and the owner's accent will all take you back to Veneto. *Pollo, pesce,* and *paste* $7.25-14. Open Mon.-Thurs. 11:30am-2:30pm and 5:30-10pm, Fri.-Sat. 5:30-10:30pm.

World Gourmet, 1917 F St. NW (371-9048), near 19th St. Though mainly known for its sandwiches ($3.70-4.50; amusing names include "World Bank" and "Guilt"), this deli also offers snacks and sweets from the world over—catering to a white-collar clientele. Open Mon.-Fri. 7:30am-7pm, Sat. 11:30am-5:30pm.

FOOD

Georgetown

The majority of Georgetown's dining options line the central thoroughfares M St. and Wisconsin Ave., where they vie for the attention and patronage of wary tourists, power-lunching execs, and snacking suburban youth. The eclectic array of eateries ranges from the pretention and expense of flashy dark-wood and polished-brass establishments to the much more affordable mixture of Indian, Ethiopian, Thai, and Vietnamese. Closest Metro stops: **Foggy Bottom-GWU and Dupont Circle.**

★ **Aditi,** 3299 M St. NW (625-6825), at 33rd St. The Sanskrit name translates as "creative power" or "abundance"; here it also means "great food." The $14 Aditi dinner is an Indian feast that will challenge any appetite; alternatively eat light with a vegetarian entree, $5-8. Meat dishes $9-13. Open for lunch Mon.-Sat. 11:30am-2:30pm, Sun. noon-2:30pm; for dinner Sun.-Thurs. 5:30-10pm, Fri.-Sat. 5:30-10:30pm.

★ **Booeymonger,** 3265 Prospect St. NW (333-4810), at Potomac St. Georgetown students and residents stop by for breakfast ($3 for the special) or a quick 'n' tasty giant sandwich (such as the Pita Pan or Tuna Turner) for under $5. The $6 dinner special (available 5pm-closing) includes a specialty sandwich, beverage, and choice of salad or soup. Free coffee refills (until 11am) jump-start your weekday morning. Open daily 8am-midnight.

Burrito Brothers, 3273 M St. NW (965-3963), at Potomac St. Value menu features tacos with beans for under $3. Crisp, fresh ingredients and plenty of vegetarian fare. Delivery (232-8646). Open Sun.-Wed. 11am-midnight, Thurs.-Sat. 11am-3am.

Busara, 2340 Wisconsin Ave. NW (337-2340), near Calvert St. Busara means "blue topaz," and the sleek, black, neon, and metallic modern decor justifies the name. This upscale Thai restaurant boasts indoor and garden seating, as well as an extensive bar. Lunch $6-8, dinner $9-15. Veggie entrees $8. Proper attire required: no jeans. Open for lunch Mon.-Fri. 11:30am-3pm, Sat.-Sun. 11:30am-4pm; dinner Sun.-Thurs. 5-11pm, Fri.-Sat. 5pm-midnight.

Café La Ruche, 1039 31st St. NW (965-2684), near M St. A spacious and pleasant French café with lovely wooden tables, blue and yellow embedded tiles, and old-fashioned street signs on the walls. Try the delicious gazpacho ($3.75) or choose from an array of quiches ($6-7), French entrees ($5-7), and desserts ($4). Lovely outdoor seating available. For carry out, call 965-2591. Open Sun.-Thurs. 11:30am-11:30pm, Fri Sat. 10am-midnight. Early-bird special Mon.-Fri. 5-7pm.

Caffè Northwest, 3251 Prospect St. NW (342-9002), near Potomac St. A mellow, arts café specializing in espresso, Italian sodas, iced drinks, and light fare. Drinks $1-3 sandwiches $4-5. The interior provides chess games and funky art in a spacious carpeted gallery, while a relaxed seating area awaits outside. Open Mon.-Thurs. 7am-midnight, Fri. 7am-1am, Sat. 8am-1am, Sun. 8am-midnight. 10% discount for students.

Caffè Sorrento, 1522 Wisconsin Ave. NW (338-2314). This small, family-owned Italian café is an oasis away from Georgetown's hubbub, with elegantly presented food and a chessboard decor. Antipasti $2-8, sandwiches $5.50-7, Italian sodas $2.25, truly delicious desserts $1-3; savor the *spumoni.* Open Mon.-Fri. 11am-10pm, Sat.-Sun. 9:30am-10pm.

Dean and Deluca Café, 3276 M St. NW (342-2500), near 32nd St. This pleasant and well-shaded outdoor café (glass-enclosed in the winter) is situated between the namesake gourmet market and Georgetown Park, tucked away from the bustle of M St Light fare, including salads and pastries. Espresso $1.35, cappuccino $1.80, beer $4 Freshly squeezed lemon- or limeade $1.80. Live jazz Fri. 6-10pm. Open Sun.-Thurs 8am-8pm, Fri. 8am-11pm, Sat. 9am-11pm. 30-min. free validated parking on lot; 2hr free with $10 purchase.

El Caribe, 3288 M St. NW (338-3121). Treasured by Cubans and Cuba-philes throughout D.C., this petite and pretty establishment is the only Washington restaurant to feature the cuisine of America's closest Communist neighbor, as well as other dishes of Latin America, the Mediterranean, and the Middle East. Tapas $5-7. Entrees $9-19 Open daily 11:30am-11pm; sometimes closes earlier on weekdays—call ahead.

Enriqueta's, 2811 M St. NW (338-7772), at Pennsylvania Ave. near 28th St. Famous for its lightly spiced, authentic Mexican cuisine. Friendly service in a bright festive environment of multi-colored chairs and tablecloths. The *mole,* Mexico's national dish ($13), is noteworthy. Entrees $11-14. Typically Mexican desserts around $3. Open Mon.-Thurs. 11:30am-2:30pm and 5-10pm, Fri. 11:30am-2:30pm and 5-11pm, Sat. 5-11pm, Sun. 5-10pm.

Fettoosh, 3277 M St. NW (342-1199), at Potomac St. Tree branches, lanterns, and black and yellow tiles adorn this fine Middle Eastern restaurant. Hummus $3, falafel $4.75. Entrees $8-15, sandwiches $3.50. Some nights feature live entertainment. **Fettoosh Express,** a fast-food version of Fettoosh and the least greasy of Georgetown's cheap Middle Eastern spots, stands 2 doors away, convenient for Georgetown students on their way home from bar-hopping. Fettoosh dining room open Mon.-Thurs 11am-11pm, Fri.-Sat. 11am-5am, Sun. 11am-1am. Fettoosh Express open Sun.-Thurs 11am-3am, Fri.-Sat. 11am-5am.

Georgetown Bagelry, 3245 M St. NW (965-1011), between Wisconsin Ave. and 33rd St. NYC-style bagel 55¢. Bagel burger $3.59, slice of pizza $1.75. Try a "pregel" (bagel-as-pretzel; $1). Open Sun.-Thurs. 7am-9pm, Fri.-Sat. 7am-midnight.

The Georgetown Dinette, 3206 O St. (337-3649), near Wisconsin Ave. Small diner run by a friendly husband-and-wife team serving fast food including hot dogs and burgers ($1-5). Open Mon.-Sat. 11am-8pm.

Gepetto, 2917 M St. NW (333-2602), near 29th St. Small Italian eatery specializing in thin crust pizza. Cheese-and-tomato pizza $11. Free pizza at the bar Mon.-Fri. 5pm-7pm. Take-out and free delivery (333-4315). Open Mon.-Thurs. noon-11pm, Fri.-Sat noon-12:30am, Sun. noon-11pm.

Hibiscus Café, 3401 K St. NW (965-0408), under the Key Bridge. The modern neon decor is worth the walk from M St. This former warehouse, serving "nouvelle Caribbean cuisine," has become almost impossibly hip, but mere mortals may still partake of pizza ($8.50-12) and beer ($4-5) while experiencing the chic, the sculptural, and the surreal. Open Tues.-Thurs. 6-11pm, Fri.-Sat. 6pm-midnight.

Houston's, 1065 Wisconsin Ave. NW (338-7760), near M St. Perfect for meat-and-potatoes lovers. The hickory-grilled hamburgers are served with a slew of shoestring fries ($7.50). Eating light is difficult here; even the salads ($6.50-8.75) may be brought home in a doggie bag. Lines are long and reservations aren't taken, so walk around Georgetown while you wait or crowd into the bar. Open Mon.-Fri. 5pm-until it closes Sat.-Sun. noon-until it closes.

Las Pampas, 3291 M St. NW (333-5151). This elegant little joint earns high praise for its Argentinian renderings of beef—arguably the best steak in town—but prices reflect the quality ($13-22). More budget-oriented travelers may opt for the "budget-conscious" section of the menu, or the dinner specials (offered around 5:30-6:30pm) with a choice of appetizer, main course, and dessert for $10. Open Mon.-Fri. noon-11pm, Sat.-Sun. noon-midnight.

Mama Maria and Enzio's, 2313 Wisconsin Ave. NW (965-1337), near Calvert St. Blue Mediterranean paintings surround you as you enjoy a $3.50 calzone, lunch pasta entree ($3.50-6), or dinner pasta ($6-9). Open daily 11am-3pm and 5-11pm.

★ **Moby Dick House of Kabob,** 1070 31st St. NW (333-4400), near M St. Souvlaki, sandwiches, and kabob served with fresh pita bread (baked in their own clay oven) or steaming rice. Vegetarian sandwiches include the Veggie Delight: fresh avocado, provolone, mushrooms, tomato, alfalfa, and spinach. Sandwiches around $4, platters and rice dishes $5-11. Mon.-Thurs. 11am-10pm, Fri. 11am-4am, Sat. noon-4am, Sun. noon-10pm.

Olympic Carry Out, 3207 O St. NW (338-2478, fax 338-2612), a block from Wisconsin Ave. Strictly delivery ($10 minimum) and take-out, serving homemade Greek and Mediterranean specialties as well as subs. Olympic-sized portions, rapid service. Gyros ($3.80), 8-inch subs ($4), and homemade desserts ($2). Open Mon.-Sat. 11am-10:30pm, Sun. noon-9:30pm.

Pad Thai, 1608 Wisconsin Ave. NW (342-3394). Pad Thai $7 at lunch, $8 at dinner. Vegetarian dishes $8-10. Lunch specials with soup $6.50-7.25; dinner entrees $8-12. Delivery within 3-mi. radius ($12 min.). Carry out available. Open Mon.-Thurs. 11:30am-10:30pm, Fri.-Sat.11:30am-11pm, Sun. 4:30-10pm.

★ **Paolo's,** 1303 Wisconsin Ave. NW (333-7353), near N St. Huge, elegant Italian dishes well worth the price (pasta $10-17, pizza $7-10, other entrees $13-17). A center seat affords a view of the chef baking a calzone in the wood-burning pizza oven as the impeccable waitstaff replenishes cold drinks and hot breadsticks. Prosciutto, Portobello, & Pesto Pizza, $9. In the summer, the black marble tables near the open front are conducive to people-watching—as well as being watched. Open Sun.-Thurs. 11:30am-1am, Fri.-Sat. 11:30am-2am.

Peacock Café and Market, 3203 Prospect St. NW (625-2740), at Wisconsin Ave. A quiet café/deli with small marble tables and a juice bar. Specialty sandwiches named after old Hollywood greats like Charlie Chaplin and Ginger Rogers; the stars are immortalized with fresh deli meats and cheeses ($3.75-6). Salads $2.50-6.25. "Mel Brooks" bagel sandwich $4. Open Mon.-Sat. 8am-10pm, Sun. 10am-10pm. Free delivery 7 daily 5-10pm ($15-min.).

★ **Ristorante Piccolo,** 1068 31st St. NW (342-7414). Just off M St., this 2-story building evokes visions of a Mediterranean landscape: a sea-blue exterior hides the warm earth-tones inside. The well-dressed, power-lunching clientele is the only reminder of the Georgetown locale. The tranquil aura of the dining room and upstairs terrace is accompanied by the pampering of a caring waitstaff. Elegant entrees include pasta, seafood, and lunchtime gourmet sandwiches (no pizza here). Lunch ($6-10), dinner ($9-17), and extraordinarily delicate tiramisu ($5). Open Sun.-Fri. 11:30am-10:30pm, Sat. 11:30am-11:30pm (sometimes midnight).

Quick Pita, 1210 Potomac St. NW (338-7482), near M St. Good, cheap Middle Eastern fare, perfect for a Quick Snack or take-out. All sandwiches under $4. Falafel $3.25, miniature pies $1.25. Free delivery in the Georgetown area after 6:30pm ($12 min.). Open Sun.-Wed. 11am-3am, Thurs.-Sat. 11am-4am.

Saigon Inn, 2928 M St. NW (337-5588), at 30th St. Slightly cheaper than Vietnam-Georgetown, its ancient rival. The peaceful, intimate rose-and-green dining room sports photographs of Haiti's and Peru's presidents, previous patrons of the Inn. The ingredients are fresh and well-prepared; the Saigon pancake ($8), a crispy crepe filled with tender meat, seafood, and crunchy bean sprouts, is their specialty. Strong, sweet Vietnamese coffee is a wonderful finish. Lunch special: 4 dishes for $4 (available until 3pm daily). Most entrees $6-9. Open Mon.-Sat. 11am-11pm, Sun. noon-11pm.

★ **Sarinah,** 1338 Wisconsin Ave. NW (337-2955), near O St. (also accessible through 3202 O St. around the corner). An inauspicious doorway leads downstairs to a tropical jungle: broad-leaved potted plants, pulpy wooden fruits, and colorful statuettes.

Delicious Indonesian food includes *satays*, grilled and skewered lamb, beef, chicken or shrimp with spicy sauces ($9-10), and vegetarian entrees ($7-8). Long list of exotic desserts ($3.25-4.25). Open Tues.-Sat. noon-3pm and 6-10:30pm, Sun. 6-10:30pm.

★ **Sushi-Ko,** 2309 Wisconsin Ave. NW (333-4187), below Calvert St. Authentic, no-frills Japanese food prepared before your eyes. The *Maki-sushi Nigiri* and *Temaki-sushi* are wonderfully affordable; each are under $5. Fish include the customary trout salmon, and tuna, as well as the more exotic *Uzara* (fish eggs with quail eggs). Order of sushi (2 pieces) $2-4.75. Open Mon. 6-10:30pm, Tues.-Fri. noon-2:30pm and 6-10:30pm, Sat. 5-10:30pm, Sun. 5-10pm. Valet parking $4.50.

Tandoor, 3316 M St. (333-3376, delivery 232-8646), near 33rd St. Authentic, spicy northern Indian cuisine. $5 lunch specials. Dinner $11-15; vegetarian entrees $7-9. Taste buds be wary: even items not marked with a red pepper may fry a tender tongue. Open daily 11:30am-2:30pm and 5:30-10:30pm.

Thomas Sweet, 3214 P St. NW (337-0616), at Wisconsin Ave. Ice cream, frozen yogurt, gourmet sandwiches, muffins, and bagels are made daily in the store. The best ice cream in D.C. by a light-year. Single-scoop $1.80. Hefty helpings of yogurt or ice cream mixed with fruit or candy $3.50-4.50. Open June-Aug. Mon.-Thurs. 9:30am-11pm, Fri.-Sat. 9:30am-midnight, Sun. 11am-11pm.

Vietnam-Georgetown Restaurant, 2934 M St. NW (337-4536), at 30th St. A relaxing and unassumingly handsome spot; serves up *cha giú*, crispy Vietnamese spring rolls ($6.45), and grilled chicken or beef on skewers ($8.45), among other things. When it's warm, dining under a canopy of trees in the extensive outdoor seating area is a pleasant option. Entrees $6-9. Open Mon.-Thurs. 11am-11pm, Fri.-Sat. 11am-midnight, Sun. noon-11pm.

★ **Zed's Ethiopian Cuisine,** 3318 M St. NW (333-4710), near 33rd St. Award-winning cuisine eaten with your hands, free from embarrassment, in the company of youthful, savvy local clientele. Basket-weave tables make for an authentic dining experience. Appetizers $4. Entrees $6-12. $5 weekday lunch specials. On a level with the excellent Ethiopian fare in Adams-Morgan. Open daily 11am-11pm.

Farragut

As with most areas, restaurants are created according to the needs and tastes of potential customers. In Farragut, the lunch-breaking businessperson lacking the luxury of time perpetuates a relationship of convenience with ubiquitous delis, fast-food joints, and street vendors. Health-conscious yuppies have incited an explosion of low-fat dining options. Establishments hawking frozen yogurt, salads, and espresso (for that mid-afternoon caffeine fix) compete for attention with bars offering happy-hour free buffets. Ethnic options are easily found as well; the area's diversity chalks variety right up there with quick service. Beware the occasional wallet-breakers, the scenes of power lunches and business dinners. Yet while the days in Farragut are filled with the hustle and bustle of a metropolis, the evenings and weekends bring a more relaxed intern- and executive-free sense of sophistication.

The Art Gallery Grille, 1712 I St. NW (298-6658), near 17th St. Metro: Farragut West. An Art Deco interior and original Erté serigraphs are juxtaposed with traditional diner stools and booths. The professional clientele enjoy various three-egg dinner omelettes ($7-9) or the Middle Eastern Pita Pocket ($8-9) while watching TV at the bar. Happy hour 5-7:30pm. DJ on Fri. nights. Outdoor seating available. Open Mon.-Wed. 6:30am-10pm, Thurs.-Fri. 6:30am-2am, Sat. 6:30am-11pm.

Café Amadeus, 1300 I St. NW (962-8686), entrance on 13th St. Metro: McPherson Square. This modern café serves traditional German dishes that vie with a smattering of Middle Eastern cuisine. Sit-down entrees $6-17, but the take-out counter offers a wide variety of more affordable sandwiches ($3-4). The house specialty are the health-conscious Hunter-Style Tikka dishes: lamb, chicken, turkey, beef, or shrimp grilled with special spices ($8-10). Happy hour (Mon.-Fri. 4pm-8pm) offers free appetizers with any drink. Open Mon.-Fri. 11am-9pm.

Casa Blanca, 1014 Vermont Ave. NW (393-4430), near K St. Metro: McPherson Square. The modest decor can be deceiving; Casa Blanca masters homemade Spanish, Mexican, Salvadoran, and Peruvian cuisine. Two tacos ($3.50) satisfy the staple-seeker, while the Peruvian *pollo a la braza*—roasted chicken with salad and fried potatoes or rice and beans ($5.50)—provides something a little less Tex-Mex. Open Mon.-Sat. 9:30am-10pm, Sun. noon-5pm.

Chesapeake Bagel Bakery, 818 18th St. NW (775-4690). Metro: Farragut West. This branch of a local chain (28 locations in the Washington area) is frequented primarily for its 45¢ bagels, but the $4-per-lb. pasta/sushi/noodle/salad bar is a celebrated attraction as well. Open Mon.-Fri. 6:30am-4:30pm, Sat. 8am-3pm.

Cup'A Cup'A, 1911 K St. NW (466-2872). Metro: Farragut North. The prime location on K St. makes this one-stop coffee shop perpetually busy; the espressos ($1-2) are particularly popular among Washington business folk. Cookies and biscotti ($1) are abundant and prime for dipping. Open Mon.-Fri. 7am-6pm, Sat. 9am-3pm.

Eye St. Café, 1915 I St. NW (457-0773). Metro: Farragut West. Middle Eastern/Italian. A high-quality, restaurant setting with café prices serves up treats such as pepper salad ($6) and *zaatar* pizza (wood-burning oven-baked, with thyme paste, roasted sesame, onion, feta, and tomato, $9); desserts include baklava ($3) and tiramisu ($5). Open Mon.-Thurs. 11:30am-3pm and 5:30-9pm, Fri. 11:30am-3pm and 5:30-10pm.

Lebanese Castle, 1120 20th St. NW (296-5666). Metro: Farragut West or Farragut North. Fine Lebanese dishes are presented in a beautiful decor and friendly atmosphere. Entrees ($9-12) include various Mediterranean and Middle Eastern dishes, from lamb kebabs to stuffed grape leaves (each dish $10). Of course, the real deal is happy hour, or "renewal hour" as translated from the Lebanese (Mon.-Fri. 5-7pm), with free appetizers. Outdoor seating available. Open Mon.-Fri. 11:30am-3pm and 5-10pm, Sat. 5:30-10pm.

Health Zone, 1445 K St. NW (371-2900). Metro: McPherson Sq. Mmm...steamed veggies and rice ($4.60). If that doesn't sound appealing, the Health Zone veggie burger ($3.70) is indeed tasty, and the veggie pizza ($4.50) likewise deserves a try. Large frozen yogurt $1.60. New age music and health-oriented quotations displayed on burlap banners complete the motif. Open Mon.-Fri. 7am-4pm.

La Prima Market Caffè, 950 14th St. NW (898-1140), near K St. Metro: McPherson Square. La Prima specializes in hot Italian dishes, gourmet pizzas ($5-7), and create-your-own sandwiches (with a "sand-wish card"; $4.30). Patio seating available. Open Mon.-Fri. 7am-5pm.

New York Gourmet Deli, 2000 L St. NW (296-8113). Metro: Farragut North. The deli of D.C. delis, due to its sheer size and vast selection. On their way to work, patrons fill up on the breakfast bar ($3 per lb.), and, at lunchtime, the same famished business folk flock to the indoor and outdoor seating, hot and cold lunch bars ($4 per lb.), and fresh deli sandwiches ($4-5). All this serve-yourself action leaves the guys behind the counter bored to death. Open Mon.-Fri. 6:30am-4pm.

Palais du Chocolat, 1200 19th St. NW (659-4244), at M St. Metro: Farragut North or Farragut West. Self-proclaimed "place for chocolate-lovers," Palais du Chocolat is an ideal source for the requisite mid-morning (and afternoon) sugar high. Chocolate may be patrons' first choice, but delicious pastries, sandwiches, quiches, and salads ($1-4) are close seconds. (Happy hour Mon.-Fri. 4-6:30pm.) Lunchtime offers a *croque monsieur* (grilled cheese, $4). The white-chocolate replicas of the Capitol dome are pure, bureaucratic bliss. Open Mon.-Fri. 8am-6:30pm.

Pan Asian, upstairs at 1018 Vermont Ave. NW (783-8899). Metro: McPherson Sq. Can't decide among Japanese, Korean, Chinese, Thai, and Filipino? Pan Asian has it all: shrimp tempura ($5), hot-and-spicy drunken noodles (noodles with minced chicken and a spicy basil sauce, $6), pad Thai, Singapore Curry Vermicelli, and more. The quiet atmosphere and filling dishes provide a satisfying respite during a busy workday. Open Mon.-Fri. 11:30am-8:30pm.

Recessions, 1700 K St. NW (296-6686)—ironically located in the basement of the Commerce building. Metro: Farragut North. Claiming to serve "too much for your money," this tick-tacky café sports old advertisements on its walls from the days when a brand-new Buick was $1000. Lunchtime means long lines; these guys don't know the first thing about recessions. Hot entrees are never more than $7 (and that includes the ½-lb. steak), and 10-oz. burgers with all sorts of toppings cost $6 or less; recent ventures include breakfast fare, including omelettes ($3) and pancakes (2 for $2). Happy hour 5-8pm. Open Mon.-Fri. 7am-10pm.

Sholl's Colonial Cafeteria, 1990 K St. NW (296-3065), in the Esplanade Mall (enter by way of 20th St.). Metro: Farragut West. One of a dying breed, Sholl's serves up good cooking on cafeteria trays: breast of lamb or roast beef $2.25, homemade pies ($1.50). These guys (and dozens of their patrons) have been around forever; their exceptionally low prices are an enduring testament to their longevity. Open Mon.-Sat. 7am-2:30pm and 4-8pm, Sun. 8:30am-6pm.

★ **The Star of Siam,** 1136 19th St. NW (785-2839), between L and M St. Metro: Farragut West or Farragut North. This critically acclaimed restaurant is a favorite of both businesspersons and true connoisseurs. The *Gang Keo-Wan*—green curry with chicken or beef, coconut milk, bamboo shoots, eggplant, and green beans ($7.50 lunch, $8.50 dinner)—will raise your oral temperature to a new extreme. Outdoor seating available. Open Mon.-Sat. 11:30am-11pm, Sun. 5-10pm.

Thai Kingdom, 2021 K St. NW (835-1700), near 21st St. Metro: Farragut West or Foggy Bottom-GWU. Pink curtains and lunchtime throngs give this place away. Ornate and overflowing with gilt decorations, buddhas, and photos of famous Thais, Thai Kingdom prides itself on its Gai Yarng Kingdom dish—grilled chicken, rice and several sauces ($6.50); the Gueyteow Phad Ki-Mao (rice noodles with basil chicken, $6) is another favorite. Open Mon.-Thurs. 11:30am-2:30pm and 5-10:30pm, Fri. 11:30am-2:30pm and 5-11pm, Sat. noon-2:30pm and 5-11pm, Sun. noon-2:30pm and 5-10pm.

★ **Tokyo Terrace,** 1025 Vermont Ave. NW (628-7304), near K St. Metro: McPherson Square. While many of Farragut's salad bars offer sushi of mediocre variety, Tokyo Terrace caters to the area's sushi-lovers and connoisseurs with a serious variety of both Japanese and Chinese fare. The Sushi Combination ($6-11) supplies a taste of everything, and the all-you-can-eat sushi, tempura, and miso soup buffet ($11; available Fri. 6-9pm) supplies *a lot* of everything. Open Mon.-Thurs. 9:30am-7:30pm, Fri. 9:30am-9pm, Sat. noon-7:30pm.

Tuscana West, 1350 I St. NW (289-7300). Metro: McPherson Square. In a modern, classy setting, the Italian cuisine can be a little pricey ($11-18 for gourmet pizza and pasta dishes), but the tasty *bruschetta* ($6) is more than enough sustenance for executive-watching—ever seen someone down three martinis at lunchtime? Happy hour also offers affordable treats: drink specials and free hors d'oeuvres. Nightly live jazz and piano. Open Mon.-Fri. 11:30am-11pm, Sat. 5:30pm-3am.

Vie de France, 1615 M St. NW (659-0992). Metro: Farragut North. French-inspired fast food includes pizza on a croissant crust ($3) and *Pain Bagnat,* a French take on the tuna sandwich ($5.50), but Vie de France is perhaps best-known simply for its fresh-out-of-the-oven French bread. Espresso drinks $1.25-2.50, cookies 90¢. Open Mon.-Fri. 7:30am-5pm, but café/deli closes at 4pm.

Whatsa Bagel, 1216 18th St. NW (293-8990), enter on Jefferson Pl. Metro: Farragut North. 50¢ bagels come in wacky daily varieties like sun-dried tomato, cheese, banana-nut, granola, "everything," and rotating specialty flavors like chocolate chip, carrot, and piña colada. Offbeat "overstuffed" bagel sandwiches include: chopped liver ($2.90) and scrambled egg ($1.50). Pizza $1.25-1.50 per slice. Open Mon.-Thurs. 7am-7pm, Fri. 7am-6pm, Sat.- Sun. 8am-3pm.

Dupont Circle

Dupont Circle's food is more expensive but more varied than that of bohemian Adams-Morgan to the north. Coffee shops, one-of-a-kind American restaurants, and a pricey *patisserie* or two complement the ethnic assortment.

Afterwords Café, 1517 Connecticut Ave. NW (387-3825), near Q St. Late-night sweets behind a bookshop. Some expensive *nouvelle* entrees, but Washington's best cakes, pies, and mousse ($3.25-6.25) are rich rewards for living the literary life. Cappuccino-lovers: come one, come all. Live music Wed. at 8pm, Thurs. at 9pm, Fri.-Sat. at 10pm. Open Sun.-Thurs. 7am-1am, Fri.-Sat. 24hr.

Bacchus Restaurant, 1827 Jefferson Place NW (785-0734), near 19th St. Entrees hover around $13, but this Lebanese den—named after the god of good times—offers tantalizing appetizers, ranging in price from $4 to $5.75 and in ingredients from okra to eggplant to pomegranate to lamb. Open Mon.-Fri. noon-2:30pm and 6-10pm, Sat. 6-10pm.

FOOD

Bua, 1635 P St. NW (265-0828, delivery 232-8646), near 17th St. A cool, spacious dining room and patio seating complements Bua's Thai cuisine. Dinner entrees $8-13 (most around $8); lunch entrees $6-7.50. Happy hour (Tues.-Sat. 5-7pm): mixed drinks and beer for $1.75. Open daily 11:30am-2:30pm and 5-11pm.

Café Luna, 1633 P St. NW (387-4005), near 17th St. Health- and self-conscious locals flock here for the extensive menu of veggie and fat-free dishes amid a foppish atmosphere. Pasta $6-8.25. Sandwiches $4-5.50. Breakfast ($2-4.25) served all day. À la carte brunch served Sat.-Sun. 10am-3pm ($5-6). Open Mon.-Thurs. 8am-11:30pm, Fri. 8am-2am, Sat. 10am-2am, Sun. 10am-11:30pm.

Café Parma, 1724 Connecticut Ave. NW (462-8771), between R and S St. Excellent Italian regional cooking served in an understated atmosphere. Fantastic entrees $6-13. Open Sun.-Thurs. 11:30am-10:30pm, Fri.-Sat. 11:30am-11:30pm.

★ **City Lights of China,** 1731 Connecticut Ave. NW (265-6688), between R and S St. Perhaps the District's best Chinese restaurant, City Lights serves carefully prepared Szechuan-Hunan standards ($9-22, most around $10) and widely acclaimed house specialties, such as the crispy fried shredded beef ($13). Appetizers include steamed dumplings with chives and pork ($4.50). Open Mon.-Thurs. 11:30am-10:30pm, Fri. 11:30am-11pm, Sat. noon-11pm, Sun. noon-10:30pm.

DC Café, 2035 P St. NW (887-5819), near 21st St., conveniently located near several of the Circle's clubs and bars. Excellent pizza (plain 10-in. pie that feeds two, $6), as well as Syrian and Mediterranean dishes. Indoor and outdoor dining areas. Free delivery ($15 min.; within a 4-block radius). Cool and cheap. Open 24hr.

Dupont Italian Kitchen, 1637-41 17th St. NW (328-3222), at R St. Delicious, no-frills Italian food at excellent prices. Pasta $4.50-7, hot sandwiches $3-4, small cheese pizza $4.50. Indoor seating and a sidewalk café. Free delivery in the Dupont Circle area. Open Mon.-Fri. noon-midnight, Sat.-Sun. noon-1am.

Dupont Down Under, entrance at Mass. Ave. and 19th. Underground pedestrian bypass offers an alternative way to cross the Circle via a multi-ethnic food court. Perfect for those on the run. Open Sun.-Thurs. 10am-9pm, Fri.-Sat. 10am-10pm.

★ **Food for Thought,** 1738 Connecticut Ave. NW (797-1095), three blocks north of the Circle. Casual coffeehouse atmosphere attracts alternative youth, and veggie dishes satisfy the healthiest appetites. Evening sets by local acoustic musicians add a Bohemian touch; open mike every Mon. 9-11:30pm. Bulletin boards announce everything from rallies to beach parties to rides to L.A. Pool table upstairs. Great chunky gazpacho (cup $3). Lunch combos with soup or salad $4.75-6.75 (Mon.-Fri. until 4:30pm), dinner $6-10. Open Mon.-Thurs. 11:30am-12:30am, Fri. 11:30am-2am, Sat. noon-2am. Sun. 5pm-12:30am.

Jolt 'N' Bolt, 1918 18th St. NW (232-0077), near S St. Espresso $1.05, cappuccino $1.75, coffee $1. In summer, they'll ice just about anything; you can enjoy it on the porch. Open Mon.-Thurs. 7am-11pm, Fri. 7am-midnight, Sat. 8am-midnight.

Lauriol Plaza, 1801 18th St. NW (387-0035), near S St. True Mexican food—no greasy *chimichangas* here—served on a charming patio by gracious waiters. Fried bananas $2.50. Many entrees amplified by rice and *frijoles* ($7-16). Free parking for patrons. Open Sun.-Thurs. 11:30am-11pm, Fri.-Sat. noon-midnight.

Pan Asian Noodles & Grill, 2020 P St. NW (872-8889), near 20th St. Oodles of noodles in every soup, sauce, and style. Vegetarian dishes upon request. Lunch $6-9, dinner $7-10. Open Mon.-Thurs. 11:30am-2:30pm and 5-10pm, Fri. 11:30am-2:30pm and 5-11pm, Sat. noon-2:30pm and 5:30-11pm, Sun. 5-10pm.

Paru's Indian Vegetarian Restaurant, 2010 S. St. NW (483-5133), near Connecticut Ave. Vegetarian fast food served southern-Indian-style in a small-diner atmosphere. Rice platters served with vegetable *pilav, raitha, paratha, papoid,* and lemon pickle ($8). Open Mon.-Sat. 11:30am-8:45pm.

★ **Pizzeria Paradiso,** 2029 P St. NW (223-1245), near 21st St. The lines are perpetually long most nights, but wouldn't you expect them to be for the best pizza in the city? The toppings are tasty and traditional—basil, prosciutto, capers—but the crispy crust is out-of-this-world. Sides include tangy *panzanella* (Tuscan bread and vegetable salad) and elegant salads. Desserts include biscotti ($3) and *gelati* ($4). Open Mon.-Thurs. 11am-11pm, Fri.-Sat. 11am-midnight, Sun. noon-10pm.

★ **The Pop Stop,** 1513 17th St. NW (328-0880), near P St. The price of a cup of coffee buys you several hours in the easy chairs upstairs at this hippest of D.C. cafés. Down-

FOOD

stairs puts a well-stocked magazine rack within reach, while the streetside patio offers some serious people-watching. The structural diversity attracts a diverse crowd, though it's weighted toward the local, gay, and young; many stop by on their way to or from bars and clubs—that espresso yields a second wind on a Saturday night. The café serves a wide variety of coffee drinks ($1-3) and sandwiches (with chips $4). Open Sun.-Thurs. 7:30am-2am, Fri.-Sat. 7:30am-4am.

Sala Thai, 2016 P St. NW (872-1144), at 21st St. Light spicy Thai fare draws locals to this modern downstairs dining room. Most lunch entrees $6 (though the delicious crispy fish goes for $8). Dinner entrees $7-13. Critics rave about the soft-shelled crabs ($13). Free delivery. Open Mon.-Thurs. 11:30am-2:30pm and 5-10:30pm, Fri. 11:30am-2:30pm and 5-11pm, Sat. noon-11pm, Sun. noon-10:30pm.

★ **Skewers,** 1633 P St. NW (387-7400, delivery 546-8646), near 17th St. Skewers defies the neighborhood tendency toward multi-ethnic menus and sticks exclusively to Middle Eastern fare, coupled with its tapestry-hung, pottery-filled interior. Chicken kabob and two side dishes, $7. Open Sun.-Thurs. 11am-11pm, Fri.-Sat. 11am-midnight.

★ **Soho Tea & Coffee,** 2150 P St. NW (463-7646); directly en route to the bars and clubs near P St. west of the Circle. This hip coffeehouse benefits from its strategic location, drawing crowds of bar-and-club-hoppers in the wee hours of the morning and serving a steady stream of patrons all day long. Veggie bowls ($4.25), sandwiches ($5.25). Espresso $1.25-3.50. Open daily 6am-4am.

Trio Restaurant, 1537 17th St. NW (232-6305), at Q St. The 1963 March on Washington planners met in this diner, nowadays popular with the gay community. Those who prefer good grub to fine dining will appreciate this sturdy standby and its hearty American meals. Sandwiches $1.75-5.75. Open daily 7:30am-midnight.

★ **Zorba's Café,** 1612 20th St. NW (387-8555), near Connecticut Ave., by the Q St. entrance to the Dupont Circle Metro. Mediterranean folk music is played for indoor and outdoor customers enjoying fantastic Greek food. The restaurant is self-service; place your order with the cashier inside. *Yero* plate (with Zorba's excellent french fries and a small salad) $5.40. Open Mon.-Wed. 11am-11:30pm, Thurs.-Sat. 11am-2:30am, Sun. noon-10:30pm.

Shaw / U District

The immediate vicinity of 14th and U St. NW, the area's edge near the **U St.-Cardozo Metro** stop, is a safe source for supreme soul food, a uniquely African-American cuisine. Visit in the daytime only.

★ **Ben's Chili Bowl,** 1213 U St. NW (667-0909), at 13th St. Self-declared "Home of the Famous Chili Dog," this venerable (30-year-old) neighborhood hangout sports photos of Bill Cosby's visit to Ben's as well as multiple shots of Denzel Washington, taken when a scene from *The Pelican Brief* was filmed here. Spicy homemade chili—on a chili dog (served with onion, mustard, and potato chips, $2), on a half-smoke ($3), or on a ¼-lb. burger ($2.50). Die-hards eat it plain: small bowl $2, large bowl $2.55. Open Mon.-Thurs. 6am-2am, Fri.-Sat. 6am-4am, Sun. noon-8pm. Breakfast served Mon.-Sat. until 11am.

★ **Florida Avenue Grill,** 1100 Florida Ave. NW (265-1586), at 11th St. From the U St.-Cardozo Metro stop, walk east on U to 11th St., then walk north up 11th St. to Florida Ave. or take the Metrobus that runs up 11th St. Small, enduring (since 1944) diner once fed famous Black leaders and entertainers. Now their framed faces beam down at hordes of regulars. An article in the first booth is about a 32-year veteran Grill server: "I'd love to serve [President Reagan] chitlins," she says. "It might straighten his head out." Fantastic Southern-style food: breakfast (served until 1pm) with salmon cakes or spicy half-smoked sausage, grits, apples, or biscuits ($2-6). Lunch and dinner dishes served with choice of two vegetables ($6.50-10). Also various dishes featuring pigs' feet. Open Tues.-Sat. 6am-9pm.

Julio's, 1604 U St. (483-8500), near 16th St. An upscale restaurant and bar with 2 floors of dining, a popular rooftop, and a pool room. All-you-can-eat lunch buffet $7 (Mon.-Fri. 11:30am-3pm). Sandwiches $6-7.25. All-you-can-eat Sun. brunch $13 (10am-3pm). Happy hour (Mon.-Fri. 5-7pm): $2 rails and drafts and free pizza Mon.-Thurs.; $1 slices Fri. Delivery Mon.-Sun. ($3). Open daily 11:30am-10:30pm.

★ **Outlaw's,** 917 U St. NW (387-3978), between Vermont Ave. and 9th St. Should be the "In-laws'." Family-run establishment crowds in regulars for real, meat-laden home-cooking. Cramped downstairs quarters open onto the kitchen, where daily specials like liver and onions (Mon.), meat loaf (Tues.), and Salisbury steak (Thurs.) are cooked up. Food is cheap, too: cornbread 50¢, dinners served with 2 vegetables $5.30-7.65, sandwiches $3.25-4.85. Take-out available. Upstairs, the Family Bar and Lounge turns out jazz tunes Tues.-Wed. Open Mon.-Fri. 11am-6pm.

Polly's Café, 1342 U St. NW (265-8385), near 14th St. Sardine-can packed neighborhood restaurant and bar caters to a mixed crowd of professionals, students, and locals. A cozy interior and a varied, reasonably priced menu draw many for Sunday brunch featuring hearty American fare (i.e. meat, potatoes, and eggs, $7-8) and a choice of brunch cocktails. Portobello mushroom steak with bean salad ($9), mixed drink pitchers ($13-17). Happy hour Mon.-Thurs. 11pm-2am knocks $1 off rails and drafts. Opens Mon.-Fri. at 6pm, Sat.-Sun. at 10am. Kitchen open Sun.-Thurs. until midnight, Sat.-Sun. until 2am.

Adams-Morgan

Adams-Morgan's jambalaya of cultures can satisfy any unusual taste, from Latin American to Ethiopian to Caribbean—all for around $10. Adams-Morgan has justifiably become D.C.'s preferred locale for budget dining, but has also recently been infiltrated by a slew of decidedly overpriced spots. Don't be taken in; good food at a good price is literally around the corner. The action spreads from 18th, Columbia, and Calvert St. NW uphill along Columbia or down 18th.

The Argentine Grill, 2433 18th St. NW (234-1818), near Columbia Rd. Chic brick, art pix, a cured cow's skin, blue fans, and a mural comprise the decor. The cook is as artful as the decorators, even with the less elaborate dishes. Lunch sandwiches are a manageable $5-7. Dinner entrees $9-19. Open Mon.-Thurs. 5:30-10:30pm, Fri.-Sat. 5:30-11:30pm, Sun. 11:30am-10:30pm.

Bukom Café, 2442 18th St. NW (265-4600), near Columbia Rd. A mellow, hip West African restaurant and bar serving up stews, sugar cane, and other specialty dishes (entrees $8-10). Bukom is a two-time "Taste of Adams-Morgan" contest winner. Live entertainment: jazz Tues. at 8pm, West African music Wed.-Thurs. and Sun. starting at 9pm, Fri.-Sat. at 10pm. Open Tues. 4pm-midnight, Wed.-Thurs. and Sun. 4pm-2am, Fri.-Sat. 4pm-3am.

Dahlak, 1769 U St. NW (332-6435), near 18th St. Dahlak may not be as fancy as its Ethiopian competitors, but the food is just as good. Individual entrees $5-7.50; combo platters ($6.50-7.25) provide a delicious variety, along with salad and, of course, *injera,* Ethiopian sour pancake bread. Lunch specials $5. Live entertainment Fri.-Sat. 10pm-2am. Open daily 11am-midnight.

★ **The Islander,** 1762 Columbia Rd. NW (234-4955), upstairs—easy to miss. Some of the best food in D.C. is made in this small Trinidadian and Caribbean restaurant, which has been winning regulars for over 15 years with its exotic but unpretentious cuisine. Curried goat ($8.75) and Calypso chicken ($8.50) are worth a try. Nine kinds of *roti* (thin pancakes stuffed with vegetables/meat) are a bargain at $3.50-7. Appetizers $1.50-4. Sweet ginger beer ($1.50). Open Mon. 5-10pm, Tues.-Thurs. noon-10pm, Fri.-Sat. noon-11pm.

Julia's Empanadas, 2452 18th St. NW (328-6232), near Columbia Rd. In this cheerful, brightly colored establishment, Julia's tasty meat- and veggie-filled pastries are "made by hand, baked with love" according to the menu; but rest assured: she uses an oven, too. Baked empanadas $2-3; fried $1.89—one's a snack, two're a meal. Delicious dessert empanadas ($2) must not be overlooked. Limited seating. Open Sun.-Wed. 11am-10:30pm, Thurs. 11am-midnight, Fri.-Sat. 11am-3am.

★ **Meskerem,** 2434 18th St. NW (462-4100), near Columbia Rd. Fine Ethiopian cuisine served in a beautiful setting: cheery yellow 3-level interior incorporates an upstairs dining gallery with Ethiopian woven tables and a view of the diners below. Lunch entrees $7.25-11, dinner $9-12. Open daily noon-midnight.

★ **Mixtec,** 1792 Columbia Rd. NW (332-1011), near 18th St. Mixtec is a cheap, friendly, and refreshing bastion of hearty Mexican food. Two bright rooms wear neat paper lanterns and wooden Mexican chairs, while a neon light flashes the specialty—*tacos al carbon.* The $3 version consists of two small tortillas filled with beef and served with three kinds of garnish. Chicken *mole* ($10). Entrees $9-10. Open Sun.-Thurs. 11am-10pm, Fri.-Sat. 11am-11pm.

Montego Café, soon to be known as **Mobay Café,** 2437 18th St. (745-1002), near Columbia Rd. The name may soon be different, but this is the same rollicking restaurant and bar, serving Caribbean food with an American twist late into the night. Seafood entrees $9-11, chicken entrees $6.75-8.50, sandwiches $4.75-6.25. Á la carte brunch ($4.50-9) served daily until 3pm. Open Sun.-Thurs. 10am-2am, Fri.-Sat. 10am-4 or 5am.

Pasta Mia Trattoria, 1790 Columbia Rd. NW (328-9114), near 18th St. Practice makes perfect, and Pasta Mia has had plenty of pasta practice—other than a few traditional appetizers and desserts, nothing but noodles are on the menu. Airy rooms and big portions ($7-9) yield an great meal. Open Mon.-Sat. 6-10:30pm.

Perry's, 1811 Columbia Rd. (234-6218), near 18th St. The awning sports a rebus. A funky modern dining room provides the backdrop for nouvelle Mediterranean/Japanese cuisine, while entrees ($10-16) and sushi (75¢-2.75 per piece) can also be savored on one of Washington's most popular rooftops, where the owners grow orange and lemon trees. Open Mon.-Sat. 6pm-1am, Sun. 5pm-1am. Kitchen closes Sun.-Thurs. at 10:30pm, Fri.-Sat. 11:30pm.

El Pollo Primo, 2471 18th St. NW (588-9551), near Columbia Rd. By their awning ye shall know them. Moist, flavorful, tender, greaseless, cheap chicken hot off a big smoky grill. Two-piece chicken dinner with tortillas, salsa, and 2 side orders $3.45, 3-piece dinner $4.40. Side orders include beans and rice ($2 each à la carte). Free delivery noon-11pm daily ($10 min.). Open daily 9:30am-10pm.

FOOD

★ **Red Sea,** 2463 18th St. NW (483-5000), near Columbia Rd. The first of Adams-Morgan's famous Ethiopian restaurants is still among the best. Appetizers include a *sambusa* pastry filled with tasty ground beef and spices ($2.50). The claret-toned surroundings provide a serene atmosphere in which to savor the traditional pancake bread, *injera,* accompanied by tender lamb, beef, chicken, and vegetable *wats.* Entrees $7-11. Open Sun.-Thurs. 11:45am-11pm, Fri.-Sat. 11am-midnight.

Saigonnais, 2307 18th St. (232-5300), near Kalorama Rd. George Stephanopolous ate here. The intimately elegant dining room harbors white-linen draped tables and tasty, reasonably priced Vietnamese fare. Lunch specials $5.50-7, dinner entrees $7.25-14.50. Delivery available. Open daily 11:30am-3pm and 5-11pm.

So's Your Mom, 1831 Columbia Rd. NW (462-3666). Deli with mock-New York sensibility (get it?!). Meats are shipped from the Big Apple itself, while fresh baked goods arrive daily from Baltimore. Huge tasty sandwiches ($3-5) are made on your choice of French, Italian, or soft sub roll (croissants cost extra). Genoa salami sandwich $4. The freshly squeezed orange juice ($2 for a large disguised as a medium) is some of the best around. Take-out only. Open Mon.-Fri. 7am-8pm, Sat. 8am-7pm, Sun. 8am-3pm.

Star of Siam, 2446 18th St. (986-4133), near Columbia Rd. Acclaimed Thai cuisine is served in an attractive second-floor dining room or on a rooftop deck. Visitors who are feeling particularly meditative may ask to kneel at a traditional low table. Light and flavorful Pad Thai $6.50-8.25. Entrees $6.25-10 at lunch, $8-13 at dinner. Delivery available daily 5-10:30pm. Open Mon.-Thurs. 5-11pm, Fri. 5pm-midnight, Sat. noon-midnight, Sun. noon-11pm.

El Tamarindo, 1785 Florida Ave. NW (328-3660), just east of the corner of Florida and 18th St. (nighttime warrants caution in this area). Superb and cheap Salvadoran and Mexican food is served into the early morning. House combination plate of appetizers presents cheese quesadillas, nachos, chicken wings, a *taquito,* and guacamole and sour cream ($6.25). Entrees run $5.50-12, with nearly all under $10. Open Mon.-Thurs. 11am-2am, Fri.-Sat. 11am-5am, Sun. 10am-5am.

Tom Tom, 2333 18th St. (588-1300). This attractive, hip restaurant and bar is graced with live music and upcoming D.C. cultural events are announced on blackboards. Tom Tom serves up tapas ($4-7) and Mediterranean fare; choose your own pasta ($6) and sauce ($3-5) for a (potentially) tasty personalized conglomeration. Kitchen open Mon.-Thurs. 5-11pm, Fri.-Sat. 5pm-midnight, Sun. noon-midnight; bar open Sun.-Thurs. until midnight and Fri.-Sat. until 2:30am.

Upper Northwest

WOODLEY PARK

A diverse group of popular eateries—some dirt-cheap, some wallet-smashing—gather on a single block of Connecticut Ave. around the Woodley Park-Zoo Metro, north of Dupont Circle and just a Calvert St. bridge away from Adams-Morgan. **Metro: Woodley Park-Zoo,** for all of the following:

The Lebanese Taverna, 2641 Connecticut Ave. NW (265-8681). Generous appetizers, many of them vegetarian ($3.50-7), and entrees are served in an outdoor or indoor setting. Lunch sandwiches ($5.50-6) are more affordable than the somewhat pricey dinner entrees ($8.75-14.50). Open Mon.-Thurs. 11:30am-2:30pm and 5:30-10:30pm, Fri.-Sat. 11:30am-2:30pm and 5:30-11pm, Sun. 5-10pm.

Rajaji, 2603 Connecticut Ave. NW (265-7344). Near-total darkness complements spicy vegetarian curries ($5-7 at lunch, $6-7.50 at dinner) and a wide selection of Indian breads $1.50-2.25. Very spicy vegetarian curries are very, very spicy. Spicy. Open daily 11:30am-2:30pm and 5:30-11pm.

Saigon Gourmet Restaurant, 2635 Connecticut Ave. NW (265-1360). Traditional Vietnamese comfort accompanies reasonable prices for appetizers (*hâ iò*, spring rolls, $3.50-4) and entrees (*bò xào xâ*, lemon grass beef, $6-10). Open Mon.-Sat. 11:30am-3pm and 5-10:30pm, Sun. 11am-3pm and 4:30-10pm.

Saigon Inn, 2614 Connecticut Ave. NW (483-8400). The new baby sibling to Georgetown's Saigon Inn is blessed with the same elegant serenity and tasty offerings. Four dishes for $4.50 (Bud and Perrier quenchers $1) 11am-3pm daily. Yummy and light vermicelli, Vietnamese-style, $6-8. Free delivery ($12 min.). Open Mon.-Thurs. 11am-10pm, Fri.-Sat. 11am-11pm, Sun. noon-10pm.

A Taste of India, 2623 Connecticut Ave. NW (483-1115), a few doors down from Rajaji. Tasty appetizers ($1-6) preface Tandoor-oven and curried entrees (lunch $6-10, dinner $6-11). A Taste of India is more mainstream than Rajaji—i.e. for Westerners who can't take the heat. Free delivery ($12 min.). Open Mon.-Fri. 11am-3pm and 5-11pm, Sat.-Sun. 11am-11pm.

Thai Taste, 2606 Connecticut Ave. NW (387-8876). D.C.'s voyeuristic black-and-neon magnet for Thai-food lovers. Mirrors at every table; patrons watch themselves eat the spicy house noodle specialty ($8) and Thai iced coffee ($2). All-you-can-eat lunch buffet $7. Dinner from $6.50. Open daily 11:30am-10:30pm.

GLOVER PARK

A ten-minute walk up Wisconsin Ave. from Georgetown proper, this area between Calvert and R St. seems to hog more than its fair share of D.C.'s top budget eateries.

★ **Austin Grill,** 2404 Wisconsin Ave. NW (337-8080). The Austin Grill sets the standard for Tex-Mex in Washington. Relying on a foundation of brilliantly prepared standards it also has a range of more inventive dishes featuring fresh and unusual meats topped with exquisite house sauces. Try the *carnitas,* melt-in-your-mouth braised pork fajitas ($9.75), or the Austin special, a pair of enchiladas striped with a trio of house sauces ($8.50). The place is small and hip, hence lines are long. The wait for a table can be made more pleasant with the Stars and Bars, a powerful margarita worth the $4.75 price. Open Mon. 11:30am-10:30pm, Tues.-Thurs. 11:30am-11pm, Fri. 11:30am-midnight, Sat. 11am-midnight, Sun. 11am-10:30pm.

★ **Faccia Luna,** 2400 Wisconsin Ave. NW (337-3132). Pizza-crust connoisseurs, this small local chain is your Mecca, your Delhi, your Jerusalem. The wood-fired oven produces a masterful harmony of crisp-yet-tender crust, accompanied by subtly seasoned sauce and steaming cheese. Forget pepperoni and top it with eggplant, spinach, or pesto. The selection also includes intriguing pastas and piping-hot calzones, and the sunlit, blond-wood booths are so pleasant that dessert on a full stomach is at least an excuse to stay a little longer. Basic pie $6.05-11.50. Toppings extra. Open Sun.-Thurs. 11:30am-11pm, Fri.-Sat. 11:30am-midnight.

Max's Best Ice Cream, 2416 Wisconsin Ave. NW (333-3111). Max's Best is pretty darn good. This old-fashioned ice cream parlor features cones at modern prices ($1.65), as well as subs and sandwiches ($1.65-5.60), including good old peanut butter and jelly ($1.65). Max and Marsha do ice cream cakes, too. Open Sun.-Thurs. 11am-11pm, Fri.-Sat. 11am-midnight; winter open daily 9am-9pm.

★ **Rocklands,** 2418 Wisconsin Ave. NW (333-2558). Rocklands serves up South Carolina/Florida-style tangy grilled barbecue. Quarter-rack of pork ribs $4.50, BBQ pork sandwich $4. If you eat in at the mahogany counter, you can raid owner John Snedden's shelf of some 100 different hot sauces; have just one or sample as extensively as your deviously promiscuous little mouth will permit. Y'all come back now, y'heah? Open Mon.-Sat. 11:30am-10pm, Sun. 11am-9pm.

CLEVELAND PARK AND TENLEY CIRCLE

No one would place Cleveland Park or Tenley Circle on the cutting edge of anything. Still, these areas have the best of both worlds: back streets nearly as quiet as the suburbs and two avenues on which good food hides from the masses.

Cleveland Park

Budget ethnicity dominates the food in otherwise Caucasian Cleveland Park, on Connecticut Ave. **Metro: Cleveland Park,** for all of the following:

Ivy's Place, 3520 Connecticut Ave. NW (363-7802). Ivy's throws together Indonesian and Thai fare, though the cuisines do not so much collide as coexist; the menu has separate Indonesian and Thai listings, none over $9. The lunch special ($6), early bird dinner special (4:30-6:30pm; $7), and dinner special ($11) include soup, appetizers, and a choice of entree. Vegetarian-friendly. Free delivery ($12 min.). Open daily noon-11:30pm.

Palais du Chocolat, 3309 Connecticut Ave. NW (363-2462). See complete listing, p. 95. Open Sun.-Tues. 8am-8pm. Wed.-Thurs. 8am-10pm, Fri.-Sat. 8am-midnight.

Wingmaster's Grill Chicken and Ribs, 3514 Connecticut Ave. NW (244-1111). Sweet, springy corn bread and other tasty, very affordable side orders (60¢-$1.50) complement the grilled chicken and ribs. Lunch and dinner samplers ($5.30 and $7.30, respectively) bring you varying combinations of grilled breasts, ribs, wings, and side orders. Open Sun.-Thurs. 11am-10pm, Fri.-Sat. 11am-11pm.

Yanni's, 3500 Connecticut Ave. NW (362-8871). Yanni's is a bright, airy neighborhood favorite serving some of the town's finest Greek food. Starters include *tzatziki,* a cool yogurt and cucumber dip ($4); heaping *souvlaki* platters ($9), include *tzatziki* as well as french fries and a Greek salad. Open daily 11:30am-11pm.

Yenching Palace, 3524 Connecticut Ave. NW (362-8200). The 1961 Cuban Missile Crisis came to an end here, when emissaries from Khrushchev and Kennedy finalized the Soviet missile removal over a Chinese banquet. Today, the handsome semicircular booths host less nail-biting diplomacy and more finger-licking feasting; the food remains great and reasonably priced. Dinner entrees $5.50-16. Lunch combinations $5.50; available until 3pm. Free delivery ($12 min.). Open Mon.-Thurs. 11:30am-11pm, Fri.-Sat. 11:30am-11:30pm, Sun. noon-11pm.

Tenley Circle

Shoppers, American University students, and local professionals frequent these places. **Metro: Tenleytown,** for all of the following:

a.k.a. Frisco's, 4115 Wisconsin Ave. NW (244-7847). This charming deli/café emulates San Francisco prototypes—it's bright, airy, and decked out in the whitest of whites. Generous sandwiches test combinations—the Berkeley ($4.05) wraps up diced turkey, olive oil, tarragon vinegar, capers, onions, lemon pepper, tomato, and sprouts in a pita. Sandwiches substitute gourmet mustards, lemon, vinegars, relishes, and other spices for generic mayonnaise and salt. Sandwiches $3.50-4.25. Salads $3-4.25. *Huge* "exploded" potatoes (50¢-$2) make a meal. Open Mon.-Fri. 11am-4pm, Sat. 11am-3pm.

Armand's, 4231 Wisconsin Ave. NW (686-9450). Chicago-style deep-dish pizza invades Washington (small triple-cheese pizza $6.35, medium $9, large $10.35). Armand's also boasts thin-crust New York-style pizza and the chain's gourmet California-style pizza with exotic toppings like Thai chicken (marinated chicken breast, peanut-ginger sauce, scallions, shredded carrots, red pepper, and bean sprouts). All-you-can-eat pizza and salad bar buffet, $5 (Sun.-Thurs. 11am-2:30pm and 9-11pm, Sat.-Sun. 10am-1pm and 9-11pm). Open Sun.-Thurs. 11am-11pm, Fri.-Sat. 11am-1am. Down the street, **Armand's take-out-only window** at 5000 Wisconsin Ave. NW (363-5500) supplies a small variety of cheaper slices ($1.40-$1.75). Open Mon.-Thurs. 11am-11pm, Fri.-Sat. 11am-midnight, Sun. noon-11pm.

★ **Cactus Cantina,** 3300 Wisconsin Ave. NW (686-7222), at Macomb St. near the Cathedral. From the Metro, take Metrobus #30, 32, 34, 35, or 36 towards Georgetown. How fresh is the food here? The kitchen doesn't even own a can opener and the salsa is no more than 30-minutes-old when it arrives at your table. Cactus Cantina is a local hangout with fantastic food, including exceptional Tex-Mex standards, like enchiladas ($7.50 for 3), or items from the mesquite-fired grill ($9.50-20). Open Sun.-Thurs. 11:30am-11pm, Fri.-Sat. 11:30am-midnight.

The Dancing Crab, 4611 Wisconsin Ave. NW (244-1882), at 41st St. Locals dive in for fresh seafood, especially crabmeat sandwiches ($7) and Maryland-style crabcakes ($15). Rotating lunch specials Mon.-Fri. until 3pm, $6-8. All-you-can-eat hard-shell blue crabs (Tues.-Thurs. $19) available seasonally. Upstairs, the Malt Shop (see **Nightlife & Entertainment,** p. 213) will pour you a cold brew. Open Mon.-Thurs. 11am-10:30pm, Fri. 11am-11pm, Sat. noon-11pm, Sun. 3-10:30pm.

Krupin's, 4620 Wisconsin Ave. NW (686-1989). This popular deli and restaurant imports many of its fine ingredients from more deli-dependent cities such as New York. Smoked fish ($10-14), matzo ball soup ($3.50), and pastrami ($6.75) all have a place on Krupin's menu. Order one of the $12-14 nightly dinner specials, including soup or salad, vegetable du jour, and choice of potato, entree, and dessert. Open daily 8am-10pm.

Mediterranean Deli, 4629 41st St. NW (362-1006), at Wisconsin Ave. This small, nondescript eatery dishes out some of the best and cheapest Mediterranean food in town. Vegetarian fare includes vine leaves—grape leaves stuffed with rice, onion, lemon, and parsley ($4.50). Sandwiches include *baba ghanoush* ($3), and falafel ($3.50). Open Mon.-Sat. 11:30am-10pm, Sun. noon-8pm.

FRIENDSHIP HEIGHTS

Restaurants become pricier as you approach Western Ave., more reasonable as Maryland grows more distant. **Metro: Friendship Heights,** for all of the following:

★ **Booeymonger,** 5252 Wisconsin Ave. NW (686-5805), at Jenifer St. A blood relation of the one in Georgetown, Booeymonger puts together elaborate sandwiches, almost all under $5. Your jaw may not fit around the Patty Hearst: turkey, bacon, melted provolone, and Russian dressing on an English muffin ($4.75). The puns are obscure (the English muffin and Russian dressing represent Hearst's Anglo-Saxon stock and conversion to Communism, respectively) but delicious. Salads $2.25-5.25. Decent and very generous breakfast special $3. Open Sun.-Thurs. 7:30am-1am, Fri.-Sat. 7:30am-2am.

Chadwick's, 5247 Wisconsin Ave. NW (362-8040). While the inside offers shade, the front greenhouse area may offer a more enjoyable dining experience. Sandwiches and burgers $6-8, salads $5-8. Sweet treats include mud pie ($4) and thick mocha milkshakes ($3). Happy hour Mon.-Fri. 4-7pm: margaritas $2, domestic bottles or glass of house wine $1.50. Open Mon.-Thurs. 11:30am-2am, Fri.-Sat. 11:30am-3am, Sun. 10am-2am.

Yosaku, 4712 Wisconsin Ave. NW (363-4453). An attractive atmosphere of black lacquered tables and an attentive, courteous staff that maneuvers around masterfully in team Yosaku baseball jerseys. Sushi bar, entrees, and noodles $5-14. Sushi á la carte; *nigiri* sushi (50¢-$2 per piece) or *maki* sushi ($2.50-4.50). Open Mon.-Thurs. 11:30am-2:30pm and 5:30-10:30pm, Fri. 11:30am-2:30pm and 5:30-11pm, Sat. 5:30-11pm, Sun. 5:30-10pm.

WORTH DRIVING TO

★ **Parkway Deli,** 8317 Grubb Rd. (301-587-1427), just over the District line in Maryland. Take 16th St. NW all the way north to East-West Hwy., turn left on East-West, then left onto Grubb. An obscure shopping center hides Washington's best deli from all but true connoisseurs, who often wait up to an hour for weekend breakfasts. Parkway has a great selection of sandwiches, deli meats, snacks and drinks, as well as a sit-down restaurant-style dining area. Try any sandwich ($3.55-6.85) or a bagel with Nova lox ($5.85); the pickle bar (free after 4pm) makes national treasures of vinegar and peppercorns. Open Mon.-Tues. 8am-9:30pm, Wed.-Fri. 8am-10pm, Sat. 7am-10pm, Sun. 7am-9:30pm.

Northeast

An area not known for its fine cuisine, Northeast offers a few budget options clustering near Catholic University. **Metro: Brookland-CUA,** for all of the following:

Colonel Brooks Tavern, 901 Monroe St. NE (529-4002), across from the Metro busloading area. From Catholic U., pick up Monroe St. at its intersection with Michigan Ave. in front of the University Center building, at the south end of campus, on 9th and Monroe St. This half-restaurant, half-bar is the casual hangout for Catholic U. students and staff alike. The entrees ($9-13) are tasty, but the pub grub is cheaper and just as good. The Colonel's favorite is a 3-story sandwich/tower of pastrami, turkey, swiss cheese, slaw, and dressing ($7). Sandwiches are washed down with a mug of Pete's Wicked Ale or Wild Goose Porter ($2.75), a more traditional premium (mug $2.25), a domestic mug ($2), or one of the brews of the month (mug $2.50). Live entertainment Tues. 7pm-closing. Free parking. Open Sun.-Thurs. 11am-2am, Fri. 11am-3am, Sat. 11:30am-3am.

Murry and Paul's Restaurant, 3513 12th St. NE (529-4078). The orange exterior and vinyl booths are misleading; the hot, filling food is tastier and more reasonably priced than at other diners, and served up by a cheerful, friendly staff. Breakfast of steak, eggs, homefries or grits, and toast $4.60. Modest selection of subs and sandwiches $1.45-6. Open Mon.-Sat. 6am-4pm, Sun. 8am-2pm.

Bethesda, MD

All those white-collar suburbanites must have exceptional taste buds, because Bethesda's concrete renaissance maintains many of the D.C. area's best eateries. Bethesda boasts about 150 restaurants; because there are so many so close together, downtown Bethesda (the area bounded roughly by Wisconsin Ave. on the east, Bethesda Ave. on the south, Rugby Ave. on the north, and Arlington Rd. and Old Georgetown Rd. on the west) almost demands a pre-dinner stroll to compare menus and ambience. **Area code: 301; Metro: Bethesda,** for all of the following:

★ **Bethesda Crab House,** 4958 Bethesda Ave. (652-3382), near Arlington Rd. This extraordinary restaurant is a little like the crabs it serves: not much to look at, but boy is it good. Camp-style tables and benches—covered in newspaper—crowd a small room and patio, but succulent all-you-can-eat crabs crowd the plates ($18, including coleslaw and corn). Also serves shrimp, lobster, and other hard-shell crawlies. One of Bethesda's great institutions, with 33 years of experience. Reservations recommended. Open Mon.-Sat. 9am-midnight, Sun. 11am-midnight.

Bob's Famous Homemade Ice Cream, 4706 Bethesda Ave. (657-2963). One of Washington's most popular local scoopers, with branches here, in Cleveland Park, and on the Hill. Bob's is small, clean, and cool. Ice cream from $1.85-3.60, brownie sundaes $4.70, and frozen yogurt $1.55-2.45. Bakery and deli selections: sandwiches $3.50-4.20. Open Mon.-Thurs. 7:30am-10:30pm, Fri. 7:30am-midnight, Sat. 11am-midnight, Sun. noon-10:30pm; call for winter hours.

Louisiana Express, 4921 Bethesda Ave. (652-6945), near Arlington Rd. White lattice and the smell of Cajun cuisine beckon one to the chicken jambalaya, a symphony of chicken, tomatoes, vegetables, spices, and rice ($5). Critically acclaimed crawfish bisque $3. Half-chicken with Cajun spices, vegetable jambalaya, and soft, soft biscuits $5.50. Sun. brunch (9am-2:30pm) offers a concoction of scrambled eggs with ham, bacon, and sausage on french bread with melted cheese. Delivery available ($15 min.). Open Sun.-Thurs. 7:30am-10pm, Fri.-Sat. 7:30am-11pm. Breakfast served Mon.-Sat. until 11am.

Paradise Restaurant, 7141 Wisconsin Ave. (907-7500, delivery 571-0111), near Bethesda Ave. "Kebab Cuisine" from a wood-burning grill. The flowers, mirrors, and intriguing colors of the dining room vie with the $7 all-you-can-eat luncheon buffet consisting of soup, 6 entrees, salad, and fruit (served daily noon-3pm) for your attention. *Sambosa,* a deep-fried pastry filled with spiced beef, 4 for $5. Cold appetizers $2-5, hot appetizers $4-7, entrees $7-13. *Baklava* $2.50. Open Sun.-Thurs. 11am-10:30pm, Fri.-Sat. 11:30am-11pm.

Persepolis Restaurant, 7130 Wisconsin Ave. (656-9339, delivery 571-0111), near Bethesda Ave. "Exquisite Persian cuisine" locked in Manichaean struggle with Paradise Restaurant across the street; everybody wins. Friendly staff delivers kebab and other Middle Eastern food. All-you-can-eat lunch buffet $7 (served daily 11:30am-2:30pm). Hummus and pita $4; *chelo kabob-e kubideh* (ground sirloin of beef with onions, saffron, and spices) $8. Take-out bargains are found at **Persepolis Express** next door (656-1313). Open daily 11:30am-10pm.

Philadelphia Mike's, 7732 Wisconsin Ave. (656-0103/4/5, delivery 571-0111 with $12 min.), near Middleton Ave. That broken bell may be the only reason to visit Philadelphia now, because Mike's has mastered the Philly cheesesteak ($3.65-7). If you don't believe us, dead-on rave reviews pass the waiting for your green-bedecked table. Burgers $3-4, breakfast subs under $2. Open Mon.-Fri. 8am-10pm, Sat. 9am-10pm, Sun. 9am-9pm.

Positano and Aldo Café, 4940-8 Fairmont Ave. (Positano 654-1717, Aldo Café 986-0042/3), near Old Georgetown Rd. Aldo's sordid past (as a garage) is revealed by ads for Walker mufflers and Pelco batteries; the garage has since been transformed into a quaint, open-air restaurant. Pasta $5.50-7.50, pizza $2-4. The adjoining **Positano,** with its Mediterranean arches and grand *palazzo* style, is more upscale and expensive, although the two restaurants share a kitchen. Pasta dishes run $6-10 at lunch, $8-13 at dinner. Both open daily 11:30am-2:30pm and 5-10pm.

★ **Rio Grande Café,** 4919 Fairmont Ave. (656-2981), near Old Georgetown Rd. Louder than Texas and more crowded than Mexico City—with reason. Diego Rivera-style murals depict Mexican beer and are lit by Christmas lights over the bar. Appetizers $3.25-9. $3 buys a huge, tasty taco; $8 buys 3. Tacos *al carbon* $12, quesadillas $5.50-9. Open Mon.-Thurs. 11am-10:30pm, Fri. 11am-11:30pm, Sat. 11:30am-11:30pm, Sun. 11:30am-10:30pm.

Steamers, 4820 Auburn Ave. (718-0661), near Norfolk Ave. Seating both indoors and on the outdoor patio. Serves fresh fish, lobster, crab cakes, shrimp, steamers, mussels, ribs, and steak. Entrees usually about $15. Medium crabs $22 per dozen. Happy hour (Mon.-Fri. 4-7pm, Sat.-Sun. noon-5pm) features drafts for $1.25, mixed drinks for $1.50. Kitchen closes Sun.-Thurs. at 11pm, Fri.-Sat. at midnight. Open Mon.-Fri. 4pm-12:30am, Sat.-Sun. noon-1:30am. The **Steamers Grill Room,** in the next room, serves lunch Mon.-Fri. beginning at 11:30am.

Stromboli Family Restaurant, 7023 Wisconsin Ave. (986-1980), near Leland St. Italian standards in a Stromboli family atmosphere. Spaghetti with tomato sauce and garlic bread $4 at lunch, $6 at dinner; subs $4.70-6. Highly touted calzone $5. Small cheese pizza $4. Delivery $1.50. Open Mon.-Thurs. 10am-10pm, Fri.-Sat. 10am-11pm, Sun. noon-9:30pm.

★ **Tako Grill,** 7756 Wisconsin Ave. (652-7030). A dangling red lantern lights the way to this modern Japanese grill, slick with glazed wood and track lighting. Young professionals struggle with chopsticks or devour excellent sushi, unfazed by mournful stares from the prominent aquarium. Unbelievable $6 lunch special stuns customers with miso soup, sprout salad, 6-piece sushi roll, rice, and an entree—it's one of the best bargains in the city (Mon.-Fri. 11:30am-2pm). Also worthwhile are the *Donburi,* steaming rice with noodles, vegetables, and grilled meat (with miso soup and sprout salad, $6). Open Mon.-Thurs. 11:30am-2pm and 5:30-9:45pm, Fri. 11:30am-2pm and 5:30-10:15pm, Sat. 5:30-10:15pm.

Tastee Diner, 7731 Woodmont Ave. (652-3970), at Cheltenhem Dr. Tastee is a classic '50s diner, populated by regulars and waitstaffed by veterans. Wooden booths, a long counter, and jukeboxes at tables—all are gloriously and anachronistically intact. Breakfast served around-the-clock: grits $1.15, hotcakes with syrup $2.65. Entrees $3-6 (most $5). Hamburgers $2-3.45. Dinner specials available Mon.-Fri. 11am-10pm, Sat.-Sun. noon-10pm. Open 24hr.

Terramar, 7800 Wisconsin Ave. (654-0888). The superb Nicaraguan cuisine is pricey (entrees around $20), but worth the stretch. Stucco columns divide the expansive chamber, lending the sense of a Latin American plaza without the summer heat. Live Latin music Fri.-Sat. nights. Reservations recommended. Open Tues. 5-10pm, Wed.-Thurs. 11:30am-2:30pm and 5-10pm, Fri. 11:30am-2:30pm and 5-11pm, Sat. 5-11pm, Sun. 5-9pm.

Takoma Park, MD

Takoma is hardly a tourist trap—there are no glitzy, gimmicky restaurants or overpriced chains to be found. When hunger strikes, while window-shopping or people-watching, you won't have to reach far into your wallet—meals are rarely over $10 in Takoma. **Area code: 301**; **Metro: Takoma,** for all of the following:

FOOD

Everyday Gourmet, 6923 Laurel Ave. (270-2270). Do it yourself or let them do it for you. Off-the-rack gourmet supplies fill one side of this clean, airy café; a counter serving coffee, baked goods, and inventive sandwiches fills the other. Sandwiches $4-5, soup $2.55, muffins $1. Open Mon.-Fri. 7am-8pm, Sat. 8am-6pm, Sun. 8am-3pm.

Mark's Kitchen, 7006 Carroll Ave. (270-1884). Like the surrounding neighborhood, Mark's is a harmonious blend of contrasting elements. American diner and Asian restaurant, meat and vegetarian dishes—all coexist in a serene, pretty atmosphere. Worthwhile Korean delights include seaweed soup ($2.25) and Korean steak ($5.50). Spinach salad with chicken teriyaki $5.50. Dumplings $2. Curried vegetables $5.50. Open Mon.-Sat. 8am-9pm, Sun. 8am-8pm.

Palais du Chocolat, 6925 Willow St. (723-4280). As you approach the center of Takoma from the Metro, Willow St. will appear mere feet before the Maryland border; head south of Eastern Ave. This industrial-looking shop in an industrial-looking building supplies its genteel sisters downtown and in Woodley Park with all things sweet. Cookies 85¢. No seating; make a picnic of the daily lunch special, which includes a sandwich, a tart, and a drink ($4.50). Open Mon.-Sat. 9am-6pm.

Takoma Station Tavern, 6914 4th St. NW. (829-1999). Just steps west of the Metro (away from central Takoma), this popular jazz club has recently started playing a new tune: lunch. Most sandwiches are $7, including the house specialty crab-cake sandwich. For finger-lickin' fun, try the $7 chicken wing basket. Happy hour (Mon.-Fri. 4-8pm) offers $1 off drinks and a free buffet. $5 cover after 7pm. Proper attire required. Open Mon.-Fri. 11:30am-2am, Sat.-Sun. 4pm-2am.

Taliano's, 7001B Carroll Ave. (270-5515). The only bar on Takoma's main drag serves up standard Italian specialties such as pasta ($5.25-7.25), calzones ($5.50), and pizza amid a checkerboard classic-diner decor. Eight-topping, 12-inch Taliano's special ($14). Half-price pizza after 5pm on Mon., and Fri.-Sat. the place mellows out to live folk, blues, and rock. Bar open Mon.-Thurs. 11:30am-midnight, Fri.-Sat. 11:30am-1am, Sun. noon-midnight. Kitchen closes 1-2hr. earlier.

Arlington, VA

If you think you've exhausted Adams-Morgan's ethnic eateries, Arlington may be the way to go. The hodgepodge of ethnic foods from Rosslyn to Ballston defies glib classification. The Clarendon area, nicknamed Little Saigon, holds not only Vietnamese but also worthwhile Japanese, Chinese, and Thai food. But even the name "Little Asia" would slight the nearby all-American establishments dishing out chili and ribs. **Area code: 703,** for all of the following:

Atami, 3155 Wilson Blvd. (522-4787, delivery 527-9000). Metro: Clarendon. Japanese Atami prepares *nigiri* (fish with *wasabi* horseradish on rice) and *maki* (rice, fish, and vegetables rolled in seaweed) sushi—platters served with miso soup, salad, and rice (lunch $6.25, dinner $10.25). Vietnamese fare also available. Open Mon.-Thurs. 11am-10pm, Fri. 11am-10:30pm, Sat. noon-10:30pm, Sun. 4-9:30pm.

Café Dalat, 3143 Wilson Blvd. (276-0935). Metro: Clarendon. Café Dalat is yet another award-winning Vietnamese restaurant in Little Saigon. This family-run establishment offers a variety of delicious dishes, all for $7-9. Large vegetarian menu. Open Sun.-Thurs. 11am-9:30pm, Fri.-Sat. 11am-10:30pm.

★ **Café Saigon,** 1135 N. Highland St. (243-6522 or 276-7110, delivery 527-9000), across from Clarendon Metro. "French" decor. Popular dishes are the grilled pork and crispy rolls (*cha gio*) on "funny" rice noodles ($8). Carnivores will enjoy the beef wrapped in beans, vermicelli noodles, wine, mushrooms, and chopped onion ($8). Open Sun.-Thurs. 10am-10pm, Fri.-Sat. 10am-11pm.

The Cambodian Restaurant, 1727 Wilson Blvd. (522-3832), near Quinn St. Metro: Court House. With lunch entrees from $5.50-7.25 and dinner entrees from $6.25-9, this restaurant is less expensive than its Vietnamese counterparts up the road. Open Mon.-Fri. 11:30am-2:30pm and 5:30-10:30pm, Sat.-Sun. 5:30-11pm.

Chesapeake Seafood Crab House, 3607 Wilson Blvd. (528-8888/8896). Metro: Clarendon. This real "seaside" crabhouse provides cheery outdoor seating, brown paper tablecloths, and hammers to break open the crab shells. Most people come here for the steamed and spiced crabs, but this "Vietnamese, Chinese, French, and American" restaurant also offers standards including fried chicken and hush puppies, as well as wacky anomalies like *Ech Xaao Lan* (curried frog legs, $10). Vegetarians can select from a whole page of appetizers, soups, and entrees. Don't confuse this place with the similarly named chain. Open daily 11am-10pm.

Delhi Dhaba, 2424 Wilson Blvd. (524-0008), not visible from the street; access through the parking lot (behind a deli/convenience store). Metro: Clarendon or Courthouse. Indian dishes are ordered at the counter, deli- (and Delhi-) style, and brought to a table. Dishes are $6 at most; most vegetarian dishes are $4.50. Hard-core budget travelers may just fill up on Indian breads (generous servings $1-2.50). Open Sun.-Thurs. 11am-10pm, Fri.-Sat. 11am-11pm.

Food Factory, 4221 N. Fairfax Dr. (527-2279, delivery 527-9000), across from Ballston Metro; entrance in back. The name is perplexing. Pakistani char-broiled kebabs put American "shish kabobs" to shame. *Nan* (tandoori bread) and skewers of chicken, beef, or lamb ($4.70-6). Above the kebabs in the display case are rows and rows of *samosas,* pastries filled with peas and potatoes ($1). All meats are *halal* (prepared according to Islamic law); the clientele is almost 100% Middle Eastern. Open Mon.-Fri. 11am-10pm, Sat.-Sun. noon-10pm.

Hard Times Café, 3028 Wilson Blvd. (528-2233, delivery 908-0700), across from Clarendon Metro. See complete listing below. Chili $4-6.40; microbrews $3-3.25. Open Mon.-Thurs. 11:30am-10:30pm, Fri.-Sat. 11:30am-11pm, Sun. noon-10pm.

Kabul Caravan, 1725 Wilson Blvd. (522-8394). Metro: Court House. The surroundings feel like a museum, thanks to the owners' fine collection of Afghan weapons, costumes, and other objects, all of which hang gracefully from the walls (and predate the Russian invasion). Entrees $8-16. Open Mon.-Fri. 11:30am-2:30pm and 5:30-11:30pm, Sat.-Sun. 5:30-11:30pm.

Little Viet Garden, 3012 Wilson Blvd. (522-9686), 1 block from the Clarendon Metro stop. Inexpensive Vietnamese food (surprise, surprise!). What sets it apart from its neighbors is its snazzy interior, featuring sleek black chairs, a padded bar, and live palm trees. Or maybe it's the outdoor seating. At any rate, the food is good; there are three $10-11 dishes on the menu; everything else is under $9. Open Mon.-Fri. 11am-2:30pm and 5-10pm, Sat.-Sun. noon-10pm.

★ **Queen Bee,** 3181 Wilson Blvd. (527-3444). Metro: Clarendon. When you see how long the line is some evenings, you'll think people are waiting for concert tickets instead of Vietnamese food. They say you can't order wrong here, although everyone orders the same spring rolls (*cha gio*) for appetizers ($2.50). Entrees $5.50-9. Open daily 11:15am-10pm.

Red Hot and Blue, 1600 Wilson Blvd. (276-7427, delivery 578-3663), under an office building near Pierce St. Metro: Court House. Pit barbecue direct from Memphis, with logo to match—two pigs sport shades, guitars, and Elvis pompadours. The late Republican media mogul Lee Atwater, among others, licked his lips over the down-home pork BBQ ribs. Regular order $9.50, full rack $16.50 (feeds two)—wet (basted with sauce) or dry (rubbed with traditional Memphis spices). Some opt for a pulled-pig sandwich ($4.50). Lines can be long on weekend nights. Open Sun.-Thurs. 11am-10pm, Fri.-Sat. 11am-11pm.

Tom Sarris' Orleans House, 1213 Wilson Blvd. (524-2929). Metro: Rosslyn. Steak and fish are the specialties in this fantastic cross between a medieval castle and a New Orleans dining room. Stained glass, thrones in the waiting area, and a suit of armor make for a strange aura when combined with curly-Q wrought iron and strings of Christmas lights. Lunch has the best deals: famed prime rib ($7, $8 at dinner), superlative crab cakes ($5). Fresh fried catfish $8. Lunch entrees $5-6. Most dinners $8-12. Open Mon.-Fri. 11am-11pm, Sat. 4-11pm, Sun. 4-10pm.

Alexandria, VA

Old Town's food scene resembles Georgetown's—though more quaint and less crowded. The city's specialties, cheap BBQ and expensive seafood, endure. **Area code: 703**; **Metro: King St.**, for all of the following (except Royal Restaurant):

Armand's Chicago Pizzeria, 111 King St. (683-0313). Armand's spacious, family-style restaurant offers an all-you-can-eat pizza buffet and salad bar (Mon.-Fri. 11:30am-2:30pm, Sat.-Sun. 11:30am-3:30pm) and midnight munch buffet (Fri.-Sat. 10:30pm-1am)—steals at $5; children 6-11 get them at half-price, under 6 free. Deep-dish pizzas ($6.50-15.25). Sandwich platters under $5. Upstairs awaits former Washington Capitals defenseman Bryan Watson's **Penalty Box** sports bar. Open Sun.-Thurs. 11:30am-11pm, Fri.-Sat. 11:30am-1am.

Lite 'n' Fair, 1018 King St. (660-6085). Ki Choi, former executive chef of the ritzy Watergate Restaurant, owns this gem disguised by a modest façade, which prides itself on its inexpensive, fresh selection of seafood. Char-broiled salmon steak ($9). Other dishes and sandwiches ($4-8) round out the menu. Free delivery 11am-2pm ($10 min.). Open Mon. 11am-3pm, Tues.-Sat. 11am-9pm.

Bob Rubin's New York Deli, 222 N. Lee St. (684-0372), at Queen St. If you can squeeze into this tiny place and onto a high chair, order up a hearty breakfast ($1.75-7.50) or a "Deli-Meister's" sandwich ($4.50-7). Breakfast served Mon.-Fri. until 11am, Sat. until 11:30am, and Sun. all day. Open Mon.-Fri. 6am-3pm, Sat. 8am-3pm, Sun. 9am-4pm.

Ecco Café, 220 N. Lee St. (684-0321), at Queen St. A wax Charlie Chaplin greets patrons of this jazzy place—which would like to think of itself as new and original. Pizzas ($7.50-9) and homemade luncheon pastas ($8-10) are served amid neon-lit portraits of the famous. Open Mon.-Thurs. 11am-11pm, Fri.-Sat. 11am-midnight, Sun. 11:30am-10pm.

The Fish Market, 105 King St. (836-5676), near Union St. This rollicking seafood restaurant seats 785 and features live ragtime piano, Broadway tunes, jazz, and acoustic guitar with enthusiastic audience participation (Thurs. 7pm, Fri.-Sat. 8pm). Six bars and a small balcony make this baby-blue building a happening 20-something hangout. Creaky floors and exposed rafters for nostalgic types. Clam chowder $2, salads $6-7, seafood sandwiches $4-7, platters $8-10. Kitchen closes at midnight. Open Mon.-Sat. 11:15am-2am, Sun. 11:15am-midnight.

Gadsby's Tavern, 134 N. Royal St. (548-1288), near King St. After touring the museum, visitors can eat off their own pewter; waiters in 18th-century dress deliver generous (but pricey) helpings of 18th-century cooking (dinner stews, colonial pies, etc. $10-20). Tasty traditional tea bread, and English trifle for dessert ($5). Delivery ($10 min.). Nightly "colonial" entertainment. Open daily 11:30am-3pm and 5:30-10:30pm. Tours Tues.-Sat. 10am-4pm, Sun. 1-5pm.

Hard Times Café, 1404 King St. (683-5340), near West St. Cincinnati (finely ground beef in a tomato sauce with cinnamon), Texas (coarsely ground chuck without tomatoes, mildly seasoned), and vegetarian chili (all $5, $4 for kids) make the HTC deservedly popular. Chili is also served atop your burger or pasta; a chili-spaghetti plate with beans, cheese, onions, and homemade cornbread ($5.70) would stuff anyone. Homemade beer-batter onion rings too. "Hot Salsa Hour" (Mon.-Fri. 4-8pm) provides free chips and salsa with discounted beers. Delivery available. Open Mon.-Thurs. 11am-10pm, Fri.-Sat. 11am-11pm, Sun. noon-10pm.

King Street Blues, 112 N. St. Asaph St. (836-8800), near King St. A tribute to the South, with its slow-smoked ribs, pork and turkey BBQ, fresh salads, and po' boy sandwiches. Low-fat, low-calorie options as well. Blue plate special ($5) changes daily: Wed. features Virginia beef stew; Thurs. fried chicken. Pub-like dining room with bar downstairs; decor includes paper-maché figures, murals, and painted *faux* shuttered windows and flower boxes. Open Mon.-Thurs. 11:30am-10pm, Fri.-Sat. 11:30am-midnight, Sun. 11:30am-10pm. Bar stays open until 1:45am.

La Madeleine, 500 King St. (739-2854). This French bakery and café serves fantastic breakfast omelettes ($5), sandwiches and pasta ($5-7), and an extensive selection of desserts ($1-2)—all with a contemporary American twist. Open Sun.-Thurs. 7am-10pm, Fri.-Sat. 7am-11pm.

Old Town Sandwich Shop, 127 S. Peyton St. (684-6775), between King and Prince St. Bagels with cream cheese $1.10, danish and breakfasts 80¢-$3.20, sandwiches $2-3.80. Perfect for a quick bite and a newspaper in the morning. Fresh food, fast service, and nothing over $4. No seating. Open Mon.-Fri. 7am-4pm.

Royal Restaurant, 734 N. Asaph St. (548-1616). Metro: Braddock Rd. Alexandria's oldest and least pretentious restaurant dishes out home-style meals and '50s jukebox hits. Sandwiches $2-7; omelettes $3.30-5 for breakfast, $5.50-5.75 for lunch or dinner; entrees $5.50-12. "Alexandria's Best Breakfast" menu $2.50-8 ($8 buys 2 eggs with steak). Those who don't want to bop to "Splish Splash" and "Under the Boardwalk" should sit on the left. You *must* try the rice pudding ($2). All-you-can-eat Sun. brunch buffet ($6.50, excludes beverages). Karaoke Fri. 7pm. Open Mon.-Sat. 6am-9pm, Sun. 7am-2pm.

The Scoop Grill and Homemade Ice Cream, 110 King St. (549-4527). Funky flavors (like bittersweet, Jack Daniels, and Adam's Apple) make this ice cream store a cut above the rest—mighty popular with families during the day and students at night. Burgers and sandwiches $2-5, freshly baked goods $1-2. Ice cream: small $2, medium $2.50, large $3. Be warned: the hours vary according to the owner's whims. Open Mon.-Thurs. 8am-11pm, Fri.-Sat. 8am-midnight, Sun. 9am-11pm.

South Austin Grille, 801 King St. (684-8969), at Columbus St. Moderately priced Tex-Mex in this cheery pastel hangout, complete with the AG signature hot pepper lights. Fajitas ($9-14), tacos ($6-7), burritos ($6-7), and very popular hot Texas chili ($5-6). Brunch ($5-9) served Sat.-Sun. 11:30am-3pm. Domestic bottled beers $2.75, imports $3.25. Kitchen closes one hour earlier than the bar. Open Sun.-Mon. 11:30am-11pm, Tues.-Thurs. 11:30am-midnight, Fri.-Sat. 11:30am-1am.

Sights

Beneath a thicket of museums and monuments lies the real Washington. The ethnically diverse neighborhoods of Adams-Morgan and Shaw beckon with exotic foods and a thriving club scene that could compete with even the likes of New York. Dupont Circle is *the* place to sit and schmooze over coffee, to hang with the eternally hip, or to discover D.C.'s large and active gay community. In Anacostia, a struggling African-American community tries to rebuild its troubled neighborhood. In Capitol Hill pubs, politicians make deals, trade gossip, and leak stories to the press. In Georgetown, preppy students and ambitious interns crowd the shops and bars, oblivious of tourists. And in Northeast and the Upper Northwest, a number of spread out residential communities beckon with their suburban charm. Before or after the inevitable Smithsonian odyssey, the rest of Washington deserves your time; away from the major attractions, *real* Washingtonians go about their business in art galleries and ethnic communities and at parks and embassies. There are plays worth seeing, music worth listening to, and streets to delight and educate the attentive pedestrian. These areas can reveal the difference (and the hidden links) between D.C.'s harbor of government and D.C.'s various homegrown cultures.

Sight-Seeing Tours

Tens of thousands of out-of-towners leave D.C. yearly without having set foot in anything but museums and monuments. If they only knew what they were missing. Guided tours cost substantially more than Metro fares, confine visitors to the central section of the city, and isolate them from actual Washingtonians. If you are nevertheless inclined to witness only the District's highlights from behind a bus window or from a duck-van, the following are some of D.C.'s most popular tour offerings.

D.C. Ducks, 1323 Pennsylvania Ave. NW (966-3825) provides an entertaining land-and-water tour of the monuments and the sights on the Mall, D.C. Ducks does it all on a van that transforms into a boat. Kids love it. (Adults $20, children 3-12 $10.) For a more traditional tour, try **open-air buses** and **trolleys.** They operate on all-day tickets, so you can get off at any stop, then get back on when another coach comes by. The most popular tour company is **Tourmobile Sight-seeing,** 1000 Ohio Dr. SW (recorded messages 554-7950 and 554-5100), near the Washington Monument. Tours (in blue-and-white buses) run between 9am and 6:30pm from mid-April to mid-September, otherwise between 9:30am and 4:30pm. For the standard 18-sight loop, get on at any stop (indicated by blue-and-white signs) and buy tickets from the driver. (Adults $12, children 3-11 $6.) Special routes travel to the Frederick Douglass home (a 2½-hr. loop; adults $6, children $3) and to Mount Vernon (daily 10am, noon, and 2pm; adults $20, children $10; price includes admission). For these routes, purchase tickets up to an hour prior to departure from booth. Combination specials available. The orange-and-green coaches of **Old Town Trolley** (301-985-3021) follow a 2-hour narrated circle with stops in downtown Washington, Georgetown, the National Cathedral, and Arlington Cemetery. Not all stops sell tickets, but passengers may board at any stop and pay at the next ticket-vending location. (Trolleys run June-Aug. Mon.-Fri. 9am-5pm, Sat.-Sun. 9am-5:30; Sept.-May Mon.-Fri. 9am-4pm, Sat.-Sun. 9am-4:30pm. Tours $18, children 5-12 $9.)

Other companies avoid the more obvious sights with specialized tours of thematically linked D.C. sights. **Scandal Tours** (800-758-8687), a comedy show on wheels, hires actors to impersonate disgraced politicians as they steer tourists from one place of infamy to the next. In good weather, the 75-minute tour whizzes past Gary Hart's townhouse, Watergate, and the Vista Hotel, where Mayor Barry was caught with his pants down ($27). Tours depart from the Old Post Office April-Sept., Sat. 1pm. Reservations required. Capitol Entertainment Services (636-9203) runs standard tours of major sights, but specializes in a three-hour **Black History Tour** through Lincoln

Park, Anacostia, and the Frederick Douglass home. (Tours begin from area hotels during the summer; call for information on winter group tours. $22, children 3-11 $12.)

For guided strolls around Adams-Morgan or Lafayette Square, try nationally recognized Anthony S. Pitch's **walking tours** (301-294-9514; fax 301-309-0753). Mr. Pitch offers a one-hour Lafayette Square tour (group of 15 people or more required; $6 per person) and a two-hour Adams-Morgan tour (Sun. at 11am; $5 per person); Georgetown tours will also be given in 1997. Also offered is a two-hour **motorized tour of The Presidents' Homes** (20-person-min. per bus; $23 per person) which visits the pre- and post-White House residences of all 17 20th-century American presidents. Call ahead for details concerning all tours.

The U.S. Capitol

It is natural enough to suppose that the center and heart of America is the Capitol, and certainly, in its outward aspect, the world has not many statelier or more beautiful edifices.

—Nathaniel Hawthorne, 1862

While the U.S. Capitol (dial 224-3121 for operator) may no longer be America's, or even Washington's, most beautiful building, and while the legislators that roam its halls may be the nation's most pervasive manifestation of cynicism, the structure's scale and style still evoke the power of the republic. (Metro: Capitol South or Union Station.) The Capitol's symmetries—along its east-west and north-south axes—suggest the legislative process' checks and balances (or perhaps the perpetual tug-of-war between the House and the Senate). As the centerpiece of government, the Capitol is perched atop Capitol Hill, and the compass stone embedded in the crypt is the origin of the city's coordinates. The three-tiered **East Front** stands opposite the Supreme Court and the Library of Congress Jefferson Building, seemingly to assimilate their respective virtues of justice and knowledge. From Jackson (1829) to Carter (1977), most U.S. presidents took their inaugural oath here, vowing to preserve, protect, and defend the U.S. Constitution. Reagan's 1981 inauguration ceremony was the first to be administered on the **West Front,** which, with its grand entrance, overlooks the National Mall. The north and south wings house the present Senate and House of Representatives, respectively; a U.S. flag over either wing denotes that the corresponding House of Congress is in session.

Amateur architect William Thornton was given the nod to design the Capitol in 1793; shortly thereafter, when Congress arrived in 1800, designer Benjamin Latrobe assessed and reassembled the interior. Congress had only begun to implement their bureaucratic behemoth when the British, on a tear of destruction, burned down the whole shebang in 1814. Charles Bullfinch replaced Latrobe in 1818, finishing the Capitol's central section with a dome made of copper-plated wood. By 1850, the building was no longer sufficiently sizable for the expanding Congress, and President Fillmore tapped Thomas U. Walter to expand the edifice and erect the rotunda. Assisted by Montgomery Meigs, Walter oversaw the 1860s construction of the awe-inspiring cast-iron dome that still stands today. At the apex of it all stands Thomas Crawford's statue, "Freedom."

Outside the West Front of the Capitol, at 1st St. NW, the 1922 **Grant Memorial** stands encircled and out-maneuvered by driveways and barricades. General Ulysses S. Grant, whose willingness to sustain huge losses led the Union Army to victory, contemplates war morosely in his battered uniform. Seven horsemen charge to the north, while three horses strain and tug a cannon through mud to the south. Henry

Forget Donkeys and Elephants...

One of the plans entered in the competition for the design of the Capitol building called for an enormous statue of a rooster, serving as the structure's zenith.

Shared took 21 years to design the 252-ft.-long memorial, hailed today—by those who notice it—as a realistic monument to the arduous and terrible aspects of battle.

THE INTERIOR

The **public entrance** is through the East Front. Lines are shortest in winter (particularly Feb.), and longest in spring, when roving bands of field-tripping middle schoolers in matching t-shirts plague the city. Between mid-March and mid-June, the wait may be as long as three hours; in summer, the wait averages about 90 minutes. Generally, Sundays and Mondays see shorter lines, as do daily lunch hours.

Above the East Front entrance is the female trio of America, Hope, and Justice (President John Quincy Adams wouldn't let Hercules, a heathen, join them), and the East Portico displays Randolph Rogers's huge bronze **Columbus Doors.** The doors mimic Ghiberti's *Gates of Paradise* in Florence but (in an uncharacteristic separation of Church and State) substitute Columbus's biography for the Bible.

The Capitol has over 10,000 visitors a day. Most get lost. The 19th-century design yields little logic, and disorientation among the symmetry requires little effort, as north becomes south becomes north; fortunately, **maps** are available from the tour desk in the rotunda. The desk is also the place to sign up for a free guided **tour,** which leave from the desk every 15 minutes from 9am to 4pm daily. Those adventurous enough to embark independently may out of necessity ask one of the 1200 Capitol Police, stationed in every corner of the building, for assistance. They know the building inside and out, and they will not hesitate to let visitors know when they have sauntered somewhere off-limits.

Inside the doors, the 180-ft.-high, 96-ft.-wide **rotunda** stretches and yawns. The *grisaille* (brown-and-white) frieze of condensed history encircles the collar of the dome, high above the floor. The frieze was largely executed by Constantino Brumidi, but was finished by others after Brumidi fell off his scaffold in 1877 and died three months later. (Interestingly, Brumidi was not permitted to sign his name anywhere in the artwork, and he compensated with a self-portrait hidden behind a tree.) In the overhead *Apotheosis of George Washington,* George occupies the center of a giant allegory, as Liberty, Victory, the 13 states, and countless virtues attend. The painting was only recently discovered after being covered up for a century by the campfire soot of Union soldiers, who used the rotunda as a barracks during the Civil War. Eight enormous paintings hang below the fresco at ground level, and depict scenes of the States' formative years. Among these paintings is John Trumbull's *The Declaration of Independence,* also featured on the $2 bill. Busts and statues of luminaries ranging from Washington himself to Martin Luther King, Jr. stare upward at the art. Statesmen from Lincoln to JFK have lain in state in the Capitol's center for three hours prior to burial; recently, in his much-publicized "Living Will," the late President Richard Nixon opted to forego this highest of national honors.

Just south of the rotunda, still on the second level, is **Statuary Hall,** the first meeting place of the House of Representatives. According to original doctrine, Statuary Hall was to hold the statues of two people from (and selected by) each state. When the concentration of 100 statues became too much weight for the room to bear, the figures had to be dispersed throughout the building. Floor plaques commemorate some of the past representatives who also occupied the Oval Office. John Quincy Adams was the first to realize that the room was a rather effective echo chamber; legend has it that Adams used to lay on his desk, "sleeping," as he listened to his political adversaries converse/plot on the other side of the room. Due to size-restraints, however, the growing House was eventually forced to move down the hall to the current House chamber, where whisperings may thrive.

North of the rotunda, visitors can find The **Old Senate Chamber.** The comparatively modest old room is reminiscent of a time when oratory from the Senate floor actually mattered—Daniel Webster, John C. Calhoun, and Henry Clay all held forth here. The chamber was restored in 1976 for the American Bicentennial celebration to look as it did when last occupied in 1859. As on the house side, the current senate chamber lies farther north, but must be accessed by way of the crypt (first) level.

Stairs lead down to the crypt level from landings on both the north and south sides of the rotunda. The **crypt** itself was built to house George Washington's body, but it lacked the space for both the bodies of George and Martha Washington, which Washington had wished to be buried together. The bodies were buried instead at Mount Vernon, and an attempt to have the bodies exhumed was thwarted by the state of Virginia (see **Mount Vernon,** page 256); as a result, the tomb remains empty today. The crypt also contains the compass stone, originally the exact center of Washington, D.C.; it is from this point of origin that the District's quadrants (NW, NE, SW, SE) are drawn. The stone ceased to be the center when Arlington was given back to Virginia and Georgetown was annexed. A statue of Abraham Lincoln, originally situated in the rotunda, now keeps vain watch over Washington's tomb. Lincoln's head has **no left ear**—the sculptor claimed that the absent feature is representative of Lincoln's unfinished life. Today the crypt houses various visitor displays, including models of original potential designs for the Capitol.

Also on the level of the crypt is the **Old Supreme Court Chamber,** where the Supremes met until they were granted their own building (and current home) across the street. While the lawyers' tables face the bench, red plush couches face the lawyers, meant for the honorable ladies of the court. The chamber has a somewhat sinister history: in 1806, the ceiling handed down its opinion on architect Latrobe's assistant, crushing him when he tried to move blocks before the masonry had dried. Restored in 1976, the room is now an architectural wonder—the curved ceiling stands without architectural support.

CONGRESSIONAL CHAMBERS

The monumentality of marble and granite can only go so far. For a glimpse of live, modern-day legislative action, visitors may climb to the **House and Senate visitors galleries,** and listen to issues debated on the floor. Americans may request a gallery pass (valid for the entire 2-year session of Congress) from the office of their representative, delegate, or senator by paying a visit or writing to him or her in advance. Foreign nationals may get passes valid for a single day by presenting a passport, driver's licence, or birth certificate (or photocopies thereof). For a House pass, they should go to the desk immediately outside the House visitors gallery. For a Senate pass, foreigners should *not* go to the Senate visitors gallery, but to the large "Appointments desk" located at the extreme North End (i.e., Senate side) of the main hallway of the crypt level of the building.

In the ceremony-laden House and Senate chambers (in separate wings of the Capitol), expect a few bored-looking elected officials failing to listen to the person on the podium who might be speaking for the exclusive benefit of home-district cable TV viewers (most members watch, or have someone else watch, the sessions on C-SPAN from their offices). Those who do attend are usually engaged in conversation with each other. Former House Speaker Tip O'Neill once ordered a cameraman to pan the empty chamber while a congressman babbled on, making evident to TV-Land that the man was orating into the void. Despite its lack of attendance, the congressional chambers are not entirely void of traditional protocol; the Vice President still technically presides over the Senate (though he is rarely present), and the Speaker of the House, called "Mr. Speaker," presides over the House (though another member of the majority party assumes his role). In the Senate chamber, notice the elementary-school style of the Senators' desks. The bigger, more ornate House chamber packs in all of official Washington every January for the President's annual televised State of the Union Address. Yet even when the chambers are nearly evacuated, they still harness enough grandeur to evoke the patriot in every American citizen. The air of formality dictates respect for the legislators on the floor—there is no talking or reading allowed in the galleries. If visitors do happen to make a little too much noise, they'll hear about it from a secret serviceman.

Debates and discussions on the House and Senate floors have become increasingly complex, and long ago ceased to be efficient methods of lawmaking. The real business of Congress is conducted in **committee hearings** all over the Capitol and the additional House and Senate office buildings. Most hearings are open to the public. The *Washington Post's* "Today in Congress" box is in the paper's A-section; the box lists hearings and their assigned rooms. Unlike in their grand chambers, here Congresspeople sit at tables across from visitors rather than two stories below them; they debate, inquire, and consider facts and laws, rather than conduct pompous, indiscernibly relevant ceremonies. Especially interesting and controversial hearings can get very crowded; most hearing rooms don't have many seats, and most of them are reserved for lobbyists and other hangers-on. Potential attenders should show up early and keep their fingers crossed.

A third way to find out what Congress is up to is to wander around the Capitol's office space for a glimpse of a few real Congresspeople and many important-looking imitations. American citizens will surely be well-received at the office of their Representative or Senator, though your chances of seeing the Member him- or herself are slight. A majority of Members have public offices in House or Senate office buildings, which lie outside the Capitol itself. If you hear a buzzer or see a red light flash, watch the Members rush to the floor for an imminent vote. To get there, you may ride the **Capitol subway,** which shunts Congressfolk, staffers, and tourists between the Capitol and the office buildings. Subways to the House offices leave from the sub-basement of the House side of the Capitol; the elevator is best reached near the far southern end of the crypt level's central hallway. Subways to the Senate office buildings leave from the basement of the Senate side of the Capitol; that elevator is best reached near the far northern end of the crypt level's central hallway.

Basement perks and shops in the Capitol and the House and Senate offices are generally open only to Members, who guard their privacy well. One favorite Congressional perk is the Members-only gym, where Democrats and Republicans alike try to get former pro-basketball standouts Tom McMillan (D-MD) and Bill Bradley (D-NJ) to play on their team. The basement of the Capitol itself once held a blacksmith shop, a water reservoir, and an 800-ton coal vault to keep the Members warm.

Some unmarked rooms on the Senate side of the Capitol are used by Senators as private **"hideaways."** The Senate Rules Committee doles out these secret second offices by seniority. Some are just oversized closets, but the best are roomy, furnished offices where esteemed legislators can spend plenty of time working *incommunicado*. Only janitors and senators know where the hideaways are—any unmarked door could have a Senator inside. They're used to being interrupted for directions, which doesn't mean you should wander around opening doors in search of hideaways (unless you just love the Capitol Police). While most legislators use their hideaways as a second office, legends remain that these lairs have often been put to less forthright uses.

The Capitol is open daily from 9am to 4:30pm (Memorial Day-Labor Day daily 8am-8pm). Tours and special assistance for **visitors with disabilities** are available from the Special Services Office in the central first floor crypt area (or call 224-4048, TDD 224-4049). Tours visit the rotunda, the downstairs crypt area, and sometimes Statuary Hall.

Too Many House Speakers in the Kitchen Spoil the...

In 1907, House Speaker Joe Cannon bestowed Congress with one of its finest traditions. Cannon commanded that his famous bean soup be served every day in the Capitol; thus, it has been on the menu ever since. Bureaucratic...*beans?*

Capitol Hill

Metro: Capitol South; Eastern Market; Federal Center; Union Station.

With the National Tourist Mecca, Congress, and the President to the west, and the city's worst slums to the south, Capitol Hill seems incongruously friendly; its townhouse-filled center (around East Capitol St. between 2nd St. and 11th St. NE/SE) gracefully accommodates blue-collar, white-collar, Black, Hispanic, Asian, and White people. Restored townhouses abut buildings in various states of decay, and Jaguars

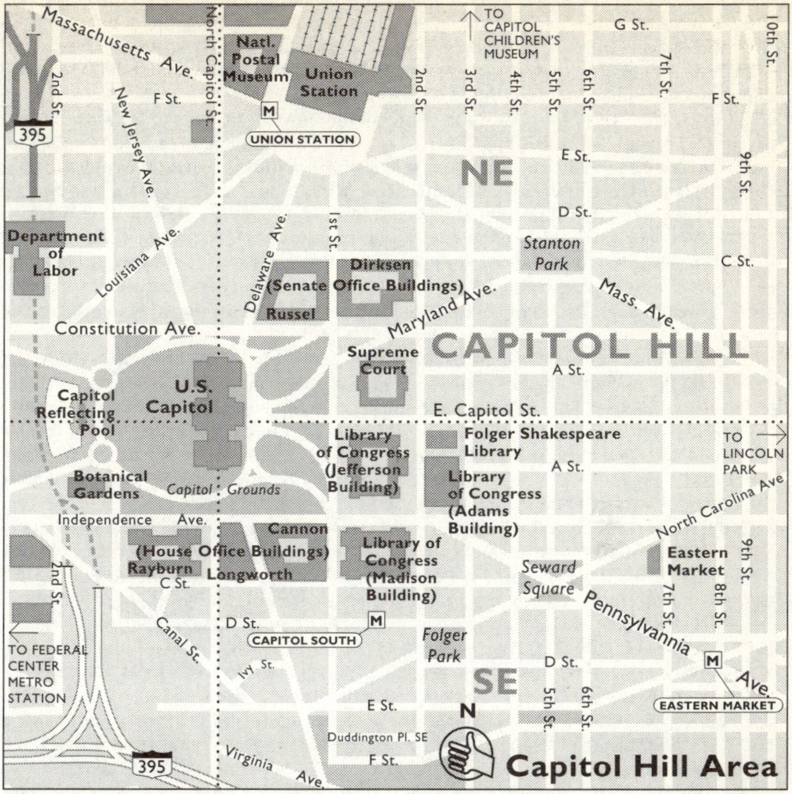

mix freely with humbler autos. Close to the Capitol building, most pedestrians are Congressional and government workers whose silk power-ties connote self-importance. East of 2nd St., corner drugstores, grocery stores, and a diner (Jimmy T's; see **Food,** p. 85) relax with the residents amid trees and lawns. You may even spot a few Congresspeople driving home, though their aides are more likely to live here than the Members themselves.

Safety in the neighborhood is indeed something of a concern; here as nowhere else, blocks can change character abruptly. Be aware of your surroundings, human and architectural. Avoid the areas east of Lincoln Park or south of Pennsylvania Ave. SE (except along 8th St.). After events at RFK Stadium, raging hordes of concertgoers proceed westward down East Capitol St.; don't be afraid to join them.

Capitol Hill's approximate boundaries are North and South Capitol streets on the west, H St. NE on the north, Lincoln Park on the east, and the Southeast-Southwest Freeway on the south. Close to the Capitol building itself cluster major sights, including the Library of Congress, the Folger Shakespeare Library, and the Supreme Court. At dusk, night-owls head for the bars and restaurants that line Pennsylvania Ave. between 2nd St. and 7th St. SE.

THE SUPREME COURT

While they're not publicly accountable—they're not elected, after all—the nine justices of the nation's highest court graciously open their courtroom to the tourist masses who stream daily from the Capitol across the street into the imposing

Supreme Court Building, 1 1st St. NE (479-3000). (Metro: Capitol South or Union Station.) When the court is in session, early risers may have a chance to see the justices in action, by staking out one of the public seats at an oral-argument session. And when the court is not in session, lectures in the courtroom introduce visitors to the history and workings of the court.

The Supreme Court wasn't always so hospitable to visitors, though, for it is only relatively recently that the court has been housed in a building of its own. From 1800 to 1935, the justices met in the Capitol, first in any empty office they could find and later in the room now known as Old Supreme Court Chamber. This chamber was so poorly illuminated that when some justices complained that a newly arrived statue of Justice depicted her without the traditional blindfold, Chief Justice John Marshall replied that it was fine—she couldn't possibly see anything in that room anyhow. In 1935, the court decided it was time to take the nation's separation of powers literally, and it moved out of the Capitol—and across the street—into the faux-Greek temple designed for it by architect Cass Gilbert.

Visitors should enter through the main entrance on 1st St., climbing the stairs flanked by James Earle Fraser's sculptures *Contemplation of Justice* (on the left) and *Authority of Law* (on the right). Nine impressive figures posture in the pediment. Three are former Chief Justices. Three are classical Greek virtues. One is a former Senator. The other two are Cass Gilbert, the building's architect, and Robert Aitken, the pediment's sculptor. The atrium is a columned chamber sporting busts of former chief justices. Straight ahead, behind the red curtain, is the Supreme Court Chamber, where the court meets to hear cases.

When the court is in session (Oct.-June), it hears oral arguments Monday through Wednesday from 10am to 3pm for two weeks of each month. Attorneys get only half an hour each to make arguments and field questions from the Nine. There is no jury: the Supreme Court, like any appeals court, doesn't decide facts; it just interprets the laws and the Constitution. **Arguments** are open to the public on a first-come, first-served basis. Seating begins at 9:30am; a line usually begins to form at 8:30am. Visitors who show up too late to be seated may walk through the standing gallery to hear some of the argument. The *Washington Post*'s A-section lists sitting schedules and cases. Be forewarned: the May and June sessions are reserved almost exclusively for reading decisions.

SIGHTS

Any time the court is not sitting, visitors can hoof through the courtroom. On these days, brief **courtroom lectures,** every hour on the half hour between 9:30am and 3:30pm, cover the history, operations, duties, and architecture of the court and its building.

The excitement continues below the court, where a larger-than-life statue of John Marshall, known as the "Great Chief Justice" around these parts, presides over an exhibit on the history of the court and its building. Around the corner from the exhibit hall, a small theater screens a 22-minute adaptation of the PBS series *This Honorable Court,* which serves up an intelligent summary of U.S. legal history as well as interviews with real live justices. The levels above the courtroom are closed to the public. In addition to offices, they contain a third-floor gymnasium where justices and their staffs ply their basketball skills above the highest court in the land. (Open Mon.-Fri. 9am-4:30pm. Free.) For more about the political role of the Supreme Court, see **U.S. Government and Politics,** p. 7.

LIBRARY OF CONGRESS

The Library of Congress, 1st St. SE (707-5000, recorded events schedule 707-8000), between East Capitol and Independence Ave. (Metro: Capitol South), has surpassed its original mission—to be Congress's library—as well as its second mission—to be the nation's library. Its current aspirations are global: it wants to be the world's library, a great repository for humankind's accumulated knowledge, with "all answers stored in a single place." The library is already the world's largest, with 26 million books and over 80 million other holdings, including Stradivarius violins, a Gutenberg Bible, newsreels, periodicals, and phonograph records. Less than a quarter of the 26 million books are in English; most aren't even in the Roman alphabet, but in Arabic, Chinese, Japanese, and other scripts.

The original library was founded in 1800, when Congress began to assemble mostly law and history books for members' personal use. The British torched them all in 1814, so Congress bought Thomas Jefferson's personal collection (6487 volumes) and started all over. An 1870 copyright law guaranteed the library a free copy of every book the United States registered, and the Library of Congress flourished. The library occupies three buildings: the 1897 Beaux Arts Jefferson Building, which hogs the display space; the 1939 Art Deco Adams Building across 2nd St.; and the 1980 Madison Building, a marble slab on Independence Ave. that is the largest office building in Washington, with 48 acres of floor space (doubling the library's space).

The **Jefferson Building,** whose green copper dome seals a spectacular octagonal reading room, is one of the most beautiful in Washington. Infrequent **library tours** leave from the Visitors Orientation Theater, just past the information desk in the lobby of the Madison Building. The theater screens an informational 22-minute video introduction to the library every half hour beginning at 9am. Currently, tours of the Jefferson Building leave from the Great Hall at 10, 11:30am, 1, 2:30, and 4pm. Tickets are free but tour spaces are limited; tickets may be obtained at the information desk in the Jefferson Building.

The Jefferson Building is like no library you have ever seen before. The Great Hall expands among grand staircases and ceiling frescoes, perpetuating the sense of enormity and grandeur felt upon entering. Once inside the great hall, the tour proceeds up the flanking staircases amid myriad paintings and mosaics of erudition. One such mosaic, seen from a second flight of stairs, depicts the Roman goddess Minerva, having put down her spear and shield, with her outstretched arm holding a list of academic disciplines to be studied. A sound-proof gallery overlooks the octagonal Main Reading Room and its 236 desks, spread out under a spectacular dome, whose apex hovers 160 feet above the floor. The dome's collar, at the top, boasts the "Stages of Human Knowledge," a painting which labels each major civilization of history and that civilization's primary contribution to mankind. The dome's windows feature the seals of each state in the Union. At the Gallery level of the Reading Room, columns sport female sculpture representing the academic disciplines; each sculpture is flanked by statues of legendary scholars and figures of said field (the statue representing art is flanked by Michelangelo and Beethoven). A syncretic statue grafts wings and Lincoln's head onto the body of Rodin's *Thinker*. The hall that was once the main entrance to the Main Reading Room is noticeably darker and more somber than the glitzy, Italian Renaissance style of the Great Hall; it was designed to situate readers in a serious, scholastic frame of mind. On the ceiling of the hall are three medallions representing Medicine, Law, and Theology—considered to be the three most educated professions of the time. The medallions are surrounded by the names of Americans distinguished in each field. Not surprisingly, "Law" is in the middle, indicating its supreme presence in the nation's capital.

One of the library's priceless possessions is the **Gutenberg Bible,** one of only three surviving copies, printed on vellum in 1455. The Bible is in near-perfect condition after restorative care during 1996.

For those with sincere scholarly interests, perhaps the best way to see the library is to do some research there. All of the vast collection, including rare items, is open to anyone of college age or older with a legitimate research purpose. Even the Main Reading Room in the Jefferson Building is open to scholars; the library is closed-stack, however—they'll bring the books to you. It's also a non-circulating library, so you must do your reading there. (Most reading rooms open Mon.-Fri. 8:30am-9:30pm, Sat. 8:30am-6pm, call 707-5000 for further information.)

Near the Library of Congress

The **Fountain of Neptune** splish-splashes in the front plaza of the Library of Congress Jefferson Building, on 1st St. between Independence Ave. and East Capitol St. You can see the 1897 fountain only from a very narrow swath of sidewalk, but it's well worth the trouble to stop and look. Wildly twisting horses flank the central figure of Neptune, turtles spit water at Nereids (high-class mermaids), Tritons (mermen) recline half-hidden in water, and twisting snakes spit water at *you* in this homage to Rome's famous Trevi Fountain.

Next to the Library of Congress Adams Building, the **Folger Shakespeare Library,** 201 East Capitol St. SE (544-4600), houses the world's largest collection of Shakespeareana. That's over 275,000 books and manuscripts. Alas, unless you've got a Ph.D. and research to do, you can't see them. You can go inside the building, though, and see the Great Hall exhibition gallery, a re-created Tudor gallery with dark oak panels and carved Elizabethan doorways. The **Shakespeare Theater** at the Folger is no longer at the Folger; the near-exclusively Shakespearean company has moved downtown to 450 7th St. NW (393-2700; see **Nightlife & Entertainment: Theater,** p. 220). During the day, tourists can peek at the theater itself, which imitates the Elizabethan Inns of Court indoor theaters, like the Blackfriars, where Shakespeare's company performed. The Folger also sponsors high-quality readings, lectures, and concerts; call for details. Recurring highlights are the **PEN/Faulkner poetry and fiction readings** and the **Folger Consort,** a chamber music group that specializes in Renaissance works and songs. Outside on the 3rd St. side of the building, tourists can stop for a rest or a quiet read in the Elizabethan **"knot" garden,** so-named because the different plants—all popular in Shakespeare's day—are arranged in intertwining patterns. (Exhibits open Mon.-Sat. 10am-4pm; library open Mon.-Fri. 8:45am-4:45pm.)

Flanking the Library of Congress and the Capitol on Constitution Ave. between Delaware Ave. and 2nd St. NE, and on Independence Ave. between 1st St. SW and 2nd St. SE, are the **House and Senate Office Buildings.** (Metro: Capitol South. Open Mon.-Fri. 8am-7pm.)

These office buildings are hardly designed for tourists—they're needed partly because so much space in the Capitol *is* designed for tourists. Nevertheless, energetic patriots could learn a lot about how Congress works by walking through one of the buildings. American citizens can find the offices of their Congresspersons without much trouble; consult the **directories** posted near all entrances and elevators. Once there, show proof of residence in your state and district and you can obtain passes to the House and Senate galleries and free information on some Washington sights. You can always ride the underground subway to the Capitol, but if you're hearing bells, save some seats for the Senators and Representatives who are being called to the Capitol for a vote.

Twentieth-century sculptor Alexander Calder's last work, *Mountains and Clouds,* occupies nine stories of the **Hart Senate Office Building**'s atrium (on Constitution Ave. NE between 1st and 2nd St.). Calder died in 1976 on the night after he met with architects to work out the sculpture's details; the $650,000 sculpture was not completed until 1986. The sculpture may be viewed in its natural light from the ground floor or from the building's various open balconies. The stable black "mountains," sculpted from sheet metal, weigh 39 tons; the mobile "clouds," made from aircraft aluminum, weigh 4300 lb. A computer controls the mobile's rotation.

Nestled beside the Hart building is the **Sewall-Belmont House,** 144 Constitution Ave. NE (546-3989). (Metro: Union Station.) One of the oldest houses in Washington is now the headquarters of the National Woman's Party. Today, a museum on the women's movement resides upstairs (see **Museums & Galleries,** p. 202).

NEAR UNION STATION

Moving northwest from the Capitol, the **Taft Memorial** stands on the triangular park between Constitution Ave., New Jersey Ave., and Louisiana Ave. NW. The 1958 statue of former Ohio senator Robert A. Taft (son of President William Howard Taft) assiduously defends a large, fluted concrete obelisk. Twenty-seven bells set into the obelisk ring like church chimes every 15 minutes.

Two blocks north of the Capitol grounds, **Union Station,** 50 Massachusetts Ave. NE (general information 371-9441) draws nearly three times as many visitors each day—50,000—as the Capitol itself. Most are there to use the Metro or hop an Amtrak train, but many come to admire Daniel Burnham's monumental Beaux Arts design, which took $25 million to erect from 1905 to 1908 and $160 million to renovate in 1988. The site of the climactic shoot-out in *The Untouchables,* the station now welcomes visitors with 120 chic shops and a glitzy food court rather than crossfire. To reach the station, walk northeast down Delaware Ave. from the Capitol or take the Metro to the Union Station. Outside, Christopher Columbus sails toward the Capitol in the large and striking sculpture that anchors the plaza. Inside, colonnades, archways, and huge domed ceilings equate Burnham's Washington with imperial Rome and the then-dominant train network with Roman roads. The station's wall tracings in the East Hall even copy examples from Pompeii. Downstairs, the train concourse is so expansive that it could hold the Washington monument horizontally. It also houses the **National Map Gallery,** the cavernous American Multi-Cinema, and lots of eateries. (Retail shops open Mon.-Sat. 10am-9pm, Sun. noon-6pm; call 842-3757 for cinema information.) For train information, see **Getting to Washington, D.C.,** p. 49.

Directly west of Union Station across 1st St. is the **City Post Office** (842-3812), another of Burnham's Beaux Arts buildings, completed in 1914. Officials lobbied for the post office to be constructed next to Union Station in order to expedite the collection and distribution of mail. Italian marble and granite constitute the exterior, which houses the new **National Postal Museum** (see **Museums & Galleries,** p. 200). The post office still operates; enter on North Capitol St. (open Mon.-Fri. 7am-midnight, Sat.-Sun. 7am-8pm).

Farther up on North Capitol is the **Government Printing Office** (512-0132), a large building in finely worked red brick. The G.P.O. now contracts out most of the government's printing needs, but still prints thousands of federal documents yearly, in addition to postcards, passports, and civil-service exams. Plant tours ended in the '60s, when someone realized that the electric forklifts, hot molten lead, and six-foot pneumatic knives could poke an eye out. The bookstore's entrance is on the North Capitol St. side of the building; the G.P.O. stocks what the government prints; there are Washington guidebooks, historical studies, and entertaining tomes only the U.S. Government could produce (e.g. *Design of Small Dams, Perspectives on John Philip Sousa,* and the *Amateur-Built Aircraft Flight Testing Handbook).* The government *Advisory Circulars,* the foreign-country guides, and the military *Back Yard Mechanics* books may even be useful. Across the hall, the **Congressional Sales Office** sells Congress' publications; the *Congressional Record* once sold out in one day when a conservative Senator, debating a bill to ban pornographic 900 numbers, inserted excerpts from some steamy recordings into his speech. (Both stores open Mon.-Fri. 8am-4pm.)

Northeast of Union Station is the **Capital Children's Museum,** 800 3rd St. NE (675-4120), a large red-brick building that looks like a city school. (Metro: Union Station.) Enter on 3rd St. between H and I St. NE (see **Museums & Galleries,** p. 201).

EAST OF 3RD STREET

Three blocks southeast of Union Station, down Massachusetts Ave. NE, **Stanton Park** offers benches, lots of shade, and a playground. An eclectic mix of white-collar lunchers, homeless loungers, and children frolicking in the playground will give you an instant sense of Capitol Hill's diversity. The park's visual anchor is a skillful equestrian statue of Nathaniel Greene, Esq., a Revolutionary War Major General. Greene rides along in Continental uniform, complete with tri-cornered hat and fringed shoulder epaulets. A 1930 windstorm once toppled horse and rider off the pedestal and onto their heads in the middle of the park.

When he first moved to D.C. after the Civil War, Black abolitionist, orator, autobiographer, and statesman Frederick Douglass lived at 316-318 A St. NE, two blocks east of the Supreme Court. Once the site of the Smithsonian Museum of African Art, the three-story gray house now houses the **Caring Institute** (547-4273), which honors benevolent Americans (open Mon., Wed., Fri. 2-4pm. $3).

From the Capitol, stroll east on East Capitol St. to see neighborhood life in an upscale part of Capitol Hill. A 10-block walk from the Capitol will bring you straight to **Lincoln Park,** a good area in which to people-watch during the day. (As with all parks downtown, however, it becomes dangerous after dark.) One statue remembers Abraham Lincoln as the Great Emancipator; the monument was supposedly constructed solely through contributions from former slaves. Another memorial, the only statue of a black woman in D.C., depicts Mary McLeod Bethune, who founded the National Council of Negro Women.

Southeast

Metro: Eastern Market; Navy Yard; Anacostia.
Southeast isn't so much a neighborhood as a geographical fact, a perfect right triangle bounded by East Capitol St., South Capitol St., and the District line. The two notable neighborhoods that crouch within Southeast's confines, Capitol Hill and Anacostia, lead a paradoxical coexistence: the Hill's famous law-absorbed offices seem like an odd companion for Anacostia's notorious crime-filled streets. But by no means should Southeast be ignored: a handful of captivating sights, including a pair of museums and some great clubs in Anacostia and the Washington Naval Yard reward street-smart walkers and confident drivers.

BARRACKS ROW

For a taste of Southeast Washington, try walking down 8th St. SE from the Eastern Market Metro stop to the **Navy Yard,** a stretch sometimes known as "Barracks Row." Although technically a part of Capitol Hill, the area has more in common—in look and feel—with the Southeast part of the District than with the Capitol and its environs. Barracks Row is usually safe during the day (Marines keep watch over some of the blocks), but don't walk it alone at night.

The **Marine Barracks,** 8th and I St. SE (433-2258), house what are nicknamed the "Eighth and Eye Marines." The head of the Marine Corps dwells at one end of the parade ground in a house built in 1806 (the British spared it when they torched D.C. in 1814). The barracks also house "The President's Own," the Marine Corps marching band that John Philip Sousa led from 1880 until 1892. The band now totes its Sousaphones on international tours. The infantry, though they served in the Gulf, are mostly here for ceremony; they march at Arlington Cemetery, stand around at White House ceremonies, and guard Camp David, the president's retreat. Visitors may not tour the grounds unaccompanied, and no official tour program exists. You may, however, be able to finagle a personal tour; ask the Marine at the guardhouse. The only sure way to see the grounds is to attend one of the **Friday evening parades,** at 8:30pm every Friday, May-Aug.

SIGHTS

NAVY YARD

Three museums and a destroyer stay ship-shape among the booms at the Washington Navy Yard. (Metro: Navy Yard.) Enter from the gate at 9th and M St. SE and ask for directions or look at the maps posted just inside. Follow the main road (9th St. SE) 1½ blocks to the big white stucco Building 58, the **Marine Corps Historical Center and Museum** (433-3840). An immediate right past the museum and then a left will put you on the road that travels past the diminutive **Navy Art Gallery** (433-3815), with its biannually changing depictions of naval activity, and down to the waters of the Anacostia River. Here, the **Navy Museum** (433-4882) in Building 76 should buoy anyone let down by the admire-but-don't-touch Air & Space Museum on the Mall; here you can climb on or in many of the display pieces.

The **U.S.S. Barry,** a decommissioned destroyer docked a few steps from the Navy Museum, offers a glimpse of maritime life. Climb aboard and a snappily dressed seaman will lead you through berths, control rooms, the bridge, the captain's quarters, and the combat center. The small mess room, the largest open area in the ship, will give you boundless sympathy for the men (and recently, women) who live cooped up in one of these machines for months at a time. Also, dig the decoy used during

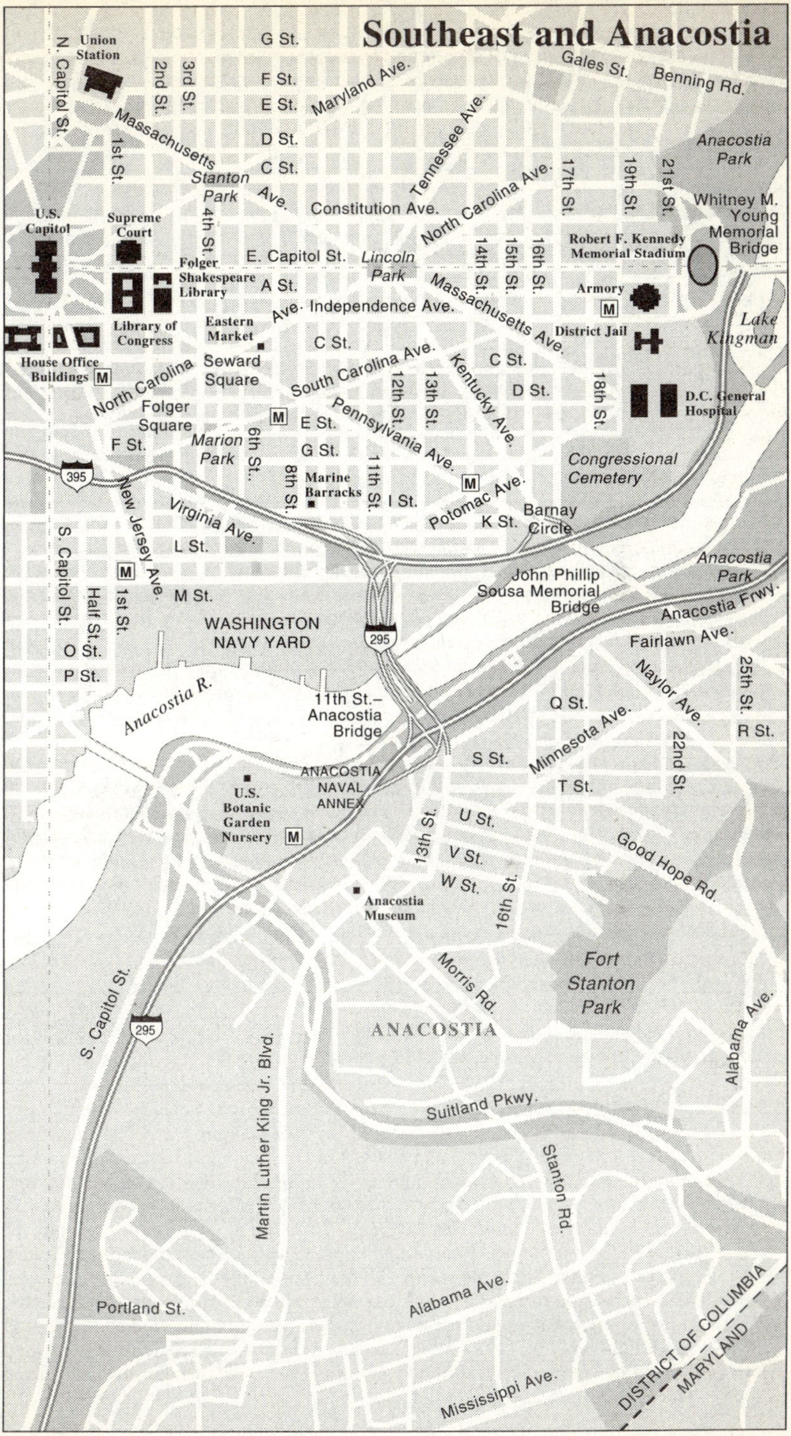
Southeast and Anacostia
Union Station
N. Capitol St.
2nd St.
3rd St.
G St.
F St.
E St.
D St.
C St.
Maryland Ave.
Tennessee Ave.
Gales St.
Benning Rd.
Anacostia Park
Massachusetts Ave.
1st St.
Stanton Park
4th St.
Constitution Ave.
North Carolina Ave.
17th St.
19th St.
21st St.
Whitney M. Young Memorial Bridge
U.S. Capitol
Supreme Court
Folger Shakespeare Library
E. Capitol St.
Lincoln Park
14th St.
15th St.
16th St.
Robert F. Kennedy Memorial Stadium
A St.
Massachusetts Ave.
Armory
Library of Congress
Eastern Market
Independence Ave.
Lake Kingman
District Jail
House Office Buildings
C St.
C St.
Seward Square
South Carolina Ave.
Kentucky Ave.
D St.
18th St.
D.C. General Hospital
North Carolina
Folger Square
12th St.
13th St.
E St.
Pennsylvania Ave.
F St.
Marion Park
6th St.
G St.
8th St.
Marine Barracks
11th St.
I St.
Congressional Cemetery
395
New Jersey Ave.
Potomac Ave.
K St.
Barnay Circle
Virginia Ave.
L St.
S. Capitol St.
Half St.
1st St.
M St.
John Phillip Sousa Memorial Bridge
Anacostia Park
Anacostia Frwy.
WASHINGTON NAVY YARD
295
O St.
P St.
Fairlawn Ave.
Naylor Ave.
25th St.
Anacostia R.
11th St.–Anacostia Bridge
Q St.
Minnesota Ave.
R St.
22nd St.
S St.
ANACOSTIA NAVAL ANNEX
T St.
U.S. Botanic Garden Nursery
13th St.
U St.
V St.
W St.
16th St.
Good Hope Rd.
Anacostia Museum
Morris Rd.
Fort Stanton Park
S. Capitol St.
295
ANACOSTIA
Alabama Ave.
Martin Luther King Jr. Blvd.
Suitland Pkwy.
Stanton Rd.
Portland St.
Alabama Ave.
DISTRICT OF COLUMBIA
MARYLAND
Mississippi Ave.

anti-submarine operations—it's a large motor that sailors threw overboard and dragged behind the ship so that noise-homing torpedoes would strike it instead of the ship's hull. (Open April-Sept. Tues.-Sun. 10am-5pm, Oct.-March 10am-4pm. Tours every 15 min. Free.)

ANACOSTIA

Anacostia began, ironically enough, as Washington's first suburb: white developers in the 1850s founded "Uniontown" on farmland across the river for settlers disturbed by the growing working-class presence on Capitol Hill. After the Civil War, one-acre plots ($200-300) sold by the Freedmen's Bureau drew freed slaves, who founded the Barry's Farm community. Blue-collar African-Americans would cross the 11th St. bridge to work by day in the city and then return at night to build their houses by fire-light. Isolation from the rest of the city built a strong community but also made Anacostia easy to ignore. As the Black population increased in the 1950s, this neglect worsened—plumbing and electricity were inadequate and housing, education, and employment opportunities grew few and far between.

Despite the opening of the Anacostia Metro station (on the green line), this neighborhood remains largely unattractive to tourists. While community residents struggle to overcome drug-related violence, progress is slow and costly. **If you prefer exploring on foot, do so here only during the day and with a friend or two.** A drive down Martin Luther King, Jr. Ave. SE is much safer, though, and equally rewarding. You can see the shards of a once-strong community for yourself; people still congregate and socialize along this central artery.

Look north from the parking lot of **Our Lady of Perpetual Help Church,** 1600 Morris Rd. SE (678-4999), across the street from the Lucy Ellen Molten Elementary School, for a good view of downtown, the Washington Monument, the Lincoln Memorial, and the Capitol. But watch out for the drug dealers; although the *Washingtonian* called this lot the best vantage point for gazing at the monuments, and the *Post* recommends it as one of the best spots for viewing the Fourth of July fireworks, they didn't mean for anyone to roam this area on foot.

Anacostia is also home to the **Anacostia Museum,** 1901 Fort Place SE (357-2700), which focuses generally on African-American history and culture (see **Museums & Galleries,** p. 201). Nearby, at 1411 W St. SE, the **Frederick Douglass Home** (426-5960) pays tribute to the great abolitionist and statesman. Also known as Cedar Hill, the house was Douglass's final residence. Douglass escaped from slavery in 1838, published the *North Star* newspaper in the 1840s, and served in the 1880s as a D.C. official and as the U.S. Ambassador to Haiti. He broke a Whites-only covenant when he bought the Old Anacostia house in 1877. Cedar Hill remains as Douglass furnished it, housing a cane belonging to Abraham Lincoln and given to Douglass by Mrs. Lincoln after the assassination. Take the Mt. Ranier B-2 bus from Howard Rd. near the Anacostia Metro station to the home. House tours (every ½hr. from 9am to 4pm) begin with a movie and continue with a walk through the house. (Open daily Nov.-April 9am-5pm; Oct.-March 9am-4pm. Free.)

The Waterfront

Yes, Virginia. D.C. has a waterfront too, a whole mile of it stretching south of G St. SW, along Maine Ave. and the parallel, smaller Water St. SW. Yachts congregate here at the **Washington Marina,** under the noses of high-priced seafood restaurants and hordes of joggers. In the summer, fairs reel in hundreds of Washingtonians, kids in tow, to check out the t-shirts and food and to ogle the boats. Theater-lovers park here for the **Arena Stage** (see **Nightlife & Entertainment,** p. 220).

The area has remained relatively untouched by the hordes of expensive shops that generally make a point of invading waterfront property; the result is a landscape with a functional, local feel. The outstanding attraction is the **Wharf Seafood Market,** between 9th and 11th St. SW and Maine Ave. NW (next to the Memorial Bridge).

Take the Metro to Waterfront, or from the L'Enfant Plaza stop walk two blocks to 9th St. SW from the exit at 7th and D St. SW and then down 9th St. (away from the Mall) to Maine Ave. No matter the season, no matter the day (except Christmas and perhaps New Year's), the vendors stand in their markets—floating platforms tied to the dock—and sell seafood galore. It's the oldest open-air seafood market in the U.S., beating out even New York's famous Fulton Fish Market; sellers have been at it here since 1794, and nothing's going to stop them now. During low tide you'll find yourself looking down at mounds of ice cubes, coral lobsters, and crawling crabs, as well as at rows of their aproned caretakers. Most fishermen sell at the wharf from about 8am to 9pm. The seafood, primarily from the Chesapeake Bay, couldn't be fresher. Be warned, however: the markets do not furnish seating, and the fishy smell packs a wallop. Benches and other spots along the waterfront provide more pleasant areas for picnicking, though they may require a bit of a walk.

At the opposite side of Water St. from the wharf, two **touring ships** sail the harbor; the *Spirit of Washington* and the *Potomac Spirit* depart from Pier 4, at 6th and Water St. SW (554-8000). See **Sports & Recreation,** (p. 225)., for details.

The Mall and Environs

Metro: Smithsonian; L'Enfant Plaza; Archives.

The Mall, the U.S.'s taxpayer-supported national backyard, was until this century D.C.'s central cipher, a vacant lot in the middle of it all. Today, it's the District's recreational lawn; on any sunny day, hundreds of natives and out-of-towners sunbathe and lounge, play frisbee or football, pummel their little brothers, or go fly a kite. The Mall serves as the hub of much of the city's activity, both governmental and tourist: adjacent to its green swaths are the **Smithsonian Museums** (p. 184), the **U.S. Capitol,** and the **White House** (connected via the Ellipse); within its boundaries are such landmarks as the **Washington Monument,** the **Lincoln Memorial,** and the **Vietnam War Memorial** (the **Jefferson Memorial** is just across the Tidal Basin). Nearby, the **Bureau of Engraving and Printing** and the **U.S. Holocaust Memorial Museum** vie with lesser-known attractions like the **U.S. Botanical Gardens.**

Just east of the Smithsonian Castle on the south side of the Mall, a musical **merry-go-round** delights all creatures great and small for only $1 a go. Thousands of people with trucks full of musical instruments and traditional cuisines congregate on the Mall in early July for the **Festival of American Folklife,** replete with evening dancing. Other occasional celebrations, like the **Fourth of July,** swamp the Mall with tents and blankets. See **Appendix: Special Events** (p. 292).

Exotic foliage from all continents and climates vegetates inside and outside the **U.S. Botanical Gardens,** 1st St. and Maryland Ave. SW (225-8333) in front of the Capitol. (Metro: Federal Center SW.) Burbling fountains, glass-covered atriums, orchids, dinosaur-era plants, and the amusing sausage tree near the entrance await amid natural glory. Guided tours are given on Tuesdays and Thursdays at 9 and 11:30am (call ahead; open 9am-5pm).

WASHINGTON MONUMENT

D.C.'s quintessential tiny, crowded, overheated elevator leads to equally tiny windows with breathtaking (read: nauseating) views. The Washington Monument inspires never-ending crowds of tourists to sacrifice their sweat, time, and patience ascending, descending, and photographing it. A vertical altar to America's first president, the marble-faced monument weighs 81,120 tons, stands on a foundation 126½ sq. ft. and 37 ft. deep, and could withstand a super-tornado blowing at 145 mph (at least that's what the experts say). Two-foot blocks of marble, along with rubble masonry, make up the base exterior; the interior support switches to New England granite about 450 ft. up, then gives way to solid marble capped by a 9-in. aluminum pyramid. In 1986, D.C. cops left bullet holes on the monument at eye-level when they gunned down a man who parked his van here, claimed it was full of dynamite, and threatened to blow up the famous structure.

For an obelisk, the monument took plenty of time and energy to build. Robert Mills' 1845 design called for a one-story, 30-column temple around the base. After Congress agreed to Mills' plan, construction began on July 4, 1848 but soon ran out of money; Alabama, which couldn't afford to send cash, contributed a stone instead, starting a trend that saved the monument. France, the Cherokee Nation, the American residents of Fu-Chow Fu, China, and over 100 other nations, states, towns, and people sent stones. When the Vatican sent a block of Italian marble in 1854, the Know-Nothings—an anti-Catholic and anti-immigrant political party—raided the grounds and stole "the Pope's stone;" afterwards, contributions dried up.

During the Civil War, the half-finished obelisk was nicknamed the "Beef Depot Monument" in honor of the cattle that Army quartermasters herded on the grounds. The monument's stone changes hue 150 ft. up: when construction began again after the Civil War and the builders returned to their favorite Maryland quarry, the layer of stones of the original color had already been used up. George Marsh, the U.S. Ambassador to Italy and an obelisk fan, nixed Mills's Doric temple in 1880 and the structure opened four years later.

The first men to ascend the monument could choose between the steam elevator and the stairs; women and children had to climb the 698 steps, since Mr. Otis's invention was considered dangerous. The stairs up the monument were a famous (and strenuous) tourist exercise until the Park Service closed them in the wake of heart attacks (on the way up) and vandalism (on the way down). The line for the elevators isn't as slow as it looks; it takes 45 minutes to circle the monument. Up at the top, tiny windows offer lookout points. From 500 ft. up, you can look down on all of D.C.'s major sights. The view from the top of the **Old Post Office** (see p. 87), however, is even better; in fact, the Washington Monument is almost more attractive when viewed from afar. Busy tourists may find their time better spent elsewhere.

The monument ascends at Constitution Ave. and 16th St. NW, west of the Mall proper and east of the Lincoln Memorial (Metro: Smithsonian). A wheelchair is available for any visitor who needs it; people with disabilities may bypass the long lines (open April-Aug. daily 8am-midnight; Sept.-March daily 9am-5pm; free).

Near Washington Monument

The **Reflecting Pool,** between the Washington and Lincoln memorials, reflects Washington's obelisk in seven million gallons of lit-up water 24 hours a day. If you lean over far enough, it might reflect you too. Based on pools at Versailles and the Taj Mahal, the Reflecting Pool's design minimizes wind ripples while maximizing poetic effect. A demonstration big enough to surround the 2000-ft.-long pool with people—such as the 1994 Gay Rights march—makes an impressive sight indeed.

Constitution Gardens stretches out north of the Reflecting Pool. The gardens are actually landfill—everything west of the Washington Monument and south of Constitution Ave. was once a swamp, but tell that to the ducks. On a weeping willow-dominated island in the park's lake, a granite and gold plate lists the signers of the Declaration of Independence.

VIETNAM VETERANS MEMORIAL

Maya Ying Lin, who designed the memorial, called it "a rift in the earth—a long, polished black stone wall, emerging from and receding into the earth. The memorial is a moving composition," she explained, "to be understood as one moves into and out of it; the passage itself is gradual, the descent to the origin slow, but it is at the origin that the meaning of the memorial is to be fully understood." While still an undergraduate at Yale, Lin beat 1400 contestants with her design. This subtlest of D.C.'s memorials changes its sheen and mood between day and night. Its granite reflects the Washington and Lincoln memorials at equal sizes.

The name of each of the 58,132 Americans who died in Vietnam is chiseled onto the stark black edifice. (Those Americans who are still missing in action have yet to be acknowledged.) Books at both ends of the structure serve as indexes to the memorial's numbered panels. Families and veterans come here to ponder and to mourn;

Korean War Memorial

On June 25, 1950, North Korea launched a surprise attack on South Korea. Twenty-one countries sent troops to help defend South Korea; China sent troops to bolster North Korea's effort. The "conflict" (it was never officially called a "war") ended with the signing of an armistice that solidified the separation of the two countries on July 27, 1953.

The three-year conflict resulted in more than 628,000 UN troops lost; over 54,000 Americans lost their lives. (For perspective, 57,000 Americans died in Vietnam over the 10 years of U.S. involvement in that conflict.)

Forty-two years after the armistice was signed, on July 27, 1995, the Korean War Memorial was dedicated. The $18 million tribute received 60% of its funding from American Korean War veterans, and made use of no federal money. Located at the west end of the Mall near the Lincoln Memorial, 19 colossal polished steel statues (14 Army men, 3 Marines, a Navy medic, and an Air Force officer) trudge up a hill, rifles in hand, an eternal expression of weariness mixed with fear frozen upon their faces. A black granite wall with over 2000 sandblasted photographic images from the war stands nearby. One edge of the wall extends into a shallow pool of water, a symbol of the Korean peninsula.

Over 8000 American soldiers are still missing due to a period of conflict that, although finally commemorated, is nevertheless "The Forgotten War."

many make rubbings of their loved ones' names from the walls. Other visitors leave letters, flowers, or more unusual objects; these items are collected by the Park Service. The National Museum of American History's "Personal Legacy" exhibit displays a sampling of some of these offerings; see **Museums and Galleries** (p. 188).

Some soldiers (and congresspeople) objected to the memorial's nonmilitary appearance, the government therefore commissioned Frederick Hart to sculpt realistic-looking (i.e., exhausted) bronze troopers emerging from an unknown battlefield. The statues seem to stare straight at the memorial's central corner, as if to apologize for breaking the silence Lin's design commands.

Three bronze figures at the east end of the memorial balance the three troopers to the west—they compose the **Vietnam Women's Memorial.** Each woman, sculpted by Glenna Goodacre in 1993, strikes a different pose; one aids a wounded soldier, another mourns a lost one, staring into his helmet. The third looks out into the sky and clutches her friend's arm as danger approaches.

The Vietnam Veterans Memorial descends into the earth northeast of the Lincoln Memorial, north of the Reflecting Pool, and south of Constitution Ave. at 22nd St. NW. (Metro: Foggy Bottom or Smithsonian.) It's entirely outdoors, so the memorial stays "open" 24hr.; park rangers leave at midnight. Call 634-1568 for information.

LINCOLN MEMORIAL

Though consensus demanded some memorial to Lincoln almost immediately after his assassination in 1865, the present marble temple wasn't built until 50 years later. The current Parthenon-like superstructure stands 80 ft. high, with simple Doric columns climbing 44 ft. to the frieze, where an inscription holds the names of the 36 states in existence during Lincoln's presidency. A massive layer of stone atop the columns lends the building the watchful solemnity of a crypt. The names of the lower 48 states wrap around the memorial's roof; a plaque at the bottom of the 130-ft.-wide stairway footnotes Alaska and Hawaii. The memorial's steps have hosted many famous gatherings; African-American soprano Marian Anderson sang from the steps here after she was barred from segregated Constitution Hall in 1939. Martin Luther King, Jr., gave his "I Have a Dream" speech to the 1963 March on Washington crowd from these same stairs. Today the base of the memorial most notably hosts vet-related vendors who find it easier to park their carts on the Lincoln Memorial's flat concrete than on the grass of the Vietnam Memorial. On the Fourth of July, throngs of fireworks-viewers clamor to the steps for the best seats in the District.

Daniel Chester French's seated Lincoln presides over the memorial from the inside, keeping watch over the Reflecting Pool, protest marchers, and Fourth of July fireworks. The stonecutting firm Picirilli Bros. couldn't find a block of marble big enough for Honest Abe; instead, it joined 28 blocks so tightly that you can barely see the seams. In American Sign Language, Lincoln's hands spell "A" and "L"—French's reminder that it was Lincoln who signed Gallaudet College (the only college in the country for deaf students) into existence. The arms of the marble seat bear Roman *fasces,* symbols of imperial power—an unfortunate choice, given Mussolini's concurrent ascension to power in Italy.

Lincoln's stirring **Gettysburg Address** graces the wall to the left of the statue. Also note his (longer) second inaugural address, given 63 days prior to his assassination, and the un-subtly corrected "engravo" where "euture" has been changed to "future." Looming above Lincoln's famous words are Jules Gurin's allegorical gold-detailed canvas murals. To the south, the Angel of Truth frees slaves, flanked by Justice and Immortality; to the north, the Angel of Truth brings the North and the South together after the Civil War, with help from Fraternity and Charity.

The memorial's interior looks best early in the morning, when the rising sun shines through the marble roof; builders soaked it in paraffin to improve its translucency. At night, Lincoln glows in electric lights; memorial-goers can watch the Washington Monument's image shimmer in the Reflecting Pool and meditate from the steps. The memorial anchors the west end of the Mall across the Reflecting Pool from the Washington Monument; from Foggy Bottom, walk south along 23rd St. NW. (Metro: Smithsonian or Foggy Bottom; it's a long walk.) Since it has no doors, the Memorial is open 24hr.; a ranger hangs around daily from 8am until midnight.

JEFFERSON MEMORIAL

> *I think this is the most extraordinary collection of talent, of human knowledge, that has ever been gathered together at the White House, with the possible exception of when Thomas Jefferson dined alone.*
>
> —JFK, addressing a gathering of Nobel Prize winners in 1962

The third member of D.C.'s white-marble triumvirate, finished in 1942, holds court due south and across the Tidal Basin from the Washington Monument. A 19-ft. hollow bronze Thomas Jefferson stands enshrined in a domed, open-air rotunda surrounded by massive Ionic columns. The memorial's graceful design, by John Russell Pope, pays homage to Jefferson's Charlottesville home, Monticello. The cherry trees (which bloom in the spring) were a gift from Tokyo to Washington in 1912.

President Franklin Roosevelt had all the trees between the memorial and the White House razed so he could watch the memorial's construction. High-society ladies tried to protect the 33 cherry trees that stood in his line of sight by chaining themselves to the trunks; the bureaucrat in charge of construction served them coffee and tea until their bladders protested, then bulldozed the trees while they were in the powder room. A path of grass is still clearly visible today, allowing the memorial's visitors a view of the White House.

Jefferson himself designed a number of neoclassical buildings during his life, including the Virginia state capitol and the quadrangle and library at the University of Virginia. Corn and tobacco, Virginia's cash crops, are visible under his coat, the tobacco forming a sort of column as a reminder of Jefferson's architectural bent. The interior walls quote from Jefferson's writings: the *Declaration of Independence,* the *Virginia Statute of Religious Freedom,* his *Notes on Virginia,* and an 1815 letter. The Declaration of Independence extract contains 11 discrepancies with the original; several of these were committed to shorten the quote so it would fit on the wall. The carved squares get smaller near the top of the dome, so the ceiling looks higher than its mere 30 ft.

Today, Jefferson's pocket of peace is disturbed by the restoration of cracked columns—the unfortunate result of time, automobile exhaust, and acid rain. The memorial remains open 24 hours, with the lights always on. Park rangers answer questions from 8am until midnight, except on Christmas (426-6822 or 425-6821). The memorial overlooks the Tidal Basin along D.C.'s southwestern edge; walk to it along the Basin's rim from Independence Ave. or 14th St. SW. (Metro: L'Enfant Plaza or Smithsonian.) Drivers should take 14th St. SW (heavily trafficked during the day).

TIDAL BASIN AREA

The Jefferson Memorial overlooks Washington's most popular man-made lake, the **Tidal Basin,** where **paddleboats** ripple in and out of Thomas Jefferson's shadow. Visitors finishing their tours of the Mint find themselves here—on a lake small enough to be entirely visible at once, but big enough to accommodate many boaters. For paddleboat rentals, see **Sports and Recreation** (p. 229).

Too famous for their own good, the Japanese **cherry trees** surround themselves with a protective ring of botanically minded tourists during the two weeks in late March or early April when most of them are in bloom along the Tidal Basin's rim. The original batch of trees, sent in 1909 from Japan as a symbol of trans-Pacific friendship, arrived bearing insects and fungi and were promptly obliterated by the Department of Agriculture. The current bloomin' wonders, received in 1912, were Japan's second try. After Japanese bombers attacked Pearl Harbor in 1941, irate Washingtonians took buzzsaws to several of the trees.

Mellow **West Potomac Park** and **East Potomac Park,** lush with trees, lawns, and sculptures, park themselves on either side of the Tidal Basin along Ohio Dr. SW. The latter is bigger, but the former is more popular. West Potomac Park holds summer polo games at 3pm on Sundays.

It's hard to spend more than 10 minutes south of the Lincoln Memorial without hearing military helicopters motoring away over the Potomac; if you see one heading due north, toward the White House, it may well contain the President.

SOUTH OF THE MALL

Millions of listeners on every continent but this one tune into the **Voice of America,** 330 Independence Ave. SW (619-3919; Metro: Federal Center SW), the U.S. government's overseas radio and TV organ. Tours start at the C St. entrance between 3rd and 4th St.; watch radio announcers at home in the studio, speaking anything from English to Dari to Uzbek. (Public tours lasting 45 min. begin Tues.-Thurs. at 10:40am, 1:40, and 2:40pm, except holidays. Reservations required.)

Bureaucrats shop till they drop in the low-ceilinged, light-bulb bastion **L'Enfant Plaza,** named for Pierre L'Enfant, D.C.'s ubiquitous original urban planner. The plaza itself is an immense underground structure that takes up an entire block between 9th and 10th St. at D St. SW. The plaza's construction threatened to topple the saw-tooth-based **Department of Housing and Urban Development,** an unhealthy looking X-shaped building on D St. SW between 7th and 9th. A long-standing HUD rumor holds that the building was designed to resemble a particularly admired Paris post office. Unfortunately, the HUD building was twice the size of Paris'; the square-cube law, which says that anything of given proportions gets weaker as it gets bigger, made the outsized HUD structure unsound from the outset.

The Mint, or the **Bureau of Engraving and Printing** (622-2000), at 14th St. and C St. SW, just southeast of the Washington Monument (Metro: Smithsonian), offers unguided tours (along claustrophobic tunnels smelling of ink) of the presses that annually print over $20 billion worth of money and stamps. Look for the bins of shredded bills. Crowd-herders fondly refer to the place as "the money factory;" and signs affixed to the presses announce "the buck starts here," taunt visitors with "Have you ever been so close and yet so far away?" and poke fun at employees: "Think how I feel: I printed my lifetime salary in a few minutes!" Skip breakfast, or expect to grow old in line. Thankfully, the wait is relieved by lots of stamps, discontinued bills, TV screens, and other displays along the way. Free Muzak, too (open Mon.-Fri. 9am-2pm; free).

Just north of the mint, at 100 Raoul Wallenberg Place SW, the **U.S. Holocaust Memorial Museum** (488-0400; Metro: Smithsonian) reminds huge crowds of the atrocities visited upon European Jews by the Nazis. See **Museums** (p. 196).

Old Downtown

Metro: Metro Center; Gallery Place-Chinatown; Judiciary Sq.; Archives-Navy Memorial; Federal Triangle.

"Old Downtown" is an arbitrary label for the area north of the Mall bounded by Constitution Ave., 2nd St., New York Ave., and 15th St. NW. Old Downtown harbors a concentration of federal businesses—many U.S. agencies and departments do their regulating thing here. But Old Downtown also fosters a thriving private sector, with a plethora of street vendors, luncheon spots, and pricey hotels to rival the few block-long department stores around Metro Center. This grudging symbiosis reflects the area's history: before government moved in, 7th St. NW was D.C.'s main commercial center. During the 1800s, it boasted the largest outdoor market (the no-longer-extant Center Market, opened in 1801) and the monumental Patent Office building. Old Downtown's eclecticism is also evident in its pedestrians: a conglomeration of tourists, professionals, bureaucrats, and the city's homeless throng the streets on weekdays. At night they find their respective havens—hotels, bars, 'burbs, and benches. Each group has its own hubs and hotspots, but not one can claim the neighborhood as its own. Public and private, foreign or native, all pursue their special interests here. Developing museums solicit aid while panhandlers negotiate territorial concessions; the cloistered members of Congress have nothing on Old Downtown.

Pennsylvania Avenue, particularly the stretch between the White House and the Capitol (now closed to commercial vehicles), and between 6th and 15th St. NW, is probably the most discussed street in Washington. New Presidents traverse it quadrennially in the Inaugural Parade, warranting the logical nickname "Street of Presidents." Most new Chief Executives ride in a limo, but Jimmy Carter showed his energy-consciousness in 1976 by walking the 16 blocks to the White House. Before and during the Civil War era, the avenue, which runs all the way from Northwest to Anacostia via the John Philip Sousa Bridge, was D.C.'s most important thoroughfare. At night, the street became "Hooker's Division," named for the hard-living Union General Joseph Hooker. Shady bars and prostitution flourished here. However, anyone who says the term "hooker" (for a prostitute) came from General Hooker's name is probably just a proud Washingtonian: the word, older than the general, most likely derives from Brooklyn (NY)'s old Red Hook district.

An array of Greco-Roman Revival federal buildings includes the **Federal Trade Commission** on 6th St., which is blessed with a profusion of outdoor sculptures. (The statue of a half-naked man wrestling a horse near the eastern doorway represents the Commission's monopoly.) Other Neoclassical structures along the avenue are the **National Archives** (between 7th and 9th), the **Justice Department** (between 9th and 10th), the taxing **Internal Revenue Service** (between 10th and 12th), and the **Interstate Commerce Commission** (between 12th and 14th). These buildings, along with the District Building and the Dept. of Commerce, form the **Federal Triangle complex,** once the site of Murder Bay, a notorious slum. The looming **FBI,** the enchantingly anachronistic **Old Post Office,** and the elegant **Willard Hotel** make their contrasting marks on the avenue's wide vistas, as does the **District Building** at 14th and D St. NW. Congress invented the Pennsylvania Ave. Development Corporation in 1972 to encourage private enterprise along the government-dominated street. The result has been a string of offices; hence, any weekday stroll up the avenue allows a simultaneous survey of Washington architecture and Washington professionals. Small parks and plazas along the length of the street offer calm resting places for exhausted walkers.

NEAR JUDICIARY SQUARE

From the Judiciary Square Metro at the 4th and D St. exit, a right turn onto D St. and a one-block walk will take you to the **D.C. Courthouse** (879-1010) at 500 Indiana Ave., at 5th St. and D St. NW. This modern building offers some insight as to how the legal system really operates. Suspects, lawyers, cops, and taxi drivers compete for sidewalk space outside, while lawyers rush up and down three levels of escalators inside, scampering to file their briefs in time. The D.C. Superior Court and the D.C. Court of Appeals share the building; confusingly, the Superior Court is the *inferior* of the two. They say Justice is blind; here, she's just oblivious to tourists. Pamphlets are available at the Public Information Desk (to the left of the entrance); visitors may ask which criminal cases they can sit in on. Alternatively, they can eat in the cafeteria on the "C" level or just ride the escalators. Whee! (Courthouse open Mon.-Fri. 8:30am-5pm; free.)

Toward the Mall, across C St. NW, the **U.S. Courthouse** (535-3555), at 333 Constitution Ave., squats in conservative austerity on the east side of John Marshall Park (Metro: Judiciary Square). At the Constitution Ave. entrance, one can see the monument to Civil War general George Meade, who led Union forces at Gettysburg and now stands guard over the courthouse building, flanked by an ecletic brigade of nymphs, Roman warriors, and a medieval knight figure in a bizarre mixture of artistic and historical contextualization. The entrance on 3rd St. affords a glimpse of the **Department of Labor.** The federal court building claims to be open to the public; even though it's legal, it's hard to shake a feeling of intrusion. Better-dressed lawyers and Constitutional issues stalk these marbled halls, which contain the Court of Appeals for the D.C. Circuit. Both civil and criminal cases are generally open to the public, depending on availability of space. The trial schedule in Room 1825 may list some interesting cases. (Courthouse open Mon.-Fri. 9am-5pm; free.) There is some metered parking available on Indiana Ave., but empty spaces are rare during the court day. In **John Marshall Park,** workaholics and alcoholics compete for a lunch bench alongside a lifelike statue of two chess players. One player looks smug, the other dismayed—checkmate. Pigeons perch on an oversized statue of Marshall, the first and perhaps most significant chief justice of the Supreme Court (who here resembles a haggard Anthony Hopkins). Across the street, facing the East Wing of the National Gallery of Art, the small bit of parkland once held the boardinghouse where poet Walt Whitman lived in 1864.

The **Canadian Embassy** (682-1740), at 501 Pennsylvania Ave. NW behind the D.C. Courthouse, deserves more than a glance (Metro: Judiciary Square or Archives-Navy Memorial). The east front, bordering Marshall Park, is a spacious court surrounded by six 50-foot columns of smooth, pale, unpolished aluminum that hold up three of the embassy's six modern floors. The Rotunda of the Provinces, on the southeast corner of the court, creates a shady platform and caps a cascading pool of water. At the embassy's Marshall Park entrance is Bill Reid's black-bronze 11,000-lb. sculpture, *The Spirit of Haida Gwaii.* The Haida are a Native-American tribe indigenous to Canada's Queen Charlotte Islands; this striking piece, perched in a pool of water, depicts a number of Haida mythical figures crammed into a canoe and paddling for their lives. Information is available in French and English at the entrance. A gallery in the embassy's basement displays rotating exhibitions of other modern Canadian art (open Mon.-Fri. 9am-5pm; free).

National Law Enforcement Officers Memorial

The National Law Enforcement Officers Memorial (Metro: Judiciary Sq.), is situated, appropriately, in Judiciary Sq. between E and F St. and 4th and 5th St. NW in front of the **National Building Museum** and directly above the Metro station. (See **Museums & Galleries,** p. 198.) Dedicated by President Bush in October 1991, the memorial's three acres recognize the service of all officers and honor the more than 13,000 federal, state, and local officers who have died in the line of duty. In the creation of his composition, architect Davis Buckley drew from Michelangelo's Piazza del Campidoglio in Rome as well as Maya Ying Lin's Vietnam Veterans Memorial just blocks away. In effecting the semi-elliptical walkway around the edge of the memorial, Buckley utilized Michelangelo's geometric solution for presenting an off-center base as centered. And in transforming the walkways into "pathways of remembrance" (with the names of fallen officers engraved in the gray marble bordering the paths), Buckley nods to Lin's design for the Vietnam memorial. A bronze lion or lioness guards each of the four entrances along the pathways while watching over slumbering cubs, conveying the responsibility, strength, and courage of those who enforce the nations's laws.

With the monument's dual role as both memorial and public park, pedestrians and casual visitors share the space with the families and friends of slain officials. As at the Vietnam memorial, rubbing-pads for etching names are available both on-site and at the National Building Museum. Remembrances left by mourners are collected and some are on display at the Visitors Center; the many letters from children are especially moving. The **Visitors Center,** two blocks west at 605 E St. NW, details the history of the memorial. (Memorial open 24hr. Visitors Center open Mon.-Fri. 9am-5pm, Sat. 10am-5pm, Sun. noon-5pm; free.)

NATIONAL ARCHIVES

The United States' founding documents can still be found at the National Archives, between 7th and 9th St., and Constitution Ave. NW (general information 501-5000, TDD 501-5404, guided tours 501-5205, library and research 501-5400; Metro: Archives-Navy Memorial). Visitors line up outside to view the original *Declaration of Independence, U.S. Constitution,* and *Bill of Rights* (often, unfortunately, ignoring the rotating exhibits that flank them). Humidity-controlled, helium-filled glass cases preserve and exhibit all three documents in the central rotunda. The writing is rather faded due to the parchments' overexposure to strong light prior to preservation concerns; now, the special laminated glass and filters protect the documents from light and give them a greenish tinge. Every night these cases sink into the floor; the documents' nightly repose in a basement vault makes them harder to steal, slower to deteriorate, and safe from nuclear attack. The dent in the metal of the casing is a reminder that, in 1986, someone tried to shatter the glass with a hammer and destroy the Bill of Rights. Also largely ignored by tourists is the 13th-century *Magna Carta,* King John of England's famous guarantee of rights to his angry barons. The document on display is one of four existing copies of the 1297 version, endorsed by Edward I. The Latin script is remarkably well-preserved and readable. The copy is the only one permanently residing in the United States, as well as the only one that is privately owned. It's now at the Archives on indefinite loan from its owner, H. Ross Perot. The *Magna Carta* was originally approved by King John in 1215, and guaranteed such fundamental rights as the right to trial by jury, equality before the law, and freedom from arbitrary arrest.

Long tiered steps, stone friezes, fluted columns, and mammoth bronze doors (1-ft. thick and 40-ft. high) reflect the fact that neoclassicist John Russell Pope, of National Gallery of Art fame, also designed the Archives. (Main exhibit area open daily April-Labor Day 10am-9pm, Labor Day-March 10am-5:30pm. Free.) The Archives will even play bits of Nixon's infamous Watergate tapes for the public, though at a safe distance from the White House. The tapes are stored, along with increasing amounts of Archives material, in a new facility, Archives II, located in College Park, MD. Most research materials are now at Archives II. (Open Mon. and Wed. 8:45am-5pm, Tues. and Thurs.-Fri. 8:45am-9pm, and Sat. 8:45am-4:45pm. Office of Administrative Services (301) 713-6400; research information (301) 713-6800 or (301) 713-6779. Researcher cards are issued upon the presentation of a photo ID; cards are valid for three years.)

The Archives preserves over four billion papers and paraphernalia pertaining to American history. Its files hold about 2% of the paper the federal government generates, including maps, patents, photographs, police journals, and census forms. A very small percentage of the Archives' possessions can be displayed at one time. The

Archives owns but does not display the *Emancipation Proclamation*, President Lincoln's slave-freeing document of 1862. Unusual items stored in the Archives include a portrait of Richard Nixon painted on a grain of rice; a red wig worn by Watergate villain Howard Hunt; and a file of *Topps* baseball cards taken as evidence in a 1960s lawsuit.

The **Microfilm Room** on the building's fifth floor allows visitors to check military records, census records, and Confederate and Revolutionary papers. Genealogy buffs tending family trees find plenty of historical fertilizer here, as do professional writers, such as Alex Haley *(Roots)*, researching their upcoming best sellers. At the Central Research Library, librarians will track the information that you need from the Archives' reams of data. (Research facilities open Mon. and Wed. 8:45am-5pm, Tues. and Thurs.-Fri. 8:45am-9pm, Sat. 8:45am-4:45pm; enter at Pennsylvania Ave. and 8th St.)

The **tour** of the Archives presents other highlights, such as the vault into which the Declaration, Constitution, et al. are lowered each night, and the patents for an "escape coffin." (Call in advance to arrange tours.) Also on display are the Reagan family census, the arrest record for John Wilkes Booth, a photo of Helen Keller with President Eisenhower, and President Nixon's 1974 letter of resignation. (Tour reservations: 501-5205; U.S. citizens may contact their congressmen instead. Tours daily at 10:15am and 1:15pm. Free. Tour-takers enter at Pennsylvania Ave. and 8th St.) "Tokens & Treasures: Gifts to Twelve Presidents," an exhibition showcasing gifts received by presidents from Hoover to Clinton, will be exhibited through January 1997. Given by governments, diplomats, and private citizens, gifts include jewelry, artwork, caricatures, and musical instruments. The "American Originals" exhibit will be on display through December 1998; items in the exhibit rotate periodically. The collection includes the cancelled check for the purchase of Alaska, the first *Superman* comic book, the Louisiana Purchase Treaty (signed by Napoleon), pictures taken from the moon, and the Supreme Court order for public school desegregation.

UNITED STATES NAVY MEMORIAL

The United States Navy Memorial (737-2300) on Pennsylvania Ave. at 8th St. NW, across Pennsylvania Ave. from the National Archives (Metro: Archives-Navy Memorial), is a popular rest and lunch spot for tourists and local workers alike. The circular memorial holds weekly **concerts** by the Navy Band (Tues. at 8pm in the summer months). Weather permitting, the U.S. Navy Ceremonial Guard Drill will perform close order drill each week (Tues. at 1pm); in the spring the memorial hosts "Lunchtime Concerts" by high school and collegiate bands and choral groups. Set into the ground is the largest-ever **stone map** of the world; the map's north is exactly aligned to the true north. Pictographs line the walls, the Naval Hymn is carved into the steps, and Stanley Bleifeld's statue *The Lone Sailor* is conducive to serene contemplation of the ocean. The **Naval Heritage Center,** the memorial's visitors center, is located at the back right of the memorial. Inside, the stairs' descent is accompanied by the "Wave Wall," which holds glass panels etched with renditions of ships. The waves lead into the Gallery Deck, another nautical room that in turn leads into the Presidents' Room. The room honors presidents who have led or served in the Navy—both Roosevelts (who served as assistant secretaries of the Navy), Kennedy, Johnson, Nixon, Ford, Carter, and Bush. The film *At Sea* flaunts high-tech graphics in the **Theater**, proximate to the Gallery Deck's entrance. The film is shown Mon.-Sat. every hour starting at 10am, 1pm on Sun. Movie tickets: adults $3.75; seniors, Plank Owners and Shipmates of the Navy Memorial, students (under age 18) and those on active military duty with ID $3. Memorial open 24hr. Visitors Center open Mon.-Sat. 9:30am-5pm, Sun. noon-5pm.

THE FBI

Like its namesake, the block-long J. Edgar Hoover FBI building, 10th St. NW at Pennsylvania Ave. (324-3000), one block west from the Navy Memorial, represents the

Shoot 'em up!

At the end of the tour, a marksman picks up an FBI-standard revolver and a German HNK-MP5 fully automatic submachine gun and blasts away at sinister cardboard evildoers. Tellingly, the largely American audience always applauds when the gunfire ends.

nadir of Washington modernism. Waiting in line for a glimpse of the interior, you may get to know it well. Once inside, serious-minded agents will guide you through the popular FBI tour, casting light on some of the organization's tricks (and none of its scandals). Tour lines form on the building's outdoor plaza; tour entrance at E St. NW (Metro: Federal Triangle or Archives-Navy Memorial).

The end of the go-go, right-wing 80s hasn't fazed the Federal Bureau of Investigation. Today's FBI still hunts Commies, druggies, homosexuals, and interstate felons with a vigor little diminished since J. Edgar Hoover's 25-year stint as its chief. Hoover earned himself, and the Bureau, a reputation by nabbing the nation's notorious criminals of the 30s and 40s, then driving the FBI through more than a decade of political espionage, homophobic innuendo, and hounding of left-wing figures. He fired all of the Bureau's female agents upon taking the helm, proclaiming that a woman would serve the FBI "over his dead body." Until Hoover's death in May 1971, the FBI's female employees were resigned to filing and photocopying. July 1971 saw the appointment of the Bureau's first female agent since the 30s.

Tourists can only access the high-security interior via a tour; tours occur as often as the guides can give them and are prefaced by a corny movie. Real FBI agents sport walkie-talkies (and a strange resemblance to flight attendants) as they whisk visitors through gangster paraphernalia and photos, relics of crime bosses, confiscated marijuana and cocaine, a display of 5000 illicit guns (including a gun disguised as a cane), old cryptographic devices, and mugshots of the nation's 10 most wanted criminals. Tourists have identified felons from their mugshots on two separate occasions; each led to an arrest. The FBI's crack team of scientists will ignore visitors as they analyze hair, blood, and DNA samples from behind plexiglass. In the wake of all this excitement, your tour-agent will probably thwart any *Twin Peaks* or *Untouchables* fantasies by announcing that 25% of all Federal agents are accountants assigned to unglamorous, white-color crimes.

In theory, parking is available near the Bureau, on 9th St. In practice, the Metro and a walk from the Mall may be better means. In June and July, crowds sometimes wait up to four hours for a tour; however, advance tickets are available from your congressmen. Tours Mon.-Fri. 9am-4:15pm; free.

Near the FBI

"Sic semper tyrannis!" shouted John Wilkes Booth as he jumped to the stage just seconds after shooting President Abraham Lincoln during a performance at **Ford's Theatre** (426-6924, TDD 426-1749), 511 10th St. NW, one block north of the FBI (Metro: Metro Center, 11th St. exit). The phrase means "Thus always to tyrants"—it's the motto of the state of Virginia, usually printed under a picture of Virginia mercilessly quashing a tyrant (presumably) with her foot. An actor, Booth had no trouble sneaking into the theater. Lincoln's April 14, 1865 appearance at *Our American Cousin* was his first time in public since the Civil War had ended. At 10:15pm, while the audience was laughing, Booth entered the President's box, shot Lincoln, then injured his leg jumping onstage. The museum below the theater runneth over with placards and portraits of Lincoln. At night, Ford's Theatre becomes a contemporary playhouse (see **Nightlife & Entertainment: Theater,** p. 222). The theater is under the jurisdiction of the National Parks Service. A ranger may be coaxed into narrating the events of the assassination for you (open daily 9am-5pm; free).

The next morning, President Lincoln passed away across the street at the **Petersen House** (426-6830), 526 10th St. NW. He slept, and later died, diagonally, in the small bed. The tiny room where he passed away now looks as it did then, and the intimacy

Don't Quit Your Day Job

Lincoln's assassination was actually part of a larger conspiracy that included plans to kill Secretary of State William Henry Seward and Vice President Andrew Johnson; it was critical to the plot that all of the killings take place simultaneously in order to diffuse security. Only Booth was "successful." Seward had recently been in a riding accident which neccessitated a neck brace—the brace courageously foiled Lewis Powell's knife. George Atzerodt simply decided at the last minute that murdering Johnson wouldn't solve anything.

of the room—its dotted white curtains, low walnut bed and bureau, and simple tumblers and pitchers—makes visitors feel like strangers at a wake. Likewise, the crowds rotating through the house create the unnerving impression that their presence, and yours, constitutes some form of sacrilege. The bloodstained pillows have been removed indefinitely for restoration (open daily 9am-5pm).

The **Old Post Office,** at Pennsylvania Ave. and 12th St. NW (606-8691, TDD 606-8694), sheathes a shopping mall in architectural wonder (Metro: Federal Triangle). Its arched windows, conical turrets, and 315-ft. clock tower are a standing rebuke to its sleeker contemporary neighbors. Completed in 1899, the Post Office Building was criticized by the *New York Times* for looking "like a cross between a cathedral and a cotton mill." The building has also been referred to as a tooth in need of extraction. Having avoided demolition in the 1950s, the wayward edifice now houses a one-room post office, some federal office space, a multi-ethnic food court, shops, and a stage. Offices rise on all four sides of a 12-story space in which tourists and businesspeople enjoy cheap but tasty meals (sushi for less than $5) and incessant musical performances. For information on the shops—collectively known as the Pavilion—call 289-4224. The National Park Service can show you around the **clock tower** (tour info 606-8691). The 15-min. tour meets every 5 min. at the glass elevators in the patio area downstairs, where food tables cluster. The view from the top may be D.C.'s best, especially since the archways are open-air (wired for safety), not glassed-in or minuscule (like the Washington Monument's). The Washington Ringing Society makes the tower chime for hours on end on Thursdays (for practice), and on federal holidays. (Tower open mid-April to mid-Sept. 8am-10:45pm; otherwise 10am-6pm. Shops open Mon.-Sat. 10am-8pm, Sun. noon-6pm.)

CHINATOWN

This five-square-block community shares enough with other cities' renditions to be worth exploring (Metro: Gallery Place-Chinatown). Start at 7th and H St. NW; the bilingual street signs and by the dragon-covered multicolored gilded archway are rather helpful landmarks. Mainland Chinese money paid for the arch in the mid-80s, sparking protests by local leaders on anti-Communist grounds. Chinatown's history resembles that of Chinese districts across the nation. After the Chinese Exclusion Act of 1882 had restricted immigration, barred Chinese aliens from most jobs, and prohibited Chinese women and children from entering the United States, the persecuted immigrants lived and worked near 4th St. and Pennsylvania Ave. NW. Two rival *tongs* (merchants' associations) formed to offer protection to Chinese-owned businesses. When government buildings displaced the old Chinatown, the *tongs* led the move to today's neighborhood.

Technically bounded by 5th, 8th, F, and I St. NW, Chinatown is slowly shrinking under the pressure of crime and rising rents, but the remaining shops and restaurants serve many first-generation Chinese immigrants. The area promises to be hugely revitalized with the construction of the gargantuan **MCI Center,** future home of the Washington Bullets and Capitals. The new arena, slated to open for the 1997-98 season, is the brainchild of Abe Pollin, owner of both teams. Pollin worked with city officials to carry out a plan that was specifically designed to benefit both businesses and area residents. While Chinatown streets are generally safe during the day, exercise extra caution at night and bring a friend or two, especially on weekends. (For a handful of the ubiquitous restaurants in Chinatown, see **Food,** p. 89.)

FROM GALLERY PLACE TO METRO CENTER

The **National Museum of American Art** and the **National Portrait Gallery** (357-2700, TDD 357-1729) share the **Old Patent Office Building,** a Neoclassical edifice two blocks long (American Art entrance at 8th and G St., Portrait Gallery entrance at 8th and F; Metro: Gallery Place-Chinatown). The NMAA houses the largest collection of American art in the world, while the NPG is a surprisingly engrossing museum devoted exclusively to portraiture. (See **Museums & Galleries,** p. 184.)

At 901 G St. NW, across 9th St. from the National Museum of American Art, is the **Martin Luther King, Jr. Memorial Library** (727-1111), the flagship of D.C.'s library system. The brick and black glass rectangular building is the only one in Washington designed by Bauhaus celeb Ludwig Mies van der Rohe. Inside, see Don Miller's mural of Rev. Dr. King, one of the United States' most important civil rights leaders, who led the nonviolent protests that helped end legal segregation. Local history aficionados will find their heaven in the Washingtoniana Room. (Open during the summer Mon., Wed., and Thurs. 10am-7pm, Tues. 10am-9pm, Fri.-Sat. 10am-5:30pm; open the rest of the year Mon.-Thurs. 9am-9pm, Fri.-Sat. 9am-5:30pm, Sun. 1-5pm; hours change frequently—call for the most recent schedule. Free.)

The building on 8th St. between H and I St. NW used to be a synagogue; now it's the **Greater New Hope Baptist Church.** Founded in 1852, Washington Hebrew (now far away on Massachusetts Ave. NW) was the first Jewish congregation in D.C. The charmingly eclectic building, erected in 1898, attracts a healthy stream of architecture buffs for its hodgepodge of styles: the juxtaposition of the twin-tower stone facade, two shades of brick, and the high silver dome reflects the diversity of faiths that have worshipped here. Although the church does not have any specific tourist program, a knock on the front door may earn you a better view of the stained-glass Star of David and the high dome.

SIGHTS

Two blocks west of the MLK library, the **National Museum of Women in the Arts,** 1250 New York Ave. NW (783-5000; Metro: Metro Center) exhibits the work of women artists in a former Masonic Temple. (See **Museums & Galleries,** p. 203.)

Just west of the NMWA, **New York Ave. Presbyterian Church,** at New York Ave., H St., and 13th St. NW (393-3700), displays relics of Abraham Lincoln's history (Metro: Metro Center). In a meeting room one floor below the sanctuary, Lincoln's failed proposal to compensate states that freed their slaves hangs above the settee where he drafted it. A room next door holds letters from Mary Lincoln to the church's then-Rev. Gurley. Seventeen Presidents have worshipped here. Modern Presidents who attended services here, including Carter and Reagan, have preferred to sit where Lincoln did. (Tours given Tues.-Sun. 9am-5pm, but visitors are always welcome.)

ALONG 14TH AND 15TH ST.

Washington's branch of the **National Aquarium,** the nation's first, cowers in the basement of the Commerce Department building, at 14th St. and Constitution Ave. NW (482-2825; Metro: Federal Triangle; enter on 14th St.). Children may stare contemplatively at the 60-odd small tanks of exotic sea creatures and delight in the "touch tanks." The saltwater fishes' vibrant colors and wild shapes (some flat as pancakes, others round as marbles) are mesmerizing. Visitors can also see the obese catfish, the four lumbering sharks (non-vegetarian, man-eating variety), and the disappointingly petite American alligators. Electric eels are disturbingly Frankenstein-esque, with skin that appears to be "stitched." Models and placards make the aquarium easy to understand. This National Aquarium is less sophisticated, and less spectacular than the one in Baltimore; many tanks are empty and the fish somehow less profound. The Aquarium was "set free" from government funds in 1982, and now depends on private donations—fed to the hungry clam at the exit—for maintenance.

(Open daily 9am-5pm. Feedings at 2pm daily: sharks Mon., Wed., Sat.; piranhas Tues., Thurs., Sun. Admission $2, children 2-10 yrs. and seniors 75¢.)

The renovated **Willard Hotel** (628-9100, fax 637-7326) spreads its silver finery over 1401 Pennsylvania Ave. NW like an engraved announcement of its century-old marriage to the rich and influential. President Grant hung out in the hotel's carpeted, chandeliered lobby, where office- and favor-seekers came to plead their cases. Ever since then, the Washington representatives of companies and causes have been called **"lobbyists."** (Now you know.) The din of suited people making deals in the lobby testifies to the fact that some things never change.

Next to Freedom Plaza, **Pershing Park** provides the corner of Pennsylvania Ave. and 15th St. NW with a refreshing pool. A statue of General John "Black Jack" Pershing, leader of U.S. forces in World War I, stands triumphant among marble slabs whose blue and pink tracings map his battles. Today the General's battle sights are a haven for youth on skateboards.

Old Downtown ends at 15th St. NW with the **Treasury Building,** a Greek Revival monolith with all the charm of an iceberg. Grim and portentous, it casts a shadow over a particularly complicated snarl of traffic. Adding insult to injury, its north wing breaks the long arm of Pennsylvania Ave. and blocks the White House from view. The stone-faced statue of Alexander Hamilton (America's first Secretary of the Treasury) offers no consolation. (To reach the President's residence, walk north along 15th St. one block until Pennsylvania Ave. reappears.) The building's imposing presence in the corporate end of Old Downtown is a constant reminder to big businesses that no matter how much money they make, the government will always have more.

White House Area and Foggy Bottom

Metro: McPherson Square; Foggy Bottom-GWU.
Before the Civil War, when most of Washington remained undeveloped, the White House anchored its own neighborhood: socialite circles and Cabinet secretaries liked to live around Lafayette Square, across from the President's House, or slightly farther up 16th St. NW. Since World War II, development on all sides has turned the White House from a center into a boundary: the blocks it occupies separate lawyer-laden Farragut to the north, government-lumbered Old Downtown to the east, Foggy Bottom to the west, and the Mall south of the Ellipse.

Though unscrupulous writers claim all of D.C. was "built on a swamp," only Foggy Bottom can truthfully carry that banner. The misty, low-lying swamp air gave the neighborhood its name before it was absorbed by heavy industry (and its fog-resembling pollutants) in the early 20th century. During World War II, while industrial contraction and government expansion swept manufacturing out of Northwest, the State Department took up quarters here at 23rd and C St. NW. Just as "the Pentagon" means the Defense Department, "Foggy Bottom" has become journalese for State; the neighborhood's old name now suggests the intellectual fog and diplomatic doublespeak in which the State Department indulges. Today's Foggy Bottom rolls from 15th St. NW to the Potomac River, and from I St. to Constitution Ave. New Hampshire Ave., Pennsylvania Ave., K St. NW, and 23rd St. NW all meet at **Washington Circle,** where ol' George is situated on his horse. Near the Mall, government departments butt headquarters with old, respectable organizations in an unbroken sprawl of gardens, columns, and statuary. Above F St., George Washington University competes for breathing room with hotels and moderately priced townhouses. Farther east, the low-rise office buildings of Farragut edge closer and closer to their target in the White House.

THE WHITE HOUSE

The White House, at 1600 Pennsylvania Ave. NW (456-7041, TDD 456-6213), isn't Versailles; the President's house, with its simple columns and expansive lawns, seems a compromise between patrician lavishness and democratic simplicity. In 1792 Thomas Jefferson proposed a contest to design the President's residence. Jefferson's own diagrams lost out to James Hoban's more regal plan when then-President George Washington judged the competition. The National Building Museum's exhibit on Washington as symbol and city describes the debate (see **Museums & Galleries,** page 198). John Adams was the first chief executive to live in Hoban's structure, and Jefferson himself became the first to build additions. All this work was ruined when the British burned down the house, and much of D.C., in 1814; First Lady Dolly Madison interrupted her dinner to flee the flames, taking with her one of Gilbert Stuart's famous portraits of Washington. The White House has boasted wheelchair access since at least 1933, when FDR, who needed it, took office. (He also installed a swimming pool.) Martin Van Buren, who fenced off the lawns, started keeping the White House gardens spic-and-span; 120 years later, Jacqueline Kennedy made the Rose Garden famous, spurring later journalists to call Gerald Ford's stay-at-home reelection effort the "Rose Garden Campaign" in 1976. (Voters, who never did promise him a Rose Garden, replaced Ford with Jimmy Carter.)

Despite remodelings in 1902 and 1948, the central third of the Executive Mansion looks more or less as Hoban planned it (he didn't design the East and West Wings). The White House is home to press conferences, state receptions, busloads of security guards, and even the occasional Presidential nap. When the President is in town, an American flag flies over his house. The President's personal staff works on his speeches and schedules and such in the West Wing, while the First Lady's cohort occupies the East Wing. The President does his own paperwork in (and sometimes makes televised speeches from) the famous Oval Office. Helicopters land on the White House lawn to whisk him away to conferences and vacations. One façade stays floodlit all night for the benefit of TV news reporters. Big lawns, fences, long driveways, and closed gates discourage terrorists; if you wait long enough, however, you may be rewarded with a glimpse of the residents through the bushes.

You may **tour** certain rooms at the White House after obtaining a free ticket at the **White House Visitors Center,** 1450 Pennsylvania Ave. NW, at the corner of 15th and E St. (Disabled visitors can go straight to the Pennsylvania Ave. entrance without a ticket.) After you get a ticket, you'll wait about 2½ hours for the tour (tours Tues.-Sat. 10am-noon; tickets distributed starting at 7:30am). American citizens can arrange a more comprehensive and intimate tour of the White House through their Congresspeople; write or call your Congressperson several months in advance.

The regular (non-Congressional) tour is guarded, but unguided; you might try posing your questions to the Secret Service guards. You'll start on the ground floor of the East Wing; the **lobby** here contains a portrait of the late Jacqueline Kennedy Onassis with roses and a sign saying "In Memoriam." The **China Room** charters the changes in American taste and style through a display of the long succession of presidential china. The **Diplomatic Reception Room** is notable for its wallpaper: Jackie Kennedy, well-known for her preservational instincts, practically ran out in front of the wrecking ball to salvage it from a derelict mansion. Upstairs, the **East Room** has been used for the wakes of those presidents who died in office. It also hosted Abigail Adams' clothesline, Susan Ford's senior prom, and Teddy Roosevelt's favorite boxing and wrestling matches, and now houses the portrait of Washington that Dolly Madison so heroically saved. The **Blue Room,** said to be the White House's most beautiful, frequently receives ambassadors paying their first formal visits to the president. The furniture set, purchased by President Monroe, is not complete; a later president thought it was ugly and sold it off. Furniture-savior Jackie Kennedy found the sofa in a garage in Georgetown. The **Red Room** is red; it also displays a painting of Philadelphia's Independence Hall that was once lost, then recovered (not, this time, by Jackie Kennedy) in Bombay, India, where it sold for $7. The **State Dining Room** entertains large groups of guests, such as the Queen of England and her entourage. Its gold and white elegance served hunter Theodore Roosevelt when he mounted his trophies there. An obsolete bomb shelter under the Treasury building, built during World War II, connects to the White House by a tunnel under the East Lawn; aides in-the-know use the tunnel as a quick exit to 15th St. NW. The White House can be reached from anywhere downtown by walking towards 16th St. NW along Pennsylvania Ave. (Metro: McPherson Square, Vermont Ave. exit.)

Near the White House

Due south of the White House, the empty grass of the **Ellipse** sometimes fills up with political demonstrators or congregating tour groups. A small granite shaft in the Ellipse bears the names of the 18 landowners who gave up their plantations for the sake of D.C.'s construction. Directly in front of the White House, where the green grass meets E St. NW, Washington's Zero Milestone provides tangible evidence of early surveyors.

Sometimes it's hard to tell the homeless, the political demonstrators, and the statues apart in **Lafayette Park,** across Pennsylvania Ave., north of the White House. All three are more-or-less permanent presences, assuming various stances that exude defiance, triumph, and grief. Clark Mills' stone-faced Andrew Jackson stands in the center of the park. All of Jackson's companion statues represent Revolutionary War heroes, reminders that the U.S. could not have won its independence without help from foreign lands. The Marquis de Lafayette joined Jackson in 1891, on the southeast (15th and Pennsylvania) corner of the park. A half-dressed woman (France?) hands him his sword. (An old joke has the lady saying, "Give me back my clothes, and I'll give you back your sword.") At the southwest corner of the park, notice Lady Liberty brandishing her sword and—oops!—nearly stabbing the American Eagle to death. Although the eagle jumps back with a screech and a squawk, Lafayette's compatriot Rochambeau doesn't notice: he's too busy pointing to the southwest. Polish Brigadier Thaddeus Kosciuszko, who fortified West Point and Saratoga for the Continental Army, defends the northeast corner, and Baron Von Steuben, who trained American troops at Valley Forge, drills pedestrians from the northwest corner (and looks like a cross between John Wayne and Elvis).

St. John's Church, at 16th and H St. NW (347-8766), at the north end of Lafayette Park, is known as the Church of Presidents; each one since Madison has dropped in at least once. The ubiquitous Benjamin Latrobe (of U.S. Capitol fame) designed it for free; look for his half-moon windows. President Clinton sometimes attends the 8:30am service (open daily 9am-3pm; tour after Sun. service).

Though Benjamin Latrobe designed it, **Decatur House,** 748 Jackson Place NW at the west end of Lafayette Park (842-0920; enter on H St.) retains mostly historical interest. (Metro: Farragut West or Farragut North.) Naval hero Stephen Decatur, the navy's youngest captain ever, defeated the Barbary Pirates and captured the top British frigate during the war of 1812 before he moved in; after only one year in his new house, Decatur died in a duel with a former military mentor. During the 1830s and '40s, hotelier John Gadsby entertained Washington's elite in the ballrooms while he kept slaves chained behind the house. In 1871 the house was purchased by Edward Beale, best remembered for having carried official news of the Gold Rush to Washington in a frontiersman disguise. The Beales were responsible for most of the later improvements to the house, including the elegant inlaid floors and "Romantic eclectic" furnishing (in evidence in the upper drawing room). The first floor, decorated in the Federal style, displays Decatur's furnishings, carefully selected to impress. The salon has big windows and a tiny fireplace, but it was well heated in the winter during cocktail hour, then called "crush or squeeze." Tours of the house last about 40 minutes. (Open Tues.-Fri. 10am-3pm, Sat.-Sun. noon-4pm. Admission $4; seniors, students, and children $2.50.)

Blair House, 1651-53 Pennsylvania Ave. NW, near the southwest corner of Lafayette Park, hosts foreign dignitaries who visit Washington; Secret Service agents and diplomatic limousines mean one's in town. President Harry Truman lived here during White House renovations; a plaque on the wrought-iron gates remembers a guard who saved him from a would-be assassin by "taking a bullet." The house is not open to the public.

On the same block, the **Renwick Gallery of the National Museum of American Art,** at 17th St. and Pennsylvania Ave. NW, devotes itself to "American craft," an

A Capital Paradox

Sign-toting demonstrators used to congregate on the White House side of Pennsylvania Ave. until the Secret Service punted them across the street. But during 1995, a number of bizarre breaches in security (one man crashed a plane into the White House; one fired a gun at the President's home; several people hopped the fence and made it onto the White House lawn before being restrained by Secret Servicemen) led to tighter security measures. Pennsylvania Ave. is now closed to commercial traffic. The plan was to reroute the masses away from the White House, but paradoxically the masses have inched even closer. Protesters and tourists now crowd the street up to the gates of the White House (exactly the opposite of what was intended). The plan did benefit someone, however—Bob Dole has made the unsuccess into a '96 campaign issue.

amazingly broad artistic category which includes all manner of original, off-beat objects. The building was designed by James Renwick, Jr., (also the architect of the Smithsonian Castle) in the style of the French Second Empire. Two rooms, the Octagon Room and the Grand Salon, are furnished in the styles of the 1860s and '70s; most of the furniture belonged to Richard Rush, a Smithsonian regent who personally carried James Smithson's 105 gold sovereign bequest from England to the United States (see **Museums & Galleries,** p. 201).

The **Old Executive Office Building,** at 17th St. and Pennsylvania Ave. NW, amazes pedestrians with its gingerbread complexity; President Truman called it "the greatest monstrosity in America." Cascades of small plain columns, tall chimneys, pediments, porches, and an endless array of mini-colonnades give the Second Empire-styled building its Baroque distinction. Cannons flank the entrance steps. The building continues to house White House staff, therefore tours are only given on Saturdays. However, gilded domes, frilly balustrades, and the Indian treaty room's marble wall panels, 800-pound bronze lamps, and gold ornamentation are worth any scheduling inconvenience. The ornate front side is currently obscured by scaffolding, as extensive roof renovation is underway (to be completed in 1997). To schedule a free tour, call 395-5895 a few weeks in advance.

WEST OF THE ELLIPSE

The **Organization of American States,** at 17th St. and Constitution Ave. NW (Metro: Farragut West), across the street from the southwest corner of the Ellipse (information 458-3000, museum/gallery 458-6016), is a Latin American extravaganza: dappled sunlight engulfs its air-conditioned center, where a fountain gurgles over greenery. The patio's tiles copy traditional pre-Colombian designs. During parades, the OAS locks up so that would-be snipers have no opportunity to take advantage of its strategic rooftop position.

The OAS's main-floor art gallery is small but fresh, displaying 20th-century art from Central and South America. Upstairs are the OAS **meeting rooms,** which hold formal sessions. The meetings, held largely in Spanish, welcome curious tourists; non-Spanish-speakers can hook up to translation machines. (Call to ask when they're in session.) Open rooms afford views of grand Tiffany chandeliers and ornately reliefed ceilings, while the **Hall of the Americas** (more of a pleasant open-air atrium than a hall), parades the flags of the OAS member nations and busts of their founders. The flags hang in alphabetical order according to their nations' Spanish names. Downstairs and outside, the God of Flowers, Xochipilli, whom the Aztecs honored with hallucinogenic feasts and sacrificial frenzies, reclines in the **Aztec Garden.** The garden path leads to the **Museum of the Americas,** a collection of art from Mexico, Peru, Brazil, and other member states. The two-story building houses a permanent collection of modern art, as well as several temporary exhibits. (OAS open Mon.-Fri. 9am-5pm; museum open Tues.-Sat. 10am-5pm. Free.)

If you can find the entrance at 1776 D St. NW, the **Daughters of the American Revolution Museum** (628-1776) will open historical doors for you—more than 33, in fact. (Metro: Farragut West, then walk south on 17th St.) The building complex is the largest block of buildings in the world entirely owned, operated, and payed for by women. A docent will show you the Beaux-Arts Memorial Centennial Hall's 33 period rooms—each room was conceived, designed, and furnished by the DARs of a different state to illuminate early American lifestyles. New Jersey's room, for instance, is furnished with the remains of a sunken ship, downed in the Battle of Red Bank. Even the anchor and chain were used; their iron has been transformed into a gargantuan lighting fixture. California's tri-cultural room incorporates Chinese vases, Mexican serapes, and American horsehair furniture. The cavernous library is now a home for books on genealogy; it once hosted the first meeting ever on the subject of arms limitation (after World War I). The DAR insignia (hanging over the obligatory portrait of George Washington) was made from a cannonball from the Battle of Saratoga. Call the DAR's Education Office for a guided tour. (Museum open Mon.-Fri. 8:30am-4pm, Sun. 1-5pm. Tours Mon.-Fri. 10am-2:30pm, Sun. 1-4:30pm. Free. Library open Mon.-Fri. 9am-4pm. Entrance for the disabled at 1775 C St.)

Adjoining the building is **Constitution Hall,** located on 18th St. between C and D St. NW (638-2661). This 4000-seat auditorium hosts concerts and ceremonies, and is also where the DAR's President General presides over her Continental Congress. Draped from the box sections of the U-shaped amphitheater are the buff and blue of the DAR State seals. Tapestries of Revolutionary moments, like the Boston Tea Party and George Washington's inauguration, dangle over the stage. The stage has been used for patriotic purposes and civic occasions, though it's most famous for an unpatriotic one: in 1939 the DAR wouldn't let African-American soprano Marian Anderson sing here, so she sang instead from the steps of the Lincoln Memorial.

The **American Red Cross,** at 17th and E St. NW (737-8300), looks out of Tiffany stained-glass windows that deserve a look. Inside the east building's bronze doors, a receptionist will point you first to a video on CPR, then up the marble staircase, where Hiram Powers' busts of Faith, Hope, and Charity reside. In the second-floor assembly room, Louis Tiffany's stained glass portrays figures from Spenser's *Faerie Queene:* Filomena, virtuous Una, and of course, Redcrosse the knight (open Mon.-Fri. 9am-4pm; free).

Once housed in the Renwick's mansion, the **Corcoran Gallery of Art,** Washington's oldest art museum, now displays works by the likes of Thomas Cole and Roy Lichtenstein in much larger, Neoclassical quarters on 17th St. between E St. and New York Ave. NW, just north of the Red Cross building. The gallery's building is considered one the country's best examples of Beaux-Arts architecture and houses American art from colonial times to the present, as well as European painting and sculpture. (Metro: Farragut West. See **Museums & Galleries,** p. 203.)

Perched on a corner and shadowed by the American Institute of Architects (AIA) building that semi-encircles it, **The Octagon,** 1799 New York Ave. NW at 18th St. (638-3105), continues the Foggy Bottom tradition of obscuring historic houses with office buildings. (Metro: Farragut West; walk down 18th St.) Arrive at the right moment and an expert will guide you around the house. The Madisons fled here when British troops torched the White House in 1814; they spared the Octagon, probably because the French ambassador flew his nation's flag over the house. Despite its name, the house is hexagonal; a tower in one corner interrupts its geometry. The table on which the Treaty of Ghent was signed is here; it's a curious furnishing, with 12 ivory-inlaid drawers marked "receipts," "bills paid," and "letters." A suicidal slave girl, Colonel Taylor's daughter, and Dolly Madison are some of the ghosts said to roam the Octagon. On display in the cellar is a collection of artifacts uncovered by recent excavations, including a colonial rangetop. The Octagon also houses temporary exhibits; recently it presented displays on the innovations of architect Bruce Goff. (Open Tues.-Sun. 10am-4pm. Admission $3, seniors and students $1.50.) Exhibits continue in the modern AIA building behind The Octagon, and the **AIA Bookstore** is worth a visit (open Mon.-Wed. and Fri. 8:30am-5pm, Thurs. 8:30am-6:30pm).

The **Department of the Interior** (208-4743) covers a square area on C St. NW between 18th and 19th and extends to D St. Franklin Roosevelt laid the cornerstone for the building in 1936, using the same trowel that George Washington employed to lay the Capitol's cornerstone in 1793. The National Park Service desk spews helpful brochures about forests and outfitters. Sign in and present ID to a guard at the main entrance on 18th and C St. and walk down the hallway. To the right is the park office; to the left is the Interior Department's museum. Enter here to learn how to make a topographic map, look at fossils, and follow dioramas portraying the "opening" of the American West. (Museum open Mon.-Fri. 8am-5pm.)

The **Federal Reserve** counts its change in a heavy-set, clean-lined building on Constitution Ave. between 20th and 21st St. NW. The Federal Reserve Board and its head, Alan Greenspan, control the nation's money supply; they decide how much dough there should be and what interest rates major banks should pay when they borrow it. The actual greenbacks sleep in regional banks in Boston, New York, Cleveland, Dallas, and San Francisco (among other cities); this building is just where the board meets and has its offices, and where some economic research takes place. Paul Cret's skimpy temple to Mammon has the settled, staid look of established wealth. An eagle on the lintel oversees the hundreds of square feet of flatness (and hundreds of rollerbladers) in front.

The **National Academy of Sciences,** at 21st and C St. NW (enter on Constitution Ave.; 334-2000), has a lot of really smart people. It also holds space for art exhibits, and a fantastic heliocentric gold-tiled dome decorated with ancient Greek philosophical figures. Dangling from its center is a bizarre pendulum swinging over an Egyptian-inspired pedestal. When all of this starts to lose its goofy novelty, ask the guard at the front desk to slide aside the massive bronze doors to reveal eight panels, each of which depicts an important scientific personality, from Aristotle to Einstein (open Mon.-Fri. 8:30am-5pm). At the corner of 22nd St. NW and Constitution Ave., the beloved physicist sits above a star map: the 28-ft. field of emerald pearl granite holds metal studs that represent the planets, sun, moon, and stars. Einstein's aphorisms are carved on the back of his bench. (Note: the man who formulated the Theory of Relativity seems to be wearing Tevas.)

Few collections of American furniture and art compare with that of the **State Department,** 21st and C St. (647-3241), whose cement HQ extends to 23rd St. (Metro: Foggy Bottom-GWU.) You must reserve a space on the 45-minute guided tour to see the inside of the State Department. The free tours fill up very quickly; call at least a month in advance. The original walls of the reception rooms were avocado-green, with floor-to-ceiling windows, wall-to-wall carpeting, and exposed steel beams. The undiplomatic decor prompted 1960s Secretary of State Dean Rusk to launch Project Americana, in which the State accumulated Boston highboys and lowboys, Chippendale chairs, paintings of Washington, and other cute items made between 1750 and 1825. There's a portrait of Thomas Jefferson in a toga; a highboy capped by a bust of political thinker John Locke; and the desk where Thomas Jefferson wrote the Declaration of Independence and Nixon signed Constitutional Amendment #26, giving 18-year-olds the right to vote. The Benjamin Franklin dining room makes a spectacle of itself in mauve and gold; the French carpet took a whole weekend to lay. (Tours of diplomatic reception rooms Mon.-Fri. 9:30, 10:30am, and 2:45pm; call for reservations. Strollers not permitted. "Tour not recommended for children under 12.")

Foggy Bottom north of F St. is the province of **George Washington University** (994-4949). The Visitor Center desk in the Academic Center, at 801 22nd St. NW (enter at H St.), gives away brochures, newspapers, and *The Big To Do*, an entertainment calendar. Dance, theater, and music flourish at GWU's Lisner Auditorium, while the school-spirited cheer for the Colonials basketball teams.

Across G St. NW from the Kennedy Center, at the western end of Virginia Ave., the looming black-and-white half-cylinders of the **Watergate** buildings (offices, apartments, and a luxury hotel) seem to bend away from the White House, toward the Potomac River. The Watergate scandal took its name from these buildings—the office space housed the Democratic National Committee's headquarters when Nixon ordered them burgled in 1972.

THE KENNEDY CENTER

Above Rock Creek Parkway, the white rectilinear **John F. Kennedy Center for the Performing Arts** (tickets and information 467-4600, TDD 416-8524) rises and glows like a marble sarcophagus. (Metro: Foggy Bottom-GWU, then walk away from downtown on H St. and turn left, or south, onto New Hampshire Ave.; pedestrian entrance off 25th St. at the end of New Hampshire Ave. NW.) Built in the late 1960s, the center boasts four major stages and a film theater; its sumptuous interior rolls out wall-to-wall red carpets under mirrors, bronze busts, and crystal chandeliers. Many nations have donated rooms, free-standing art, and other materials in memory of JFK. Student tickets, sometimes well-discounted, make taking in a show here possible on most budgets. Before entering the Kennedy Center, stop at the parking lot to marvel at A. Teno's 1976 contorted statue of Don Quixote. Stop again to view Jurgen Weber's bronze reliefs, located outside the east ends of the Hall of Nations and Hall of States, respectively (see below).

Almost everything in the Kennedy Center has a self-explanatory name. State flags hang in the **Hall of States** in the order in which they joined the Union. There is an **Information Desk** just inside the entrance, and the **American Film Institute Theater** is on the right (for more on the theater, see **Movies,** p. 222). The west end of the Hall lends equipment for the hearing impaired (free). In the **Hall of Nations,** the flags of all nations with which the U.S. has diplomatic relations hang in alphabetical order. Both grand halls lead to the **Grand Foyer,** which could swallow the Washington Monument with room to spare. A rather unsavory 7-ft. bronze bust of JFK stares up at 18 ponderous Swedish chandeliers.

In the **Concert Hall,** an audience of 2750 can hear up to 200 classical musicians. The President's box includes a reception room and a banner with his seal, which hangs from the balcony when he deigns to attend. The impressive organ has over 4144 pipes. The stage was a gift from over 692 high school, college, and community organizations from the U.S., Canada, Britain, and Japan. In return, the stage frequently hosts high school and youth ensembles, giving them the opportunity to perform in a major venue; free concerts and children's performances are also offered. The National Symphony Orchestra calls the KenCen Concert Hall home. Visitors kick back in the **Israeli Lounge** on the Box Tier of the Concert Hall (that means just outside it and up the stairs). The lounge's vivid turquoise, red, yellow, and olive ceiling depicts musical instruments. Admire the Hebrew message inlaid (in 24-carat gold) in the wooden wall mosaic; intricate sepia sketches adorn the other walls. Carved from a 700-year-old tree, 12-ft.-high, intricate Nigerian doors lead into the **African Room.** Tapestries, ornate bowls, print cloth, and reliefs show off the continent's traditions.

If rehearsals are not in progress, you may visit the opulent, all-red **Opera House** and sink your feet into its plush velvet carpet. Snowflake-shaped chandeliers, gifts from Austria, cover a 70-ft.-diameter circular space and require 1735 electric light bulbs. Japan's more sensible gift, the red silk curtain, adds to the grandeur. A Waterford crystal chandelier, with 4000 perfectly matched prisms, hangs from 22-carat gold-leaf ceiling panels in the **South Opera Lounge.** This lounge also holds two handwoven Spanish tapestries, copies of paintings by Goya. When red turns to purple on the roof level, you're near the **Terrace Theater,** an acoustic marvel and home to an excellent chamber-music series. Art scattered about the center's levels ranges from blast-damaged sheet metal polished to a glow to tapestries depicting the seven days of creation. Greece donated a bronze casting of a statue discovered beneath the Aegean Sea. Henri Matisse designed France's gift, a set of blue-and-white tapestries.

The **Eisenhower Theatre** is the smallest of the main-floor theaters, seating only 1100 people. The steep angle at which the seats—which are made of East Indian laurel wood—meet the stage can be somewhat unnerving. Comic operas, Classical Greek plays, and small productions are performed here.

The Roof Terrace Restaurant would bankrupt almost anyone, though a walk along the outdoor **roof terrace** is free. Unfortunately for acrophiles, the roof and other portions of the building are undergoing renovations (to be completed mid-1997). Generally, the roof offers unbeatable views of the Watergate complex, the Gothic spires of Georgetown, and Roosevelt Island.

Excellent disabled access includes provisions for sight- and hearing-impaired audience members; all theaters are wheelchair-accessible. (Center open daily 10am-midnight. Free tours 10am-1pm, every 15min. Parking in the commercial basement lot available for short- and long-term visits. Parking for events demands a flat rate of $8. Half-hour parking available before 6pm, free with purchase of a ticket for a Kennedy Center event.)

Georgetown

The heights in this neighborhood, above the Potomac River, are very picturesque and are free, I should conceive, from some of the insalubrities of Washington.

—Charles Dickens, American Notes (1842)

Metroless: closest stations are Foggy Bottom-GWU and Dupont Circle (both followed by a 15-min. walk).

At once residential and commercial, bustling Georgetown offers a much-needed respite to those wearied by the gleaming white halls of power and colossal monuments that are Washington's tourist industry staples. Two-by-four restaurants and overpriced shops, rowdy saloons, and a smattering of nightclubs crowd together along Wisconsin Avenue and M Street NW, anxious for the patronage of tourists, students, and Georgetown's upscale locals alike. To the west, Georgetown University students study and quaff kegs a mere bus ride away from the residence of their alma mater's most famous alumnus, Bill Clinton (class of '68). Georgetown serves its eponymous university well, obliging students with all-night food and late-night record stores, international newspapers and magazines, and easy access to the bastion of bureaucracy just over the Pennsylvania Ave. bridge.

Bustling during the day, Georgetown at night becomes a kaleidoscopic fête of cruising scenesters. Walk M St. or Wisconsin Ave. on a summer Saturday night to appreciate that peculiar brand of skin-tight Georgetown glamour which owes more to Miami Beach than to Washington.

Residential Georgetown is a genteel neighborhood with brick-lined streets and sweeping trees, placid and distant from the rapid pace of worldly Washington. Close-set townhouses respectfully defer to gracious mansions; privacy is protected by hedge barriers and ivy. Though increasingly withdrawn from public display, a slow Southern way of life has carried on here since the Federal period. The young and hip, the fashionable and powerful, may fly from one trendy area to the next, but old historic Georgetown endures.

In 1702 Queen Anne of England granted the "Rock of Dumbarton," a huge tract of land, to Ninian Beall. By the 1730s the Beall family was complaining to the colonial government about "squatters" on its land at the edge of the Potomac. The "squatters"—Scottish merchants—founded the town of George, after George II of England. The town was incorporated in 1789, the year of the inauguration of Georgetown University. The port brought the new town commerce and people; as the farthest point up the Potomac to which a ship could travel, Georgetown proved ideal for the sorting and shipping of tobacco from Virginia and Maryland. Incidentally, not until the 1800s were the Bealls fully paid for their land.

Georgetown has been referred to as the "parent of the Federal City" since Suter's Tavern (a no-longer-extant local watering hole), was thought to have hosted George Washington and his cohorts as they negotiated the establishment of a capital city. (The same pub was later used by Pierre L'Enfant and Andrew Elicott when the two were laying out plans for the Capital.)

As the only existing town within the District's limits, Georgetown was the logical hangout for Washington's first bigwigs—while much of central Washington remained unbuilt, Georgetown prospered. Most of its Federal-style buildings were erected between 1780 and 1830, when the port was thriving. You can still distinguish the smaller townhouses below Dumbarton St., built for the workers, from the larger houses of upper Georgetown (around R and S St.). This historically prestigious area, previously known as "Georgetown Heights," is now called "Old Georgetown" and has been designated as a national historic district.

Georgetown's incarnation as a harbor town was colorful but short-lived. Trade and exports had increased dramatically after the revolution; growth in entertainment and lodgings attracted travelers. The town became so busy that in 1790 the town fathers had to ban free-running pigs and chickens from the streets. In 1828 President John Quincy Adams turned the first shovelful of dirt for the Chesapeake & Ohio (C&O) Canal. However, the same day that Adams opened the canal dig, workers in Baltimore drove the first spike for the Baltimore and Ohio Railroad, whose steam-driven efficiency KO'd the C&O as a commercial route. Although the canal still thrived in the 1870s, steamships of the following decade couldn't fit into the harbor; after an 1889 flood, ports such as those in Baltimore and Norfolk—not to mention Southwest Washington—rendered Georgetown's harbor obsolete. The canal survives as part of the national park system; long-winded bicyclists have replaced barge-pulling mules along its towpaths.

Washington's free Black population nearly doubled between 1830 and 1861: D.C.'s first Black congregation, the still-active Mt. Zion United Methodist Church, was also an Underground Railroad station for slaves on their way to a free Canada. Yet, despite its proximity to the Union capital, White Georgetown was a determinedly Confederate city during the Civil War, buzzing with Southern spies.

As Georgetown's economy faltered, working-class Black families took quarters in historic mansions subdivided into apartments. Employed as domestics, cooks, and stable attendants to the remaining estates, more than 1000 families occupied "Herring Hill" (south of P St. between Rock Creek Park and 29th St.), so called because residents subsisted on fish from the harbor. In the early 20th century Georgetown was racially integrated and unfashionable; the first Washington zoning act labeled it "industrial." But when FDR's New Deal (masterminded by his "Brain Trust" at 3238 R Street) and World War II nearly doubled the number of federal jobs, the new white-collar (and white) civil servants invaded Georgetown. Black families sold their homes, and African-American culture moved downtown.

Today only the rich can afford the inflated real estate, and only the chic feel the need to do so, though lately the neighborhood has been more prestigious than popular. The history of those who have resided in Georgetown is indicative of the shifting political winds; John F. Kennedy lived here as a U.S. Senator (at 3260 N St.), as did Senator John Warner and his wife Liz Taylor. A smattering of rent-controlled apartments around Georgetown are inhabited largely by the unmonied; some of the townhouses between M St. and R St. have been subdivided and rented out to Georgetown University students and gaggles of interns, though others nearby may hide lovely inner courtyards and Warhols in every bathroom. Hollywood has found the area's geography interesting, if not irresistible: movies set partly in Georgetown include *The Exorcist* and *St. Elmo's Fire.*

ORIENTATION

Wisconsin Ave. and **M St.** are the main thoroughfares, and their intersection (Washington's oldest) centers the neighborhood. Address numbers on Wisconsin Ave. start below M St. and go up as the avenue goes north (in this area, uphill). Numbered streets run parallel to Wisconsin and perpendicular to M, increasing east to west. For most of its Georgetown length, K St. is directly under the Whitehurst Freeway and thus hard to find on maps. (At twilight, enjoy the *Blade Runner*-style view of the looming Whitehurst.) East of Georgetown is the K St. Business District and, north of that, the Dupont Circle neighborhood; Rock Creek Park provides a clear boundary. M

SIGHTS

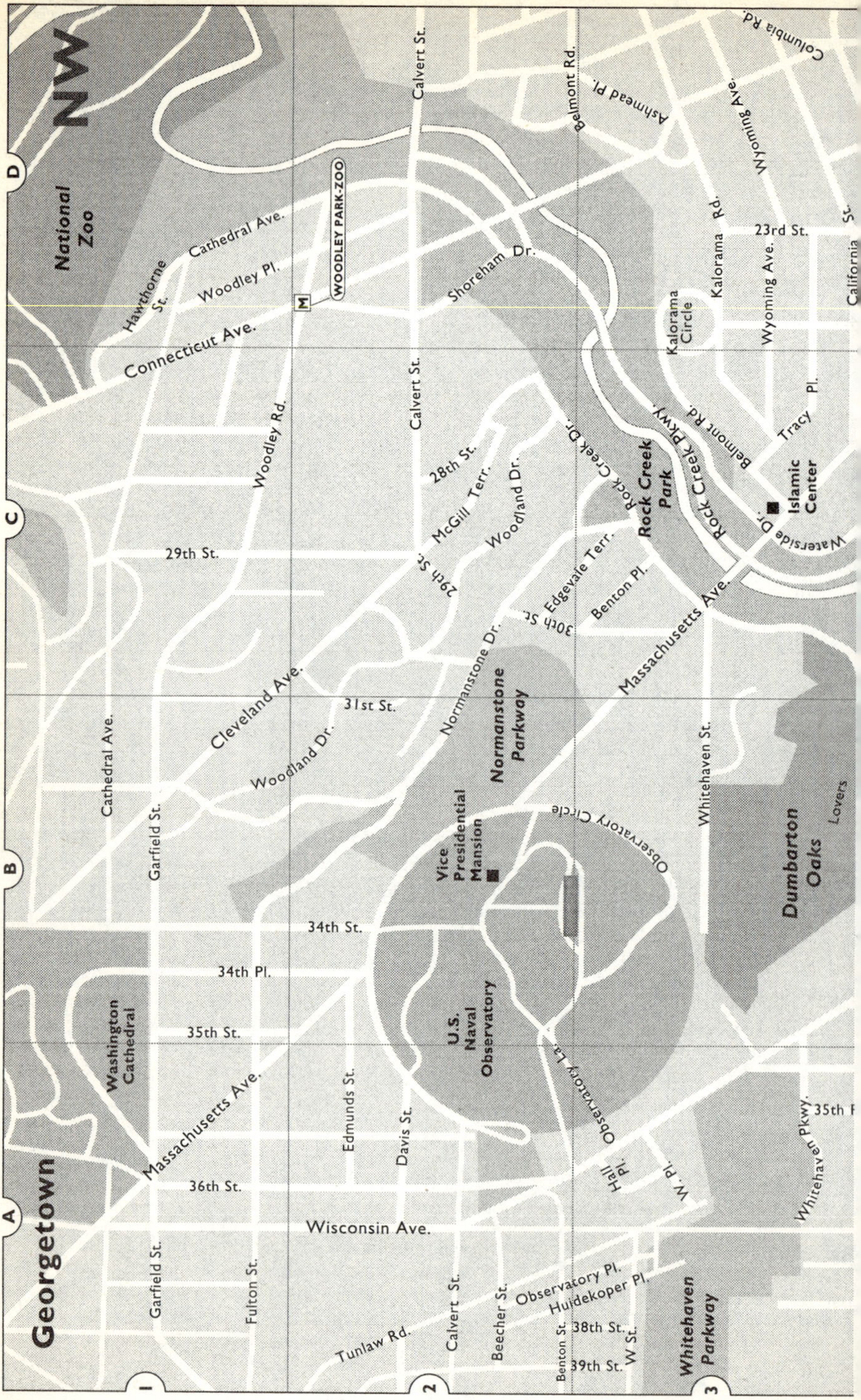

NW
National Zoo
Georgetown
Washington Cathedral
U.S. Naval Observatory
Vice Presidential Mansion
Normanstone Parkway
Rock Creek Park
Dumbarton Oaks
Whitehaven Parkway
Islamic Center
Kalorama Circle
WOODLEY PARK-ZOO
M
Connecticut Ave.
Cathedral Ave.
Woodley Pl.
Hawthorne St.
Shoreham Dr.
Calvert St.
Belmont Rd.
Ashmead Pl.
Columbia Rd.
Wyoming Ave.
Kalorama Rd.
23rd St.
California St.
Tracy Pl.
Waterside Dr.
Rock Creek Pkwy.
Rock Creek Dr.
Woodley Rd.
28th St.
McGill Terr.
Woodland Dr.
29th St.
Edgevale Terr.
30th St.
Benton Pl.
Massachusetts Ave.
Cleveland Ave.
31st St.
Normanstone Dr.
Whitehaven St.
Lovers
Observatory Circle
Garfield St.
34th St.
34th Pl.
35th St.
Edmunds St.
Davis St.
Observatory La.
Hall Pl.
W. Pl.
35th Pl.
Whitehaven Pkwy.
36th St.
Wisconsin Ave.
Fulton St.
Tunlaw Rd.
Calvert St.
Beecher St.
Observatory Pl.
Huidekoper Pl.
38th St.
Benton St.
W St.
39th St.
A
B
C
D
1
2
3

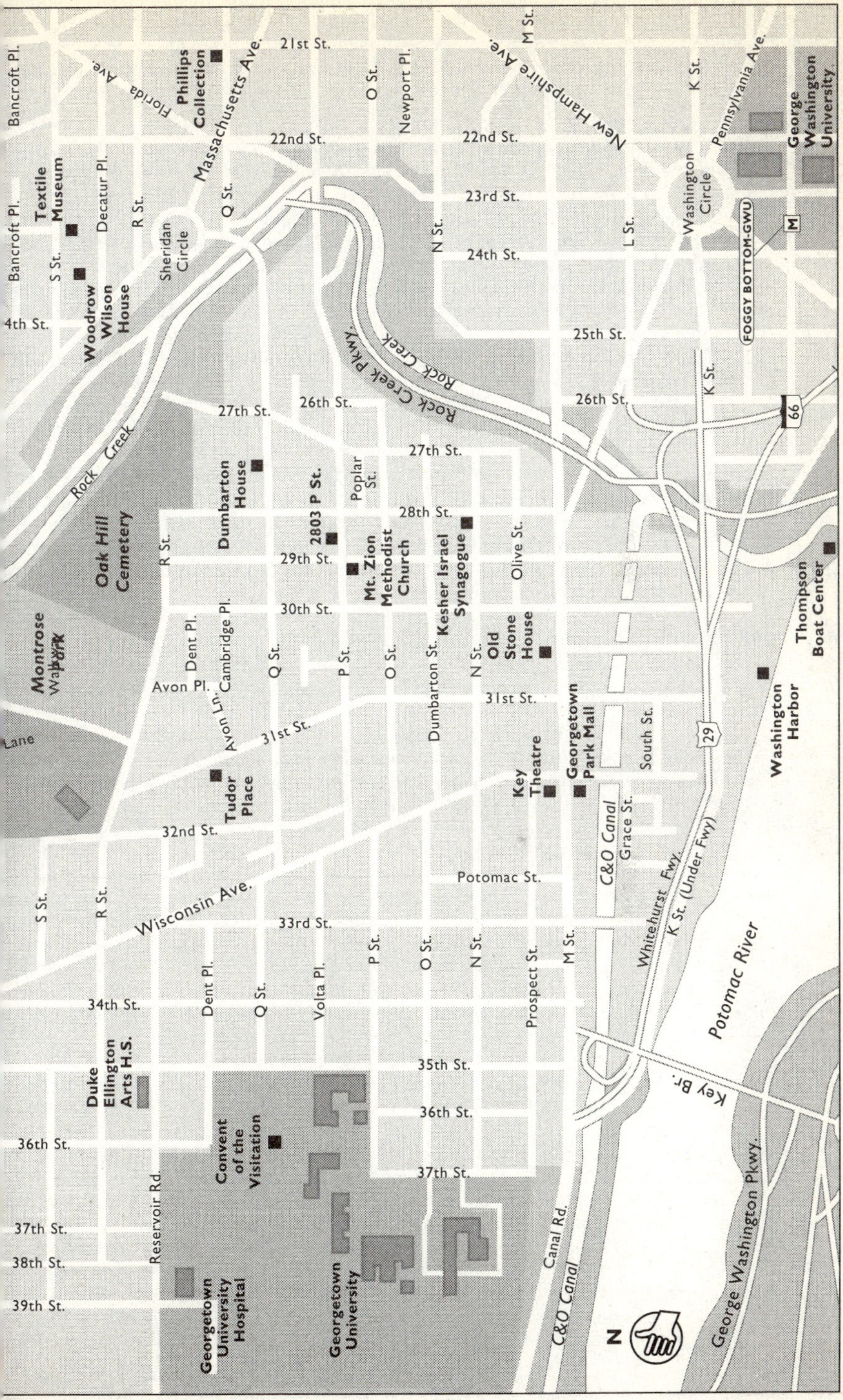
Phillips Collection
Textile Museum
Woodrow Wilson House
Sheridan Circle
Massachusetts Ave.
Florida Ave.
New Hampshire Ave.
Pennsylvania Ave.
Washington Circle
George Washington University
FOGGY BOTTOM-GWU
M
Rock Creek
Rock Creek Pkwy.
Oak Hill Cemetery
Montrose Park
Dumbarton House
2803 P St.
Mt. Zion Methodist Church
Kesher Israel Synagogue
Old Stone House
Tudor Place
Key Theatre
Georgetown Park Mall
Washington Harbor
Thompson Boat Center
C&O Canal
Whitehurst Fwy.
K St. (Under Fwy)
Potomac River
Key Br.
George Washington Pkwy.
Canal Rd.
Wisconsin Ave.
Duke Ellington Arts H.S.
Convent of the Visitation
Georgetown University Hospital
Georgetown University
Reservoir Rd.
Bancroft Pl.
S St.
Decatur Pl.
R St.
Q St.
P St.
O St.
N St.
M St.
L St.
K St.
Newport Pl.
Poplar St.
Olive St.
Dumbarton St.
Dent Pl.
Cambridge Pl.
Avon Pl.
Avon Ln.
Volta Pl.
Prospect St.
Potomac St.
Grace St.
South St.
Lane
21st St.
22nd St.
23rd St.
24th St.
25th St.
26th St.
27th St.
28th St.
29th St.
30th St.
31st St.
32nd St.
33rd St.
34th St.
35th St.
36th St.
37th St.
38th St.
39th St.
29
66
N

St., Pennsylvania Ave., P St., and Q St. are the only ways to Georgetown for pedestrians coming from downtown or Dupont Circle. West of Key Bridge, M St. becomes Canal Road (leading to Bethesda, MD), and neon and brick abruptly yield to the trees and vines of Glover Archibold Park.

GETTING THERE

If you try to **park** your car in Georgetown, you may not have time to do anything else—weekends are particularly infamous. Try 35th St. near the university (particularly promising in summer), farther north around R and S streets, or Georgetown's eastern edge on the other side of Wisconsin Ave., around 28th St. Garages are wallet-draining (and frequently full) but are conveniently located near the center of town. On weekend nights, choose a block and drive around in circles, scrounging for a place—raucous teens will miraculously arrive and drive their Mercedes off to the suburbs.

The nearest **Metro** stop, Foggy Bottom-GWU, is about eight long blocks from the center of Georgetown. When you exit the station, you'll find yourself facing 23rd St. NW. Turn left down 23rd and walk clockwise around Washington Circle against traffic until you reach Pennsylvania Ave.; then trudge down Pennsylvania over the bridge and to M St. From Dupont Circle, just follow P St. west, past Rock Creek Park, or, alternatively, walk southwest on New Hampshire Ave. and take a right onto M St. **Metrobuses** #30, 32, 34, 35, and 36 run from M St. up Wisconsin past Dumbarton Oaks and up to the Friendship Heights Metro and the Maryland border. Metrobuses tagged D2 and D4 travel from Union Station to Georgetown via Dupont Circle. From Adams-Morgan, take the #42 bus (at Columbia Rd.) to Dupont Circle, then switch to the #G2 bus (at 20th and P St.) to Georgetown.

No Way Down

When Kevin Costner, in the movie *No Way Out,* escaped Pentagon nasties by racing deep into the bowels of the "Georgetown Metro," D.C. audiences laughed out loud. Persistent rumors claim that the Georgetown Citizens' Association vetoed a Georgetown Metro stop, illogically voting to clog their streets with other people's autos just to keep away carless proletarians. In fact, a Georgetown subway would have posed a prohibitive engineering problem—a 90-degree turn in an underground tunnel just at the water's edge.

HISTORIC GEORGETOWN

Away from Wisconsin Ave. and M St., genteel Georgetown is rife with old townhouses and historic properties. Many of these locations open themselves up to the curious public, while others, like their reclusive residents, reveal no more than their aristocratic façades. The **Dumbarton Oaks** estate, at 1703 32nd St. NW between R and S St. (recorded information 339-6401, tour information 342-3212), includes two must-see sights: the mansion/museum, which displays Byzantine and pre-Columbian art, and the magnificent terraced gardens. (See **Museums & Galleries,** p. 204.)

Martha Washington's granddaughter slept at **Tudor Place,** 1644 31st St. (965-0400), between Q and R St. Martha Custis Peter used the $8000 that her step-grandfather, George Washington, willed her to purchase the property at 1644 31st St. and build this Neoclassical house, completed in 1816 and designed by William Thornton, an amateur architect whose previous credits included work on the U.S. Capitol. From what is now the dining room, Mrs. Peter and a friend watched the British torch Washington in 1814. The property passed through six successive generations until the last owner, Armistead Peter III, formed a foundation that opened the house to the public in 1984. The house and garden are not period museums but have been maintained as they were lived in by Mr. Peter, including a pigeonhouse complete with rare white pigeons with feathered feet. The required tour lasts about an hour; the gardens are open to visitors afterwards. (Open by reservation only; tours Tues.-Fri. 10, 11:30am, 1, and 2:30pm. Sat. every hour 10am-3pm. $6, $5 for students and seniors, $3 for children under 12; gardens open Mon.-Sat. 10am-4pm; during April, May, Sept., and Oct., the garden is open on Sun. afternoons for self-guided tours.)

The Federal-style **Dumbarton House,** 2715 Q St. (337-2288), displays 18th- and 19th-century furniture and decorative arts, and serves as headquarters for the National Society of the Colonial Dames of America. Check out the "cow china," pieces made with a pattern copied from a family member's drawing. Chinese porcelain was finer than any manufactured in America at that time; people would send their drawings to China where artisans would copy the pattern. Dolley Madison stopped here while fleeing from the British in 1814; some of her letters and belongings are on exhibit. You can relax in the garden free of charge, or let a genteel "dame" guide you around the immaculate house. (Guided tours Tues.-Sat. 10am-12:15pm; closed July and Aug. Admission $3, $2.50 each in groups of 10 or more; students free.)

2803 P St. seems like every other house on the block. The fence seems like every other fence. But every stake of the **Gunbarrel Fence** is really a 1767 Charlevoix rifle barrel, with the rifle stocks buried in the retaining wall. Reuben Dawes, a stonecutter, built three houses (numbers 2803 to 2811) on this block of P St. in 1843, and used surplus Mexican War rifles to build his cheap fence. Some of the fence stakes have a small notch near the top—the rifle sight.

Mount Zion Methodist Church, 1334 29th St. (234-0148), was founded in 1816 by a group of 125 African-Americans. The church was a stop on the Underground Railroad; passengers sometimes hid in a vault on the Old Methodist Burying Ground (later to become the Mount Zion/Female Union Band Cemetery) a few blocks away. Today Mount Zion's congregation remains full and active, and its interior is just as it was in 1800. Behind the church, at 2906 O St., the **Community House,** erected in 1810-11, holds old records, manuscripts, and photographs of past congregants, including Leontine Kelly, the first black woman to become a bishop. To see the Community House and Church, call ahead to make an appointment. The **Mount Zion Cemetery** and **Female Union Band Cemetery,** both at 27th St. NW and Mill Road NW, behind Q St., remain open to the public. In 1842 the Female Union Band, a benevolent association of women, purchased this plot for the burial of free blacks, thus establishing the first African-American cemetery in D.C. The Mt. Zion Methodist Church later rented (and renamed) the Old Methodist Burying Ground next to it "for the sum of one dollar in hand." The two cemeteries are not distinguishable today; both are sadly decayed and overgrown. However, you can still read some of the gravestones.

Unfortunately, Georgetown's only synagogue, the **Kesher Israel** at 2801 N St. NW, is not open for tours. Built in 1911 by local merchants, it does, however, offer services every morning and evening as well as a useful information line. Call 333-4808 for the latest on local **Kosher restaurants** and special hotel discounts (available to Kesher Israel congregants). The office administrator (333-2337), around the corner at 1308 28th St., is another helpful source of information.

The only surviving pre-Revolutionary building still standing in Washington, the **Old Stone House** at 3051 M St. (426-6851) has been restored and refurbished with reproductions and relics of pre-Revolutionary Georgetown. Low doorways and lumpy beds provide an accurate indication of the colonists' height, as well as a sense of the rough "comfort" of colonial living. Rumors that Pierre L'Enfant lived here while designing the city helped convince Congress in 1950 to protect the house. The National Park Service demonstrates 18th-century cooking, bread-baking, candle-making, and fabric-spinning every so often (house open Wed.-Sun. 9am-5pm; tiny garden open April-Sept.; free).

Flag-lovers may be disappointed by the **Star-Spangled Banner Monument** at **Francis Scott Key Park** (at the southwestern corner of 34th and M St.); it's merely a circular trellis-like structure. The park marks the former site of Francis Scott Key's house with some benches and wild roses. But the namesake bridge over the **C&O Canal** affords a picturesque view of the sandy towpath.

GEORGETOWN UNIVERSITY

When Archbishop John Carroll learned where the new capital would be built, he rushed to found Georgetown University (main entrance at 37th and O St.), which opened in 1789 as the United States' first Catholic institution for higher learning. Reacting against the religious persecution which forced him to seek his own education in Europe, Carroll was anxious to welcome students of varied backgrounds, and even early Georgetown classes boasted a religious mixture that would turn many modern universities green with envy. (In spite of this religious tolerance and diversity, women were only admitted as recently as 1969.) Father Patrick Healy, who became President of Georgetown in 1873, was the first Black American to hold a Ph.D. Healy re-organized the college and graduate schools and began construction of the central Healy building (the one with the clock tower). Though today approximately 50% of the 6000 undergraduates are Catholic and a Jesuit brother resides in every dorm, students of many creeds and nations attend. Georgetown's College of Arts and Sciences is just one of five undergraduate programs—the other four are somewhat more pre-professional: Business, Foreign Service, Language and Linguistics, and Nursing. The distinctions are purely academic, however: students of the several schools live, study, and party together. In addition to the five undergraduate schools, the University contains three graduate schools—Law, Medicine, and the Graduate School of Arts and Science. All facilities are located on the main Georgetown campus with the exception of the Law School (which makes its home in the midst of the nation's law-making bodies). With several dormitories as well as newly renovated apartment "villages" surrounding the U., Georgetown students have a substantial array of living options to choose from. On-campus living is required for the first two undergraduate years, guaranteed for three years, and possible for all four. Many students prefer to live off campus in the many townhouses that line the narrow, brick-paved streets which surround the U.

Georgetown's student body encompasses the usual array of "types"—jocks, pre-professional grinds, intellectuals, and foreign politicos—but its proximity to the nation's political heart means a preponderance of the politically bewitched. The students constitute a wealthy, chi-chi crowd; and the campus has a decidedly preppy, conservative tilt.

With a strong focus on undergrad teaching, classes are quite small, averaging 50 students. Mild winters give way to the oppressive heat and humidity of the D.C. summers during which the campus fills with high school debaters and the ambitious, power-hungry young interns who watch and discuss CNN and C-Span religiously.

The vast selection of bars and clubs in the neighborhood lures many students to popular haunts such as Winston's, Champions, and the Tombs. Drinking and partying, like at most colleges, are favorite Georgetown pastimes.

The basketball team, perennial contender for the national college title (they won in 1984), plays at the USAir Arena (formerly the Capital Centre) in Landover, MD, since crowds are far too large for a college gym. (Call 301-350-3400 for information.) Purchase tickets through Ticketmaster (432-7328) or through the campus Ticket Office (687-4692) or Athletic Department (687-2449).

The Campus

With the exception of a few old buildings owing their design to Flemish Renaissance and English Gothic, most campus architecture—largely constructed in the last two decades—is firmly rooted in the postmodern aesthetic. The recent and largely red-brick structures make a concerted effort to blend in with their setting, but this admirable endeavor meets with variable success. Enter through the **main gate** (located on 37th St., across from its intersection with O St.) and get maps and directions from the student in the **information booth** to the left. The Gothic splendor of **Healy Hall** lies straight ahead, as does the statue of Archbishop John Carroll in the center of **Healy Circle.** Healy and Copley Lawns lie to your left and right respectively. During warm weather, these lawns are a major social gathering ground. They for-

What's a Hoya?

Georgetown **teams** are called Hoyas, which supposedly derives from the old, half-Greek, half-Latin cheer *hoya saxta,* "what rocks," developed back when students were forced to study both languages. Tour leaders on campus further test the gullibility of prospective students by explaining that the correct answer to the question: "What's a *Hoya?*" is "Yes." Famous Hoyas have included pro basketball player Patrick Ewing, New York prelate John Cardinal O'Connor, Supreme Court Justice Antonin Scalia, and Senate Majority Leader George Mitchell (D-Maine).

merly held the university football field and students used to sit along the old stone wall which helps to enclose the quadrangle to cheer (*Hoya saxta!"* of course). Almost every Georgetown student takes a photo seated in John Carroll's lap at some point during their undergrad years. To the left is the **Lauinger Library;** built in memory of an alum who perished in Vietnam, it was erected as a modern counterpart to Healy. With 2.2 million volumes, it's the main repository of the university's library materials. Lauinger's reading room is open daily until 2am and 24hr. during exam periods. To the right of the lawns lies the Gothic **White Gravenor,** named for two of America's first Jesuits, which houses the **Office of Undergraduate Admissions** (687-3600 in Rm. 103). Campus tours begin here; call to reserve a spot. Look for the hands on the **Healy Hall clock;** you might have little luck. Each year seniors (attempt to) steal them and ship them to someone famous.

Through Healy lies the smaller and quieter **Dahlgren Square.** A fountain and the **Dahlgren Chapel** lend a more meditative atmosphere to this secondary campus quadrangle. Facing the chapel, to the right is a small white balcony from which Lincoln addressed troops during the Civil War.

Turn right at Healy Hall and walk past Copley Hall (on your left) until you reach the new **Intercultural Center (ICC),** a ziggurat-like, modern red brick building overlooking a small cemetery on campus—a peculiarly touching juxtaposition. Past the ICC, cross the bridge to your left to reach **Leavey Center,** the infinitely helpful student union. The building houses an **Information Center** (687-1457), and bulletin boards in the hall leading towards the **bookshop** (687-7482) advertise apartments for rent, job openings at the University, and furniture sales. The bookshop is your source for Hoya paraphernalia (open Mon.-Fri. 8:30am-8pm, Sat.-Sun. 11am-5pm). The G.U. Student Federal Credit Union resides inside, as do some **fast food joints**. At night the center fails as the student hangout it was envisioned to be; the place can be more deserted than the library.

Outside of Leavy, in front of Henley Village is the **Georgetown U. Transportation Service (GUTS)** shuttle bus stop. The shuttle runs about every 15 minutes during the academic year to nearby Metro stops in Rossyln and Dupont Circle.

SOUTHERN GEORGETOWN

For an aesthetic fix, pretend to shop for other people's art in **Spectrum Gallery,** 1132 29th St. NW (333-0954), an artists' cooperative owned and run by 29 local artists. Pick up a *Galleries* guide at any local gallery and look for an opening at the Spectrum—they're open to the public. Postcards and posters are also for sale (open Tues.-Sat. 11am-6pm, Sun. noon-5pm).

Retired from commercial use since the 1800s, the **Chesapeake & Ohio Canal** (301-299-3613) extends 185 mi. from Georgetown to Cumberland, MD. Nature abounds along the **C&O Canal towpath** (below and parallel to M St.), the dirt road along which trusty mules once pulled barges on the canal. The benches under the trees around 30th St. make a prime city lunch spot. After Georgetown, the C&O changes from a polluted relic suitable for romantic strolls to a clean waterway whose towpath accommodates gamboling families and mountain-bikers. Kayakers often practice on the water; fishermen sometimes walk the trails in search of trout or bass. The towpath, a flat and wide sandy path, grows monotonous after a few miles of running,

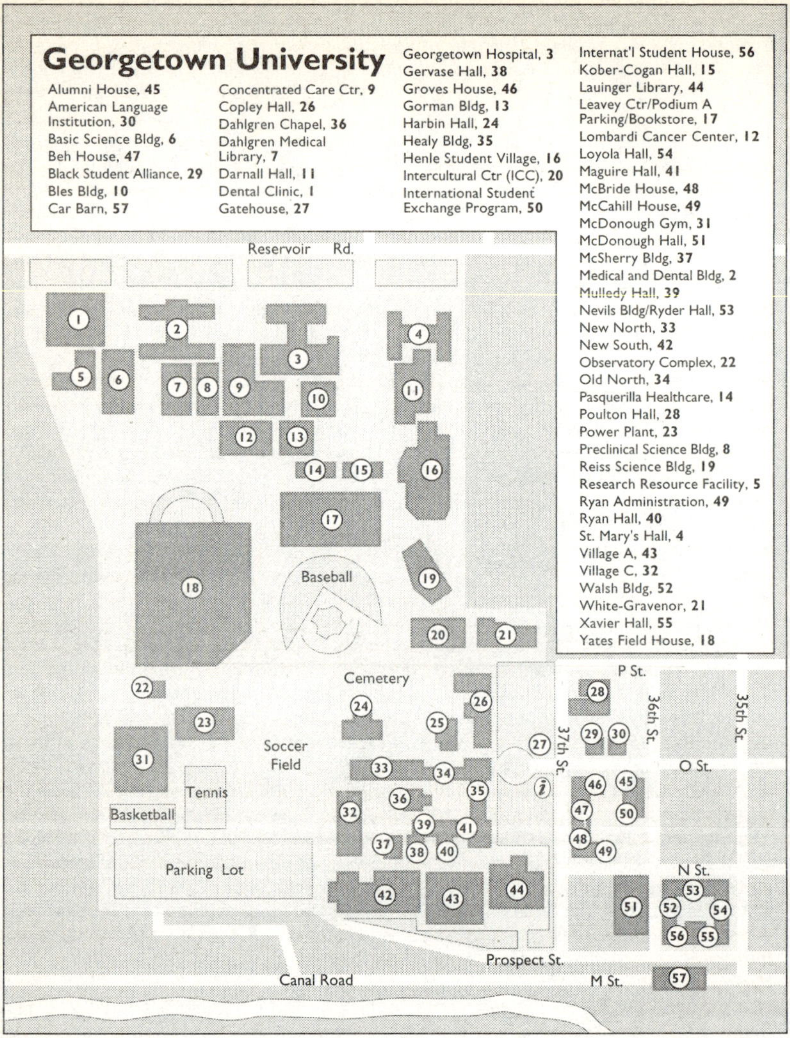

walking, or biking, though the uniformity is broken by long bridges, small, man-made and natural waterfalls, and historical spots. To reach the canal's relatively unspoiled bits without straying too far from public transportation, take the **D4 bus** out along Macarthur Blvd., then turn left and walk through the subdivisions until you reach the canal.

Too tired to walk along the canal? *The Georgetown,* a **C&O Canal boat** (472-4376), may be your ticket. Huge mules pull the passenger-filled boat down the canal; National Park Service guides wear 19th-century costumes, guide the boat through a lock, and explain the history of the canal. Board (and pay) for the 90-minute ride at the canal's **Visitor Center** (653-5190 or 301-299-3613; in emergencies, call the U.S. Park Police at 619-7300), south of M St. at 1057 Thomas Jefferson St. NW. (Boats leave from April to mid-Sept. Wed.-Sun. 10:30am, 1pm, and 3pm. From mid-Sept. to Oct. Wed.-Fri. 1 and 3pm; Sat. 10:30am, 1, 3, and 5pm; Sun. 10:30am, 1, and 3pm.

Rides $5, seniors and children $3.50.) The Visitor Center also provides information on horseback riding, fishing, camping, hiking, biking, and picnicking. Each summer from June to August there is a series of free "Concerts on the Canal." For dates and details, call 703-866-7164.

Farragut

Metro: Farragut North; Farragut South; McPherson Square.
Dupont Circle and Foggy Bottom melt imperceptibly into this glass-walled business district, bounded roughly by N, I, and 15th St. NW on the north, south, and east (respectively), and by 21st St. on the west. With government wrapped up in its own affairs just a few Metro stops to the east, lawyers, lobbyists, and other professionals labor on behalf of every interest group around. The 13-story height limit prevents New York-style claustrophobia from plaguing the District, but white-collar joggers, honking taxicabs, and street vendors hawking everything from $1 hot dogs to $3 silk ties to $100 wool rugs all conform to the corporate arena. Connecticut Avenue, K Street, New Hampshire Avenue, and 17th Street boast most of the retail and hotel hubbub, while several sights hover around M Street and Rhode Island Avenue. The business of Washington is best observed on a walk down Connecticut Avenue between N and K streets; E. J. Applewhite called it "a monotonous uniformity of office buildings poured out like ice cubes."

For a kaleidoscopic glimpse of Washington, old and new, take the Vermont Ave. exit from the McPherson Square Metro and walk northeast (toward N St. NW) on Vermont Ave. **Thomas Circle** features an amusing Union General Thomas sticking his chin out indignantly as his horse sneezes—the two have been frozen in this uncomfortable position since 1879. Vermont Ave. yields to a quiet residential neighborhood where two museums fight a war of ideas: The **Bethune Museum and Archives,** 1318 Vermont Ave. NW (332-1233; Metro: McPherson Square), chronicles the life of leader and civil rights activist Mary McLeod Bethune (see **Museums and Galleries,** p. 205), while two doors down the **Confederate Memorial Hall** commemorates the Southern cause during the Civil War. The Romanesque hall, at 1322 Vermont Ave. NW, once housed Confederate veterans. The impassioned docents speak dolefully of "those Yankees" and lament the statues of Union Generals Thomas and Logan, which taunt the Hall from nearby traffic circles (open by appointment; call 483-5700 for information; free).

At 1601 Massachusetts Ave. NW, the **Australian Embassy** (797-3000) welcomes visitors to exhibits that change approximately every month. Australian accents and electric doors can be inconceivably fun (open Mon.-Fri. 9am-4:30pm; free).

As Rhode Island Ave. heads west to M St., Farragut takes a break from business to wrestle with more existential questions. The **B'nai B'rith Klutznick National Jewish Museum,** at 1640 Rhode Island Ave. NW (857-6583; Metro: Farragut North; see **Museums and Galleries,** p. 205.), contests **St. Matthew's Cathedral,** 1725 Rhode Island Ave. NW (347-3215), one block away. St. Matthew's vibrant, vaulted ceiling frescoes and candle-filled chapels embrace worshippers for Sunday Mass in Latin (10am) and Spanish (1pm). (Guided tour Sun. 2:30-4:30pm. Free.)

On the corner of M St. and 17th St. NW, the **National Geographic Society Explorer's Hall** occupies the first floor of its pin-striped building (857-7588, group tours 857-7689, N.G. Society 857-7700; Metro: Farragut North). The museum proffers interactive films, a live parrot, a miniature hands-on (!) tornado, a huge globe, and fascinating changing exhibits, often by *National Geographic* magazine's best photographers. Recent displays include "Africa's Dinosaur Castaways," featuring a 25-ft. dinosaur skull, and a virtual reality exhibit that will supplement your D.C. visit with a side trip to Rome's St. Peter's Basilica (open Mon.-Sat. 9am-5pm, Sun. 10am-5pm; wheelchair access; free).

From M St., head east and make a right onto 15th St. to tour the **Washington Post** in its domineering tan building at 1150 15th St. NW (334-7969; Metro: Farragut North). Spin controllers, press secretaries, leakers, and flacks in this media-conscious

"I got my job through the Washington Post"

In the room where top editors decide which news will lead *The Post* everyday is a steel plate covered with ink that is two-decades old: "Nixon Resigns." It's the biggest headline ever printed in "the president's newspaper."

The Post made it happen and they know it. And, be you a visitor or staffer, they won't let you forget it. Older editors wandering the fifth floor newsroom of the downtown headquarters have been overheard breaking out into verbatim renditions of the Senate Watergate hearings. Young reporters offer up reverent inquiries as semi-retired former Executive Editor Ben Bradlee works the room.

Some say the *Post* hasn't progressed much from its glory days when it felled a president. Still, most industry observers consider it the best metropolitan daily in the country. It's the most widely read paper (in terms of readers who live within its intended geographic region), putting it well ahead of the *NY Times* in "penetration." Circulation is amplified by the fact that the newsstand price is a mere 25¢—a price well below what it takes in ink and paper to produce the product.

Tour-takers (if it's not 2 or 6pm when 20 or so top editors are debating important decisions) may wander into the conference room and be greeted by not only the Nixon plate and a library of books penned by *Post* reporters and editors, but with a Watergate memento that reveals the depth of recognition upon which the *Post's* continuing obsession is based. On the right wall as you enter the room, framed along with an inlaid signed photo, is a graphic of the slogan for a major 1970s classified-ad sales campaign. The slogan: "I got my job through the *Washington Post*." The signature: Jerry Ford.

town make the well-respected *Post* their #1 target. You'll see the hectic news room, enormous presses, and the mock-brick-floored mailroom. (One-hour tours Mon. 10, 11am, 1, 2, and 3pm. Reservations necessary. Children must be in the fifth grade or older. Free.)

L and M St. lead toward the shops and office buildings of Connecticut Avenue. A shortcut from 17th to Connecticut Ave. and Desales St. will bring you through the long, elegant, marble lobby of the **Mayflower Hotel,** 1127 Connecticut Ave. NW (347-3000; Metro: Farragut North). Warren & Wetmore, who built New York City's Grand Central Station, also designed this High Society gem, nicknamed the "grand dame" of Washington hotels. The grand ballroom was the site of every inaugural ball from Presidents Coolidge to Reagan. Gleaming gold-colored fixtures recall the Roaring Twenties, when this hotel was the largest in the United States.

Picnickers may enjoy the (occasional) summer sounds of flute duets and jazz sax players in **Farragut Square,** three blocks south of Connecticut Ave. on 17th St. between I and K St. NW. The statue, staring off into the distance, spyglass in hand, is Admiral David Farragut, the man who coined: "Damn the torpedoes—full speed ahead!" (The reference belongs to the Battle of Mobile Bay, Alabama in 1864, when "torpedoes" meant floating mines.)

Washington's golden age of outdoor statues lasted for 50 years after the Civil War; everything that you could possibly want to know about the War Between the States is evident in D.C.'s public sculpture. **McPherson Square,** where Vermont Ave. meets I, K, and 15th St. NW, promotes the memory of Gen. James McPherson, who commanded an army during Sherman's scorched-earth march through Georgia.

One block away between 13th, 14th, K, and I St. NW, **Franklin Square's** shady benches invite you to contemplate the protruding belly of Revolutionary War Commodore of the Navy John Barry; his coat is unbuttoned to afford a prime view.

Dupont Circle

Metro: Dupont Circle.

Dupont Circle's character has run a complete cycle, from prestigious to trendy to pricey. Once titled Washington's most diverse neighborhood, the Circle and its envi-

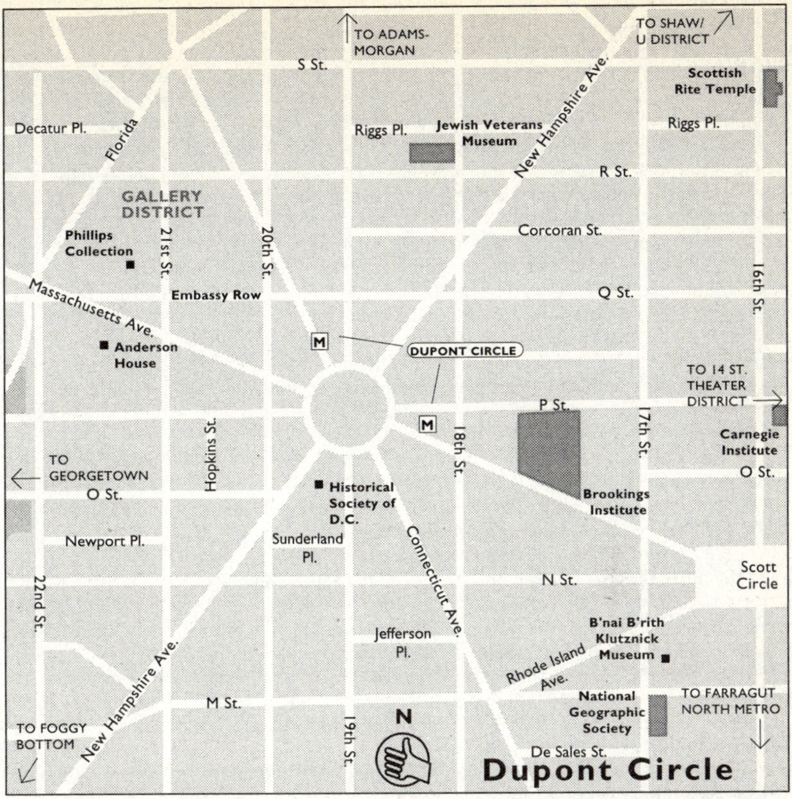

rons remain a haven for Washington's artsy, international, and gay communities. The neighborhood's mix of businesses and wayward pleasures makes for aesthetic delight but a zoning commission's headache; artists, ambassadors, antique dealers, beggars, bike messengers, booksellers, and committees all congregate within a few blocks north of N St. As the night moves in, the street crowds shift from lunching lawyers to café-hopping couples. Along Connecticut Ave. north of the Circle, hot-shot staffers of the *New Republic* stroll nervously past buzz-cut gay activists from ACT UP and OUT! (D.C.'s equivalent of Queer Nation). Sidewalks scream timely social messages stenciled with spray-paint. West of Connecticut and along Massachusetts Ave., embassies flap their flags, while lobbyists flap their mouths in nearby townhouse offices. Those tired of the fast lane can relax with new art in the many galleries or ogle Old Masters in the Phillips Collection.

In its residential and commercial development, Dupont Circle was a late bloomer. No one lived on its streets until after the Civil War. When the growth spurt hit, however, change came quickly. Big-spending, fast-acting Boss Shepherd took *de facto* charge of the city in 1871, then poured money into the area around his Dupont Circle home. The Circle itself became a federal park (it still is), Connecticut Avenue was paved, and railroad tracks ran up it from downtown. When the British built their new legation at Connecticut Ave. and N St. in 1874, the millionaires' race to Dupont Circle began. The area kept its social prestige until the 1940s, by which time Washington's segregated Black elite had built a parallel neighborhood of its own, "Striver's Row" along U St. near 17th. As the rich fled the city, hippies moved in and made Dupont their own during the '60s and '70s, until rising real estate prices and gentrification drove them out.

The Dupont Circle neighborhood presses eagerly against its boundaries at 16th, 24th, N and S St. NW. Its only Metro stop, helpfully named Dupont Circle, will put you within walking distance of everything in the area. The **D2, D4, and D8 buses** pass 20th and P St. on their way to Georgetown, while the **42** and **N** buses head up Connecticut Ave. and the **S2 and S4** speed down 16th St. Parking at night is nearly impossible except along Massachusetts Ave.; if you must drive around during the day, try the neighborhood's eastern edge (near 16th St.) and pray. Massachusetts Ave. runs through the Circle northwest-southeast, linking Old Downtown with the placid National Cathedral area. New Hampshire Ave. zooms through on its way from the Kennedy Center to NE and Takoma Park. Connecticut Ave. runs almost, but not quite, north-south to (and under) the Circle, between downtown and the zoo; Florida Ave. branches off from Connecticut Ave. at S St. and heads for neighborhoods with more dangerous reputations. Columbia Rd. splits up with Connecticut just afterwards and steers itself towards Adams-Morgan and Mt. Pleasant. Pedestrians leaving the Dupont Circle Metro can head up Connecticut for shopping and dining, up Massachusetts Ave. for embassies, northwest (between the two) for art, east to the slightly run-down but earnest 14th St. theater district, or south to the bustling charmlessness of Farragut.

The heart of the neighborhood throbs in **Dupont Circle** itself, a grassy hub for the incoming spokes of six avenues and streets. Admiral DuPont's millionaire descendants moved his statue to Delaware; a fountain adorned by semi-nude goddesses now hosts the chess players, lunching office workers, drug dealers, and herds of spandex-clad bike messengers who populate the island.

At the **Christian Heurich Mansion,** 1307 New Hampshire Ave. NW (785-2068), the Historical Society of Washington, D.C. leads visitors through the German-American beer baron's "castle on the Rhine." Exquisite woodwork renders the Romanesque mansion worth a scan. Visitors may catch a glimpse of the decorative arts, architecture, and domestic life of turn-of-the-century Washington. (Mansion, Historical Society research library, Washingtonia Bookstore, and a changing exhibit area all open Wed.-Sat. 10am-4pm. Call ahead to arrange group tours. Admission $3; students, seniors, and children $1.50.)

The eastward leg of Mass. Ave., toward Farragut, is flanked by embassies. The prestigious **Brookings Institute** at 1775 Massachusetts Ave. NW acts as a liberal stronghold and appropriate buffer between the Circle's alternative activism and the business buffs to the east. Richard Nixon once contemplated blowing up the files at Brookings, whose influence has declined since its Kennedy-era glory days. Your favorite resident academic can be found via the interactive computer in the lobby.

EMBASSY ROW

Massachusetts Ave. between Dupont Circle and Observatory Circle is also called **Embassy Row.** Before the 1930s, Washington socialites lined the avenue with their extravagant edifices; status-conscious diplomats found the mansions perfect for their purposes, and embassies and chanceries moved in by the dozen. Major industrialized nations have designed their own compounds (Great Britain and Japan) or moved away from downtown for more room (France and Germany); smaller or poorer countries occupy the still-grand townhouses. Identify an embassy by the national coat-of-arms or flag out front; identify an international scandal by reporters on the sidewalk. The ornate **Indonesian Embassy,** 2020 Massachusetts Ave. (293-1745), once belonged to the McLean family, the last private owners of the infamous Hope Diamond (now housed at the National Museum of Natural History).

From Massachusetts Ave., turn right onto 21st St. for the **Phillips Collection,** 1600 21st St. at Q St. NW (387-2151), the first museum of modern art in the U.S. and the classiest non-Smithsonian showplace in town (see **Museums**, p. 205).

A little further along Massachusetts, pass through the grand arched and gravel-paved entrance of **Anderson House,** 2118 Massachusetts Ave. NW (785-2040 ext. 16) next to the Ritz-Carlton Hotel, to see the **Museum of the Society of the Cincinnati** and its pervasive egg-and-dart design along the outside moldings. The house retains the robber-baron decadence and original furnishings of U.S. ambassador Larz Anderson, who built it in 1902-5 (open Tues.-Sat. 1-4pm; free).

Via still more embassies, Massachusetts eventually circumnavigates **Sheridan Circle** at 23rd St. NW. General Philip Sheridan looks dashing and equestrian in the Circle's arboreal center. A small raised plaque on the sidewalk of the Q St. side of the Circle commemorates ex-Chilean ambassador Orlando Letelier, who was killed in 1976 by a car bomb along with Ronni K. Moffitt. Letelier represented the Marxist government of Salvador Allende, which dictator Pinochet overthrew with CIA help in the same year. After the assassination was featured on the TV show *America's Most Wanted* four years ago, the culprit was apprehended. From the Circle, the **Dumbarton Bridge** leads 23rd St. pedestrians over Rock Creek Park to Georgetown via a pair of powerful but dejected-looking bronze buffalo.

Several embassies later, Massachusetts makes one last stop before crossing Rock Creek Park into Upper Northwest, at the **Islamic Center,** 2551 Massachusetts Ave. NW (332-8343). Flags line the entrance to this brilliant white building, whose stunning designs stretch to the tips of its spired ceilings. Ambassadors of several Islamic nations (Egypt, Iran, Turkey, and Afghanistan) founded the mosque after World War II. Visitors may enter the mosque, but note that shorts are not allowed and women must cover their heads and wear sleeved clothing (no short dresses allowed). (Open daily 10:30am-5pm. Donation requested. Prayers held 5 times daily.)

On the other side of Rock Creek Park, Massachusetts Ave. links some particularly striking embassies, including those of Brazil, Norway, and Britain, before it reaches the Vice President's mansion and the Naval Observatory.

GALLERY AREA

From the Q St. exit of the Dupont Circle Metro, walk one block north on Connecticut Ave. to R St. to reach many of Dupont Circle's 25 art galleries, which cluster between 21st and 22nd St. (see **Galleries** on p. 206).

Turn right from R St. onto 22nd St.; then walk up the hill past Decatur Pl. to the tiny fountain and spreading **Spanish steps.** Take the steps to S St., turn left, pass the embassies of Laos, Ireland, and Myanmar (formerly Burma), and enter the **Textile Museum,** 2320 S St. NW (667-0441). It's the world's largest repository of rare and valuable textiles, with over 15,000 holdings, of which only a few are shown at a time. The museum boasts strong collections of carpets from Asia, antique pieces, and contemporary work from the world over (open Mon.-Sat. 10am-5pm, Sun. 1-5pm). The **Arthur D. Jenkins Library** contains an immense collection of literature and visual resources on the textile arts (open Wed.-Fri. 10am-2pm; free, suggested donation $5). A few doors away, the **Woodrow Wilson House,** 2340 S St. NW (387-4062), preserves the memory of former president Woodrow Wilson with a detailed and informative tour of his house and belongings, enlivened by snippets of personal history. The aging and embittered Wilson spent his last year here after the Democrats lost the White House in 1920. Today, a 20-min. film and a one-hour tour introduce visitors to the nation's last great intellectual president and the only one to have taken up residence in Washington after leaving office. (Open Tues.-Sun. 10am-4pm. Admission $5, students $2.50, seniors $4, under 7 free. Wheelchair access.)

East of Fondo del Sol on R St., the **National Museum of American Jewish Military History,** 1811 R St. NW (265-6280), offers surprisingly rich displays on a seemingly thin subject. The museum is under the auspices of the Jewish War Veterans of the U.S.A., a key organization in the civil rights movement. Particularly unnerving are the yellowed pamphlets (part of the moving World War II exhibit) from American Nazi parties denouncing the veterans. Upcoming exhibits include "Women in the Military: A Jewish Perspective" (open Mon.-Fri. 9am-5pm, Sun. 1-5pm; free). Continue east on R St. to discover the **House of the Temple,** 1733 16th St. NW (232-3579). Flanked by 33-ft. columns, guarded by turbaned sphinxes, utilized by Scottish Rite Masons, and designed by John Russell Pope, the ancient-looking temple struts imposingly among the apartments and offices of lower 16th St. Pope's design copies the Mausoleum at Halicarnassus, one of the Seven Wonders of the Ancient world. The lengthy tour

(1½hr. or more) is a fascinating look at the quasi-religious aspects of this secretive selective society (open Mon.-Fri. 8am-4pm. Last tour at 2pm. Free).

Shaw / U District

Metro: Shaw-Howard University; U St.-Cardozo.
Shaw was once the address of choice for important African-American senators (Reconstruction-era Sen. Blanche K. Bruce), poets (Jean Toomer and Langston Hughes), musicians (Duke Ellington), journalists, and lawyers. These American legends and their cohorts developed the "Striver's Section," along U St. between 7th and 15th St. NW; businesses on 7th St. boomed. Music lovers of every color and creed crowded into the Howard Theater; the nearby Lincoln Theater was the first theater in the area to show movies to an integrated audience. Fashion flourished in Shaw in the '30s and '40s when stepping out meant dressing up. Desegregation in the 1950s played taps for the theaters—as other parts of the city were opened up to the black middle class, Shaw's population and influence were reduced. The final blow came in 1968, when news of the assassination of Martin Luther King, Jr. touched off three days of looting, smashing, and burning along 14th St., 7th St., and H St. NW—the former arteries of Black D.C.

Shaw today is best viewed along its edges, in the Logan Circle neighborhood along 13th St. NW above M St. (Greater Shaw runs roughly between 14th and North Capitol and between M St. and Florida Ave. NW.) U St. has become a major east-west artery, originating at the intersection of Florida Ave. and 18th St. NW (the no-man's land between Adams-Morgan and Dupont Circle) and extending to the Howard University campus. Some blocks still show the effects of the '68 riots. Run-down tenements, boarded-up and abandoned buildings, and crumbling storefronts abound. Violence, usually drug-related, threatens even the residents hanging out on their stoops. Shaw becomes deserted away from its business center. Areas around housing projects are especially dangerous. Exercise caution and travel in groups.

But don't give up on Shaw— give it your attention at mealtime or in the evenings, when safe areas offer spectacular dining and entertainment options. The Howard Theater remains a half-demolished marquee, but the Lincoln was bought and restored by the city and reopened in February of 1994. Venerable neighborhood institutions like Ben's Chili Bowl and the Florida Avenue Grill have, like their customers, weathered the troubles for decades. Meanwhile, the long-delayed Shaw Metro stations have finally opened. U St. itself, a haven for prostitution in the '70s and '80s, has become a destination for the ever-roaming hip. Youthful types head west on U St. to boogie, read poetry, or fatten up on Sunday brunch. Some of the city's best clubs and bars are in the U; simply take a cheap taxi ride home. (See **Nightlife & Entertainment,** on p. 211.) For soul-food restaurants, which serve Southern-derived, pork-and-greens-heavy cuisine unique to African-American culture, see **Food and Drink: Shaw/U District** (p. 98).

Howard University (806-6100), whose roughly 20-block campus slopes northeast from 7th and W St. NW, is America's most historically important black university (Metro: Shaw-Howard Univ.). From the Metro, walk north on 7th St., which changes into Georgia Ave. (a 20-min. walk). The 89-acre campus stretches to the east along 7th and Georgia. (Be very careful walking on 7th and Georgia St. at night, and do not walk alone.) Founded in 1867 to help newly freed slaves, the university was named for Gen. Oliver Otis Howard, head of the Freedmen's Bureau after the Civil War. The private research university now has 12,000 students, most of them African-American. Late Supreme Court Justice Thurgood Marshall, ex-New York City Mayor David Dinkins, and novelist Toni Morrison are only a few of Howard's zillions of famous alums. The campus has one of D.C.'s highest elevations—and a great view of downtown. Two-hour campus tours (including a videotape presentation and question-and-answer session) are available from Monday to Friday between 10am and 3pm by appointment only (call 806-2900 for scheduling). The university library at 500 Howard Pl. (on the Howard campus; 806-7250) is open to the public; its **Moorland-**

Springarn Research Center maintains the largest collection of black literature in the United States (open Mon.-Thurs. 8am-midnight, Fri. 8am-5pm, Sat. 9am-6pm, Sun. 12:30-9pm; limited hours during summer months).

Adams-Morgan

Metroless: closest stations are Woodley-Park Zoo (15-min. walk) and Dupont Circle (20-min. walk).

Though Dupont Circle remains the most bohemian of Washington's neighborhoods, sometime in the late '80s the mantle of multicultural hipness passed to Adams-Morgan. Immigrants from Mexico, El Salvador, and Ethiopia have amplified the diversity in an area already defined by its conglomerate of ethnic identities. Slick dance, world beat, and rickety do-it-yourself punk venues start up, change names, and fold each year in Adams-Morgan; even older square folks have long ago discovered that a wreath of fantastic **ethnic food** circles 18th, Columbia, and Calvert St. NW. A wealth of street carts and **secondhand stores** line Columbia Rd. east of 18th St.; visitors enjoy strolling, shopping, and browsing among them in the daytime.

Poorly served by public transportation, Adams-Morgan also suffers from a dearth of parking spaces, especially at night, when the streets tend to jam. The best bet is to make the pilgrimage from the Metro; from the Woodley Park-Zoo Metro stop, walk south (downhill) on Connecticut Ave. (those who exit the Metro station via the escalator are already facing this direction). After a short block and a left turn (eastward), walkers are lifted stories above Rock Creek Park's treetops by the Duke Ellington Bridge—three blocks away from Adams-Morgan's center, the five-pronged meeting place of Columbia and 18th. Florida Avenue NW divides Dupont from Adams-Morgan on the south; Connecticut Ave. lines its western side. Church-clogged 16th St., the wide east edge, leaves Adams-Morgan behind for rougher streets; a vague north boundary, Harvard St., bears Adams-Morgan into Mount Pleasant, where a similar, but poorer mix of immigrants and young white-collar types survives. The area west of 16th St., especially during the day, is relatively trouble-free.

Kalorama Park, nicknamed "dog-walk park," is a grassy triangle between Columbia Rd., 19th St., and Kalorama Rd. It houses benches, trees, a small park shelter, a playground, and basketball and tennis courts that local youths often use as soccer fields. Children rollerskate down the hill to 19th St.

Columbia Road between 16th and 18th St. is packed with **street vendors,** selling African and Latin American wares as well as fresh fruit during the summer. Salsa music blares from stands whose proprietors hawk cassettes of other Latin beats.

Three churches defend the broad intersection of Harvard, 16th, and Columbia Rd. NW. Watchful pedestrians can see the round tower, pillars, and pilasters of the **National Baptist Memorial Church** all the way from 18th St. Across the street is the **Unitarian All Souls Church,** an important venue for all-ages hard-core shows since the mid-'80s. The 1921 church closely resembles the 1721 Church of St.-Martin-in-the-Fields in London, a model for Anglican parishes all over the world. The severely vertical **Unification Church** (a former Mormon Temple) reads its *Washington Times* across 16th St. from All Souls.

Grocery stores abound in Adams-Morgan, as the Hispanic residents support small corner *bodegas* filled with Latin American staples. The selection of items is a sight in itself. At least one of these places warrants a walk-through (see **Shopping,** p. 234).

Meridian Hill Park lies off 16th Street between W and Euclid St. NW. High retaining walls run the two-block length of the park, which encloses a high hill carved into a rectangular, 900-ft. esplanade complete with a long, impressive waterfall. For all its grand landscaping, however, the park is rather sinister; high walls and the hill block any escape except to W or Euclid St., making the lawns a mugger's playground. Visitors should explore in groups during the day and leave the grounds to the squirrels at night.

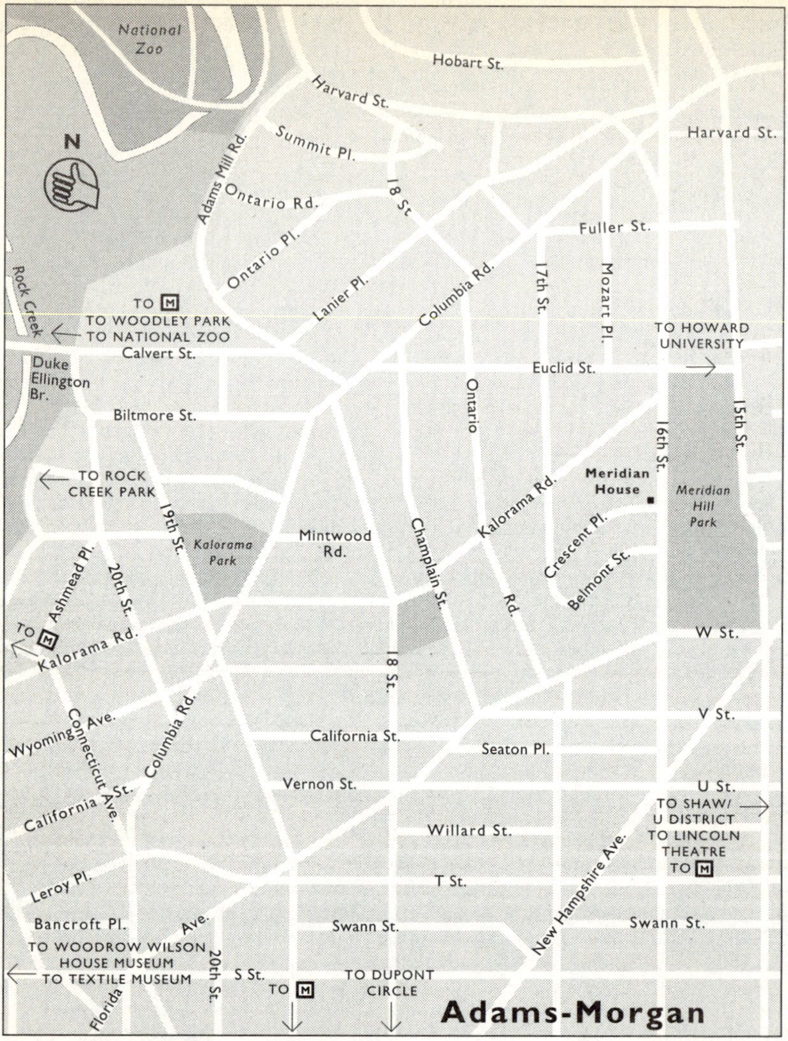

Upper Northwest

Metro: Woodley Park-Zoo; Cleveland Park; Van Ness-UDC; Tenleytown-AU; Friendship Heights.

Immense Upper Northwest (the portion of D.C.'s northwest quadrant west of Rock Creek Park and north of Georgetown) is home to a gaggle of suburban (and largely indistinguishable) residential communities. There are no discrete boundaries between these neighborhoods, though Fessenden St. NW may be said to divide **Tenleytown** from **Friendship Heights,** Quebec St. to cut between the **Cathedral area** and **Glover Park,** and R St. to separate the latter from Georgetown. Connecticut Ave. parallels Wisconsin Ave., but is somewhat more urbane. City politicians call Upper Northwest "west of the park;" the well-educated and well-to-do residents stay close to their professional contacts, living in the twilight zone between city and suburb. These neighborhoods are Washington, D.C.'s most prolific in terms of trees, parks, and private schools. The **National Cathedral** and the **National Zoo** are Upper Northwest's outstanding sights.

GETTING THERE & GETTING AROUND

The L1 and L2 **Metrobuses** shuttle up and down Connecticut Ave., linking Chevy Chase, MD with Dupont Circle and Farragut; the Van Ness-UDC, Cleveland Park, and Woodley Park-Zoo Metro stations are all stops along the bus route. The #30, 32, 34, 35, or 36 buses can shuttle you all the way up Wisconsin Ave. from Georgetown; at the District line in Friendship Heights, a central Metrobus terminal allows travelers to change buses to go into Maryland. **Metro stations** are located at Woodley Park, Cleveland Park, Van Ness (on Connecticut Ave.), Tenley Circle (Tenleytown), and Friendship Heights. Once there, these neighborhoods are easy to get around in. Most of the cross streets fit into D.C.'s alphabetical-order scheme: letters, then two-syllable names, then three-syllable names.

Connecticut Ave. connects Dupont Circle to Woodley Park, the Zoo, Cleveland Park, and finally the District line at Chevy Chase Circle. Wisconsin Ave. NW runs north from Georgetown past the Cathedral, through Tenley Circle and the Friendship Heights area, and on to Bethesda, MD.

Massachusetts Ave. runs northwest from downtown and Dupont Circle to the Cathedral (at Wisconsin Ave.), past American University, and north to the District line at Westmoreland Circle. Nebraska Ave. connects residential areas, running southwest-northeast from American University to Wisconsin Ave., Connecticut Ave., and finally to Military Road and Rock Creek Park.

Western Ave., the District's northwest border, meets Wisconsin in Friendship Heights at what was once measured as the city's most polluted intersection. Military Road marches east from Wisconsin and Western to Connecticut, through Rock Creek Park, and on to 16th St. NW.

NATIONAL ZOO

The first giant pandas left China for Washington's National Zoological Park (673-4800) as a gift from Mao to Nixon. But after years of tragically unsuccessful attempts to birth a baby panda in captivity, Ling-Ling died in 1992. Condolence cards and well wishes from around the world are still posted on the **Panda House** windows, blocking much of the view for the vertically challenged. Ling-Ling's mate Hsing-Hsing remains alone (and reportedly depressed) in the Panda House, unable to escape the adoring scrutiny of camera-toting crowds.

But Hsing-Hsing is hardly the only reason to visit the National Zoo; after the obligatory pilgrimage to the Panda House, visitors can watch the fish and monkeys in the cageless **"Amazonia"** exhibit, wander through the **rainforest** exhibit, or play St. Francis by strolling through the skyscraper-sized bird cage. The zoo aims to enshrine its captives in environments they enjoy; some exhibits even maintain their own wooded islands.

The Zoo spreads eastward from Connecticut Ave. a few blocks uphill from Calvert St. NW and the Woodley Park-Zoo Metro; the entrance is at 3000 Connecticut Ave. NW. Connecticut Ave. from the Cleveland Park Metro is a more level though longer route. In good (i.e., not sweltering) weather, pedestrians might enjoy walking up Connecticut Ave. from Dupont Circle (about 16 blocks). Drivers can park their worldly transport vehicles inside the Connecticut Ave. entrance.

Occupying a swath of land liberated from Rock Creek Park, the zoo is criss-crossed with walking paths. All paths are segments of either the blue **Valley Trail** (marked with bird tracks) or the red **Olmsted Walk** (marked with elephant tracks), but the "footprints" have faded considerably. The posted signs may provide more useful guidance. The more level Olmsted Walk explores land-animal houses, while the Valley Trail winds among the bird and sealife exhibits. Ambitious visitors who don't want to miss a thing may traipse along one trail from the entrance to the far end of the zoo, near the lion-tiger hill, where they can pick up the other trail and return to the entrance. The non-linear layout and its lack of sightlines make a **map** invaluable; they are available from the **information office** in the Education Building, near the main (Connecticut Ave.) entrance (open May-Sept. 9am-6pm, Oct.-April 9am-5pm). It is possible to see all of the exhibits in a long morning or afternoon, and it is certainly more satisfying to linger a little longer than to rush through in search of the major attractions.

Valley Trail descends to the great **flight cages,** where many birds spread wide their wings. One cage is devoted exclusively to eagles, who need the room in order to breed successfully. Cranes, mallards, and herons shine in the tranquil artificial wetlands, while sinister-eyed bongos with tufts of hairy feathers range on the hill. Children can get a closer look at their flighty friends in the indoor **bird house** and the spooky **bat cave,** or watch the playful **seals** and **sea lions** eat lunch and have their teeth brushed with seafood-flavored toothpaste (11:30am daily).

Along Olmsted Walk, rhinos, giraffes, and obscure pachyderms stretch out and stress out in a concrete barn. The boxed-in **elephants** stand around in unhealthy-looking tiny spaces, usually indoors. Visitors flock with open mouths and pointing fingers to the **Great Ape House,** where they are either tactfully ignored or obligingly entertained by the cosmopolitan primates on the other side of the glass. The Great Ape House, with its statues of animals on the roof, was once the main zoo building, back when vacationing circus animals made the zoo's winter population bulge. In the seriously crowded split-level **Panda House, feeding times** (11am and 3pm) provide the best glimpse of Hsing-Hsing. **Invertebrates** (starfish and sea urchins and such) get their own house, the only one of its kind.

The zoo has made recent efforts to bring its scientific operations into the public eye; in Sept. 1995, it opened a new research facility for primates next to the Reptile House. **Think Tank** enables visitors to watch zoo biologists study animal behavior. The monkeys are free to climb along the wire back and forth between Think Tank and the Ape House, and scientists plan to chart their movements to study their social behavior. The **Cheetah Conservation Station** chronicles cheetahs' disappearance from the wild (cheetahs' poor level of reproduction is partly due to low DNA variance and low-quality sperm). Almost any large animal that can stand the climate will be found outdoors; the polar bears are probably sweating worse than you are. Herd animals, like the okapi, frequent the fenced-off hillsides. Small animals, like lizards, still live indoors. The overdue shift from bare concrete and black iron to natural settings tends to hide the residents from the visitors; the free-ranging tamarins at the zoo swing freely (though often obscured) from limb to limb.

Some of the houses contain kid-centered learning laboratories; the bird house nests the **Bird Resource Center** (open Fri. 10am-1pm and Sat.-Sun. 10am-2pm). **Summer Serenade concerts** by the U.S. Navy Band take place on certain evenings; call the zoo for information. Both trails claim wheelchair access, though it's easier to wheel down Olmsted Walk. The zoo is accessible by bike from the Rock Creek bike path, but bikes must be locked up upon arrival. Single- or double-strollers and baby carriers can be rented at information stations; wheelchairs are also available. (Auto parking $4 for 1st 3 hrs., $2 per hr. thereafter, $10 max. Free handicapped parking in lots B and D. Zoo grounds open daily 8am-8pm, Oct.-April 8am-6pm; buildings open daily 9am-6pm, Sept.-March 9am-4:30pm. Free. Scheduled feedings listed at information desk; audio tours also available.)

Near the Zoo

Next door to the zoo at 3133 Connecticut Ave. NW, the **Kennedy-Warren Apartments** thrived as some of Washington's fanciest addresses during the 1930s. The Egyptian-themed roof adornments and exterior panels on this three-structure, block-long building merit some serious stares, as does the garden out front.

Up Connecticut Ave., at 3400 International Drive NW, **Intelsat headquarters** (944-6800) gleams like a science-fiction ant colony. (Metro: Van Ness-UDC.) Intelsat is a cooperative satellite producer supported by 121 countries; a high-tech tour orbits the ground floor. Visitors pass under prototypes of the Intelsat satellites and watch a

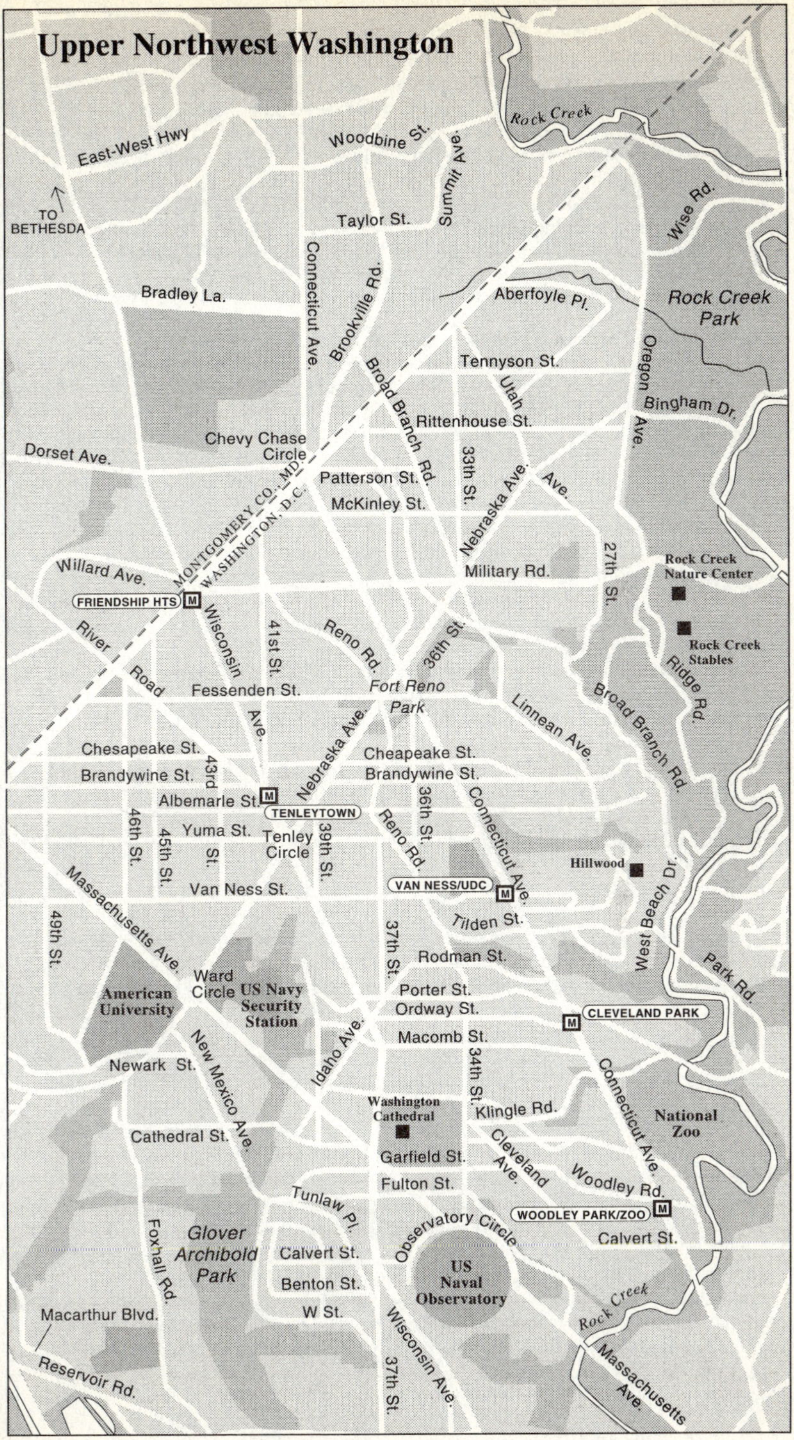
Upper Northwest Washington
East-West Hwy
Woodbine St.
Summit Ave.
Rock Creek
TO BETHESDA
Taylor St.
Wise Rd.
Connecticut Ave.
Brookville Rd.
Bradley La.
Aberfoyle Pl.
Rock Creek Park
Tennyson St.
Broad Branch Rd.
Utah
Oregon Ave.
Bingham Dr.
Rittenhouse St.
Chevy Chase Circle
Dorset Ave.
Patterson St.
33th St.
Nebraska Ave.
Ave.
McKinley St.
MONTGOMERY CO., MD.
WASHINGTON, D.C.
Willard Ave.
Military Rd.
27th St.
Rock Creek Nature Center
FRIENDSHIP HTS
Wisconsin Ave.
River Road
41st St.
Reno Rd.
36th St.
Rock Creek Stables
Ridge Rd.
Fessenden St.
Fort Reno Park
Linnean Ave.
Broad Branch Rd.
Chesapeake St.
Cheapeake St.
Brandywine St.
43rd St.
Brandywine St.
Albemarle St.
TENLEYTOWN
Nebraska Ave.
Reno Rd.
36th St.
Connecticut Ave.
46th St.
45th St.
Yuma St.
Tenley Circle
39th St.
Hillwood
Massachusetts Ave.
Van Ness St.
VAN NESS/UDC
West Beach Dr.
49th St.
Tilden St.
37th St.
Rodman St.
Park Rd.
American University
Ward Circle
US Navy Security Station
Porter St.
Ordway St.
CLEVELAND PARK
New Mexico Ave.
Idaho Ave.
Macomb St.
Newark St.
34th St.
Connecticut Ave.
Washington Cathedral
Klingle Rd.
National Zoo
Cathedral St.
Cleveland Ave.
Garfield St.
Fulton St.
Woodley Rd.
Tunlaw Pl.
WOODLEY PARK/ZOO
Observatory Circle
Calvert St.
Foxhall Rd.
Glover Archibald Park
Calvert St.
US Naval Observatory
Benton St.
Rock Creek
W St.
Wisconsin Ave.
Macarthur Blvd.
Massachusetts Ave.
Reservoir Rd.
37th St.

hokey, take-it-with-a-grain-of-salt introductory film (though the end does contain some fantastic special effects). This fascinating bastion of technology looks as though it came straight out of *Star Trek*. (One-hour tours by appointment only.)

Hillwood, 4155 Linnaean Ave. NW (686-5807), once the mansion of General Foods heiress Marjorie Meriweather Post, now displays her jewels—not just shiny earrings and necklaces but a wing of Russian decorative arts, coins, and Fabergé eggs said to be the largest outside Russia. You may have to sell your own jewels to see it, though—a two-hour tour of the newly remodeled collection costs $10. Outside, 25 acres of gardens replicate England, Japan, and imperial Russia in begonian glory. (A visit to the garden is included in the tour price, or $2 for the garden alone. Open Tues.-Sat.; tours by appointment only. Reservation office open Mon.-Fri. 9-11:30am, 1:30-3pm.)

WASHINGTON NATIONAL CATHEDRAL

The Cathedral Church of Saint Peter and Saint Paul, also called the **Washington National Cathedral,** at Massachusetts and Wisconsin Ave. NW (537-6200, recorded information 364-6616), took a long time getting off the ground: more than a century passed between 1791, when George Washington proposed (in a move characteristic of the separation between Church and State) "a great church for national purposes," and 1893, when Congress empowered a foundation to build the thing. The questions concerning where to put the cathedral—and in which style to build it—occasioned more church-state conflict: some called the chosen site, 57 acres on Mount St. Albans (D.C.'s highest point), too far from government buildings. Others complained that the planned Gothic style would clash with downtown's neo-Athenian architecture. In any event, the well-kept grounds keep the business world (if not the Wisconsin Ave. traffic) at a distance.

SIGHTS

Building the cathedral (the world's sixth-largest) took over 80 years, from 1907 until 1990, though the interior spaces have been in use for decades. As Gothic architecture dictates, the cathedral has the shape of a cross, with the nave in the main body of the church, the apse at the altar, and the transepts forming the cross-piece. Indiana limestone is the only structural material here; all details were carved from the walls by hand. Even the soaring ceiling slabs were constructed on location; artisans hovered more than 100 feet above the floor while they sculpted them.

The cathedral has always endeared itself to official Washington. At the cornerstone-laying ceremony in 1907, President Theodore Roosevelt showed up to speak, and every U.S. president since has dropped by. Even in this political city, however, the cathedral has risen majestically to its religious functions. Rev. Martin Luther King, Jr. preached his last Sunday sermon from the Canterbury pulpit; more recently, another Nobel Peace Prize winner, the Dalai Lama, spoke here. Writers, as well as speakers, have taken note of the cathedral: Margaret Truman's *Murder in the Cathedral* was set in Bethlehem Chapel. Christmas and Easter services attract plenty of tourists and quite a few dignitaries. Regular Episcopal services are open to the public (Mon.-Sat. 7:30am, noon, and 4pm; Sun. 8, 9, 11am, and 4 and 6:30pm; also Sept.-June and special occasions Sun. 10am. Only the Sun. 11am service takes place in the main upper church).

Cathedral **maps** are available at the northwest entrance. (The **wheelchair ramp** and **restrooms** are also near this entrance.) The free 45-minute guided **tour,** led by purple-hatted docents, is supplemented by visits to the lower crypt level and upper Observation Gallery. (Tours available Mon.-Sat. 10am-3:15pm every 15 min., Sun. 12:30-2:45pm, except on holidays. Suggested donation $2 adults, $1 children.)

President Woodrow Wilson's tomb juts from the south aisle (under the window commemorating him). Immediately to Wilson's right is the cathedral's most unusual stained-glass window, a blue and red **spacescape** donated by a former NASA director; an actual moon rock is embedded in the center of the window. Others buried here include blind and deaf education pioneer Helen Keller; her companion and teacher Anne Sullivan Macy; Larz Anderson, capitalist, diplomat, and builder of Anderson House; and Cordell Hull, secretary of state during World War II. The bulk of those who rest here forever are cathedral workers and artists; after devoting their lives to the cathedral, many wanted to remain here always. Stone carvings and statues depict, not surprisingly, biblical figures. One of the best, the **Statue of Christian Majesty** surrounded by all the angels and archangels, sits behind the High Altar.

The **crypt level** harbors the Bethlehem Chapel, the Chapel of St. Joseph of Arimathea, and the Resurrection Chapel. The Chapel of the Good Shepherd awaits flocks on this level as well and stays open until 10pm. (Enter from the west end of the cathedral at night.) Caution: the stairs to the crypt level are not user-friendly to handicapped persons and may exhaust or distress those with mobility problems.

An elevator ride (the elevator is located near the main doors of the west entrance) to the top floor of the **Pilgrim Observation Gallery** won't run you into any pilgrims, but you will see Washington—from the highest vantage point in the city. The cathedral's **museum** is to the left of the elevator; one display explains cathedral vocabulary, gratifyingly clearing up any confusion between "grotesque" and "gargoyle."

The **Bishop's Garden** near the South Transept, resembling a medieval walled garden, is a sanctuary for herbs and roses (open daily until dusk). Though the garden is technically closed at night, young Washingtonians have taken midnight strolls here for years. The lights illuminating the fountain cast flowing shadows against the cathedral, yielding the perfect romantic retreat. Education returns to the Middle Ages at the well-connected **National Cathedral School** for Girls (NCS), established in 1899, and **St. Alban's School** for Boys, founded in 1905; both educate on the Cathedral grounds. NCS's Hearst Hall relaxes in a softer Italian Renaissance style, while St. Alban's Gothic excess matches the cathedral (and the school environment). According to ex-headmaster Canon Charles Martin, "St. Alban's exists to help boys not into the Kingdom of Harvard but into the Kingdom of Heaven."

Children and families "build" parts of their own cathedrals at the **Medieval Workshop** (537-2930); they can carve stone, see how a stained-glass window is created, or mold a gargoyle out of clay (open July-Sept. Mon.-Fri. 1-4:30pm, and year round Sat. 11am-2pm). June and July host an irregular schedule of **outdoor classical music concerts. The Cathedral Choristers** sing Mondays through Wednesdays at 4pm during the school year. **Organ demonstrations** take place Wednesdays at 12:30pm, and recitals on Sunday afternoons. Call for specific dates and schedules. In late September or early October an **Open Hours day** resounds with organ music, choral recitals, and the only chance all year to climb the tower and see the carillon.

Public transportation will take you to the cathedral, but not without a little hassle. (Metro: Tenleytown, then take the #30, 32, 34, or 36 bus toward Georgetown; or walk up Cathedral Ave. from the equidistant Woodley Park-Zoo Metro.) Driving from downtown, take Massachusetts Ave. north and turn right on Wisconsin Ave.; the cathedral is on your immediate right. Parking is free but limited to the lot between the northwest and North Transept entrances and on the streets on or near the grounds. (Cathedral proper open May-Aug. Mon.-Fri. 10am-9pm, Sat. 10am-4:30pm, Sun. 12:30-4pm; Sept.-April Mon.-Sat. 10am-4:30pm, Sun. 12:30-4pm. Call about disabled and hearing-impaired access.)

GLOVER PARK

Busy with physicists and astronomers during the day, the **U.S. Naval Observatory** (recorded information 762-1467, reservations (for groups of 15 or more only) 762-1438) opens up—sort of—for guided tours on Monday nights (except federal holidays) at 8:30pm. Enter the South Gate on Observatory Circle across from the New Zealand embassy. **Parking** is available outside the gate on Observatory Circle, near the British embassy. The gate opens at 8pm, but hopefuls should show up by 7:30pm—only the first 90 people are allowed in, and as many as 30 spots may be reserved. Visitors must show ID and pass through a metal detector upon entering and are not allowed to leave until the 1½-hour **tour** is over, either due to spying concerns or fear of damage to the equipment. The tour has three parts: a ½-hour video, a visit to a 12-inch refracting telescope in order to view celestial objects, and a look at the atomic clock. Some visitors will be immensely intrigued by the observatory's science and history, others may not want to sacrifice an all-too-fleeting glimpse of the night sky. Appropriate the observatory's timekeeping functions and set your watch by its **atomic clock**—call 762-1401 for the official U.S. hour, minute, and second. The grounds of the observatory are closed to the public at all other times, in part for the security and privacy of the Circle's other tenant: the Vice President. The looming, white **Vice Presidential Mansion** is best viewed from the intersection of Massachusetts Ave. and 34th St., though even here high fences and dense foliage conceal it rather effectively.

Across the street from Al's place, Norwegian diplomats beat the heat in their ultramodern embassy, a green glass and copper edifice that looks as though it was giftwrapped in a chain-link fence. Along with the embassy of Cape Verde next door, the Norwegian embassy marks the end of the stretch of Mass. Ave. known as "Embassy Row" which begins southeast of Dupont Circle.

Heading west on Calvert St. and taking a right on Wisconsin offers the ultimate diplomatic snub. The **Russian embassy** compound on the left, behind high stone walls and higher fences is most definitely off-limits to all comers. The embassy's location, on top-dollar property near the summit of Mount St. Albans, incensed Cold Warriors when construction began in the early '80s. Smile domestically for the security cameras as you walk by.

TENLEY CIRCLE

Sidwell Friends School, at Wisconsin Ave. and Rodman St. NW, is recognizable by the tennis courts visible from the street. The school, reaffirming its history of educating offspring of the D.C. powerful (past parents include Bob Woodward, Tim Wirth, David Brinkley, and Bill Bradley), became the talk of the town with the arrival of First Daughter Chelsea Clinton. Farther up at Wisconsin and Davenport, rival **Georgetown Day School** studies and plays in a tile-faced building that appears plagued with the measles. Both schools lay claim to liberal philosophies and hefty tuitions. Across Wisconsin Ave., public **Woodrow Wilson High School** serves a diverse student body who tend to hang out in **Fort Reno Park,** across Chesapeake St. at 40th St. NW. Summer punk shows in the park include embarrassing amateurs and brilliant local talent alike, sometimes on the same evening.

Few of these high school students stay in the neighborhood after graduation, but college could be as close as just down the street at **American University,** which fans out behind Ward Circle at Massachusetts and Nebraska Ave. NW. Among AU's few attractions are its affordable performing-arts events. The movies shown to film classes during the school year are free to visitors; some are landmarks in the history of cinema. (See **Nightlife & Entertainment,** p. 222.) Theater, dance, and musical events at AU proliferate, but their quality varies; contemporary composers-in-residence may offer performances at low ticket prices. Call 885-2787 for more information on performing arts at AU.

South of American University, hills and forests hide opulent homes along prestigious **Foxhall Road.** Glover Archibald and Battery Kemble parks rise only blocks away. A few houses, such as that of philanthropist David Lloyd Kreeger, hide their custom architecture behind concrete fences that are up to a city-block in length. Few tourists come this far west of Georgetown, but the neighborhood's relative isolation and botanical proliferation make it perfect for an afternoon stroll.

An afternoon stroll is out of the question at the **Israeli Embassy,** 3514 International Dr. NW at Reno Rd., several blocks east of Tenley Circle (Metro: Van Ness-UDC). You'll recognize it by what's not there: lacking the ornate coat-of-arms, the statuary, and the refurbished-mansion look that normally signal an embassy, the Israeli delegation works securely inside a chunky concrete building whose heavy construction and difficulty of approach represent the last word in anti-terrorist architecture. During the Gulf War, the embassy received an extra round of security from circling Secret Service cars.

FRIENDSHIP HEIGHTS

The words "Friendship Heights" conjure up the secret addiction of many Washingtonians—ritzy boutiques and *faaabulous* buys. Exit signs inside the Metro station point you in the direction of different stores. The exit at Western Ave. and Military Rd., deposits shoppers on street level to ponder the choices. Like the neighborhood itself, the shopping areas are a hybrid of suburbia and metropolis, blocks of street-level shops with sprawling malls nearby.

Beside this shopping mecca, the nostalgic **Washington Dolls' House & Toy Museum** cavorts at 5236 44th St. NW (244-0024), one block west of Wisconsin Ave., next to the Jenifer Mall. Six rooms inside showcase a carefully researched collection of antique dolls, dolls' houses, toys, and games. The collection captures American social history (some international pieces are also displayed), reliving the antediluvian days when little girls were presented with dolls and tiny play kitchens to prepare them for Domestic Life. Numerous miniaturized buildings are displayed here, from Mexican mansions to the U.S. Capitol. (Admission $4, seniors $3, children under 12 $2. Open Tues.-Sat. 10am-5pm, Sun. noon-5pm.) At night after the stores close, their **parking lots** stay open—a convenience to Wisconsin Ave. diners.

Bethesda, MD

Metro: Bethesda.

Bethesda lets out a relaxed, self-satisfied yawn as it stretches west of Wisconsin Ave. from the District's Maryland border to the National Institutes of Health. Born of a boondocky crossroads in the early, agrarian days of Montgomery County, a wave of suburban housing shook the sleepy, rattletrap cowtown out of its past and set it down again on the edge of this century. Soon enough, immigrants were boring wells here and calling this soil their own. In no time, various exquisite cuisines and a healthy crop of new cultural offerings had made Bethesda an important social center. In the last decade, real-estate has become high-priced and scarce, as sites have been snatched up for corporate complexes and gracious residences. But some of Bethesda's mid-century charm does remain, however hidden; it will take some sniffing to uncover the stubbornly rundown diners and silvery Art Deco shopfronts.

A visit to Bethesda should include shopping, exploring, contemplating urban design, and, most importantly, eating well and cheaply; the lack of major sights hardly precludes a trip here. Upon arrival, visitors walk through a collection of outdoor modern sculpture. Bill Wainwright's *Rainbow Forest,* an aluminum-disc sculpture, sways securely above the Bethesda Metro's top escalator, sporting obscure holograms. The bright yellow aluminum sculpture on the plaza itself is Mary Ann Mears's *Beacon.* In the open plaza just outside the Metro, crowds of up to 500 dance away Friday nights between May and September (6pm to 9pm). Dancing fashions range from business suits to zebra prints to unfortunate spandex outfits. From Thanksgiving to February, outdoor ice-skaters figure-eight around the plaza.

A short block south of the Metro station, the old, small, and stoney-faced **Bethesda Post Office,** 7400 Wisconsin Ave., glowers at the encroaching mass of steel and glass (301-441-2664; open Mon.-Fri. 8am-6pm, Sat. 8:30am-1pm). Directly north of the post office is the *Madonna of the Trail,* a 1929 stone memorial to the mothers of covered-wagon days. A detour west off Wisconsin Ave. will bring you to **Hampden Square,** an attractive condo and office complex at 4801 Hampden Lane. Around the base of the building, a shady courtyard gives the illusion of seclusion. The columns around it suggest a Mediterranean grotto, while Tom Supensky's blue ceramic *The Wave* suggests, well, the Mediterranean. Raymond Kaskey's *Neptune,* a concrete rendering of the god's face, entrances children from a nearby wall.

The **Montgomery Farm Women's Cooperative Market,** at 7155 Wisconsin Ave. (301-652-2291), a low white building near Bethesda Ave. can barely hold its bustling farmer's market (Wed. and Sat. 7am-3pm). The cooperative, begun in 1932, is still run entirely by farmers; the first man joined its governing board in 1968.

NATIONAL INSTITUTES OF HEALTH

Like rats in a maze, some 3500 researchers in white coats scurry among NIH's 45 buildings and 316 acres. Their quest: cures for cancer, AIDS, and their ilk—and perhaps a Nobel Prize or two along the way. Most of the action takes place in labs that are closed to the public, but the biologically curious can still wander around the expansive grounds, located between Wisconsin Ave. (Rte. 355) and Old Georgetown Rd. just inside the Beltway in Bethesda (Metro: Medical Center). For a more purposeful stroll, pick up a free, 1½-hr. tour cassette and player from the **Visitor Information Center,** building 10, room B1C-218, under a three-story atrium in the building's center (301-496-1776). **Building 10** is the largest on the campus. You can reach the glass and brick behemoth on foot from the Metro, or by hopping on an NIH "campus shuttle" bus at the station. The Visitors Center also experiments with a slide show, videotaped exhibits, a working lab, and guided **tours.** (Visitors Center open Mon.-Fri. 8:30am-5pm. Tours Mon., Wed., and Fri. at 11am.) Also on the lower level of Building 10 in room BIL-101, the **Foundation Bookstore** sells medical sketch books and notebooks, anatomical charts, stethoscopes, and blood-pressure cuffs (open Mon.-Fri. 8:30am-4pm). Many people come to the Visitors Center for literature on specific areas of disease research; more information can also be found in the **National Library of Medicine,** the world's largest library devoted to a single subject (301-496-6095. Free tours Mon.-Fri. 1pm; meet in the lobby of Building 38A. Main reading room open Mon.-Fri. 8:30am-5pm, Sat. 8:30am-12:30pm. History of Medicine reading room open Mon.-Fri. 8:30am-5pm; library has database, "Internet Grateful Med," available on the World Wide Web. Materials for on-site use only.)

Rock Creek Park

City-weary voices crying out for wilderness can rejoice in the 15 mi. of hiking trails and bridle paths in Rock Creek Park. More like a managed forest than a landscaped city park, the 2100-acre green is a leafy home for joggers, park rangers, and bustling wildlife. (Supposedly, Charles de Gaulle once mistook it for the French Embassy's new backyard.) This opiate for nature addicts takes the shape of a bent syringe, with the needle pointing at the Kennedy Center and the plunger west of 16th St. NW, at the District's northern tip. **Rock Creek Parkway,** which becomes Beach Drive north of Klingle Rd. NW, winds through the park from north to south alongside its watery namesake. Some of the forest trails run near the parkway, which offers a noisy reminder of nearby city traffic, but the tiny bridges and sporadic creeks keep wilder sections of the park to themselves.

Thanks to plentiful shady trees, it's about 10 degrees cooler inside the park than outside. Along Rock Creek Pkwy., starting at Calvert St. and Connecticut Ave., is a 1½-mi. "Parcourse" **exercise trail,** complete with 18 **workout stations** where you can push-up, pull-up, and sit-up to your heart's content (and benefit). A four-mi. run starts where Rock Creek Pkwy. crosses under Connecticut Ave.; run north toward Pierce Mill and then retrace your route. In upper Rock Creek Park, there's a standard 11-mi. run from Beach Dr. to Tilden St. to East-West Hwy. in Chevy Chase. Cyclists will find plenty of **bicycle trails** crisscrossing the park and plenty of signs pointing them out. These same cyclists compete with rollerbladers for control of Beach Dr. from 7am on Saturdays until 7pm on Sundays, when the park closes its gates to motorized vehicles for most of its length north of Broad Branch Rd. Parking is plentiful at lots throughout the park, and sporadic grassy knolls along Beach Dr. are designated as daytime **picnic spots.** Camping in Rock Creek Park, however, is always illegal, probably dangerous, and mostly impossible anyway.

The remains of several **Civil War Forts** are interspersed throughout the grounds; the park also boasts tennis courts and a golf course, open to the public (for a fee). Activities are offered at **Pierce Mill,** a restored gristmill, and the **Art Barn** (mill open Wed.-Sun. 8am-4:30pm; barn open Wed.-Sun. 10am-5pm). During the summer, per-

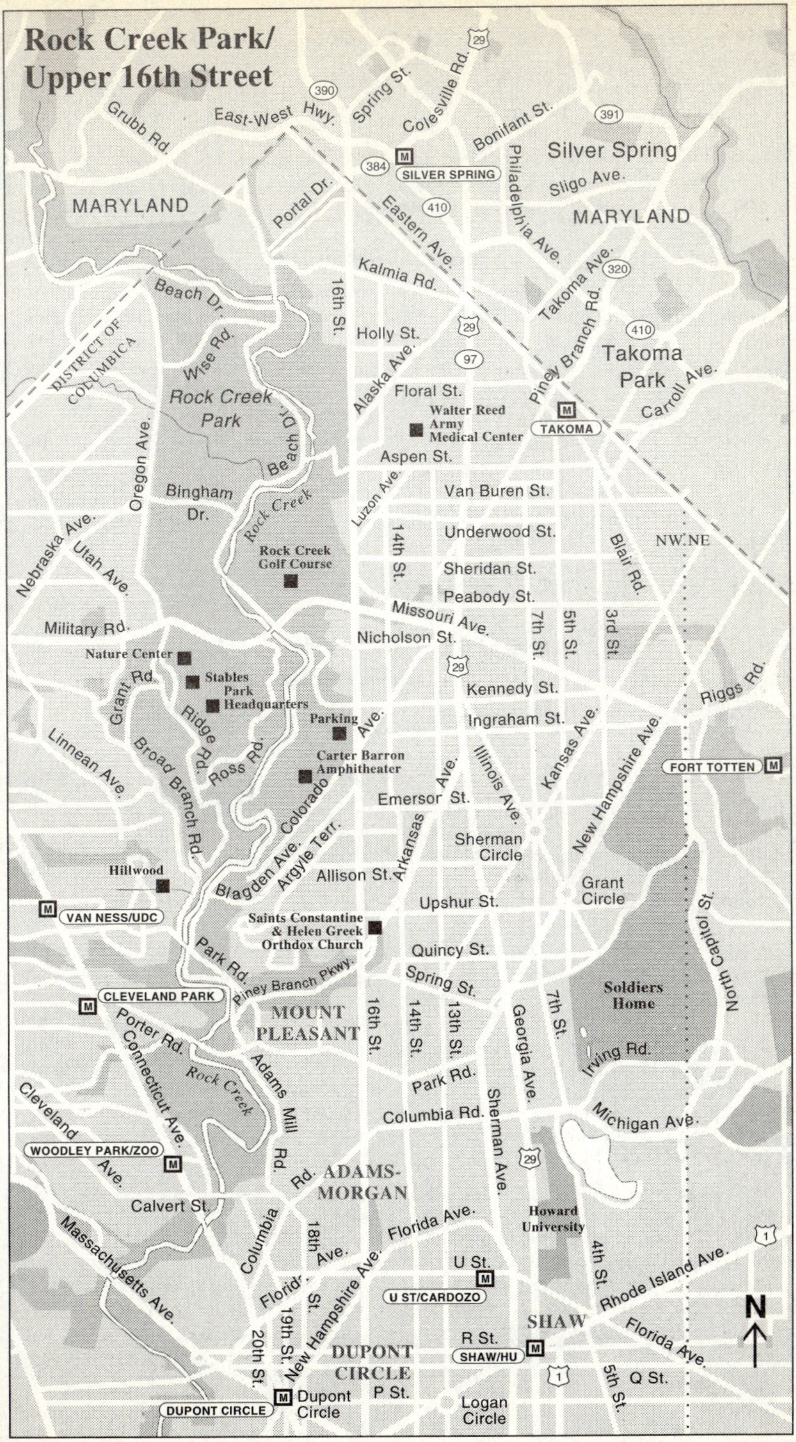
Rock Creek Park/
Upper 16th Street
MARYLAND
Grubb Rd.
East-West Hwy.
390
Spring St.
Colesville Rd.
29
Bonifant St.
391
Silver Spring
384
SILVER SPRING
Sligo Ave.
410
Portal Dr.
Eastern Ave.
Philadelphia Ave.
MARYLAND
Kalmia Rd.
16th St.
Takoma Ave.
320
Beach Dr.
Holly St.
29
410
Piney Branch Rd.
Takoma
Park
Carroll Ave.
DISTRICT OF COLUMBIA
Wise Rd.
Alaska Ave.
97
Floral St.
Rock Creek
Park
Walter Reed
Army
Medical Center
TAKOMA
Oregon Ave.
Beach Dr.
Aspen St.
Bingham
Dr.
Luzon Ave.
Van Buren St.
Rock Creek
Underwood St.
Blair Rd.
NW NE
Nebraska Ave.
Utah Ave.
Rock Creek
Golf Course
14th St.
Sheridan St.
Peabody St.
Military Rd.
Missouri Ave.
7th St.
5th St.
3rd St.
Nicholson St.
Nature Center
29
Grant Rd.
Stables
Park
Headquarters
Kennedy St.
Riggs Rd.
Parking
Ingraham St.
Ridge Rd.
Linnean Ave.
Broad Branch Rd.
Ross Rd.
Carter Barron
Amphitheater
Illinois Ave.
Kansas Ave.
New Hampshire Ave.
FORT TOTTEN
Colorado
Ave.
Emerson St.
Arkansas Ave.
Sherman
Circle
Argyle Terr.
Blagden Ave.
Allison St.
Hillwood
Grant
Circle
Upshur St.
VAN NESS/UDC
Saints Constantine
& Helen Greek
Orthdox Church
Quincy St.
North Capitol St.
Park Rd.
Spring St.
Piney Branch Pkwy.
Soldiers
Home
CLEVELAND PARK
MOUNT
PLEASANT
16th St.
14th St.
13th St.
Georgia Ave.
7th St.
Porter Rd.
Irving Rd.
Connecticut Ave.
Rock Creek
Adams Mill
Rd.
Park Rd.
Cleveland
Ave.
Columbia Rd.
Sherman Ave.
Michigan Ave.
WOODLEY PARK/ZOO
29
Rd.
ADAMS-
MORGAN
Calvert St.
Columbia
18th
Ave.
Florida Ave.
Howard
University
1
Massachusetts Ave.
U St.
4th St.
Rhode Island Ave.
Florid
St.
New Hampshire Ave.
U ST/CARDOZO
N
19th St.
SHAW
Florida Ave.
20th St.
DUPONT
CIRCLE
R St.
SHAW/HU
1
5th St.
Q St.
DUPONT CIRCLE
Dupont
Circle
P St.
Logan
Circle

SIGHTS

formances are given at the outdoor **Carter Barron Amphitheater;** see **Nightlife and Entertainment** for details (p. 207).

Park **information** can be had by mail, by phone, or in person from the park's **Nature Center,** at 5200 Glover Rd. NW (426-6828/9; http://www.nps.gov), which also screens films (Sat.-Sun. at 11am) and offers a planetarium show (Sat.-Sun. at 1 and 4pm, Wed. at 3:45pm). Various "Ranger's Choice" events are also offered on Saturdays and Sundays; monthly schedules are available from the Nature Center (open Wed.-Sun. 9am-5pm). Horse rentals are offered by the **Rock Creek Horse Center** (362-0117); bikes, canoes, and rowboats are rented at **Thompson's Boat House** (333-4861). For more information, see **Sports and Recreation** (p. 225). In an **emergency,** call the park police (619-7300).

Near Rock Creek Park

The **Walter Reed Army Medical Center** is home to the **National Museum of Health and Medicine,** Building 54, 6825 16th St. NW (202-782-2200), near Rock Creek Park. Scientists and scholars here study assassinations, birth defects, military doctors, and medical anomalies (take an S2 or S4 bus up 16th St. from downtown, or a 52 or 54 bus from the Takoma Metro Station). Presidents Lincoln and Garfield, both shot while in office, get their own displays. The **actual bullet that ended Lincoln's life** is on display as well as a **skull fragment** and a lock of his hair. The pathology displays, which are accompanied by case histories of the unfortunate subjects, are some of the most unusual exhibits in the museum. A **grisly skeleton** whose fused bones keep the adult owner frozen in a seated position is just one of the creepy items in the Walter Reed closets (open daily 10am-5:30pm; free).

SIGHTS

Takoma Park, MD

Metro: Takoma.

Takoma Park straddles two lines. One is the D.C. line; half its own town, half a Washington neighborhood, Takoma Park aspires simultaneously to small-town coziness and subdued hipness. The other line divides the '60s generation from their yuppie successors: neighbors' tie-dyes and suit-and-ties coexist in a happy compromise. Colorful bungalows, trees, and roomy Victorian houses dominate the idyllic streetscape. Crystals, tiny Ozark harps, and South American cotton clutter the retail scene and fit the low-key, neo-Woodstock dress code. As any resident could tell you, the town declared itself a nuclear-free zone during the mid-'80s height of Reaganism, joining Berkeley, CA, and Madison, WI. Recently, both Takoma breeds pulled together to push for environmental reform.

There are no major sights this removed from downtown, but Takoma Park still merits a stroll, not to mention **window-shopping.** For Takoma Park's commercial heart, head up Carroll St. from the Takoma Metro and into the town proper, where Carroll St. becomes Carroll Ave. on the left and Laurel Ave. on the right. The shops are open all week, though the people-watching is certainly prime on weekends. (See **Shopping,** p. 231, for stores in this area.)

Northeast

> *As you move about the city you will see that outlying tracts of land, once the broad receptacles of dead animals and where no better scavengers appeared than the buzzards or the crows, have been reclaimed and added to the city and made to blossom like the rose.*
>
> —Frederick Douglass, Lecture on the National Capital (1877)

Metro: Rhode Island Ave., Brookland-CUA, Ft. Totten, Minnesota Ave., Deanwood.

Northeast Washington is too big to be a neighborhood. The triangle formed by North Capitol St., East Capitol St., and Eastern Ave. (for most of Northeast, the District line) encloses over a quarter of the District's land area, including parts of Capitol Hill (covered under that section), Takoma Park, and some lesser-known middle-class neighborhoods. Many parts of Northeast have been overwhelmed by the crack epidemic, especially near the Prince George's County line and east of the Anacostia River. On the other hand, **Catholic University** guards (and landscapes) its acres north of Michigan Ave. off North Capitol St., while the **National Arboretum** and **Kenilworth Gardens** landscape (and guard) even more space east of Capitol Hill.

North Capitol St. cruises from the Capitol to the northern tip of the D.C. diamond at startlingly high speeds for city driving. Four roads run roughly parallel through Northeast on a southwest-northeast diagonal: Maryland Ave., which shoots out from the Capitol, eventually intersecting with the larger Bladensburg Rd. (which continues through the Maryland border); New York Ave., home of the cheap-motel strip; Rhode Island Ave.; and meandering Michigan Ave., which leads to the Catholic U. area. Maryland Ave. is the southernmost of the quadruplets. 13th St., which becomes Brentwood Rd. south of Rhode Island Ave., slices through the middle-class Brookland neighborhood. South Dakota Ave. parallels the District line, while off-again, on-again Eastern Ave. follows the line itself. Northeast sights are spread out all over the quadrant; visitors should expect to spend a significant amount of time driving or riding the Metro to and from them.

NATIONAL ARBORETUM

The National Arboretum, 3501 New York Ave. NE (245-2726; main entrance at 24th and R St. NE), is the United States' organic library of trees and flowers. Nearly 10 mi. of roads crisscross some 444 acres of land, which sprout flora ranging from crabapples to crapemyrtles. Every passing month in spring or summer sees flowers and blooms explode in a different corner of the arboretum. The May azaleas are particular favorites, as are the April cherries. Detailed information and brochures about seasonal highlights available from **Arbor House** (the visitors center).

A few attractions, such as the gargantuan **herb garden,** draw visitors year-round, but none more so than the arboretum's world-class stock of **bonsai** (the Japanese term for artistic potted plants) and **penjing** (the Chinese term for tray landscapes). While bonsai art tends to solely feature the miniature tree, penjing often incorporates rocks, figurines, boats, and pagodas. Gardens, pavilions, and wooden tables exhibit more than 130 miniature flora, many of which are not only rare but also incredibly expensive (some bonsai cost over $10,000) and difficult to sustain.

From the bonsai collection, visitors will notice what seems to be an ancient Roman ruin sitting atop a hill at the center of the arboretum. The columns in question actually had a more local, though no less distinguished, origin—they once spanned the East Portico of the Capitol. Completed in 1826, the **Portico** was dismantled in 1958 to make room for an addition to the Capitol; the twenty-two columns were held in storage until 1984, when they were moved to the arboretum.

The arboretum is large enough to deem a drive through it worthwhile, although a long, leisurely stroll is undoubtedly the best way to proceed. Bicycling is another option. If at all possible, visitors should drive to the arboretum, since the surrounding area is somewhat dangerous; **parking** is readily accessible inside the R St. entrance. The hopelessly carless can Metro themselves to Stadium-Armory, take the B2 bus to the intersection of Bladensburg Rd. and R St., and walk east on R. (Open daily 8am-

Bonsai!

Love of the bonsai has engendered an international network of fanciers, cultivators, and weirdos: in July 1991, a mysterious thief nabbed a $1000 bonsai from the Arboretum and then returned it three days later in improved condition—it had been pruned rather expertly. Go figure.

5pm; July-March Mon.-Fri. 8am-5pm, Sat.-Sun. 10am-5pm. Bonsai collection open daily 10am-3:30pm. Free. **Arbor House** open Mon.-Fri. 8am-4:30pm, April-June daily 8am-4:30pm. Gift shop open daily March-Dec. 10am-3pm.) Schedules of special events, from bonsai demonstrations to flower arrangement displays, are available at Arbor House.

THE REST OF NORTHEAST

Across the Anacostia River from the National Arboretum, **Kenilworth Aquatic Gardens,** Anacostia Ave. and Douglas St. NE (426-6905), does for aquatic plants what the arboretum does for trees (Metro: Deanwood). Dozens of ponds sacrifice their surfaces to thousands of lilies, lotuses, and hyacinths. The gardens look best in July and Aug., when the tropical plants bloom, and unless you have a fondness for unadorned lily pads, come in the morning before the midday heat closes up the complex flowers. The paths amid the ponds warrant at least a half-hour stroll, while the .7-mi. **river trail,** which leads to the last natural marsh on the Anacostia River, requires an hour. The floating flora accompany a virtual army of turtles, frogs, waterfowl, muskrats, raccoons, and opossums. (A few blocks from the gardens, more dangerous infantry hold periodic turf wars. Watch your step.) But within the gardens, visitors are enveloped in a soothing cocoon of tranquil, natural beauty; the gardens are sadly undervisited and it is easy to imagine yourself the sole inhabitant of wild rainforest or coastal wetlands. The 77 acres of Kenilworth Marsh are a rest stop for tremendous numbers of migrating birds of all kinds. A **Visitors Center** offers pamphlets and brochures, an exhibit on the history of the gardens, and an aquarium exhibit. Metro-riders should get off at the Deanwood stop, tramp over a green-cage bridge, and head straight down Douglas St. The entrance is at Anacostia Ave. and Douglas St. Drivers should take New York Ave. NE out of the city and hang a right on Kenilworth Ave. just after crossing the District line; signs direct to the gardens. (Open daily 7am-4pm; Visitors Center open daily 8am-4pm. Tours Sat.-Sun. and holidays at 9am, 11am, and 1pm.)

Catholic University, Michigan Ave. and 4th St. NE (319-5200), is an urban anomaly, a campus in, but not of, the city. (Metro: Brookland-CUA.) The suburban grade-school architecture that greets visitors at the edge of the campus nearest the Metro is misleading; not far beyond lie the sort of Gothic buildings, creeping foliage, and spacious quadrangles that you might expect of a small-town college. The school doesn't offer guided tours; guests may wander freely. Periodically posted campus maps will keep you oriented, and are available at the information desk on the first floor of University Center East, at the southern end of campus. The **Information Center** is open Mon.-Thurs. 8:30am-10pm, Fri. 8:30am-9pm, Sat. 3-9pm, Sun. 1-9pm. Alums include Chris and Susan Sarandon, as well as John Voight—who, as a student, painted the basketball court. A portion of the floor is on display near the information desk. Leading programs include drama, philosophy, and of course, religion and canon law. Those who earn a masters or doctorate in Catholic theology from CUA. get their degrees signed by the Pope. Buildings like the Marian Scholasticate and Salve Regina Hall will remind you that you're at a school where 80% of the students, and most of the professors, are Catholic. CUA's Hartke Theatre puts on arias for a professional-quality Summer Opera series. See **Nightlife & Entertainment** (p. 219) for more information.

Pedestrians won't miss the **Basilica of the National Shrine of the Immaculate Conception** (526-8300), located on the edge of the Catholic U. campus at Michigan Ave. and 4th St. NE. (Metro: Brookland-CUA.) After all, it's the eighth largest church in the world, and the largest Catholic church in the western hemisphere (take that, St. Patrick's). The shrine's striking, boundary-crossing architecture catches eyes too, as Romanesque arches support stark, Byzantine-flavored façades and a blue-and-gold onion dome that seems straight from Kiev. The bell tower beside the main entrance is cleverly disguised as an Islamic minaret. The interior continues the architectural mix 'n' match, as some 59 kneeling chapels dedicated to the Virgin Mary line the walls of the main Church and crypt level. Many of them are decorated with stained-glass windows and colorful, intricate mosaics—part Byzantine, part Romanesque, and part neither. Funded partially by children who have mailed in pennies, the

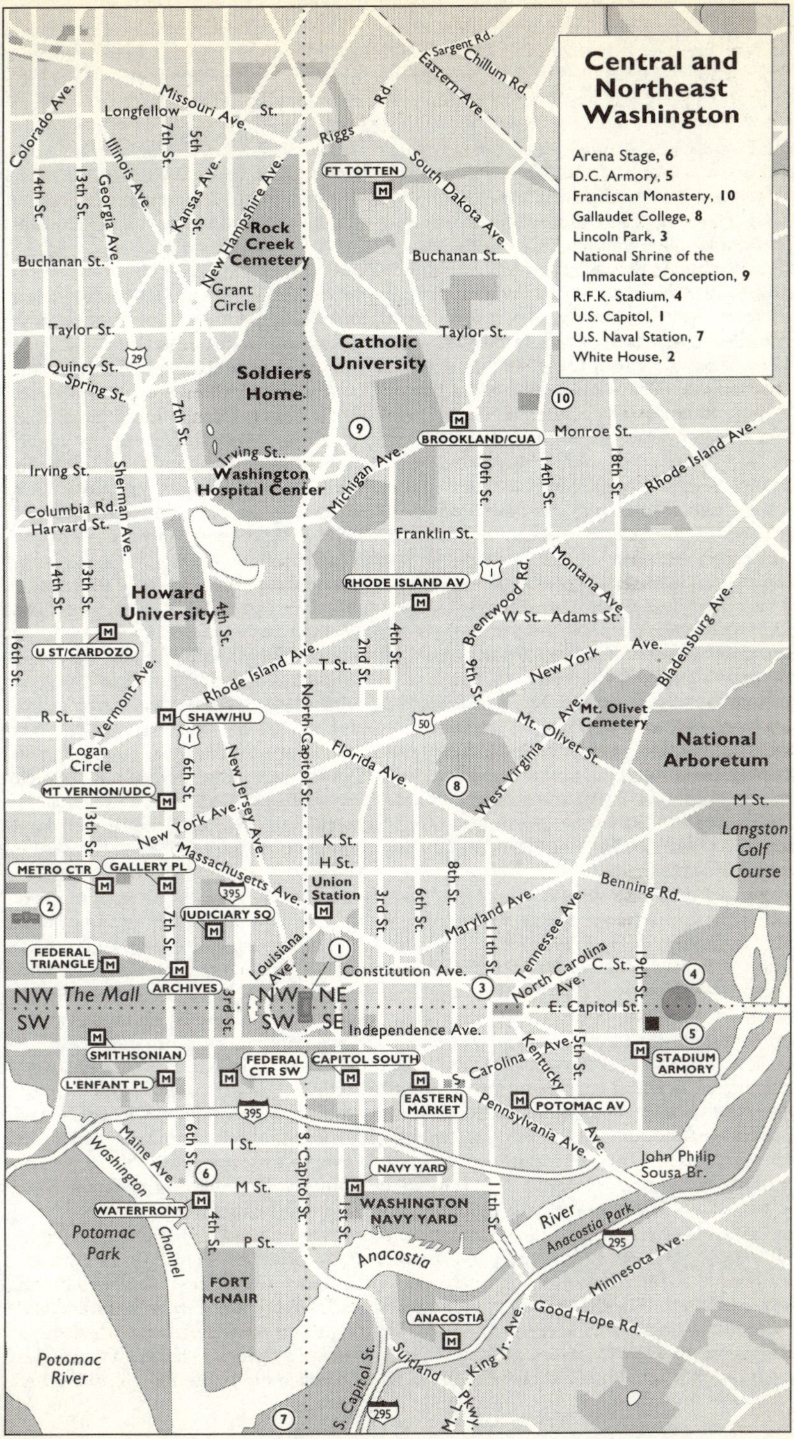
Central and Northeast Washington
Arena Stage, 6
D.C. Armory, 5
Franciscan Monastery, 10
Gallaudet College, 8
Lincoln Park, 3
National Shrine of the Immaculate Conception, 9
R.F.K. Stadium, 4
U.S. Capitol, 1
U.S. Naval Station, 7
White House, 2
Rock Creek Cemetery
Grant Circle
Soldiers Home
Catholic University
Washington Hospital Center
Howard University
Logan Circle
Mt. Olivet Cemetery
National Arboretum
Langston Golf Course
Union Station
The Mall
Washington Navy Yard
Fort McNair
Potomac Park
Potomac River
Washington Channel
Anacostia River
Anacostia Park
John Philip Sousa Br.
FT TOTTEN
BROOKLAND/CUA
RHODE ISLAND AV
U ST/CARDOZO
SHAW/HU
MT VERNON/UDC
METRO CTR
GALLERY PL
JUDICIARY SQ
FEDERAL TRIANGLE
ARCHIVES
SMITHSONIAN
L'ENFANT PL
FEDERAL CTR SW
CAPITOL SOUTH
EASTERN MARKET
POTOMAC AV
STADIUM ARMORY
NAVY YARD
WATERFRONT
ANACOSTIA
NW NE SW SE

SIGHTS

National Shrine hosts weekly masses, which most CUA students attend. The Basilica may be reached by walking straight across the CUA campus from the Metro; the main entrance is at street level on the front side of the shrine, to the right of the stairs leading up to the Upper Church. (Basilica open April-Oct. daily 7am-7pm, Nov.-March 7am-6pm; **tours** Mon.-Sat. every hour on the hour 9am-3pm; Sun. every hour on the half hour 1:30-4pm. Free. Upper Church masses held Sat. 5:15pm; Sun. 9am, 10:30am, noon, and 4:30pm. Crypt Church mass held Sun. 7:30am; Latin mass 1:30pm. Weekday masses held 7am, 7:30am, 8am, 8:30am, 12:10pm, and 5:15pm in the Crypt Church. Call about holiday services.) Handicap access, wheelchairs, and free parking are available.

The peaceful **Franciscan Monastery,** 1400 Quincy St. NE (526-6800), brings a little bit of the Holy Land to America. (Metro: Brookland-CUA.) Some 700 years ago, the Roman Catholic Church entrusted the Franciscans with the guardianship of the Holy Land's most precious tombs and temples, and the monastery commemorates that duty with replicas of these shrines spread throughout the church and the surrounding grounds. The arched entrance at the corner of Quincy and 14th St. leads directly to the main entrance, above which rises stately Byzantine architecture. A maze of glass display cases proceeds to the waiting area, adorned with gilded copes and chasubles, where visitors may wait for a tour led by a Franciscan monk. Alternatively, those who do not desire a tour may set out independently in the main church, and see the first of the many religious replicas—a model of Jesus' Sepulcher, including the rolling rock he pushed away in the Resurrection. Red lights lead to **murals** depicting Christ and the Apostles, as well as to a three-dimensional mural of the crucifixion. The advantage of taking the tour is that it also leads visitors downstairs to the replicas of the Roman **catacombs,** where holy relics and wall mosaics trace Bible stories. On deposit in the reliquaries are a collection of St. Benigus's bones wrapped in cotton; a statue of St. Cecilius, whom soldiers tried unsuccessfully to decapitate; and a statue of St. Sebastian—a popular subject of Renaissance painters—who miraculously survived being shot full of arrows by Roman soldiers. Outside the monastery are the explorable well-tended **gardens** and replicas of a number of noted tombs and grottos. The beautiful **Rosary Portico** or **Cloister Walk** winds around the garden, displaying plaques on which prayers are engraved in many languages. From the Brookland-CUA Metro, take an H2 or H4 bus or walk across the Michigan Ave. bridge, continue for about 2 blocks, and then turn right on Quincy St. (Open Mon.-Sat. 9-11am and 1-4pm, Sun. 1-4pm. Free. **Tours** leave every hour. Free parking in two lots on 14th St. Wheelchair accessible.)

Rock Creek Cemetery (829-0585) harbors monuments and gravestones between New Hampshire Ave. NW and North Capitol St. (Metro: Fort Totten; enter at Rock Creek Church Rd. and Webster St. NW.) Section E of the cemetery contains Augustus Saint-Gaudens's **Adams Monument.** Henry Adams's wife Marian committed suicide by drinking photographic chemicals. Saint-Gaudens's bronze figure—hooded, cloaked, and seated—depicts her. Commonly called "Grief" instead, the statue seems to recall universal human pain (open daily 7:30am-dusk).

Gallaudet University, 800 Florida Ave. NE (651-5000, TDD 651-5000), established in 1864, is still the world's only university for the deaf. (Metro: Union Station.) Protesters shouting and signing "Deaf President Now" made national news in 1989; the students subsequently got a deaf president, Dr. I. King Jordan, and the deaf community got more nationwide media attention than ever before. An exhibit in the Visitors Center (651-5050) behind College Hall on the right shows several short films and videotapes and an array of photographs (open Mon.-Fri. 9am-5pm; free).

Arlington, VA

Metro: Crystal City; National Airport; Rosslyn; Arlington Cemetery; Court House; Clarendon.

Arlington abandoned Washington in 1846 when Virginia snatched back its contribution to the Federal City. Nevertheless, Arlington's inclinations remain Washingtonian.

SIGHTS

Four bridges to downtown D.C. serve as Arlington's above-ground umbilical cords—a reminder that it endures as the Last Colony's first colony. While buildings in Washington can't rise higher than the Capitol dome, corporate high-flyers take power trips in Rosslyn's skyscrapers, which lie just across the Potomac from Georgetown. Arlington's suburban status also yields more land for the taking: Arlington Cemetery, National Airport, and the Pentagon would be unthinkable in the capital on account of their sheer size. South or west of these behemoths of business and government, thousands of commuters find Arlington's modest houses convenient. Several Asian and Hispanic communities call Arlington County home.

ORIENTATION

The Arlington Visitors Center, 735 18th St. (358-5720 or 800-677-6267) will answer your questions and give you armloads of brochures (Metro: Crystal City; open daily 9am-5pm). If you try to drive in Arlington for any length of time, you'll probably get lost. The original, D.C.-esque street plan featured two- and three-syllable streets in alphabetical order (Upton, Vermont, Wakefield, Woodstock, Abingdon, Buchanan) running roughly north-south and crossed by east-west numbered streets. While these streets exist, they are often only a few blocks long; some end and pick up again miles from where they began. Add the network of non-parallel numbered routes, highways, and boulevards—designed to move commuters from downtown D.C. to their Fairfax bungalows—and you have non-linear, mind-bending insanity. These disorienting major roads include I-395 and the Columbia Pike (Rte. 244) in South Arlington, Arlington Blvd. (Rte. 50), Wilson Blvd., and Washington Blvd. (Rte. 237). I-66 can take you *through* Arlington, but not *to* much of it.

Fortunately, the Metro and Metrobus can take you where you want to go. Buses cruise down Columbia Pike, Arlington Blvd., and Wilson Blvd. Check with the Metro (637-7000) before you make the trip. The Metro's Orange Line can shuttle you out to most of Arlington's hotspots for ethnic cuisine. The major sights, Arlington Cemetery and the Pentagon, are just across the river at the Metro stops named for them. If you get really lost, check streets signs for "N" (north of Rte. 50, or Arlington Blvd.) or "S" (south of it). The **area code** in Arlington is **703.**

SIGHTS

Rosslyn is just what D.C.'s designers were trying to avoid. In this mess of skyscrapers, the Gannett/*USA Today* building looms so large that it is routinely blamed for the navigational blunders of airplanes landing at National Airport.

Crystal City, another concrete community of offices and condos, resides (like real crystal) half-underground. Its miles of underground tunnels connect block upon block of buildings, and the Metro will bring you straight to a massive underground shopping mall, **Crystal Underground.** Three air-conditioned, underground blocks away from the Metro in Building 3 of Crystal Plaza (follow the signs to "Plaza 3"), the **Patent and Trademark Office** (on the third floor) has all the country's millions of patents on file. On the lobby level is the dinky **National Inventor's Hall of Fame,** which honors Alexander Graham Bell, Charles Goodyear, Louis Pasteur, Samuel Morse, and others. Check out G.M. Pratt's 1877 sewing machine. Special events take place on National Inventors Day, which falls on or near February 11 (Thomas Edison's birthday). (Open Mon.-Fri. 8am-8pm. Free.)

The four galleries at the **Arlington Arts Center,** 3550 Wilson Blvd. (524-1494), near the Virginia Square Metro, contain paintings, drawings, sculptures, and mixed-media pieces, most of which are for sale. Classes are available in life drawing, painting, and other media. Call about fall programs like Thursday evening seminars and discussion groups, as well as the periodic poetry readings, most of which require some sort of fee (open Tues.-Fri. 11am-5pm, Sat.-Sun. 1-5pm; free).

ARLINGTON NATIONAL CEMETERY

The silence of Arlington National Cemetery honors those who sacrificed their lives in war. The 612 acres of rolling hills and tree-lined avenues hold the bodies of U.S. military veterans—from five-star generals to unknown soldiers. As the largest military cemetery in the U.S., Arlington National Cemetery holds 200,000 veterans and their dependents. The hundreds who visit each day aren't exactly tourists—a walk through the cemetery's endless rows of white headstones is too solemn an experience to be confused with sight-seeing. Still, marble monuments to nurses and military groups often cross the line, sliding into memorial kitsch.

Robert E. Lee once owned an estate covering most of the cemetery grounds, but the general had to abandon his land when he moved to Richmond with his family to serve the Confederacy. Since the Lee family couldn't show their faces to pay property taxes on the land (because they would have been arrested), the Union government seized the property. Major General Montgomery Meigs, who hated the Lees for joining the South, began to bury Union troops in places like Mrs. Lee's rose garden so that the family could never reclaim their estate. Since then, many prominent soldiers have come to rest in peace in Arlington. Pierre L'Enfant, who laid out Washington, was reinterred here along with soldiers from the Revolutionary War and the War of 1812. His grave on the hillside in front of Arlington House, Lee's former residence, overlooks the city he designed. General Philip Sheridan, who fought for the Union in the Civil War, lies near Confederate General Lee's former home; the Arlington Memorial Bridge symbolizes the reunification of the country by connecting the Lincoln Memorial with Arlington House.

Among the plain headstones of World War I soldiers lies General of the Armies John J. Pershing, commander of U.S. forces during World War I, who asked to be buried among his men. Second World War heroes include Generals George C. Marshall and Omar Bradley. Gen. Daniel "Chappie" James, who flew 78 missions in the Vietnam War, was the highest-ranking African-American officer to date: a four-star general in the Air Force. Arlington also holds Joe Louis, the longest-lasting world heavyweight boxing champion in history, and Abner Doubleday, the supposed inventor of baseball, at whom the first shot in the Civil War was fired. Arctic explorers Robert E. Peary and Richard Byrd lie on the same hallowed ground as Supreme Court Justices Earl Warren and Oliver Wendell Holmes. Presidents Taft and Kennedy round out the cemetery's list of honored tombs.

Tombstones note the war in which the soldier fought. A sunken shield represents service in either the Civil War or the Spanish-American War. Pointed headstones signify Confederate soldiers and can be found around the Confederate Memorial in section I-23. Each day, an average of 15 burials take place; during each ceremony, the flag at Arlington House stands at half mast. For some high-ranking officers, a caisson carrying the casket leads the funeral procession.

Take the **Metro** to Arlington Cemetery. To **drive** from downtown Washington, take Independence or Constitution Ave. and turn left onto 23rd St. to cross the Arlington Memorial Bridge. Visitors from Virginia and Maryland have a variety of options, but the easiest is probably the Beltway (I-495) to the Virginia side of the George Washington Pkwy., then the Arlington Memorial Bridge. **Cyclists** coming from the Mt. Vernon Trail should look for a turnoff just south of the Arlington Memorial Bridge; follow it to the cemetery. The cemetery is free. Hours are April-Sept. 8am-7pm, Oct.-May 8am-5pm. Parking costs $1.25 per hour for the first three hours and $2 for each additional hour.

Before you enter the main gate, stop by the **Visitors Center** near the parking area. The information booth at the center of the building (692-0931) dispenses explanatory, gridded maps of the grounds. Winding paths are intended to provoke contemplation and reflection, but may induce fatigue as well; the short-winded should take the Tourmobile (tour $4, children 3-11 $2). Temporary passes to drive into the cemetery can also be obtained here. They will look up the location on microfiche and give

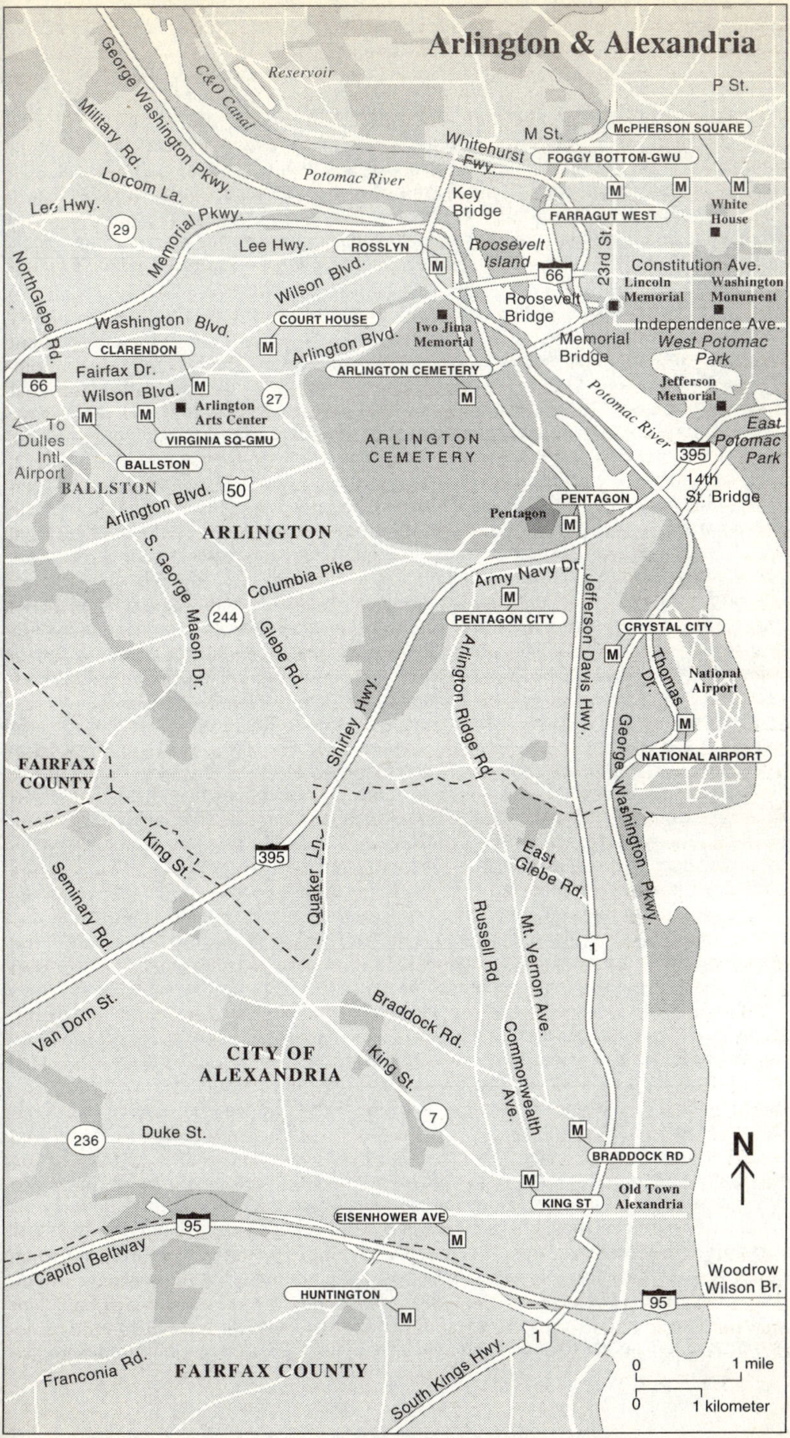
Arlington & Alexandria
Reservoir
C&O Canal
P St.
M St.
McPHERSON SQUARE
Whitehurst Fwy.
FOGGY BOTTOM-GWU
George Washington Pkwy.
Military Rd.
Potomac River
Lorcom La.
Lee Hwy.
29
Memorial Pkwy.
Key Bridge
FARRAGUT WEST
White House
Lee Hwy.
ROSSLYN
Roosevelt Island
23rd St.
Constitution Ave.
66
Lincoln Memorial
Washington Monument
NorthGlebe Rd.
Wilson Blvd.
Roosevelt Bridge
Washington Blvd.
COURT HOUSE
Two Jima Memorial
Independence Ave.
Arlington Blvd.
Memorial Bridge
West Potomac Park
CLARENDON
Fairfax Dr.
66
ARLINGTON CEMETERY
Wilson Blvd.
27
Jefferson Memorial
Potomac River
Arlington Arts Center
East Potomac Park
To Dulles Intl. Airport
VIRGINIA SQ-GMU
ARLINGTON CEMETERY
395
14th St. Bridge
BALLSTON
BALLSTON
50
PENTAGON
Arlington Blvd.
Pentagon
ARLINGTON
S. George Mason Dr.
Columbia Pike
Army Navy Dr.
244
Glebe Rd.
PENTAGON CITY
CRYSTAL CITY
Jefferson Davis Hwy.
Arlington Ridge Rd.
Thomas Dr.
National Airport
Shirley Hwy.
George Washington Pkwy.
NATIONAL AIRPORT
FAIRFAX COUNTY
King St.
395
East Glebe Rd.
Seminary Rd.
Quaker Ln.
Russell Rd
Mt. Vernon Ave.
1
Van Dorn St.
Braddock Rd.
CITY OF ALEXANDRIA
King St.
Commonwealth Ave.
7
236
Duke St.
BRADDOCK RD
N
KING ST
Old Town Alexandria
EISENHOWER AVE
95
Capitol Beltway
Woodrow Wilson Br.
HUNTINGTON
95
1
Franconia Rd.
FAIRFAX COUNTY
South Kings Hwy.
0
1 mile
0
1 kilometer

SIGHTS

you instructions on how to get there. Those wishing to find the grave of a loved one should visit the **Arlington Information Center.**

The Grounds

The **Kennedy Gravesites** hold President John F. Kennedy and his brother, Senator and Attorney General Robert F. Kennedy. John Kennedy's wife, Jacqueline Kennedy Onassis, and two of their children who died shortly after birth are also buried here. JFK supposedly once stood near Arlington House, and, seeing the spectacular view of Washington, declared, "I could stay here forever." The Purple Heart he won in World War II earned him just that privilege. The Eternal Flame, lit by his widow at his funeral, flickers above his simple memorial stone. Famous sentences from his inaugural speech are inscribed on a low wall near the site, reminding all who pass of the soaring eloquence of speechwriter Ted Sorensen. RFK's famous words are similarly inscribed near his more modest grave: the statesman wished for nothing more than a wooden cross to mark his final resting place.

The **Tomb of the Unknowns** honors servicemen who died fighting for the U.S. Unidentified soldiers from World Wars I and II and the Korean and Vietnam Wars lie under the white marble sarcophagus overlooking the city. The famous inscription reads, "Here rests in honored glory an American soldier known but to God."

The tomb is guarded 24 hours daily by delegations from the Army's Third Infantry, who sport woolen dress blues, white gloves, and bayonets. You can watch the ritualized **changing of the guard** every hour on the hour from October to March and every half hour from April through September. The towering sentinels take 21 steps and then turn to face the tomb for 21 seconds to symbolize the 21-gun salute, the highest military honor. **Memorial Amphitheater** is closed for repairs, but will eventually resume its Easter Sunrise, Memorial Day, and Veterans Day services. Memorials near the amphitheater include the **Space Shuttle Challenger Memorial,** the **Iran Rescue Mission Memorial,** the **War Correspondents Memorial,** and the **Canadian Cross of Sacrifice,** remembering U.S. citizens in the Canadian Armed Forces.

SIGHTS

"A rose is a rose is a rose," wrote Gertrude Stein; in the same vein, what seems to be a ship's mast rising out of the ground is a **ship's mast rising out of the ground.** The mast belonged to the *U.S.S. Maine,* which exploded in the harbor of Havana, Cuba, in 1898. The rallying cry "Remember the Maine!" helped start the Spanish-American War, though no one knows whether the Spanish caused the explosion. Polish statesman and musician Ignace Jan Paderewski was interred in the memorial until Poland became "free." He was returned to his homeland in June of 1992.

The **Confederate Memorial,** a goodwill gesture commissioned in 1900, set aside an area for the burial of Confederate troops. The memorial itself shows the female representation of Peace facing south and holding a plow and a pruning hook. Inscribed around the base is the passage from Isaiah, "They shall beat their swords into plowshares, and their spears into pruning hooks." A bronze frieze surrounding the base depicts Confederate soldiers leaving home, and then returning in defeat. A **Civil War Memorial** lies along Crook Walk near Arlington House; more American soldiers died in this war than in any other. The bones of 2111 soldiers who fell in the Battle of Bull Run and along the route to Rappahanock lie beneath the stone sarcophagus; the remains were never identified, but the soldiers' names and deaths were recorded in the Archives.

The restored pastel-peach **Arlington House** was originally built in 1802 by George Washington Parke Custis, Robert E. Lee's father-in-law and distant relative. Self-guided tour information is available from one of the women in antebellum costume inside. The parlor connects through a series of arched doorways to the Family Dining Room. Up the narrow staircase, the girls' dressing room, playroom, and bedrooms contain antique dolls and clothing. Colonel Robert E. Lee penned his resignation from the United States Army in his bedchambers. Downstairs, you can see the White Parlor and the Morning Room, where paintings of George Custis lean against an easel. The storeroom, conservatory, and Lee's office close the tour. (You won't find Lee's grave

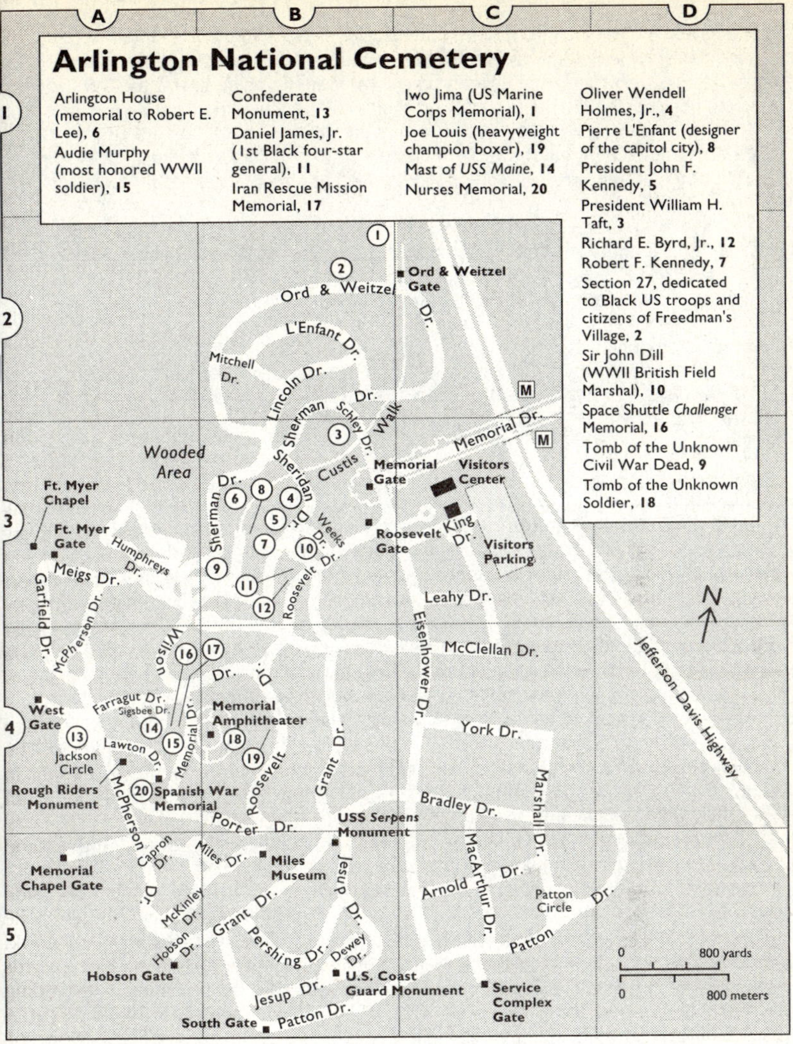

in Arlington Cemetery: he chose to be buried at the southern college he helped to found, Washington & Lee, in Lexington, Virginia.)

Near the Cemetery

If you continue down Custis Walk in front of Arlington House and leave the cemetery through Weitzel Gate, you can walk to the **Iwo Jima Memorial.** On the way lies President William Howard Taft's grave, to the left of the path in section 30. The walk from Weitzel Gate to the memorial takes 20 minutes, so you may prefer to drive to the junction, located between Arlington Blvd. and Ridge Rd., especially on hot days. Or, take the Metro to Rosslyn and walk for five minutes east on Ft. Myer Dr. until you reach Arlington Blvd.; the memorial will be on your left. Its design is based on Joe Rosenthal's Pulitzer Prize-winning photograph of six Marines straining to raise the

U.S. flag on Iwo Jima's Mount Suribachi. The island saw 6321 U.S. soldiers die in battle in February 1945, including three of the men the memorial depicts. Admiral Nimitz's comment on the battle, "Uncommon valor was a common virtue," adorns the statue's base. The U.S. flag is real, but the "flagpole" is a lead pipe—just as in the photo. The memorial became a gay cruising area in the '70s; today, the Marine Corps Marathon begins here each year, and military concerts and parades take place in the summer on Tuesdays from 7pm until 8:30pm. (For information on the memorial, call 202-619-7222.)

Near the Iwo Jima Memorial (just walk in the direction that the marines are leaning) rises a rectangular 127-ft.-high tower that houses the **Netherlands Carillon** (285-2598), a set of 49 bells made in Dutch foundries to commemorate Holland's liberation from the Nazis on May 5, 1945. The carillon is played from June to August on Saturdays between 6pm and 8pm, as well as on national holidays; in April, May, and September it rings on Saturdays from 2pm to 4pm. If the bells are ringing, you can climb the towers and enjoy the view or watch the *Carillomeurs* do their stuff. A park ranger briefs the crowd on carillons one half hour before performances. Two bronze panthers guard the bells, and the grounds bloom with more than 15,000 tulips each spring.

THE PENTAGON

If the Washington Monument's smooth obelisk symbolizes the vigor of the American nation and the Capitol's Classical dome represents the dignity of democratic government, the Pentagon's mass of concrete shows just how huge a military bureaucracy can get. On July 17, 1941, the War Department gave its planners one weekend to design a building that would hold all the capital's military offices. On Monday morning, the architects returned with the familiar five-sided behemoth, which was designed to fit between two highways; objections to the original site within Arlington Cemetery forced a move to Hell's Bottom, swampy government-owned land next to the Potomac. A work force of 13,000 toiled 24 hours a day for 16 months to create the steel-reinforced concrete edifice. Thanks to FDR's stipulation that no marble be used in the thing's construction, the resulting polygon cost "only" $50 million to build, a savings to taxpayers who were paying that much in rent every eight years for the military's old offices.

SIGHTS

When the military moved in May 1942, the building's one completed wing was too small. Today, many of the Pentagon's offices and corridors are still empty—there's more room than they'll ever need (we hope). As chief avatar of the military-industrial complex, the Pentagon was the natural target of the mammoth anti-Vietnam War march of 1968, which inspired poems by Robert Lowell and Norman Mailer's famous book *The Armies of the Night.* Some marchers tried to exorcise the "war demon" supposedly kept in check by the building's mystical shape. TV coverage of the marchers, who joined hands to form a huge ring around all five sides, exhibited to the rest of the country the extent of anti-war feeling.

Today the world's largest office building boasts the world's largest parking lot and a bus terminal longer than most trains. The Pentagon has five sides, five stories, five concentric hallways, a five-acre courtyard in the center, ten radial hallways, four zip codes of its own, and $400 toilet seats. Two-and-a-half Washington Monuments would fit across it lengthwise. Twenty-six thousand civilians, soldiers, and sailors sprawl over 6.5 million sq. ft. They take the Metro or park their 8770 cars in 16 parking lots. They climb 131 stairways and ride 19 escalators to walk through 17½ mi. of corridors. Yet it takes no more than seven minutes to walk between any two points in the building—*if* you know how to read the address: 2E651, for example, is on the second floor, ring E, near corridor 6, room 51.

You'll never have the chance to get lost on the **guided tour,** though. The public had free run of the place until 1972, when somebody bombed a bathroom. Now all visitors must sign in, walk through a metal detector, be X-rayed, show proper identification, and stick with the tour. The tour guide walks backwards to keep an eye on the visitors and keeps the pace so brisk that the tour is like a military music video: lots of pictures whizzing by, but very little information. Attentive tour-takers can nonetheless learn a lot with their eyes. Between the memorials and exhibits, the myriad uniforms, the private shopping mall, and the motorized mini-mail carts, you'll discover the achievements, attitudes, structure, and sheer size of the United States defense establishment.

A corny film will show you the **War Room**—whose large screens light up with maps and data during national emergencies—and the **National Command Center,** but you'll never get to these basement chambers yourself. However, if you've seen *Dr. Strangelove* or *War Games*, you can already guess what they look like.

The **Commander-in-Chiefs' Corridor** depicts each U.S. president beside a montage of drawings and newspaper headlines. Another display models famous aircraft; its most recent addition is a model of the **Stealth bomber,** whose low-altitude flight eludes radar while its high price ($500 million per plane) provokes disgust. Used in the U.S. invasion of Panama and in the Persian Gulf War, the Stealth is one of several technically secret projects that the tour guide will discuss. Look for the **Delta Force** patch on display; the government won't even acknowledge the existence of this secret anti-terrorist team, but the Pentagon exhibits its insignia anyway.

Endless corridors commemorate exceptional soldiers. Hallways celebrate military topics including General George Marshall, women in the military, and Vietnam POWs. An array of flags and a memorial to valiant dogs ends your tour. Look out the window at the **hot dog stand** in the middle of the courtyard; it's called **"ground zero"** because during the cold war the Soviets thought it was a strategic nuclear weapons control room and planned to bomb it first if war should have erupted.

Tours are **free** and given every half hour on weekdays between 9:30am and 3:30pm, except on federal holidays; from October to May, the 10:30am, 1:30pm, and 3pm tours are eliminated. Be ready to go 10 min. early; there is a mandatory briefing. No reservations are necessary, but large groups and those with special needs may reserve tours by calling 695-1776. All persons must present a photo ID. Acceptable photo IDS are passports, drivers licenses, college IDs, and International Student ID Cards. Try coming early in the morning to avoid the lines and to fit in the 1-½-hour tour before lunch. No facilities for meals are available, *nor are restrooms open to the public during the tour.* The Pentagon has its own Metro stop; one of the Metro escalators leads directly to the tour office. The Pentagon hankers down inside a triangle formed by three highways—Rte. 110 and 27 and I-395; those who must drive here should take the 14th St. Bridge from D.C. to I-395 and find the Pentagon exit about 15 seconds into Virginia. Visitor parking is available but limited, and the walk from the lot takes a few minutes; enter through Corridor One at the South Parking Entrance.

ROOSEVELT ISLAND

The Theodore Roosevelt Memorial Association felt that their boy deserved better than the standard statue-and-pedestal memorial package. To commemorate the popular hunter, conservationist, and president, they purchased an entire 88-acre island which, with Congress's consent, became Roosevelt Island in 1932. Now a wilderness preserve, the island squats in the Potomac River just west of Foggy Bottom, a mere 15 minutes from downtown. To transform the place from "swamp" to "memorial," Congress erected an impressive statue of Roosevelt and a parking lot, but not much else. The island's natural ruggedness is itself a fitting memorial to the man famous for starting the Panama Canal, leading the charge up San Juan Hill during the Spanish-American War, negotiating an end to the Russo-Japanese War, and expressing his great love for the outdoors by regularly disappearing into the forest, seeking solitude and things to shoot.

Add to Roosevelt's list of accomplishments the establishment of the U.S. Forest Service and the creation of Shenandoah, America's first national park. The island which bears his name today contains swamp, marsh, and forest habitats which host such critters as turtles, muskrats, cottontails, and foxes (also look for Redwing Blackbirds, whose calls contrast strangely with the noise of cars rushing over Roosevelt Bridge). Woody climbers and epiphytes hang from the trees, jungle-style. The island's 3 mi. of

trails require an hour to hike; wide, flat paths make the long walks relaxing. More adventurous walkers may follow smaller subsidiary trails, literally off the beaten path. Rocky **beaches** reward those who find them with views of the Kennedy Center and environs, across the river. On weekends, local fisherfolk cast off from here into the murky waters of the Potomac, where swimming is most emphatically for fish only. (Explorers beware: the narrow footpaths leading to the beaches tend to be cobwebby and lined with nettles.) Even harder to find than the beaches are the **restrooms,** hidden in the delicately designated "comfort station," a brown lodge at the southwest corner of the island near Theodore Roosevelt Bridge.

The **memorial** lurks just west of the center of the island's northern half. The design by Eric Gugler includes a 17-foot bronze statue of Roosevelt (executed by Paul Manship) in front of a 30-foot slab of granite reminiscent of *2001: A Space Odyssey.* In front is an oval terrace surrounded by a moat spanned by a series of footbridges. Four 21-foot granite "tablets" are inscribed with juicy Roosevelt soundbites, among them: "There are no words that can tell the hidden spirit of the wilderness" and "Keep your eyes on the stars, but remember to keep your feet on the ground."

Rangers will give combined nature-and-history summertime **tours** if called seven days in advance; call 703-285-2600 for arrangements. For a rundown of the ever-shifting hours and services, call 426-6922 or 703-285-2598.

From Washington, drive across the Roosevelt Bridge, take a right onto the George Washington Parkway's northbound lanes, and exit into the Roosevelt Island lot; if you see Key Bridge, you've missed it. Public transportation enthusiasts should take the Metro to Rosslyn, then walk down N. 19th St. and look for footbridges across the highway spaghetti on the Virginia shore; or, you could walk across Key Bridge from Georgetown and follow the Mt. Vernon Trail along the river. There is a footbridge at the parking lot which all visitors must cross to get to the island. Sadly, bikes are not allowed on the island, although there is a bike rack in the parking lot.

Alexandria, VA

Metro: Braddock Road; King Street.

When Scottish tobacco merchants founded Alexandria in 1749, they did not have "quaint" in mind; its location on the Potomac River seemed perfect for bundling up and shipping out the great weed from down south. Though included in the land grant that created D.C. in 1791, Alexandria stayed an independent-minded (and very Southern) shipping town—when Virginia removed it from the District of Columbia in 1846, one resident reported "great rejoicing and cannon firing." When Washington ballooned after World War II, the spreading wave of bedroom communities crashed over the town. It didn't become a tourist sight until the '80s, when Old Town re-cobblestoned the streets, rebricked the sidewalks, installed gardens and patios, restored over 1000 old façades, and invited tall ships and contemporary shops to share the 1700s atmosphere. On weekends, half of northern Virginia joins a smattering of tourists to shop, stroll, and dine. Old-time sailors might enjoy some of the many pubs and clubs, but sophisticated jazzers, angst-ridden teens, and modern singles will all find some appropriate nightlife.

ORIENTATION

Old Town Alexandria lies in the square formed by Oronoco St. on the north, the Potomac River on the east, Gibbon St. on the south, and Alfred St. on the west. Restaurants, bars, art galleries, and shops nestle here in a perpetually charming state. Old Town's streets form a grid; north-south streets are randomly named, while east-west streets in central Old Town are royally named (King, Prince, Duke, Queen, etc.). Street layout in the rest of Alexandria has all the sense of a bowl of pasta; I-395 cuts Alexandria off from Arlington to the north, and the Beltway rushes along its southern border. King St. (Rte. 7) connects I-395 to Old Town, and the George Washington Pkwy. runs nearly along the river until Old Town, then becomes Washington St. To find Old Town from the King St. Metro, walk down King St. (to your left as you leave

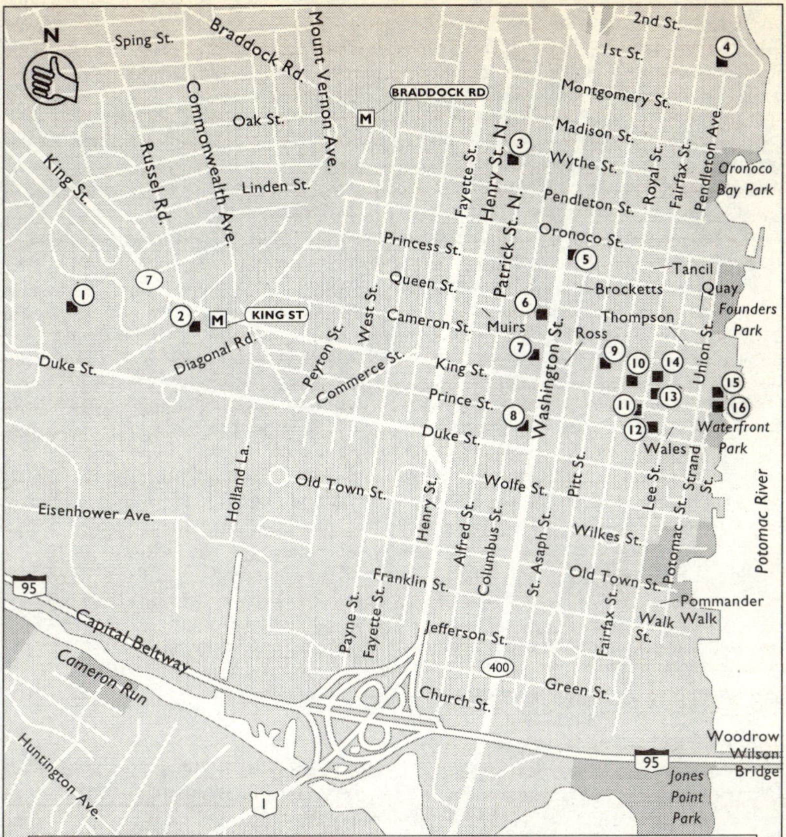

Alexandria, VA Old Town & Vicinity

Alexandria Archaeology, **16**
Alexandria Union Station, **2**
Athenaeum, **12**
Black History Resource Center, **3**
Carlyle House, **14**
Christ Church, **7**
Gadsby's Tavern/ Museum, **9**
George Washington Masonic Memorial, **1**
Lee's Boyhood Home, **5**
Lloyd House, **6**
Lyceum, **8**
Market Square, **10**
Ramsey House/Visitor Center, **13**
Stabler-Leadbeater Apothecary Shop, **11**
Torpedo Factory, **15**
Waterfront Museum, **4**

the Metro; walk away from the tracks, not under them). A DASH bus also runs from the Metro to Old Town at random intervals. **DASH** runs throughout the city (75¢) and to the Pentagon ($1). Call 370-DASH for more info. Drivers should take the East King St. exit from the George Washington Pkwy.; Old Town is about 20 minutes from downtown D.C. The **area code** for Alexandria is **703.**

SIGHTS

King Street is the main thoroughfare through Old Town. It's the king of streets for eating seafood and visiting art galleries and shops. The galleries huddle closer to the Metro, while the restaurants, like lemmings, cluster closer and closer to the river. Each Saturday the town hosts a morning fair, complete with waterfront activities, riverboat rides, and a **Farmer's Market** at 301 King St. in Market Square (370-8723; market open 5-9am). Fresh baked goods, meats, produce, and handicrafts are sold in the brick arcades, replete with fountains, trees, and hanging baskets, on the south plaza of the city hall. Beware of visiting Alexandria on a spring or summer weekend; you may find yourself barred from many museums and houses by the hundreds of weddings that take over every picturesque place in town.

The **Lyceum** information center, at 201 S. Washington St. (838-4994), shows exhibitions and audio-visual presentations for the visitor who wants in-depth historical contextualization of many of the walking tour's sites. The brick and stucco Greek Revival building has been a military hospital, a private home, and an office building. Its collection of period objects includes prized Alexandria silver. (Open Mon.-Sat. 10am-5pm, Sun. 1-5pm. Free parking is available. Travelers with disabilities should call to take advantage of the Lyceum's resources. Tours are offered, some in Braille, but call in advance to make arrangements.) George Washington and Robert E. Lee both prayed at **Christ Church,** 118 N. Washington St. (549-1450) at Cameron St., a red-brick Colonial building with a domed steeple. Its quiet, shady cemetery with well-tended gardens is an inviting rest stop for modern-day visitors. Nearly as bright as the outdoors on a sunny day, the interior of the church has stark white walls, an unusual domed window behind the altar, and hand-lettered tablets containing the Apostle's Creed and the Lord's Prayer (open Mon.-Fri. 9am-4pm, Sun. 9am-noon, Sun. 2-4:30pm; guided tours are available; free).

Built in 1794, the authentically Victorian **Lloyd House,** 220 N. Washington St. (838-4577), is primarily a genealogical library, but visitors might enjoy the drawing rooms and exhibits full of old models of clipper ships, paintings, and antique books (open Mon.-Sat. 9am-5pm; tours available; free).

Restored to its 18th-century good looks, **Gadsby's Tavern,** 134 N. Royal St. (838-4242), shows how budget travelers did it 200 years ago (when as many as 4 people would be assigned to a bed). Upstairs, large ballrooms are still used for special functions, while the stairless minstrels' gallery recalls the revelry of days past. (Open Oct.-March Tues.-Sat. 10am-4pm, Sun. 1-4pm. Admission $3, children 11-17 $1.)

The **Stabler-Leadbeater Apothecary Shop and Museum,** 105-107 South Fairfax St. (836-3713), the second-oldest in the country, still operates. Martha Washington's letter requesting castor oil hangs in a glass case. Old-time druggists used the shop's hundreds of colorful hand-blown bottles, mortars and pestles, powders, eyeglasses, weights, and scales (and probably appreciated the Gothic detailing on the shelves), as the high-pitched recording will attest. The museum has recently undertaken a massive project to sort through old order slips—soon it will be known just who was sick—and from what. Senators Daniel Webster, Henry Clay, and John Calhoun supposedly had some "drug store" conversations here. And Robert E. Lee was hanging out here when he received the message to stop John Brown's insurrection at Harper's Ferry. The gift shop sells antique apothecary items. (Open Mon.-Sat. 10am-4pm, Sun. 1-5pm. Admission $2, students $1, under 11 free.)

Restored so faithfully that even its vivid colors are deemed authentic, the **Carlyle House,** 121 North Fairfax St. (549-2997), home of Scottish merchant John Carlyle, showcases Alexandria's favorite century. Carlyle patterned his home after those in 18th-century Scotland and northern England. Tours start in the basement, where the servants lived; the white-plaster, stable-like rooms look nothing like the ornate upstairs. The second-story floors show off *trompe l'oeuil* "marble," along with the requisite exquisite antique furniture. The last room has been left unrestored, with beams and wall exposed just as they were found. (Open Tues.-Sat. 10am-4:30pm, Sun. noon-4:30pm. Tours given on the ½hr. Admission $3, seniors and students $1, under 10 free.) The gazebo and garden in the back serve as a public park—a good choice for an intimate picnic.

Alexandria's oldest house, the **Athenaeum,** 201 Prince St. (548-0035), holds local and touring art shows as well as the Alexandria Ballet (379-8997). The rose-colored building, with its large, round columns and dignified pediment, merits attention; notice how its Greek Renaissance flair differs from the surrounding Colonial architecture. (Open Wed.-Fri. 11am-4pm, Sat.-Sun. 1-4pm.)

Over 160 artists paint, draw, and sculpt in public on two floors of the **Torpedo Factory,** 105 N. Union St. (838-4565). With 83 studios, five galleries, an art school, and an archaeology lab, the art world has conquered the World War I-era munitions factory, leaving the former occupants only a small exhibit and an inert torpedo. Works from just about every mode of artistic creation await aesthetic completion or financial commodification in the myriad workshops, most of which are open to visitors. A quick walk across the wharf behind the Torpedo Factory will lead you to its **Food Pavilion.** High quality cheap eats are complemented by an understandably artsy interior. (Open daily 8am-midnight. Torpedo Factory open daily 10am-5pm. Suggested-donation box. Wheelchair access.)

On the third floor of the factory, **Alexandria Archaeology,** 105 N. Union St. (838-4399), the city's urban archaeology lab and museum, displays 18th- and 19th-century artifacts (open Tues.-Fri. 10am-3pm, Sat. 10am-5pm, Sun. 1-5pm).

George Washington slept in the guest room of **Robert E. Lee's Boyhood Home,** 607 Oronoco St. (548-8454) near Asaph St. The Revolutionary War hero, "Light Horse" Harry Lee, was the first to lease this home in 1812; Robert E. Lee went to the Quaker school next door. Most of the Lees' belongings are at Washington and Lee University, but on display are one of America's first indoor kitchens and a set of miniature furniture (carpenters' method of advertising). United Mine Workers president John L. Lewis lived here from 1927 to 1969. Candlelit tours are offered in December. (Open Mon.-Sat. 10am-4pm, Sun. 1-4pm. Admission $3, students 10-17 $1.)

Over 37 different Lees inhabited the **Lee-Fendall House** at 614 Oronoco St., across from Robert E. Lee's Boyhood Home. The suburban-esque white-and-black mansion was constructed by Philip Fendall in 1785 on land once owned by man-about-Alexandria "Light Horse" Harry Lee. Tours feature yet more Lee family knick-knacks and documents, for those who just can't get enough. (Open Tues.-Sat. 10am-4pm, Sun. noon-4pm. Last tour 3:45pm. Admission $3, students $2, under 12 free.)

The **Black History Resource Center,** 638 N. Alfred St. (838-4356; enter on Wythe St.), is housed in the Robert H. Robinson Library, originally for blacks only. Built in 1940 after local African-Americans staged the nation's first "sit in" to protest the segregation of the library system, the center today showcases paintings, photographs, and other memorabilia that untangle black history in Alexandria. A printed walking tour lists historical sights, including several churches, the Franklin and Armfield Slave Market, and the house of George Seaton, a free black master carpenter who was elected to the city council and state legislature in the 1870s. (Open Tues.-Sat. 10am-4pm. Wheelchair access.)

The **George Washington Masonic National Memorial,** at 101 Callahan Drive (683-2007), at the top of King St., rises 400 ft. over Alexandria. The lofty Greek-temple-style portico supports a steep pyramid. Look for the careful blending of all five orders of Classical architecture: Doric, Ionic, and Corinthian on the three exterior levels of the tower, Composite in Memorial Hall, and Tuscan in Assembly Hall. Inside, the ninth floor claims to reproduce parts of King Solomon's Temple. Another five floors of exhibitions celebrate George Washington and Masonry. Murals of George Washington celebrating St. John's Day and laying the Capitol's cornerstone as well as a 370-year-old Persian rug valued at $1 million are on display. A 330-ft. observation deck provides a fair view of the city. To go above the second floor, you must take the (free) 70-minute tour (open daily 9am-5pm; tours are given on the half hour in the morning, and on the hour in the afternoon).

Museums & Galleries

The Mall

For information on D.C.'s first citywide Museum Bus, transportation accessing both museums on the Mall and throughout the Washington area, see **Essentials: Getting Around,** page 60.

Smithsonian Museums

The Smithsonian is the catalogued warehouse of American cultural memorabilia. Words that might describe this country—grand, hegemonic, diverse—are equally appropriate to this mammoth museum and research institution. The world's largest museum complex (comprised of 16 museums, in addition to the National Zoo) stretches out—not even in its entirety—along Washington's longest lawn, the Mall. Nine of the Smithsonian museums flank the Mall (the **Museum of American History, Museum of Natural History, Air and Space Museum, Hirshhorn Museum and Sculpture Garden, Arts and Industries Building, Museum of African Art, Arthur M. Sackler Gallery, Freer Gallery,** and the **Smithsonian Castle**), while four additional museums are located less than a mile away (**Renwick Gallery, Museum of American Art, National Portrait Gallery,** and the **Postal Museum**). Elsewhere in D.C. are the **Anacostia Museum** (page 201) and the **National Zoological Park** (page 159). The Smithsonian's **Cooper-Hewitt, National Museum of Design** and **National Museum of the American Indian** reside in New York City.

The institution's scientists are similarly situated in a variety of outposts, classifying and investigating in faraway laboratories ranging from Panama to Nepal to Arizona. Smithsonian curators manage over 139 million objects, most of which you'll never see. Scientists and historians worldwide take an interest in the millions of beetles, thousands of works of art, and hundreds of airplanes that make the Smithsonian Institution outstanding in both the arts and sciences, not to mention tourism. With such a massive collection at hand, the Smithsonian can assemble almost any exhibit it chooses: individual halls and chambers may be filled with gleaming minerals, orbital satellites, teenage fashions, or models by Rodin. Tourists throng the Mall to see the dinosaurs at Natural History, the Apollo XI capsule at Air and Space, and the luminous pyramids next to the East Wing building—many, in fact, don't budget enough time to see much else. The sensible visitor will take at least three days to roam the 13 Smithsonian buildings, the **National Gallery of Art,** and the **U.S. Holocaust Museum** on and near the National Mall.

The Smithsonian began as the magnanimous idea of British scientist James Smithson. The chemist had never visited America, but his will left 105 bags of gold sovereigns to "found at Washington, under the name of the Smithsonian Institution, an establishment for the increase and diffusion of knowledge among men." (Had Smithson's nephew had children, they would have inherited the gold instead.) Congress voted to take the money, British though it was, in 1836. The Smithsonian Institution was established in 1846; the red-brick, Victorian "Castle" was its first permanent home, as well as the home to bachelor scientists who boarded there along with the institution's growing collections. The Victorian-with-a-vengeance Arts and Industries Building, the second-oldest structure, initially opened its doors at President Garfield's inaugural ball in 1881; the rest of the Mall splits neatly into domed neoclassical sprawl (Natural History, National Gallery's West Wing, Freer) and smooth, geometric modernity (Air and Space, East Wing, American History, Hirshhorn). Since 1980, new museums have had to hide below ground, the casualties of space limitations. Substantial portions of the Sackler Gallery and Museum of African Art crawl under stone entrance pavilions behind the Castle.

ORIENTATION AND PRACTICAL INFORMATION

Nine Smithsonian buildings, the National Gallery of Art, and the U.S. Holocaust Museum immediately flank the Mall (see The Mall Area color insert map or D.C.'s Museums and Monuments map for a visual orientation). On the north side, to the left as you face the Capitol from the center of the Mall, are the National Gallery of Art's East Wing and West Wing, the National Museum of Natural History, and the National Museum of American History. Closest to the Capitol on the right is the National Air and Space Museum, then the Hirshhorn, and then the Arts and Industries Building. The red Smithsonian Castle hides the Sackler Gallery and the National Museum of African Art in its dainty backyard garden. Next door is the Freer Gallery. Completing the lineup of museums on the west side of the Castle is the U.S. Holocaust Museum, nestled in the southwest corner of the Mall, farther up past the Dept. of Agriculture on Independence and 14th. Tour-bus-congested Jefferson and Madison Drives run east-west along the Mall. The Smithsonian Metro stop isn't always the best way to reach a given museum; L'Enfant Plaza is closer to Air and Space and the Hirshhorn. Federal Triangle is closer to Natural History and American History, and Archives-Navy Memorial is closer to the National Galleries of Art. Parking in or north of the Smithsonian complex is nearly impossible. Some on-street spaces south of Independence Ave. SW may be available, but *caveat conductor:* one wrong turn onto the SE-SW Freeway, and you may be irrevocably Virginia- or Anacostia-bound.

All Smithsonian museums are **free** and **wheelchair-accessible;** many offer written information in French, German, Spanish, Italian, Japanese, Chinese, Arabic, and Portuguese. Smithsonian museums are open daily from 10am to 5:30pm (except for the Anacostia Museum, which closes at 5pm), with extended spring and summer hours determined annually. Some museums are closed winter weekends.

Time is an invaluable thing to a Smithsonian visitor; too many visitors give up longed-for hours among the airplanes just to say they've seen the Abstract Expressionists (or vice versa). An hour in one museum is better spent than an hour dashing through three, especially when the extent of one's interest causes an hour to seem like five minutes. Call 357-2700 (TDD 357-1729) Mon.-Fri. 9am-5pm, Sat.-Sun. 10am-4pm to contact a Smithsonian operator for **information** on all the museums. For recorded information on tours, concerts, lectures, films, and performance art, call 357-2020 (Spanish 633-9126). You may also write the Smithsonian at Smithsonian Information, Smithsonian Institution, MRC 010, Washington, D.C., 20560, or visit the Smithsonian Home Page on the World Wide Web at http://www.si.edu. Information desks in the Castle and the museums distribute the **Smithsonian Guide for Disabled Visitors;** however, the volunteer staff is seldom available before 10am or after 4pm. Most museums have two main entrances, one from the Mall and one from Constitution or Independence Ave.; the latter is often easier for wheelchairs to negotiate. Visitors with disabilities can call a specific museum prior to their visit and obtain more extensive literature and assistance. Sight- or hearing-impaired visitors may call 786-2942 to arrange for interpreted tours.

SMITHSONIAN CASTLE

The **Smithsonian Castle,** 1000 Jefferson Dr. SW (357-2700, Dial-a-Museum recording 357-2020, TDD 357-1729), holds no real exhibits, but it does have information desks and two small theaters that continuously play a 20-minute introductory movie. Information on all Smithsonian buildings is offered at the castle, via **touch-sensitive computer screens.** The Castle also contains a **crypt** that holds James Smithson's body (he finally made it to America after all). The whole crypt was moved from Genoa, Italy in 1904. Near the crypt is the symbolic **Smithsonian mace** (a silver staff with a ball at the end of it) and a display about the varieties of zinc that Smithson identified and had named after him. The building itself, designed by James Renwick, Jr., is crowned by 11 towers, no two of which are the same. This intentional asymmetry and integration of different architectural styles conveys either the originality or the indecisiveness of the Castle's creator. The posh-looking, roped-off hallways lead to Smithsonian offices

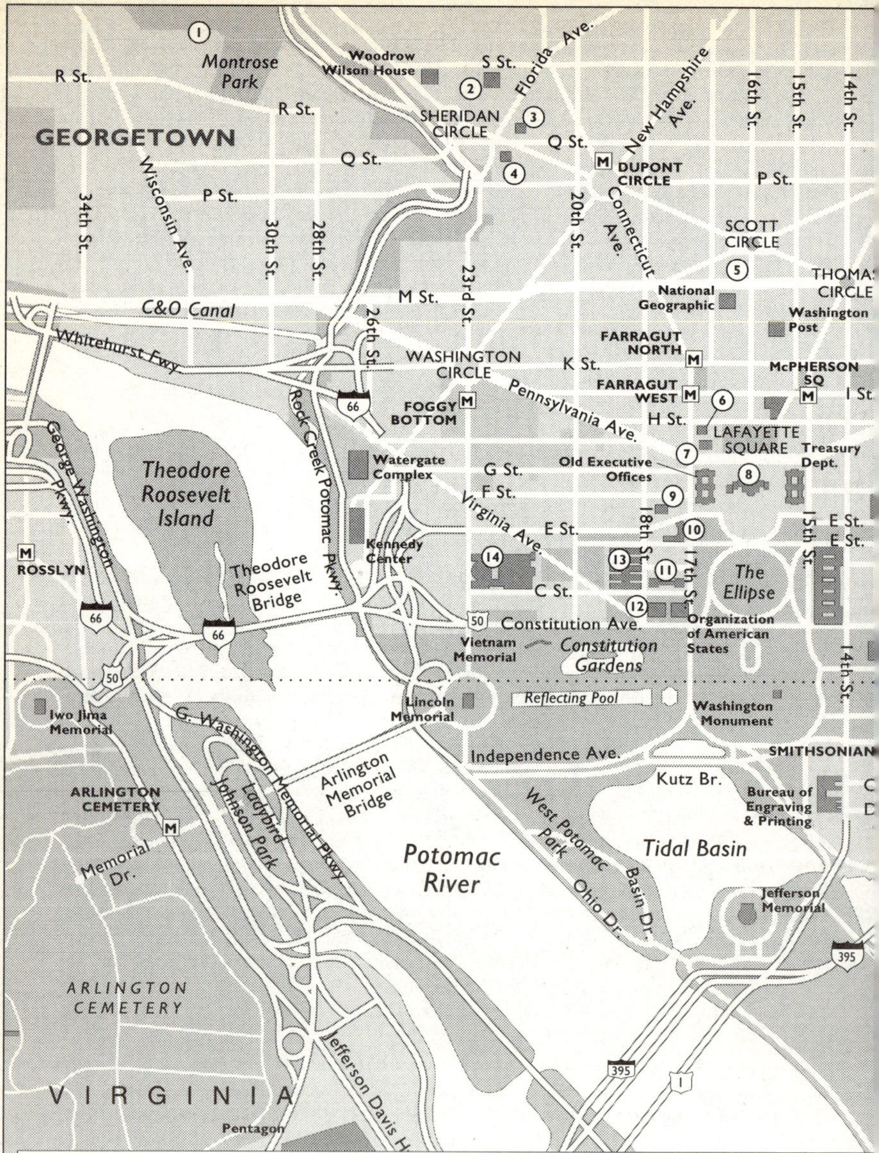

Museums & Galleries

Anderson House, **4**

Arthur M. Sackler Gallery, **25**

Arts and Industries Building, **27**

B'nai B'rith Klutznick Museum, **5**

Capital Children's Museum, **31**

Capitol Building, **32**

Corcoran Gallery of Art, **10**

D.A.R. Museum/ Continental Hall, **11**

Decatur House, **6**

Dumbarton Oaks, **1**

Diplomatic Reception Rooms, **14**

Folger Shakespeare Library, **34**

Ford's Theatre, **16**

Freer Gallery of Art, **23**

Hirshhorn Museum and Sculpture Garden, **28**

Interior Department Museum, **13**

Library of Congress, **33**

Museum of Modern Art of Latin America, **12**

National Air and Space Museum, **29**

- National Archives, **20**
- National Building Museum, **18**
- The National Gallery of Art, **30**
- National Museum of African Art, **26**
- National Museum of American Art, **17**
- National Museum of American History, **22**
- National Museum of Women in the Arts, **15**
- National Museum of Natural History, **21**
- National Portrait Gallery, **19**
- Navy Memorial Museum, **35**
- Octagon Museum, **9**
- Phillips Collection, **3**
- Renwick Gallery, **7**
- Smithsonian Castle, **24**
- Textile Museum, **2**
- White House, **8**

and services for "associates" (who pay annual dues to be members of the museum). (Open daily 9am-5:30pm, information desk open daily 9am-4pm.)

NATIONAL MUSEUM OF AMERICAN HISTORY

Henry Ford once said that "history is bunk." The National Museum of American History prefers to think that history is junk: several centuries' and thousands of artifacts' worth of machines, textiles, photographs, vehicles, harmonicas, guns, fiber-optic cable, hats, and uncategorizable American detritus reside here behind plexiglass and plaques. When the Smithsonian inherits a quirky artifact of popular culture, like Dorothy's slippers from *The Wizard of Oz* or Archie Bunker's chair, it is likely to find its home here. The museum, opened in 1964, was named the National Museum of History and Technology until 1980, and a certain techno-focus remains evident in halls such as "A Material World" or "Information Age." Recently, the museum has attempted to present a less two-dimensional account of American cultural and political history; some of the most powerful exhibits are those that "present challenging ideas about our country's past" (see "Field to Factory," below). The most famous displays are individual objects, such as the original Star-Spangled Banner; but the crowds around these Smithsonian staples shouldn't distract from the more informative halls of this national attic.

Enter the boring rectilinear building from the Mall or from 14th St. and Constitution Ave. NW. (Metro: Smithsonian or Federal Triangle.) **Maps** are available from an information desk. As in the other major Smithsonian museums, lingering is most enjoyable when it's done in front of what one *really* wants to see; to see all of the exhibits properly takes at least a full day, but three hours should suffice for a more selective, personalized tour.

On the second floor, the Mall entrance brings you face to face with the swinging **Foucault's pendulum.** Fixed in a single plane of perpendicular motion, it knocks over pegs set up in a circular pattern and thereby proves that the Earth rotates.

When Francis Scott Key, detained on a ship in Baltimore Harbor, saw an American flag fly over Fort McHenry at dawn on September 14, 1814, he knew British invaders had failed to take Baltimore; the elated Key sat down and wrote **"The Star-Spangled Banner,"** the U.S.'s unsingable (read: octave-and-a-half vocal range) national anthem. There has been talk of National Anthem turnover; some patriotic songbirds find "America the Beautiful" both more appealing and appropriate. The enormous flag that inspired the nevertheless-enduring anthem now hangs behind the pendulum on the museum's second floor.

From the building's crowded center, visitors can turn left for 20th-century African-American history in "Field to Factory." This exhibit includes a detailed description of the experiences of African-Americans who migrated to northern states after the Reconstruction, as well as a chronicle of the civil rights movement. At one point, in order to proceed from one part of the exhibit to the next, visitors must pass through a doorway divided into two different sides, one marked "Colored" and the other "White." To the right is an exhibit on 18th-century European-American history, entitled "After the Revolution." Also to the right, "First Ladies" traces the evolution of the role of Presidential wives from parlor socialites to political allies. Immediately to the left of the flag, "American Encounters" marks the quincentenary of Columbus's landmark visit to North America by depicting cultural interactions in the American Southwest since 1539. Outside the entrance to the "Field to Factory" exhibit is the famous "topless" statue of George Washington. Horatio Greenough, in Florence, carved the figure at the request of Congress in 1832; the statue was so big the Capitol's doors had to be removed to drag George inside, and so heavy it threatened to collapse the Capitol's floor. The sculpture was reinstalled outdoors, where snow collected in his lap and on his bare chest. Brrr. The Smithsonian finally acquired the boondoggle in 1908.

Specialized collections of musical instruments, coins, and military paraphernalia dominate the third floor. "A More Perfect Union" chronicles the World War II internment of Japanese-Americans in faithful and compassionate detail. Honestly and consciously eschewing wartime euphemism, the exhibit analyzes the government's disregard of its victims' Constitutional rights and its implications of a race-based definition of citizenship. The museum has been especially careful to present the human toll; interactive videos of survivors and photographs of the camps are prominently displayed. In one life-size photograph of a Japanese-owned grocery store that was forced to close, a sign in the window ironically reads: "Many thanks for your Patronage. Hope to serve you in Near Future. God be with you till we meet again." The third floor also houses the stirring "Personal Legacy," a sampling of some of the 25,000 items that mourners have left at the Vietnam Memorial, including a decorated Christmas tree, a wedding ring, and a lonely teddy bear, worn with age. The collection is on indefinite loan from the National Parks Service.

The mechanically inclined will love the first floor, where entire galleries enshrine in plexiglass displays of electricity, trains, cars, clocks, and power tools. "A Material World" occupies the central first floor, along with the museum bookstore. Electronics reign in "Information Age"; clunky early computers like EDSAC give way to microprocessors and high-definition TV. The interactive displays throughout the exhibit allow visitors to make copies of their own fingerprints, attempt currency trade, and discover who lives in their home ZIP code. The recently opened "Science in American Life" serves up a brief history of the nation's scientific progress and its cultural implications, from the tabletop science of the 19th century through the science of genetic engineering and the futuristic quest for the perfect tomato.

The sprawling **bookstore** on the lower level sells quality Smithsonian jazz and folk records, in addition to the usual museum memorabilia. An old-fashioned, functioning U.S. Post Office and a 1910-style **ice cream parlor** (located in the Palm Court resting area) also enliven the first floor. The museum hosts year-round special events, including dance, music, and lectures. Splendid silent (or occasionally, simply forgotten) **films** are screened in the Carmichael Auditorium, often for free. Schedules are available at the information station near the first-floor exit. In the summer, the Carmichael Auditorium plays host to **free public concerts** by the Smithsonian Jazz Masterworks Orchestra; event tickets are free, but must be obtained in advance. For tickets or more information, call the Smithsonian Resident Associate Program (357-3030). Write to *Events*, Room MBB66 MRC 646, National Museum of American History, Smithsonian Institution, Washington, D.C. 20560 for a comprehensive pamphlet of the museum's happenings and activities. Museum open daily 10am-5:30pm; extended summer hours determined annually.

"Hey kids, do that again!"

Who says the Smithsonian doesn't have a sense of humor? One display features a camcorder-toting tourist who is wearing a rather loud, "monument-print" shirt.

NATIONAL MUSEUM OF NATURAL HISTORY

The Neoclassical, golden-domed Museum of Natural History, built in 1911 at 10th and Constitution Ave. (Metro: Smithsonian or Federal Triangle), speculates upon the earth and its existence in two and a half large, crowded floors of exhibits. As with the Museum of American History, several hours of gazing time are required in order to do the halls justice. When the museum was conceived, "natural history" exclusively meant geology and biology; the rarely seen tag "and National Museum of Man" licensed the curators to add anthropology exhibits (some displays have women in them, too). Corridors, cases, dioramas, and hanging specimens reflect the Victorian mania to kill, collect, catalogue, and display. Among the dusty specimens of birds and mammals and the endless dioramas of "native peoples" are some real jewels: from minerals like the Hope Diamond to educational gems such as the scampering, iridescent arthropods in the recently remodeled Orkin Insect Zoo. Children will appreciate this museum for its many low-to-the-ground view windows and displays, as well as the signs begging visitors to "Please Touch!"

Inside the stone-floored entrance, the largest African elephant ever captured stands under dome-filtered sunshine, amid the hubbub of running children and slack-jawed tourists. Above visitors' heads, colored banners point out the various exhibits. The entrance rotunda is open to the second floor; it is therefore fairly easy to find most attractions even without the aid of the **map,** which is nonetheless available from the **information desk** to the right of the pachyderm at the entrance. The $3 "self-guided audio tour," narrated by Meryl Streep, is less valuable than a genuinely *self*-guided tour.

The "History of Life" exhibit is just to the right of the Mall entrance, behind the information desk. The central hallway can barely accommodate the huge dinosaur skeletons that rear, hover, and wait to strike. One intriguing exhibit allows visitors to pretend that they are archaeologists examining—via remote camera—a partially excavated fossil, and displays the materials necessary for further study. Next door, "Life in the Ancient Seas" contains big fish with teeth as well as turtles the size of a coffee table. One display case, set off by itself, initially seems to house an immense round fish—eventually it becomes clear that it is actually a giant fish's *head*.

Inside the Ice Age rooms, the giant ground sloth, the saber-toothed tiger, and the woolly mammoth await; a swift waltz through "Fossil Plants" affords a look at the surprisingly colorful petrified trees. The "Human Evolution" display offers one of many disclaimers scattered throughout the museum (the staff has discovered that their exhibits are often inaccurate, sexist, and biased). More of these disclaimers are posted among the "Mammals" and "Birds" displays across the rotunda; the disclaimers are perhaps most necessary, however, in the exhibits on native cultures (Asian, African, Pacific, South American, and indigenous North American), where displays include a Maori getting his backside tattooed, and the procedure undertaken by the Shuar of eastern Ecuador in order to shrink their enemies' heads. A sign states that some of the displays are drawn from present-day life, while some are historical in the temporally removed sense; they have apparently been placed in the same exhibit, which does little to distinguish the two. The native cultures displays continue on the second floor, as do the dead animals; "Reptiles" and "Bones" are significantly less stimulating than a visit to the zoo. The **Insect Zoo** is worth a glance, however, if only for the fact that many of its exhibits are living, including giant cockroaches (a lively bunch), exotic millipedes, and walking sticks (invisibly still). Unfortunately, the second floor mineral wing is temporarily closed, due to reopen in mid-1997. The museum kept the celebrity of the collection on display, however; visitors can still line up for a glimpse of the famously cursed **Hope Diamond.**

Kids can touch nearly everything in the **Discovery Room** (357-2287), hidden beyond the Sea Life at the end of the Hall of North American Mammals. The room contains a human skeleton and various bones and stones to handle. The Education Center at 357-2747 can arrange a group visit. Entrance to the Discovery Room requires a ticket, most effectively obtained at the door 15 min. before the room opens; in the busy season, passes usually run out by early afternoon (open Tues.-Fri. noon-2:30pm, Sat.-Sun. 10:30am-3:30pm).

The less-used Constitution Ave. entrance leads to the ground floor, the designated area for temporary exhibitions. An escalator hauls visitors up and down from the rotunda. Docents give free guided **tours** of the museum daily at 10:30am and 1:30pm from September to June. (357-2700, TDD 357-1729; museum open daily 10am-5:30pm; extended hours determined annually.)

NATIONAL AIR AND SPACE MUSEUM

The National Air and Space Museum, on the south side of the Mall between 4th and 7th St. SW (Metro: L'Enfant Plaza), is best described as **big.** The museum is colossal in the expanse and scope of its topics; the individual exhibits themselves can soar stories from foundation to rooftop. The museum offers close encounters with the pinnacles of scientific achievement, eliciting awe that is indescribable. While other museums excel at recreating the reality of daily life or displaying the expansion of individual genius, Air and Space captures and holds those rare moments that collectively awed or inspired humanity. DC-3s loom over visitors while 80-ft. rockets balance in a pit that reaches from basement to skylight; films come to life on a five-story IMAX screen while exhibits take you into unknown galaxies and show you the dark side of the moon.

Of course, the scale of the museum is commensurate with the scale of the achievements it commemorates. Before 1903, human beings had never left the surface of the planet by mechanical means—the Wright brothers did so that year in a rickety biplane which now hangs in the museum's entrance gallery. But by 1969—just 66 years later—humans had the know-how to leave the Earth's surface far behind, and on July 20, Neil Armstrong and Buzz Aldrin landed on the moon in a rickety lunar module, a duplicate of which is on display in the museum.

The scope of the history and the size of the exhibits have combined to make Air and Space the most popular museum in the world, drawing some 7.5 million visitors each year. Everyone is bound to be fascinated by something—it becomes impossible to see everything. **Brochures** and a **map** are available at the information desk, and can aid in planning out a day's visit. A **film** in the middle of the day may be just the thing for tired legs. A guide leads free **tours** of the museum at 10:15am and 1pm daily from the tour desk in the entrance gallery. Several shorter visits might be best, though the whole museum can be sampled in three hours if raced through.

Air and Space's best exhibits are, well, its biggest—the actual planes and crafts from all eras of flight. The **Wright brothers' biplane** in the entrance gallery looks intimidated by its younger kin. Actual planes and rockets congregate in Galleries 100 (Entrance), 114 (Space Hall), and 102 (Air Transportation). Here are the **Skylab** space station, the **Apollo XI** command module, and the **DC-7.** Early jet planes park on the ground in Gallery 106 (Jet Aviation). The duplicate lunar lander has touched down outside the cafeteria. Gallery 103 houses the controversial **Enola Gay** exhibit.

Soak up the science in Gallery 207 (Exploring the Planets), which details what is known about the earth's eight orbital buddies, as well as how we know it. Gallery 211 highlights the images of flight and space appropriated in the arts, from Wagner's "Evening Star" (from the opera *Tannhauser)* to rock group KISS's star-shaped makeup. Gallery 102 is your ticket to Commercial Air Transportation, with old airliners like the Douglass DC-3 and an exhibit about air-traffic control that may be better than the real thing: the plastic mannequins can never go on strike.

Few exhibits are interactive; most are there to be stared at, period. One exception is Gallery 213 (Beyond the Limits), where visitors can use a computer program to design their own airplane; another is Gallery 203 (Sea-Air Operations) where visitors can pilot a fighter, try to land it on a carrier, and, probably, crash or sink—via computer. With the aid of films, interactive displays, and a simulated Martian environment, an exhibit in the museum entitled "Where Next, Columbus?" (Gallery 209) brings an historical perspective to issues dealing with past and future space exploration, solar sails, and human contact with extraterrestrials.

Air and Space takes an understandable interest in mass-market science fiction. One gallery test-flies the **U.S.S. Enterprise** from Star Trek. Around such galleries, of course, genuine technology and detailed explanations show how real spacecraft are designed. The atmosphere is educational and at times militaristic, but various video displays, the IMAX films, and the Star Trek exhibit can be a galaxy of entertainment for those wearied by endless facts and figures.

IMAX movies give spectators vertigo in the Langley Theater, home of the five-story movie screen. The perennially popular "To Fly," an aerial tour of America from balloons to spaceships, shows with three rotating films. Headsets translate some IMAX films into other languages. (Films run 10:10am-5:25pm. Tickets $4, youth (2-21yrs.) and seniors $2.75; available at the box office on the museum's ground floor.)

The **Einstein Planetarium** harbors a 70-foot starry dome. The standard show, "The New Solar System" will introduces new and current concepts of the universe. (Shows run every 40 min. 11am-5pm. Tickets $4, children, youth, and seniors $2.75; available at the box office on the second floor near the Spirit of St. Louis.)

Self-guided **cassette tours** are available in English and several other languages ($3.50, students and seniors $3). 24-hr. information 357-1686; museum open daily 10am-5:30pm; extended hours determined annually.

HIRSHHORN MUSEUM AND SCULPTURE GARDEN

If you're convinced that art ended with Picasso, stay away from the Hirshhorn Museum and Sculpture Garden—home to the modern, post-modern, and post-post-modern—at 8th St. and Independence Ave. SW (357-2700, TDD 357-1729). The reinforced circular structure perches on four piers 14 ft. above the ground to create a plaza area for the display of sculpture. The four-story, squat concrete cylinder on stilts has outraged traditionalists since 1966. Each floor consists of two concentric circles: an outer ring of rooms and paintings, and an inner corridor of sculptures. From the inner circle, windows face the courtyard and its penny-collecting fountain. (The staff apparently finds this layout simple enough to absolve them of any obligation to provide a floor plan at the information desk.)

Built around immigrant philanthropist Joseph Hirshhorn's gifts, the museum still carries the flavor of personal preference rather than institutional design. Of the museum's architecture, S. Dillon Ripley, former secretary of the Smithsonian, once said, "If it were not controversial in almost every way it would hardly qualify as a place to house contemporary art, for it must somehow be symbolic of the material it is designed to encase."

The Hirshhorn's best shows feature art since 1960; no other gallery or museum in Washington even pretends to keep up with the Hirshhorn's avant-garde paintings, mind-bending sculptures, and mixed-media installations. The halls are packed with the art of 20th-century artists from Calder to Kelly to de Kooning to Stella; even visitors who could supply the missing first names might fall in love with some unknown work. But innocents of modernism need not fear: the work of artists like Georgia O'Keefe, René Magritte, Max Ernst, Jackson Pollack, Edward Hopper, and Joan Miró is intermingled with the more intimidating art by lesser-known artists.

The museum claims the world's most comprehensive set of 19th- and 20th-century Western sculpture, including small works by Rodin and Giacometti. The collection also includes pieces by Renoir, Degas, Matisse, Gaugin, and Picasso. The second and third floors show changing parts of the museum's permanent collection. The lowest level gathers temporary exhibits, an auditorium, and a film on the appreciation of modern art (subtitled for the hearing impaired; comfy chairs for everybody).

Outdoor sculpture shines in the courtyard of the museum, with aluminum, steel, bronze, silver, and red creations set up artfully along the stony pavement. From across Jefferson Ave., the sunken sculpture garden perplexes picnickers. Enter the Hirshhorn through the revolving doors at Independence Ave. (Museum open daily 10am-5:30pm. Sculpture Garden open daily 7:30am-dusk. Tours of the museum Mon.-Sat. 10:30am, noon, and 1:30pm; Sun. 12:30pm. Sculpture tours for the blind and sign-language tours also available. Call 357-3235 for tour information.)

ARTS AND INDUSTRIES BUILDING

Between the Castle and the Hirshhorn, the Arts and Industries Building is an exhibition of an exhibition, the 1876 Centennial Exhibition of American technology in Philadelphia. After the exhibition had ended, most of the foreign exhibitors donated their shows to the U.S. government to save themselves the cost of shipping them home. Congress ordered the Smithsonian to house the inherited objects (over the museum's objections) and paid for the Arts and Industries Building, America's first national museum. The museum's exterior is a polychromatic, multi-style chaos of gables, arches, rails, shingles, bricks, and windows—singularly reflective of the Victorian drive for more, bigger, and "better."

On the inside, the dust that has gathered on some of the old-fashioned glass cases is part of this museum's surprising charm. Light fare, such as furniture and candy-making equipment, congregates near the Mall entrance; further inside, heavier machinery—like an old-fashioned elevator and generator—will delight advocates of steam power. The **Discovery Theater** presents plays especially for children, such as *The Velveteen Rabbit* and *Little Red Hen.* An **experimental gallery,** facing Independence Ave. on the other side of the main fountain, showcases innovative (and usually interactive) exhibits from individuals, museums, and non-profit organizations around the world. Exhibition space is available through an application process and serves as a testing ground from which exhibitors learn how to improve their shows before taking them on tour. The museum has also lent space to other Smithsonian exhibits, most recently the "Visual Journal: Harlem and D.C. in the Thirties and Forties."(Museum open daily 10am-5:30pm. Discovery performances Tues.-Fri. 10 and 11:30am, Sat. 11:30am and 1pm. Admission $5, Resident Members $4, groups of 10 or more $3.50 per person. Reserve by calling the box office at 357-1500 (voice and TDD) Mon.-Fri. 10am-4pm.)

NATIONAL MUSEUM OF AFRICAN ART AND ARTHUR M. SACKLER GALLERY

Built in 1987, the National Museum of African Art and the Sackler Gallery hide their non-Western treasures underground, behind the Castle and below the beautifully landscaped four-acre **Enid A. Haupt Garden.** The Garden is as carefully crafted and meticulously sculpted as the art beneath it. Its main entrance faces Independence Ave. and 10th St. SW (garden opens at 7am, closing hours Memorial Day-Sept. 30 8pm, Oct.-Memorial Day 5:45pm. Metro: Smithsonian). Both museums have two underground exhibit levels and connect to both the International Gallery and the S. Dillon Ripley Center three stories underground. Halls allow visitors to walk among the Sackler, the African, and the Freer (see below). The museums access the outside world through paired postmodern pavilions in the Haupt Garden; if you face the Castle, the Sackler entrance will be on your left, the African entrance on your right.

The **National Museum of African Art,** 950 Independence Ave. SW (357-4600, TDD 357-4814), collects, catalogues, polishes, and shows off artifacts from Sub-Saharan Africa, offering insight into cultures where craftsmanship and artistic creativity go hand in hand, and where texture, color, form, and iconography are regularly incorporated into even the simplest of everyday objects. Entering the first-level central hall, you are greeted by a **slit-gong,** a drum in the shape of an unidentifiable animal. Permanent exhibits include a collection of bronzes from what is today Nigeria and assorted pottery. There are also pieces by contemporary African artists. The second floor houses temporary exhibits (open daily 10am-5:30pm; hour-long tours Tues.-Thurs. at 1:30pm, Sat.-Sun. at 11am, 1pm). A calendar of events lists changes in the tour schedule and is available at the information desk.

The small **International Gallery,** 1100 Jefferson Dr. SW (357-1300), inside the S. Dillon Ripley Center, continually offers new and thoughtful temporary exhibits. Recent exhibits have featured lithographs from a politically transformed Eastern Europe, and "Talents of the Brush," featuring entrants in the Jill Sackler Chinese calligraphy competition.

The **Arthur M. Sackler Gallery,** 1050 Independence Ave. SW (357-2041, TDD 786-2374), showcases Sackler's extensive collection of art from China, South and Southeast Asia, and Persia. Illuminated manuscripts, Chinese and Japanese paintings from many centuries; carvings and friezes from Egypt, Phoenicia, and Sumeria; Hindu gods, jade miniatures, and other such works repose in low light and air-conditioned majesty. Permanent displays include "Monsters, Myths, and Minerals," and "Sculpture of South and Southeast Asia." Exhibits occasionally have excellent self-guided tour materials for children under 12. Call for tour information. The **Sackler Library** (357-2091), on the second level, is open to the public Mon.-Fri. 10am-5pm. (Museum open daily 10am-5:30pm.)

FREER GALLERY

The Freer Gallery of Art, on the Mall at Jefferson Dr. and 12th St. SW, is an anomaly among the Mall's voluminous, showy structures. A fraction of the size of most Smithsonian museums, the Freer quietly displays an ostensibly odd combination of Asian and American art. However, the latter betrays the former's influences. (For example the paintings and designs of James McNeill Whistler employ an East-Asian aesthetic his opulent and spectacular "Peacock Room," is ruled by the kimono-clad "Princess from the Land of Porcelain.") A sequence of connected galleries surround an elegant courtyard and lead visitors from the American art past Japanese, Korean, Chinese Buddhist, South Asian, and Islamic works. Careful attention has been paid to the restoration and presentation of these works; a recent exhibition detailed "The Life of a Japanese Painting." If properly restored, these paintings should not need treatment for another 300 years. Recently connected to the Sackler via a new shared exhibition gallery, the Freer collection (comprising over 26,000 objects) is as richly historical and fabulously opulent as its neighbor's—Chinese bronzes, precious manuscripts jade carvings, and so forth reward hour upon hour of viewing and consideration. Its unusual combination of Eastern and Western art, and the beautiful permanent collection and thoughtful temporary displays all come together in exquisite harmony (open daily 10am-5:30pm; free **tour** daily at 1:30pm).

■ National Gallery of Art

The National Gallery of Art and the **U.S. Holocaust Memorial** are not technically Smithsonian constituents; however, their proximity to the institution and the Mall lends them an informal association.

NATIONAL GALLERY OF ART: WEST BUILDING

The National Gallery (737-4215, TDD 842-6176) houses and hangs its world-class jumble of pre-1900 art in a domed marble temple to Western Tradition designed by the Pope himself—John Russell Pope, whose more-reverent-than-thou columns and stairs also adorn the National Archives and the Jefferson Memorial. The original, Ionic-style National Gallery building (now known as the West Wing) was conceived, proposed, financed, and named by financier Andrew Mellon, who realized that other collectors would be more likely to donate to a gallery if it didn't bear his name. The West Wing and the East Wing collectively constitute North America's most popular art museum, with over six million visitors annually (next is the Metropolitan Museum of Art in New York, with four million). The West Building holds works by El Greco, Raphael, Rembrandt, Vermeer, and Monet, among many others.

The West Wing building can be accessed from the Mall or from the entrance at 6th St. and Constitution Ave. NW. (Metro: Archives-Navy Memorial.) At the Constitution Ave. entrance are noteworthy zodiac symbols on an outdoor Mellon fountain. Both portals leave visitors in the round central "court" under the dome, where black marble pillars and a fountain celebrate the god Mercury. Sculpture-saturated hallways lead right (east) and left (west) from the Mall entrance to the exhibition rooms. Usually, the rooms to the east of the rotunda house French, British, and American paintings while the galleries on the west hold Italian, Dutch, Spanish, German, and Flemish works. The West Building has been undergoing roof and skylight replacement; exhibits may be temporarily relocated. The **information desk** to the left (west) of the rotunda can provide specific locations. Museum floor plans are also available from the information desk. In the same room, visitors can access the **"Micro Gallery,"** the museum's interactive computer system. Visitors may view and learn about more than 1700 of the works in the permanent collection, or even design and print a **personal tour map.**

This museum's contents read like an encyclopedia of Western art. Every room houses recognizably famous works, from the two-dimensional gold-leaf pre-portrait paintings of the Middle Ages to the rough strokes of Impressionism to bold American landscapes. The West Building hangs its canvases in lots of small rooms rather than a few big ones—an undeviated walk from one end to the other can cause a visitor to miss most of the works. West and East Garden Courts relieve the potential monotony of the Old Masters with fountains, ferns, sunlight, and benches. Leonardo da Vinci's earliest surviving portrait (and the only painting by that artist in the U.S.), *Ginevra de' Benci,* is the main attraction in the startlingly fine collection of Italian Renaissance art. Auguste Renoir's *Girl with a Watering Can* and other well-known French Impressionist pieces hang in Galleries 85-93 across the rotunda from the Italian works. The museum's prize rooms are a hall of knock-'em-dead Dutch masters with a few of the world's 30-odd Vermeers, and a room exclusively featuring Jan Van Eyck's *The Annunciation.* Early 20th-century American works begin in Gallery 70; a plethora is found in the East Wing.

Throngs of youths admire Salvador Dali's science-fictional *Last Supper* in the turn of the stairway between the underground concourse and the first floor of the West Wing; the lower level harbors relatively low-key collections of sculpture (including a room full of Rodins), prints and drawings, and temporary exhibits.

Even the cheapest connoisseur can exult in the museum's guided tours, gallery talks, free classical music concerts, and general profusion of special events, whose mercurial schedules are available at the information desk in the rotunda (as well as in the East Wing). Vocal, piano, and chamber music concerts take place most Sundays evenings between October and June at 7pm in the West Garden Court (call 842-6941 for the schedule); most events are free but seating is limited (open Mon.-Sat. 10am-5pm, Sun. 11am-6pm).

NATIONAL GALLERY OF ART: EAST BUILDING

Completed amid much fanfare in 1978, the "East Wing" of the National Gallery of Art (737-4215) houses (and sometimes hides) much of the museum's plentiful 20th-century collection. I. M. Pei's celebrated design is itself a work of art. The smooth marble four-story gallery outlines high, interlocking triangles, glass-topped to flood the atrium with sunlight. On one hand, the building is at once calming and innovative; the design accommodates large-scale works—by Alexander Calder, Anthony Caro, and others—created especially for the new structure. On the other hand the impressive atrium houses no art; the East Wing is utterly inefficient as an exhibit space. Whereas the West Building sacrificed beauty in an attempt to house large collections, Pei filled potential gallery space with air to make the design pleasingly bright and spacious; he succeeded, but not without a price.

The building has drawn huge crowds to its celebrated temporary exhibitions. The Prince and Princess of Wales were at the head of the queue for 1985's "Treasure Houses of Great Britain"; more recent visiting collections have included the contemporary works amassed by local philanthropists Robert and Jane Meyerhoff (rooms entirely devoted to works by Rothko, Johns, Rauschenberg, and others).

Enter the East Wing from Constitution Ave., Pennsylvania Ave. at 4th St. NW, the Mall, or the gallery's West Building (via the underground moving walkway). (Metro: Archives-Navy Memorial.) The immense red and black Calder mobile hanging in the entrance hall is the gallery's trademark; it quietly recalls the knife-edge exterior of the building itself, one of the sharpest corners in modern architecture. Believe it or not, two galleries for temporary exhibits are tucked into the corners of the ground floor; finding them is a challenge. Other temporary-exhibit galleries lurk on the mezzanine and upper levels. A **directory** can be found on the ground floor, and a **floor plan** is available from information.

The East Wing hangs its permanent collection in two places. A spacious gallery on the 4th St. side of the upper level currently holds most of the European works, including over a dozen by Picasso, representing most of his stylistic phases, and nearly as many by Matisse. In the gallery's early rooms, Surrealists including Miró, Magritte, and Man Ray play with your mind while Fauves such as Derain assault your retina with brash, colorful brushstrokes. To track the post-war shift of the art world's gravitational center from Europe to America, you'll have to shift as well, to the gallery downstairs on the Concourse level. Here you'll find Warhol's 32 Campbell's soup can paintings and a couple of Lichtenstein's comic-like Pop canvases, as well as more recent works by lesser-known artists. The Concourse level is also home to Matisse's famous giant paper collages, which can be viewed only at certain hours to minimize light damage (Mon.-Sat. 10am-2pm, Sun. noon-4pm). At the very top of the building, on the tiny and triangular Tower level, is the carefully arranged assortment of sculptures by the technologically inspired American sculptor David Smith, whose works involve sophisticated and futuristic welding techniques and were meant to be viewed from a variety of perspectives.

To see the East Wing properly takes at least an hour and a half, excluding sufficient time for appreciation of the building's exterior. Outdoors, between the West and East Buildings, a scattering of glass pyramids (skylights for the underground restaurant) and a sleek fountain complement the hip architecture of the building itself (open Mon.-Sat. 10am-5pm, Sun. 11am-6pm).

■ U.S. Holocaust Museum

The U.S. Holocaust Memorial Museum, 100 Raoul Wallenberg Place SW (488-0400; Metro: Smithsonian), opened in April of 1993 after more than a decade of preparation. The project was the brainchild of Carter administration advisors, and in 1979, Carter himself asked Holocaust survivor and author Elie Wiesel to plan the museum. The federal government threw in a piece of land, and the U.S. Holocaust Memorial Council began private fundraising efforts to pay for the building's construction.

In a 1989 address to the council, President George Bush declared that "this building will testify more powerfully than any words to the importance of protecting freedom and dignity for all people." The museum project has been hailed over the years by three more Presidents and thousands of government officials, clergymen, and lay leaders as a necessity for a country whose living memory of the Holocaust years is rapidly fading and becoming increasingly distorted. In this vein, testaments of President Dwight D. Eisenhower are immortalized on plaques throughout the museum—upon visiting Nazi concentration camps in Europe after World War II, President Eisenhower vowed to stand as witness to the savagery so that Holocaust allegations would never be charged to "propaganda."

The museum's prominent and symbolic site—close to the Mall and within view of the Washington Monument and Lincoln Memorial—inevitably places the museum, and its subject matter, in the midst of America's archives and in the context of its history. Unlike Europe, where the history of the Holocaust is told in aging synagogue-museums or in the worn buildings of former concentration camps, the new U.S. museum is uniquely suited to its audience. Its displays move beyond mere historical narrative; visitors are *made* to experience events from a more personal and immediate perspective. Those entering the **permanent exhibition** are given a card with a photo and description of an actual Holocaust victim. The card chronicles the changes in that individual's life over the course of the war. A "Tower of Photos" surrounds observers in another part of the hall, inundating them with pre-Holocaust photos of an entire village. Invariably, it is the pictorial evidence, the photos of individual faces, which forces upon the potentially detached observer an emotional connection with the documented events. The museum assumes ignorance on the part of its visitors and gives them the whole story, beginning on the fourth floor (accessible by elevator) with **"Nazi Assault, 1933-39,"** which chronicles not only the rise of Nazism, but also the events leading up to the war in Europe and the history of anti-Semitism from the beginnings of Christianity onward. Via film footage, artifacts, and clearly written descriptions, the exhibit guides observers through the increasingly explicit persecution of German Jews in the years preceding the second world war. Vistors are made to experience the progression towards genocide and the exhibit's assertion that the passive acceptance of the German populace made it all possible. A 13-minute video chronicles the Nazi rise to power in the 1920s and '30s. **"The Final Solution, 1940-44"** is less forgiving; a black-and-white film (shown behind walls too high for small children to peek over) shows barbaric medical experiments performed by Nazi doctors. In full view, still photos and dioramas depict Jews and others being rounded up and sent to concentration camps, then exterminated in gas chambers or at gunpoint. One photo shows a sea of women's hair, shorn off prisoners to be sold and eventually used as a manufacturing fiber. Victims' personal items, on loan from Holocaust museums in Poland and Germany, are also displayed here. Finally, **"Aftermath—1945 to the Present"** brings it all together. Films show Soviet, British, and American troops entering the concentration camps, shocked by the mass graves and emaciated prisoners they encounter. A wall lists the names of those who heroically defied the Nazis to save Jewish lives, while more films and tapes bear the chilling testimony of Holocaust survivors.

Throughout the permanent exhibition, instances of U.S. and world callousness to the plight of the Jews are justifiably condemned. One display discusses FDR's refusal to bomb the extermination facilities at Auschwitz, despite pleas from American Jews. At the end of the permanent exhibit is the entrance to the free-standing octagonal **Hall of Remembrance,** with its eternal flame symbolically placed within the museum to emphasize the central theme of the exhibits—to never forget.

James Ingo Freed used forms derived from the Holocaust itself to create a building that is as much about the Holocaust as the exhibits it contains. Set between the neoclassical Bureau of Engraving and Printing and the Victorian Auditor's Building, the museum brings together the materials of both neighboring buildings—limestone and red brick—with the forms of the concentration camp guard towers (in the four glass-topped "towers" that line the north side of the building) and the ovens in which prisoners died (as the arched brick portals in the Hall of Witness). The center beam of the steel-and-glass skylight ceiling of the Hall of Witness runs at a diagonal, giving the whole room a warped feeling.

The "Americanization" of the Holocaust embodied in this museum—both its presence in the capital and its conscious efforts to engage American crowds—has led critics to contend that the museum is just "one more American theme park," complete with interactive computer set-ups and video displays, films that play and replay atrocities for each new slew of visitors, and shiny, visually striking exhibits that entertain as much as they educate. Yet even detractors must give credit to the fine presentation of a vast amount of material in a coherent, sensitive, and ultimately effective exhibit. While most of the museum is inappropriate for the very young, children should be encouraged to explore the **"Remember the Children"** exhibit on the first floor (no ticket required). Here, the story of the fictitious Holocaust survivor Daniel is told through his diary entries and depictions of his homes before the war, in the ghetto, and in a concentration camp. Children can open Daniel's drawers, lift up his blankets, and open windows to see how Daniel lived both "before" and "after" the institution of anti-Semitic laws. The museum also houses a resource center for teachers and the **Wexner Learning Center,** where visitors conduct research on Holocaust topics through computers and interactive films.

Massive overcrowding has forced the museum to require all visitors to the permanent exhibition to have **tickets.** To acquire tickets on the same day as your visit, get in line before 9am at the 14th and C St. entrance. Otherwise, it's safer to buy tickets through TicketMaster two weeks in advance (in D.C. call 432-7328; in MD 410-481-7328; in VA 703-573-7328; out of region 800-551-7328) and submit to the agency's $4 service charge (tickets are free for those who stand in line). Tickets are good for admission to the exhibition *at certain times only;* try to get an early time, if possible. You don't want to be rushed as you make your way through the exhibits, and crowds often necessitate a wait for a good view of the more popular displays.

The museum sits on a parcel of land between 14th St. and Raoul Wallenberg Place SW (a portion of 15th St. renamed in honor of Raoul Wallenberg, the Swedish diplomat who saved thousands of Hungarian Jews from the Nazis), just south of Independence Ave. Don't try to see everything in one day; allow at least four hours for the briefest of breeze-throughs. (Museum open daily 10am-5:30pm.)

Outside the Mall

SMITHSONIAN MUSEUMS

Old Downtown: National Building Museum

It's only proper that an architectural marvel should house the National Building Museum (272-2448), which towers above F St. NW between 4th and 5th St. (Metro: Judiciary Square, directly across from the F St. exit). In 1881, Congress asked military engineer Montgomery Meigs to design a cheap brick building for the 1500 clerks of the Pension Bureau. The bureaucrats lucked out: Meigs's Italian-inspired edifice remains one of Washington's most beautiful. A terra-cotta frieze, 3-ft. high and 1200-ft. long, frames an endless parade of Union soldiers arriving to collect their pensions; the frieze includes doctors, wounded soldiers, and artillery pieces amid the crowds of infantry. Caspar Buberl, sculptor of the frieze, was inspired by early photographer Eadweard (not Edward) Muybridge, who analyzed the motions of walking and running. Inside, the expansive **Great Hall** exhibits a sort of budget opulence. On one hand, its eight Corinthian columns are among the world's largest; life-sized busts peer down from 244 wall niches; and a terra-cotta fountain is 28 ft. in diameter. The Great Hall—big enough to hold a 15-story building—may even cause visitors sensitive to scale, spectacle, and splendor to gasp involuntarily. But on the other hand, the columns are brick (their "marble" surface required 4000 gallons of rose paint) and the roof, partly corrugated metal, rests on iron supports. Meigs wanted to fill the niches with busts of prominent Americans; to stay within his budget, however, he had to revise his plans and base the busts on Smithsonian life masks of Native Americans. In 1984 the busts "were discarded" and replaced with 244 replicas of eight models by artist Gretta Bader of "American Builders."

Architecture is not the museum's only preoccupation, however. It honors American achievements in urban planning, construction, and design, and explores these achievements' social and philosophical implications. Subjects of recent temporary exhibitions have included the barn as cultural icon, the effects of commercial architectural photography, and the history and symbolism of American fences.

"Washington: Symbol and City," one of the N.B.M.'s first permanent exhibits, records D.C.'s dual history. Half the exhibit concerns the planning of monuments and central Washington; the other half deals with D.C.'s residential areas. Other highlights include models of the rejected designs for the Washington Monument and the chance to design your own Capitol Hill rowhouse. The exhibit raises the perennial question of how the federal, private, business, tourist, and symbolic aspects of the city are, and should be, prioritized.

The museum also sponsors free lunchtime **concerts** (at 12:15pm), generally by chamber and jazz ensembles or military bands, on selected Wed. and Thurs. afternoons in the Great Hall. (Museum open Mon.-Sat. 10am-4pm, Sun. noon-4pm; open until 5pm daily during summer months). Tours Mon.-Fri. 12:30pm, Sat.-Sun. 12:30pm, 1:30pm. Excellent handicap access, including assistance for visually impaired visitors. Free, but suggested donation: adults $3, students and seniors $2.

Old Downtown: National Museum of American Art and National Portrait Gallery

The National Museum of American Art and the National Portrait Gallery (357-2700, TDD 357-1729) share the **Old Patent Office Building,** a Neoclassical edifice two blocks long (American Art entrance at 8th and G St., Portrait Gallery entrance at 8th and F; Metro: Gallery Place-Chinatown). Washington's ubiquitous Greek temple motif, complete with Doric columns, seems more appropriate to these cultural shrines—which moved here in 1968—than to the 19th-century bureaucrats the Patent Office once employed. Robert Mills, architect of the Washington Monument, designed the more delicate, less imposing south wing (now the Portrait Gallery). The American Art is recognizable due to the glistening fiberglass cowboy (*Vaquero)* in its company, while the Portrait Gallery is marked by its hanging banners—the two areas are connected by a courtyard, in which visitors may bask in the sun.

National Museum of American Art

This museum, housing the largest collection of American art in the world, is as expansive and eclectic as the cultural legacy it is meant to represent. The surprisingly deserted corridors contain a pleasantly diverse and disorganized selection from the museum's hoard of major 19th-century painters' and folk and ethnic artists' colonial, impressionist, and photographic works, as well as a smattering of contemporary innovators. Of course, the expected Gilbert Stuarts aren't lacking, either.

D.C. janitor James Hampton stayed up nights in an unheated garage for 15 years to assemble the *Throne of the Third Heaven of the Nations' Millennium General Assembly.* Now on permanent display down the corridor to the left of the main entrance, this array of sculptures may permanently alter your spiritual life. *Time* has called it "the finest work of visionary religious art produced by an American." The throne comprises 177 objects, including ruined furniture, electrical cables, and dead light bulbs sheathed in aluminum and gold foil. No one exhibited or even knew of the work until years after Hampton's death in 1964. The *Throne*'s framework of religious symbolism and its cryptic writing system have yet to be decoded; mere mortals will just stare, dumbfounded.

Other pieces on a similarly grandiose scale include Paul Feeley's six-foot-tall gold fiberglass *Jack,* and Thomas Moran's gargantuan canyon landscapes in the second-floor lobby. The museum's "Art of the American West" room (first floor) offers 19th-century depictions of Native Americans, including important works by Native American artists. Selections from what the NMAA calls the finest collection of African-American art of any general museum are displayed on the second and third floors.

The third floor showcases 20th-century work, and, like much of the museum, warrants more attention that it gets. The Lincoln Gallery was originally designed as the Patent Office exhibition room and served its country as a makeshift hospital during the Civil War. Today, it houses works by everyone from Franz Kline to Georgia O'Keefe to Roberta Rauschenberg. Exhibits rotate regularly.

Free tours are given Mon.-Fri. at noon and Sat.-Sun. at 2pm. Temporary exhibitions are given real weight at the NMAA; they give the museum a chance to show off elements of its immense collection normally forced into storage by lack of display space (the NMAA owns over 35,000 works). Wheelchair access at 9th and G; sign language tours and oral interpreters available on request (786-2942, TDD 786-2414). Museum open daily 10am-5:30pm.

Directly above the Portrait Gallery and accessible via the NMAA's third floor modern art collection is the **Great Hall,** once the largest room in the United States. Its gilded American Victorian Renaissance walls were witness to Lincoln's second inaugural ball in 1865. Now restored to its antebellum splendor, the hall fufills the building's original purpose by displaying patent models.

National Portrait Gallery

If a museum devoted exclusively to portraiture sounds monotonous, think again; the wide range of media, periods, styles, and people represented make the narrow halls of the National Portrait Gallery more like a museum of the American character. Portraits in the gallery come in all shapes and sizes, from a miniature superimposition of P.T. Barnum's head on a beetle's body (thus rendering the curiosity king a "humbug") to a life-sized painting of opera star Marian Anderson in a long red gown. A caricature of Rachmaninoff shows the Russian composer pensively playing piano; nearby, depictions of Theodore Roosevelt are exceptionally prolific.

Corridors have themes such as "Poets and Painters"; athletes and other modern celebrities are also represented. The collection also holds photographs, though it prefers to acquire "portraits taken from life sittings." A rare daguerreotype of a young Frederick Douglass reflects the photographic technique's formative years.

The gallery's temporary exhibits and unmarked rooms are more fun and offbeat than the staid permanent collections, which include a **Hall of Presidents** (2nd floor) and the **Meserve Collection** (3rd floor), containing Matthew Brady's Civil War photos of Lincoln. The expected dryness of the **Galleries of Notable Americans** is relieved by portraits whose conservatism is so extreme that they become amusing. A portrait of **Pocahontas** painted when she was living in England (circa 1595-1617) presents a stuffy maiden in velvet with a Protestant's lace cuff around her neck; Davey Crockett is also depicted in a surprisingly austere manner, looking more like a State Representative than a fur-trapper. The gallery also boasts a life-sized portrait of Samuel Clemens (Mark Twain), an image of Elizabeth Cady Stanton looking very clever, a bust of Geronimo, and a portrait of Mary Cassatt painted by Edgar Degas.

NPG museum **tours** on a walk-in basis or by request (357-2920). Museum open daily 10am-5:30pm. Wheelchair access near the garage at 9th and G St. Free.

Capitol Hill: National Postal Museum

Established in 1993, the National Postal Museum (357-2700, TDD 357-1729), located on the lower level of the City Post Office at 1st St. and Massachusetts Ave. NE (Metro: Union Station), is the latest jewel in the Smithsonian crown, and it has learned from the institution's previous mistakes. While other Smithsonian museums bombard visitors with an indigestible amount of information—often in painfully small fonts—the Postal Museum delivers an intelligent and accessible summary of the nation's postal and philatelic history. In under an hour, visitors can navigate a replica of the forest paths used by the nation's first mailmen, and create work for current mailmen by addressing, stamping, and mailing their very own National Postal Museum postcards. An escalator accesses the museum from the center of the cavernous lobby of the City Post Office. Look up as you ride down: three airmail planes hang far overhead in the 90-ft.-high atrium. The display at the foot of the escalator, "Moving the Mail," is dedicated (not surprisingly) to the vehicles used to transport mail. It features some of the museum's larger pieces, including the red-white- and-blue "long-life vehicle" standard on the streets today, and a more dated railway mail car where visitors can try their hand at sorting the mail. Also in this area, free postcards are available from kiosks where visitors generate an addressed postcard, put it through one of the metering machines (the stamp will still cost you 20¢—the U.S.P.S. draws the line at free postage), and drop it through a slot to mail it off.

A number of passages radiate off this main hall, each containing a separate exhibit; the passage directly opposite the escalator is probably the best place to start. The exhibit there, "Binding the Nation," tells the early story of the postal system. As every mail aficionado can tell you, neither rain nor sleet nor dark of night can stay these couriers from their appointed rounds. But the rounds were much tougher going before the advent of motorized mail trucks and electronic ZIP code scanners, as this display makes eminently clear. The exhibit covers the history of the postal system from Colonial times to the Civil War. Not surprisingly, the Pony Express gets big play, but the gallery's entrance recreates the King's Best Highway, the roadless postal route that ran between New York and Boston in the 1670s (a path that has since become the motel-infested Route 1). At a computer video terminal inside the exhibit, visitors can attempt to choose the best mail route between various U.S. cities in the 1800s.

The next gallery, "Customers and Communities," picks up where "Binding the Nation" left off. The "Rural Free Delivery" section displays the five winners of a contest to find the most unusual RFD mail boxes—the replica of the U.S. Capitol held at arm's length by Uncle Sam is a classic. The exhibit ends with a section on postal oddities, including the charred remains of the Craig, Alaska Post Office, collected and stored in a jar and the letter-carrier uniform worn by Cliff Clavin, everyone's favorite oedipal oddity, on the late TV series *Cheers*.

Across the main hall, "The Art of Cards and Letters" displays examples of wartime correspondence from U.S. military conflicts, including the Persian Gulf War. Letter-writing stations are available for those so inspired. "Stamps and Stories" overflows

Capital Children's Museum

Release your Smithsonian-induced tension by touching and feeling every exhibit in this huge interactive experiment of a museum, located at 800 3rd St. NE (675-4125), directly behind the Union Station parking lot, in a large red-brick building that looks like a city school (Metro: Union Station). Visitors can grind and brew their own hot chocolate while trying on ponchos in the two-story mock-up of a Mexican plaza, write with a quill and ink, print a simple plate with a printing press, walk through the life-sized cave, and leave a mark on the wall in the shadow theater. A model town lets children play in a miniature community complete with a bus to drive, a manhole to descend, and a working telephone system. The museum also has a high-tech animation exhibit, which teaches the basic principles of cartoon-making and even lets kids be filmed against an animated background, à la Roger Rabbit. On weekends, the museum sponsors an acclaimed Holocaust education program for children, led by Holocaust survivors; call for details. (Open daily 10am-5pm. Admission $6, seniors $4, children under 2 free. All children must be accompanied by an adult.)

with the museum's renowned collection of philatelic rarities (including the priceless "Inverted Jenny") as well as a smaller collection of overexcited philatelists.

The museum's **Discovery Center** is adjacent to the exhibition galleries and offers daily activities and projects for children and adults, from deciphering a bar code to solving a postal crime. The **Library Research Center,** with more than 40,000 volumes and manuscripts, is the world's largest postal-research facility. The center houses a specimen study room, an audio-video viewing room, and a separate library of rare books. The library facilities are available to scholars and the interested public by appointment only (633-9370). The museum also houses a gift shop, a stamp store, and (surprise) a fully functional post office.

Maps are available at the **information desk.** Special **tours** for groups may be arranged in advance by calling 357-2991 (Mon.-Fri. 10am-3pm). To arrange tours for persons with visual or hearing impairments, call 786-2942 (TDD 786-2414) one week in advance (Mon.-Fri. 10am-3pm). Sign language and oral interpreters for programs other than tours are available by calling the same number two weeks in advance. The museum is open daily 10am-5:30pm. (Free.)

Southeast: Anacostia Museum

1901 Fort Place SE (287-3369, Sat.-Sun. 357-2700). Metro: Anacostia. (Walking here from the Metro can be dangerous; take a cab.) Founded in 1967 in a former movie theater and later moved to modern quarters, this Smithsonian "neighborhood museum" holds temporary exhibits on African-American history and culture. In 1996, the museum exhibited "Down through the Years," an all-encompassing collection of works that outlined the museum's history; the exhibit prefaced renovations to be made on the building (the museum is scheduled to reopen sometime late 1996-early 1997—call to confirm). At other times, call or pick up a flyer at the Smithsonian Castle (on the Mall) to see what's showing. A small museum store sells cards, posters, and books by and about African-Americans. To reach the museum by car, take MLK Ave. SE to Morris Rd., turn left on Morris (which becomes Erie St., then Fort Pl.); by bus, take the W-1 or W-2 on Howard Rd. near the Anacostia Metro and ride to the museum's doorstep at Fort Place (open daily 10am-5:30pm; free).

Dupont Circle: Renwick Gallery

At 17th St. and Pennsylvania Ave. NW, the Renwick Gallery (357-1300, 357-2531) fills its Second Empire mansion with some of D.C.'s most interesting art. (Metro: Farragut West.) This Smithsonian-owned gallery says it displays "American craft," but its holdings aren't just for macramé buffs. The first floor's temporary exhibits often show fascinating mixed-media sculptures, tapestries, and constructions by important contemporary artists. Upstairs, the **Grand Salon** and the **Octagon Room** display epic 19th- and early 20th-century works in grand style. These rooms, however, are not indicative of the museum's true bent; the second floor displays contemporary "craft." Although many pieces in the collection rotate, look for two of the Renwick's most arresting works: Wendell Castle's 1985 *Ghost Clock* and Larry Fuente's 1988 *Game Fish.* The former, at first glance simply a grandfather clock with a sheet thrown over it, was actually carved from a single piece of mahogany; the latter is a huge sailfish trophy ingeniously plastered with children's toys. The first-floor displays rotate every few months (open daily 10am-5:30pm; wheelchair access; free).

CAPITOL HILL

Sewall-Belmont House

Just a few blocks from Washington's largest museums sits a small, intimate museum, quietly dedicated to the achievements of women. Nestled beside the Hart Senate office building, Sewall-Belmont House, 144 Constitution Ave. NE (546-3989), holds a museum of the U.S. women's movement, as well as the offices of the National Woman's Party. (Metro: Union Station.) Travelers who have battled the Smithsonian crowds will appreciate the peace and attention granted here. When visitors arrive, the sole guide on duty greets them at the door, puts out a "Tour in Progress" sign, and whisks them off for a personal tour of the premises. Along the way, visitors may admire some of the oldest digs in Washington; the house was built in 1800 by Robert Sewall, incorporating parts of a house dating to 1680. Treasury Secretary Albert Gallatin was one of the first to reside in the house, and in 1803, he negotiated the Louisiana Purchase from a front room because he despised the 20-minute carriage ride to the Treasury Building. In 1814, American resistance troops fired upon camping British soldiers from the house's top floors. The irked and pyromaniacal British set the house ablaze, as they did to most of official Washington, but a fortuitous rainstorm spared most of the building. Restorations returned it to tip-top shape, and in 1929, the National Women's Party bought the house for its headquarters.

Most of the tour focuses on the NWP's fight for suffrage, as well as on the life of Alice Paul, who founded the party in 1913. The main hall, referred to as the "Hall of Fame," holds busts of noted suffragettes and feminists Susan B. Anthony, Lucretia Mott, and Elizabeth Cady Stanton, as well as a life-sized statue of Joan of Arc. Sybil Luddington is shown on the horse she rode on the night of April 26, 1777, to warn the militiamen in Danbury, CT of an impending attack by the British. Her ride was twice as long as Paul Revere's and, unlike Revere, she did not get caught by the British. At the end of the hall hangs the large yellow-and-purple banner used to picket the White House for suffrage in 1917. Other rooms contain art and photographs related to the women's movement as well as beautiful period furnishings, including the sort of rope bed whose fickle tension apparently gave rise to the expression "sleep tight." (House open Tues.-Fri. 10am-3pm, Sat. noon-4pm. For a tour, simply go up the front staircase and ring the bell. Free.)

SOUTHEAST

Navy Museum

You can play Popeye at this refreshingly hands-on paean to things naval, located in Building 76 at the Navy Yard (433-4882). Metro: Eastern Market. Visitors climb inside the space capsule, man the huge ship guns (3-in., 50-caliber), squeeze into a bathysphere used to explore the sea floor, or give orders on the bridge. Fondle the life-sized replicas of "Little Boy" and "Fat Man," the atomic bombs detonated over Japan at the close of WWII. Alvin and Trieste undersea vehicles hang from the ceiling next to Navy airplanes, while countless model ships are laid up in glassy drydocks—the American craft are up to 14 ft. long, and their anachronistic opponents include a 1916 Austro-Hungarian warship and a Greek trireme. Next door, technology steams on at the unpretentious **Museum Annex.** Just a small building full of old submarines, the Annex shows off the Intelligent Whale, a hand-propelled submarine the Navy bought in 1869. Run your hands along the Seehund, a well-designed mini-sub the

Nazis used for coastal defense in the days of World War II. (Museum open Mon.-Fri. 9am-4pm, Sat.-Sun. 10am-5pm.)

Marine Corps Historical Museum and Navy Art Gallery

The **Marine Corps Historical Museum,** in Building 58 at the Navy Yard (433-3534; Metro: Navy Yard), marches through Marine Corps time from the American Revolution to the present. Twenty exhibit cases tout the actions, guns, uniforms, and swords of marines from the halls of Montezuma to the shores of Kuwait. The 1996 special exhibit commemorated the 50th anniversary of WWII, and in addition to the photo of men raising the American flag at Iwo Jima, the museum has the actual flag itself (complete with bullet holes). (Open Mon., Wed.-Thurs., and Sat. 10am-4pm, Fri. 10am-8pm, Sun., noon-5pm.) Nearby, in Building 67 (433-3815), the one-room **Navy Art Gallery** hangs paintings of naval action, all by talented sailors and "combat artists." These specialized artists sailed, ate canned rations, and braved gunfire with the sailors, all to record on canvas the action on board. Exhibits change every six months (open Wed.-Fri. 9am-4pm, Sat.-Sun. 10am-4pm).

OLD DOWNTOWN

National Museum of Women in the Arts

The National Museum of Women in the Arts, 1250 New York Ave. NW (783-5000; Metro: Metro Center), suffers slightly from the architectural constraints of its home. The bottom two floors were once a Masonic Temple, and a hunt for the museum's permanent collection, which begins on the third floor, feels like an initiation rite. From outside, the NMWA resembles the neighboring office buildings; inside, sweeping staircases, pink marble, and celestial chandeliers are better suited to a mansion than a museum. The ground floor contains the museum shop and information desk. A second-floor balcony harbors changing displays.

An alternative to the elevator is to climb the stairs, traverse the balcony, and ascend the spare, hidden staircase to the third floor. There are many Renaissance and Baroque paintings as well as 19th- and 20th-century samples; particularly enjoyable are the vital "still"-lifes of Rachel Ruysch (1644-1750), last of the great Dutch fruit and flower painters. The *salonière* Elisabeth Vigée-Lebrun (1855-1842) was court painter to Marie Antoinette; when she applied for admission to the Royal Academy, critics wondered whether her beautiful work had been done by a man.

Women artists have come into their own in the last 100 years, and the permanent collection proves it with works by Mary Cassatt, Georgia O'Keeffe, Lilla Cabot Perry, and Alma Thomas. Helen Frankenthaler's expansive landscape-esque canvas compels a visit. The comparatively young museum invites a flood of temporary exhibitions; the museum listings in *City Paper* or the *Washington Post* Weekend section will entice you further (open Mon.-Sat. 10am-5pm, Sun. noon-5pm; suggested donation $3, seniors and students $2).

FOGGY BOTTOM

Corcoran Gallery of Art

Once housed in the Renwick's mansion, the Corcoran (638-3211, 638-1439, or 638-1070), Washington's oldest art museum, now exhibits in much larger, Neoclassical quarters on 17th St. between E St. and New York Ave. NW. (Metro: Farragut West.) Frank Lloyd Wright called it "the best-designed building in Washington." The Corcoran shows off American artists like portraitist John Singer Sargent, impressionist Mary Cassatt, and seascape master Winslow Homer. An air of medieval romance is provided by Thomas Cole's 1841 *Return from the Tournament,* on display in the North Atrium, and Louis-Maurice Boutet de Monvel's gold-leafed series on Joan of Arc, which begins on Clark Landing. Montana Senator Clark donated many of the Corcoran's more interesting 19th-century pieces, as well as the wildly baroque **Salon Doré,** a gaudy gold-leaf room that the Senator had transported from its early 18th-century Parisian home to his equally flagrant New York palace.

The Corcoran also houses a fine selection of contemporary American art, displaying such greats as Willem de Kooning and Ellsworth Kelly. Look for Andy Warhol's 1973 *Mao* as well as a slew of Roy Lichtenstein pieces. Four major exhibitions, not necessarily modern, sweep the second floor yearly. In 1988 the Corcoran reneged on its promise to house a touring exhibit of photography by the late Robert Mapplethorpe; the ensuing uproar over homophobia, obscenity laws, and federal funding of the arts rendered the Corcoran notorious and made Mapplethorpe one of the best-known names in photography.

Free **tours** are given daily at noon and on Thursdays at 7:30pm. Free **jazz concerts** take place in the Hammer Auditorium every Wednesday at 12:30pm. (Open Mon., Wed. and Fri.-Sun. 10am-5pm, Thurs. 10am-9pm. Suggested donation $3, families $5, students and seniors $1, under 12 free.)

GEORGETOWN

Dumbarton Oaks

This 16-acre estate, at 1703 32nd St. NW between R and S St. (recorded information 339-6401, tour information 342-3212), is all that remains of the original Rock of Dumbarton property, out of which settlers once carved the town of George. The mansion/museum's attractive displays showcase Byzantine and pre-Columbian art, and the terraced gardens are the best cheap date in town. The inscription in the courtyard reads, "Art is a haven from misfortunes for mankind"; Dumbarton Oaks' beauty and splendor are sufficiently convincing.

The mansion (not to be confused with the entirely separate Dumbarton *House*) has switched names and styles frequently since its construction in 1801. Robert and Mildred Bliss renovated it to accommodate the library and collections, then donated the house and gardens to Harvard University, Mr. Bliss's alma mater, in 1940. The imposing gates and the solemn hush of the Dumbarton Oaks building's entrance can be forbidding, but the cold, scholarly atmosphere hides treasures. The **Garden Library** gathers rare books, reference materials, and illustrations related to landscape architecture, garden history, and botany. To the dismay of a flower-enthused public, few pieces are on display—in fact, research facilities are only open to scholars with appropriate credentials (academia thrives in Dumbarton Oaks; the estate has resident scholars and awards fellowships annually).

The **Byzantine Collection** contains floor mosaics, bronzes, ivories, ecclesiastical silver, and jewelry, mostly from the Byzantine Empire (CE326-1453). The numerous Roman small-scale portraits are worth noting, particularly the exquisite *Millefiori* (literally, "thousand flowers"), or mosaic glass cameos. The unfinished faces of the figures carved on a Roman sarcophagus here have led experts to believe that in large warehouses, sarcophagi were often made and then stored, to be personalized when eventually ordered. The gallery, Philip Johnson's 1963 design, holds Robert Bliss's **pre-Columbian art** collection; the eight circular glass pavilions, arranged like flower petals around a fountain, vie in beauty with the art they contain. If you stand in the center of one of the round rooms and talk, only you can hear the echoes. The gallery includes carvings and tools from the Aztec and Mayan civilizations, displayed in natural light against the backdrop of the woods outside.

Textiles from the pre-Inca Huari civilization dating back to the 6th century are also here, preserved by the climate's extreme dryness. The **Music Room** displays El Greco's *The Visitation.* Igor Stravinsky's *Dumbarton Oaks* concerto premiered here for the Blisses' 30th wedding anniversary in 1934. Subscription concerts, for the Dumbarton Oaks Friends of Music, still take place in the room every winter (collections open Tues.-Sun. 2-5pm; suggested contribution $1, otherwise free).

The **Dumbarton Oaks Gardens,** at 31st and R St., inside the gates of the estate, demand at least an hour's worth of attention. The formal gardens only occupy 10 acres of the original estate; 27 acres of Dumbarton Oaks Park, 10 acres of the Danish

Embassy, and 6 acres of estate buildings and grounds insulate the garden from the outside world. Even in winter, the "bones" of the garden are serene and lovely: some trees were chosen and planted specifically for the distinctiveness of their branches when bare. A 2-mi. trail that leads through Rock Creek Park up to the National Zoo offers an invigorating walk, but the steep, rocky, and staircased paths are not easily wheelchair- or stroller-navigable. (Zoo info. 673-4800. Gardens open daily April-Oct. 2-6pm, Nov.-March 2-5pm. Admission $3, seniors and children $2; Nov.-March free. Season (April-Oct.) passes available: individual $25, family $40.)

FARRAGUT

The Bethune Museum and Archives

At 1318 Vermont Ave. NW (332-1233; Metro: McPherson Square), the Bethune Museum commemorates the life of educator, leader, and pioneer civil rights activist Mary McLeod Bethune with exhibits on the first and second floors and a ½-hour video. The townhouse that holds the museum once served as headquarters for the National Council of Negro Women, which Bethune founded. One of 17 children of former slaves, she grew up to be the founder of a college, FDR's head of the Division of Negro Affairs, and a leading member of the NAACP, among other things. The museum chronicles her achievements and emphasizes her determination throughout a career that spanned two decades and four presidential administrations. The house is also home to the extensive **Archives for Black Women's History.** (Open Mon.-Fri. 10am-4pm, Sat. by appointment. Archives open by appointment. Free.)

B'nai B'rith Klutznick National Jewish Museum

This thoughtful museum, at 1640 Rhode Island Ave. NW (857-6583; Metro: Farragut North), contains Jewish cultural and ritual objects, including George Washington's famous letter to a Newport, Rhode Island synagogue which contains the first statement enunciating America's commitment to religious and ethnic toleration. The drawings by Auschwitz survivor David Wainapel are particularly gripping. A wall of archives is available, and the rotating exhibits are fascinating. The security guard and accompanying bulletproof glass aren't just evidence of paranoia: terrorists held over 100 people hostage in the B'nai B'rith building in 1977. (Open Sun.-Fri. 10am-5pm, except Jewish holidays. Suggested donation $2, seniors, students, and children $1.)

DUPONT CIRCLE

Phillips Collection

The Phillips Collection, at 1600 21st St. at Q St. NW (387-2151), houses the first and one of the finest modern art collections in the United States. Its founder, Duncan Phillips, was a graduate of Yale and heir to a family steel company with money to spend and impeccable taste in art. Opened in 1921 by Phillips in the family mansion, the museum is now home to some 2500 pieces of art, only a fraction of which can be shown at any given time. The works on display are thus something of an ever-changing, collective work of art, harboring a larger structure and logic as curators attempt to mesh the works with each other and with whatever temporary exhibits occupy the galleries. Each individual gallery is hung with an internal logic as well; discerning the connections may require a Ph.D. in art history in some cases, but well-informed docents can help out.

Enter the museum through the new **annex** at 1612 Massachusetts Ave., added when the collection grew too large for Phillips' original Victorian mansion at 1600 Massachusetts Ave. Walk through the annex's three floors before crossing over to the original mansion and descending through three more. On the first floor as you enter is one of the few relatively permanent installations—the **Rothko room.** Other such rooms include a **Klee room** and, most famously, a **Renoir room** holding Renoir's masterpiece *Luncheon of the Boating Party.* The third floor of the annex is generally reserved for temporary exhibits. The stroll up the annex and down through the original mansion is a delightful parade of works by Delacroix, Matisse, van Gogh, Mondrian, Degas, Miró, Gris, Kandinsky, Turner, Courbet, Daumier, Prendergast, O'Keefe, and Hopper—to name a few. "Artful Evenings," with live music and gallery talks, occur during the summer every Thurs. 5-8:30pm; admission is $5. (Open Tues.-Wed. and Fri.–Sat. 10am-5pm, Thurs. 10am-8:30pm. Sun. noon-5pm. Admission Sat.-Sun. $6.50, students and seniors $3.25, under 18 free. Tues.-Fri. admission by contribution.)

Art Galleries

Contained in an area northwest of **Dupont Circle,** Washington's art gallery district is bounded by Connecticut Ave. on the east, Florida Ave. on the west, and Q St. to the south. The neighborhood houses about 25 galleries displaying everything from contemporary photographs to tribal crafts; most of the galleries reside in townhouses on otherwise residential streets. Nineteen galleries have organized themselves into **"Galleries of Dupont Circle."** They publish a map of member galleries and hold a joint **open house** the first Fri. of each month (except Aug.) from 6-8pm. Call 232-3610 for more information. These "First Fridays" are the best way to discover D.C.'s local art scene. You can also explore the contents of the galleries almost any afternoon of the week, though many galleries have variable hours (or are closed) during the summer; call ahead. Most galleries will also schedule appointments outside of regular hours. A stroll down R St. puts nine of the galleries directly in your path.

The gallery district is readily accessible from the Q St. exit of the Dupont Circle Metro station. North of the Circle, on Connecticut Ave., the **Kathleen Ewing Gallery,** upstairs at 1609 Connecticut Ave. (328-0955), provides a glimpse of 19th- and-20th century American and European photography. The gallery favors striking juxtapositions of contemporary photos with earlier works (open Wed.-Sat. noon-5pm).

Continuing north on Conn. Ave., turn left onto R St., the main drag of the gallery area. The R St. galleries cluster together on either side of 21st St., complementing one another's styles and exhibits. **Gallery K,** 2010 R St. (234-0339), boasts contemporary art in all media displayed in three rooms and two floors (open Tues.-Sat. 11am-6pm). Downstairs from Gallery K is **Africa** (745-7272), whose traditional African tribal masks and pottery contrast sharply with the modern sculptures in the gallery above (open Tues. 2-6pm, Wed.-Sat. noon-6pm). At the end of the block near 21st St., the **Robert Brown Gallery,** 2030 R St. (483-4383), covers its white walls with prints and paintings by contemporary international artists. Exhibits change every six weeks (open Tues. and Fri.-Sat. noon-6pm, Wed.-Thurs. noon-5pm).

Across 21st St., the townhouse-*cum*-gallery trend continues with the **Washington Printmakers Gallery,** 2106½ R St. (332-7757), the only D.C. gallery devoted exclusively to original prints (open Tues.-Sat. 11am-5pm, Sun. noon-5pm). **The Studio** (232-8734) and **Anton** (328-0828) galleries share a home at 2108 R St. Both contain the works of local and international painters and sculptors; the Anton particularly prides itself on its emphasis on women artists. You'll know the building by the pseudo-sign in front bearing the word "Studio." (The Studio open Wed.-Sat. noon-5pm. Anton open Tues.-Sat. noon-5pm.)

Perhaps the most popular R St. attraction, **Fondo del Sol Visual Arts Center,** 2112 R St. NW (483-2777), is a bilingual, artist-run visual feast. Occupying the nebulous territory between gallery and museum, it showcases Latino and other minority art in a four-story townhouse. Fodo del Sol often features works by Native American, Afro-American, and immigrant American artists in addition to the more frequent Hispanic art displays. Daily video programs, as well as occasional special programs are also presented (open Tues.-Sat. 1:30-5:30pm; admission $3, students $1, children free). Rounding out the R St. art spaces is the highly focused **Burdick Gallery,** 2114 R St. NW (986-5682), which houses a collection of Eskimo sculptures and graphics (open Tues.-Fri. noon-6pm. Sat. 11am-5pm).

Nightlife & Entertainment

Just about everyone should be able to find a play, performance, concert, club, or flick to suit his or her taste in D.C. Major culture purveyors, especially the **Kennedy Center,** make up for high ticket prices with **student discounts** and frequent low-cost or free events. Smaller **theaters** do things a little differently, and often more cheaply, along 14th St. and elsewhere. **Chamber music** emanates from seasonal midday concert series, often at the same museums and churches you might sight-see. And of course in Washington, like everywhere else, **drinking** is always a big hit.

Washington teems with **special events** (see the **Appendix,** p. 292); many of them involve theater, music, dance, or movies, such as the American College Theater Festival, Filmfest D.C., various outdoor military band concerts, Adams-Morgan Day, Malcolm X Day, the Blues Festival, Gay Pride Day, and the Folklife Festival.

Bars and Live Music

Most of the bars in Washington feature some type of live music. If you don't mind a young crowd, squeeze into a local pub for rock, punk, reggae, R&B, and folk; the D.C. punk scene is, or at least was, one of the nation's finest. To see what's up with local bands, just look at *City Paper.* (Also see **Washington, D.C.: An Introduction: Music,** p. 12.) The **9:30 club** is the leading venue, and many of the best shows are cross-generational (and fairly safe) gatherings in churches, rented halls, or at Fort Reno. Flyers advertise small theaters and rock-related events around Dupont Circle and Adams-Morgan—**Second Story Books,** 20th and P St. NW, is a good source for event announcements. (Metro: Dupont Circle.) Go-go music is best experienced at outdoor gatherings, but **Breeze's** in Northeast is a fine indoor venue.

Like any large city, Washington has arenas where devotees shell out over $20 for a little live MTV. The biggest events hit sports arenas: **RFK Stadium** in the summer and the **USAir Arena**—formerly the Capital Centre—year-round (see **Sports and Recreation,** p. 225). The newest of D.C.'s live-act venues, the **Capitol Ballroom,** 1015 Half St. SE (703-549-7625; Metro: Navy Yard) is a colossal concert hall that seats 2000 and admits all ages. Opened in July 1995, the Ballroom boasts an impressive lineup of big-name alternative bands and small-name, big-draw local groups. Tickets run $5-35, and are available from TicketMaster (432-7328) and **ProTix** (800-955-5566). Doors open at 7pm. The **Wolftrap Filene Center,** 1551 Trap Rd., Vienna, VA (703-255-1900), approx. 45 min. from D.C., hosts acts ranging from Peter, Paul, and Mary to the Miami City Ballet. Ticket prices range according to the performance, though lawn seats are generally $10 cheaper than pavilion seats. Tickets are available through ProTix (in VA: 703-218-6500). Popular bands (Pearl Jam, in 1996) also play the **Meriweather Post Pavilion** (410-730-2424/5/6), at Rte. 29 Columbia Pike in Columbia, MD, less than an hour from D.C. or Baltimore. Lawn tickets run $15-25, seats inside run $20-100. For tickets, call the Pavilion, TicketMaster, or ProTix.

George Washington University sponsors shows in **Lisner Auditorium,** 21st and H St. NW (202-994-1500). Lisner hosts plays and rock concerts by well-known "alternative" acts (like Weird Al Yankovic); tickets are sometimes free and never cost more than $25. Call in advance for prices and purchase locations.

On summer Saturdays and Sundays, jazz and R&B shows occupy the outdoor, 4200-seat **Carter Barron Amphitheater,** set into Rock Creek Park at 16th St. and Colorado Ave. NW (426-6837; tickets around $16).

From late June to late August, rock, punk, and metal preempt soccer-playing at **Fort Reno Park** (282-1063), at Chesapeake and Belt St. NW above Wisconsin Ave. (Metro: Tenleytown Circle.) Most concerts feature two or three groups; some ragged amateurs, some seasoned scenesters, and some wonderful, crunchy-rock and-rol ers—all accompany your frisbee-playing. Consult *City Paper* for schedules.

CAPITOL HILL

★**Hawk 'n' Dove,** 329 Pennsylvania Ave. SE (543-3300). Metro: Capitol South. A Hi institution since 1967, when its several rooms separated pro- and anti-Vietnam Wa clients ("hawks" and "doves"). Wood-paneled walls hold antique signs, railroa lights, vintage neon signs, and even a brass bar. Interns hang out while the neigh bors watch sports and singles watch each other; as in '67, different rooms serve di ferent crowds (one room is for non-smokers). The three buildings, all over 10 years old, have been a blacksmith shop, a salt-water taffy plant, and D.C.'s first ga station. DJ Sat. nights. Happy hour Mon.-Thurs. 4-7pm. Sandwiches $4-6.50. Bee $1.75 and up. 14 kinds of bottled beer and 11 drafts available. Midnight breakfas served Mon.-Thurs. 11pm-1am, Fri.-Sat. 11pm-2am ($7, with steak $9). Sat.-Sun brunch (10am-3:30pm) offers Screwdrivers, Mimosas, or Bloody Marys for $2 Open Sun.-Thurs. 10am-2am, Fri.-Sat. 10am-3am.

Kelley's "The Irish Times," 14 F St. NW (543-5433). Metro: Union Station. Wal out of Union Station and take a right turn onto Mass. Ave.; F St. shoots off to you left at the intersection with North Capitol. Irish street signs, the *Irish Times,* an Joyce on the wall give the pub an authentic Irish feel, but the mood is quickl dashed by the hordes of noisy Georgetown law students. This is the site of th annual June marathon *Ulysses* reading (see p. 294). Live music Tues.-Sat. starting a 8:30pm. Happy hour (Mon.-Fri. 3-7pm): drafts $2, bottled beers $3.50. Open Sun Thurs. 9:30am-2am, Fri.-Sat. 9:30am-3am.

Taverna the Greek Islands, 307 Pennsylvania Ave. SE (547-8360). Metro: Capito South. First-floor bar complements two floors of dining with comfortable servic and a jovial young crowd. Look for fresh mint sprigs from the boss's garden i vases at the bar. Happy hour (Mon.-Fri. 3:30-7:30pm) brings $1.85 mixed drink and $1 draft beer. Bar offers a sandwich special every night (except Sun.) afte 7:30pm. Open Mon.-Sat. 11am-midnight, Sun. 4-10pm.

Tune Inn, 331½ Pennsylvania Ave. SE (543-2725). Metro: Capitol South. Unpreten tious fun has meant slumming at the Tune Inn since 1933; *Esquire* calls it one o America's 100 best bars. Clients range from Congressional staffers to constructio workers to students. Walls hold mounted fish, game heads, and sports trophies Sandwiches under $5. Beer $1.50 for draft, $2.25 for bottles. Open Sun.-Thurs 8am-2am, Fri.-Sat. 8am-3am.

The Li'l Pub, 655 Pennsylvania Ave. SE (543-5526). Metro: Eastern Market. Neigh borhood pub distinguished by a friendly and diverse crowd (black and white, ga and straight), yellow stucco walls, and a large framed photo of a customer bein accosted by a stripper. Pool tournament every Thurs. in the large back room; win ners receive a Pub gift certificate. Drafts from around $1. Microbrews $3.50. 50¢ o more off drinks during happy hour (Mon.-Fri. 3-8pm). Open Mon.-Thurs.11am 2am, Fri.-Sat. 11am-3am, Sun. 1pm-2am.

Jenkins Hill Pub, 319 Pennsylvania Ave. SE (544-4066). Metro: Capitol South. Don' let the stained glass over the downstairs bar distract you from the ESPN-tuned TV that hang at either end. Of course, serious sports fans head upstairs, where a large screen TV competes with two pool tables and a dartboard for their attention. A third bar downstairs, the **Underground,** features live music Wed.-Sun. Drink prices vary among the bars: drafts start at $1.75, bottled beer at $2.50, mixe drinks at $3.25. Fri.-Sat. 3-7am Jenkins serves tea, coffee, and breakfast. Open Sun. Thurs. 11am-2am, Fri.-Sat. 24hr.

OLD DOWNTOWN

Capitol City Brewing Company, technically 1100 New York Ave. NW (628-2222) enter on the corner of 11th and H St. Metro: Metro Center. Get sloshed the yuppi way: drink microbrew. Massive copper vats of beer—see what's on tap. Half pint $2.80, pints $4. Open daily 11am-2am.

Stoney's Restaurant, 1307 L St. NW (347-9163), near 13th St. Metro: Farragu North. Everyone's a regular here—or at least is treated like one. Half bar, hal greasy spoon, Stoney's serves up ½-price steak-and-cheese on Mon., burgers on Tues., and pizza on Wed. during the lengthy happy hour (4pm-midnight). Despite the name, the place is a bustling bar. Open daily 9am-1am.

WHITE HOUSE AREA AND FOGGY BOTTOM

Mr. Henry's Washington Circle, 2134 Pennsylvania Ave. NW (337-0222). Metro: Foggy Bottom-GWU. Plush red wallpaper and centuries-old *Sunday Telegraph* clippings—all in chronological order—grace this pseudo-Victorian saloon. Sit near the jukebox and control the music; Mon.-Sat. there's also an outdoor porch area for eating or sordid carousing. Happy hour (4-7pm) features $1 drafts and $1.50 rails. Open Mon.-Thurs. 11am-2am, Fri. 11am-3am, Sat. 5pm-3am.

Quigley's, 1825 I St. NW (331-0150), enter through the mall or the outside world. Metro: Farragut West. Relax upstairs or boogie down below. Business-types crowd into this large, upscale spot. Drafts $2, bottled beers $3. Save about $1 during happy hour (Mon.-Fri. 4-7pm). Thurs.-Sat. brings occasional live music with a $5-15 cover. Open Mon.-Thurs. 11:30am-10pm, Fri.-Sat. 11:30am-3am.

Lulu's New Orleans Café, 1217 22nd St. NW (861-5858), at M St. Metro: Foggy Bottom-GWU or Dupont Circle. As schizophrenic as Flicks (see p. 210); its alternate personality is the **Deja Vu** dance club. Happy hour (Mon.-Fri. 4-7pm) offers drink specials and free food (like blackened shrimp, chicken fingers, and Cajun catfish), making Lulu's a favorite summer-intern hangout. DJ plays progressive and rock for Deja Vu dancers Sun.-Thurs. 8pm-2am and Fri.-Sat. 8pm-3am. Live jazz accompanies Sun. à la carte brunch (10am-4pm). Fri.-Sat. karaoke at 7pm. Bar is open Mon.-Thurs. 4pm-2am, Fri. 4pm-3am, Sat. 8pm-3am, Sun. 8pm-2am.

GEORGETOWN

★**Old Glory,** 3139 M St. NW (337-3406). This open-front restaurant features Southern cuisine by day and becomes a hot spot for the young/young-at-heart by night. Drafts $2.50-3.25, bottled beer $3-6. Mixed drinks $3.50-4. Specialties include "White Lightning" or "Old Glory Slush" drinks. Live rock and blues Sat.-Thurs. Open Sun.-Thurs. 11:30am-2am, Fri. 11:30am-12:30am, Sat. 11:30am-2:30am.

★**The Tombs,** 1226 36th St. NW (337-6668), at Prospect St.; entrance to the right of 1789 Restaurant. Recognize the bar? Designers for the movie *St. Elmo's Fire* based a stage set on it. Georgetown students as well as some high profile clientele (Clinton, Beau Bridges, Chris O'Donnell) drop in for burgers and beer. $2-3 cover on Sun. nights (DJ and dancing). Mixed drinks $3.25 and up. Open Mon.-Thurs. 11:30am-2am, Fri. 11:30am-3am, Sat. 11am-3am, Sun. 9:30am-2am.

★**The Bayou,** 3135 K St. NW (333-2897), under the Whitehurst Freeway in Georgetown; take any #30 Metrobus to M St. and walk 2 blocks down Wisconsin Ave. Bands on their way up and bands on their way down, with a rough 'n' ready crowd that loves them all. Music varies from metal and rock to blues and jazz. Comedy at 6:30pm Sat. Most shows 18+; the rest all ages. Cover $3-20. Reggae on Sun.; Mon. is Grateful Dead night ($4). Box office open 8pm-midnight. Open Sun.-Thurs. 8pm-1:30am, Fri. 8pm-2:30am, Sat. 6:30pm-2:30am, but call ahead; no band means no Bayou.

The Saloun, 3239 M St. NW (965-4900), near Potomac St. Two of the best things in life: live jazz by local musicians every night and 75 different kinds of beer (18 on tap). Draft $4, bottled beer $4.25. Appetizers $1.25-6. Attracts a late-20s and 30s crowd. Cover weeknights $2, Fri.-Sat. $3. Open Sun.-Thurs. 5:30pm-2am, Fri.-Sat. 5:30pm-3am.

Garrett's, 3003 M St. NW (333-1033), near 30th St. Up the street from Charing Cross; fluid movement between the two. G-town's most popular bar is a body-to-body, all-night frat party. The "Hemingway" rhino, an integral part of the decor, was shot by one of Ernest's wives. Cute railroad-themed menu offers Gorgonzola bread for $3. Beer and mixed drinks $3. Happy hour (Mon.-Fri. 5-7pm): ½-priced drinks, beer, house wine. Wed. nights ½-priced microbrews. Open Mon.-Thurs. 11:30am-2am, Fri.-Sat. noon-3am, Sun. noon-2am.

J. Paul's, 3218 M St. NW (333-3450), near Wisconsin Ave. King of the Georgetown restaurant/saloons for its broad-based appeal—it even has its own award-winning brand of amber lager (pint $4.25). Open Sun.-Thurs. 11:30am-1:30am, food serv until 11:30pm; Fri. 11:30am-2:30am, food served until midnight; Sat. 10:30a 11:30pm. Hours may vary slightly in the winter.

Charing Cross, 3027 M St. NW (338-2141), near 30th St. Collegians pound bee early here, then head down the street to Garrett's. Clean-cut prep-school types a the norm, but interns fill in for departed collegians. During summer months, a se by the open front will let you listen to drinkers' condescending remarks abo passersby. Standard Italian fare; entrees $7-14. Draft beer $2, bottled $2.50-3.5 Mixed drinks $3-4.25. Happy hour Mon.-Fri. 4-8pm. Charing Cross ale $2. Op Sun.-Thurs. 11:30am-2am, Fri.-Sat. 11:30am-3am, Sun. 5pm-1:30am.

Mr. Smith's, 3104 M St. NW (333-3104), near 31st St. A generally convivial atm sphere pervades this self-proclaimed "friendliest saloon in town," a popular nigh spot and active singles scene. Menu includes sandwiches and grill items. Featur live bands of all musical persuasions Fri. and Sat. nights upstairs and a piano bar c the ground floor. $1 draft weekdays 4-7pm. Mixed drinks $3.25-6. Open Sur Thurs. 11:30am-2am, Fri.-Sat. 11am-3am.

Champions, 1206 Wisconsin Ave. NW (965-4005), at the end of an alley near M S Strapping jocks abound. Signed photos of sports stars are on the wall, Redski (football) and Capitals (hockey) players stop by, and the "big game" is always c TV. Around 11pm young singles (mid-20s to mid-30s) replace aging armchair qua terbacks. Europeans come by to gawk, and can you blame them? Happy hour Fri. 10pm. Live music on Sun. and dancing every night. No cover, but a one-drink mi imum on weekends. Draft $2.60, bottled beer $4.10. Open Mon.-Thurs. 5pm-2an Fri. 5pm-2:30am, Sat. 11:30am-3am, Sun. 11:30am-2am.

FARRAGUT

★**Crow Bar,** 1006 20th St. NW (223-2972). Metro: Farragut North or Farragut Wes Everyone from bikers to businessmen stops by for the house brew, Crow Be ($3.75, $3 during happy hour). The "Forbidden Planet" space-age dance roo (open Thurs.-Sat. 9pm-close) heightens the off-beat decor, featuring a plaster-an paper-maché Lady Liberty who leads you upstairs. Two floors; a game room featu ing foosball and pool; and a patio. Happy hour 4-7pm. Open Mon.-Thurs. 11:30ar 1:45am, Fri. 11:30am-2:45am, Sat. noon-2:45am, Sun. noon-1:45am.

Acme, 1207 19th St. NW (833-2263). Metro: Farragut North. "Think globally, drir locally," says this friendly local hangout. Pool room upstairs is quieter and mo removed from the hubbub of the bottom two floors. DJ and dancing Thurs.-Sa nights. Happy hour (Mon.-Fri. 4-7pm) pleases patrons with $6 pitchers and ½-pric nachos on Wed. Tues. features a live blues band with no cover, and $2 domest beers during happy hour. Open Sun.-Thurs. 11:30am-1:30am, Fri.-Sat. 11:30an 2:30am.

The Madhatter, 1831 M St. NW (833-1495), near 19th St. Metro: Farragut North c Farragut West. Packs 'em in every night of the week. Starts hopping during happ hour (Mon.-Fri. 4-7pm; $1.50 rails and a free buffet) and stays happening until clo ing. DJ Tues.-Sun. beginning at 9pm. Open Sun.-Thurs. 11:30am-1:30am, Fr 11:30am-2:30am, Sat. 10:30am-2:30am.

Flicks, 1160 20th St. NW (296-8644). Metro: Farragut West, Farragut North, or Fogg Bottom-GWU. Flicks, a full-time saloon, moonlights on the weekends as a danc club. Covered from floor to ceiling with movie photos, this joint caters to colleg crowds during the year and a more eclectic group in the summer. Cover: Thur during the academic year $8 with open bar, Fri. $5, Sat. $10. Happy hour (Mon.-Fr 4-8pm): $1.50 rails. Open Mon.-Fri. 11am-2am, Sat. 11am-3am.

DUPONT CIRCLE

★**Brickskeller,** 1523 22nd St. NW (293-1885), between P and Q St. Metro: Dupo Circle. THE place for beer. If you drank a different beer every day, it would st take you nearly two years to work your way through Brickskeller's list of over 60 brews—the world's largest beer selection. Six continents and some sixty countri contribute brews representing virtually every style of beer in existence, from com mon ales and lagers to smoked beers and oatmeal stouts. Go down under with

Van Diemens lager from Australia ($4.50), or Middle Eastward with a bottle of Maccabbe from Israel ($3). The saloon's original "beer-tails" are mixed drinks made with beer, like the house classic Black Velvet (stout and champagne, $4.50) or the Ruddy Mary (with beer instead of vodka, $3.25). Bi-monthly beer-tasting events feature brewers plugging their potables ($24 for the night; call ahead for schedule and reservations). 21+. Open Mon.-Thurs. 11:30am-2am, Fri. 11:30am-3am, Sat. 6pm-3am, Sun. 6pm-2am.

★**The Fox and Hounds,** 1537 17th St. NW (232-6307). Metro: Dupont Circle. Local residents proclaim the jukebox the best in D.C. Early-20s crowd races to the patio for strong drinks and shoulder-to-shoulder company, while a mellower, more diverse crowd makes conversation inside. Happy hour features $1.75 domestic beers, $1.50 rails, and free chips and salsa (Mon.-Fri. 4:30-6:30pm). Regular drink prices are also low: most bottled beers are $2.50. Open Mon.-Thurs. 11am-2am, Fri. 11am-3am., Sat. 10am-3am, Sun. 10am-2am. Patio closes at midnight.

★**Planet Fred,** 1221 Connecticut Ave. NW (331-3733 or 466-2336). Between the eclecticism of the clientele and the craters, neon spacescape, and lava lamps decking the walls, a trip to Planet Fred may feel like an alien experience. Occasional live bands pack in wall-to-wall punks, while Wed. night's "Drag Freak Bingo" draws a zany bunch ($7 cover) and "Female Trouble" every other Sun. is an ever-popular lesbian dance party. Sun. is also rockabilly night; Mon. offers free salsa lessons (7-9pm) and $2.75 margaritas; Thurs. is DJ dancing and $10 all-you-can-drink; Fri.-Sat. cost $5 for DJ dancing. Happy hour (Mon.-Fri. 4-7:30pm) includes $1.50 drafts and $1.75 rails. Open Sun.-Thurs. 11:30am-2am, Fri. 11:30am-3am, Sat. 8pm-3am.

The Big Hunt, 1345 Connecticut Ave. NW (785-2333). You won't have to hunt for long in this jungle-painted mega-bar to find the features that make it one of the hottest spots in town. Everything about this place is big: the beer list (27 on tap, mostly microbrews), and the crowd (everyone from yuppies to couriers). Pool, too. Don't miss the lively happy hours (Mon.-Fri. 4-7:30pm), when Rolling Rock, Coors, and rail drinks are all $1.75. Open Mon.-Thurs. 11am-2am, Fri. 11am-3am, Sat. noon-3am, Sun. 4pm-2am.

Capo's, 1722 Connecticut Ave. (462-8771), between R and S St. Metro: Dupont Circle. An attractive new bar attached to Café Parma draws on a top-notch kitchen to offer a top-notch happy hour: all-you-can-eat antipasto with a $4.50 min. drink purchase. If you don't believe it, check out the spread in the window. Drinks are cheap then, too, with domestic drafts going for $3 and rails and wine for $2.75. Happy hour Mon.-Fri. 5-7:30pm and daily 10:30pm-close (drinks only). Bar open Mon.-Thurs. 11:30am-1am, Fri.-Sat. 11:30am-1:30am, Sun. 11:30am-midnight.

The Childe Harold, 1610 20th St. NW (483-6700), near Connecticut Ave. Metro: Dupont Circle. One of the last real saloons in Washington has served up burgers and beer in shadowy red-brick splendor since 1967. A pricey restaurant with the same name resides upstairs while the mixed bohemian and professional crowd revels downstairs, especially at happy hour (Mon.-Fri. 3-7pm), which discounts all rails ($2.25), Rolling Rocks ($1.75), and house wines ($2). Fri.-Sat. 10pm-2am Harold fosters a "Stepchilde" nightclub, with $2 Rolling Rock and no cover. 21+. Open Sun.-Thurs. 11:30am-2am, Fri.-Sat. 11:30am-3am.

El Bodegón, 1637 R St. NW (667-1710, delivery 546-8646), near 17th St. Metro: Dupont Circle. As close to Spain in America as you'll get. Cool stucco walls hung with pottery and tile. Garlic, peppers, and curing hams (complete with little cups to catch the drippings) dangle from wood beams. Live flamenco music and dancing Thurs.-Sat. at 8pm. Enjoy the show and the atmosphere—forget the entrees ($15-25) and nosh on *tapas* instead—little Spanish appetizers that go for $3.50-8. *Empanadillas* (pastries stuffed with spiced ground beef) $3. Open daily 11:30am-2:30pm and 5-11pm.

SHAW / U DISTRICT

★**9:30 club,** 815 V St. NW (concert line 393-0930, tickets 265-0930). Metro: U St.-Cardozo; use the Vermont Ave. exit. D.C.'s most established local and alternative rock venue (since the legendary D.C. Space closed down) is now in a new location. Occasionally $3 to see three local bands; $5-20 for nationally known acts, which often sell out weeks in advance. Crowd ages and styles vary according to concert line-up (under-21 admitted and hand-stamped). Cash-only box office open Mon.-Fri. 1-6pm, until 11pm on show-days, Sat.-Sun. 6-11pm. Door time Sun.-Thurs. 7:30pm-midnight, Fri.-Sat. 9pm-2am. 50¢ surcharge for advance tickets from 9:30 club box office. Tickets also available from ProTix (800-955-5566).

★**Asylum in Exile,** 1210 U St. NW (319-9353; 232-9354 for information). Metro: U St.-Cardozo. An alternative to D.C.'s bigger and badder band clubs. Asylum's tendency to book less-known live musicians has made it Washington's most-overlooked nightspot. The death-goth decor doubles as an intimate setting, with DJ dance beats and an outdoor patio. Bands Wed.-Fri.; acoustic music Wed. for no cover. $3 cover on Thurs., $5 on Fri. When there's no band, there's still drinking and dancing. Nightly specials 8-11pm, with varying $2 pints and $2 Rolling Rock pitchers on Tues. 18+. Open Sun.-Thurs. 8pm-2am, Fri.-Sat. 8pm-3am.

The Black Cat, 1831 14th St. NW (concert line 667-7960, bar 667-4490), between S and T St. Metro: U St.-Cardozo. One of Washington's best live music venues turns its stage over to a variety of alternative and folk bands. The Red Room offers pool, pinball, and 12 beers on tap (no cover in the Red Room even when there's a show in the main room). Happy hour (Fri.-Sat. 6-7:30pm) takes $1 off all drinks. Some shows free, most $5-10. Open Sun.-Thurs. 8pm-2am, Fri.-Sat. 6pm-3am.

Las Cruces, 1524 U St. NW (328-3153). The King lives on at this restaurant/bar/shrine to Elvis which celebrates New Mexican cuisine. Regulars come here for made-to-order enchiladas ($5.75-6.50), 50¢ pints of Rolling Rock during Elvis happy hour (daily 5:43-7:30pm), and the frozen margaritas ($5). Altar to Elvis in the backroom. Open Tues. 11:30am-2am, Wed.-Thurs. 11am-2am, Fri. 11am-3am, Sat. 12:30pm-3am, Sun. noon-2am. Sun.-Thurs. kitchen closes at 11pm, Fri.-Sat. at midnight.

ADAMS-MORGAN

Mr. Henry's, 1836 Columbia Rd. NW (797-8882), near 18th St. Dark bar with dark wood furniture; gay and straight clientele. Mr. Henry discovered Roberta Flack here. Nightly live entertainment. Open mike Tues.-Wed. and $7 minimum; bands every other day, with $5 cover and comedy on Thurs. Sat. DJ after 11pm. Draft beer $2.25. Appetizers $3.75-4.25. Sandwiches $4.75-6. Happy hour (Mon.-Sat. 4-8pm): 75¢ off drinks. Cover Fri.-Sat. $7.50. 21+. Open Mon.-Thurs. 4pm-2am, Fri. 4pm-3am, Sat. 10am-3am, Sun. 9am-2am.

Cities, 2424 18th St. NW (328-7194), between Belmont and Columbia Rd. Cities' packed restaurant and bar stays hip, or tries to, by changing decor and menu every year or so to mimic a different city—*nel 1996, sono Firenze, Italy!* The chef keeps her job through all the culinary mutations; the chic decor hints at out-of-budget-range entrees. DJ Fri.-Sat. after 10pm. Beer $4, mixed drinks $5. Open Mon.-Thurs. 5pm-2am, Fri.-Sat. 5pm-3am.

Café Bukom, 2442 18th St. NW (265-4600), near Columbia Rd. A mellow, funky West African restaurant and bar. Live entertainment by West African bands, usually starting at 10pm. Beer $3.50-4. Open Tues. 4pm-midnight, Sun. and Wed.-Thurs. 4pm-2am, Fri.-Sat. 4pm-3am.

Kala Kala, 2439 18th St. NW (232-5433), near Columbia Rd. In a fit of self-important frenzy, new-kid-in-town Kala Kala pronounces "one world, one bar" to all. The music—be it live or Memorex—is always African or reggae; call for the live events schedule. DJ Wed.-Sun. Happy hour (daily 5-9pm) features 2-for-1 drafts and rails—but the mild malt liquor Ngoma from Togo is worth a swig. Open Wed.-Sun. 7pm-2am, Fri.-Sat. 7pm-3am.

Chief Ike's Mambo Room, Chaos, and Pandemonium, 1725 Columbia Rd. (Chief Ike's 332-2211, Chaos 797-4637, and Pandemonium 797-4637), near Ontario Rd., about 2½ blocks from 18th St. Downstairs at Chief Ike's, pub-style American food ($4.25-10, most under $5) accompanied by live R&B Mon.-Tues. and DJ Wed.-Sat. Up a long red staircase are Chaos and Pandemonium, 2 tumultuous rooms featuring alternative music and pseudo-Japanese decor. Pool table in Pandemonium. Usually no cover and $1 off all drinks during happy hour (daily 4-8pm). Beer $3; rails $3.50. Prices higher when a band plays. 21+. Chief Ike's open Sun.-Thurs. 4pm-2am, Fri.-Sat. 4pm-3am. Chaos and Pandemonium open Sun.-Thurs. 6pm-2am, Fri.-Sat. 6pm-3am.

UPPER NORTHWEST

★**Oxford Tavern "Zoo Bar,"** 3000 Connecticut Ave. NW (232-4225), across the street from the zoo. Metro: Woodley Park-Zoo. Washington's oldest saloon with a cheery wildlife mural and a bright neon subtitle, but Steely Dan and Duke Ellington are still on the jukebox (so everything is alright). They say the first time you come in here is the last time you'll be a stranger, and it's true: tourists, locals, and regulars mix and mingle at happy hour (Mon.-Fri. 3-7pm) and chug $1.50 drafts, $2.50 rails, and $1.75 domestics. A DJ plays on Fri. nights, and live jazz, rock, and blues bands hold forth Tues.-Thurs. and Sat. At other times, the jukebox offers an unparalleled 7 plays for a dollar. Open Sun.-Thurs. 9:30am-2am, Fri.-Sat. 9am-3am.

Ireland's 4 Provinces, 3412 Connecticut Ave. NW (244-0860). Metro: Cleveland Park. Draws a family crowd to communal tables and small stage with nightly Irish and folk music; soloists on Sun.-Mon. croon traditional ballads, while groups Tues.-Sat. get the crowd's feet tapping—and sometimes dancing. Mon. night football viewing draws area locals, too. Happy hour (Mon.-Thurs. 5-8pm and Fri. 4-8pm) discounts everything from domestics ($2.50) to imports ($3.25) to rails ($2.50), and of course Guinness ($2.50). Outdoor café-style seating, too. Cover varies. Open Sun.-Thurs. 4pm-2am, Fri.-Sat. 4pm-3am.

Nanny O'Brien's, 3319 Connecticut Ave. NW (686-9189). Metro: Cleveland Park. The across-the-street neighbor and arch rival of the 4Ps, Nanny's reputedly serves the best Guinness in town. The crowd is a three-way mix of locals, AU students, and D.C.'s young Irish population. Cheap drinks and free buffet at happy hour (Mon.-Fri. 4-8pm): $1.50 domestic bottles and drafts, $2.50 import bottles and drafts, $1.75 mixed drinks and house wine. Nightly traditional Irish music; highlights include a Mon. open-mike session and Wed. performances of Irish countryside dances. Open Sun.-Thurs. 4pm-2am, Fri.-Sat. 4pm-3am.

The Malt Shop, 4611 Wisconsin Ave. NW (244-9733), at 41st St. above the Dancing Crab. Metro: Tenleytown. The place for a brew and The Game with the regulars. In the good old days, the Redskins drank here after taping "Redskin Sideline" down the street at WUSA-TV. They didn't want to say they were going to a bar, and instead said they were going to a malt shop; hence the name. Pictures of famous 'Skins abound on the theme wall. Drafts $2.25, imported bottles $2.50, pitchers $6.50. During happy hour, bartender Rosie serves up $2 drafts and $2.25 domestics and rails; she's almost as much of a Malt Shop institution as the 'Skins themselves once were. Open Mon.-Fri. 4pm-12:30am, Sat.-Sun. noon-1:30am.

Quigley's, 3201 New Mexico Ave. NW (966-0500), three blocks southeast of the AU campus. Metro: Tenleytown. American restaurant by day: burgers ($6.50), sandwiches ($5-8), and salads ($5.50-8); American U. hangout by night. Students come for ½-price burgers and chicken sandwiches on Sun. nights (6-11pm). Last Mon. of each month brings ½-price food to the bar (5-8pm). Happy hour (Mon.-Fri. 4-7pm) means $1.50 pints of Bud, $1.75 house wine, $2 rails, and discounted appetizers. Sat.-Sun. all day $2.50 varying specials. Live bands Tues.-Sun. Open Mon.-Thurs. 11:30am-1:30am, Fri. 11:30am-3am, Sat.-Sun. 11am-2:30am.

NORTHEAST

Breeze's Metro Club/Deno's, 2335 Bladensburg Rd., NE (526-8880). Go-go got going here, and it keeps the beat with local live bands (19+, cover $5-12). No alcohol served. Parking provided. Open Wed.-Thurs. 9pm-2am.

Kitty O'Shea, 3514 12th St. NE (832-3945). Metro: Brookland-CUA. A larger-than-life painted leprechaun by the door greets the locals who come here to shoot pool and guzzle mugs of the bar's 31 beers; multiple signs declare that "work is the curse of the drinking classes." Domestic pitchers $5 every day until 11pm. Good, greasy fare includes giant appetizers ($2.25-5), baskets of miniburgers ($4.25), and the self-proclaimed best cheesesteaks in town ($5). Open Sun.-Thurs. 3pm-1:30am, Fri.-Sat. 3pm-2:30am.

Colonel Brooks Tavern, 901 Monroe St. NE (529-4002). Metro: Brookland-CUA. Pick up Monroe St. at its intersection with Michigan in front of the University Center building, at the south end of Catholic U.'s campus. Fine food draws crowds by day, fine beer draws crowds by night. A handful of local microbrews tops the list

ENTERTAINMENT

(mug $2.75, pitcher $12.50), but they'll serve up the usual Bud if they have to (mug $2, pitcher $8.50). Live entertainment (Dixie band, jazz, and blues) Tues. after 7pm. Open Sun.-Thurs. 11am-2am, Fri. 11am-3am, Sat. 11:30am-3am.

BETHESDA, MD

Tequila Sunrise Café, 7940 Wisconsin Ave. (907-6536). This outdoor cantina, bar, and patio wouldn't fail as a movie set. Happy hour (Mon.-Fri. 4-7pm) offers $1 off drinks and a buffet of free appetizers. Bottled beer $3.25. Mixed drinks $3.50-5. Open Sun.-Mon. 4:30pm-1am, Tues.-Thurs. 11:30am-1am, Fri.-Sat. 11:30am-2am.

Parker's, 4824 Bethesda Ave. (654-6366, delivery 571-0111), near Woodmont Ave., 2 blocks from Wisconsin Ave. A family restaurant, local hangout, and bar. Burgers and sandwiches $5.50-7. Daily specials on both food and drink. Happy hour (Mon.-Fri. 5-7pm) beams with ½-priced appetizers. Drafts start at $3, mixed drinks at $3.25. Sat. live music. Open Mon.-Sat. 11am-2am, Sun. noon-1am (Aug. Sun. 5pm-1am).

Bethesda Theater Café, 7719 Wisconsin Ave. (656-3337). Metro: Bethesda. 2 blocks north of the Metro. Crack open a cold one while Schwarzenegger cracks heads. Nibble on a tasty burger while T-Rex munches on a slimy lawyer. Beer, wine, and deli food are served while you watch slightly aged first-run movies from cushy chairs at low-lying tables. B.T.C. evokes the days when going to a movie was a great social event instead of a chance to watch glorified TV with 300 of your closest friends. Sun. and Tues. are no-smoking days. Admission Sun.-Thurs. $3.50, Fri.-Sat. $4.50. Matinees always $1.50. Beers from $1.90, wine from $3.75 per glass, 12-in. pizza $7. Amusingly named sandwiches, like One Flew Over the Turkey Breast, $4.75-6. Popcorn $1.50. 21+. Call or consult local papers for movies and showtimes. Plan to arrive a ½-hr. early for tickets on Sun. and weeknights, 45 min. early Fri.-Sat.

TAKOMA PARK, MD

Taliano's, 7001B Carroll Ave. (270-5515). The only bar on Takoma's main drag. After 5pm on Mon. it's ½-price pizza night, and Fri.-Sat. the place mellows out to live folk, blues, acoustic, and rock music. Bar open Mon.-Thurs. 11:30am-midnight, Fri.-Sat. 11:30am-1am, Sun. noon-midnight. Kitchen closes 1-2hr. earlier.

ARLINGTON, VA

★**Bardo,** 2000 Wilson Blvd. (703-527-9399). Metro: Court House. One block east (downhill) from the Metro. This is the bah where William Kennedy Smith got a beatin' from a bounsah. Hugely popular 20-something haunt is the self-proclaimed "largest microbrewery on the continent." At least 11 types of Bardo microbrews on tap. Happy hour (weekdays before 8pm and all day Sun.) offer $1.50 mugs and $2 pints of Bardo beer. Billiard room with 24 tables opens daily at 5pm. Free brewery tours Thurs. 7pm. Open Mon.-Fri. 11:30am-2am, Sat. 1pm-2am, Sun. 4:30pm-2am.

Galaxy Hut, 2711 Wilson Blvd. (703-525-8646). Metro: Clarendon. Limited liquor but exotic beers: over 50 to choose from. Local art decorates the walls, ceiling, and table tops. Entertainment provided by a 100-CD jukebox. Live music and poetry readings on weekends. Open Mon.-Fri. 5pm-2am, Sat.-Sun. 7pm-2am.

Iota, 2832 Wilson Blvd. (703-522-8340). Metro: Clarendon. A destination mostly for its performances of every style and genre. Microbrews $3.50-4.25, 31 bottled beers start at $2.80. Tunes almost every night from 9pm on. Happy hour (Mon.-Fri. 4-7pm): $1.50 microbrews and $1 off rails and drafts. Open Mon.-Fri. 4pm-2am, Sat.-Sun. 11am-2am.

ALEXANDRIA, VA

219 Basin St. Lounge, 219 King St. (703-549-1141). Metro: King St., a 20-min. walk. Local tavern sells $2.50 drafts and $3 rails. Live piano Tues.-Wed. at 8:30pm, jazz Thurs.-Sat. at 9pm. Open Mon. 11am-midnight, Tues.-Thurs. 11am-1:30am, Fri.-Sat. 11am-2am, Sun. 10am-midnight.

Ireland's Own, 132 North Royal St. (703-549-4535). Metro: King St. High-spirited pub and restaurant whose nightly live Irish entertainment fills Old Town's largest patio. Even the owner sings along on weekends. A visit from Ronnie hasn't been forgotten: a sign reading "Reagan's corner" hangs on a beam near the bar, and souvenir postcards of the event are for sale. Happy hour (Mon.-Fri. 4-7pm) features $1.50 domestic drafts, $3.25 imports, free buffet, and other assorted discounts. Drink prices rise when the entertainment begins (Sun.-Thurs. at 8pm, Fri.-Sat. at 9pm). Don your green, take a look at the "Blarney Room," and clap along. Open Mon.-Sat. 11am-1:30am, Sun. 10:30am-1:30am.

Laughing Lizard Lounge, 1322 King St. (703-548-2582), upstairs from the Stage Door. Metro: King St. Young crowd rocks loudly past 1am. Spontaneous dancing to rock or reggae in the back room. Order lizard legs (small $5, large $7). Bud on tap $3, rails $3.75. Happy hour Mon.-Fri. 5-7pm. Mon.-Thurs. open-mike, Fri.-Sat. live jazz and blues or occasional comedy. Cover: comedy $6, jazz $3. Downstairs deli feeds hungry masses of people daily until 1:30am. Open daily 5:30pm-2am.

Tiffany Tavern, 1116 King St. (703-836-8844), near S. Fayette St. Metro: King St. Homey and laid-back with a mellow crowd. Mon. and Wed.-Thurs. nights are open-mike, usually featuring talented local folk singers. Bluegrass dominates. Heavy wood interior and big bar. Happy hour (Mon.-Fri. 5-7pm): $1.50 drafts, $2 domestic beers, $2.25 rails. Sandwiches $5-7, catfish nuggets $5.50 (plus a crabmeat omelette for $6.25). Entrees $7-9 for lunch, $7-12 for dinner. Irish music Tues. nights, bluegrass/country Fri.-Sat. nights. Open Mon.-Thurs. 11:30am-2:30pm and 5pm-midnight, Fri. 11:30am-2:30pm and 5pm-2am, Sat. 5pm-2am.

Jazz and Blues

Washington has a surprisingly large, diverse, and thriving jazz and blues scene. With so many clubs from which to choose (in most sections of the city), there's one for virtually everyone's budget. A free lunchtime jazz series takes place downtown at the **Corcoran Gallery,** 17th St. between E St. and New York Ave. NW (638-3211), in the Hammer Auditorium every Wednesday at 12:30pm. (Metro: Farragut West or Farragut North.) The **Kennedy Center** and the **Smithsonian Museums** also sponsor free jazz shows.

★**Madame's Organ,** 2003 18th St. NW, near Florida Ave. in Adams-Morgan. (667-5370). The neon sign above the door shouts "Sorry, we're open" and in flows an eclectic clientele that can only be described as fab. Pink walls, dark red lighting, and wolf skins greet patrons. This blues club features live music nearly every night, with Sat. reserved for "a DJ from outer space" (Sept.-May). Cover $3. Drafts $2.50, mixed drinks $3.50. Open Sun.-Thurs. 6pm-2am, Fri.-Sat. 6pm-3am.

★**Vegas Lounge,** 1415 P St. NW (483-3971), four blocks east of Dupont Circle. Metro: Dupont Circle. Tiny tables, dim red lights, and a devoted crowd of regular patrons and performers give this blues den its Vegas air. Professional jam sessions Tues.-Wed. (otherwise known as "open-mike nights," but these guys play like pros) and bands Thurs.-Sat. (cover $5-9) churn out an assortment of styles the manager, "Dr. Blues," enthusiastically describes as Chicago-meets-New Orleans. Happy hour (Tues.-Sat.) offers $1 off beers. Be careful in this area at night. Open Tues.-Thurs. 7pm-2am, Fri.-Sat. 7pm-3am.

Blues Alley, 1073 Rear Wisconsin Ave. NW (337-4141), in an actual alley, below M St. in Georgetown. Cool jazz in an intimate supper club dedicated to the art. The club's music society sponsors a youth orchestra to nurture new talent. Past performers include Mary Wilson of the Supremes and Wynton Marsalis. Ticket prices $13-38. $7 food-or-drink minimum. Creole cuisine (entrees $14-19) served from 6pm. Beer $4, mixed drinks $5 and up. Upscale casual dress; some sport tuxes on big nights. Shows at 8 and 10pm. Call for reservations and prices.

One Step Down, 2517 Pennsylvania Ave. NW (331-8863), near M St. Metro: Foggy Bottom-GWU. More casual and less expensive than Blues Alley. Jukebox well-stocked with jazz. Local jazz Wed.-Mon., out-of-town talent Fri.-Sat. Daily happy hour features 90¢ drafts 3pm-7pm. Cover $5 weeknights, $10-15 weekends. Open daily 10:30am-2am.

★**Café Lautrec,** 2431 18th St. NW (265-6436), in Adams-Morgan. Spot this chic establishment from a distance by the enlarged mural of a Lautrec print painted across the front of this converted townhouse. Live jazz nightly. Tues. is Brazilian night. Fri.-Sat. features bartop tap dancing (hehhehheh). $6 min. per person once the music starts. Beer $3.25-5.75. Open Sun.-Thurs. 5pm-2am, Fri.-Sat. 5pm-3am.

Takoma Station Tavern, 6914 4th St. NW (829-1999). Metro: Takoma. A largely African-American crowd appreciates quality jazz Mon.-Sat., and reggae on Sun. Two large, tidy bars serve a generous, four-shot Long Island Iced Tea that'll knock you off your stool. Open Mon.-Fri. 11:30am-2am, Sat.-Sun. 4pm-2am.

City Blues, 2651 Connecticut Ave. NW (232-2300). Metro: Woodley Park-Zoo. Local blues and jazz musicians toot and strum daily in the bay window of this townhouse *cum* restaurant. Dinner entrees are a little pricey ($9-18), but you can come to just sway by the bar and nurse a drink. Fri.-Sat. after 9pm $5 cover (no cover for diners). Brunch Sat.-Sun. 11am-3pm. Live music Sun.-Thurs. at 8:30pm, Fri.-Sat. at 9:30pm. Open Sun.-Thurs. 11:30am-2am, Fri.-Sat. 11:30am-3am.

Wharf, 119 King St. (703-836-2834) in Alexandria. Metro: King St. Jazz/blues bar. $2.75 drafts, $3.25 rails. Mon. and Fri.-Sat. live jazz, Tues.-Thurs. blues, Sun. folk or pop. Music starts at 8:30pm on Mon., 9pm Tues.-Thurs., and 9:30pm Fri.-Sat. Cover: Mon. and Fri.-Sat. $5, Tues.-Thurs. and Sun. $3. Downstairs restaurant open daily 4pm-11pm. Open Mon.-Thurs. 9pm-1am, Fri.-Sat. 7pm-1:30am.

Dance Clubs

Let's Go has the most up-to-date club listings you'll find anywhere. These are *the* places to go. But, alas, dance clubs in D.C. have been known to fold as fast as honest congressfolk. So call ahead. And beware: some clubs move too fast to be caught in print. You might catch these transient gems in the pages of *City Paper;* more likely you'll just see a flyer posted somewhere in Georgetown or Dupont Circle.

SOUTHEAST

★**Tracks,** 1111 1st St. SE (488-3320). Metro: Navy Yard. The hottest dance club in D.C. Two dance floors, three bars, a patio, an outdoor volleyball court, and a set of bleachers overlooking the main dance floor (all packed into an old warehouse) ensure that there's something for every type of club-goer to do. Thurs. is college night: alternative youth with baggy pants and small knapsacks pay the $5 cover to enjoy the open bar 9-10:30pm. Fri.'s music is deep house with no cover 8-9pm, $5 9-10pm, $8-10 after 10pm; bar serves $1 drinks and $4 pitchers until midnight in the summer. Sat. is gay. Sun. brings R&B and hip-hop with a $2 cover after 7pm. Both are free and run 4-8pm. At 8pm, the club opens for an evening of house beats with a $3 cover until 9pm, $3-5 9-11pm, and $5 after 11pm. All drinks $2.25. Women's night last Tues. of every month; no cover before 9pm, $10 after. Doors open at 8pm with no cover before 9pm, $3 after. Secured parking nearby. Open Thurs.-Fri. at 9pm, Sat. 8pm, Sun. 7pm; no set closing time. Always 18+.

OLD DOWNTOWN

The Ritz, 919 E St. NW (638-2582), near 9th St. Metro: Gallery Place-Chinatown. Rumored to be the largest club on the East Coast, the Ritz boasts 5 clubs and music for every kind of crowd. The Gallery is strictly reggae; live jazz by candlelight in a moody-blues atmosphere downstairs. Sun. 18+ college night. Wed. reggae with $5 cover. Fri. rave night. Fri.-Sat. no cover before 8:30pm, $10 cover after; proper attire required. Dress on other nights is casual but fashionable—no sneakers. Open Wed. 9pm-4am, Fri. 5pm-4am, Sat. 9pm-4am, Sun. 10pm-4am.

Coco Loco, 810 7th St. NW (289-2626), between H and I St. Metro: Gallery Place-Chinatown. Chic Brazilian restaurant lends its bright, mosaic-tiled floor to DJ-driven salsa, merengue, and samba dancing every Thurs.-Sat. beginning at 10pm. No food during nightclub hours: the kitchen has to close to make room for the countertop Brazilian dance show (Fri.-Sat.). Cover: Thurs. $10, no cover before midnight; Fri.-Sat. $10 for men, $5 for women. Thurs. 18+. Dress is casual, but you might want to look like you just left the office. Nightclub open Thurs. 11pm-2:30am, Fri.-Sat. 11pm-3am.

FOGGY BOTTOM

Deja Vu, 1217 22nd St. NW (861-5858), at M St. Metro: Foggy Bottom-GWU or Dupont Circle. DJ plays progressive and rock Sun.-Thurs. 8pm-2am and Fri.-Sat. 8pm-3am. Fri.-Sat. $3 cover. For info, see **Bars** (p. 209).

GEORGETOWN

★**The Tombs,** 1226 36th St. NW (337-6668), at Prospect St.; entrance to the right of 1789 Restaurant. $2-3 cover Sunday nights for DJ and dancing, 10pm-2am. For more information, see **Bars** (p. 209).

★**Winston's,** 3295 M St. NW (333-3150), near 33rd St. So many men, so little hair. Marines and Navy soldiers come for R&R. Georgetown, American, and George Washington University folk crowd in too for a lively dance scene every night of the week. 18+. $3 cover weekends. Beer $1.50-3. Mixed drinks $3-4. No tank tops. Open Sun.-Thurs. 8pm-2am, Fri.-Sat. 8pm-3am.

Crazy Horse, 3259 M St. NW (333-0400). The college-military crowd shows up for pop music upstairs, hip-hop downstairs on Fri.-Sat. nights. Live music on Sun. Happy hour Fri.-Sat. 9-11pm. Beer, mixed drinks $3. 18+, $4-5 cover. Open Sun., Wed.-Thurs. 9pm-2am, Fri.-Sat. 9pm-3am.

Sports Fans, 3287 M St. NW (338-7027). A sports bar that doubles as a dance club; a plastic football player bursts through the wall as fans head downstairs to boogie to Top 40 hits. Cover $6 on Tues. with 10¢ drafts; $7 on Wed. with open bar on drafts; Thurs. is college night with $5 cover for women, $6 for men and open bar for all. Fri.-Sat. 2-for-1 on domestic beers 8-10pm and no cover before 9:30pm. Otherwise Fri.-Sun. $10 (women free on Sun.), and an open bar for all. Sun. night $1 cover, $1 any drink. Open Sun., Tues.-Thurs. 9pm-2am, Fri.-Sat. 8pm-3am.

Champions, 1206 Wisconsin Ave. NW (965-4005), at the end of an alley near M St. Strapping jocks abound. Dancing every night after 9pm. No cover, but there's a one-drink minimum on weekends. See **Bars** (p. 209) for more information.

FARRAGUT

★**Forbidden Planet,** 1006 20th St. NW (223-2972), at the **Crow Bar** (see p. 210). Metro: Farragut North or Farragut West. This space-age dance room of a hip bar is one of the most densely populated nightspots in the city. Open Fri.-Sat. 9pm-2am.

★**Zei,** 1415 Zei Alley (842-2445), between H and I St. NW. Metro: McPherson Square. Attire is "funky to formal," and the students and yuppies who frolic here treat it like a fashion show. Mon. is "Groove," an 18+ house dance party with open bar 10-11pm and a $5-8 cover; "Wax" on Tues. churns out funk and acid jazz to an 18+ crowd for $3-7; Wed. is $5 for reggae with $2.50 drinks until 11pm, 21+; Thurs. is "Paradiso" with an open bar 10-11pm and international dance beats for an 18+ crowd and a cover of $8; Fri.-Sat. DJs spin Top 40 dance music for a 21+ crowd and $10 cover. Open Mon.-Thurs. 10pm-2am, Fri.-Sat. 10pm-3am.

The Madhatter, 1831 M St. NW (833-1495), near 19th St. Metro: Farragut North or Farragut West. Packs 'em in every night of the week. DJ Tues.-Sun. beginning at 9pm. Open Sun.-Thurs. 11:30am-1:30am, Fri. 11:30am-2:30am, Sat. 10:30am-2:30am. For more information, see **Bars** (p. 210).

Flicks, 1160 20th St. NW (296-8644). Metro: Farragut West, Farragut North, or Foggy Bottom-GWU. Flicks, a full-time saloon, moonlights on the weekends as a dance club, 10pm-2am. Cover: Fri. $5, Sat. $10. See **Bars** (p. 210) for more info.

DUPONT CIRCLE

★**Planet Fred,** 1221 Connecticut Ave. NW (331-3733 or 466-2336). Between the eclecticism of the clientele and the craters, neon spacescape, and lava lamps decking the walls, a trip to Planet Fred may feel like an alien experience. Thurs. is DJ dancing and $10 all-you-can-drink; Fri.-Sat. cost $5 for DJ dancing. Daily happy hour (5-8pm) with varying specials blasts out of this world with 99¢ Rolling Rocks on Fri. Open Sun.-Thurs. 11:30am-2am, Fri. 11:30am-3am, Sat. 8pm-3am. For more information, see **Bars**, p. 210.

SHAW / U DISTRICT

★**Bent,** upstairs at 1344 U St. NW (986-6364), near 13th St. Metro: U St.-Cardozo. Big Dali clocks melt off the roof, about to slip onto the pavement below. More surrealism awaits you inside with a heterogeneous mix of gay and straight, black and white, male and female. The silver walls sweat with riotous disco dancing. Happy hour (Thurs.-Fri. 6-9pm) with free fondue and salsa, $2 rails, and $1.50 Rolling Rocks. Wed.-Sat. DJ '70s-90s disco grooves with a $2 cover after 11pm. Sun. '70s funk soul with no cover but $7 all-you-can-drink. Open Wed. and Sun. 9pm-2am, Thurs. 6pm-2am, Fri. 6pm-3am, Sat. 9pm-3am.

Utopia, 1418 U St. NW (483-7669), near 14th St. Metro: U St.-Cardozo. This SoHo-style "bar and grill, art and eat" joint hosts free dancing in the back for a young and eclectic group of locals. The North African art in the front was painted by owner Jamal Sahri himself; the back room features a rotating exhibit. Lunch, brunch, dinner, and happy hour (Mon.-Fri. 4-8pm and Sun.-Thurs. 10pm-2am: draft $2-3, bottled beer $2, rail drinks $3). Thurs. live Brazilian music, Sun. live blues and jazz. Open daily 11am-2am.

State of the Union, 1357 U St. NW (588-8810), near 14th St. Metro: U St.-Cardozo. This restaurant/bar/dance club's name is a play on words: patrons step inside to confront busts of Karl Marx and other Soviet regalia. Music of the jazzier genre: jazz, blues, salsa, acid jazz, and hip-hop reign. Happy hour (Mon.-Fri. 5-8pm) offers $2 Rolling Rocks, $3 Sam Adams, $3.75 mixed drinks. Mon. is live jazz in the front room, Tues. is live acid jazz in the back, Wed. alternates between world beat and poetry readings, Thurs. jazz and reggae, Fri.-Sat. deep house. Sun. brunch 11:30am-3pm. The back room has a removable wall for summertime patio action. Usually no cover; when there is one, it's only after 10:45pm. 21+. Open Mon.-Thurs. 5pm-2am, Fri.-Sat. 5pm-3am, Sun. 11:30am-3pm and 5pm-2am.

Manute Bol's Spotlight, 1211 U St. NW (265-5833). Metro: U St.-Cardozo. Owned by and named for a former Washington Bullets' hoopster, this classy club draws dance fiends, jazz musicians, and b-ball fans alike to its African art-bedecked bar and lounge. Warm up during happy hour (Mon.-Fri. 4-9pm) with 2-for-1 domestic drafts and free appetizers from 5 to 7pm. Mon. oldies, Tues. DJ dancing with a $5 cover, Wed. open mike, Thurs. live blues, Fri. live jazz, Sat. DJ house, and Sun. live jazz and blues. Usually no cover, sometimes $5 on DJ nights. Proper attire required on weekends. Open Sun.-Thurs. 11am-2am, Fri.-Sat. 11am-3am.

ADAMS-MORGAN

★**Club Heaven** and **Club Hell,** 2327 18th St. NW (667-4355), near Columbia Rd. Hell is downstairs, Heaven is upstairs—the ground-floor Italian restaurant must be *il Purgatorio.* In Hell, smoke blurs the funky gold tables and loud music emanates from spooky, yellow-backlit masks (every high schooler's dream of a New York café and bar). Heaven looks rather like an old townhouse: scuffed wood floor, comfy couches, a small bar, and three TVs, but the dance floor throbs to pounding beats and Heaven's back patio is crowded with timid souls who can't take the noise. Thurs. '80s dance party in Heaven with $4 cover. No cover other nights. Domestic beer $3, imports $3.75; $1 off during happy hour (daily 6-8:30pm in Hell). Dancing starts about 10pm. Heaven open Sun.-Thurs. 10pm-2am, Fri.-Sat. 10pm-3am. Hell open Tues.-Thurs. 9pm-2am, Fri.-Sat. 6pm-3am.

Rancho Deluxe, 2218 18th St. NW (745-2478). Skulls, human and animal, and assorted Latin Americana come together at this popular club, where DJs spin progressive dance tunes every night except Wed. Music starts at 10:30pm. Happy hour (daily until 9pm): $1 off all drinks. Domestic beers $3, imported $4. Open daily 5:30pm-1:30am.

UPPER NORTHWEST

★**Oxford Tavern "Zoo Bar,"** 3000 Connecticut Ave. NW (232-4225), across the street from the zoo. Metro: Woodley Park-Zoo. A DJ plays on Fri. nights until 3am. No cover. See **Bars** (p. 213) for more information.

Classical Music

D.C. is home to the well-respected **National Symphony Orchestra.** They perform at the **Kennedy Center,** 25th St. and New Hampshire Ave. NW (416-8000), which is to say that their tickets are normally on the expensive side ($22-47). On the other hand, the whole Kennedy Center half-price-tickets rigmarole applies to NSO performances. The NSO also gives three free concerts a year in celebration of particular holidays: Memorial Day, the Fourth of July, and Labor Day. Many other free concerts enliven the summer; see **Special Events** (page 292) for specifics. The **Washington Opera** (416-7890) also calls the Kennedy Center home. Chamber music in the Kennedy Center is more often cheap or free, especially during December's furious round of events, which culminate in the pre-Christmas *Messiah* sing-along.

The **Library of Congress,** 1st St. SE (concert line 707-5502), sponsors free (though tickets are required) concerts at the **Lincoln Theater** (328-6000). Concerts sometimes feature valuables from the library's collection, like a Stradivarius violin.

The **Summer Opera Theater Company** (526-1669, summer box office 319-4000), in Catholic University's **Hartke Theater,** runs a summer opera series better than anyone has a right to expect. Operas run in June and July; call for exact dates and ticket prices. Ushers and volunteers see the shows for free—call in advance. The **Wolftrap Filene Center**'s opera company vocalizes amid nature in the center's outdoor pavilion (see **Live Music,** p. 207).

The **Washington National Cathedral's Summer Festival of Music** (537-6200) draws crowds to free concerts (mostly chamber and choral music) in June and July. **The Phillips Collection,** 1600-1612 21st St. at Q St. NW (387-2151), provides an appropriate setting for chamber music and classical piano concerts—along with the occasional jazz show—each Sunday from September to May at 5pm (free with museum admission). Check the *Washington Post's* Weekend section for information. **The Society of the Cincinnati at Anderson House,** 2118 Massachusetts Ave. NW (785-2040), next to the Ritz-Carlton Hotel (Metro: Dupont Circle), also hosts free chamber music concerts (year-round; call for schedule), by various artists, and on the 2nd and 4th Tuesdays of every month (Oct.-May), by the Air Force Chamber Players. All concerts are at 1:30pm, and seating is on a first-come, first-served basis._From October to May, **Dumbarton Concert Series** sponsors chamber, choral, jazz, and Celtic concerts in an intimate, historic candlelit hall in **Dumbarton Church,** 3133 Dumbarton St. NW (965-2000), near Wisconsin Ave. in Georgetown. (Admission $22-28, student and senior discounts available; reserve at least one week in advance). The **Smithsonian museums** (357-2700) also host a smorgasbord of classical performances; grab a schedule at the Smithsonian Castle on the Mall.

Comedy Clubs

Chelsea's, 1055 Thomas Jefferson St. NW (298-8222), in the Foundry Building below M St. in Georgetown. Home of the **Capitol Steps,** a renowned political-satire troupe composed of Congressional staffers, whose proximity to the absurd spectacle of national government inspires them to write and perform political parody. Has included such favorites as "Fools on the Hill" and "the Joy of Sax." Tickets $30 without dinner, $45 with dinner. Capitol Steps performs most Fri. at 8, Sat. at 7:30pm; doors open 2hr. earlier. Open Sun.-Mon. and Wed.-Thurs. 9pm-2am, Fri.-Sat. 10pm-4am. Live bands: Sun. Persian, Mon. Ethiopian, Wed. Arabic, Thurs.-Sat. Latin. Cover Wed., Fri.-Sat. $10, other nights free.

The Improv, 1140 Connecticut Ave. (296-7008) in New Downtown. Metro: Farragut North. Cheap, wacky comedy for a youthful crowd. Tues.-Thurs. shows $10, Fri.-Sat. $12. Shows at 8:30 and 10:30pm.

Pool Halls

Buffalo Billiards, 1330 19th St. NW (331-7665). Metro: Dupont Circle. Across from the 19th St. Metro exit. The mothership of the new chain lines up 33 tables (including D.C.'s only regulation snooker table) in a cleaner, classier version of an old-fashioned saloon. Regular rates $5 per hour per person, $10 for two, $12 for 3, $14 for 4. Lower rates during slow daytime hours, higher during peak weekend hours. Full bar and food service available. Happy hour (Mon.-Fri. 4-8pm, Sat.-Sun. 1-7pm): $2 domestic pints and $2.50 rails. Open Mon.-Thurs. 4pm-2am, Fri. 4pm-3am, Sat. 1pm-3am, Sun. 1pm-1am.

Atomic Billiards, 3427 Connecticut Ave. (363-7665), in the heart of Cleveland Park. Metro: Cleveland Park. The funkiest of places, with a Jetsonian space-age mural behind the bar, vintage furniture lining the walls, and board games to bide the wait for one of the six tables. Same rates as Buffalo's. Limited bar service with beer and abundant coffee drinks. Limited food service includes grilled-cheese sandwiches ($2.50) and potato chips. $2 longnecks until 8pm every day. Open Mon.-Thurs. 4pm-1am, Fri. 4pm-2am, Sat. noon-2am, Sun. noon-midnight.

Babe's Billiards Café, 4600 Wisconsin Ave. NW (966-0082), in Tenleytown. Metro: Tenleytown-AU. A bright, windowed pool hall/restaurant. Happy hour (daily 3-7pm): $1.50 domestic beers, ½-price appetizers and pool $3.60 per person per hour. After 7pm pool $6.60 per person per hour. Late-night breakfast served 1 hr. before closing. Open Mon.-Thurs. 3pm-3am, Fri.-Sat. 3pm-4am.

Georgetown Billiards, 3251 Prospect St. NW (965-7665), in Georgetown. This independent pool hall has been claimed by Georgetown U. students as their official hangout/snack bar. 19 tables; rates vary. Happy hour (Mon.-Fri. 4-8pm). Open Mon.-Thurs. 4pm-2am, Fri.-Sat. 1pm-3am, Sun. 2pm-1am.

Theater

Arena Stage (488-3300), 6th St. and Maine Ave. SW, is often called the best regional (non-New York) theater company in America (Metro: Waterfront). The 45-year-old theater has its own acting company and three performance spaces: the Kreeger Theater and Fichandler Stage present high-quality new and classic plays, and the Old Vat Theater holds smaller, more experimental performances. (Tickets $21-45; for the Fichandler and Kreeger, $12-18, seniors 15% off, students 35% off; ½-price tickets usually available 90min. before start of show.) Visual and hearing aids are available, in addition to wheelchair access. The box office is generally open Mon.-Sat. 10am-7pm, Sun. noon-7pm.

The prestigious **Shakespeare Theatre,** at the Lansburgh, 450 7th St. NW (box office 393-2700; Metro: Archives-Navy Memorial), at Pennsylvania Ave., offers a Bard-heavy repertoire. The 1996-97 season (fall-spring) includes *Henry VI, Antony and Cleopatra, As You Like It,* and Eugene O'Neill's *Morning Becomes Electra.* Call months in advance for reservations, ticket prices, performance times, and discounts for students and seniors. Standing-room tickets (currently $10) are available two hours prior to performance. (Call at least 24hr. in advance to arrange disabled access.) If you are in town during June, try to take advantage of the Shakespeare's unique annual "Free for All" free performance series. For two weeks every summer, the company gives free performances at the **Carter Barron Amphitheater** in Rock Creek Park. The shows always draw capacity crowds, so be sure to obtain tickets in advance from the Shakespeare Theatre box office, Carter Barron box office, or the *Washington Post.* Call 628-5770 for details, or consult the *Post.*

At 25th St. and New Hampshire Ave., the **Kennedy Center's** (416-8000) innumerable performing-arts spaces include two theaters, the Terrace Theater and the Theater Lab. The highest-grossing play in the history of the center, *Shear Madness* still packs in the crowds and keeps 'em laughing. The "Something New" series takes the conservative center over the edge into performance art. Though tickets get expensive (many range from $10 to $65), most Kennedy Center productions offer half-price tickets right before the start of an event and earlier on the day of performance to students, seniors, military personnel, handicapped persons; call 467-4600 about discount tickets. The Kennedy calendar is dotted with listings of free events, such as the American College Theater Festival, which showcases free performances of top college productions (see **Annual Events,** p. 293).

Thespians thrive in Washington's **14th St. theater district,** where tiny repertory companies explore and experiment with truly enjoyable results. *City Paper* provides very good coverage of this scene. If tickets are out of your price range, don't despair; **usher.** All of the regular companies need unpaid help in the aisles, and once the paying crowds are inside, ushers usually watch the play for free. Call the theaters as far in advance as you can. Woolly Mammoth, Studio, the Source, and the Church St. Theaters dwell in a potentially dangerous neighborhood east of Dupont Circle, near or on 14th St. NW between P and Q St.; not all the action is on stage, and not all the commerce goes on in ticket booths. Don't come here alone at night.

TICKETplace, 730 21st St. NW (842-5387), at George Washington University's Lisner Auditorium, 21st and H St. NW. Metro: Foggy Bottom-GWU. Sells ½-price (plus 10% surcharge) day-of-show tickets for theater, music, dance, and special events on a walk-up basis. Cash only. (Also some full-price advance sales for cash or credit card.) Open Tues.-Fri. noon-6pm, Sat. 11am-5pm.

Woolly Mammoth, 1401 Church St. NW (393-3939). Metro: Dupont Circle. Take P St. east, away from the Circle, to 14th St. Make a left on 14th and another left on Church St. The theatre is the poorly marked building on your immediate right. Intense, daring productions by local playwrights, performed by local artists. The theater encourages would-be playwrights to send in manuscripts for readings. Box office open Mon.-Fri. 10am-6pm, Sat. 11am-6pm, Sun. 10am-2pm. Many cheap deals, including "far side seats," and occasional pay-what-you-can shows. Tickets $22; $5 discount for students, seniors, and groups of eight or more.

Studio Theater, 1333 P St. NW (332-3300). Metro: Dupont Circle. All types of drama and comedy on two stages (Mainstage Wed.-Sun. and Second Stage Wed.-Sat.). Tickets for Second Stage are $15 Wed.-Fri., $20 Sat.; for Mainstage $18-23.50 Wed.-Thurs. and Sun., $24.50-29.50 Fri.-Sat. Students with ID and seniors $5 off Mainstage shows; students can sometimes get ½-price tickets ½-hr. before Mainstage shows. Call about ushering or group discounts. Box office open Mon.-Wed. 10am-6pm, Thurs.-Sun. 10am-9pm.

The Source Theater, 1835 14th St. NW (462-1073), between S and T St. Metro: U St.-Cardozo. The Source is 14th St.'s oldest, most established "alternative" theater. Produces the Washington Theater Festival every summer at various D.C. locations, in addition to its regular assortment of Off-Broadway shows. Shows Wed.-Sun.; tickets $12, sold through ProTix (800-955-5566). Two-for-one specials on Wed. Students and seniors $2 off with advance purchase. Half-price student rush tickets available ½hr. before curtain. Call for information on ushering programs; ushers watch for free. Box office open Mon.-Fri. noon-6pm, Sun. noon-3pm.

Church St. Theater, 1742 Church St. NW (265-3748). Metro: Dupont Circle. A variety of drama ranging from Shakespeare to experimental to experimental Shakespeare. Tickets $15-18, with student and senior discounts decided on a show-by-show basis. Performances Wed.-Sat. at 8pm and Sun. at 7pm. Box office opens 1hr. before showtime.

National Theatre, 1321 Pennsylvania Ave. NW (628-6161). Metro: Metro Center or Federal Triangle. Big-name, big-budget theater often hosts visitors from Broadway, and the ticket prices reflect it ($35-65). But the fall-spring "Monday Night at the National" program puts on a variety show for free (information 783-3372), while old movies occasionally pop up as part of the "Summer Cinema" program on Mon. "Saturday Morning at the National" is a free series of kids' events. Half-priced tickets available for students, seniors (65 and over), military, and the disabled Tues.-

Wed. (usually at 8pm) and Sun. matinees (2pm). Call in advance for help for sight- or hearing-impaired.

Lincoln Theater, 1215 U St. NW (328-6000), directly across from the U St.-Cardozo Metro. Built in 1920, the Lincoln hosted such acts as Pearl Bailey and Duke Ellington, and was the first theater in the area to show movies to an integrated audience. For its historical significance, the city bought the decaying theater and restored it; the Lincoln reopened in Feb. 1994 to feature various musical and comedy acts. Tickets $25-40. Box office open Mon.-Fri. 10am-6pm, Sat. noon-8pm, and on show days until showtime, or buy through TicketMaster (432-7328).

Warner Theatre, 1299 Pennsylvania Ave. NW (628-1818). Metro: Metro Center or Federal Triangle. A recently refurbished ornate relic of its days as a vaudeville showhouse, the Warner now hosts high-priced concerts and plays ($20 and up). Tickets available at the box office (open Mon.-Fri. 10am-4pm, Sun. noon-3pm) or from TicketMaster (432-7328).

Ford's Theatre, 511 10th St. NW (347-4833). Metro: Metro Center, 11th St. exit. The theater where President Lincoln was assassinated now hosts musicals and big-budget shows. Tickets $24-36 (Sat. is the most expensive). Rush tickets available at the box office for seniors (55+) and students 1hr. before showtime ($15). Groups of 20 or more get 15-25% discounts (call 638-2367). Box office open Mon. 10am-6pm, Tues.-Fri. 10am-8pm, Sat. noon-8pm, Sun. noon-5pm.

Stage Guild, Carroll Hall, 924 G St. NW (529-2084). Metro: Metro Center or Gallery Place. A horseshoe-shaped balcony, high stage, and unbolted floor seats in this former school auditorium give set designers a rare opportunity to experiment. Four plays in the Sept.-May season. Mon.-Fri. and matinees $18, Sat.-Sun. $20. Call 48hr. in advance for group rates (10 or more qualify for ½-price tickets).

GALA Hispanic Theatre, 1625 Park Rd. NW (234-7174), in rickety Mount Pleasant; walk northeast on Columbia to 16th, turn left and walk three blocks to Park Rd. Turn left; GALA is behind the Sacred Heart school. The national award-garnering *Grupo de Actores Latino Americanos* presents four plays by modern or classical Latin American or Spanish authors each season (Sept.-June). Plays are in Spanish, with a simultaneous English translation provided via headset. Also hosts the *Poesía en Escena* series, a program of poetry presented from the stage. Tickets $18, students and seniors $16, groups of 10 or more $12. Productions Thurs.-Sat. 8pm, Sun. 4pm. Reservations recommended; call Mon.-Fri. 10am-4pm.

Movies

D.C. is awash with movie theaters; *Let's Go* lists those with unusual agendas or discounts. Check the *Post's* Style or Show sections for all the film that's fit to print.

The Smithsonian's **Hirshhorn Museum** (357-2700), on the Mall at Independence Ave. and 8th St. SW, runs three separate weekly (or so) free film series: foreign and independent films at night (usually at 8pm), documentaries about modern art, and animated matinees for kids. *Calendar* brochures are available at the Hirshhorn, and should contain the film schedule. The Smithsonian's **Museum of American History** also hosts classic and art films, sometimes with a pre-flick talk. The excellent **American Film Institute** (828-4000), at the Kennedy Center, shows classic American, foreign, and avant-garde films, usually two per night.

American University film classes show movies most nights on a varying schedule, free and open to the public; for a schedule, call 885-2040 (8:30am-5pm).

Bethesda Theater Café, 7719 Wisconsin Ave. (656-3337). See p. 214.

Key Theatre, 1222 Wisconsin Ave. NW in Georgetown (333-5100), near Prospect St. (1 block north of M St.). First-run art films every critic raves about. Subtitled films and exclusive showings offer plenty of chances to polish up your French. Admission $7, over 65 $4, children $3, first show of the day $4.

Outer Circle, 4849 Wisconsin Ave. NW (244-3116), across the street from Safeway. Metro: Tenleytown. First-run foreign films, some exclusive engagements. If the Key isn't showing it, this place is. Admission $7.25, seniors and children $4.25. All shows before 6pm $4.25.

Dance Performances

The Dance Place, 3225 8th St. NE (269-1600). Metro: Brookland-CUA. Experimental studio and theater leaps with dance, performance art, and/or music nearly every weekend (Fri.-Sat. at 8pm and April-Oct. Sun. at 7pm, Oct.-March 4pm). Controversial performers like Holly Hughes and hot, new choreographers and companies make their D.C. debuts here. Native American, Japanese, and ethnic groups join the commotion. Each June the **Dance Africa D.C. Festival** explodes with hourly free traditional dance performances from all over Africa, accompanied by an outdoor food-and-crafts market. Regular performances $10, students and seniors $8, children under 18 $5. Ushers watch for free (call for information).

Gay, Lesbian, and Bisexual Nightlife

Since Dupont Circle is the nucleus of activity for D.C.'s gay community, most of the drinking, dining, and dancing options congregate to the east of the Circle along 17th St. and west of it on P St. between 21st and 22nd. While some may not explicitly cater to gay clientele, they draw mostly gay patrons anyway. **Soho Tea and Coffee, Café Luna, The Pop Stop,** and **Trio** in the Circle all serve largely gay clientele.

The Annex, 1415 22nd St. NW (296-0505). Enter through Badlands (same address). Video and pool room is the quieter cousin of one of D.C.'s hottest dance clubs. The obvious choice for those who like the clean-cut crowd but prefer the bar atmosphere. Fri. night karaoke led by local drag queens. $5 cover. Open Fri.-Sat. 8pm-3am.

★**Badlands,** 1415 22nd St. NW (296-0505), near P St. This peach-colored monolith of a building hosts a young crowd serious about dancing which moves to the beat of Top 40, dance, and house music. Tues. is ½-price night; a $2 cover goes to charity. Thurs. is college night; cover is $3. Cover Fri.-Sat. $5. Expect to wait in line Fri.-Sat. Open Sun.-Thurs. 9pm-2am, Fri.-Sat. 9pm-2:45am.

★**The Circle Bar,** 1629 Connecticut Ave. NW (462-5575). Metro: Dupont Circle. A three-in-one social emporium with a ground-floor restaurant, a top-floor bar, and an underground dance club. All three draw a young, professional, racially mixed crowd. Happy hour (Mon.-Fri. 5-9pm) drops Bacardi and Skyy Vodka prices to $2, while Sat.-Sun. happy hour (11am-10pm) keeps all vodka prices at $2. Wednesday is ladies' night. Open Sun.-Thurs. 11am-2am, Fri.-Sat. 11am-3am.

DC Eagle, 639 New York Ave. NW (347-6025). Metro: Mt. Vernon Sq. Busy leather bar whose faithful patrons come early to drink and stay late to dance. Happy hour (Mon.-Fri. 6-9pm) with $1.25 rails and domestic beers. Two pool tables on two floors. Open Mon.-Thurs. 6pm-2am, Fri. 6pm-3am, Sat. noon-3am, Sun. noon-2am.

The Edge, 56 L St. SE (488-1200). Metro: Navy Yard. Around the corner from **Tracks.** Male entertainment warehouse with 6 bars, 2 dance floors, a snack bar, and game room. Wed. draws a racially diverse 20- to 30-something male crowd ($6 cover before 11pm, $8 after); Thurs. is ladies night with $1 drafts and $8 cover. Fri.-Sat. nights cater to a Black male crowd ($5 cover). Sun. "Pecs on the Deck" has no cover 4-7pm, and fills up fast with...er...pecs. Secure parking in nearby lots. Open Mon., Wed.-Thurs. 7pm-2am, Fri.-Sat. 7pm-4am.

Escalando!, 2122 P St. NW (822-8909). Metro: Dupont Circle. Amid neon lights, flashing mirrors, and walls emblazoned with colossal multicolored chili peppers, a predominantly Latino male crowd takes the floor for dancing and drinking. On the weekends, women join the fun. Free salsa and merengue lessons Mon. at 9pm; drag shows at midnight Sat.-Sun. Cover $5. Open Mon. 4pm-2am, Tues.-Thurs. and Sun. 11am-2am, Fri.-Sat. 11am-3am.

★**Fraternity House,** at 2122 P St. rear NW (223-4917), in the alley between 21st and 22nd St. The "Frat House" attracts an ethnically mixed crowd of young gay men. Ladies' night held once a month. Strobe lights, disco balls, videos, and hard-core house beats pump and flicker as the guys dance the night away amid mirrored walls. Happy hour (Mon.-Fri. 4-9pm) features $1.50 domestic beer. Specials every weeknight, like ½-price Tues. and $1 domestics on Wed. No cover for video bar;

downstairs cover $3. Open Mon. 4pm-3am, Tues.-Wed. 4pm-2am, Thurs. 4pm-4am, Fri. 4pm-5am, Sat. 8pm-5am, Sun. 8pm-2am.

★**Hung Jury,** 1819 H St. NW (279-3212). Metro: Farragut West. Believe it or not, no one's hung here. Lesbians from all over D.C. from 30-something couples to singles scoping the scene spend their weekend nights bopping to Top 40. $5 cover. Men must be accompanied by a woman to enter; gay men are admitted but occasionally must "prove" they're gay. Shooter $1. "Grab bags" (whatever a bartender pulls out of a box) $1.50. Open Fri.-Sat. 9pm-3:30am.

★**J.R.'s,** 1519 17th St. NW (328-0090). Metro: Dupont Circle. Upscale but down-home brick and varnished-wood bar, with wood floors, stained glass windows, and a DJ in a choir stall overlooking the tank of "guppies" (gay urban professionals). Happy hour (Mon.-Thurs. 2-8pm, Fri. 2-9pm): $2 domestic bottled beer, Sat. noon-8pm and Sun. all day: 75¢ vodka. A relaxed neighborhood bar by day, at night it becomes *the* place for S&M (stand and model)—if you're into that sort of thing. Mon.-Thurs. 3pm-2am, Fri. 2pm-3am, Sat. noon-3am, Sun. noon-2am.

Mr. P's, 2147 P St. NW (293-1064), near 22nd St. Metro: Dupont Circle. Oldest gay bar in the Circle pleases die-hard regulars with free chips and salsa, $2 beers, and $2.25 mixed drinks. In the evenings, male patrons spill out onto the patio bar and head upstairs to the video bar to dance the night away (video bar 9pm-close). Two-for-one rails on Wed. and $5 unlimited drafts on Sun. after 4pm. Open Mon.-Thurs. 3pm-2am, Fri.-Sat. 3pm-3am, Sun. noon-2am.

Phase One, 525 8th St. SE (544-6831). Metro: Eastern Market. Lesbian club with casual atmosphere draws women of all ages and styles for dancing. Pool tables, video bar, DJ. Beer $2.25. No cover Sun.-Thurs., $5 Fri.-Sat. Open Sun.-Thurs. 7pm-2am, Fri.-Sat. 7pm-3am.

★**Planet Fred,** 1221 Connecticut Ave. NW (331-3733 or 466-2336). Metro: Dupont Circle. Between the eclecticism of the clientele and the craters, neon spacescape, and lava lamps decking the walls, a trip to Planet Fred may feel like an alien experience. Occasional live bands pack in wall-to-wall punks, while Wed. night's "Drag Freak Bingo" draws a zany bunch ($7 cover) and "Female Trouble" every other Sun. is an ever-popular lesbian dance party. Sun. is also rockabilly night; Mon. offers free salsa lessons (7-9pm) and $2.75 margaritas; Thurs. is DJ dancing and $10 all-you-can-drink; Fri.-Sat. cost $5 for DJ dancing. Happy hour (Mon.-Fri. 4-7:30pm) includes $1.50 drafts and $1.75 rails. Open Sun.-Thurs. 11:30am-2am, Fri. 11:30am-3am, Sat. 8pm-3am.

Remington's, 639 Pennsylvania Ave. SE (543-3113). Metro: Eastern Market. A gay country-western nightclub and Top 40 video bar. Large dance floor on the first floor. Carpeted upstairs features posters of James Dean, a pool room and bar. Happy hour Mon.-Wed. 4pm-2am, Thurs.-Sun. 4-8pm. Free country-western dance lessons Mon.-Wed. at 8:30pm. Cover $3 Fri.-Sat. after 9pm. Open Sun.-Thurs. 4pm-2am, Fri.-Sat. 4pm-3am.

★**Tracks,** 111 First St. SE (488-3320). Metro: Navy Yard. One of the hottest straight dance clubs in D.C., Tracks becomes *the* hottest gay dance club in D.C. on Sat. nights. No cover 8-9pm, $5 9-11pm, $7 after 11pm. Two dance floors, three bars, patio, outdoor volleyball court. Opens Sat. 8pm with no set closing time. See p. 216 for more information.

Trumpets, 1603 17th St. NW (232-4141), on the corner of 17th and Q. Metro: Dupont Circle. Thirty-something, clean-cut, and professional men use this restaurant and lounge more for eating and meeting than drinking or dancing. New Age decor with sheet metal bolted to the walls gives this place a little hipness to which its happy hour (Mon.-Fri. 4-8pm) adds $1 rails and domestic drafts and $3 imports and premiums. Daiquiri bar on patio in summer. Wed. is women's night. Wheelchair access on Q St. Open Sun.-Thurs. 4pm-2am, Fri.-Sat. 4pm-5am.

Ziegfeld's, 1345 Half St. SE (554-5141). Metro: Navy Yard. Young and older gays and lesbians take turns attending Ziegfeld's nightly dance shows. Cover $6. Open Thurs. and Sun. 9pm-2am and Fri.-Sat. 9pm-3am.

Sports & Recreation

When it comes to the wide world of sports, Washington, D.C. takes a characteristically self-conscious approach: many of the city's politicos, professionals, and interns are far more concerned with the condition of their bodies than with the condition of their nation. This is not to say that professional athletics are altogether neglected; the Redskins have historically enjoyed a very devoted following, while the Capitals and Bullets have drawn recent interest due to the performances of some rising young stars. Without a doubt, however, the gems of the Washington sports scene are the Georgetown Hoyas, who regularly graduate players into the NBA (see Georgetown University, p. 148).

Nevertheless, none of these pro teams exerts the same daily influence on the lives of most Washingtonians as do recreational athletics. Joggers, bikers, and rollerbladers are forever competing for the capital's streets and footpaths. During the summer months, there isn't a sport more important than softball on the Mall; interns and professionals in their 20s and 30s grab a glove and a bat and compete in both informal leagues and pick-up games. In D.C., the city's ethic is reflected in its sports—the nation's movers and shakers maintain the same participatory attitude on the ball field as they do in the corporate field.

Spectator Sports

BASEBALL

While D.C. packs in the hard-hitters where national politics are concerned, it falls short when it comes to the national pastime. The city hasn't had a major league baseball team since 1970, when the Washington Senators (perhaps best known for their role in *Damn Yankees*) left to become the Texas Rangers. Although Washington has been content to play godparent to the **Baltimore Orioles** for the past 25 years, there has been a recent movement to bring an expansion team to the greater D.C. area. For the time being, thousands of Washingtonians will continue to commune to beautiful **Camden Yards** (410-547-6234) in order to catch some Major League action (see Entertainment and Nightlife, p. 258). Tickets for O's games range from $3 (standing room) to $25 (reserved boxes).

BASKETBALL

When it comes to hoops, the NCAA generally has more to offer Washingtonians than the NBA. The **Washington Bullets,** the city's professional team, have a long tradition of losing, a trend which has only recently begun to reverse itself. You can almost always catch the action between November and April at the **USAir Arena,** 1 Harry S. Truman Dr., Landover, MD, between Landover Rd. and Central Ave. Take the Beltway to exits 15A or 17A and follow the signs. Tickets range from $12 to $40, and are available for most weeknight games; call the **ticket office** at 301-622-3865. The real stars are the college teams, and the **Georgetown Hoyas** lead the pack by fielding a consistently good team every year. Tickets $5-15. Call 301-350-3400 or 687-4692 for information.

FOOTBALL

Despite their politically incorrect name, the **Washington Redskins** are a source of pride and joy for avid D.C. sports fans and seemingly disinterested residents alike. Three-time Superbowl champions ('82, '87, '92), the 'Skins draw crowds to **Robert F. Kennedy Stadium,** 2400 East Capitol St. SE (547-9077), for season games September through December. Regular season tickets are difficult to come by; they've sold out for each of the last 28 years. Preseason tickets are occasionally available from the **RFK**

ticket office (546-2222) for $35-50. If you're desperate for tickets, call a local ticket agency, but be willing to spend $50-100 for merely average seats.

HOCKEY

The **Washington Capitals** don't exactly dominate the high-speed game of hockey, but have managed to bring respect to a once-lowly franchise by making it to the post-season for the past two years. Faithful fans turn up at the USAir Arena for home games during the October-April season. Tickets ($12-45) are almost always available (except for "big games" on weekend nights). To order, call 301-386-7000.

SOCCER

Buoyed by swelling youth interest and the recent 1994 World Cup, soccer has undergone a meteoric rise in popularity over the past few years, culminating in the start of a new American league, **Major League Soccer (MLS).** Since the league's inception in 1996, Washingtonians have wasted no time learning what the rest of the world has known for decades—no other sport can compare to *futbol*. Despite some early mascot problems (many thought their eagle-and-ball insignia was too reminiscent of fascist symbolism), the **Washington, D.C. United** have had a promising first season, selling out record crowds if not yet captivating television audiences. Led by star U.S. attacker John Harkes, the United overcame some early season losses to become a surprise playoff contender. The United play at **RFK Stadium** (547-9077) from mid-April through September.

Participatory Sports

The Bob Dole "stairmaster-in-the-office" workout is a common mode of exercise for Washington's elite. Extra-office action often involves a consciousness of physique and a certain relevance of political clout that serve as a testament: having heavily borrowed from the ancient Greeks in designing its monuments and crafting its republican forms of government, Washington employs their athletic ethic as well. A stroll down the jogger-infested Mall during a weekday lunch hour will confirm that D.C.'s policy-makers exercise more than just their political influence. If you're unconvinced that the city takes recreation as seriously as legislation, call the **Department of Recreation and Parks** (673-7660 or 673-7671) for detailed proof.

BICYCLING

Cycling enthusiasts will love Washington's street plan for its long blocks and wide avenues, but Washington won't love them back: the crazy antics of bike messengers have bred hatred in most city drivers. Stay off the streets and sidewalks during the day, but pick any of the numerous bike paths and you can't go wrong. One of the best options is the **Mount Vernon Trail,** an 18-mi. trail which starts on Theodore Roosevelt Island and follows the Potomac River and the George Washington Parkway to its namesake, George Washington's scenic mansion. Another is the **C & O Canal Towpath,** a 184-mi. stretch that links Georgetown to Cumberland, MD. For more cycling ideas, try useful publications like the ADC's **Washington Area Bike Map** or the longer distance **Greater Washington Area Bike Map,** available at local book and sporting stores. Cyclists should always take precautions; wear a helmet.

City Bikes, 2501 Champlain St. NW (265-1564), near the 18th St. and Columbia Rd. intersection in Adams-Morgan. Mostly mountain bikes and hybrids. Bikes $10 per hr., $25 per day, $90 per week. Tandems $10 per hr., $40 per day. Locks and helmets free. Children's seats and trailers. $400 credit-card deposit required, or cost of bike in cash. Open Mon.-Wed. and Fri.-Sat. 10am-7pm, Thurs. 10am-9pm, Sun. noon-5pm.

Thompson Boat Center, 2900 Virginia Ave. NW (333-4861), at the intersection of Rock Creek Pkwy. and Virginia Ave. Metro: Foggy Bottom-GWU. 18-speed mountain bikes $6 per hr., $22 per day. $10 deposit required with ID. Rentals must be returned by 7pm. Open May-Aug. Mon.-Fri. 6am-8pm, Sat.-Sun. 7am-7pm; Sept.-Oct. and March-April daily 6am-7pm.

Big Wheel Bikes, 315 7th St. SE (543-1600). Metro: Eastern Market. Mountain bikes for $5 per hr., $25 per business day; 3-hr. min. For an extra $5, you can keep the bike overnight. Major credit card required for deposit. Open Tues.-Fri. 11am-7pm, Sat. 10am-6pm, Sun. 11am-5pm.

Better Bikes (293-2080), will deliver a bike anywhere in the D.C. area. 10-speeds $25 per day, $95 per week; mountain bikes $38 per day, $125 per week. Helmet, map, backpack, locks, and breakdown service included. $25 deposit; driver's license, credit card, or passport required for collateral. Cash only. Open 24hr.

Fletcher's Boat House, 4940 Canal Rd. NW (244-0461). On the C&O towpath. *Bicycles can be used only on canal towpath.* $4 per hour (2-hr. min.), $12 per day. ID necessary as deposit. Open Mon.-Fri. 9am-7:30pm, Sat.-Sun. 7:30am-7:30pm. No rentals after 5pm. Hours vary seasonally and depend on weather.

Bike the Sites, Inc., 3417 Quesada St. NW (966-8662), offers tours complete with bicycles, helmets, and equipment; licensed tour leaders; and a "unique perspective" of the nation's capital and surrounding areas. Tours lead 2-15 people, leave from/return to major hotels or near Metro stations, and range from $25 (1-hr. Early Bird Fun Ride) to $65 (day-long Civil War Battlegrounds Ride); prices, start times, and locations vary seasonally—call for specific information.

BOATING

Cruises

Potomac **boat trips** include meals and entertainment and are priced accordingly. For less money, visitors may take a 90-min. **monument tour.** The **Potomac Riverboat Company** (703-684-0580) runs cruises April-Oct., Tues.-Sun. Tours depart from the city pier in Old Town Alexandria (adults $14, seniors $13, children ages 2-12 $7).

Dandy Restaurant Cruise Ship, 0 Prince St., Alexandria (703-683-6076), offers a variety of elegant cruise experiences. Lunch cruises Mon.-Sat. and Champagne Brunch cruise on Sun. range from $26 to $30 and last 2½ hours. The nightly dinner and dancing cruises ($50-58; 3hr.) boast a five-course gourmet meal and a spectacular view of D.C.'s monuments.

Spirit of Washington, at 6th and Water St. SW (554-7447). Metro: Waterfront. The *Spirit of Washington* hosts lunch ($27-33) and dinner cruises ($49-59) Tues.-Sun. and moonlight cruises ($23) Fri. and Sat. nights. The outings feature live bands and narrated tours of the city. Cruises depart from Pier 4.

Boat Rentals

If cruises are too expensive, stuffy, or sedate for your blood, grab an oar, rent a boat, and take to the waters yourself. If there are two or more mates in a boat, *everyone* should be able to swim (or at least have a life preserver). All aboard.

Fletcher's Boat House, 4940 Canal Rd. NW (244-0461). Canoes $17 per day, rowboats $15 per day. No rentals after 5pm. Open Mon.-Fri. 9am-7:30pm, Sat.-Sun. 7:30am-7:30pm.

Thompson Boat House, (333-4861), Rock Creek Pkwy. and Virginia Ave. NW. Canoes $6 per hour, $20 per day. Sea kayaks $7 per hour, $24 per day. Double kayaks $20 per day. Shells available with certification. ID required. Boats must be returned by 7pm. Open Mon.-Fri. 6am-8pm, Sat.-Sun. 7am-7pm.

Tidal Basin Boat House, 1501 Maine Ave. SW (484-0206), will send you **paddle-boating** across D.C.'s cherry-tree-lined man-made lake. 2-seaters $7 per hour; 4-seaters $14 per hour. Boats must be returned by 8pm. Open daily 10am-7pm.

Jack's Boats, 3500 K St. NW in Georgetown below Key Bridge (337-9642). Canoes and rowboats $5 per hour, $25 per day. Open Mon.-Fri. 9am-8pm and Sat.-Sun. 8am-8pm.

BOWLING

Perhaps due to their blue-collar reputation, bowling lanes are scarce inside the largely white-collar District; a crack at the pins usually requires a trek to the suburbs.

Bowl America, 8616 Cameron St. in Silverspring, MD (301-585-6990). The closest lanes to D.C. 10-pin bowling. $3 per game per person. Shoe rental $2. Open Mon.-Fri. noon-9pm, Fri.-Sat. 9am-1:30am, Sun. 9am-4pm.

Shirley Park Bowl, 2945 S. Glebe Rd. in Arlington (703-684-5800). Take 395 south and get off at exit 7. Mon.-Fri. $1.50 per game until 6pm, $3 afterward. Sat.-Sun. $2 per game until 6pm, $3 afterward. Open Tues.-Sun. 24hr. Sun. 9am-midnight, Mon. 9am-2am.

GOLF

A favorite pastime for D.C.'s social and political elite, golf is mostly confined to the grassy greens and rolling hills of the city's exclusive country clubs. The following, however, are a few public courses open to PGA Tour pros, wealthy businessmen, and hackers looking for an inexpensive round:

Robert F. Kennedy Stadium (397-8638). Metro: Stadium-Armory. Mon.-Fri. 9 holes $9, 18 holes $15. Sat.-Sun, 9 holes $12, 18 holes $19. Club rentals $6-10. Pull carts $3. Riding carts $12-18. Open during daytime hours.

Rock Creek Park (882-7332), at 16th St. and Rillenhouse NW. Green's fees same as at RFK Stadium's. Club rentals $6-8. Pull carts $3. Riding carts $12-19. Open daily 5:30am-8pm during the summer; call for winter hours.

East Potomac Park Golf Course (863-9007), on Ohio Dr. Rates are similar to RFK and Rock Creek's.

Mini-Golf Modern Art

As unlikely as it sounds, local Baltimore artists have designed a visually stunning 18-hole miniature-golf course. Located at the base of the power plant (at 601 E. Pratt St.) in Baltimore's Inner Harbor, **Art Links** (410-244-1200) assimilates artistically interpreted Baltimore landmarks into the spirit of mini-golf. The course includes holes inspired by Fort McHenry, Edgar Allen Poe, and the Baltimore & Ohio Railroad. Utterly devoid of plastic, the course attracts children, avid golfers, and art connoisseurs alike (open 10am-10pm daily; admission $5).

HIKING

Nature lovers will be impressed with the number of hiking trails in the greater metropolitan area. In addition to the **C&O Canal Towpath** and the **Mt. Vernon Trail** (see **Bicycling**), **Rock Creek Park** contains a network of hiking trails (282-1063 or 426-6829). The **George Washington Carver Nature Trail** starts from the Anacostia Museum, 1901 Fort Pl. SE (287-3369) and meanders for 7 mi. Virginia's **Great Falls Park** (703-285-2965) boasts 16 mi. of footpaths. Open daily in summer, 7am-dusk. Vistors center open daily in summer 9am-6pm. The small but scenic **Roosevelt Island** (703-285-2598) preserves wildlife and about 2 mi. of trails.

HORSEBACK RIDING

Those with romantic hopes of galloping across woodlands at breakneck speeds will find their hopes dashed at the **Rock Creek Park Horse Center,** 5110 Glover Rd. NW (362-0117). Guided 1-hr. trail rides are walk-only, so you'll probably find yourself astride a mild mare instead of a swift stallion. $21 per person; must be at least 12 yrs. old. Sat.-Sun. at noon, 1:30, and 3pm. Reservations necessary.

ICE SKATING

When winter hits hard, there's **free ice skating** on the Reflecting Pool in front of the Lincoln Memorial and on the C&O Canal. If these options aren't available, try the **National Sculpture Garden Rink,** 9th and Constitution Ave. NW (371-5342; Metro: Smithsonian). Admission $4.50, rental $2.50.

JOGGING

Those who choose to traverse Washington on their own unaided feet will find the **C&O Canal Towpath** and **Rock Creek Park** jogger-friendly–at least before dusk (for more information on staying safe on foot, see page 31). Near the **Tidal Basin,** on the **Mt. Vernon Trail,** and along the **Mall** are especially good areas to jog. Serious runners may want to enter the **Marine Corps Marathon** on Nov. 1, which commences at the Iwo Jima Memorial and goes through most of downtown D.C. ($21 entrance fee). If a marathon sounds daunting, check the *Washington Post* "Weekend" section for upcoming races.

ROLLERBLADING

To see D.C. on wheels but without a car, try the latest high-profile fad in fun and fitness. If you want some company, meet the **Washington Area Rollerskaters** in the parking lot off Beach Dr. in Rock Creek Park Sat. at noon for a social skate through the park, or in front of the White House at 9th and Constitution Ave. Sun. at 12:30pm and Wed. at 6:30pm for a city skate. Call 466-5005 for details. Rent at **City Bikes,** at 2501 Champlain St. NW (265-1564). ($10 per hour, $25 per day. Helmet and pads included. Open Mon.-Wed. 10am-7pm, Thurs. 10am-9pm, Sat. 10am-7pm, Fri. and Sun. noon-5pm.)

SOFTBALL

After a hard day's work, young professionals and interns flock to the Mall to participate in informal league softball games. Teams and leagues are primarily determined according to the players' professions—aspiring journalists from *The Washington Post* play those of *The New Republic,* while lobbyists bunt to congressional staffers. Pick-up games also abound for those without political or corporate affiliation. A great way to meet people, softball is a key component in the Washington sub-culture of schmoozing.

SWIMMING

Beaches

The best D.C.-accessible beaches are at the **Delaware seashore,** a 3-hr. drive from the city. If the sweltering heat is too much, do what most of the city does on summer weekends—leave. But if you haven't the money or mobility to make the exodus, there are plenty of public pools where you can beat the heat.

Pools

Pools can be found in nearly every neighborhood. The facilities themselves are generally clean and safe; many of the surrounding areas are not. When choosing a pool, it is best to stick to the same cautionary procedures you might use when choosing an accommodation: don't swim anywhere you wouldn't sleep. The following are several pools easily accessible by the Metro. Other, less accessible (but recently renovated) pools include **Francis** (25th and N St. NW) and **Upshur** (14th and Upshur St. NW). Both are outdoor facilities. All pools open Mon.-Fri. 1-8pm, Sat. Sun. noon-7pm (some may open earlier). Call the **Aquatics Branch** of the Dept. of Recreation and Parks at 576-6436 for more complete listings.

Wilson, Nebraska Ave. and Chesapeake St. NW (282-2216). Metro: Tenleytown-AU. Indoor facility open during the summer: Mon.-Fri. 10-11am, noon-1:15pm, and 7-8pm for laps; general public swim Mon.-Fri. 1:30-5:30pm, Sat. noon-4pm. Free.

Capitol East Natatorium, 635 N. Carolina Ave. SE (724-4495). Metro: Eastern Market. Indoor pool; lap lanes always in effect. Summer hours Mon.-Fri. 6:30-9am, 1-5pm, 6-7pm (until 9pm on Tues., Thurs., Fri.); Sat.-Sun. 10am-5pm. Call in advance (pool often fills to 200-person capacity). Free.

Georgetown, 34th St. and Volta Pl. NW (282-2366). Metro: Tenleytown or Friendship Heights, then take #32, 34, or 36 bus to Wisconsin in Georgetown. Outdoor pool; lap lanes always in effect. Open Tues.-Fri. 1-8pm, Sat.-Sun. noon-7pm. Free.

TENNIS

Although most Washingtonians who play tennis do so seriously at a private club, D.C. still offers several **public tennis courts** in **Rock Creek Park,** at 16th and Kennedy NW (722-5949), and at **East Potomac Park,** 1090 Ohio Dr. SW (554-5962). Hard, clay and indoor courts. Summer rates range from $3.25 to $8 for hard/clay courts and $11-14 for indoor courts. Open Mon.-Fri. 7am-10pm, Sat.-Sun. 7am-8pm. Call for winter hours.

Gay and Lesbian Sports and Recreation

D.C. Strokes Rowing Club, P.O. Box 39076 (371-8897). Washington area group with competitive, recreational, and novice rowing programs for gay men and lesbians interested in the sport. Basically a bunch of young, fit gay men and women who love to row. Annual dues $30 or month long introductory ($50) and recreational ($60) programs. Call for further information.

Crew Club, 1321 14th St. NW (319-1333). Metro: McPherson Square. Social/recreational facility, health club, and gym for gay males looking to work up a sweat. Weight gym, lockers, showers, tanning, and game room. No alcohol. Admission $19. Tues. half price 8am-midnight. Wed. college night ($12 with college ID). Open 24hr.

Shops & Services

Shopping Malls

Georgetown would like to think that it has mastered the art of mall-building—the ritzy **Georgetown Park,** 3222 M St. NW, near Wisconsin Ave., shines even underground with brass galore and 150 stores, including J. Crew and Williams Sonoma (298-5577; open Mon.-Sat. 10am-9pm, Sun. noon-6pm). The grandiloquent green Edwardian interior is a bit overwhelming, but waterfalls and air-conditioning create a climate-controlled oasis for weary travelers. Glance up at the escalators; aside from leading you just where you don't want to go, they're the same ones Kevin Costner sprinted down in *No Way Out* before jumping on the fictitious Metro. To get to Georgetown Park, take the Metro's Red Line to Friendship Heights, then ride any of the 30-series buses south on Wisconsin Ave. Alternatively, ride the Orange Line to Foggy Bottom and walk 20 min. westward into Georgetown. **Mazza Gallerie,** 5300 Wisconsin Ave. (686-9515; open Mon.-Fri. 10am-8pm, Sat. 10am-6pm, Sun. noon-5pm; Metro: Friendship Heights) and **Chevy Chase Pavilion,** 5335 Wisconsin Ave. (686-0937; open Mon.-Fri. 10am-8pm, Sat. 10am-6pm, Sun. noon-5pm; Metro: Friendship Heights), certainly give Georgetown a run for its money. The **Fashion Centre at Pentagon City,** 1100 S. Hayes St. in Arlington (703-415-2400; open Mon.-Sat. 10am-9:30pm, Sun. 11am-6pm; Metro: Pentagon City) is another contender. The **Ballston Common Mall,** 4238 Wilson Blvd. between Stuart and Randolph St. (703-243-8088, open Mon.-Sat. 10am-9:30pm, Sun. noon-6pm), offers everything you need (and don't need) one block from the Ballston Metro. Two more clones are **Tyson's Corner Center,** 1961 Chain Bridge Rd., McLean, VA (703-893-9400; open Mon.-Sat. 10am-9:30pm, Sun. 11am-6pm), and **Tyson's Galleria,** Capital Beltway, Exit 11-B, McLean, VA (703-827-7730; open Mon.-Sat. 10am-9pm, Sun. noon-6pm). Take the Metro's Orange Line to West Falls Church for both; from the Metro, take bus 28A, 28B, 5S, or 3B to Tyson's Corner Center, or a shuttle (Mon.-Fri. 6:40am-8:40pm; 75¢) to Tyson's Galleria. Both Tyson's solicit shoppers at Rte. 7 and Rte. 123, off the Beltway at exit 10B or 11B. The **Montgomery Mall,** 7101 Democracy Blvd., Bethesda, MD (301-469-6000; open Mon.-Sat. 10am-9:30pm, Sun. 11am-6pm), has emerged as one of suburbia's most popular. Metro: Grosvenor; then Montgomery County bus #47. Finally, there's **White Flint Mall,** 11301 Rockville Pike, Rockville, MD (301-231-7467; open Mon.-Sat. 10am-9:30pm, Sun. noon-6pm; Metro: White Flint).

Department Stores

When genteel **Woodward & Lothrop** succumbed to bankruptcy in 1995, it was the end of an era in Washington retail. "Woodies" was the last Washington-based department store; its demise followed that of Raleigh's and Garfinckel's, conforming to a dominant trend across the country—national and global chains are overwhelming Washington's local retailers.

Lord & Taylor, 5255 Western Ave. NW (362-9600), on the corner of Jenifer St. and Western Ave. near Mazza Gallerie. Open Mon.-Fri. 10am-9pm, Sat. 9am-7pm, Sun. 11am-6pm. Also at: White Flint Mall (301-770-9000). Metro: White Flint. Open Mon.-Thurs. 10am-9:30pm, Fri. 10am-10pm, Sat. 9am-9:30pm, Sun. 11am-6pm.

Filene's Basement at Mazza Gallerie (966-0208). Open Mon.-Sat. 10am-9pm, Sun. noon-6pm. Also at: 1133 Connecticut Ave. NW (872-8430). Metro: Farragut North. Open Mon.-Sat. 9:30am-8pm, Sun. noon-5pm.

Hecht's, 12 St. and G NW (628-6661). Metro: Metro Center. Open Mon.-Fri. 10am-8pm, Sat. 9am-8pm, Sun. noon-6pm. Also at Friendship Heights Metro. Open Mon.-Thurs. 10am-9:30pm, Fri. 10am-10pm, Sat. 9am-10pm, Sun. 11am-7pm.

Whatever happened to Dinner and a Movie?
Tiffany & Company, at 8045 Leesburg Pike and 5500 Wisconsin Avenue in Friendship Heights, was recently named **"Best Place for a Third Date"** by *Washingtonian* magazine. The magazine's "resident expert" explains: "Listen, this is Washington. The negotiations could take forever. You've got to cut to the chase." Perhaps Tiffany & Co. will pop the investment question and cash in on Vegas-inspired drive-thru matrimony.

Nordstrom, 1400 S. Hayes St. in Arlington (703-418-4488). Metro: Pentagon City. Open Mon.-Sat. 10am-9:30pm, Sun. 11am-6pm. Also at the Montgomery Mall in Bethesda (301-365-4111). Open Mon.-Sat. 10am-9:30pm, Sun. 11am-6pm.

Macy's, 1000 S. Hayes St. in Arlington (703-418-4488). Metro: Pentagon City. Open Mon.-Sat. 10am-9:30pm, Sun. 11am-6pm.

Bloomingdale's at the White Flint Mall (301-984-4600). Open Mon.-Sat. 10am-9:30pm, Sun. noon-6pm.

Bookstores

Atticus Books, 1508 U St. (667-8148), near 15th St. Metro: U St.-Cardozo. Used-book store with a good selection of foreign-language and academic books. Paperbacks half off cover price. Open Mon.-Sat. 11am-7pm, Sun. 11am-6pm.

Booked Up, 1204 31st St. NW (965-3244), near M St. in Georgetown. Lends a sense of walking into someone's private library and feeling underdressed for the occasion. Rare and antique books $15-20,000 each. Open Mon.-Fri. 11am-3pm, Sat. 10am-12:30pm.

Capitol Hill Books, 657 C St. SE (544-1621). Metro: Eastern Market. Right around the corner from Eastern Market. A small, inviting used-book store covering all subjects, with strong gay-studies and black-studies sections. Check the carts out front for good paperback bargains. Open Tues.-Fri. 11:30am-6pm, Sat.-Sun. 9am-6pm.

★**Chapters,** 1512 K St. NW (347-5495), in Old Downtown. Metro: McPherson Square. High-quality downtown bookstore satisfies literati stranded in la-la-lawyer-land. Browse away—they answer the phone with a whisper so as not to disturb you. Chapters is D.C.'s premier location for literature; the thoughtful collection is augmented by capsule recommendations and reviews from the owners and staff. Offers scheduled lectures, readings, authors' book-signings, and ½-price book sales. Open Mon.-Fri. 10am-6:30pm, Sat. 11am-5pm.

Chuck and Dave's Books, Etc., 7001 Carroll Ave. (301-891-2665), in Takoma Park. Road atlases and maps, postcards of Yeats and Camus, newspapers like the *Village Voice,* a decent academic book collection, and a good selection of periodicals. A semi-annual ½-price sale enables book buyers to practically walk off with the merchandise. Skylights make for cozy browsing. Open Mon.-Fri. 10am-8pm, Sat. 10am-7pm, Sun. 10am-5pm.

Idle Time Books, 2410 18th St. NW (232-4774), between Belmont and Columbia Rd. in Adams-Morgan. One of the largest (three floors) used-book stores in the city, with great prices. Impressive art magazine section. Open daily 11am-10pm.

Kramerbooks, 1517 Connecticut Ave. NW (387-3825). Metro: Dupont Circle. Every respectable city needs a late-night bookstore, and Washington has Kramerbooks, open all night Fri.-Sat. Browsers explore the extensive fiction and history sections before slipping past the cookbooks into **Afterwords Café** and bar in back. Open Mon.-Thurs. 8am-1am, Fri. 8am-Mon. 1am.

Kulturas, 1741 Connecticut Ave. NW (462-2541), near R St. Metro: Dupont Circle. Piles up secondhand books, records, and vintage clothing in friendly haphazardness. Paperbacks go at half the original price. Paintings-of-the-month (by local artists) spruce up the back of the store. Open Mon.-Sat. 11am-9pm, Sun. 11am-7pm.

The Lantern Bryn Mawr Bookshop, 3160 O St. NW (333-3222), near Wisconsin Ave. in Georgetown. Great big gobs of used books, from rare first editions to chintzy romance novels, all priced to move. Managed by charming grannies with a passionate love of books. Hardcover (from $6) and paperbacks (from $1) share shelf space with some old jazz and classical records ($1). Open Mon.-Fri. 11am-4pm, Sat. 11am-5pm, Sun. noon-4pm.

Logic and Literature Book Shop, 1209 31st St. NW (625-1668), between M and N St. in Georgetown. Used and rare books bought and sold. Specializes in history, science, literature, art, and philosophy. Open Mon.-Tues. noon-5:30pm, Wed.-Fri. 11:30am-6pm, Sat. 11am-6pm.

Luna Books, 1633 P St. NW (332-2543), on the third floor above Café Luna and Skewers. Metro: Dupont Circle. Bookstore/coffeehouse moonlights as a "Democracy Center," which means your average patron is an activist and the major activity is political discourse. Discount nonfiction and political texts, as well as discussion groups offered. Open Mon.-Fri. 11am-10pm, Sat.-Sun. noon-11pm.

Mystery Books, 1715 Connecticut Ave. NW (483-1600 or 800-955-2279). Metro: Dupont Circle. Agatha Christie, Dorothy Sayers, Ellis and Elizabeth Peters—it's all here in addition to book signings, newsletters, catalogues, and "Crime and Nourishment" gift baskets. Open Mon.-Fri. 11am-7pm, Sat. 10am-6pm, Sun. noon-5pm.

National Organization for Women (NOW) Bookstore, 1615 K St. NW (467-6980), in Old Downtown. Metro: McPherson Square. Books, T-shirts, decals, and postcards with the twin themes of diversity and equality. Browse through the colorful emblems of egalitarianism. Open Mon.-Fri. 10am-6pm.

The Old Forest Bookshop, 3145 Dumbarton St. NW (965-3842), between 31st St. and Wisconsin Ave. in Georgetown. A small house full o' books; mostly general-interest literature, history, and art. Hardcovers as marked, paperbacks half the original price. Open Sun.-Mon. noon-6pm, Tues.-Sat. 11am-7pm.

Olsson's Books and Records, 1239 Wisconsin Ave. NW (book info. 338-9544, music info. 338-6712), in Georgetown. Also in Old Downtown, Dupont Circle, Alexandria, and Bethesda. Local chain with great selections in literature, travel, and history; music section offers classical, blues, jazz, gospel, and world recordings. Open Mon.-Thurs. 10am-11pm, Fri.-Sat. 10am-midnight, Sun. 11am-11pm.

Second Story Books, 2000 P St. NW (659-8884), at the corner of 20th St. Metro: Dupont Circle. Thousands of used books. Open daily 10am-10pm.

United States Government Bookstore, 1510 H St. NW (653-5075), near 15th St. Metro: McPherson Square. Pamphlets galore: the most tiresome or most exciting reading material you've ever encountered. Open Mon.-Fri. 8:30am-4:30pm.

Yawa, 2206 18th St. NW (483-6805), between Kalorama Rd. and Wyoming Ave. in Adams-Morgan. Specializes in African and African-American literature; greeting cards, incense, and jewelry. Open Mon.-Sat. 11am-9pm, Sun. noon-6pm.

Yes!, 1035 31st St. NW (338-7874), near M St. in Georgetown. Alternative paths to health of body and soul: an affirmative experience for all who enter. Enormous selection of books on Krishna, acupressure facelifts, diet and nutrition, metaphysics and tarot, massage technique, astrology, martial arts, and Jungian studies. Also, a nirvana-oriented music collection (not the band) featuring Gregorian chants and meditation music. Free coffee for browsers. Call 800-YES-1516 (937-1516) for free catalog. Open Mon.-Thurs. 10am-7:30pm, Fri.-Sat. 10am-8pm, Sun. noon-7pm.

Yesterday's Books, 4702 Wisconsin Ave. NW (363-0581), at Chesapeake St. Metro: Tenleytown. Used books (nearly 30,000) of every conceivable kind, from politics to literary criticism to gay studies. Coffee, cake, and chairs for your browsing pleasure. Open Mon.-Thurs. 11am-9pm, Fri.-Sat. 11am-10pm, Sun. 1-7pm.

Clothing Stores

If you're a young prepster looking for that perfect Polo shirt, you'll be in ecstasy among the collegiate choices in Georgetown. All the old standbys are within walking distance from each other. **Benetton,** 1200 Wisconsin Ave. NW (625-0443). Open Mon.-Thurs. 10am-9pm, Fri.-Sat. 10am-10pm, Sun. 11am-8pm. **Banana Republic,** 3200 M St. NW (333-2584). Open Mon.-Sat. 10am-10pm, Sun. 11am-8pm. **The Gap,** 1258 Wisconsin Ave. NW (333-2805). Open Mon.-Thurs. 10am-9pm, Fri.-Sat. 10am-10pm, Sun. 11am-8pm. **J. Crew,** 3222 M St. NW (965-4090). Open Mon.-Sat. 10am-9pm, Sun. noon-6pm. **Patagonia,** 1048 Wisconsin Ave. NW (333-1776). Open Mon.-Fri. 10am-8pm, Sat. 10pm-6pm, Sun. 11am-5pm. **Urban Outfitters,** 3111 M St. NW

(342-1012). Open Mon.-Thurs. 10am-10pm, Fri.-Sat. 10pm-11pm, Sun. 11am-8pm. For a somewhat more unique shopping experience:

Clothes Encounters (...of a Second Kind), 202 7th St. SE (546-4004). Metro: Eastern Market. Across from Eastern Market, on the corner of North Carolina. Consignment shop for designer women's clothing. Pick up nearly new dresses and accessories at a third of the new price. Open Mon.-Wed. and Fri. 11am-6pm, Thurs. 11am-7pm, Sat. 10am-6pm, Sun. noon-4pm.

Commander Salamander, 1420 Wisconsin Ave. NW (337-2265), near O St. in Georgetown. Drop in, tune in, turn on. Offbeat clothing from grunge wear to outrageously extreme vinyl/plastic/polyester fashions. Open Mon.-Thurs. 10am-10pm, Fri.-Sat. 10am-11pm, Sun. 11am-8pm. Closes 1hr. earlier winter weekdays.

Hats In the Belfry, 1237 Wisconsin Ave. NW (342-2006), across from Prospect St. in Georgetown. Hats average about $25, but range to $400! When the hot Washington sun beats down, they can charge as much as they want and still find a market. This is where people buy that Cat-in-the-Hat hat. Open daily 10am-10pm.

Kobos Afrikan Clothiers, 2444 18th St. NW (332-9580), in Adams-Morgan. Elegant, intricate clothing and authentic items for adults and children, imported from Africa. Open Mon.-Thurs. 11am-7pm, Fri.-Sat. 11am-8pm, Sun. noon-7pm.

Man For All Seasons, 321 7th St. SE (544-4432). Metro: Eastern Market. On the same block as Eastern Market. Consignment shop for designer men's clothes offering stylish suits, shirts, and shoes for half the original price. Open Tues.-Wed. and Fri. 11am-6pm, Thurs. 11am-7pm, Sat. 10am-6pm, Sun. 12:30-4:30pm.

Rage Clothing, 1069 Wisconsin Ave. NW (333-1069), in Georgetown. Faded, ripped, acid-washed, stone-washed, and studded—look no further for classic old jeans. Open Mon.-Thurs. 11am-9pm, Fri.-Sat. 11am-10pm.

Rainbow Artwear, 3001 M St. NW (333-3914), in Georgetown. Eclectic array of beautiful, colorful, handcrafted clothing made from natural fibers. Open Mon.-Wed. 11am-8pm, Thurs. 11am-9pm, Fri.-Sat. 11am-9:30pm, Sun. noon-6pm.

Secondhand Rose, upstairs at 1516 Wisconsin Ave. NW (337-3378), near P St. in Georgetown. Consignment shop for designer women's clothing, shoes, and accessories; merchandise by designers such as Donna Karan, Ralph Lauren, Yves St. Laurent, Chanel, and Anne Klein at less than a third of the original price. Open Mon.-Sat. 10am-6pm. Closed Mon. July-Aug.

Gay, Lesbian, and Bisexual Shops and Services

Lambda Rising, 1625 Connecticut Ave. NW (462-6969), between Q and R St. Largest selection of gay and lesbian literature in the world, including lots of gay and lesbian travel guides. T-shirts ($15-20) and novelty items also available. Serves as an info. center and ticket outlet for concerts and events. Helpful and friendly staff. Occasional book signings and live music. Open daily 10am-midnight.

GLIB BBS, a computerized information and communications service. Call 703-578-GLIB with your computer and a modem. Features on-line chatting, Internet e-mail, message boards, and databases filled with information on bisexual, gay, and lesbian D.C. Free to members/financial supporters of a gay community group, $60 per year otherwise. Definitely worth a look. Demo sessions at Lambda Rising.

Lammas, 1426 21st St. NW at P St. (775-8218). Extensive selection of feminist and lesbian literature. Open Mon.-Sat. 10am-10pm, Sun. 11am-8pm.

The Leather Rack, upstairs at 1723 Connecticut Ave. NW (797-7401). All the leather gear you could possibly want, need, or imagine. A largely gay clientele. Wall of whips ($7-26) and paddles ($20-30). 18+. Open daily 10am-11pm.

Grocery Stores

Addisu Gebaya, 2202 18th St. NW (986-6013), in Adams-Morgan. The smell of incense mingles with that of Ethiopian herbs and spices in this tiny grocery; also stocks clothes, jewels, and magazines. Open Mon.-Sat. 9am-10pm, Sun. 9am-9pm.

Arlington Farmer's Market, at the Arlington Courthouse (Courthouse Rd. and Clarendon Blvd.). Metro: Court House. Farmers sell their fresh fruits, vegetables, flowers, and baked goods. All items must have been produced within a 100-mi. radius, so you know it's the real stuff. Open Sat. 7am-noon.

Da Hua Market, 623 H St. NW (371-8888). Metro: Gallery Place-Chinatown. Chinese market with fresh vegetables as well as almost every canned and bottled good a Chinese kitchen would need. Chicken feet, dried squid, seaweed, and a wide variety of Ramen noodle meals for budgeteers. Open daily 10am-8pm.

El Gavilan, 1646 Columbia Rd. NW (234-9260), between Ontario Rd. and Mozart Pl. in Adams-Morgan. A popular but small store; two aisles crammed with Latin, African, and West Indian groceries all the way up to the ceiling. Open Mon.-Sat. 9am-10:30pm, Sun. 9am-8:30pm.

Firehook Bakery, 106 N. Lee St. (703-519-8020), between King and Cameron St. in Alexandria. Metro: King St. Bread baked daily, in such off-beat flavors as green olive and sage ($4 per loaf). Loaves $1.50-5. Day-old bread ½-price on Mon. Open Mon.-Fri. 7am-7pm, Sat. 7am-6pm, Sun. 8am-6pm.

Jerusalem Butcher, 2116 18th St. NW (265-7100), in Adams-Morgan. Upstairs from Merkato Market. Kosher deli and groceries, cooking supplies, and seasonings. Fresh *halal* meat. Open daily 10am-9pm.

Merkato Market, 2116 18th St. NW (483-9499), near California St. in Adams-Morgan. Down a flight of stairs—look for the green sign. Named for the huge market in Addis Ababa, the Ethiopian capital. Small, airy store with 2 low-rise aisles stocked with Ethiopian food; spices are their specialty. Open daily 9am-10pm.

Middle East Market, 7006 Carroll Ave. (301-270-5154), in Takoma Park. Metro: Takoma. Noodles and cracked wheat ($2). Spices and foodstuffs difficult to obtain elsewhere. Open Mon.-Fri. 10am-7pm, Sat.-Sun. 10am-5pm.

Tivoli Gourmet and Pastry, 2 locations, both in Arlington: 901 Stuart St. (703-528-5200), at the entrance to the Ballston Metro; and 1700 Moore St. (703-524-8902), at the entrance to the Rosslyn Metro. Breathtaking pastry displays, quick quiches, pasta salads, and sandwiches at lunch time, as well as a beautiful selection of cheeses, fresh-baked crusty breads, wines, and meats. Gargantuan cookies 85¢-$1.10 each, muffins 85¢. Open Mon.-Sat. 7am-8pm, Sun. 8:30am-3:30pm.

HEALTH FOOD

Cash Grocer Natural Foods, 1315 King St. (703-549-9544), near West St. in Alexandria. Metro: King St. Walk in past an overflowing bulletin board and piles of health-oriented pamphlets. Vitamins, hand-dipped candles, bulk nuts, and organic produce. Open Mon.-Fri. 10:30am-6:30pm, Sat. 9:30am-6:30pm.

Food For Health, 3804 Wilson Blvd. (703-524-4499), in Arlington. Metro: Virginia Sq./GMU. Vitamins and diet books; wheat germ ($2) and seaweed ($3). Candy (ironically) awaits at the counter. Open Mon.-Sat. 10am-7pm, Sun. noon-6pm.

Yes! Natural Gourmet, 1825 Columbia Rd. NW (462-5150), near 18th St. in Adams-Morgan. Fat-free, meat-free, oil-free, salt-free, sugar-free concoctions. Open Mon.-Sat. 9am-8pm, Sun. noon-6pm. Also at: 3425 Connecticut Ave. NW (363-1559). Metro: Cleveland Park. Open Mon.-Sat. 9am-8pm, Sun. noon-6pm.

Record Stores

Atticus Books, 1508 U St. (667-8148), near 15th St. Metro: U St.-Cardozo. Used books and a good selection of music. Records $1-20, $3-4 on average; CDs $3-9. Open Mon.-Sat. 11am-7pm, Sun. 11am-6pm.

CD Mania, 1083 Wisconsin Ave. NW (337-4979), upstairs at the corner of M St. in Georgetown. New, used, buy-sell-trade. They say they'll beat anyone's price on a new CD. Open Sun. noon-8:30pm, Mon.-Thurs. noon-10pm, Fri.-Sat. noon-11pm.

House of Musical Traditions, 7040 Carroll Ave. (301-270-9090), in Takoma Park. Metro: Takoma. The House boasts a superior instrument collection of everything that ever went twang, wang, bong, boom, or shaka laka from Thailand to Portland. An international collection of folk, rock, and bluegrass music, with tapes and CDs from Ireland, Britain, Hungary, and the Smoky Mountains (among others). Tickets for area folk concerts are available (prices vary; shows usually held at the Silver Spring Unitarian Church). They also repair instruments. Open Tues.-Wed. noon-7pm, Thurs.-Fri. noon-8pm, Sat. 11am-7pm, Sun. 11am-5pm.

The Record Mart, upstairs at 217 King St. (703-683-4583), between Lee and Fairfax St. in Alexandria. Metro: King St. Ascend a staircase plastered with an impressive collage of music posters to reach this shop jam-packed with music aficionados and great used music (mostly LPs). Pick up information on monthly buy-sell-trade conventions. Open Sun.-Thurs. 10am-9pm, Fri.-Sat. 10am-10pm.

12" Dance Records, 2010 P St. NW (659-2010), above the Subway restaurant. Metro: Dupont Circle. Dim lights and a disco ball will make you want to stop awhile. Open Mon.-Thurs. and Sat. noon-9pm, Fri. noon-11:45pm, Sun. 1-6pm.

Military Surplus

Sunny's Affordable Outdoor Store, a Baltimore-based chain with several Washington locations. All sorts of camping equipment and army-like outdoor clothing.

In **Old Downtown:** 917 F St. (737-2032). Metro: Gallery Place-Chinatown. Open Mon.-Sat. 8:30am-6:30pm, Sun. 11am-5pm.

In **Georgetown:** 3342 M St. NW (333-8550). Open Mon.-Wed. 10am-7pm, Thurs.-Fri. 10am-8pm, Sat. 9am-7pm, Sun. 11am-5pm.

In **Farragut:** 1416 H St. NW (347-2774). Metro: McPherson Sq. Open Mon.-Sat. 8:30am-6:30pm, Sun. 11am-5pm.

Specialty and Unusual Shops

CAPITOL HILL

Fairy Godmother, 319 7th St. SE (547-5474). Metro: Eastern Market. On the same block as Eastern Market. Sells games, books, and toys for the young and young at heart. Has blocks ($33) for budding architects, language tapes ($5-20) for budding diplomats, and a large social-studies section for budding senators. Open Mon. noon-6pm, Tues.-Fri. 11am-6pm, Sat. 10am-5pm.

Woven History, 311 7th St. SE (543-1705). Metro: Eastern Market. Beautiful handwoven, vegetable-dyed rugs from over 30 countries ($35-8000+); copper and tile artwork. Many pieces are woven by refugees from Nepal, Pakistan, and India; a portion of the proceeds goes toward the Cultural Survival Rug Weaving Project (dedicated to supporting refugee communities). Open Tues.-Sun. 10am-6pm.

GEORGETOWN

Babbling Books, 1651 Wisconsin Ave. NW (342-1202). Actually part of Washington Video. Books-on-tape for rent, essential for that long drive or ride. Three-day rentals $3.50-6, 7-day rentals $7-10. Return the tapes by mail for an additional $5; on Sun. rent 2 tapes for the price of 1. Open Mon.-Thurs. 10am-10pm, Fri.-Sat. 10am-11:30pm, Sun. noon-10pm.

Fair Trade Market, 1519 Wisconsin Ave. NW (965-4164), between P and Q St. A nonprofit organization that creates jobs for artisans in developing countries, Fair Trade Market offers thousands of handmade items: toys, crafts (carved wooden boxes from India $10), clothing, and cards. A cross-reference guide details each product. Free organic coffee. Open Tues.-Sun. 11am-6pm.

Grafix, 2904 M St. NW (342-0610). Vintage posters, old prints, and custom framing. Unframed pictures from antique magazines start at $5; the cabinets hide scores of affordable, unusual prints. Open Mon.-Fri. 11am-6pm, Sat. 11am-5pm.

Movie Madness, 1222 Wisconsin Ave. NW (337-7064), near M St. As many movie and music posters as can fit into a 15-by-12-ft. room, from recent hits to old idols like Marilyn Monroe and James Dean. Postcards for the frugal. Movie stills: color $4.50, black-and-white $3. Poster prices $5-20. Open Mon.-Thurs. 11am-9pm, Fri.-Sat. 11am-10pm, Sun. noon-7pm.

The Pleasure Place, 1063 Wisconsin Ave. NW (333-8570), near M St. in Georgetown. Kinkier underwear than Frederick's of Hollywood and sex toys you'd expect to find on 14th St. Stock up on panties, pasties, and massaging oils. 19+. Open Mon.-Tues. 10am-10pm, Wed.-Sat. 10am-midnight, Sun. noon-7pm.

S&A Beads, 3143 N St. NW (337-2204), in Georgetown. A spacious setting for a wide variety of domestic and imported beads. String your own. Open Mon.-Thurs. 11am-7pm, Fri.-Sat. 11am-8pm, Sun. 11am-6pm.

FARRAGUT

Capitol Coin and Stamp Co. of Washington, D.C., 1701 L St. NW (296-0400). Metro: Farragut North. This small store specializes in items of philatelic interest, political pins, posters, and banners. Probably the only place where you can still buy a Barry Goldwater doll ($45) or a Cuomo/Iacocca pin. Spoof paraphernalia abounds for the disenchanted. Open Mon.-Fri. 10am-6pm, Sat. 10am-5:30pm.

The Map Store, 1636 I St. NW (628-2608), across from Farragut Square. Metro: Farragut West. Maps ($2.50-13), globes, road atlases, and guides for the traveler. And, of course, *Let's Go* books galore. Stop here before hitting the road. Open Mon.-Fri. 9am-5:30pm, Sat. 10am-4pm.

DUPONT CIRCLE

Backstage, Inc., 2101 P St. NW (775-1488), at 21st St. Metro: Dupont Circle. A veritable caucus of rubber politicians greets thespians as they enter D.C.'s only theater store, which trafficks in everything from scripts and scores to costumes and criticism. Open Mon.-Wed. and Fri.-Sat. 10am-6pm, Thurs. 10am-7pm.

The Pleasure Place, 1710 Connecticut Ave. NW (483-3297), near R St. Metro: Dupont Circle. See complete listing above. Open Mon.-Tues. 10am-10pm, Wed.-Sat. 10am-midnight, Sun. noon-7pm.

SHAW/ U DISTRICT

Boutique Mikuba, 1359 U St. NW (483-6877), near 14th St. Metro: U St.-Cardozo. A crowded store specializing in African art, jewelry, and clothing. Open Mon.-Thurs. 11:30am-9pm, Fri. 11am-11pm, Sat. 11am-9pm.

ADAMS-MORGAN

Oya's Mini Bazaar/Beads Outlet, 2420 18th St. NW (667-9853). Stacked to the ceiling with crafts and accessories from around the world. Woven handbags, wooden beads, toys, and jewelry at great prices. Open daily 12:30-11pm.

Peruvian Silver House, 2438½ 18th St. NW (387-7528). Silver jewelry, Aztec, Mayan, Ethiopian, and Mexican crafts. Open daily noon-9pm.

ALEXANDRIA, VA

Angie's Doll Boutique, 1114 King St. (703-683-2807), at Fayette St. Dolls, dolls, dolls: from the most exquisite to the latest Barbie. Beware of browsing with a 7-yr.-old. Open Tues.-Sat. 11am-5:30pm.

Bavarian Alps, 924 King St. (703-683-3994), at Patrick St. The tackiest German gift store you've ever seen, and proudly so: wall-to-wall steins and nutcrackers. The red door is open Tues.-Sat. 10am-6pm, Sun. noon-5pm.

Birds in the Cage, upstairs at 110 King St. (703-549-5114), near Union St. A smattering (mess?) of vintage ball gowns, jewelry, antiques, pop art, and birds in cages. Clock repair. Irregular hours; in general, open Mon.-Thurs. 11am-9pm, Fri.-Sat. 11am-midnight, Sun. 11am-9pm.

John Crouch Tobacconist/The Scottish Merchant, 215 King St. (703-548-2900), between Fairfax and Lee St. "If it's not Scottish, it's *crap!*" Kilts, pipes, clan memorabilia, smoking paraphernalia, and Scottish travel guides. Open Mon.-Thurs. 10am-10pm, Fri.-Sat. 10am-11pm, Sun. 11am-9pm.

The Washington Antiques Center, 209 Madison St. (703-739-2484), in Alexandria. More than 20 antique dealers in one place, all selling 18th- to early 20th-century doodads. Weekends mean free parking. Open daily 11am-6pm.

Daytripping from D.C.

The torrid sun and oppressive humidity of Washington summers can really drain those unaccustomed to the city's sweltering temperatures. With a Congressman's fortune (vacation days, that is) and the desire for a quick respite from the scorching pavement, an urban dweller can jump in a car, turn up the radio, and head out to the cool serenity of the Atlantic or the shade of the lush Virginia countryside. Baltimore, Richmond, and Charlottesville lend an urbane change of pace. (A note to those without a car: most of these places can be reached by train or bus.)

Listed below are the D.C.-area getaways covered in this book. The more distant destinations might be considered weekend trips.

Annapolis, MD: 45min.-1hr. driving; 40min. by bus.
Baltimore, MD: 45min. driving; 30-40min. by train; 55min. by bus.
Fairfax County, VA: 30min. driving; 1hr. by tourbus; 1½hr. by boat.
Shenandoah National Park, VA: 1hr. and 10min. driving.
Charlottesville, VA: 2½hr. driving; 2¼hr. by train; 2½hr. by bus.
Richmond, VA: 2hr. driving; 2hr. by train; 2¼hr. by bus.
Williamsburg, VA: 3hr. driving; 3¼hr. by train; 4hr. by bus.
Jamestown, Yorktown, and the James River Plantations, VA: 3hr. driving.
Virginia Beach, VA: 4hr. driving; 5hr. by train; 6½hr. by bus.
Harpers Ferry, WV: 1½hr. driving; 1hr. by train.

THE REST OF MARYLAND

Once upon a time, the picturesque, shellfish-rich estuary of Chesapeake Bay ruled the Maryland economy. On the rural eastern shore, small-town Marylanders captured crabs and raised tobacco. Across the bay in Baltimore, workers ate the crabs, loaded ships, and ran factories. Then the federal government expanded, industry shrank, and Maryland had a new, more slender core: not the bay, but the Baltimore-Washington Parkway. Suburbs grew up and down the corridor, Baltimore revitalized, and the Old Line State acquired a new, liberal urbanity. As D.C.'s homogenized commuter suburbs swell beyond the limits of Maryland's Montgomery and Prince Georges counties, Baltimore revels in its immensity while Annapolis, the capital, remains a small-town commune for sailors. The mountains and mines of the state's western panhandle—geographic and cultural kin to West Virginia—are to this day largely undeveloped. If anything brings this state together, it may be a sense of proportion: forests and fields encompass but never overwhelm, rivers and islands are not too big to be thoroughly explored, and cities are too small to engulf even the most provincial of tourists.

Annapolis

One of the premier yachting communities in the U.S., Annapolis walks the fine line between nostalgia and anachronism. With its brick-paved sidewalks and narrow streets, the historic waterfront district retains its 18th-century appeal despite the presence of ritzy boutiques and pricey retail stores. The capital of Maryland, Annapolis seems less concerned with modern legislative decisions than with commemorating past statesmanship with plaques and restored historical houses. Crew-cut "middies" (a nickname for Naval Academy students, or "midshipmen") mingle with longer-haired students from St. John's and couples on weekend getaways. Indeed, Annapolis caters to the military, intellectual, and financial elite.

Settled in 1649 with the rest of Maryland, Annapolis was declared the capital in 1694. The ubiquitous fine Georgian houses once held colonial aristocrats (and their slaves). Annapolis made real history when the Continental Congress ratified the

Treaty of Paris here in 1784, making official the end of the American Revolution. After its 1783-1784 stint as temporary capital of the U.S. (hot on the heels of Philadelphia, New York, and Trenton, NJ), Annapolis relinquished the national limelight in favor of a more tranquil, yet equally wealthy existence.

PRACTICAL INFORMATION AND ORIENTATION

Visitor Information: Annapolis and Anne Arundel County Conference & Visitors Bureau, 26 West St. (268-8687). Open daily 9am-5pm. On-the-spot questions can be answered at the **information desk** at the State House (841-3810). Desk open daily 10am-5pm.

Greyhound/Trailways: (800-231-2222). Buses stop at the MTA at the **football field** at Rowe Blvd. and Taylor Ave. Tickets are available from the bus driver; cash only. To: **Washington, D.C.** (2 per day, 1hr., $7.50); **Philadelphia** (2 per day, 7½hr., $42); **Baltimore** (2 per day, 3hr., $9).

Mass Transit Administration: (539-5000, Mon.-Fri. 6am-9pm, customer service rep. available). To: **Baltimore** Express #210 runs Mon.-Fri. (1hr., $2.85); local #14 runs daily (1½hr., $2.25). Call for times. Buses leave from St. John's and College Ave. and St. John's and Calvert St. Exact change required.

Public Transportation: Annapolis Dept. of Public Transportation (263-7964). Operates a web of city buses connecting the historic district with the rest of town. Buses run Mon.-Sat. 5:30am-10pm, Sun. 8am-7pm.

Taxi: Annapolis Cab Co. (268-0022); **Checker Cab** (268-3737).

Help Lines: Rape and Sexual Assault Crisis Center: 222-7273. **Youth Crisis Hotline:** 800-422-0009. **Poison Center:** 800-492-2414. All lines 24hr.

Emergency: 911

Post Office: One Church Circle (263-9292). Open Mon.-Fri. 8:30am-5pm. **ZIP Code:** 21401.

Area Code: 410.

Annapolis lies southeast of U.S. 50 (also known as U.S. 301), 30 mi. east of D.C. and 30 mi. south of Baltimore. From D.C. take U.S. 50 east. In D.C., 50 begins at New York Ave. and can be accessed from the Beltway. From Baltimore, follow Rte. 2 south to U.S. 50 west, cross the Severn River Bridge, then take Rowe Blvd.

The city extends south and east from two landmarks: **Church Circle** and **State Circle.** School St., in a blatantly unconstitutional move, connects Church and State. Maryland Ave. runs from the State House to the Naval Academy. Main St. (where food and entertainment congregate) starts at Church Circle and ends at the docks. Those who should happen to lose their bearings in Annapolis (it's difficult to do) can reorient themselves by looking for the State House dome or St. Anne's spire. Annapolis is compact and easily walkable, but finding a parking space—unless in a lot for a fee or in the public garage ($5-8 per day)—can be tricky.

ACCOMMODATIONS

Bed and breakfasts abound in this self-consciously quaint town, while motels are harder to come by; either way, it's going to cost you. The Visitors Information Centers have brochures on B&Bs and hotels in the area. Rooms should be reserved in advance, especially for the busy summer months. **Bed and Breakfasts of Maryland** (800-736-4667, ext. 15) aids in arranging accommodations in Annapolis. To travel in pairs is the most economical choice; two people share a room for only $5-15 more than the single rate in most of these establishments. Some rates fluctuate depending on demand; it's to your advantage to ask around and sound unconvinced.

Gibson's Lodgings, 110 Prince George St. (268-5555). One block from city dock on Randall St. Gibson's offers a patio and spacious common parlors for relaxing in elegance. With only 6 rooms, the 200-year-old Patterson House is the cheapest of the 3 buildings. Complimentary continental breakfast, free courtyard parking, and conference facilities provided. Singles $58-98, doubles $68-113. Roll away beds for a 3rd person $15 extra. 40% discount during off-season (Jan. 3-Feb. 28).

Daytripping Area
To Breezewood, PA
To Harrisburg, PA
PENNSYLVANIA
70
81
Cumberland
Hagerstown
48
Morgantown
522
70
Martinsburg
81
Stony River
50
50
Harpers Ferry
340
220
Potomac River
50
7
Winchester
219
WEST VIRGINIA
32
Elkins
33
28
55
17/50
15
81
17
50
Front Royal
66
Manassas
Warrenton
211
MONONGAHELA NATIONAL FOREST
250
211
SHENANDOAH NATIONAL PARK
BLUE RIDGE MTNS.
522
Culpeper
17
33
Harrisonburg
GEORGE WASHINGTON NATIONAL FOREST
220
250
81
Fredericksbu
Waynesboro
64
Charlottesville
N. Anna
29
VIRGINIA
Blue Ridge Pkwy.
Clifton Forge
Lexington
Buena Vista
James R.
33
64
81
15
Amherst
Buckingham
60
60
Appomattox R.
Lynchburg
360
Roanoke
460
Burkeville
460
Altavista
360
360
Roanoke R.
85
15
29
Meherrin R.

To Harrisburg, PA
To York, PA
Philadelphia
To NYC
PENNSYLVANIA
ARYLAND
NEW JERSEY
Shenandoah R.
Aberdeen
Edgewood
Betterton
Frederick
Towson
Essex
Baltimore
Rockville
Wheaton
Bowie
Bethesda
Annapolis
Arlington
WASHINGTON, D.C.
Alexandria
Dover
Delaware Bay
DELAWARE
Lewes
Rehoboth Beach
Cambridge
Salisbury
Ocean City
Lexington Park
Potomac River
Rappahannock R.
Chesapeake Bay
Pocomoke City
Assateague Island
Chincoteague
Mattaponi R.
Richmond
York R.
ATLANTIC OCEAN
N
Hopewell
Williamsburg
Petersburg
Colonial Heights
James R.
Hampton
Newport News
Cape Charles
Chesapeake Bay Bridge-Tunnel
Cape Henry
Virginia Beach
Nottoway R.
Portsmouth
Norfolk
0
30 miles
45 km

Scotlaur Inn, 165 Main St. (268-5665), atop Chick and Ruth's Delly. Ten guest rooms with A/C, color TVs, and private baths grace this homey "bed & bagel," which is less fancy than some of the other B&Bs, but far more affordable. Mammoth breakfasts are available from Chick & Ruth's (see listing under **Food**). Check-in 2pm; check-out 11am. Rates vary with room ($55-75, $5 per extra person) special rates are sometimes available.

Dolls' House Bed and Breakfast, 161 Green St. (626-2028). One block off Main St. Each of 3 rooms has a theme; charming Victoria and Sun rooms with private hall baths sleep 1 or 2 for $85, while the Nutcracker Suite sleeps up to 6 for $140 ($110 as a double). The wicker-furnished front porch vies with a beautiful back deck and garden. Check or cash only.

EconoLodge Annapolis, 2451 Riva Rd. (224-4317), 2½mi. from Historic Annapolis. With rooms starting at $69, it's hard to find the "econo" in EconoLodge. Rooms have cable TV and VCR; continental breakfast is included.

FOOD

Middleton Tavern, 2 Market Space (263-3323), at Randall St. by the dock. Established in 1750 and frequented by members of the Continental Congress, Middleton Tavern sports stuffed trophies, Revolutionary War muskets, and a Civil War uniform hanging from exposed beams. Excellent "appetizer" pastas easily make a full meal ($7). Delicious seafood lasagna $8; burgers and sandwiches $5-8. Nightly music gets the crowd rocking as they gulp down oysters from the raw bar. Open Mon.-Fri. 11:30am-1am, Sat.-Sun. 10am-1am. Fri.-Sat. piano bar upstairs; Sun. local jazz and blues. Food served daily until midnight.

Chick & Ruth's Delly, 165 Main St. (269-6737). With dishes satirically named for local and national politicians, this deli is truly an Annapolis institution, having served the city all-day breakfast for over 30 years. Omelettes ($3-6), corned beef sandwiches ($4), and malted milkshakes ($2.50) highlight an inexpensive and delicious menu. Open 24hr.

New Moon Café, 137 Prince George St. (280-1955). The only place in Annapolis to find a creative cup of coffee, a healthful meal, and a Eurocafé atmosphere all under the same roof. Menu is organically inclined. Moon Burger (non-fat, all-soy) $4.75. Turkey dog $3.75. Extensive coffee selection ($1-3). Monday nights offer poetry readings starting at 7pm. Open Mon.-Fri. 9am-3pm and 5pm-midnight, Sat.-Sun. 8am-midnight.

City Dock Café, 18 Market Space (269-0969), at Pinkney St. Cool, calm coffeehouse adds sophistication to Annapolis with its Frank Lloyd Wright-esque interior and great espresso drinks ($1-3). The quiche and gazpacho please tourists and regulars alike. Open Mon.-Thurs. 6:30am-10pm, Fri. 6:30am-midnight, Sat. 7am-midnight, Sun. 7am-10pm.

Buddy's Crabs & Ribs, 100 Main St. (626-1100), on the 2nd fl. above Banana Republic. A bright, sterile, touristy warehouse o' seafood; Buddy's offers a variety of all-you-can-eat buffets for breakfast, lunch, and dinner ($6-8). Happy hour features $1.50 domestic drafts (weekdays 4-7pm). Appetizers $3.50-12, entrees $9-19. Open Mon.-Thurs. 11am-10pm, Fri.-Sat. 11am-11pm, Sun. 8:30am-10pm.

Mum's, 136 Dock St. (263-3353), at the dock. This waterfront bar and restaurant sports a jukebox and $5-8.50 sandwiches. Wild mushroom and roasted garlic pizza ($5.75) and the cajun-style tuna steak sandwich ($7) are surprisingly well done. DJs and live bands provide music nightly. Open Mon.-Fri. 8:30am-2am, Sat.-Sun. 9am-2am.

Storm Bros. Ice Cream Factory, 130 Dock St. (263-3376). A great view of the ships at the dock accompanies the enticing 45 flavors of ice cream and 3 flavors of yogurt. $1.15 for a scoop, $2 for 2, $2.35 for 3. Open Mon.-Fri. 10:30am-11pm, Sat.-Sun. 10:30am-midnight.

Carrol's Creek Bar & Café, 410 Severn Ave. (263-8102), in the Annapolis City Marina Complex, across the Eastport Bridge from Annapolis proper. Wed. night attracts yachting enthusiasts to a fantastic view of the finish line. Carrol's is a favorite for Texas BBQ shrimp (from the Lite Fare menu, $8). Weekdays 4-7pm happy hour boasts 95¢ 10-oz. beers and $2 pints and rails, in addition to a complimentary buffet. Open daily 11:30am-10:30pm.

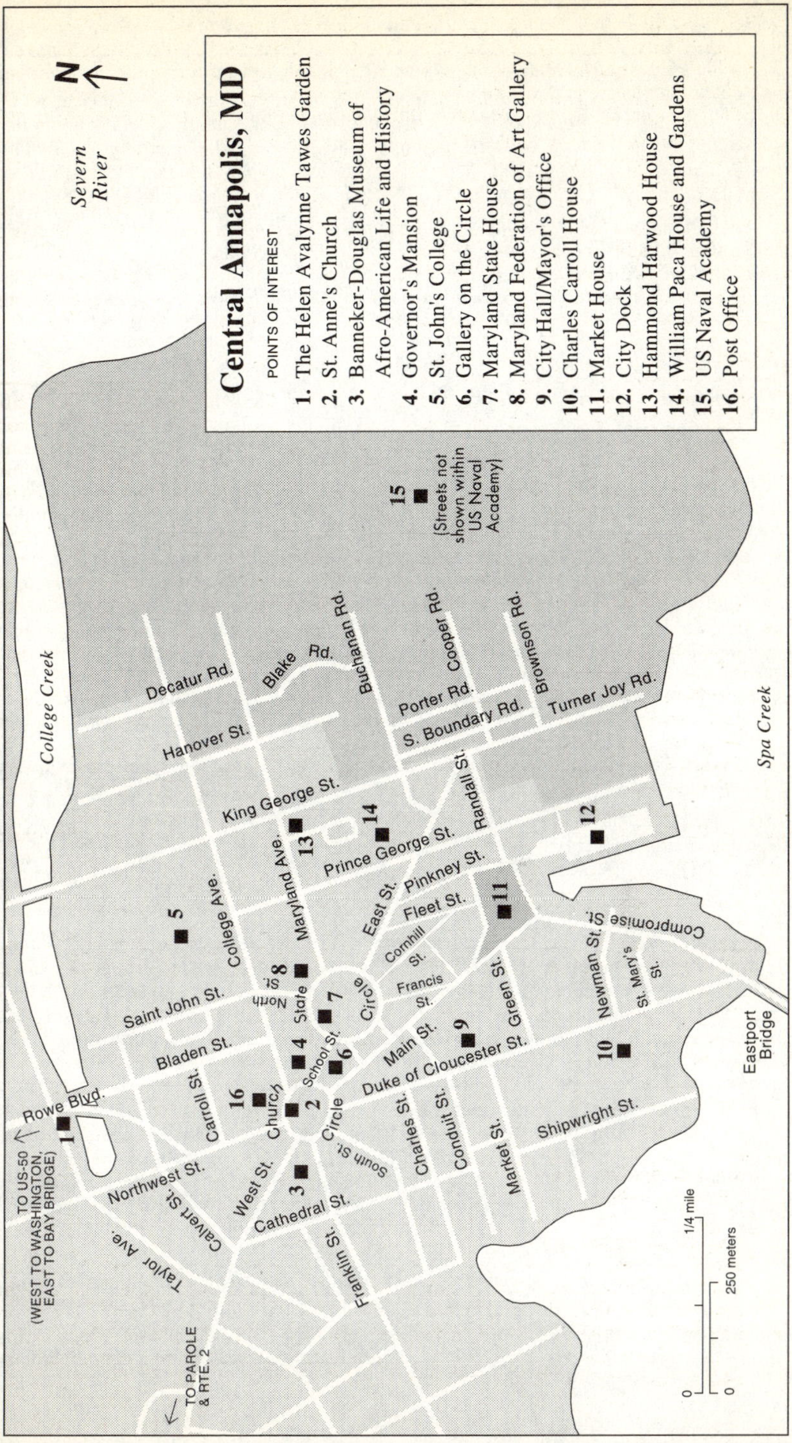

DAYTRIPPING

SIGHTS

Inside the Corinthian-columned **State House,** Maryland maps and brochures are available at the information desk, where helpful volunteers are on hand to answer questions. Built from 1772 to 1779, it's the oldest working state house in the nation, and served as the U.S.'s capitol building from 1783 to 1784. The *Treaty of Paris* was signed here on January 14, 1784. Visitors can explore the history exhibits and silver collection, or watch the state legislature bicker (in two exquisitely adorned marble halls) if the senators and delegates are in session (from the 2nd Wed. in Jan. until mid-April). (Open daily 9am-5pm; free tours at 11am and 3pm.)

From State Circle, Maryland Ave. meets up with the historic **Hammond-Harwood House,** hovering at 19 Maryland Ave., at King George St. (269-1714). This elegant 1774 building, the last one designed by Colonial architect William Buckland, retains period decor right down to the candlesticks. (Open Mon.-Sat. 10am-4pm, Sun. noon-4pm. Tours on the hr.; last tour 1hr. before closing. Admission $4, ages 6-18 $3. AAA discounts: admission $3.50, students $2.50. Uniformed armed service personnel free.) The garden in the back can be enjoyed for free.

A right onto King George St., then another onto Martin St. reveals an unimposing parking lot and the sign for the **William Paca Garden,** 42 East St. (263-5553). The end of Martin St. is the site of the well-preserved fire department; a right turn onto East St., past the Brice House, and another right onto Prince George St. brings one to the entrance to the companion museum, the **William Paca House,** 186 Prince George St. (263-5553). William Paca, an early governor of Maryland, was one of the signers of the *Declaration of Independence.* Visitors to his beautifully restored estate will find a 1765 grandfather clock still ticking inside and trellises, water lilies, and gazebos outside. Preservationists rescued the garden from beneath a bus station and parking lot. Tours are given when enough people have gathered; those interested should arrive at least an hour before closing. (House open daily 10am-4pm, Sun. noon-4pm; Jan.-Feb. Fri.-Sat. 10am-4pm, Sun. noon-4pm. Admission to house $4, garden $3. Both $6.) **Joint tickets** ($9) are also available for both the Hammond-Harwood and William Paca houses.

The smell of food and the sound of tourists may lure you down Pinkney St. towards the **City Dock.** Restaurants and tacky tourist shops line the waterfront, a convenient **information kiosk** answers questions, and boats leave on maritime tours from April to the first week in October (Mon.-Fri. every hour 11am-4pm, Sat.-Sun. every hour 11am-6pm). Naval Academy ships (in summertime skippered by fresh-faced plebes) ply the waters. The civilian yachtsmen can be seen congregating, drinking beer, and flexing—the docks easily earn their nickname, "Ego Alley."

Dedicated to the preservation of Maryland's African-American heritage, the **Banneker-Douglass Museum** (974-2893), at 84 Franklin St., adjacent to Church Circle, is named after two eminent black Marylanders: Benjamin Banneker and Frederick Douglass. The museum is housed in the Victorian-Gothic Mount Moriah African Methodist Episcopal Church, and in turn houses temporary exhibits and photographs concerning African-American cultural history (open Tues.-Fri. 10am-3pm, Sat. noon-4pm; free).

From Church Circle, a walk along College Ave. past St. John's St., and a left turn puts you on the campus of **St. John's College** (founded in 1696 as King William's School). This small, liberal arts college is the third oldest in the nation (after Harvard and William and Mary) and graduates each of its students from the same academic program, the Great Books curriculum. Implemented in 1937, the curriculum dictates a four-year program of required courses including math and science, languages, music, and the study of tomes by great authors from Homer to Freud. The campus is home to the **Liberty Tree,** a presence perhaps older than the college; the giant tulip poplar has witnessed everything from the treaties of Indians and colonists to the rallies of revolutionaries to the encampment of Union soldiers. The tree's name, though derived from the 16th-century territorial resolutions, is just as appropriate to an event

Sandy Point

Sometimes sitting on the dock and contemplating the water can get a little old. A 15-minute drive east on Rte. 50 (crossing the Severn River Bridge) will bring recreational activities-seekers to exit 32, and **Sandy Point State Park**. During the summer months, for a $2 per person entrance fee (Wed. ½ price), park visitors can barbecue, picnic, and swim. **Jet ski rentals** (410-757-7500) are $45 for ½hr., $65 for a full hr. Rentals available from mid-May to mid-Sept., Mon.-Fri. 11am-5pm, Sat.-Sun. 10am-6pm. $250 deposit or credit card required. The park is open every day of the year except Christmas and Thanksgiving, approx. 6am-9pm during summer months, and approx. 8am-5pm during the winter. Call 410-974-2149 for specific hours and additional information.

that continues to take place in its shade: St. John's annual springtime commencement.

College Ave. can be followed further to King George St., which leads to an institution whose name typifies Annapolis: the **U.S. Naval Academy.** At the U.S. Naval Academy, harried, short-haired "plebes" (first-year students) in official sailor dress try desperately to remember the words of Navy fight songs while the rest of the undergraduates, "middies" (midshipmen), go about their business (which often includes bonking the plebes on the head and other, less loving punishments). President Jimmy Carter graduated from Annapolis; more recently, the institution has made headlines for expelling its gay and lesbian students.

Named for George Bancroft, founder of the first Naval school, **Bancroft Hall** houses the entire student body in an imposing stone structure about three blocks long, making it one of the world's largest dormitories. The mammoth steps, stonework, and arched entryways suit its function as a cathedral of imparted wisdom and discipline. In the yard outside Bancroft Hall, visitors can witness the middies' noon lineup and formations. Traditionally, kissing the bronze statue of Tecumseh that stands out front garners good luck. (The rest of Bancroft Hall is closed to tourists.)

A couple of Japanese torpedoes sit at the north end of **Dahlgren Hall** (they reside outside as a general reminder of enemy threat). The hangar-like hall harbors a gymnasium, ice rink, and café, in addition to a huge model sailing ship and a yellow water-landing biplane that hang from the arched ceiling.

King Hall, the academy's gargantuan mess hall, turns madhouse at lunchtime, serving the entire brigade in under four minutes. On summer Saturdays, wedding after wedding (sometimes one per hour) take place in the Academy's **chapel;** middies, however, aren't allowed to marry before graduation. As the married couples leave the chapel, they walk beneath the raised swords of eight male classmates; and the woman, if she is a civilian, is greeted by a ninth with "Welcome to the Navy, Ma'am" (open to visitors Mon.-Sat. 9am-4pm, Sun. 1-4pm).

Elsewhere on campus, the Naval Museum in **Preble Hall** houses two rooms of naval artifacts (open Mon.-Sat. 9am-5pm, Sun. 11am-5pm; free). Antique swords, model ships, and the personal belongings of American prisoners of war are among the most fascinating exhibits. Walking tours of the academy begin at the **Armel-Leftwich Visitors Center** (263-6933) located in the Halsey Field House at the end of King George St. (Call for information on tour times. $5, seniors $4, students $3.) Throughout the summer, the academy provides entertainment for the general public, from parades and sporting events to movies and concerts. The schedule of events is published in the *Trident,* the academy's newspaper, which can be obtained for free at the visitors center.

NIGHTLIFE

Locals and tourists generally engage in one of two activities: wandering along City Dock or schmoozing/boozing at upscale Annapolitan pubs. Theater-goers can check out **The Colonial Players, Inc.**, 108 East St. (268-7373; performances Thurs.-Sun. at 8pm, additional Sun. show at 2:30pm. Thurs. and Sun. $7 (students and seniors $5),

The Games People Play

Although never mistaken for an athletic powerhouse, St. John's college nevertheless has an interesting sports tradition all its own. Each year, the undergrads of St. John's engage in a contest of pure athletic prowess—**Spartan Madball.** The game, a distant cousin of Capture-the-Flag, has only three rules: no shoes, no weapons, and no motor vehicles. Freshmen and juniors side up against sophomores and seniors, and the game is over either when one of the teams wins or someone is taken to the hospital—whichever comes first.

Of course, with the Navy in town, St. John's is overshadowed on most playing fields. The one exception? Croquet. Each year the local rivals do battle with mallets, and St. John's is the perennial winner. In Annapolis, Army-Navy may be a high-caliber rivalry, but to the students of St. John's, it is a victorious afternoon on the croquet green that awards the license to brag.

Fri.-Sat. $10.) Bars and taverns line downtown Annapolis, drawing crowds every night. The fact that you just had dinner at the **Middleton Tavern** shouldn't stop you from partying there later. The same is true for **New Moon Café,** where local jazz bands perform sporadically.

McGarvey's, 8 Garden St. (263-5700). This traditional dark-wood saloon is a favorite watering hole among the locals. Mon. and Wed. happy hour (10pm-2am) features buffalo wings, 32-oz. drafts for $2.75, and 10-oz. mugs for $1. Thurs. offers a $1.50 special on Aviator microbrew. A remarkable atmosphere is created by authentic pilot helmets, Casablanca circulation systems, and a candlelit mezzanine level. Open Mon.-Sat. 11:30am-2am, Sun. 10am-midnight.

Armadillo's, 132 Dock St. (268-6680). Armadillo's caters to a casual, comfortable clientele; happy hour (3:30-6:30pm) offers $1 buffalo wings, Mexican pizza, jalapeño bullets, and discounted beer. Their entertainment hotline (626-1551) provides information on the nightly live music, starting at 9:30pm. 21+ upstairs. Open daily 9am-1:30am.

Ram's Head Tavern, 33 West St. (268-4545). Beer connoisseurs, midshipmen, and tourists enjoy 160 different kinds of beers, including microbrew from Germany, England, and—of course—the U.S. Happy hour (weekdays 4-7pm) provides free food and reduced prices on drafts. Steaks ($14-22) are a popular form of sustenance. Open Mon.-Sat. 11am-2am, Sun. 10am-2am.

Marmaduke's Pub, Severn Ave at 3rd. 15-min. walk down Compromise St. across from the Eastport Bridge. Sailors flock here Wed. nights to watch videos of their sailboat races and enjoy the beer-and-burger special ($5). Happy hour (4-7pm nightly) features discounted rails and $1 Miller and Rolling Rock beers. Weekend piano bar offers showtunes upstairs for a $3 cover. Open daily 11:30am-2am.

Buddy's Late Night Annapolis, 30 Hudson St. (266-5888). The first and only dance club in town boasts the biggest bar and dance floor in the state. Buddy's rocks to Top 40 tunes and attracts all ages and types despite its distance from the center of town. It's big, bright, and always busy. Nightly beer specials. 21+. Free before 10pm; cover: Wed. $3; Thurs. $3 for men (free for women), Fri.-Sat. $6. Open Wed.-Sat. 8:30pm-2am.

Baltimore

Of the external embellishments of life there is a plenty there—as great a supply, indeed, to any rational taste, as in New York itself. But there is also something much better: a tradition of sound and comfortable living.

—H.L. Mencken, On Living in Baltimore, 1926

Seventy years later, Mencken's Baltimore-New York City parallel still holds true. Baltimore maintains a well-touristed waterfront district adjacent to its commercially oriented downtown—though on a scale much smaller than that of the Big Apple. And amidst Baltimore's modern, industrial harbor are reminders of a distinguished past and a glorious present: historic stone drawbridges compete with new steel structures, and the old Baltimore & Ohio Railroad contrasts with the sleek, glass-windowed skyline. Modern Baltimore still serves as Maryland's urban core, and old-time, shirtsleeve Bawlmer endures in the quiet limelight of Anne Tyler's novels and John Waters' films. Near the downtown skyscrapers, old ethnic neighborhoods like Little Italy front Baltimore's signature rowhouses, whose unique façades are microcosms of the larger city—polished marble stoops represent the shiny Inner Harbor, while straightforward brick fits the gritty urban environs, many of which are experiencing hostile race relations. But Baltimore's treasures—the National Aquarium, Camden Yards, and crabs—more than atone for its shortcomings; the city retains a tradition of "sound and comfortable living" seasoned with tourism.

PRACTICAL INFORMATION AND ORIENTATION

Visitor Information: Baltimore Area Visitors Centers, 300 W. Pratt St. (659-7000 or 800-282-6632), at S. Howard St. 4 blocks from Harborplace. Provides a map, armfuls of pamphlets, and *Quick City Guide* (a quarterly glossy with excellent maps and events listings). Open daily 9am-5:30pm. An often crowded **information booth** on the west shoreline of the Inner Harbor, between the Light St. Pavilion and the National Aquarium, offers similar info. Open daily 9am-5:30pm.

Travelers Aid: 685-3569 (Mon.-Fri. 8am-4:30pm), 685-5874 (hotline staffed Mon.-Fri. 4:30-11pm, Sat.-Sun. and holidays 8am-11pm). Two desks are situated at the Baltimore-Washington Airport (859-7209; open Mon.-Fri. 9am-9pm, Sun. 1pm-9pm). Direct-line telephones are at Penn Station and at the Greyhound terminal.

Baltimore-Washington International Airport (BWI): 859-7111. On I-195 off the Baltimore-Washington Expressway (I-295), about 10mi. south of the city center. Use BWI as a gateway to Baltimore or Washington, D.C. Take MTA bus #17 to the N. Linthicum Light rail station. Airport shuttles to hotels (724-0009) run daily every ½hr. 5:45am-11:30pm ($10 to downtown Baltimore, $15 round-trip). For D.C., shuttles leave every hr. 5:45am-11:30pm ($21-29). Trains from BWI Airport run to Baltimore ($5; at $3.25, **MARC** trains are considerably cheaper but also slower and only run Mon.-Fri.). To Washington, D.C. ($10; MARC $6).

Amtrak: Penn Station, 1500 N. Charles St. (800-872-7245), at Mt. Royal Ave. Easily accessible by bus #3 or 11 from Charles Station downtown. Trains run about every ½hr. to: New York ($58-74, Metroliner $99), Washington, D.C. ($16-18, Metroliner $22), and Philadelphia ($31-36, Metroliner $58). On weekdays, two **MARC commuter lines** connect Baltimore to D.C.'s Union Station (859-7400; 800-325-7245). The Penn line runs out of Penn Station (and stops at BWI airport), while the Camden line runs out of Camden Station, at the corner of Howard and Camden St. near Oriole Park. Both are $5.25 one-way, $9.50 round-trip. Ticket window open daily 5:30am-9:30pm, self-serve open 24hr. (credit card only).

Greyhound: 2 locations: downtown at 210 W. Fayette St. (752-1393), near N. Howard St.; and at 5625 O'Donnell St. (744-9311), 3mi. east of downtown near I-95. Frequent connections to: New York (one-way $23.50, round-trip $39), Washington, D.C. ($6, round-trip $12), and Philadelphia ($12, round-trip $20).

Public Transport: Mass Transit Administration (MTA), 300 W. Lexington St. (bus and Metro schedule info. 539-5000, recorded info. 333-2700, 800-543-9809), near N. Howard St. Operator available Mon.-Fri. 6am-9pm. Bus, Metro, and light-rail service to most major sights in the city; service to outlying areas is more complicated. Some buses run 24hr. Metro operates Mon.-Fri. 5am-midnight, Sat. 6am-midnight. Light rail operates Mon.-Fri. 6am-11pm, Sat. 8am-11pm, Sun. 11am-7pm. Base fare for all of these $1.25, but may be higher depending on distance traveled. Transfers 10¢. Bus #17 runs from the N. Linthicum light-rail to BWI.

Water Taxi: (563-3901 or 800-658-8947) Stops every 8-18min. (every 40min. Nov.-March) at the harbor museums, Harborplace, Fells Point, Little Italy, and more. An easy, pleasant way to travel to Baltimore's main sights, especially in summer—service continues until 11pm or midnight. Price varies; a pass for a full day of unlimited rides usually runs $3.50 for adults, $2.25 for children 10 and under.

Taxi: Yellow Cab (685-1212); **Royal Cab** (327-0330).

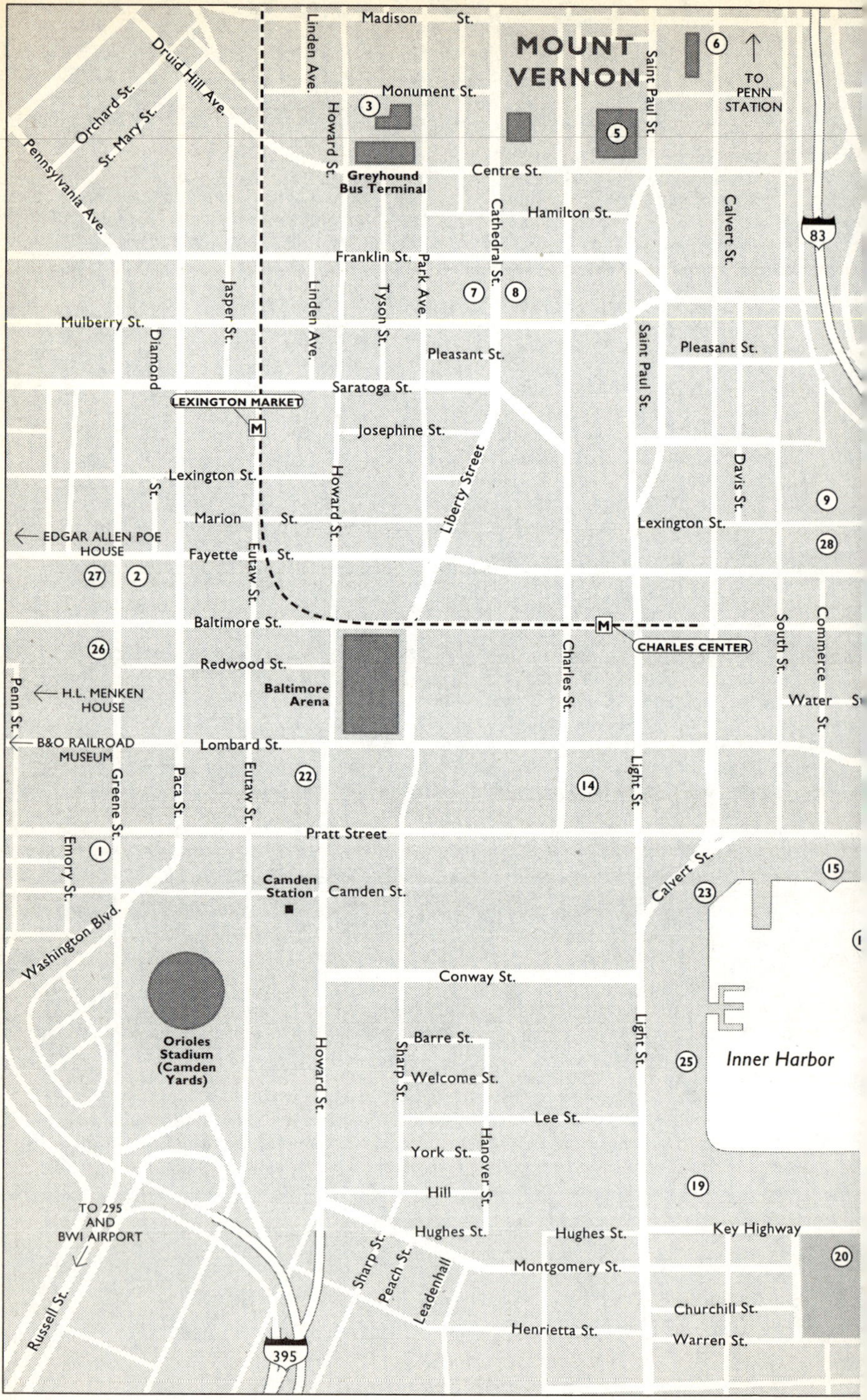
MOUNT VERNON
TO PENN STATION
Madison St.
Monument St.
Centre St.
Hamilton St.
Franklin St.
Mulberry St.
Pleasant St.
Saratoga St.
Josephine St.
Lexington St.
Marion St.
Fayette St.
Baltimore St.
Redwood St.
Lombard St.
Pratt Street
Camden St.
Conway St.
Barre St.
Welcome St.
Lee St.
York St.
Hill
Hughes St.
Montgomery St.
Henrietta St.
Churchill St.
Warren St.
Key Highway
Druid Hill Ave.
Orchard St.
St. Mary St.
Pennsylvania Ave.
Linden Ave.
Howard St.
Cathedral St.
Park Ave.
Tyson St.
Jasper St.
Diamond St.
Saint Paul St.
Calvert St.
Davis St.
Liberty Street
Eutaw St.
Charles St.
Light St.
South St.
Commerce St.
Water St.
Penn St.
Greene St.
Paca St.
Emory St.
Washington Blvd.
Russell St.
Sharp St.
Peach St.
Leadenhall
Hanover St.
Calvert St.
Greyhound Bus Terminal
LEXINGTON MARKET
CHARLES CENTER
Baltimore Arena
Camden Station
Orioles Stadium (Camden Yards)
Inner Harbor
EDGAR ALLEN POE HOUSE
H.L. MENKEN HOUSE
B&O RAILROAD MUSEUM
TO 295 AND BWI AIRPORT
83
395
M
1
2
3
5
6
7
8
9
14
15
19
20
22
23
25
26
27
28

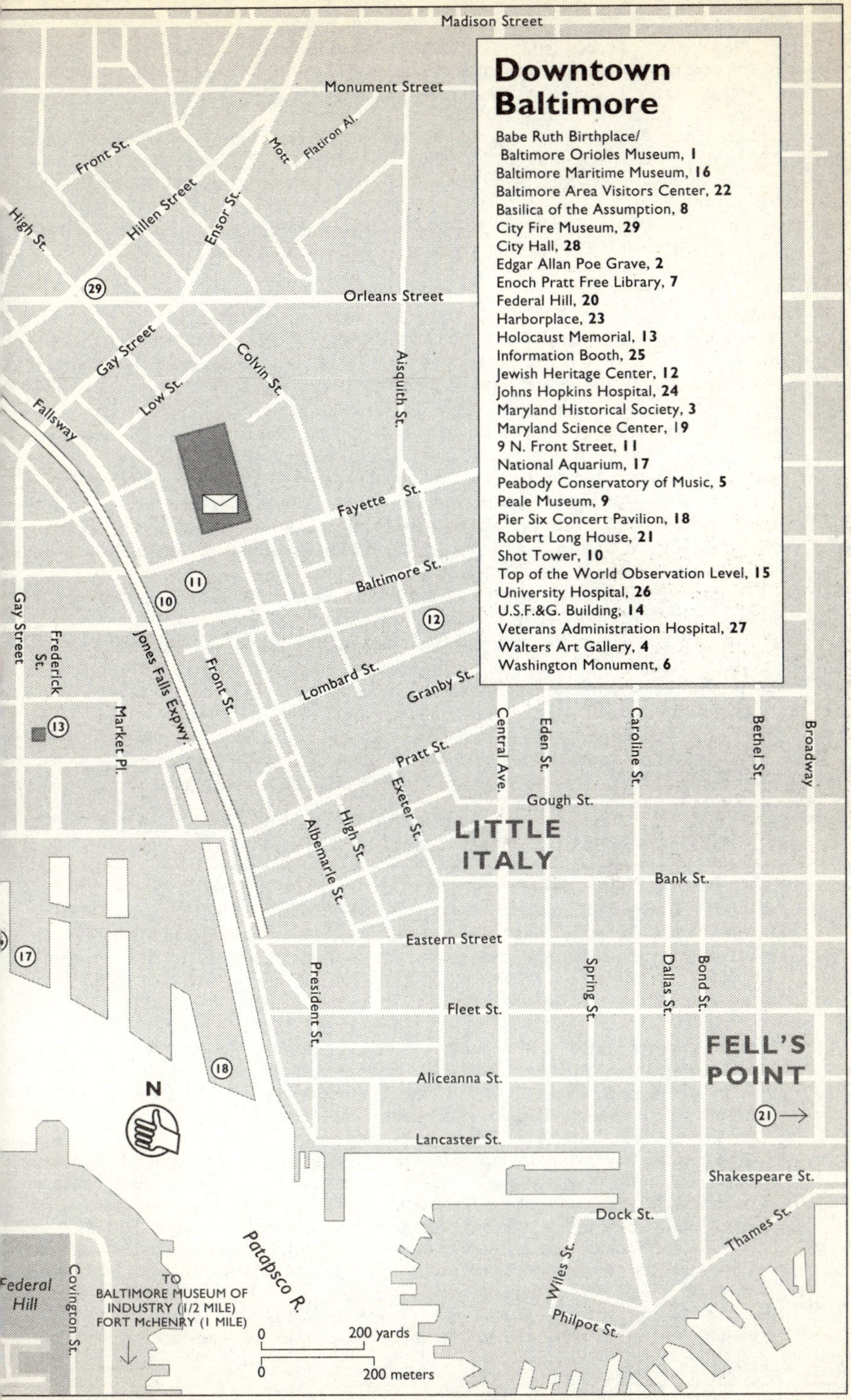
Downtown Baltimore
Babe Ruth Birthplace/
Baltimore Orioles Museum, 1
Baltimore Maritime Museum, 16
Baltimore Area Visitors Center, 22
Basilica of the Assumption, 8
City Fire Museum, 29
City Hall, 28
Edgar Allan Poe Grave, 2
Enoch Pratt Free Library, 7
Federal Hill, 20
Harborplace, 23
Holocaust Memorial, 13
Information Booth, 25
Jewish Heritage Center, 12
Johns Hopkins Hospital, 24
Maryland Historical Society, 3
Maryland Science Center, 19
9 N. Front Street, 11
National Aquarium, 17
Peabody Conservatory of Music, 5
Peale Museum, 9
Pier Six Concert Pavilion, 18
Robert Long House, 21
Shot Tower, 10
Top of the World Observation Level, 15
University Hospital, 26
U.S.F.&G. Building, 14
Veterans Administration Hospital, 27
Walters Art Gallery, 4
Washington Monument, 6
Madison Street
Monument Street
Front St.
Mott
Flatiron Al.
High St.
Hillen Street
Ensor St.
Orleans Street
Gay Street
Colvin St.
Aisquith St.
Low St.
Fallsway
Fayette St.
Baltimore St.
Gay Street
Frederick St.
Jones Falls Expwy.
Front St.
Lombard St.
Granby St.
Market Pl.
Pratt St.
Central Ave.
Eden St.
Caroline St.
Bethel St.
Broadway
Exeter St.
Gough St.
High St.
Albemarle St.
LITTLE ITALY
Bank St.
Eastern Street
President St.
Spring St.
Dallas St.
Bond St.
Fleet St.
FELL'S POINT
Aliceanna St.
N
Lancaster St.
Shakespeare St.
Dock St.
Thames St.
Wiles St.
Philpot St.
Patapsco R.
Federal Hill
Covington St.
TO BALTIMORE MUSEUM OF INDUSTRY (1/2 MILE) FORT McHENRY (1 MILE)
0 200 yards
0 200 meters

Car Rental: Thrifty Car Rental, BWI Airport (859-1136), and 2042 N. Howard St. (783-0300), 9 blocks from Penn Station; also call 800-367-2277 (24hr.). Economy cars from $35 per weekday and $185 per week. Unlimited mileage in MD and bordering states. Under 25 $15 extra per day. Must be 21 with a credit card. Airport branch open daily 6am-11pm.

Help Lines: Suicide Hotline (531-6677). **Sexual Assault and Domestic Violence Center** (391-2396). **Gay and Lesbian Switchboard** (837-8888), gay bars, meetings, and special events; operators daily 7-10pm, recording all other times.

Emergency: 911.

Post Office: 900 E. Fayette St. (347-4425). Open Mon.-Fri. 7:30am-9pm, Sat. 8:30am-5pm. **ZIP Code:** 21233.

Area Code: 410.

Baltimore is plagued with one-way streets. Baltimore Street (which runs east a few blocks north of the Inner Harbor) and Charles Street (which runs north from the west corner of the Harbor) divide the city into quarters. Streets parallel to Baltimore St. have "West" or "East" tacked onto their names, depending on which side of Charles St. a given block is. North-south streets are dubbed "North" or "South" according to their relation to Baltimore St. Interstates and signs deposit tourists at the **Inner Harbor,** near the corner of Pratt and Charles. The museum-laden **Mount Vernon** neighborhood—reached by city buses #3, 9, and 11—occupies Charles St., north of the Inner Harbor, around Monument and Centre Ave. **Little Italy** hangs its hat a few blocks east of the Inner Harbor, past the Jones Falls Expressway; a short walk or drive east to Broadway, a right (south) turn, and another short trip (a few blocks) brings you to happening, bar-happy **Fells Point.**

Baltimore dangles in central Maryland, 100 mi. south of Philadelphia and about 150 mi. up the Chesapeake Bay from the Atlantic Ocean. The Jones Falls Expressway (I-83) halves the city with its southern end at the Inner Harbor, while the Baltimore Beltway (I-695) circles the city. I-95 cuts across the southwest corner of the city as a shortcut to the wide arc of that section of the Beltway. During rush hour, these interstates slow to a crawl. Blue and green signs direct drivers to tourist attractions. To drive from Washington, D.C. to Baltimore, take the Capital Beltway (I-495) to I-95 at exit 27 or to the Baltimore-Washington Expressway at exit 22. The two highways run roughly parallel. The Russell St. exit accesses the Inner Harbor. Without traffic, the trip takes less than an hour.

ACCOMMODATIONS AND CAMPING

Expensive chain hotels dominate the Inner Harbor; for more reasonable options, call **Amanda's Bed and Breakfast Reservation Service,** 1428 Park Ave. (225-0001 or 800-899-7533). The personalized service will match you with B&Bs in private homes, small inns, or yachts that suit your needs, whether you're allergic to cats or desire a private bath. Rates begin at $50 a night. Reservations are recommended (call Mon.-Fri. 8:30am-5:30pm, Sat. 8:30am-noon).

Baltimore International Youth Hostel (HI-AYH), 17 W. Mulberry St. (576-8880), at Cathedral St. in the historic Mount Vernon neighborhood. Near bus and Amtrak terminals. Take MTA bus #3 or 11 along Charles St. Elegant, centrally located 19th-century brownstone harbors 48 beds in spacious dorm rooms, as well as full kitchen and laundry services. The lounge sports marble fireplaces, a TV, and a baby grand piano. Super-friendly managers are a great source of information about Baltimore. A/C in bedrooms and fans aplenty in common areas. Max. stay 3 nights (may be extended with manager's approval). Curfew 11pm, but house keys available for rent ($2). Members $13, nonmembers $16. Free baggage storage and linens. Mastercard and Visa accepted. Reservations recommended, especially in the summer. Those allergic to cats should consider other accommodations. Visitors shouldn't walk alone near here at night.

Duke's Motel, 7905 Pulaski Highway (686-0400), in Rosedale off the Beltway. The bulletproof glass in the front office is nothing to incite fear—all the neighborhood's motels have it. Duke's is a gem amidst a slew of less desirable motels, and probably the only place worth staying at on the Pulaski Hwy. motel strip. Simple, clean rooms have A/C, carpeting, and cable TV. Suitable only for people with cars. Singles $36-41, doubles $41-46. $3 key deposit and ID required.

Quality Inn Inner Harbor, 1701 Russell St. (727-3400 or 800-221-2222), near the Beltway in unfashionable South Baltimore, about 1mi. from Inner Harbor. Standard rooms, cable TV, and pool are provided, in addition to a complimentary continental breakfast. Most suitable for those with cars (the area is rather dangerous at night). Singles $60, doubles $70. Weekend rates: singles $65, doubles $75. $40 tourist rate with coupon obtained at the visitors center (subject to availability). AARP/AAA members, military and government personnel 10% discount.

Mount Vernon Hotel, 24 W. Franklin St. (727-2000), near Cathedral St. in Mount Vernon. Standard, comfortable rooms with A/C. Terrific location. Singles from $70, doubles from $85. Parking $6 per day.

Capitol KOA, 768 Cecil Ave. (410-923-2771 or 987-7477; fax 923-3169), near Millersville. Half-way between D.C. and Baltimore. See **Camping** on p. 79 for info.

FOOD

Virginia may be for lovers, but Maryland is for crabs—every self-respecting restaurant offers **crab cakes,** and most claim to serve Baltimore's best.

The **Light Street Pavilion** at **Harborplace,** Pratt and Light St. (332-4191), has manifold foodstuffs to suit every tourist—that's why they all come here. **The Fudgery** hands out free samples every hour and never fails to attract hordes of tourists with entertaining displays (open Mon.-Sat. 10am-9pm, Sun. 10am-6pm). **Lexington Market,** 400 W. Lexington (685-6169) at Eutaw St., provides an endless variety of produce, fresh meat, and seafood, as well as food stalls cheaper than those at Harborplace (open Mon.-Sat. 8:30am-6pm; take the subway to Lexington Station or bus #7). **Cross Street Market,** between S. Charles and Light St. in South Baltimore, provides produce, as well as one of the best raw bars in the city. In Fells Point, the two-building **Broadway Market** sits square in the middle of S. Broadway St., about three blocks from the dock (open Mon.-Sat. 7am-6pm). **One World Café,** at 904 S. Charles St. (234-0235) in the Federal Hill district, serves vegetarian cuisine to those desperately seeking an alternative to seafood.

Mount Vernon

Mount Vernon manages to squeeze in a tremendous number of restaurants among its art galleries and conservatories, and virtually all are to be found on N. Charles St., within the blocks on either side of Baltimore's Washington Monument.

Akbar, 823 N. Charles St. (539-0944). Excellent Indian food served at not-so-excellent prices (entrees $10-15). The value is in the $7 all-you-can-eat lunch buffet (Mon.-Fri. 11:30am-2:30pm), the $9 all-you-can-eat weekend brunch buffet (Sat.-Sun. noon-3pm), and samplings of the wide selection of Indian breads ($1.50-2.75). Open Mon.-Thurs. 11:30am-2:30pm and 5-11pm, Fri. 11:30am-2:30pm and 5-11:30pm, Sat. noon-3pm and 5-11:30pm, Sun. noon-3pm and 5-11pm.

Buddies, 313 N. Charles St. (332-4200). Patrons fill up on the extensive salad bar (over 80 items; $3 per lb.; Mon.-Fri. 11am-2:30pm) and pile-driving sandwiches ($5-8.50). A jazz quartet draws locals and visitors of all ages (Thurs.-Sat. 9:30pm-1am). Domestic beer $1.70, mixed drinks $2.75. Happy hour Mon.-Fri. 4-7pm offers 2-for-1 drinks. Wed. karaoke (beginning at 8:30pm). Free delivery ($10 min.; limited area). Open Mon.-Thurs. 4am-10pm, Fri. 11am-2am, Sat. 1pm-2am.

Buttery Restaurant, 531 N. Charles St. (837-2494), near E. Centre St. This out-of-the-way little diner serves up cheap eats around-the-clock. Pancakes $2-4, hamburgers $3.40, sandwich platters $2.40-4.35. Open 24hr.

The Helmand, 806 N. Charles St. (752-0311). Despite the white linen tablecloths, there's nary a thing on the menu over $10. Acclaimed by some local magazines as one of the 10 best restaurants in the city, this Afghan restaurant serves authentic dishes in which meat garnishes vegetables and yogurt sauces garnish all. An appetizer must-try is the *kaddo borani,* pan-fried and baked baby pumpkin in a yogurt-garlic sauce. Open Sun.-Thurs. 5-10pm, Fri.-Sat. 5-11pm.

Kristo's, 206 W. Saratoga St. (727-3378), close to the HI-AYH hostel. Kristo's offers great, cheap, take-out fare. An 8-in. personal pizza with 2 toppings and a soda is only $3.60 (with coupon from take-out menu). Half-subs $3-5, whole $6-10. Sandwiches $2-4, pasta $4-6. Free delivery ($6 min.; limited area). Area can be dangerous at night. Open Mon.-Sat. 11am-2am, Sun. 11am-11pm.

Louie's Bookstore Café, 518 N. Charles St. (962-1224), just up the street from the youth hostel. In front, an upscale, intellectual bookstore flaunts extensive sections on music and literature. In back, a lively café/bar/restaurant mixes well-tailored concertgoers with scruffy indie-rock locals and tourists. Lunch is cheap, but the dinner scene is groovier, with nightly live guitar, flute, piano, or violin music (8pm-midnight). Sandwiches and burgers about $5-8. Entrees $8-10. Vegetarian dishes and desserts are Louie's specialties. Open Mon. 11:30am-midnight, Tues.-Thurs. 11:30am-12:30am, Fri.-Sat. 11:30am-1:30am.

Martick's Restaurant Francais, 214 W. Mulberry St. (752-5155). You must ring the bell to enter, but once you sit down and eat you'll never want to leave. The strawberry and red onion salad ($5) is the ideal preface to the blackened lamb ($13); desserts include a fantastic bread pudding. All of Martick's dishes are layered with flavor, and despite the outer disrepair of the place, this restaurant has it where it counts—the delicious cuisine.

Little Italy and Fells Point

From Baltimore's historic districts, take bus #7 or 10 from Pratt St. to Albemarle St. and **Little Italy,** or ride bus #7 or 10 to Broadway—a four-block walk to **Fells Point.**

Amicci's, 231 S. High St. (528-1096). Slick black-and-white walls sport slick black-and-white photographs and paisley tablecloths present heaping portions of excellent Italian fare. The best bargain in Little Italy serves 11 pasta dishes under $10, and not one dish over $13. *Pane Rotundo* and *Ziti La Rosa* both feature shrimp and are not to be missed. Open Sun.-Thurs. noon-9pm, Fri.-Sat. noon-11pm.

Bertha's Dining Room, 734 S. Broadway (327-5795), at Lancaster. The bumper stickers say "Eat Bertha's Mussels": black-shelled bivalves ($7.75-10) served upon butcher-block tables, and best coupled with chunky vegetable mussel chowder (cup $1.75). Jazz bands play for local crowds Tues.-Wed. and Fri.-Sat. nights. 20 kinds of beer on tap (½-pint $2.50, pint $3.50). Afternoon tea Mon.-Sat. 3-4:30pm offers scones, tarts, and other pastries (tea reservations necessary; call one day in advance). Wheelchair access. Kitchen open Sun.-Thurs. 11:30am-11pm, Fri.-Sat. 11:30am-midnight. Bar until 2am.

Café Mundo, 1623 Thames St. (675-7105). The Euro-decor makes for a comfy dessert café with pastries made on the premises ($2-4). Cool caffeine comes in the form of an an iced cappucino ($1.75), and elegant sandwiches ($4-5) come with a free cookie. Salads also $4-5. Open Sun.-Fri. 11am-6pm, Sat. 11:30am-10pm.

Fells Point Diner, 435 S. Broadway (327-0715), at Eastern Ave. If you need a break from the more expensive restaurants in Fells Point, the pink booths and long pink counter of this clean, cheap diner will be a welcome sight. Daily specials from $6. Breakfast specials $2-5. Locals' favorites include french toast ($3), crab cakes ($4.50-12), and spinach pie with Greek salad ($5.75). Open daily 8am-4am.

Lee's Homemade Ice Cream, 821 S. Broadway (276-4556), at the corner of Thames St. A Baltimore institution with a national claim to fame: Lee's invented "cookies and cream." Cones $1.80-$4.10. Skyscraping sundaes from $3. Open Mon. noon-9pm, Tues.-Wed. 11am-9pm, Thurs. and Sun. 11am-11pm, Fri.-Sat. 11am-midnight.

Luigi Petti, 1002 Eastern Ave. (685-0055), near S. Exeter. One of Little Italy's most attractive restaurants. Mama Marie's homemade pastas $11-13, shrimp scampi $7.50, veal chop, and fresh lobster are *favoriti.* Pianist plays Thurs.-Sun. evenings. Outdoor patio and bar. Lunch menu available Mon.-Sat. until 3pm. Open Mon.-Thurs. 11:30am-midnight, Fri. 11:30am-1am, Sat. 12:30pm-1am, Sun. 12:30-10pm. Bar open daily until 2am.

Farther Out

★**Ikaros,** 4805 Eastern Ave. (633-3750), 2mi. east of downtown; take bus #10. Like its tragic namesake from Greek mythology, this restaurant is fallen from heaven. Creating a romantic, Mediterranean atmosphere, this Baltimore institution has been serving the city's best *souvlaki* ($5) for 27 years. The Greek salads ($6-7) are a meal in themselves. Other specialties are the *mousaka* ($8.50) and *kalamari* ($11). Open Sun.-Mon. and Wed.-Thurs. 11am-10pm, Fri.-Sat. 11am-11pm.

Haussner's, 3242 Eastern Ave. (327-8365), at S. Clinton; take bus #10. An East Baltimore institution. 700 oil paintings crowd the huge dining room, including copies of Rembrandt, Gainsborough, Whistler, and Homer. Haussner's central European cuisine includes fresh pig knuckles and *Sauerbraten* (meat stewed in vinegar and juices) $10.60, sandwiches $3.75-12. Big, big portions. The strawberry pie ($3.75), and other freshly baked goods can be taken out. Long pants preferred after 3pm. Open Tues.-Sat. 11am-10pm.

SIGHTS

Inner Harbor

Most tourists start at the Inner Harbor, and all too many finish there. Baltimore's generally gray and functional harbor terminates with a colorful bang in a five-square-block body of water bounded on three sides by the National Aquarium, Harborplace, the Maryland Science Museum, and a bevy of boardable old and new ships. **The Clipper City** (539-6277), a beautiful topsail schooner, provides a scenic, two-hour jaunt around the Inner Harbor. The cruise offers a full bar to those aboard, as well as an opportunity to see the 19th-century replica raise its sails. (Departs Mon.-Sat. at noon and 3pm. $12, children $2. Fri.-Sat nights Calypso sails and Sun. brunch sails also offered; call for details.)

The **National Aquarium,** Pier 3, 501 E. Pratt St. (576-3800), makes the whole Inner Harbor worthwhile. The museum's intelligent spiral lay-out makes it impossible to miss any of the aquatic wonders as one ascends to the 157-ft. glass-pyramid roof. "Wings in the Water" allows those entering to peer down on some 50 species of rays (including the playful manta) before beginning the ascent. Levels two, three, and four spiral over central tanks and through various aquatic communities, including Atlantic sea cliffs inhabited by cheeky puffins and a lush kelp forest. The Children's Cove on level four lets kids and adults handle intertidal marine animals in the **Touching Pool.** Level five (inside the glass pyramid) is a steamy tropical rainforest; piranhas, parrots, and a pair of two-toed sloths peer through the dense foliage. To exit, visitors descend a remarkable four-story series of ramps inside a 13-ft.-deep, doughnut-shaped tank. The tank simulates a coral reef and is inhabited by sharks of all shapes and sizes—it's like scuba-diving without getting wet. On ground level, an enclosed bridge leads to the **Marine Mammal Pavilion,** which contains dolphins and whales, with an amphitheater featuring performances à la Sea World. The eerie new exhibit "Jellies: Phantoms of the Deep" features jellyfish of multifarious types. To avoid long lines for Aquarium tickets, arrive before 9am; on weekends and other busy days, you will have to buy a ticket from the booth outside and return at the time printed on the ticket (usually ½hr. later, but up to 3½hr. in summer). Tickets can also be purchased in advance from TicketMaster (481-7328 before 3pm in Baltimore, 202-432-7328 in Washington, D.C.). Expect to spend three hours in the Aquarium. Excellent disabled access through separate entrance; call ahead. (Open March-Oct. Sun.-Thurs. 9am-6pm, Fri.-Sat. 9am-8pm; Nov.-Feb. Sat.-Thurs. 10am-5pm, Fri. 10am-8pm. The aquarium lobby lists slide shows and feeding times. Admission $11.50, seniors $9.50, children 3-11 $7.50, under 3 free.)

Several ships bob in the harbor by the aquarium; most belong to the **Baltimore Maritime Museum** (396-3453), at Piers III and IV. While waiting to enter the aquarium, visitors may board the U.S.S. Torsk submarine (which sank the last WWII Japanese combatant ships), the lightship Chesapeake, and the Coast Guard cutter Taney.

(Open Mon.-Fri. 10am-5pm, Fri.-Sat. 9:30am-6pm; winter Fri.-Sun. 9:30am-5pm. Admission $4.50, seniors $4, children under 13 $1.75, active military free.)

If imitation is the sincerest form of flattery, **Harborplace** is Baltimore's most flattered building. When then-mayor Schaefer and developer James Rouse decided to make the Inner Harbor tourist-friendly, they started by building an air-conditioned shopping mall at the water's edge; Harborplace is the first and maybe the best of the pier-pavilions, which can now also be found in New York, Detroit, and San Francisco. Crowds flock to Harborplace's Pratt Street and Light Street Pavilions, and the Gallery, across the street on the corner of Pratt and Light St., for a little wharf-side shopping and air-conditioned bliss (332-4191; open Mon.-Sat. 10am-9pm, Sun. 10am-6pm).

At the Inner Harbor's far edge lurks the **Maryland Science Center,** 601 Light St. (685-5225), where children can learn basic principles of chemistry and physics cleverly disguised as hands-on games and activities. The Energy Place wears them out with pulleys and levers, while the Structures exhibit allows them to explore the arts and architecture of building. The IMAX Theater's five-story screen and 38-speaker sound systems stun audiences. The Davis Planetarium's 50-foot dome is equally impressive (both are included in the price of admission). Summer weekend afternoons yield long lines. (Open Memorial Day-Labor Day Mon.-Thurs. 10am-6pm, Fri. and Sun. 10am-8pm; Sept.-May Mon.-Fri. 10am-5pm, Sat.-Sun. 10am-6pm. Admission $9, ages 4-17, seniors and military $7, under 4 free.)

Some of Baltimore's best-restored homes lie to the west of Federal Hill. **Montgomery Street** is perhaps the best example, with its grand façades and cobblestone streets. To the east along Key Highway, dilapidated warehouses loom along the shore. The former oyster cannery at 1415 Key Highway holds the **Baltimore Museum of Industry** (727-4808) in one of its warehouses. (Take bus #1 or the Water Taxi.) Guides will lead you through a functional belt-driven machine shop, let you print a handbill on an 1880 press, and pass around a weighty pair of shears once used in Baltimore's flourishing clothing trade. Also worth checking out is the steam tugboat *Baltimore.* (Open Tues.-Fri. and Sun. noon-5pm, Sat. 10am-5pm; Sept.-May Tues. and Thurs.-Fri. 10am-5pm, Wed. 10am-5pm and 7-9pm, Sat. 10am-5pm. Admission $3.50, students, children, and seniors $2.50, families $12, under 6 free.)

Fort McHenry National Monument (962-4290), located at the foot of E. Fort Ave. off Rte. 2 (Hanover St.) and Lawrence Ave. (take bus #1), commemorates the fort's victory against British forces in the War of 1812, a triumph which inspired Francis Scott Key to write "The Star-Spangled Banner." A flag flies over the fort all day, but *the* flag hangs in the Smithsonian Museum of American History in Washington (see page 188). Take the #1 bus or a narrated cruise from Finger Pier in the Inner Harbor (round-trip $5, children 2-11 $3.75). (Open daily 8am-8pm; Sept.-May 8am-5pm. Admission $2, seniors and under 17 free. Wheelchair access; film close-captioned for the hearing-impaired. Ample parking.)

West Baltimore

A few museums dwell among the rowhouses west of the Inner Harbor. The **Babe Ruth Birthplace and Baltimore Orioles Museum,** 216 Emory St. (727-1539; take bus #31), off the 600 block of W. Pratt, remembers the "Sultan of Swat." Some exhibits pitch to diehards only, like the alcove recalling each of his 714 home runs. Others take a swing at a wider audience with Maryland baseball memorabilia, including a series of rotating exhibits on Baltimore's beloved Orioles. (Open daily 10am-5pm, on game nights until 7pm; Nov.-March 10am-4pm. Admission $5, seniors $3, ages 5-16 $2, under 4 free.)

Babe Ruth would happily call a shot or two at the sparkling new **Oriole Park at Camden Yards** (547-6234), just west of the Inner Harbor at Eutaw and Camden St. Flying in the face of the recent sporting trend to build large, impersonal stadiums on the outskirts of cities, Baltimore decided to construct an intimate, vintage-style stadium on an old industrial yard in the heart of downtown. By so doing, the city now claims one of the most attractive parks in baseball. If the O's aren't playing an afternoon home game, visitors can take a behind-the-scenes tour of the stadium, including

Cognac and Roses

A short-lived, mustached, opium-addicted 1830s author, Edgar Allan Poe virtually invented the horror tale and the detective story. His most famous works include *The Tell-Tale Heart* and *The Pit and the Pendulum.* He also penned macabre, extravagantly vacant poems like *The Raven* and *Annabelle Lee.* Poe wrote for money. He never envisioned his stories would be lauded as innovative and captivating; he considered them trash.

You probably won't hear a beating heart at the **Edgar Allan Poe Grave** where the divine Edgar sleeps evermore in the Westminster Churchyard (706-7228), at Fayette and Greene St. (Guided tours every 1st and 3rd Fri. evening at 6:30pm and Sat. morning at 10am. Reservations required. Tour $4, under 12 and seniors $2.) Every year on the anniversary of Poe's death (Oct. 7, 1849), a mysterious visitor dressed in black decorates his grave with cognac and roses. (Cemetery open during daylight hours.) Edgar Allan Poe was born at the **Edgar Allan Poe House** (396-7932), in a somewhat seedy area at 203 N. Amity St., near Saratoga St. (bus #15 or 23). The tour ushers Poe-heads through the writer's biography and around the tell-tale original furniture. (Poe house open Wed.-Sat. noon-3:45pm; Aug.-Sept. Sat. noon-3:45pm. Admission $3, under 13 $1.)

the clubhouses, dugouts, press box, and scoreboard. (Tours leave hourly Mon.-Fri. 11am-2pm, on the ½-hour Sat. 10:30am-2pm and Sun. 12:30-2pm. Admission $5, seniors and children under 12 $4.)

Itself once a station for the Baltimore & Ohio Railroad, the **B&O Railroad Museum,** 901 W. Pratt St. (752-2490; take bus #31), looks out on train tracks where dining cars, Pullman sleepers, and mail cars park themselves for the touring frenzy. Inside the museum, three films chug along through the history of railroads. The enormous Roundhouse captures historic trains and full-scale replicas thereof, including the 1829 "Tom Thumb," the first American steam-driven locomotive. Don't miss the extensive model-train display. (Open daily 10am-5pm. Admission $6, seniors $5, children 5-12 $3, under 5 free. Train rides on weekends cost an additional $2. Trains parked outside are free.)

The **H.L. Mencken House,** 1524 Hollins St. (396-7997) near Gilmore St. (reached by bus #2 or 31), commemorates the wit whose *American Spectator* improved the vocabularies and soured the outlooks of thousands of 1920s readers. A film strip highlights the writer's career. (Open Sat. 10am-5pm, Sun. noon-5pm. Other times by appointment only. Tours Sat.-Sun. on the hour. Admission $2, seniors and children 4-18 $1.50, under 4 free.)

East Baltimore

In the eastern section of downtown, the **City Life Museums** line up in **"Museum Row"** at 800 E. Lombard St. (396-3523). The **Shot Tower,** at the corner of E. Fayette St. and Jones Falls Expwy, should be visible in this area; it looks like a huge smokestack; molten lead, dropped from the top, shaped itself into shotgun pellets as it fell and cooled. The City Life complex may be entered through the first of the museums—**Carroll Mansion,** which belonged to Charles Carroll, signer of the *Declaration of Independence.* The mansion depicts the lifestyle of a mid-19th-century upper-class family. In contrast, **1840 House,** the rowhouse next door, was home to a craftsman's family during the same time period. The **Center for Urban Archaeology** explores the methods archaeologists use to unearth artifacts from the city's past in local digs. One of the center's more famous digs turned up the foundations of one of Baltimore's oldest and largest breweries—practically in the center's own backyard. To explore the malty ruins in **Brewers Park,** right across Lombard St., pick up an explanatory pamphlet at the center. (Open Mon.-Sat. 10am-5pm, Sun. noon-5pm. Admission $5 to all Museum Row sites, children 4-18 and seniors $3.50, under 4 free. A $6 package includes admission to all Museum Row sights as well as the Peale Museum and H.L. Mencken House.)

The jewel in the crown of the City Life Museums, the recently built **Blaustein Center,** features displays on Baltimore's social history. The museum attempts to recreate the atmosphere of a Baltimore neighborhood circa 1920, as well as harness the modern city in a changing "Community Gallery" exhibition. Dramatic presentations based on oral histories and letters of Baltimoreans are also highlights (admission is an additional $1 for this exhibition).

A few blocks north of Museum Row sits a City Life straggler—the **Peale Museum,** 225 Holliday St. (396-1149). Portrait painter Rembrandt Peale built the museum in honor of his father Charles Wilson Peale in 1814, making it the oldest museum building in the U.S. A permanent exhibit of more than 40 portraits painted by the Peale family (Rembrandt was just the most famous son) as well as some traveling exhibits are housed there. (Open Tues.-Sat. 10am-5pm, Sun. noon-5pm. Admission $2, children 4-18 and seniors $1.50, under 4 free.)

The **Jewish Heritage Center** is a three-building complex located at 15 Lloyd St. (732-6400). On the left, the **Lloyd Street Synagogue,** built in 1845, was Maryland's first synagogue; the **B'nai Israel Synagogue,** the building on the far right, was founded in 1876 to preserve Orthodox religious practices; and between the two synagogues, the **Jewish Historical Society of Maryland** has established a library and museum to house documents, photographs, and changing exhibitions reflecting the history of Maryland's Jewish community. Formed in 1960, the center makes its home in the heart of East Baltimore, where Maryland's first Jews settled. (Open Tues.-Thurs. and Sun. noon-4pm, other times by appointment. Library open by appointment. Admission $2, children under 12 free. Free parking for visitors off Watson St.) A few blocks away on a hillside at Gay and Water St., the concrete **Holocaust Memorial** remembers the six million Jews who died in concentration camps during WWII. On the other side of the hill, facing Lombard St., a statue of flames engulfing the bodies of the Nazis' victims is shocking, especially after the less visceral symbolism of the memorial.

Mount Vernon

The Mount Vernon neighborhood, a mix of hip and stiff-upper-lip, is one of Baltimore's cultural cores. Its center is Baltimore's own **Washington Monument,** designed by Robert Mills, who later planned the more famous one in D.C. The older monument, which is more easily mistaken for an Islamic minaret than for the monument on the Mall, displays a 16-ft.-tall, toga-sporting General Washington resigning his commission as commander of the Continental Army. Carved atop a 160-ft. column, the statue suggests that Washington never lost his poise—he seems unaware of his precarious position atop the tower. The 228-step climb to the top allows a view of the surrounding neighborhood and distant Inner Harbor. (Open Wed.-Sun. 10am-4pm. Free. Take bus #3 or 31 up N. Charles St. to reach the sights in this area.) A few blocks south of the Washington Monument, the **Basilica of the Assumption** basks at the corner of Cathedral and Mulberry St. Benjamin Latrobe, who helped design the U.S. Capitol, planned the Basilica in 1806. The first Roman Catholic church in the United States, it mixes Greek Revival lines with an octagonal base and Kremlin-style twin onion domes. The Basilica purports to be the "Mecca" of the American Catholic. (Open Mon.-Fri. 7am-5pm, Sat.-Sun. 7am-6:30pm. Free tours available at noon on Sun. Call 727-3564 to arrange for other times.)

Baltimore's best museum, **The Walters Art Gallery,** 600 N. Charles St. at Centre (547-9000), keeps one of the largest private collections in the world, spanning 50 centuries in three buildings. The 19th-century collection—mostly paintings—congregates on the 4th floor of the 1974 building and includes a small but worthwhile Impressionist collection featuring Manet's *At the Café* and Monet's *Springtime.* The remaining floor space holds later additions to the collection, including a superb ancient art collection, two Fabergé eggs, and a 4th-century Byzantine vase carved from a single piece of agate. Like other museums of this scope, the Walters is too large to be seen in its entirety; pick up a map and trace out a battle plan. The museum's most esteemed possession is the Ancient Art collection on the second level, with sculptures, jewelry, and metalwork from Egypt, Greece, and Rome. Seven marble sarcophagi with intricate relief carvings are of a type found in only one other collection, that of the National Museum in Rome. The third floor holds medieval art, especially jewelry and metalwork, from the Byzantine, Romanesque, and Gothic periods. Paintings on the third and fourth floors give a nod to every European style between the 12th and the 19th centuries. Try not to miss the Hackerman House, the flashy addition to The Walters on the third floor. Rooms filled with dark-wood furniture, patterned rugs, and plush velvet curtains accumulate art from China, Korea, Japan, India, and Southeast Asia. The early Buddhist sculptures from China are very rare, as are the Japanese decorative arts of the late-18th and 19th centuries. Some of the finest examples of the often-copied Ming Dynasty Peachbloom Vases can be found here. The Gallery houses the **Walters Film House,** screening new and classic independent and foreign films on Fri. at 7:30pm. (Open Tues.-Sun. 11am-5pm. Admission $4, seniors $3, students and children under 18 free; free on Sat. before noon. Tours Wed. 12:30pm and Sun. 2pm.)

Mount Vernon's artistic and commercial communities join forces on **"First Thursdays,"** neighborhood festivals of public music, art, and extended shopping hours during 5-7:30pm on the first Thursday of every month.

The Johns Hopkins University

Approximately three mi. north of the harbor on N. Charles St. (bus #3, 9, or 11), **Johns Hopkins University** spreads out from 33rd St. The beautiful campus lies on a 140-acre wooded lot that was originally the Homewood estate of Charles Carroll, Jr., the son of a signer of the *Declaration of Independence.* Free campus tours are available at the Office of Admissions in Garland Hall (Mon.-Fri. 10am, noon, and 3pm; call 516-8171 to confirm times). Two historic houses administered by the university also lie on or near the campus. **Homewood** (516-5589), the elegant house belonging to Carroll, displays a fine collection of 18th- and 19th-century furnishings, some original to the house; **Evergreen House** (516-0341), seated on 26 acres one mi. north of the main campus at 4545 N. Charles St., shows the mansion, private theater, carriage house, and gardens of Ambassador John Work Garrett and family. (Homewood open Tues.-Sat. 11am-5pm, Sun. noon-4pm; admission $5, students and seniors $4, children 6-18 $2.50, under 6 free; tours hourly 10am-3pm. Evergreen open Mon.-Fri. 10am-4pm, Sun. 1-4pm; same admission rates apply; tours hourly 10am-3pm.) The **Lacrosse Hall of Fame Museum,** 113 West University Parkway (235-6882), squats at the end of the Johns Hopkins lacrosse fields, and houses uniforms, trophies, and equipment from over 350 years of the sport's history. (Open Mon.-Fri. 9am-5pm; March-May Mon.-Fri. 9am-5pm, Sat. 10am-3pm. Admission $2, students $1.)

To the west of campus at N. Charles and 31st St., the **Baltimore Museum of Art** (396-7100) picks up where the Walters leaves off, exhibiting a fine collection of Americana and modern art, including several pieces by Andy Warhol. The collection also impresses with works by Matisse, Picasso, Renoir, and Van Gogh. Two adjacent **sculpture gardens** of 20th-century art make wonderful picnic grounds. (Open Wed.-Fri. 10am-4pm, Sat.-Sun. 11am-6pm. Admission $5.50, students and seniors $3.50, ages 7-18 $1.50, under 7 free. Thurs. free. Metered parking available. Wheelchairs available.) In residence at the museum, the **Baltimore Film Forum** shows classic and current American, foreign, and independent films on Thursdays and Fridays at 8pm (admission $5, students and seniors $4); pick up a schedule at the museum or call 889-1993.

The Baltimore Zoo (366-5466) off of I-83, exit 7, is very proud of its new Chimpanzee Forest exhibit, which includes swinging monkeys and snapping crocodiles. It also features a spectacular Palm Tree Conservatory, and a lake surrounded by lush greenery. The top-rated zoo features "African Watering Hole," a simulated savannah with elephants, Siberian tigers, and a waterfall. The Children's Zoo imports animals from nearby farms and the Maryland wilds, such as otters and crafty woodchucks. Children can also ride a carousel and a "zoo choo" train (rides $1.25). (Zoo open

Mon.-Fri. 10am-4pm, Sat.-Sun. 10am-5:30pm; everything closes at 4pm in winter. Admission $7.50, seniors and ages 2-15 $4, under 2 free.)

ENTERTAINMENT AND NIGHTLIFE

The **Pier Six Concert Pavilion** (625-4230), at Pier VI at the Inner Harbor, presents big-name music nightly from late July through Sept. Tickets are available at the pavilion or through TeleCharge (625-1400, 800-638-2444) during the summer ($15-30). Pier V, near Harborplace, affords free eavesdropping. The **Baltimore Symphony Orchestra** plays at Meyerhoff Symphony Hall, 1212 Cathedral St. (783-8000), from Sept. to May and during their July Summerfest. (Tickets $15-45; box office open Mon.-Fri. 10am-6pm, Sat.-Sun. noon-5pm, and 1hr. before performance.) The Lyric Opera House down the street at 140 W. Mt. Royal, near Cathedral St. (727-6000), hosts the **Baltimore Opera Company** from Oct. to April. Broadway hits get a tune-up from Oct. through July at the **Morris Mechanic Theatre,** 25 Hopkins Plaza at Baltimore and N. Charles St. (625-1400). All these venues are wheelchair-friendly.

The **Theatre Project,** 45 W. Preston St. near Maryland St. (752-8558), experiments with theater, poetry, music, and/or dance Wed. through Sat. at 8pm and Sun. at 3pm. (Ticket prices $5-14. Box office open Tues. noon-5pm, Wed.-Sat. 1-9pm, Sun. noon-4pm. Call to charge tickets.) The **Arena Players** (728-6500), a black theater group, show musicals, comedies, drama, and dance at 801 McCullough St. at Martin Luther King, Jr. Blvd. The **Left Bank Jazz Society** (466-0600) sponsors jazz shows Sept.-May; call for schedules and information.

The **Showcase of Nations Ethnic Festivals** (837-4636, 800-282-6632) celebrates Baltimore's ethnic neighborhoods with a different culture featured each week from June through Sept. Though somewhat generic, the fairs are always fun, hawking international fare along with the requisite and inescapable crab cakes and beer. Most events take place at Festival Hall, at W. Pratt and Sharp St.

The beloved **Baltimore Orioles** now play at their new stadium at Camden Yards, just a few blocks from the Inner Harbor at the corner of Russell and Camden St. (see **Sports and Recreation: Baseball,** page 225). The city idolizes the team's Cal Ripken, Jr., who has played in more consecutive games than any other player in the history of baseball. The Orioles will be joined by the **Ravens** in 1997, when Baltimore gets a second chance at professional football. The Ravens, formerly the Cleveland Browns, will play in **Memorial Stadium** until a new venue is built.

Bars and Clubs

Baltimore Brewing Co., 104 Albermarle St. (837-5000), just west of the Inner Harbor on the outskirts of Little Italy. Brewmaster Theo de Groen has captured the hearts and livers of Baltimoreans with his original and distinctive lagers, brewed right on the premises in the large brass tuns that loom behind the bar. The Weizen and Märzen styles are especially good, but keep an eye out for the spicy seasonals. Beer connoisseurs will *enjoy* this place. Happy hour daily 4-7pm with $2 ½-liters of beer. Specializes in hearty German fare ($7-14), although they offer a number of cheaper sandwiches and snacks. Open Mon.-Thurs. 11am-11pm, Fri.-Sat. 11am-midnight.

Bohaeger's, 515 S. Eden St. (563-7220) in Fells Point. Hopping bar becomes a happenin' dance club on the weekend, where patrons chug $2.25 drafts on the huge outdoor patio. Happy hour (Fri. 5-7pm) takes 50¢ off all drinks and offers a free buffet. Thurs. ladies' night (ladies' drinks $1, no cover). DJ music starts at 8pm Thurs.-Sat. Open Tues.-Fri. 11:30am-2am, Sat.-Sun. 3pm-2am.

Cat's Eye Pub, 1730 Thames St. (276-9085), in Fells Point. *Playboy* thinks this is the best bar in Fells Point, and so do the regulars (an older crowd) who pack it every night for live blues, jazz, folk, or traditional Irish music (beginning at 9pm). There's no cover, but prices go up when the band strikes it up (every night and twice Sat.-Sun.). Over 25 different drafts and 60 bottled beers. Happy hour 4-7pm brings slight price reductions. Live blues Sun. 3-8pm. Open daily 1pm-2am.

8 X 10, 10 E. Cross St. (625-2000). As the name implies, this bar is *small.* But, it's popular, and overflowing with locals. Local bands play everything, including blues, reggae, and jazz. Cover $8-12. Open nightly 9pm-2am.

Green Turtle, 727 Broadway (342-4222). Green Turtle is popular with the Baltimore college crowd, and anyone else interested in tanking up for next-to-nothing. 20 beers on tap. Cheap $1.25 drafts are even cheaper (85¢) during happy hour (Mon.-Fri. 4-7pm and all night Wed.). Open daily 11:30pm-1:30am.

Hammerjacks, 1101 S. Howard St. (481-7328). This commercial concert venue is *the* place in Baltimore for nationally recognized bands. Tickets are often on sale through TicketMaster (659-7625). Show times vary; call for more information.

John Steven's, 1800 Thames St. (327-5561), near Ann St. in Fells Point. This acclaimed restaurant/bar, named after the owner's son's teddy bear, offers the expected sandwiches and seafood, as well as American sushi like the "Bawlmer roll" (backfin crab with avocado and scallions, $7.50). Beer $3, rails $2. Classical and jazz (on CD) are the music genres of choice and are ideal for the shaded patio in back. Open Sun.-Thurs. 11am-11pm, Fri.-Sat. 11am- midnight.

Louie/Louis, at the corner of Howard and Cross (727-2005). A hip crowd moves with the urban progressive and techno beats at this small-time dance club. Thurs. and Sat. are 18+ with an open bar. Cover: $6. Open Thurs.-Sat. 10pm-2am.

Max's on Broadway, 735 S. Broadway (675-6297), at Lancaster St. in Fells Point. Max's attracts a more sedentary crowd than most bars. Once a grungy venue, it is now one of Baltimore's best beer bars, with 24 taps and over 200 different bottled brews. Happy hour Mon.-Fri. noon-8pm brings $1-2 drafts. Open daily noon-2am.

The Midtown Yacht Club, 15 E. Centre St. (837-1300), just off N. Charles in Mount Vernon, two blocks from the hostel. One of the only pub-style bars in the neighborhood draws locals and English tourists longing for home with its daily specials, such as $5 domestic pitchers on Thurs. Happy hour (Mon.-Sat. 5-7pm, Sun. 9pm-2am) drops drink prices. 11 beers on tap. Open daily 11am-2am.

Orpheus, 1003 E. Praits St. (276-5599). This Art Deco establishment is a serious dance club attracting an eclectic crowd. Tues. is Rave Night with a $7 cover; Thurs. is Gothic Night with a $5 cover, Fri. is house or alternative dance with a $5 cover; Sat. is '70s, '80s, and '90s dance mix with a $3 cover; Sun. is 18+ with deep house and a $5 cover. Open Tues. and Thurs.-Sun. 9pm-2am.

Wharf Rat Bar, 801 S. Ann St. (276-9034), near Lancaster St. in Fells Point. A friendly bar with 29 beers on tap, including five of their very own "Oliver Ales." Stunning happy hour deal lets you quaff a ½-pint of 3 different drafts for only $3. Mon.-Sat. 11:30am-1am.

Gay and Lesbian Bars and Clubs

Allegro, 1101 Cathedral St. (837-3906), corner of Chase St. in the theater district. A young crowd gathers in this popular gay nightspot when the DJ starts spinning tunes at 9pm; disco and house music played nightly. Tues. is men's night; Thurs. is women's night; Wed. is "mixed energy" dance music; drag shows happen one Mon. per month. Sat. is always a theme night (like "Construction Party"). Cover Fri. and Sun. $3. Happy hour (Mon.-Sat. 6-10pm and Sun. 4-10pm) features ½-priced domestics and rails. Open Mon.-Sat. 6pm-2am, Sun. 4pm-2am.

Central Station, 1001 N. Charles St. (752-7133), on the corner of Eager St. (within walking distance of both Hippo and the hostel). This pub, with pool tables downstairs and a beautiful restaurant upstairs, is the place to be before the dance floors heat up elsewhere. Cheap fare: hamburgers and pizza $5 (5-11pm). Happy hour (daily 4-8pm) discounts drinks. Open daily 11:30am-2am.

Hippo, 1 W. Eager St. (547-0069); in a fantastic location, near the hostel and Mt. Vernon Hotel. Baltimore's largest and most popular gay bar provides pool tables, videos, and a packed dance floor. First Sun. of every month Ladies' Tea (6-10pm), Thurs. Men's Night. Cover Thurs.-Fri. $3, Sat. $5. On Thurs., cover buys "drink chips" redeemable for $3 worth of drinks. Happy hour Mon.-Fri. 4-8pm. Saloon open daily 3pm-2am. Dance bar open Wed.-Sat. 10pm-2am. Video bar open Thurs.-Sat. 10pm-2am.

Eastern Shore

The long arm of land known as the Eastern Shore is claimed by Maryland in the north and Virginia in the south. Though the Chesapeake Bay is the only physical divide between the shore and its mother states, the gulf between these areas is cultural as well. The Eastern Shore harbors a lifestyle last found in most of Virginia and Maryland decades ago. Untouched marshlands and expansive fields punctuate the forests and dunes of this tranquil landscape. Here, tractors are more common than commuters on the roads, and wild ponies still go unpenned. The Eastern Shore is a remarkable port of American natural history, a wilderness which is truly sublime.

ASSATEAGUE, MD AND CHINCOTEAGUE, VA

Local legend has it that horses first came to Assateague Island by swimming ashore after escaping a sinking Spanish galleon. Though less romantic, a more likely story is that a few centuries ago, several miserly mainland farmers put their horses out to graze on Assateague to avoid taxes and fencing expenses. Whatever their origins, the descendents of Assateague's original horses, the famous wild ponies, now roam free across the unspoiled beaches and forests of the island.

Assateague Island is divided into three parts. The **Assateague State Park** (410-641-2120), Rte. 611 in southeast Maryland, is a two-mi. stretch of picnic areas, beaches, bathhouses, and campsites. (Park open daily April-Oct. 8am-sunset. $2 per person for day use, seniors free. Campsite registration 8am-11pm. Sites $20; reservations available only in one-week blocks, Sat.-Sat.) The **Assateague Island National Seashore** claims most of the long sandbar north and south of the park and has its own campground (sites $12, Nov.-mid-May $8) and beaches, most of which are inaccessible by car. The **ranger station** (410-641-3030) here distributes free back-country camping permits, but only before 2pm; arrive early. The **Barrier Island Visitors Center** (410-641-1441), Rte. 611, provides an introduction to the park and gives day-use information (visitors center open daily 9am-5pm; $4 entrance fee per car). Of the meandering one-mi. nature trails, the Forest Trail offers the best viewing tower, but the Marsh Trail (ironically) has fewer mosquitoes (bring repellent).

The **Chincoteague National Wildlife Refuge** stretches across the Virginia side of the island. Avid bird-watchers flock here to see rare species such as peregrine falcons, snowy egrets, and black-crowned night herons. During slack tide (the last Wed. in July), the Chincoteague wild ponies are herded together and made to swim from Assateague to Chincoteague Island, where the local fire department auctions off the foals the following day. The adults swim back to Assateague and reproduce, providing next year's crop. Thus, the best time for pony-sighting on Assateague Island is in mid-July, just before they're sold. For more info., visit the **Chincoteague Refuge Visitor Contact Station,** on the island (804-336-6122; open daily 9am-4:30pm; admission $4 per car). The **Wildlife Loop** begins at the visitors center and provides ideal pony-viewing (open to people 5am-sunset; open to cars 3pm-sunset).

The best way to get to Assateague Island is by car—buses and taxis can be sporadic. If a car is out of the question, take **Carolina Trailways** (410-289-9307) to Ocean City, via daily express or local routes from Greyhound stations in Baltimore ($22) and Washington, D.C. ($36.50). From Ocean City, take a taxi to Assateague (289-1313; about $20). Carolina Trailways also runs buses from Salisbury, MD, and Norfolk, VA, stopping on U.S. 13 at **T's Corner** (804-824-5935), 11 mi. from Chincoteague. For more area info, call or write to the **Chincoteague Chamber of Commerce,** P.O. Box 258 (6733 Maddox Blvd.), Chincoteague, VA 23336 (804-336-6161; open summer daily 9am-4:30pm, after Labor Day Mon.-Sat. 9am-4:30pm).

THE REST OF VIRGINIA

If Virginia seems obsessed with its past, it has good reason: many of America's formative experiences—the white settlement of North America, the shameful legacy of the slave trade, American independence, the aristocratic farsightedness of the early U.S., and even the Civil War—all took root in Virginia. English colonists founded Jamestown in 1607; the New World's first black slaves joined them unwillingly 12 years later. While George Washington was still battling Native Americans in the French and Indian War, Thomas Jefferson wrote about religious and political freedom in the colonial capital, Williamsburg. Washington later returned to deal the British a table-turning defeat at Yorktown. Virginian James Madison traveled to Philadelphia in 1787 with drafts of the *Constitution,* and Virginian George Mason led the Bill of Rights campaign. Meanwhile, eastern Virginia's Tidewater aristocracy dominated the state for a century with its rigid, gracious culture of slave-dependent plantations—a culture that imploded during the Civil War, when Union and Confederate armies pushed one another around Virginia on the way to Appomattox.

While eastern Virginia celebrates its Revolutionary and Confederate history, Shenandoah National Park and the geologically stunning caverns of the west provide a respite from the state's barrage of nostalgia (and heat). The western region is not entirely without history, however; Jefferson's masterpieces (UVA and Monticello, in Charlottesville) and Harpers Ferry provide bastions of culture.

Virginia has, for the most part, pulled up its Old Southern roots for a more cosmopolitan existence; Virginia is home to many of D.C.'s political elite, as plantation life yields to the equally strong traditional influence of government. Still, Virginia relishes its role as the cradle of American independence and an icon of Southern culture, without hesitating to flaunt its singular place in history.

Fairfax County

Fairfax County's tourists travel back in time to the 18th-century charm of porticoes, porches, and well-pruned presidential gardens. But the warm and fuzzy colonial haven of tourism has little to do with the everyday lives of the people who reside here. This largest of Washington's suburbs prospered throughout the '80s as white- and blue-collar immigration transformed farms into suburbs, country roads into congested six-lane highways, and vacant lands into office complex upon shopping mall upon parking lot. Some fear uncontrolled development will turn Fairfax into a post-modern City of Quartz, à la L.A. Democratic County Executive Audrey Moore, elected to beat back the real-estate moguls, has yet to placate the county's commuter voters in the face of a rough economy. Meanwhile, the people keep moving in. Reston, once one of the nation's most successful "planned communities," now boasts its very own juvenile delinquents and an outdoor shopping plaza not unlike a sterilized Georgetown.

The traffic engineer's 20th-century vision is indeed a far cry from the County's historical fodder. When Philadelphia was still the nation's capital, aristocratic planters like George Washington and George Mason lived on Fairfax country estates and profited from Virginia's omnipresent cash crop, tobacco. In the 1780s, the anti-federalist pressures that produced the *Bill of Rights* emerged first and most loudly from these Virginia slave-owners. One farm is even responsible for D.C.'s historically unpopular location. According to legend, George Washington, asked to pick a spot along the Potomac for the new national capital, chose the land closest to Mount Vernon, his home. Few of Fairfax County's colonial-era plantations still produce crops, though its southern and western reaches preserve plenty of rural land. Some green space opens up to the public; parks and forests near the Potomac offer peace away from the sight-seeing circuit.

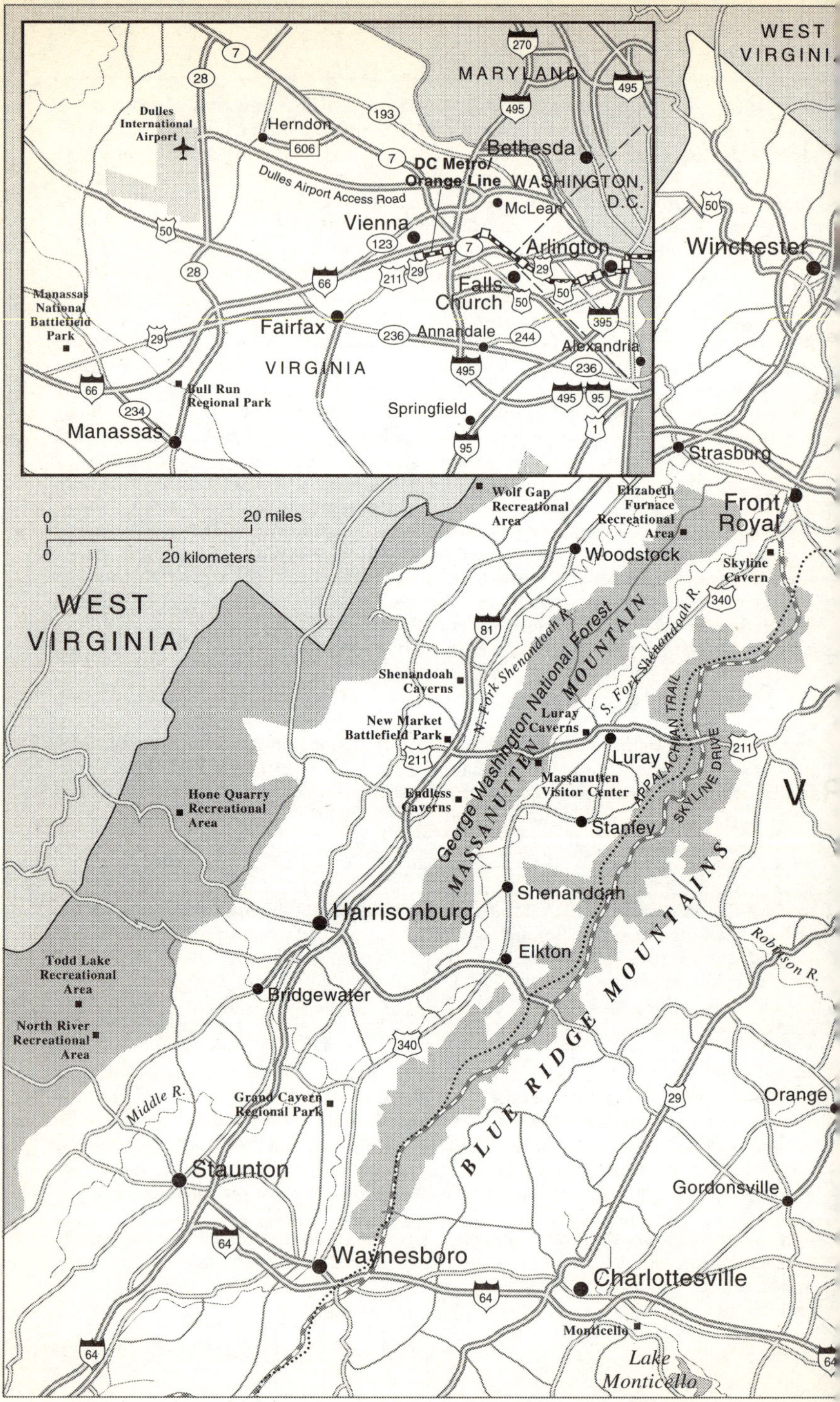
MARYLAND
WASHINGTON, D.C.
Dulles International Airport
Herndon
Dulles Airport Access Road
DC Metro/ Orange Line
Bethesda
McLean
Vienna
Arlington
Falls Church
Fairfax
Annandale
Alexandria
VIRGINIA
Springfield
Manassas National Battlefield Park
Bull Run Regional Park
Manassas
WEST VIRGINIA
Winchester
Strasburg
Front Royal
Wolf Gap Recreational Area
Elizabeth Furnace Recreational Area
Woodstock
Skyline Cavern
0 20 miles
0 20 kilometers
WEST VIRGINIA
Shenandoah Caverns
New Market Battlefield Park
N. Fork Shenandoah R.
George Washington National Forest
MASSANUTTEN MOUNTAIN
S. Fork Shenandoah R.
Luray Caverns
Luray
APPALACHIAN TRAIL
SKYLINE DRIVE
Massanutten Visitor Center
Endless Caverns
Hone Quarry Recreational Area
Stanley
Shenandoah
Harrisonburg
Elkton
BLUE RIDGE MOUNTAINS
Robinson R.
Todd Lake Recreational Area
North River Recreational Area
Bridgewater
Middle R.
Grand Cavern Regional Park
Orange
Staunton
Gordonsville
Waynesboro
Charlottesville
Monticello
Lake Monticello

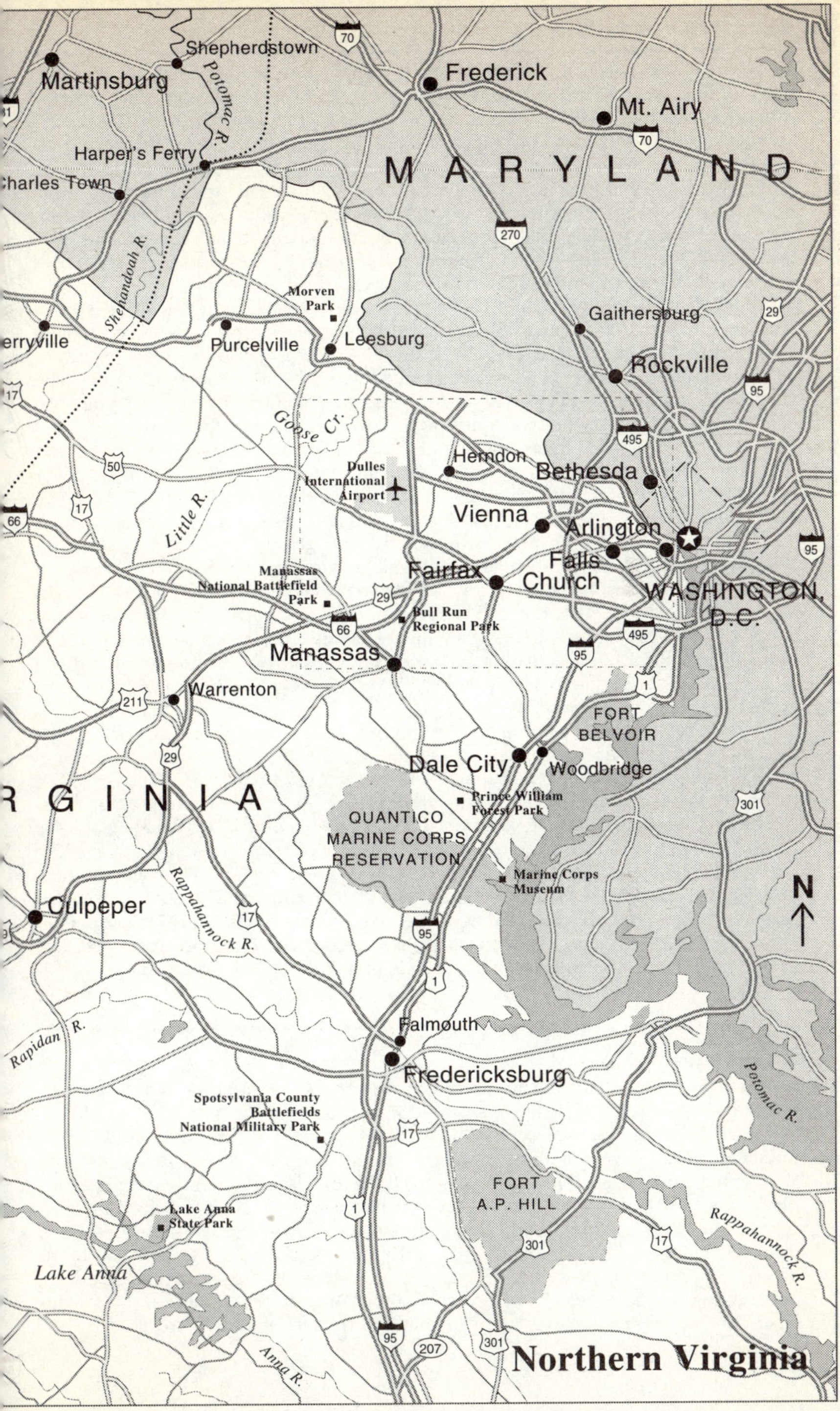
Northern Virginia
MARYLAND
RGINIA
Shepherdstown
Martinsburg
Potomac R.
Frederick
Mt. Airy
Harper's Ferry
Charles Town
Shenandoah R.
Morven Park
Leesburg
Purcelville
Gaithersburg
Rockville
Goose Cr.
Herndon
Dulles International Airport
Bethesda
Vienna
Arlington
Little R.
Manassas National Battlefield Park
Fairfax
Falls Church
WASHINGTON, D.C.
Bull Run Regional Park
Manassas
Warrenton
FORT BELVOIR
Dale City
Woodbridge
Prince William Forest Park
QUANTICO MARINE CORPS RESERVATION
Marine Corps Museum
Culpeper
Rappahannock R.
Rapidan R.
Falmouth
Fredericksburg
Spotsylvania County Battlefields National Military Park
FORT A.P. HILL
Lake Anna State Park
Lake Anna
Anna R.
N

GETTING AROUND

Given the vast expanse of Fairfax County, in conjunction with the scarcity of public transportation accessing each of its corners, the easiest way to get from place to place is undoubtedly by car. However, as some of the roads in Fairfax County can often be confusing to newcomers and residents alike, it may be better to leave the maneuvering to someone else. The **Metro**'s Blue and Yellow Lines serve the southeastern portion of Fairfax, leaving the sole Orange Line to transport daily commuters from the northern stretch of the county. This service, however, leaves the central part of Fairfax County inaccessible by rail. Metrobuses, in conjunction with **Fairfax Connector Buses** (call 703-339-7200 for fare, route, and scheduling information), pick up most of the slack in the remaining areas of the county.

If, however, you are undaunted by Fairfax County's roads, keep in mind that some warrant at least a little drivewise wariness. Perhaps most essential to both commuters and tourists, the **Capital Beltway**'s eight lanes (I-495 west of Springfield, I-95 east of it) encircle the nation's capital and are plagued with the city's congested traffic. The George Washington Parkway, quite possibly the most scenic drive in the Washington area, winds southward along the bluffs high above the Potomac River from the northwest tip of the Capital Beltway towards Alexandria, where it becomes Mount Vernon Memorial Parkway. It ends in southeastern Fairfax County at Rte. 1, the Jefferson Davis Highway, which runs parallel to I-95 from Arlington to Richmond. Heading north, I-95 becomes I-395 inside the Beltway. Duke St. in Alexandria travels west to become the Little River Turnpike (Rte. 236). Lee Highway (Rte. 29) and Arlington Boulevard (Rte. 50) run east-west—from Arlington to Fairfax City and beyond—to the Manassas National Battlefield Park, site of two civil war battles. In northern Fairfax County, Georgetown Pike (Rte. 193) is a cross-river extension of the MacArthur Boulevard in NW Washington, providing a winding trip through the forest and among the multi-million dollar homes of Great Falls and McLean. For those who intend to travel by air, the Dulles Access Road serves as a link from I-66 and the Capital Beltway to **Dulles International Airport.**

If you do plan to drive, call your destination whenever possible and ask for detailed directions. Remember that Fairfax's roads, though numerous enough to stymie long-time Washingtonians, are still far too few to handle rush-hour traffic. On weekdays, driving to Fairfax from D.C. between 4 and 7pm, or vice versa between 6 and 9am, can be troublesome. During these hours, parts of I-66 become HOV, which stands for "High Occupancy Vehicle"; you're asking for a hefty ticket if you're caught in an HOV lane without the requisite number of people in your car (look for the backseat mannequins and inflatable dolls which some desperate commuters use to circumvent this rule). Recently, I-66 was expanded from four to eight lanes, with an HOV-2 (2-person min.) lane on either side. This expansion has eased the congestion somewhat, but Fairfax commuters continue to hit the road in great numbers during rush hours.

SIGHTS

Mount Vernon

Mount Vernon is the former home of our most revered founding father: George Washington, the nation's first president, slept here, ate here, farmed here, and, in the end, died here. As Commander-in-Chief of the Continental Army, Washington was forced to travel extensively throughout the nascent nation, sometimes leaving Mount Vernon for years on end. However, despite all the time Washington spent in Philadelphia, New York, or on horseback at the head of an army, he always returned "home," which was never anything but his beloved abode overlooking the Potomac River. A talented decorator and courteous host, Washington dedicated the greater part of his life to beautifying the interior of his mansion and sculpting the surrounding gardens. Washington would no doubt be pleased to see that nearly two centuries after his death, his estate is maintained just as he might have had it kept. The mansion is spotless and the gardens well-tended, sustaining the love for the estate that Washington himself fostered, and welcoming over a million visitors each year.

The busloads of tour groups that flock to Mount Vernon's main entrance gate may seem discouraging, but be assured: there is plenty of room inside to diffuse the throngs. **Complimentary maps** are available just inside the entrance gate; though the mansion itself is easy to find, other interesting and important outbuildings, such as George and Martha Washington's tomb, may not be apparent. The estate's grounds merit at least an hour-long stroll. If you choose to begin your visit with the tour of the mansion, don't be daunted by the enormous line at the entrance; it moves surprisingly quickly.

The mansion's Georgian exterior warrants attention as one approaches the entrance. From far away, the façade passes for stone; in fact, clever builders painted the pine boards and then sprinkled the wet wood with sand to give the house a stony face.

The tour (which is not given to herded groups of visitors, but rather to a continuous line that flows from room to room within the mansion) begins in the formal dining room, most likely where the Washingtons entertained their guests. Through the room, shuffle out the back door to the piazza—which affords both a breathtaking view of the Potomac and a cool breeze—and back into the main entrance hall of the mansion. Here, enclosed in a glass case, is the key to the Bastille (the 18th-century prison relic of the French Revolution), given to Washington in 1790 by the Marquis de Lafayette, a close friend of the Washington clan. Other rooms on the first floor include the common parlor, in which Martha Washington's granddaughter Nelly Custis cultivated her taste and talent in the 18th-century music of the harpsichord. The second floor of the mansion boasts ten bedrooms, including the room in, and bed on which, George Washington slept and later died—of acute epiglottitis.

The walk-through tour ends downstairs in Washington's study, pantry, and kitchen; the kitchen stood apart from the mansion so that stove-incited fires wouldn't spread to the rest of the estate. Behind the kitchen, follow the gravel path which leads to **George and Martha Washington's tomb:** stone sarcophagi housed in a mausoleum and guarded by a sturdy iron gate. Other Washington family members are also buried in the graveyard, and nearby is the quiet, gravestone-less "slave burial ground," including a deserved memorial to Washington's slaves, who numbered greater than any other planter's slaves in Northern Virginia at that time.

On the uphill retreat from the tombs, explore the **botanical gardens** on the grounds adjacent to the mansion. While the upper garden is a well-manicured botanical fête, the lower garden seems more like a field of crops. Mount Vernon's outside field (the entire estate included thousands of acres of land) once produced tobacco, and later, corn, wheat, and smokeable marijuana, after Washington learned of the dangers that tobacco cultivation caused to the grounds' soil. Only the corn remains at the **Mount Vernon Museum,** near the slave quarters' greenhouse next to the upper garden to the left of the house; on display are more interesting relics, including Washington's swords and toothbrush, Martha's wedding slippers, and Houdon's 1785 bust of our nation's first president.

Those busloads of tour groups do tend to get a bit overwhelming during the summer season; weekday mornings are the best bet during these months. (Open daily April-Aug. 8am-5pm; Sept.-Oct. and March 9am-5pm; Nov.-Feb. 9am-4pm. Admission $8, over 62 $7.50 (ID required), children 6-11 (accompanied by an adult) $4. Call 703-780-2000 for more information.)

Getting There

To drive to Mount Vernon, take the George Washington Parkway south towards Mount Vernon (the Pkwy. becomes the Mount Vernon Hwy. in Alexandria). If you are coming off the Capital Beltway, be sure to take the exit for Rte. 1 North towards Mount Vernon. Immediately after the exit ramp, follow the brown signs for Mount Vernon, making a right on Franklin St. and then another right on Washington St., which eventually becomes Mount Vernon Hwy. after it crosses the Beltway. Follow

Mount Vernon Hwy. south for eight miles until you reach the circular drive at the estate's entrance gate. Bear left or right; parking in the Mount Vernon lot is free for four hours. Mount Vernon is also accessible by public transportation; take the **Metro**'s Yellow Line to Huntington and catch the Fairfax Connector 101 bus at the north end of the station (the ride is approx. 20min. long; call 703-339-7200 for schedule info.). A slightly more expensive yet more enjoyable and scenic option is reaching Mount Vernon via riverboat. The *Spirit of Washington,* which runs from the end of March through the end of September, leaves from the dock at Maine Ave. in Washington for a 75-minute ride to the landing at Mount Vernon, where passengers have two hours to stroll the grounds before boarding for the return trip. (Cruises leave for Mount Vernon mid-June to late Aug. Tues.-Sun. 9am and 2pm, 9am only in spring and fall. Round-trip fare, including Mount Vernon entrance fee, $23; senior citizens $21; children $14. For more information, call 202-554-8000.)

Pope-Leighey House and Woodlawn Plantation

Two houses—one old, one new—sit on the grounds of Woodlawn Plantation like bookends, holding between them the span of American architectural history. The original Georgian-style Woodlawn mansion, completed in 1806, still anchors the 2000-acre lot, but it is now joined by Frank Lloyd Wright's simple and modern Pope-Leighey House, completed in 1940 and moved to this site in 1964.

From the main parking lot, a clear path leads to Woodlawn, but a sign for Pope-Leighey House directs across the parking lot and into the woods. Take the road less traveled and admire Pope-Leighey first; plantations loiter on every Virginia street corner, but only one other Frank Lloyd Wright house of this kind is open to the public. By 1997, the house should be newly restored; it has been moved back about 30 feet due to a loose foundation. Post-restoration plans are for a manicured garden in the L-shape of the house itself, completing the exterior impression of Pope-Leighey.

The **Pope-Leighey** place is one of Wright's Usonian houses, designed for inhabitants of moderate means ("Usonia" was utopian author Samuel Butler's acronym for the United States of North America). Commissioned in 1939, the $7000 house held the four-member family of Laurent Pope, a Washington newspaper writer. When Pope relocated to work for the New York Times, he sold the house to Mr. Robert Leighey, a Fairfax County attorney. Finally, when devious highway planners sent Rte. 66 through the house's original location in Falls Church, VA, Mrs. Leighey rescued it by donating it to the National Trust for Historic Preservation in 1964. The house was moved to its present site on the grounds of Woodlawn Plantation.

The 25 Usonian houses Wright built follow his famous design precepts in their organic unity with their environment: here cypress, glass, and brick blend with the surrounding forest. Note the house's modern form—unlike many of his contemporaries, Wright's houses never seem dated. Part of Wright's genius was his attention to detail: notice the kitchen cabinets, which all open away from the window to eliminate shadows on the shelves behind. Wright was also concerned with privacy: the windows along the house's façade are high up in order to let light in without affording a view of the interior.

The **guided tour** probes the interior. Pope-Leighey covers only 1200 sq. ft., but Wright's design lends an impression of vast area. Wright's interiors exemplify his "destruction of the box" with freely flowing space. Patios and large windows at either end make the living and dining rooms seem to extend outdoors. The modern geometric furniture is made of plywood; Wright intended it as furniture most people could afford to build for themselves. The bedrooms also seem deceptively large because their closets hold, and hide, the bureaus. (Seek no storage space under the house's flat roof; Wright considered attics and basements wasteful.) Wright also created and revolutionized the carport, a key feature of the modern house.

A carport fixture would have been of little use at **Woodlawn Plantation**, a wedding present from George Washington to Nelly Custis, his adopted daughter, and Lawrence Lewis, his nephew. Custis lived with the Washingtons at Mount Vernon and she met Lewis when Washington asked him to come to Mount Vernon and serve as a secretary. Married by candlelight on February 22, 1799, George Washington's last birthday, the couple soon engaged William Thornton, the architect of the U.S. Capitol, to design and build a house on the land Washington had bequeathed them. Besides 2000 acres of his Mount Vernon lands, Washington's gift included his grist mill and a distillery.

The tour of the exquisitely preserved, five-part Georgian mansion begins in the master bedroom and the back portico, featuring a view of Mount Vernon in the distance (the five tall oak trees on the horizon mark Mount Vernon's location). The first-floor includes the main hall, the front entrance of which was used for visitors while the back entrance was used to greet river travelers. The furniture from this hall was often removed in order to accommodate Nelly Custis's penchant for dancing. Off the main hall is the music room; its peculiar ceiling was raised a foot for the sake of better acoustics. The first floor is peppered with the extremely complex and detailed needlework of Nelly Custis, present on footstools and various other accessories. The upstairs consists mainly of bedrooms, including one that was frequently occupied by the Marquis de Lafayette, a close friend of George Washington. The most well-lit room upstairs is Nelly Custis's study, in which she most likely sat occupied with her needlework. While descending the stairs and entering the gift shop as the tour draws to a close, take note of the stitched image (of two mourners in front of a grave) hung on the wall. If you look at the reflection in the situated mirror, one of the mourners mysteriously disappears and an angel appears above the grave.

After the tour and a visit to the gift shop, any extra time can be spent leisurely strolling in the gardens; the well-tended and pruned lawns and gardens' beauty magnifies the essence of this classic, Federal-period Virginian plantation. (Woodlawn open March-Dec. daily 9:30am-4:30pm with the last tour at 4pm; admission $6, students through 12th grade and seniors $4. Pope-Leighey open daily March-Dec. 9:30am-4:30pm; admission to Pope-Leighey House $6, students through 12th grade and seniors $4. Wheelchair access limited; call 703-780-4000 for details.)

Getting There

To drive to Pope-Leighey House and Woodlawn Plantation, continue down Mount Vernon Hwy. from Mount Vernon until you reach Rte. 1, also called Richmond Hwy. The driveway to the Woodlawn parking lot is right across the intersection. If you are coming from Gunston Hall, take Gunston Rd. and turn right onto Rte. 1. Then turn left at the light marking the intersection with Mount Vernon Hwy. By public transportation from Washington, take the Metro Yellow Line to Huntington and catch the 9B Metrobus, which leaves approximately every half hour from the north end of the station. The bus will ultimately wind its way along Rte. 1; get off at the intersection with the Mount Vernon Hwy./Old Mill Rd.

Gunston Hall

This well-preserved plantation is worth the extra 20 minutes on the road. Thankfully skipped by the Tourmobile route, Gunston Hall (703-550-9220) gives a relaxed tour, which focuses as much on 18th-century living as on the plantation's one-time owner, George Mason. Especially appealing to travelers with children, Gunston Hall will prove less crowded and as interesting as its more famous neighbor.

George Mason traded political thoughts with George Washington and James Madison, two other Virginia plantation aristocrats; but after they revolted against British rule, George Mason found the alternatives almost as revolting. With the outbreak of the American Revolution, the Second Continental Congress called for each colony to establish its own constitution. Mason prefaced Virginia's, the first of its kind, with his own document—the *Virginia Declaration of Rights.* Three weeks after the appearance of the *Virginia Declaration,* Thomas Jefferson used similar wording in the *Declaration of Independence.* Mason refused to sign the *U.S. Constitution* because it had no bill of rights; he helped convince Congress to add the first ten amendments (the *Bill of Rights)* to the *Constitution.*

The wait for the 20-minute guided tour (it leaves from the front porch of the house every half hour), can be spent exploring the **museum** in the visitors building. The displays provide short, informative discussions about the life of the Mason family at Gunston Hall, using the family as a springboard from which to discuss 18th-century colonial life. An 11-min. video introduction to Mason's life plays on demand.

The view of the driveway from the front porch of the house is fantastic; Mason had his driveway lined with almost 200 magnolia trees—hence the name Magnolia Avenue. The trees are lined and pruned with such precision that only some are visible from the front porch. From the outside, the house appears rather small and modest, its Georgian austerity not providing the same grandeur as that of Mount Vernon's mansion. The interior, however, lends a striking sense of roominess. Note the symmetry of the house, an essential element of Georgian style. For example, the hallway on the left side of the main hall is balanced on the right by a door behind which there is no room. The downstairs also features the bedroom where George Mason's beloved wife Ann slept and died (at the age of 39). The upstairs deviates from traditional Georgian style; it does not have the same four-room pattern as does the ground floor. His second floor consisted of eight rooms along a dormitory-style hallway, in order to accommodate his nine children.

Behind the house, an English boxwood garden grows in formal geometric patterns. One can stroll through the quiet garden or walk down to the wharf on the Potomac River. The area abuts the Mason Neck National Wildlife Refuge; the bird-watching is prime. In the meadow in front of the house, a breed of stunted sheep from Hog Island (in the Chesapeake Bay) hasn't evolved much since the 18th century. Gunston Hall also sports the requisite schoolhouse, kitchen, laundry, smokehouse, and dairy. A special celebration each year observes **George Mason Day,** Dec. 11. A **Kite Festival** in March numbers among other annual events; call for more info.

Gunston Hall is open daily from 9:30am to 5pm, with tours every half hour; the last tour begins at 4:30pm and the grounds close at 6pm. (Admission $5, adults 60 and over $4, students grades 1-12 $1.50.) Gunston Hall is in the process of becoming wheelchair-accessible; call to check on the progress.

Getting There

The only practical way to reach Gunston Hall is by car. Follow the directions to Mount Vernon, and pick up Mount Vernon Memorial Hwy. where George Washington Memorial Pkwy. ends—at the circular driveway of Mount Vernon. Drive on Mount Vernon Hwy. until you hit Rte. 1, also called Richmond Hwy. You'll pass Fort Belvoir, but keep going until you hit Gunston Rd. (Rte. 242). A few miles down the road on your left is Gunston Hall. Parking is free and plentiful.

The Rest of Fairfax

Near George Mason's house, strain your neck bird-watching at the aptly named **Mason Neck National Wildlife Refuge,** a mile down Gunston Rd. (Rte. 242) from Gunston Hall (open 8am-dark; free). Hike through forest, grasslands, and marshes while trying to photograph bald eagles, great blue herons, beavers, and otters. (No fires, camping, hunting, or fishing allowed.) Even more enjoyable than the Wildlife Refuge—and just a little further down the road—is the **Mason Neck State Park.** Perched directly on the banks of the Potomac River, the visitors center and adjacent picnic areas provide a relaxing and scenic setting, as the acres of forest land give way to the waterfront. (State Park open daily dawn-dusk; admission $1 per vehicle weekdays, $2 per vehicle weekends and holidays.)

The Wildlife Refuge may bore the skedaddle out of kids; an alternative can be found at the **Pohick Bay Regional Park** (703-339-6100), also along Gunston Rd. The facilities include the largest swimming pool on the East Coast, a marina with sail- and paddleboat rentals, an 18-hole golf course, miniature golf, picnic tables, a 4-mi. bridle path, and 200 campsites. (Open daily 8am-dark, swimming pool open only Memorial Day-Labor Day. Admission $4 per vehicle, $8 per vehicle with 10 or more passengers.

Swimming fee $3.25, children 2-11 and adults over 59 $2.75. **Golf green** (339-8585) fees Mon.-Thurs. $20, Fri.-Sun. $24.)

Breathtaking views of the Potomac River abound throughout all 800 acres of **Great Falls Park** (703-285-2966). The Park's main attraction is its 16 miles of hiking trails along the forested pathways beside the river. Hiking maps are available at the informative Visitors Center just inside the entrance gate. From the falls overlook, only a short walk from the visitors center, the map will lead along the riverbanks to the remains of a canal that George Washington's Potomac Company built in the late 1700s, in order to facilitate trade between Washington and the Ohio Valley. One can also witness the ruins of Matildaville, a late 18th-century town that once flourished with the influx of trade down the Potomac River.

Hiking is not the only attraction at Great Falls. Visitors can also indulge in kayaking and whitewater rafting—but only experienced boaters should attempt the rushing river. Serious **rock climbers** get vertical on Great Falls' bare granite; the Park Service asks all climbers to register first at the Visitors Center. Many people enjoy scrambling over the rocks that line the river, though the Park Service would rather they kept to the paths; every so often someone tumbles sidelong into the Potomac. Park rules forbid any swimming in the Potomac, and for good reason—the churning river claims about seven lives a year. Special **ranger walks** are offered daily throughout the year; contact the Visitors Center for information.

If **fishing** lures you, come here to catch and eat catfish or carp; cast your line between the two overlook points to the right of the Visitors Center. Anyone over 16 must have a fishing license. Call the Visitors Center in advance for a list of locations in Virginia and Maryland where you can purchase one. Forget about taking a Metrobus here. To drive to Great Falls, take the Beltway I-495 to exit 13, then Georgetown Pike (Rte. 193) west. Turn right at Old Dominion Drive (Rte. 738). (Open daily dawn-dark. Entrance fee $4 per vehicle, $2 per person without a vehicle, free for those under 16 and the disabled.)

A little further out of town but easily accessible by car, the **Reston Animal Park,** at 1228 Hunter Mill Rd., Vienna VA (703-759-3636), will undoubtedly satisfy that everlasting childhood desire to feed and play with animals. Located in a wide open field behind a row of contemporary homes (seemingly out of place in this rural setting), the park features everything from pigs to zebras to elephants. New arrivals include a Siberian tiger cub and a few ring-tailed lemurs. "Intra-park transportation" includes elephant rides ($3), pony rides ($1.50), and a wagon ride (included in the admission ticket) which explores the grounds and the bison. From Washington, take the Beltway (I-495) to the Dulles Toll Road (west); exit 5 is Hunter Mill Road. From Great Falls, turn right onto Georgetown Pike (Rte. 193). After several miles, take a left onto Springvale Rd. After crossing Leesburg Pike (Rte. 7), turn left on Hunter Mill Rd. The park is on the right. (Open summer Mon.-Fri. 10am-5pm, Sat.-Sun. 10am-6pm; spring and fall Mon.-Fri. 10am-3pm, Sat.-Sun. 10am-5pm. Admission $8, seniors and children 2-12 $7. Mon.-Tues. $6 for all. Animal food 50¢ per cone.)

Among the fields and homes of suburban Langley is the most interesting Washington sight you'll never see. The new headquarters of the **Central Intelligence Agency,** which supervises Uncle Sam's spy network, is most emphatically closed to tourists. One in every $200 spent on new government buildings must pay for "public art"; though its grounds are hardly public, the CIA headquarter's builders had sculptor Jim Sanborn create a flat, green wall-like sculpture stamped with thousands of letters and numbers. Only ex-CIA head William Webster and Sanborn know their secret meaning. Nonviolent mass protests occasionally (every two years or so) block the CIA's driveways, keeping the beagles from driving to work.

Shenandoah National Park

Shenandoah National Park was America's first great natural reclamation project; in 1926, Congress authorized Virginia to purchase a 280-acre tract of over-logged, over-hunted land. The small population of reclusive trappers were relocated and President

Franklin D. Roosevelt dedicated the park to wildlife preservation in 1936. The experiment remains one of his greatest successes; today, residents include not-so-reclusive deer, bears, and other critters who make their home in the lush forest that has prospered over the last 60 years. Fields have given way to woodland, transforming the park into a spectacular ridgetop preserve. A trip along its spine via Skyline Drive allows glimpses of the Blue Ridge Mountains, the fertile plains below, and some of the park's furry and inquisitive inhabitants.

Shenandoah's natural beauty comes in the form of sweeping vistas and an abundance of life. On clear days, drivers and hikers can see miles of unspoiled ridges and treetops, home to more plant species than all of Europe. In the summer, the cool mountain air offers a respite from Virginia's oppressive heat and humidity. Early in June, see the blooming mountain laurel in the highlands. In the fall, Skyline Drive and its lodges are choked with tourists who come to enjoy the magnificent autumn foliage. Of course, outdoorsmen can be found almost any season, trekking along the Appalachian Trail. The narrow park stretches almost 75 mi. along the Blue Ridge Mountains, parallel to and south of the wilder George Washington National Forest.

PRACTICAL INFORMATION

Park Information: 999-2243 (daily 8am-4:30pm), 999-3500 for 24-hr. recorded message. Mailing address: Superintendent, Park Headquarters, Shenandoah National Park, Rte. 4, P.O. Box 348, Luray, VA 22835.

Dickey Ridge Visitors Center: Mile 4.6 (635-3566), closest to the north entrance. Daily programs. Open April-Nov. daily 9am-5pm. **Byrd Visitors Center:** Mile 51 (999-3283), in the center of the park. Open April-Oct. daily 9am-5pm. Byrd offers an historical-minded museum and movie; both stations offer exhibits, free hiking pamphlets, daily weather updates, and ranger-led nature hikes.

Emergency (in park): 800-732-0911, or contact the nearest ranger.

Area Code: 540.

Shenandoah's amazing technicolor mountains—bluish and covered with deciduous flora in the summer, streaked with brilliant reds, oranges, and yellows in the fall—can be enjoyed from the many overlooking areas along **Skyline Drive** (speed limit 35 mph), which runs 105 mi. south from Front Royal to Rockfish Gap. (Miles along Skyline Dr. are measured north to south, beginning at Front Royal.) The rest stops provide picnic areas for hikers; map boards also carry data about trail conditions. The drive closes during and following bad weather. Most facilities also hibernate in the winter. (Entrance $5 per vehicle, $3 per hiker, biker, or bus passenger, disabled persons free; pass is good for 7 days and is necessary for re-admittance.)

Containing park regulations, trail lists, and a description of the area's geological history, the *Park Guide* ($2) is invaluable to those on an extended visit. Few brochures are displayed, but rangers will provide free literature upon request.

Greyhound (800-231-2222) sends buses once per morning from D.C. to Waynesboro, near the park's southern entrance ($40 one-way), but no bus or train serves Front Royal. Rockfish Gap is only 25 mi. from Charlottesville on Rte. 64. You can also drive to Shenandoah from D.C.; take Rte. 66 west to 340 south to Front Royal.

ACCOMMODATIONS AND CAMPING

The **Bear's Den (HI-AYH)** (554-8708), located 35 mi. north of Shenandoah on Rte. 601 South, provides a woodsy stone lodge with two 10-bed dorm rooms and one room with one double bed and two bunk beds. Drivers should exit from Rte. 7 onto Rte. 601 South; after ½ mi., turn right at the stone-gate entrance, and proceed up the hostel driveway for another ½ mi. No bus or train service is available. The hostel has a dining room, kitchen, on-site parking, and a laundry room. The proprietor sells snacks, drinks, and hiking and camping supplies. (Check-in 5-10pm. Front gate locked and quiet hours begin at 10pm. Check-out 9:30am. $12, nonmembers $15. Camping $6 per person. Reservations recommended; write Bear's Den (HI-AYH), Postal Route 1, Box 288, Bluemont, VA 22135.)

The park maintains two affordable lodges: motel-esque rooms within cabin-esque exteriors. **Skyland** (999-2211, 800-999-4714), Mile 42 on Skyline Drive, open April-Oct., offers brown and green wood-furnished cabins ($46-79, $5-7 more in Oct.) and slightly more upscale motel rooms ($77-88; open April-Nov.). **Lewis Mountain,** Mile 57 (999-2255 or 800-999-4714), also gets cabin fever with a set of its own ($52-55, $7 more in Oct.). Reservations are necessary; call up to six months in advance.

The park service also maintains three major **campgrounds: Big Meadows** (Mile 51); **Lewis Mountain** (Mile 58); and **Loft Mountain** (Mile 80). All have stores, laundry facilities, and showers (no hookups). Heavily wooded and uncluttered by mobile homes, Lewis Mountain makes for the happiest tenters. Sites at Lewis Mountain and Loft Mountain $12, at Big Meadows $14 with reservation. Reservations possible only at Big Meadows (800-365-2267).

Back-country camping is free, but you must obtain a permit at a park entrance, visitors center, ranger station, or the **park headquarters** (see Practical Information above) halfway between Thornton Gap and Luray on U.S. 211. Since open fires are prohibited, bring cold food or a stove; boil water or bring your own—some creeks are oozing with microscopic beasties. Illegal camping carries a hefty fine. Hikers on the **Appalachian Trail** can make use of primitive open shelters, three-sided structures with stone fireplaces, strewn along the trail at approximate 7-mi. intervals. Shelters are reserved for hikers with at least three nights in different locations stamped on their camping permits; casual hikers are banned from them. $1 per night donation. The **Potomac Appalachian Trail Club (PATC)** maintains six cabins in back-country areas of the park. You must reserve in advance by writing to the club at 118 Park St., SE, Vienna, VA 22180-4609, or calling 703-242-0693. Bring lanterns and food; the cabins contain only bunk beds, water, and stoves. (Sun.-Thurs. $3 per person, Fri.-Sat. $14 per group; one group member must be at least 21.)

HIKES AND ACTIVITIES

The **Appalachian Trail** runs the length of the park. Trail maps and the PATC guide can be obtained at the visitors center (see **Practical Information,** p. 270). The PATC puts out three topographical maps ($5 each), each of a different part of the park. When purchased as a package, the maps come with a trail guide, descriptions, and suggestions for budgeting time ($16). Brochures covering the hikes are free. Overnight hikers should keep in mind the unpredictability of mountain weather. Be sure to get the park service package of brochures and advice before a long hike.

Both park visitors centers offer a variety of **programs:** talks on local wildlife, short guided walks among the flora, and lantern-lit discussions of the mountaineers' culture and lifestyle in the evening. Slide presentations introducing the park's many natural wonders are given regularly.

Old Rag Mountain, five mi. from Mile 45, is 3268 ft.—not an intimidating summit—but the 8.8-mi. loop up the mountain is deceptively difficult. This 6-8-hr. hike is steep, involves scrambling over and between granite, and at many points flaunts disappointing "false summits." Bring lots of water, energy food, and stamina. Camping is banned above 2800 ft. (The National Park Service charges $3 to Old Rag hikers 16 and older, unless they have already paid the Shenandoah admission fee.) The **Whiteoak Canyon Trail** beckons from its own parking lot at Mile 42.6. The trail to the canyon is easy; the six waterfalls and trout-filled streams below are spectacular. (A five-day non-resident permit can be purchased at the waysides for $6.50. The visitors center lists rules governing trout fishing.) From Whiteoak Canyon, the **Limberlost** trail (5-mi. round-trip) slithers into a hemlock forest. At Mile 51.4, **Lewis Spring Falls Trail** takes only ¾-mi. to reach a gorgeous array of falls—the closest to Skyline Drive in the whole park. The trail descends farther (about an hour's walk) to the base of the falls, where water drops 80 ft. over the crumbling stone of an ancient lava flow. **Hogback Overlook,** from Mile 20.8 to Mile 21, bristles with easy hikes and idyllic views of the smooth Shenandoah River and Valley. At **Dark Hollow Falls,** Mile 50.7, a 1½-mi. hike takes you to the base of scenic cascades.

Take a break from hiking or driving at one of Shenandoah's seven **picnic areas,** located at Dickey Ridge (Mile 5), Elkwallow (Mile 24), Pinnacles (Mile 37), Big Meadows (Mile 51), Lewis Mountain (Mile 58), South River (Mile 63) and Loft Mountain (Mile 80). All have tables, fireplaces, water fountains, and comfort stations.

Outside the Park

Western Virginia boasts some of the most stunning geological formations in the east. Discovered in 1878, **Luray Caverns** (743-6551) features a "Stalagpipe Organ." (Follow the billboards on U.S. 211; exit 264 off I-81. Admission $12, children 7-13 $6, under 7 free. $1 AAA discount.) Admission to antique carriage and car museum is included (open daily 9am-6pm). The **Shenandoah Caverns** (477-3115) tout iridescent stalactites and stalagmites, with Rainbow Lake and the amusing Capitol Dome among the underground formations thriving in the year-round 56°F air. Take U.S. 211 to Newmarket, get on I-81 North, go four mi. to the Shenandoah Caverns exit, and follow the signs for the caverns—not the town of the same name. (Accessible to disabled persons. Admission $8, ages 8-14 $4, under 8 free. Open mid-April-mid-June and Labor Day-Oct. 9am-6pm, other times 9am-5pm.) **Skyline Caverns** (635-4545 or 800-635-4599), in Front Royal, has built a reputation on its anthodites, whose white spikes defy gravity and grow in all directions at the rate of an inch every seven-thousand years. The caverns are 15 min. from the junction of Skyline Drive and U.S. 211. (Open mid-June-Aug. daily 9am-6pm; spring and fall Mon.-Fri. 9am-5pm, Sat.-Sun. 9am-6pm; winter daily 9am-4pm. Admission $10, ages 6-12 $5.)

The area north of the park is home to several vineyards which offer pleasant picnic spots. **Piedmont Vineyards** (687-5528) offers free tours and samples of its ten vines. From U.S. 50 West, take Rte. 626 at Middleburg; from I-66, take Rte. 245 North, then a right at The Plains and a left onto Rte. 626 North. If a scenic paddle floats your boat, contact the **Downriver Canoe Co.,** Rte. 613 (Indian Hollow Rd.), Bentonville (635-5526 or 800-338-1963). From Skyline Drive Mile 20 follow U.S 211 west for eight mi., then north onto U.S. 340, 14 mi. to Bentonville. Turn right onto Rte. 613 and go one mi. (Prices vary with length of trip. 3-mi. trips $29 per canoe; 3-day trip $122/canoe. Kayak and tube trips also available. 25% discount weekdays.)

Charlottesville

The renowned renaissance man Thomas Jefferson, when writing his own epitaph, was careful to point out his role as "father of the University of Virginia." The college he founded sustains Charlottesville economically, geographically, and culturally, perpetuating both a community of writers—such as Pulitzer Prize-winning poet Rita Dove—and a community of pubs. But UVA is only one of many feathers in Jefferson's cap; Monticello, a cleverly constructed Classical mansion, was designed and built by Jefferson over a 40-year period. Even the friendly, hip, and down-to-earth population of this Blue Ridge foothills town seems to embody the third U.S. President's dream of a well-informed, culturally aware citizenry which chooses to live close to the land. Indeed, it is largely because of Jefferson that Charlottesville is the intellectual capital of Virginia.

PRACTICAL INFORMATION AND ORIENTATION

Visitor Information: Chamber of Commerce, 415 E. Market St. (295-3141), within walking distance of Amtrak, Greyhound, and town. Open Mon.-Fri. 9am-5pm. **Charlottesville/Albermarle Convention and Visitors Bureau,** P.O. Box 161, Rte. 20 near I-64 (977-1783). Take bus #8 ("Piedmont College") from 5th and Market St. Arranges same-day discount accommodations; Monticello, Michie Tavern, and Ash Lawn-Highland combo. tickets ($17, seniors $15.50, under 12 $7.50). Open daily March-Oct. 9am-5:30pm, Nov.-Feb. 9am-5pm.

University of Virginia Information Center, at the rotunda in the center of campus (924-7969). Brochures, a university map, and tour information. Open daily 9am-4:45pm. Students in **Newcomb Hall** (924-3363) provide a student locator service.

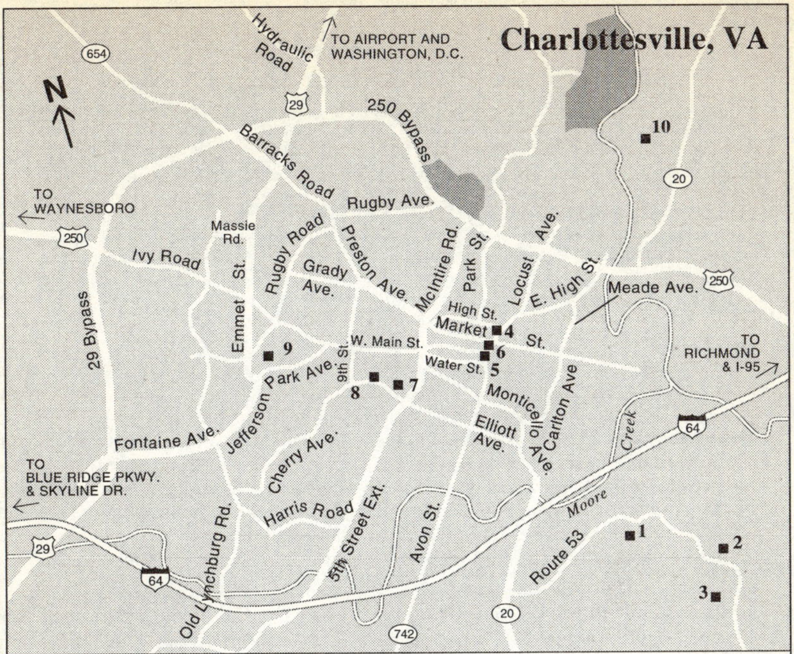

1. Michie Tavern
2. Monticello
3. Ash Lawn-Highland
4. Historic Court Site
5. Downtown Mall
6. City Hall
7. Greyhound/Trailways Bus Terminal
8. Southern Train Station (Amtrak)
9. University of Virginia
10. Rivanna Park

Open daily 8am-10pm. The larger **University Center** (924-7166), off U.S. 250 West, is home to the campus police. Transport schedules, entertainment guides, and hints on budget accommodations. Campus maps. Open 24hr.

Amtrak: 810 W. Main St. (800-872-7245, 296-4559), 7 blocks from downtown. To Washington, D.C. (1 per day, 3hr., $28); New York (1 per day, 7-8hr., $94); Baltimore (1 per day, 4hr., $45); and Philadelphia (1 per day, 5½hr., $68). Open daily 5:30am-9pm.

Greyhound: 310 W. Main St. (295-5131), within 3 blocks of downtown. To: Richmond (1 per day, 1½hr., $17); Washington, D.C. (3 per day, 3hr., $29); Norfolk (1 per day, 4hr., $32); Baltimore (4 per day, 4-5hr., $41); and Philadelphia (3 per day, 7-11hr., $48). Open Mon.-Sat. 7am-8:30pm, Sun. noon-8:30pm.

Public Transport: Charlottesville Transit Service (296-7433). Bus service within city limits. Maps available at both info. centers, Chamber of Commerce, and the UVA student center in Newcomb Hall. Buses operate Mon.-Sat. 6:30am-6:30pm. Fare 60¢, seniors and disabled 30¢, under 6 free. The more frequent UVA buses technically require UVA ID, but in practice, a studious look usually suffices.

Taxi: Yellow Cab, 295-4131. 25¢ 1st one-sixth-mi., $1.50 each additional mi.

Help Lines: Region 10 Community Services Hotline, 972-1800. **Lesbian and Gay Hotline,** 971-4942. UVA-affiliated. Open Mon.-Thurs. 5-9pm.

Emergency: 911. **Campus Police:** dial 4-7166 on a UVA campus phone.

Post Office: 513 E. Main St. (978-7610). Open Mon.-Fri. 8:30am-5pm, Sat. 10am-1pm. **ZIP Code:** 22902.

Area Code: 804.

Charlottesville streets are numbered east to west, using compass directions; 5th St. N.W. is 10 blocks from (and parallel to) 5th St. N.E. Streets running east-west across the numbered streets are neither parallel nor logically named. C-ville has two downtowns: one on the west side near the university called **The Corner,** and **Historic Downtown** about a mile east. The two are connected by **University Avenue,** running east-west, which becomes **Main Street** after the Corner ends at a bridge. Rte. 64, which runs east-west all the way to Richmond, is Charlottesville's main feeder.

ACCOMMODATIONS AND CAMPING

Emmet St. is home to dozens of fairly generic hotels and motels (A/C, cable TV; rates ranging from $40-55) which tend to fill up during summer weekends and big events during the school year.

Budget Inn, 140 Emmet St. (U.S. 29) (293-5141), near the university. Singles $42, doubles $46. $1 off in winter. Each additional person $5. Senior discounts. Office open daily 8am-midnight.

EconoLodge, 400 Emmet St. (296-2104). Singles $45, doubles $49.

Charlottesville KOA Kampground, Rte. 708 (296-9881 for info., 800-336-9881 for reservations). From Charlottesville, take U.S. 29 south to Rte. 708 southeast. All campsites are shaded. Rec hall with video games, a pavilion, and a pool (open daily 10am-8pm); free movies and laundry facilities. Fishing and pets allowed. Sites $17, with water and electric $21, full hookup $23. Open March 15-Nov. 15.

FOOD

The Corner neighborhood near UVA boasts bookstores and countless cheap eats, with good Southern grub in Charlottesville's unpretentious diners. The Emmet strip is lined with fast food franchises (which go hand-in-hand with the glut of cheap motels). The Downtown Mall (off-limits to cars; see Sights) serves more upscale fare.

The Hardware Store, 316 E. Main St. (977-1518), near the middle of the outdoor "mall." Slightly off-beat bar atmosphere: beers served in glass boots, appetizers in miniature basketball courts, and condiments in toolboxes. American grille and an eclectic set of entrees, from *ratatouille gratinée* ($5.75) to crepes both sweet ($2-5) and savory ($6-7). Sandwiches ($3-7). Quality desserts. Open Mon.-Thurs. 11am-9pm, Fri.-Sat. 11am-10pm.

Macado's, 1505 University Ave. (971-3558). Great sandwiches ($4-5), a handful of entrees ($5-7), and homemade desserts are surrounded by walls full of UVA football memorabilia. Pool tables, pinball, and foosball. Happy hour 4-7pm. Upstairs is a rockin' bar where Edgar Allen Poe once lived. Tell-tale jukebox. Open Sun.-Thurs. 9am-1am, Fri.-Sat. 9am-2am.

Littlejohn's, 427 University Ave. (977-0588). This deli serves students great sandwiches ($3-6), soups, and gigantic muffins ($1.10). The Nuclear Sub ($4) is a potent combo of barbecued beef, coleslaw, and melted cheese calculated to cause internal meltdown. Large selection of beers and NYC photos. Open 24hr.

Coupe DeVille's, 9 Elliewood Ave. (977-3966). Students cross the road for specialty chicken (½ rotisserie chicken $6.50). Burgers $5-6. Open Mon.-Fri. 11:30am-2pm and 5:30-10pm, Sat. 5:30-10pm. Pub open Mon.-Sat. 10pm-2am.

SIGHTS

Most activity on the spacious **University of Virginia** campus clusters around the **Lawn** and fraternity-lined **Rugby Road.** Jefferson watched the university being built through his telescope at Monticello; return the gaze with a glimpse of Monticello from the Lawn, a terraced green carpet that is one of the prettiest spots in American academia. Professors live in the Lawn's pavilions; Jefferson designed each one in a different architectural style. Lawn tours, led by students, leave on the hour from the Rotunda from 10am to 4pm; self-guided tour maps are provided for those who prefer to find their own way. **The Rotunda** (924-7969) once housed a bell that was shot for the crime of waking students up early. (Free tours daily; call for times. Open daily 9am-4:45pm.) The **Bayley Art Museum,** Rugby Rd. (924-3592), features visiting exhibits and a small permanent collection including one of Rodin's casts of *The Kiss* (open Tues.-Sun. 1-5pm).

The **Downtown Mall,** about five blocks off E. Main St., is a brick pedestrian thoroughfare lined with restaurants and shops catering to a diverse crowd. A kiosk near the fountain in the center of the mall has posters with club schedules.

Jefferson oversaw every stage of development of his beloved **Monticello** (984-9800), a home that truly reflects the personality of its creator. The house is a Neoclassical jewel filled with fascinating innovations (such as a fireplace dumbwaiter to the wine cellar) compiled or conceived by Jefferson. A unique all-weather passage links the kitchen and dining room so that neither rain nor snow nor gloom of night could keep dinner from its appointed rounds, while an indoor compass registers wind direction via a weathervane on the roof. The cleverly laid-out grounds include orchards and flower gardens, and afford magnificent views in every direction. (Tours offered daily. Wheelchair accessible. Open daily March-Oct. 8am-5pm; Nov.-Feb. 9am-4:30pm; tickets $8, seniors $7, ages 6-11 $4, students $3, Nov.-Feb $1.)

Minutes away (take a right turn to Rte. 795) is **Ashlawn** (293-9539), the 500-acre plantation home of President James Monroe—a close friend of Jefferson. (Open daily 9am-6pm; Nov.-Feb. daily 10am-5pm; tour $6, seniors $5.50, children 6-11 $3.)

Down the road from Monticello on Rte. 53 is **Michie** (Mick-ee) **Tavern** (977-1234), with an operating grist mill, a general store, and a tour of the 200-year-old establishment (open daily 9am-5pm; $5, under 6 $1).

ENTERTAINMENT AND NIGHTLIFE

The town loves jazz, likes rock, and thrives on pubs. Ubiquitous posters in the Downtown Mall and the free *Charlottesville Review* can tell you who plays where and when. In the **Box Gardens** behind Ashlawn June-Aug., English-language opera and musical theater highlight the **Summer Festival of the Arts** (293-4500, open Tues.-Sun. 10am-5pm; call for shows and ticket prices). Ashlawn hosts **Music at Twilight** on Wed. evenings ($10, seniors $9, students $6), including New Orleans jazz, Cajun music, blues, and swing. During the school year, the town cheers for the **UVA Cavaliers,** who compete in the intense Atlantic Coastal Conference (ACC) against perennial powers Duke, North Carolina, and Florida State Universities.

The Max, 12 11St. SW (295-6299). One of the largest and most popular bars in the city. Tues. features Top-40 DJ and dancing (cover: men 21+ $4, women 18+ $3); Wed. is 2-steppin' and line dancing with free lessons until 9:30pm ($4 cover); Thurs.-Sat. brings live bands of all genres next door to **Trax.** (For information about live shows call 295-TRAX.; $5 cover for men.) Drafts $1.85. Open Tues., and Thurs.-Sat. 8pm-2am, Wed. 7pm-midnight.

Outback Lodge, 917 Preston Ave. (979-7211). Happenin' pub with a pool table, foosball, and a jukebox. Philly cheesesteak ($5) and fajitas ($8) are popular, as is happy hour (Mon.-Fri. 4-7pm). Live music Wed.-Sat. with a cover $2-10. Call for bands, times, and exact cover. Open Mon.-Fri. 11am-2am, Sat.-Sun. 5pm-2am.

Eastern Standard, 102 Old Preston Ave. (295-8668), at the Downtown Mall near the Omni Hotel. Drafts $2.75. DJ house beats Sun., beginning at 11:30pm ($2 cover). Open Tues.-Thurs. 5pm-midnight, Fri.-Sun. 5pm-2am.

Dürty Nelly's, 2200 Jefferson Park Ave. (295-1278). Bar/deli. More than 50 beers: domestic drafts $1.50, $1.10 during happy hour (Mon.-Fri. 4-7pm). Tues. nights and weekends feature live music with a $2-4 cover. Open daily 11am-2am.

Tryangles, 212 W. Water St. (246-8783). The only gay bar in the city. Entrance requires a $25 membership which entitles you to free admission Sun.-Thurs. Fri.-Sat. features a DJ and dancing ($3 cover). Domestic drafts $1.25. Open Sun.-Thurs. 9pm-1am, Fri.-Sat. 9pm-4am.

Richmond

Once the capital of the rebel Confederacy, Richmond is by no means shy when it comes to its history. Civil War leaders Robert E. Lee and Stonewall Jackson are worshipped through Richmond's museums and restored homes, which showcase anything and everything Confederate. But Richmond is not entirely mired in its own history; indeed, Richmond honors a significant African-American heritage as well, commemorating such figures as entertainer Bill "Bojangles" Robinson, banker Maggie Walker, and tennis Hall-of-Famer Arthur Ashe (see page 280). With districts like the sprawling, residential Fan and formerly industrial Shockoe Bottom, this state capital sports its more inclusive, renovated 20th-century face.

PRACTICAL INFORMATION AND ORIENTATION

Visitor Information: Richmond Visitors Center, 1710 Robin Hood Rd. (358-5511), exit 78 off I-95/64, in a converted train depot. Helpful 6-min. video introduces the city's attractions. Walking tours and maps of downtown and the metro region. Can also arrange for same-day discounted accommodations. Open Memorial Day-Labor Day daily 9am-7pm; off-season 9am-5pm.

Amtrak: far away at 7519 Staple Mills Rd. (264-9194, 800-872-7245). To: D.C. (8 per day, 2hr., $18-23); Williamsburg (8 per day, 1¼hr., $9-10); Virginia Beach (2 per day, 3hr., $16-19, the last 3rd of the trip is on a shuttle); New York City (8 per day, 7hr., $81); Baltimore (5 per day, 3hr., $26-31); and Philadelphia (5 per day, 4¾hr., $38-48). Taxi fare to downtown $12. Open 24hr.

Greyhound: 2910 N. Boulevard (254-5910 or 800-231-2222). 2 blocks from downtown; take GRTC bus #24 north. To: D.C. (16 per day, 2½hr., $10-12); Charlottesville (2 per day, 1½hr., $18); Williamsburg (8 per day, 1hr., $11); Norfolk (10 per day, 3hr., $16); New York City (26 per day, 6½hr., $53); Baltimore (8 per day, 3½hr., $22); and Philadelphia (9 per day, 7hr., $40).

Public Transport: Greater Richmond Transit Co., 101 S. Davis Ave. (358-4782). Maps available in the basement of City Hall, 900 E. Broad St., and in the Yellow Pages. Buses serve most of Richmond infrequently, downtown frequently; most leave from Broad St. downtown. Bus #24 goes south to Broad St. and downtown. Fare $1.15, transfers 15¢. Seniors 50¢ during off-peak hours. Free trolleys provide dependable, if limited, service to downtown and Shockoe Slip daily 10am-4pm, with an extended Shockoe Slip schedule 5pm-midnight.

Taxi: Veterans Cab Association (329-3333); **Yellow Cab Co.** (222-7300).

Help Lines: Traveler's Aid, 643-0279 or 648-1767. **Rape Crisis Hotline,** 643-0888. **Psychiatric Crisis Intervention,** 648-9224. **Gay Information,** 353-3626. **AIDS/HIV Info.,** 359-4783. Mon.-Fri. 8am-6pm, Sat. noon-5pm, Sun. noon-8pm.

Emergency: 911.

Post Office: 1801 Brook Rd. (775-6133). Open Mon.-Fri. 7am-6pm, Sat. 10am-1pm. **ZIP Code:** 23219.

Area Code: 804.

Imaginative locals have invented novel names for Richmond's neighborhoods. **Carytown** is an upscale district in the northwest between Thompson St. and the Boulevard. The **Fan**, named for its dubious resemblance to a lady's fan, is bounded by the Boulevard, I-95, Monument Ave., and Virginia Commonwealth University, and harbors many of Richmond's oldest homes. **Jackson Ward,** in the heart of downtown (bounded by Belvedere, Leigh, Broad, and 5th St.), and **Shockoe Slip** and **Shockoe Bottom** to the east, are more urban areas. **Broad St.,** not Main St., is the city's central artery, and the streets that cross it are numbered from west to east. Both I-95, leading north to Washington, D.C., and I-295 encircle the urban section.

ACCOMMODATIONS AND CAMPING

Budget motels in Richmond cluster on **Williamsburg Rd.,** the edge of town, and along **Midlothian Turnpike,** south of the James River; however, public transport (see Practical Information above) to these areas is infrequent at best. The farther from

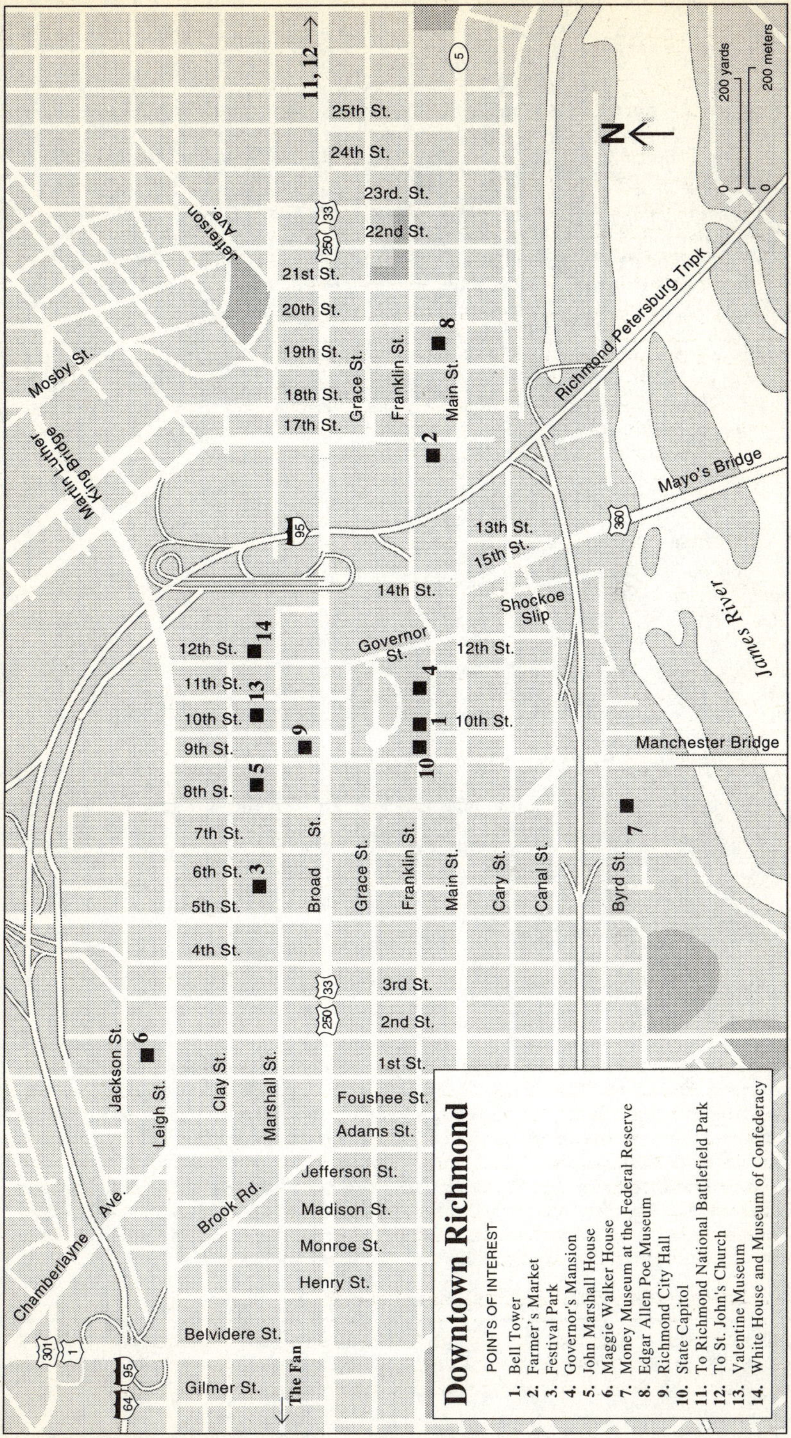
Downtown Richmond
POINTS OF INTEREST
1. Bell Tower
2. Farmer's Market
3. Festival Park
4. Governor's Mansion
5. John Marshall House
6. Maggie Walker House
7. Money Museum at the Federal Reserve
8. Edgar Allen Poe Museum
9. Richmond City Hall
10. State Capitol
11. To Richmond National Battlefield Park
12. To St. John's Church
13. Valentine Museum
14. White House and Museum of Confederacy
N
0 200 yards
0 200 meters
James River
Mayo's Bridge
Manchester Bridge
Shockoe Slip
Richmond Petersburg Tnpk
Martin Luther King Bridge
Mosby St.
Jefferson Ave.
Chamberlayne Ave.
Brook Rd.
The Fan
25th St.
24th St.
23rd. St.
22nd St.
21st St.
20th St.
19th St.
18th St.
17th St.
15th St.
14th St.
13th St.
12th St.
11th St.
10th St.
9th St.
8th St.
7th St.
6th St.
5th St.
4th St.
3rd St.
2nd St.
1st St.
Foushee St.
Adams St.
Jefferson St.
Madison St.
Monroe St.
Henry St.
Belvidere St.
Gilmer St.
Jackson St.
Leigh St.
Clay St.
Marshall St.
Broad St.
Grace St.
Franklin St.
Main St.
Cary St.
Canal St.
Byrd St.
Governor St.
11, 12

downtown you stay, the less you pay. The **visitors center** (see **Practical Information,** above) can reserve accommodations, sometimes at $10-20 discounts.

Massad House Hotel, 11 N. 4th St. (648-2893), five blocks from the capitol, in the commercial downtown area. Shuttles guests via a 1940s elevator to clean rooms with shower, A/C, and cable TV. Massad offers some of the only inexpensive rooms downtown. Singles $43, doubles $46.

Cadillac Motel, 11418 Washington Hwy. (798-4049), 10mi. from the city. Take I-95 to exit 89. Sparse rooms with A/C and cable TV. Singles $36, doubles $45.

Executive Inn, 5215 W. Broad St. (288-4011), 3mi. from center of town; take bus #6. Once the Red Carpet Inn, Executive still sports the same red carpet in its grand (by motel standards), slightly faded rooms. Provides A/C, cable TV and a pool/health club. Singles $43, doubles $45-49. Weekly rate $165 (7 nights).

Pocahontas State Park, 10301 State Park Rd. (796-4255), 10mi. south on Rte. 10 and Rte. 655 in Chesterfield. Offers showers, biking, boating, picnic areas, and a huge pool. Sites $11. No hookups. Pool admission $2.25, ages 3-12 $1.75. Open year-round. For free reservations, call 225-3867 or 800-933-PARK.

FOOD

At once a college town and a Southern capital, Richmond offers cheap student eateries and affordable down-home fare. At the **farmers market,** outdoors at N. 17th and E. Main St., pick up fresh fruit, vegetables, meat, and even a pot swine. For student haunts, head for the area around Virginia Commonwealth University (VCU), just west of downtown; for fried apples, grits, and cornbread, try downtown itself.

Coppola's, 2900 W. Cary St. (359-6969). A popular NYC-style deli crowded with happy locals and Italian food. Dinners ($5-7) and fantastic sandwiches ($3-6). Outdoor seating available. Open Mon.-Wed. 10am-8pm, Thurs.-Sat. 10am-9pm.

3rd St. Diner, at the corner of 3rd and Main (788-4750). Old-time locals on the mint-green balcony are served cheap eats—the $2.25 breakfast special (2 eggs, biscuit or toast, and homefries, grits, or Virginia fried apples), or dinner sandwiches ($3-6)—by tattooed waitresses in combat boots. Open 24hr.

Texas-Wisconsin Border Café, 1501 W. Main St. (355-2907). Owned by a pair of art professors, this isn't your typical Tex-Mex place; the walls feature monthly exhibits of local artwork. The cuisine is more traditional, with chili (bowl $4) and fajitas ($8). At night the café rolls up the rug to become a popular bar. During the school year, Sat. brunches offer live music. Open daily 11am-2am.

Oceans, 414 E. Main St. (649-3456), serves excellent, filling breakfasts and lunches. All items under $5. Open daily 7am-2:30pm.

Bottom's Up, 1700 Dock St. (644-4400), at 17th and Cary. This popular hangout serves the best pizza in Richmond ($8, will feed two) and will ply you with drinks after dark (drafts $1.50-3, bottles $2.75-3.25). Open Mon.-Wed. 11:30am-11pm, Thurs. 11:30am-midnight, Fri. 11:30am-2am, Sat. noon-2am, Sun. noon-11pm.

SIGHTS

Ever since Patrick Henry declared "Give me liberty or give me death" in Richmond's **St. John's Church,** 2401 E. Broad St. (648-5015), this river city has been quoting, memorializing, and bronzing its heroes; actors recreate the famous 1775 speech (on Sundays, from the last in May to the first in Sept., at 2pm). You must take a tour to see the church. (Tours Mon.-Sat. 10am-3:30pm, Sun. 1-3:30pm; $3, seniors $2, students under 18 $1.) The Thomas Jefferson-designed **State Capitol,** at 9th and Grace St. (786-4344), is a Neoclassical masterpiece that served as the home of the Confederate government during the Civil War and today houses the only statue of George Washington for which the first President ever actually posed (open daily 9am-5pm; Dec.-March Mon.-Sat. 9am-5pm, Sun. 1-5pm). **Monument Avenue,** a boulevard lined with trees, gracious old houses, and towering statues of Confederate heroes, is a virtual Richmond memory lane. Robert E. Lee faces his beloved South; Stonewall Jackson scowls at the Yankees. The recently commissioned statue of local hero Arthur Ashe provides an anomalous, though inspiring, addition to the avenue.

The **Court End** district stretches north and east of the capitol to Clay and College St. and guards Richmond's most distinctive historical sights. The **Museum of the Confederacy,** 1201 E. Clay St. (649-1861), is the world's largest Confederate artifact collection. The main floor leads visitors through the military history of the Great War of Northern Aggression; the basement displays guns and over 500 flags of the Confederacy; and the top floor houses temporary exhibits on such topics as slave life in the antebellum South. The museum also runs one-hour tours through the **White House of the Confederacy** next door (ask at the museum desk). Statues of Tragedy, Comedy, and Irony grace the White House's front door. (Museum open Mon.-Sat. 10am-5pm, Sun. 1-5pm; tours of the White House Mon., Wed., and Fri.-Sat. 10:30am-4:30pm, Tues. and Thurs. 11:30am-4:30pm, Sun. 1:15-4:30pm. Admission to museum $5, seniors $4, students $3, under 6 free; for the White House $5.50, seniors $4.50, students $3.50; for both: $8, $5, $3.50.)

The **Valentine Museum,** 1015 E. Clay St. (649-0711), enamors visitors with exhibits on local and Southern social and cultural history, plus the South's largest collection of costumes and textiles. Admission price includes a tour of the Neoclassical **Wickham-Valentine House** (built in 1812) next door. (Museum open Mon.-Sat. 10am-5pm, Sun. noon-5pm; house tours on the hr., 10am-4pm. Admission $5, seniors and students $4, children 7-12 $3.) Combination tickets to the Museum of the Confederacy, White House of the Confederacy, Valentine Museum, and **John Marshall House** (which contains period and family furnishings of the Chief Justice) cost $11, seniors and students $10, ages 7-12 $5 (tickets available at any of the sights, which are all within walking distance of each other). John Marshall House, at 818 E. Marshall St. (648-7998), is open Tues.-Sat. 10am-5pm, Sun. 1-5pm.

East of the Capitol, follow your tell-tale heart to the **Edgar Allan Poe Museum,** 1914 E. Main St. (648-5523). Poe memorabilia stuffs five buildings, including the **Stone House,** the oldest extant structure within the original city boundaries. (Open Tues.-Sat. 10am-4pm, Sun.-Mon. noon-4pm. Admission $5, seniors $4, students $3.)

Four blocks from the intersection of Monument Ave. and N. Boulevard rests the Southeast's largest art museum, the **Virginia Museum of Fine Arts,** 2800 Grove Ave. The Museum contains pieces ranging from ancient Egyptian works to Picasso and Warhol to Fabergé's ornate Russian eggs. (367-0844; open Tues.-Sat. 11am-5pm, Thurs. 11am-8pm in the North Wing Galleries, Sun. 1-5pm; $4 donation requested).

The **Maggie L. Walker National Historic Site,** 110½ E. Leigh St. (780-1380), commemorates the founder and president of the oldest surviving black-operated U.S. bank. Physically disabled and the daughter of an ex-slave, Walker spent her life fighting for black women's rights (tours Wed.-Sun. 9am-5pm. Free.) The **Black History Museum and Cultural Center of Virginia,** 00 Clay St. (780-9093), showcases rotating exhibits (open Tues. and Thurs.-Sat. 11am-4pm; $2, children $1).

To the west lies the **Science Museum of Virginia,** 2500 W. Broad St. (367-1080). The museum houses more than 250 hands-on exhibits, and most prominently, the **Universe Theater,** which doubles as a planetarium and an Omni theater. (Museum open Mon.-Sat. 9:30am-5pm, Sun. noon-5pm. Planetarium and Omni shows daily; call for times. Admission $4.50, seniors and children 4-17 $4. $2-3 extra for shows.)

The **Shockoe Slip** district from Main, Canal, and Cary St. between 10th and 14th St. features fancy shops in restored and newly painted warehouses, but few bargains. **Cary St.,** from the Boulevard to Thompson St., is crowded with vintage clothing stores, antique boutiques, and entertaining crowds.

ENTERTAINMENT AND NIGHTLIFE

One of Richmond's most entertaining and delightful diversions is the marvelous old **Byrd Theater,** 2908 W. Cary St. (353-9911). Movie buffs buy tickets from a tuxedoed agent, are ushered into an opulent, chandeliered theater and treated to a pre-movie concert, played on an ornate and cavernous Wurlitzer organ that rises out of the floor. All shows 99¢; on Saturdays the balcony opens for $1 extra. **Free concerts**

Arthur Ashe

On July 11, 1996, the city of Richmond unveiled a stirring memorial to Arthur Ashe on Monument Ave. The monument, which depicts the AIDS victim with a tennis racket in one hand and books in the other, surrounded by smiling children, marks a significant step forward for the former Confederate capital. The statue stands in stark contrast to such traditional Southern heroes as Jeb Stuart, Robert E. Lee, and Jefferson Davis. Ashe's prowess on the tennis court was secondary to his humanism; he devoted much time to bringing tennis programs to the inner city, providing others with the same opportunity that he turned into a Wimbledon victory—the only one that has ever gone to a black man.

abound near the farmers market at N. 17th and E. Main St. in the summer; check *Style Weekly,* a free magazine available at the visitors center. Baseball fans can watch the minor-league Richmond Braves (Atlanta's AAA affiliate) for a fraction of major-league prices (field boxes $7, reserved seats $5, general $4). Nightlife enlivens Shockoe Slip and sprinkles itself in a less hectic manner throughout the Fan.

Tobacco Company Club, 1201 E. Cary St. (782-9555). This local institution caters to 25+ professionals, with dance tunes, hip-hop, and a happy hour (upstairs, 5-7pm): cheap beer and a free buffet. Open Tues.-Sat. 8pm-2am; rarely a cover.

Matt's British Pub and Comedy Club, at 1045 12th St. (643-5653), pours out a bit of Brit wit Fri. at 8 and 10:30pm and Sat. at 8 and 11pm. Microbrews and drafts $2.75-$3.60, rails $3.40. Open Mon.-Sat. 1:30pm-2am, Sun. 4pm-2am.

Penny Lane Pub, 207 N. 7th St. (780-1682). Irish tavern with live bands nightly—traditional Irish music on Fri. Cuisine includes Bangers 'n' Mash ($10), fish 'n' chips ($8), and Cornish pastries ($10). Open Mon.-Sat. 11am-2am, Sun. 4pm-2am.

Flood Zone, 11 S. 18th St. (643-6006), south of Shockoe Slip, hosts both big-name and off-beat local rock bands. Ticket office open Tues.-Fri. 10am-6pm. Tickets $6-20, depending upon the show.

Paramyd, 1008 North Blvd. (358-3838). One of Richmond's few gay bars is a hopping gay dance club on weekends. Happy hour Mon.-Fri. 6-9pm. Drafts $2. Fri.-Sat. cover varies, Sun. $4.

Broadway Café, 1624 W. Broad St. (355-9931). Gay watering hole. Drafts $1.35-1.45. Appetizers around $4. Open Mon.-Sat. 6pm-2am, Sun. 7pm-2am.

Williamsburg

At the end of the 17th century, when women were women and men wore wigs, Williamsburg was the capital of Virginia. Home of Peyton Randolph, the President of both the First and Second Continental Congresses, the city seemed destined for national prominence. But Randolph died, and during the Revolutionary War, the capital moved to Richmond, along with much of Williamsburg's grandeur. After a century-long malaise, the depressed city was rescued in 1926 by John D. Rockefeller, Jr., who showered the troubled spots with money and restored a large chunk of the historic district as a colonial village. His foundation still sustains the restored, five-by-seven-block town-within-a-town called **Colonial Williamsburg,** where fife-and-drum corps march in the streets and wheelwrights, bookbinders, and blacksmiths go about their tasks using 200-year-old methods.

Street-side performers, evenings of 18th-century theater, and militia reviews are just part of everyday business in Williamsburg. Yet, although the ex-capital claims to be a faithfully restored version of its 18th-century self, don't look for dirt roads, open sewers, or African slaves. Williamsburg also prides itself on **William and Mary,** the second-oldest college in the United States. Physically, the countryside is gorgeous; rich forests and dense coastal marshes are veined with small creeks running into the James River. Outside Williamsburg, Virginia's other big tourist sights (**Jamestown, Yorktown,** and **Busch Gardens**) lie in wait.

PRACTICAL INFORMATION AND ORIENTATION

Visitor Information: Williamsburg Area Convention & Visitors Bureau, 201 Penniman Rd. (253-0192), ½mi. northwest of the transportation center. Free *Visitor's Guide to Virginia's Historic Triangle*. Open Mon.-Fri. 8:30am-5pm. **Tourist Visitors Center,** 102 Information Dr. (800-447-8679), 1mi. northeast of the train station. Tickets and transportation to Colonial Williamsburg. Maps and guides to historic district, including a guide for the disabled, upstairs. Info. on prices and discounts on Virginia sights, downstairs. Open daily 8:30am-8pm.

Transportation Center: 408 N. Boundary St. across from the fire station at the end of the road. **Amtrak,** 229-8750 or 800-872-7245. To: New York (1 per day, $56, 7½hr.); Washington, D.C. (1 per day, $29-34, 3½hr.); Philadelphia (1 per day, $40, 6hr.); Baltimore (1 per day, $33-40, 5hr.); and Richmond (1 per day, $10-12, 1½hr.). Open Tues.-Thurs. 7:15am-2:45pm, Fri.-Mon. 7:15am-9:30pm. **Greyhound/Trailways,** 229-1460. Ticket office open Mon.-Fri. 8:30am-6pm, Sat.-Sun. 8:30am-2pm. To: Richmond (7 per day, $11, 1hr.); Norfolk (8 per day, $11, 2hr.); Washington, D.C. (7 per day, $29, 4hr.); Baltimore (via D.C.; 7 per day, $48, 6hr.); Virginia Beach (4 per day, $15, 2½hr.). **James City County Transit (JCCT),** (220-1621). Service along Rte. 60, from Merchants Sq. in the historic district west to Williamsburg Pottery or east past Busch Gardens. Operates Mon.-Sat. 6:15am-6:20pm. Fare $1 plus 25¢ per zone-change; exact change required.

Bike Rentals: Bikes Unlimited, 759 Scotland St. (229-4620), rents for $10 per day, with $5 deposit (includes lock). Open Mon.-Fri. 9am-7pm, Sat. 9am-5pm, Sun. noon-4pm. **Bikesmith of Williamsburg,** 515 York Rd. (229-9858), rents single-speed bikes at $8.50 per 4hr., $11.50 per day. Open Mon.-Sat. 10am-6pm.

Taxi: Williamsburg Limousine Service (877-0279). To Busch Gardens or Carter's Grove $6 round-trip. To Jamestown and Yorktown $15 round-trip. Call between 8:30am-10pm.

Emergency: 911.

Post Office: 425 N. Boundary St. (229-4668). Open Mon.-Fri. 8am-5pm, Sat. 10am-2pm. **ZIP Codes:** 23185 (Williamsburg), 23690 (Yorktown), and 23081 (Jamestown).

Area Code: 804 (Hampton Rd. peninsula area: 757).

Williamsburg lies some 50 mi. southeast of Richmond between Jamestown (10mi. away) and Yorktown (14mi. away). The Colonial Parkway, which connects the three towns, has no commercial buildings along its route, helping to preserve an unspoiled atmosphere. Travelers should visit in late fall or early spring to avoid the crowds, high temperature, and humidity of summer. Signs lead to the Visitors Center, which offers information, tickets, and free parking.

ACCOMMODATIONS AND CAMPING

Budget motels line Rte. 60 west and Rte. 31 south. Avoid the expensive hotels operated by the Colonial Williamsburg Foundation. A cheaper, friendlier, and more comfortable alternative is guest houses. All expect you to call ahead.

Only five minutes from the historic district, **Lewis Guest House,** 809 Lafayette St. (229-6116), rents several comfortable rooms, including an upstairs unit with private entrance, kitchen, and bath as a single ($25) or double ($30). The friendly proprietor keeps a very short, yappy dog. A few doors down is the **Carter Guest House,** 903 Lafayette St. (229-1117). Two spacious rooms each have two beds and a shared bath. (Singles $25, doubles $26-30.) Be forewarned: Mrs. Carter —a woman of *very* traditional Southern values—will not let unmarried men and women sleep in the same bed. Hotels around the historic district, especially chain- or foundation-owned hotels, are not cheap. The **Southern Inn,** 1220 Richmond Rd. (229-8913), a 10-minute walk from William & Mary, has clean, ordinary rooms with colonial-looking façades and a pool (singles and doubles $35; office open daily 8am-1pm, 4-11pm).

Several campsites blanket the area. **Anvil Campgrounds,** 5243 Moretown Rd. (565-2300), 3mi. north of the Colonial Williamsburg Information Center on Rte. 60, boasts 73 shaded sites, a swimming pool, bathhouse, recreational hall, and store. (Sites $15, with water and electricity $23, full hookup $25.)

FOOD AND DRINK

Most of the authentic-looking "taverns" are overpriced and packed with sweaty tourists. For a fraction of the cost, you can still enjoy a colonial culinary experience by fixing a picnic with food from the **Williamsburg Shopping Center,** at the intersection of Richmond Rd. and Lafayette St. Rte. 60 also contains a bevy of fast-food places and far more pancake houses than any sane person might expect.

Beethoven's Inn, 467 Merrimac Trail (229-7069). Great sandwiches, subs, and other light fare with music-related names. Try the Titanic Sub, a combination of turkey, roast beef, grilled veggies, and feta cheese ($5.50). A variety of board games passes the wait for your food. Open Mon.-Sat. 11am-9pm, Sun. noon-8pm.

Chowning's Tavern, Duke of Gloucester St. (229-1000, ext. 2816). If you absolutely insist on eating in the historic district, you can wait in line for stew, sandwiches, or the misleading "Welsh Rabbit (Rarebit)," bread in cheese-and-beer sauce with ham (lunch entrees from $6, dinner from $15.25). The prohibitively expensive dinner here is redeemed by post-10pm affordable gambols: costumed waiters serve mixed drinks and sandwiches, sing 18th-century ballads, and teach patrons how to play outdated dice and card games. Open daily 11am-midnight.

College Delly Restaurant, 336 Richmond Rd. (229-6627), faithfully delivers sandwiches and 10-inch subs ($3.25-4.25). The "Holly" (a bacon, roast beef, and turkey sub) serves one hungry person or two delicate ones for $4. Free delivery (limited area, 6pm-1am). Open daily 10am-2am.

Green Leafe Café, 465 Scotland St. (220-3405), next door to Paul's Deli. Always mellow, Green Leafe cultivates a subdued atmosphere while serving sandwiches and salads ($3.50-5.50) and swaying on Tues. (after 9pm) to the quiet sounds of live folk music. The café's slogan is "Life's too short to drink bad beer." You won't get any here: 20 delicious brews on tap, including savory Virginia micros ($3 per pint, $3.25 per bottle). Sun. "Mug Night" (32-oz. mugs for the cost of 16-oz. pints). Open daily 9am-2am.

The Old Chickahominy House, 1211 Jamestown Rd. (229-4689), rests over a mile from the historic district. Share the antiques and dried-flower decor with pewter-haired locals whose ancestors survived "Starvation Winter" in Jamestown. Miss Melinda's "complete luncheon" includes Virginia ham served on hot biscuits, fruit salad, a slice of delectable homemade pie, and iced tea or coffee ($5). 20 to 30-min. wait for lunch. Open daily 8:30-10:15am and 11:30am-2:15pm.

Paul's Deli Restaurant and Pizza, 761 Scotland St. (229-8976), a lively summer hangout for errant, leftover W&M students, sells crisp stromboli for 2 ($6.15-9) and filling subs ($4-5). Nightly specials on pasta and seafood; Wed.-Sat. 7-9pm features ½-price on selected beer. Great jukebox. Open daily 10:30am-2am.

Sakura, 601 Prince George St. (253-1233), is popular with W&M students—weeknights they get 2-for-1 with their IDs. If you can't scare up a student, try the affordable lunches ($5-6.50). Japanese meals are prepared before your eyes, with an impressive, entertaining display of cutlery skill. Open Mon.-Fri. 11:30am-2pm and 5-9pm, Sat.-Sun. 5-10pm.

SIGHTS

Unless you plan to apply to W&M, you've probably come to see the restored gardens and buildings, crafts, tours, and costumed actors in the historic district also known as **Colonial Williamsburg.** The Colonial Williamsburg Foundation (CWF) owns nearly everything in the historic district, from the **Governor's Palace** to the lemonade stands and even most of the houses marked "private home." A **Patriot's Pass** allows unlimited admission for one year, in addition to special programs and discounts ($33, children 6-12 $19, under 6 free). The **Basic Plus Ticket** is valid for two consecutive days, offering unlimited access to all sights except **Basset Hall**—the restored 18th-century home once inhabited by the Rockefellers ($29, children 6-12 $17, under 6 free). The **Basic Admission Ticket,** good only on the day of purchase, allows access to everything but the museums and **Carter's Grove** ($25, children under 12 $15, under 6 free). Tickets are available at the **CWF Visitors Center** (220-7645; open daily 8:30am-8pm).

Though the historic district does not require a ticket (for no charge you can walk the streets, ogle the buildings, march behind the fife-and-drum corps, lock yourself in the stocks, and use the restrooms), the experience of immersing one's self in sights and speaking with the "People of the Past" should not be undervalued. Some old-time shops that actually sell goods—notably the **Colonial Post Office** and **M. Dubois Grocer** by the Palace Green—are open to the public. Two of the buildings on the CWF map, the **Wren Building** and the **Bruton Parish Church**—are made to look like regular exhibits but in fact are free. The weekly *Visitor's Companion* lists all outdoor events, evening programs, and provides a map of the colonial area.

The real beauty of Colonial Williamsburg lies in interacting with its history; "People of the Past" include Martha Washington, Thomas Jefferson, and other once-local men and women. The trade shops afford a wonderful opportunity to learn from skilled artisans such as cabinet-makers and smithies, as well as actors who are eager to talk about the growing conflict between the colonies and Britain. (Watch out for the bartender in **Raleigh Tavern;** he readily upbraids "urchins" with poor manners.)

Those willing to pay shouldn't miss the **Governor's Palace,** on the Palace Green. This mansion housed the appointed governors of the Virginia colony until the last one fled in 1775. Reconstructed Colonial sidearms and ceremonial sabers line the reconstructed walls, and the extensive gardens include a hedge maze (open daily 9am-5pm; separate admission $17). Most sights in town are open 9:30am-5:30pm; a complete list of hours is provided in the *Visitor's Companion.*

Spreading west from the corner of Richmond and Jamestown Rd., **The College of William & Mary** is the second-oldest college in the U.S., having educated Presidents Jefferson, Monroe, and Tyler. The **Sir Christopher Wren Building** (built in 1695, two years after the college received its charter), also restored with Rockefeller money, is the nation's oldest classroom building. Nearby, the shops at **Merchant Square** sprawl a hair's breadth from the historic district.

Busch Gardens, Water Country: USA, and the Anheuser-Busch Brewery

When you've filled your colonial quotient, head to **Busch Gardens: The Old Country** (253-3350), three mi. east of Williamsburg on Rte. 60. You'll be flung, splashed, and throttled by the various shows and rides. Each section of the park represents a European nation; trains and sky-cars connect the sections. Recently opened is **Escape from Pompeii,** a water coaster ride which re-creates the city's destruction by Mt. Vesuvius. **Questor** brings roller coasters into the video age, with the world's largest flight simulator. **Drachen Fire** and **Loch Ness Monster** are two enduring coaster classics. Williamsburg Limousine serves Busch Gardens (see **Practical Information** above). (Open April-mid-June and Sept.-Oct. daily 10am-7pm; mid-June-Aug. Sun.-Fri. 10am-10pm, Sat. 10am-midnight. Admission $30, children 3-6 $23. $5 off after 5pm. A three-day ticket ($45) is good for both Busch Gardens and Water Country: USA. Parking $4.) Owned and operated by Busch Gardens (and about 2mi. away), **Water Country: USA** is a mammoth 40-acre water park to end all water parks. (Open weekends in May and June-Sept. 10 10am-dusk. Admission $22, kids 3-6 $16, under 3 free. After 3pm, $12 for all.)

A free monorail from Busch Gardens takes you to the **Anheuser-Busch Brewery** (253-3036). Self-guided walking tours include visits to the brewhouse, the high-speed packaging lines, and the newest promotional displays. The **Hospitality Center** offers free beer and pizza, in addition to gift shops, films, and a gallery of artifacts from the company's history. (Accessible from I-64. Open daily 10am-4pm. Free.)

Jamestown, Yorktown and the James River Plantations

The founding of Jamestown in 1607 marked the first permanent English settlement in the New World; Britain's tradition of democracy quickly took root, as the first representative legislature was elected in 1619 (ironically, 1619 also saw slaves first brought to the New World). Just 20 mi. away, Yorktown marks the spot where the colonists essentially forced the British out of the colonies for good. The National Park System provides free, well-administered visitors' guides to the two areas. **Williamsburg Limousine** (877-0279) offers daily round-trip transportation from Williamsburg to Jamestown, Yorktown ($15), and Carter's Grove ($8), but if you can, bike from South England St. in Colonial Williamsburg along the one-way, 7-mi., wooded **Carter's Grove Country Road** to Carter's Grove and the other James River plantations. The unlined **Colonial Parkway** to both Jamestown and Yorktown makes a beautiful biking route.

JAMESTOWN

The capital of Virginia for 72 years (until 1699), Jamestown was settled in 1607 by an intrepid, if greed-driven, group of 104 men and boys. Searching for gold or a trade route to the Far East, the group found an area rich only in soil. The settlers perpetually battled starvation as they invested their energy in the harvesting of tobacco. Burned in the 1676 Bacon's Rebellion, all that remains of colonial Jamestown are a few brick foundations and related artifacts.

Accommodations

Few accommodations are closer than Williamsburg, which is 13 mi. away. An exception is the **Carrot Tree Kitchens and Lodging,** 1782 Jamestown Rd. (229-0957), with fancifully decorated, comfortable rooms and 30 wooded backyard camp sites ($30-45). Guests enjoy free breakfast goodies from the bakery next door.

Sights

At the **Jamestown National Historic Site** you'll see the remains of the 1607 English settlement as well as exhibits explaining colonial life. The **visitors center** (229-1733) offers a film and 30-min. "living history" walking tours (free with site admission), during which a guide portraying one of the colonists describes the Jamestown way of life. Among other sights, you'll visit the **Old Church Tower,** built in 1639 and the only 17th-century structure still standing, as well as a statue of **Pocahontas,** the famous daughter of Chief Powhatan, who saved Captain John Smith from excursion. Call ahead for tour information; "living history" guides get occasional off-days.

Those inclined to further explore independently may rent a 45-min. **audio tape** ($2) and drive or hike the 5-mi. **Island Loop Route** through woodlands and marsh, keeping an eye out for white-tailed deer. In the remains of the settlement itself, archaeologists work to uncover the original site of the triangular **Jamestown fort.** Over 50,000 artifacts have been unearthed already, some of which are on display at **Dale House.** At the **Glasshouse** (open daily 8:30am-6pm), workers dressed in 17th-century garb work in an attempt to replicate the glassware that were briefly blown on the settlement. The remains of the original glasshouse are nearby. The National Historic Site (229-1733) is open daily 9am-6pm; off-season 8am-4:30pm. The park opens and closes a half hour before the visitors center does. The entrance fee is $8 per car, $2 per hiker or bicyclist.

The nearby **Jamestown Settlement** (229-1607) is a museum commemorating the settlement with changing exhibits, a reconstruction of James Fort, a Native American village, and full-scale replicas of the three ships that brought the original settlers to Jamestown in 1607. The 20-min. "dramatic film" lives up to its name and fills tourists in on the settlement's history, including an embarrassed treatment of settler relations with the indigenous Powhatan tribe. (Open daily 9am-5pm. Admission $9, children 6-

12 $4.25, under 6 free. Combination ticket (good for Yorktown Victory Center as well) $12.50, children under 12 $6, under 6 free.)

JAMES RIVER PLANTATIONS

Built near the water to facilitate the planters' commercial and social lives, these country houses buttressed the slave-holding Virginia aristocracy. Tour guides at **Carter's Grove Plantation,** six mi. east of Williamsburg on Rte. 60, describe the restored house and fields. The last owners doubled the size of the original 18th-century building while maintaining the colonial "feel." The complex also includes reconstructed slave quarters and an archaeological dig. The brand-new **Winthrop Rockefeller Archaeological Museum,** built unobtrusively into a hillside, provides a fascinating case-study look at archaeology. (Plantation open Tues.-Sun. 9am-5pm; Nov.-Dec. 9am-4pm. Museum and slave quarters open March-Dec. Tues.-Sun. 9am-5pm. **Country Road** (8-mi. one-way scenic route from Carter's Grove to the historic district) open Tues.-Sun. 8:30am-4pm; Nov.-Dec. 8:30am-3pm. $13, kids 6-12 $9, free with CWF Patriot's Pass (229-1000 ext. 2973 for information).

Berkeley Plantation (829-6018), halfway between Richmond and Williamsburg on Rte. 5, was—contrary to popular belief—the site of the first official Thanksgiving in 1619, and later saw the birth of President William Henry Harrison. Union soldiers camped on the grounds here in 1862; one of them wrote the famous bugle tune *Taps.* The beautiful, terraced box-wood gardens stretch from the original 1726 brick building to the James River. (House and grounds open daily 8am-5pm. Admission $8.50, seniors $6.65, ages 6-12 $9. Grounds only $5, seniors $3.60, ages 6-16 $2.50.)

Shirley Plantation (829-5121 or 800-232-1613). Follow Rte. 5 west from Williamsburg, or east from Richmond. Surviving war after war in colonial times, and, incredibly, Reconstruction, this 1613 plantation has a Queen Anne-style mansion unrivaled by other area plantations. Currently occupied by the 10th and 11th generations of the Hill-Carter family, the mansion contains all of its original silver, portraits, and furniture. A unique, three-story staircase is seemingly devoid of any source of support. (Open daily 9am-4:30pm. Admission $7.50, 13-21 $5, 6-12 $3.75, over 60 $6.50.)

YORKTOWN

The British defeat at **Yorktown** signaled the end of the Revolutionary War. British troops led by General Charles Lord Cornwallis seized the town for use as a port in 1781, but were stranded when 17,000 American and French infantry surrounded them and the French fleet blocked the British Navy's rescue attempt. Colonists and French troops attacked and the British surrendered—a devastating blow to the British cause. The Yorktown branch of **Colonial National Park** (898-3400) vividly re-creates the significant last battle with an engaging film, dioramas, and a smart-looking electric map (behind the information center). The **visitors center** loans out tape cassettes and players ($2) for the listening pleasure of those driving the battlefield's 7-mi. automobile route. Walking the battlefield lends a sense of just how close the enemy trenches were (visitors center open daily 8:30am-6pm; last tape rented at 5pm). The **Yorktown Victory Center** (887-1776), one block from Rte. 17 on Rte. 238, offers a museum brimming with Revolutionary War items and an intriguing "living history" exhibit: in an encampment in front of the center, a troop of soldiers from the Continental Army of 1781 takes a well-deserved break from active combat (open daily 9am-5pm. $6.75, kids 6-12 $3.25).

Virginia Beach

After years of attracting a cruising collegiate crowd, Virginia Beach is shedding its playground image and maturing into a family-oriented vacation spot. While the beach and boardwalk still draw hundreds of students, nightlife venues are being systematically pushed off the main drag by the town's inhabitants; residents have become so concerned about crime and youthful irreverence that they recently had security cameras installed on the boardwalk, a measure which has made the area an extremely safe community, relative to its size. But Virginia Beach is no retirement community; it remains a beach town, with the usual honky-tonk menagerie—shops, fast-food joints, and motels—that often besmirch touristed seaside towns.

PRACTICAL INFORMATION

Tourist Office: Virginia Beach Visitors Center, 2100 Parks Ave. (437-4888 or 800-446-8038), at 22nd St. Information on budget accommodations and area sights, as well as the Virginia Beach Bikeway Map. Open daily 9am-8pm; Labor Day-Memorial Day 9am-5pm.

Trains: Amtrak, (245-3589 or 800-872-7245). The nearest station, in Newport News, provides free 45-min. bus service to and from the corner of 24½ and Pacific St., but you must have a train ticket to get on the bus. To: Washington, D.C. ($42, 6hr.); New York City ($85, 10hr.); Philadelphia ($70, 8½hr.); Baltimore ($49, 7hr.); Richmond ($18, 4hr.); Williamsburg ($13, 2hr.).

Buses: Greyhound, 1017 Laskin Rd. (422-2998 or 800-231-2222). Connects with Maryland via the Bridge Tunnel. To: Washington, D.C. ($35, 6½hr.); Richmond ($23, 3½hr.); Williamsburg ($14, 2½hr.).

Public Transportation: Virginia Beach Transit/Trolley Information Center (640-6300). Info. on area transportation and tours, including trolleys, buses, and ferries. The **Atlantic Avenue Trolley** runs from Rudee Inlet to 42nd St. (summer daily noon-midnight; 50¢, seniors and disabled 25¢, day passes $2.50). Other trolleys run along the boardwalk, the North Seashore, and to Lynnhaven Mall.

Bike/Moped Rental: Atlantic Convenient Mart (491-6143), at 28th St. and Atlantic Ave. Bikes $3 per hr., $13 per day. In-line skates $5 per hr., $15 per day. Open daily 7am-midnight. **Moped Rentals, Inc.,** 21st St. and Pacific Ave. Mopeds $23.50 per 1½hr. Open in summer daily 10am-midnight.

Emergency: 911.

Post Office: (428-2821), 24th St. and Atlantic Ave. Open Mon.-Fri. 8am-4:30pm.

ZIP Code: 23458.

Area Code: 757.

Virginia Beach is hard to get to, but easy to get around. Drivers from the D.C. area may take I-64 east from Richmond through the Hampton Roads Bridge Tunnel into Norfolk, then get on Rte. 44 (the Virginia Beach-Norfolk Expressway), which leads straight to 22nd St. and the beach. From the northern coast (near Ocean City, MD), take Rte. 13 south through the Chesapeake Bay Bridge Tunnel (toll $10). Follow Rte. 60 East into the Virginia Beach resort community. In Virginia Beach east-west streets are numbered; north-south avenues (Atlantic and Pacific comprise the main "drag") are parallel to the beach.

ACCOMMODATIONS

The number of motels in Virginia Beach is unreasonably high; unfortunately, so are most of the rates. Atlantic Ave. and Pacific Ave. buzz with activity during the summer and boast the most desirable hotels; reserve as far in advance as possible. If you're traveling in a group, look for "efficiency rate" apartments, which are rented cheaply by the week (see below).

Angie's Guest Cottage-Bed and Breakfast and HI-AYH Hostel, 302 24th St. (428-4690), ranks as the best place to stay on the entire Virginia Coast. Barbara Yates (a.k.a. "Angie") and her team welcome guests with exceptional warmth. (Check-in 10am-9pm. Memorial Day-Labor Day $12.50, nonmembers $15.50; off-season $8.50, nonmembers $11.50. Overflow camping at off-season rates. Kitchen and lockers available. Linen $2. Reservations helpful, but not required. Open April 1-Oct. 1, March with reservations.) In the bed and breakfast, rooms ($54-78) have A/C and shared baths. Accommodations at the **Ocean Palms Motel** (428-8362), 30th St. and Arctic Ave., consist of two-room apartments with refrigerators ($30-45 per night). Right next door, the **Cherry Motel,** 2903 Arctic Ave. (428-3911), rents tidy one- and two-bedroom apartments by the day and by the week, each with four beds and a kitchen.

(May 15-June 15 one-bedroom $300, two-bedroom $375; June 16-Labor Day $375/ $525. Daily rates from $50.) The **TraveLodge,** at 4600 Bonney Rd. (473-9745), just off Rte. 44 (exit 3-B), offers a special $40 rate Sun.-Thurs. Only eight miles from the seashore, this motel offers cable TV, an outdoor pool, a fitness center, and complimentary continental breakfast.

Camp at the **First Landings** (481-2131, reservations 490-3939), about eight mi. north of town on U.S. 60, where choice sites go for $19. Because of its desirable location amid sand dunes and cypress trees, the park is very popular; call two to three weeks ahead (during business hours) for reservations. (Park open 8am-dusk. Take the North Seashore Trolley.) **KOA,** 1240 General Booth Blvd. (428-1444 or 800-665-8420), runs a quiet campground with open sites and free bus service to the beach and boardwalk. The campground may be hard to find; keep your eyes peeled for the red and yellow KOA sign. (Sites $24, with electricity $26, with full hook-up $33; comfortable and spacious one-room cabins $46.)

FOOD, DRINK, AND NIGHTLIFE

Junk-food aficionados will love Virginia Beach. Beyond the neon glare, **The Jewish Mother,** 3108 Pacific Ave. (422-5430), dotes on her customers with deli sandwiches ($4-6), omelettes ($5-7), salads ($4.75-6.50), and an array of delicious desserts. At night the restaurant becomes a popular (and cheap) bar with live music; happy hour (4-7pm) features $1-1.50 domestic drafts. The Wed. night "Blues Jam" is popular. (Cover $3-5; Thurs. no cover for "ladies." Open Mon.-Fri. 8:30am-3am, Sat. 8am-3am, Sun. 7:30am-3am.) **The Raven,** 1200 Atlantic Ave. (425-1200), lays out tasty seafood (blackened tuna recommended) and steaks in a tinted-glass greenhouse, or outdoors. (Sandwiches and burgers $5-7, dinners $12-17. Happy hour Sat.-Sun. noon-3pm: Bloody Marys and mimosas $1.50. Open daily 11:30am-2am.) **Giovanni's Pasta Pizza Palace,** 2006 Atlantic Ave. (425-1575), serves tasty, inexpensive Italian pastas, pizzas, and hot grinders. (Lunches and dinners $5-8. Open daily noon-11pm.)

Organic produce, vegetarian goodies, vegan-philosophy, and a particularly tasty Garden Burger ($5) are available at **The Heritage Store,** 314 Laskin Rd. (428-0100; open Mon.-Sat. 10am-7pm, Sun. 12-6pm). At Laskin Rd. and Baltic Ave., the **Farm Fresh Supermarket** salad bar, stocked with fresh fruit, pasta salads, and desserts ($3 per lb.), is a cheap and equally healthy alternative (open 24hr.).

At night the beach becomes a haunt for lovers. **Chicho's** (422-6011), on Atlantic Ave. between 20th and 21st St., is one hot spot left from the days when bars clustered near the water. (Dress code: T-shirts, shorts, tight dresses, tanned skin.) Bartenders shout over the din of videos of surfing competitions and bungee jumping (open Mon.-Fri. 5pm-2am, Sat.-Sun. 1pm-2am; no cover charge). Increasingly, the bar scene has retreated from the main arteries to places like **H_2O,** 1069 19th St. (425-5684). Massive columns filled with burbling blue water flank the walls and give the club the atmosphere of a posh, tasteful fish tank. A $3-5 cover lets you mingle with other tanned and well-groomed fish. (Open daily 11am-3pm for lunch, 5pm-10pm for dinner, 5pm-2am for drinks. Live DJ and a dance floor.) Across the way, at 1900 Pavilion Dr. (on the first floor of the Radisson Hotel), **The Bayou** (422-8900) will drown you in the deafening sounds of live alternative bands five nights a week (cover $3-5; open daily 6pm-2am). The **Virginia Beach Amphitheater** (368-3000 for listings, 872-8100 or 262-8100 for tickets), on Concert Dr., off Princess Anne Rd., hosts big names in rock, folk, and pop music—including the Eagles and James Taylor—and seats up to 20,000 people.

WEST VIRGINIA

Harpers Ferry

Harpers Ferry's stunning location—at the junction of the Potomac and Shenandoah rivers—has time and again provided a beautiful backdrop to the events of history. This town witnessed John Brown's famous 1859 raid on the U.S. Armory—an attempt to start a war to liberate the slaves. Although Brown and his group of martyrs were captured, and in some cases, killed, the raid brought the nation's sharp moral divisions over slavery to the revolutionary forefront. (Ironically, Storer University—one of the U.S.'s first integrated colleges—was founded upon the Armory's paymaster's quarters in 1865, and endured for more than 80 years.) No longer a revolutionary hotbed, Harpers Ferry today provides excellent hiking, biking, canoeing, rafting, and surveying of nature's beauty. Thomas Jefferson called the view from a Harpers Ferry overlook "worth a voyage across the Atlantic," and while that may seem a bit extreme, if you're already across it's certainly worth the journey.

PRACTICAL INFORMATION

Park Information: 535-6223. Mailing address: Harpers Ferry National Historical Park, P.O. Box 65, Harpers Ferry, WV 25425.

Visitors Center: (304-535-6298) just inside the park entrance off Rte. 340. Open daily 8am-5pm, Memorial Day-Labor Day 8am-6pm. The center offers information on area hiking, lodging, and food, as well as free historical literature. Admission fee $5 per car, $3 per hiker or bicyclist; good for 7 consecutive days. Free parking. A bus shuttles from the parking lot to town every 15min.

West Virginia Welcome Center: (535-2482), across the street from the entrance to Harpers Ferry, unaffiliated with the town but great for in-state travelers; get information on accommodations, restaurants, and activities such as white-water rafting. Open daily 9am-5pm.

Emergency: 911, or contact a ranger at 535-6455.

Area Code: 304 (in West Virginia; 301 in Maryland).

Harpers Ferry makes a convenient daytrip (via car) from Washington. (Bikers with several days to spare may prefer the beautiful C&O Towpath to the 1½-hr. drive.) Take I-270 north to Rte. 340 West. **Amtrak** (800-872-7245) goes to Harpers Ferry (station is on Potomac St.) from D.C. only in the afternoon and back to D.C. in the morning. Reservations *required* ($15 one-way, $24 round-trip, depending on availability). The **Maryland Rail Commuter (MARC)** (800-325-7245) trains offer a cheaper and more frequent rail-ride; on Mon.-Fri., two trains run to Union Station in D.C. and three return to Harpers Ferry. ($6.75, seniors, disabled travelers, and children 5-15 $3.50. Ticket office open Mon., Wed., and Fri. 6am-9pm, Tues. and Thurs. 5am-8pm. You can also buy tickets on the train, for $3 extra if the ticket window is open.) The closest **Greyhound** bus stations are half-hour drives away in Winchester, VA, and Frederick, MD.

ACCOMMODATIONS AND FOOD

Hikers can try the**Harpers Ferry Hostel (HI-AYH),** 19123 Sandy Hook Rd. (301-834-7652), at Keep Tryst Rd. in Knoxville, MD, for cheap accommodations. Meet a rugged through-hiker or two about halfway along their 2020-mi. Appalachian Trail odyssey. This renovated auction house, standing high above the Potomac, has 28 beds in two large dormitory rooms, and two smaller rooms with 11 beds. Train service is available to Harpers Ferry, two mi. from the hostel, and Brunswick, three mi. away. Proprietor will pick you up at the station for $5, although the two-mi. hike is spectacular. (Lockout 9:30am-5pm. Check-in 7:30am-9am and 5-9pm; curfew 11pm. Limited parking. Members $11, non-members $14. Sleepsack $1. Camping $6 per member or ATC hiker, $9 per non-member; includes use of hostel kitchen and bathrooms. Max. stay 3 nights. 50% reservation deposit.)

The **Hillside Motel,** 340 Keep Tryst Rd. (301-834-8144) in Knoxville, MD, has 19 rooms that are just what you'd expect for their low rates; singles $30, doubles $35.

You can **camp** along the C&O Canal, where sites lie five mi. apart, or in one of the five Maryland state-park campgrounds lying within 30 mi. of Harpers Ferry (for more information, call the ranger station 301-739-4200). **Greenbrier State Park** (301-791-4767) lies a few miles north of Boonsboro on Rte. 66 between exits 35 and 42 on I-70 ($16; open April-Nov.). Far closer is the commercial **Camp Resort,** Rte. 3, Box 1300 (304-535-6895), adjacent to the entrance to Harpers Ferry National Park (sites $25 for 2 people, with water and electric hookup $28; each additional person $4, under 17 $2; registration fee $3 per person). They also rent cabins: $75 for a two-room cabin that sleeps eight.

Unfortunately, the stature of Harpers Ferry's restaurants doesn't match up to the area's rank in history; Rte. 340 is chock full of fast food, and the gigantic Food Lion is a great resource for hikers and bikers looking to stack up. The restaurants on historic High St. are also predictable; walk down Potomac St. instead. Here you'll find the **Little Ponderosa** (535-2168), which dishes out barbecue sandwiches and platters ($5-10) in an old train car (open Mon.-Thurs. 8am-5pm, Fri. 8am-8pm, Sat.-Sun. 7:30am-6pm). The **Back Street Café** (304-725-8019), also on Potomac St., doubles as a burger joint (burgers and hot dogs under $2.25) and an offbeat guide service; the very popular "Ghost Tours" of the town are offered weekend nights. (Tours May-Nov. 8 Fri.-Sun. 8pm; reservations recommended in Oct; tours cost $2. Call Shirley at 725-8019. Café open daily 10am-5pm.) A few three-speed bikes are for rent near the Back Street Café ($3 per hr. and $15 per day).

HIKES AND ACTIVITIES

Park rangers at the visitors center provide free 45-min. to one-hr. tours, daily from 10:30am to 4pm throughout the summer. In addition, the park offers occasional battlefield demonstrations, parades, and other dramatic re-enactments of Harpers Ferry's history (call 304-535-6298 for the schedule).

The bus from the parking lot stops at **Shenandoah Street,** where visitors may browse through the renovated blacksmith's shop (you'll wince as the blacksmith hammers at furnace-fired iron), ready-made clothing store, and general store; the stores contain replicas of 19th-century goods. Guides in period costume explain the vagaries of the Industrial Revolution. A turn onto High St. reveals many of Harpers Ferry's most interesting exhibits. **Black Voices from Harpers Ferry,** on the corner of High and Shenandoah St., is an exhibit on the history of local African-Americans from slavery to Storer University. Also on High St., the **Civil War Story** chronicles the town's role in the national conflict through displays and a 20-foot time line.

Uphill, stairs on High St. follow the Appalachian Trail to **Upper Harpers Ferry.** Ascend past **Harper's House,** the restored home of town founder Robert Harper; **St. Peter's Church,** where a sagacious pastor flew the Union Jack during the Civil War to protect the church; and **Jefferson's Rock,** where Tom had his Atlantic-crossing inspiration. At the top of the climb moulders **Storer University,** one of America's first desegregated colleges (closed now for over 40 years due to bankruptcy).

Visitors hoping to reconcile history with nature may hike or boat. The **Maryland Heights Trail** offers some of the best views in the Blue Ridge Mountains, including formidable cliffs and glimpses of crumbling Civil War-era forts and bivouacs. Climbers must register at the Visitors Center. The **Bolivar Heights Trail** follows a Civil War battle line and features trail-side exhibits and a three-gun battery. The **Appalachian Trail Conference Headquarters** (304-535-6331), at the corner of Washington and Jackson St., offers catalogues to its members featuring good deals on hiking books, as well as trail information and a maildrop for hikers. (Open May-Oct. Mon.-Fri. 9am-5pm, Sat.-Sun. 9am-4pm; Nov.-mid-May Mon.-Fri. 9am-5pm. Membership $25, seniors and students $18. Write to P.O. Box 807 or call.) The less adventurous can walk along the

Chesapeake & Ohio Canal Towpath, off the end of Shenandoah St. and over the bridge. The Towpath is also popular with bikers and hikers.

Water fanatics may contact **Blue Ridge Outfitters** (304-725-3444), a few miles west of Harpers Ferry on Rte. 340N in Charles Town; they arrange excursions ranging from four-hour canoe trips on the Shenandoah to three-day white-water raft rides on Virginia's toughest waterways (weekdays, canoe or a seat on a ½-day raft trip from $45). (Open daily 8am-7pm.) **River & Trail Outfitters** (301-695-5177), 604 Valley Rd. at Rte. 340, in Knoxville, MD, rents canoes, inner tubes, and rafts in addition to organizing guided trips (canoes $45 per day, raft trips $45 per person, tubing $28.50 per day). It also organizes weekend ($199) and day ($60) cross-country ski trips. Call for reservations. Open daily 9am-5pm. Of course, if you're staying at the hostel, tubing (and upstream transportation) are provided for free.

Antietam National Battlefield

A few miles north of Harpers Ferry, the bloodiest one-day battle of the Civil War was fought at Antietam. On September 17, 1862, 12,410 Union and 10,700 Confederate soldiers lost their lives as Confederate General Robert E. Lee tried and failed to overcome the army of Union General George B. McClellan. However, McClellan's typical failure to follow the retreating Confederates and crush them decisively tainted the victory, and eventually led to his relief of duty. Still, the nominal Union triumph provided President Lincoln with the opportunity to issue the Emancipation Proclamation, freeing all slaves in those states still in rebellion against the U. S. on January 1, 1863. The **visitors center** (301-432-5124) has a museum of artifacts used in the battle, free maps for self-guided tours of the battlefield, and tapes for rent ($5) with a detailed account of the battle. Park rangers explain with dramatic gusto the retreats and advances of the battle, providing visual aids (Civil War mortars and shells). (26-min. film 9am-5pm on the hr.; center open daily May-Sept. 8:30am-6pm, Oct.-April 8:30am-5pm; battlefield fee $2, family $4). To get to Antietam from Harpers Ferry, take Rte. 340 N. to Sandy Hook Rd. From Sandy Hook, take a right onto Harpers Ferry Rd. Follow Harpers Ferry Rd. to Sharpsburg, take a right on East Main St., and a quick left onto Rte. 65 N; Rte. 65 N leads to Antietam.

Appendix

■ Climate

The U.S. uses the Fahrenheit **temperature scale** rather than the Centigrade (Celsius) scale. To convert Fahrenheit to Centigrade temperatures, subtract 32, then multiply by 5/9. 32°F is the freezing point of water, 212° is its boiling point, and room temperature hovers around 70°.

	Average High	Average Low	Average Precipitation
January	42°F	27°F	3.4 in.
February	44°	28°	3.0
March	53°	35°	3.6
April	64°	44°	3.3
May	75°	54°	3.7
June	83°	63°	3.9
July	87°	68°	4.4
August	84°	66°	4.3
September	78°	59°	3.7
October	67°	48°	2.9
November	55°	38°	2.6
December	45°	29°	3.1

■ Area Telephone Codes

Alexandria, VA	703
Annapolis, MD	410
Baltimore, MD	410
Charlottesville, VA	804
Delaware	302
Fairfax County, VA	703
Harpers Ferry, WV	304

Jamestown and Yorktown Plantations, VA	804
Ocean City, VA	410
Richmond, VA	804
Shenandoah National Park, VA	540
Virginia Beach, VA	804
Washington, D.C.	202
Williamsburg, VA	804

To call between points in the D.C. metropolitan area that have different area codes (e.g., D.C. and Arlington), you must dial the area code, even though it's a local call. Unless otherwise noted, all telephone numbers in this book have a 202 area code.

■ U.S. Holidays

Martin Luther King, Jr.'s Birthday is celebrated on the third Monday in January (Jan. 20 in 1997), **Presidents Day** on the third Monday in February (Feb. 17). **Memorial Day,** falling on the last Monday of May (May 26), honors all U.S. citizens who have died in wars and signals the unofficial start of summer. Halfway through the summer, **Independence Day** explodes on July 4, when Americans celebrate their independence from England with barbecues, strawberry shortcake, and fireworks. Summer unofficially ends with another long weekend, **Labor Day,** on the first Monday of September (Sept. 1). **Columbus Day** comes on the second Monday in October (Oct. 13). **Thanksgiving,** the fourth Thursday of November (Nov. 27), celebrates the arrival of the Pilgrims in New England in 1620. The holiday season peaks at **Christ-**

mas (Dec. 25) and runs through **New Year's Day** (Jan. 1). Most public agencies and offices and many businesses close on these holidays.

■ Special Events

A D.C. year brims with special events; periodic parades, orations, and festivals block off streets and clog the Mall with booths, banners, and droves of people.

Remember that some of the best (and, by definition, the most spontaneous) special events do not get planned a year—or even a week—in advance and cannot be listed in *Let's Go.* Outdoor rock concerts, demonstrations, marches, and rallies, promoted by street posters and word of mouth, can leap into existence only days after the news events that inspire them.

THE FOURTH OF JULY

On the nation's birthday, the capital throws a day-long celebratory bash. In mid-morning, "colonial" troops carry out military maneuvers to the tunes of patriotic favorites, and a costumed orator reads the nation's birth certificate, the *Declaration of Independence,* from the steps of the National Archives at 7th St. and Constitution Ave. NW (National Archives Public Events Information: 501-5000). At noon, a noisy demonstration of Colonial-era militia segues into the old-fashioned **Fourth of July parade** (Washington, D.C. Convention and Visitors Association: 789-7000), along Constitution Ave. to 17th St. NW. (Throngs line the sidewalks by 11:30am; arrive early.) High school bands, veterans, baton twirlers, horses, and marchers from as far away as South America celebrate the country's existence.

The **National Symphony** (416-8100) plays on the Capitol's West Lawn from 8pm on, but the capital's **fireworks** (fuses are lit at 9:20pm), are best observed from the grounds of the Washington Monument. Bring friends and a blanket, arrive by 6:30pm for a decent spot, and face west (away from the Capitol, towards the Lincoln Memorial). For a memorable if slightly guilty and somewhat nepotistic pleasure on Independence Day, **befriend a White House intern** and squeeze an invitation to the White House Lawn; spread out in front of the balcony for a front-row view of the President and his family. If none of these options pans out, try the Jefferson Memorial: your view is less likely to be obstructed there than at the Mall.

SUMMER-LONG EVENTS

Marine Corps Tuesday Evening Sunset Parades (parade information: 433-6060). Late May-Aug at the Iwo Jima Memorial, with the U.S. Marine Drum and Bugle Corps and Silent Drill team. Metro: Arlington Cemetery. Tues. 7pm. Parking available (for a fee) at Arlington Cemetery; free shuttle service from Arlington Cemetery Visitors Center 5-7pm with 8-9pm return service. Parade is free and open to the public; no reservations necessary.

Marine Corps Friday Evening Parades (parade information: 433-6060), May-Aug. at the Marine Barracks, 8th and I St. SE. Metro: Eastern Market. The Eighth and Eye Marines advance at 8:45pm sharp: Marine Corps Band members, a procession of soldiers, the Marine mascot (a bulldog), and a spotlit figure bugling *Taps* into the night. Free, but be sure to reserve over three weeks in advance. *Reservations must be made in writing;* call for address and further information.

Military Bands Summer Concert Series, June-Aug. at the Washington Monument and U.S. Capitol. Call for exact dates and locations: Army (703-696-3399), Navy (433-2525), Air Force (767-5658), Marines (433-4011). 8pm. Free.

Navy Band Concerts, (737-2300). June through Labor Day, 8pm on Tuesday evenings at the U.S. Navy Memorial. Metro: Archives-Navy Memorial.

ANNUAL EVENTS

Martin Luther King Jr.'s Birthday, observed Jan. 20 (619-7222). Wreaths laid and the "I Have a Dream" speech re-spoken at the Lincoln Memorial. Choirs, guest speakers, and military color guard. Free.

Robert E. Lee's Birthday (and his father's), Jan. 26 (703-548-8454). Metro: Arlington Cemetery. At Arlington House, Lee's former residence. 19th-century music, birthday cake, and a show of the house. 1-4pm. Admission $3, children 11-17 $1.

Abraham Lincoln's Birthday, observed Feb. 12 (619-7222). Laying down of wreaths and booming out of the Gettysburg address from the cold steps of the Lincoln Memorial. Free.

Chinese New Year Parade, mid-Feb., down H St. NW between 5th and 8th St. Metro: Gallery Place. Firecrackers, lions, drums, and dragons make the normally tame streets of Chinatown—all 6 of them—explode with delight. Free.

Mount Vernon Open House, Feb. 19 (703-780-2000). Free admission to Mount Vernon, fife and drums on the green, and the obligatory wreath-laying.

George Washington's Birthday Parade, Feb. 19, through Old Town Alexandria (703-838-4200). Metro: King St. Free.

U.S. Army Band Anniversary Concert, Jan. 30 at 8pm, at the Kennedy Center (703-696-3399). Metro: Foggy Bottom-GWU. Top brass and choral music. Free.

St. Patrick's Day Parade, March 17, downtown on Constitution Ave. NW. A celebration of all things green. Dancers, bands, bagpipes, and floats. Free.

U.S. Botanical Gardens' Spring Flower Show, March-April (225-8333). Metro: Federal Center SW. Colorful and refreshing. Free.

Smithsonian Kite Festival, April 5 (357-3244). Metro: Smithsonian. Go fly a kite or watch designers of all ages at the Washington Monument grounds compete for prizes and trophies from 10am-4pm. Free.

National Cherry Blossom Festival, March 30 to April 13, all over town; contact the festival committee (547-1500), or just read the *Washington Post.* Official Washington becomes ecstatic over the Japanese blossoms, expected to appear during these weeks. Enthusiasts parade down Constitution Ave. NW from 7th to 17th St. (call for exact date). Other events (some free) include fireworks, a fashion show, free concerts in downtown parks, the Japanese Lantern Lighting Ceremony, the Cherry Blossom Ball, and annual marathon.

Easter Sunrise Service, Easter Sun., at Arlington Cemetery (703-607-8052). Free.

White House Easter Egg Roll, on Easter Mon. on the White House South Lawn (456-2200). Metro: McPherson Sq. or Metro Center. For kids 6 and under. Famous egg roll usually brings out the president and the press for perfect photo-ops with all-American kids; you'll have to stand in line. Eggs provided; entertainment scheduled. Enter on East Executive Ave. Call for hours. Free.

American College Theater Festival, late-April, at the Kennedy Center (416-8000). Metro: Foggy Bottom-GWU. A jury chooses the nation's best college shows, which go up at the Kennedy Center. All shows are free; line up the Friday before at 10am in the Kennedy Center's Grand Foyer, or just show up that night.

Smithsonian Craft Show, late-April, at the National Building Museum (357-4000). Metro: Judiciary Square. A sales exhibition of fine hand-crafted objects; 100 exhibitors in fiber, ceramics, glass, jewelry, leather, metal, paper, textiles, and wood, chosen by experts. Call for admission rate.

Duke Ellington's Birthday Celebration, April 20 at Freedom Plaza, 13th St. and Pennsylvania Ave. NW (331-9404). Metro: Federal Triangle. The late D.C.-born jazz legend deserves this celebration, which prominently showcases his music. Special events and workshops continue throughout the week. Free.

Shakespeare's Birthday Celebration, April 20 at the Folger Shakespeare Library, 201 E. Capitol St. SE (544-7077). Metro: Capitol South. Exhibits, plays, Elizabethan music, food, and children's events. Free.

Department of Defense/Joint Services Open House, mid-May; call for exact dates (301-568-5995, 301-981-4424). The Andrews Air Force Base, in Camp Springs, MD, opens up for visitors and aerobatics. Army parachutists plummet and recover; Blue Angels and Golden Knights demo teams zoom and swerve under the clouds. Don't try this at home. To reach the base, take the Beltway (I-95) to exit 9. Turn right onto Allentown Rd. and follow the signs. Free.

Malcolm X Day, May 21 in Anacostia Park along the Anacostia River in SE (fax 543-1649). A day-long festival honoring the slain black leader. Food, speakers, and "Harambe Village" (three tents of exhibits) complement gospel, African, Caribbean, blues, and go-go music. Free.

National Symphony Orchestra Memorial Day Weekend Concert, Sunday at 8pm on the West Lawn of the U.S. Capitol (416-8100 or 800-444-1324). Free.

Memorial Day Jazz Festival, May 26, in Old Town Alexandria, VA (703-838-4844). Local big bands. Noon-8pm. Free.

Memorial Day Ceremonies at Arlington Cemetery, May 27 (703-607-8052). Metro: Arlington Cemetery. Wreaths at John F. Kennedy's tomb and at the Tomb of the Unknown Soldier, and services in Memorial Amphitheater. Free.

Memorial Day Ceremonies at the Vietnam Veterans Memorial, May 27 (619-7222). Wreath-laying, speeches, bands, and a keynote address. Free.

Dupont-Kalorama Museum Walk Day, early June (667-0441). Metro: Dupont Circle. Eight museums north of Dupont Circle seek publicity, including the Textile Museum, Anderson House, and the Fondo del Sol Arts Center. Music, historic house tours, food, crafts, etc. Free.

Gay Pride Day, in June. Metro: U St.-Cardozo. Huge march through downtown for gay and lesbian consciousness, visibility, and rights. Starts at 16th and W St.; ends in a festival at the Francis School, 24th and 25th St. Check *The Washington Blade* for exact dates and related events. Fabulous and free.

Philippine Independence Day Parade and Fair, June 3 (call the Philippine Embassy at 467-9300). Parade: Pennsylvania Ave. NW from 4th St. to 13th St. Fair: Freedom Plaza at 13th St. and Pennsylvania Ave. Free.

Dance Africa D.C., mid-June at Dance Place, 3225 8th St. NE (269-1600). Metro: Brookland-CUA. Hourly traditional dance performances from all over Africa, accompanied by an outdoor food and crafts market. Free.

Bloomsday Marathon Ulysses Reading, begins June 15 at Kelly's Irish Times pub, 14 F St. NW (543-5433). Metro: Union Station. Annual read-through of Joyce's 2nd published novel draws crowds of literary and Irish notables. Starts around 11am on Saturday morning and continues through the night. Hear the final gasps of "yes I said yes I will yes" sometime around 10pm on Sunday. Bring along a copy of the novel to follow along. Yes, it's free, yes, it's free, yes.

Festival of American Folklife, weekends in late-June and early July, on the Mall (357-2700). Huge Smithsonian-run fair demonstrates the crafts, customs, food, and music of selected states and foreign countries to over a million visitors, with musicians, performers, and craftspeople imported from featured regions. Free.

Rotary Club Crab Feast, late-July, at the Navy-Marine Corps Stadium, Annapolis. (410-263-8686). The largest crab feast in the world. Call for admission rate.

Virginia Scottish Games, the last weekend in July (July 26th and 27th in 1997). At 3901 W. Braddock Rd. in Alexandria, VA, on the grounds of Episcopal High School (703-838-4200). Free shuttle from King St. Metro back to the games. 2-day annual Scottish festival is one of America's largest, with Highland dancing, kilts, tartans, sheepdogs, bagpiping, national professional heptathlon, animal events, fiddling and harp competitions, as well as Scottish foods, goods, and genealogy. Advance tickets $9 for 1 day, $15 for 2. Regular tickets $10 for 1 day, $17 for 2. Ages under 15 free with adult, $1 without.

Hispanic Festival, in late July on the Washington Monument grounds; call for exact date (835-1555). Metro: Smithsonian. Free food, music, dance, theater, and other cultural contributions from 40 Latin American nations.

Latin and Jazz Festival, in late June at Freedom Plaza, 13th St. and Pennsylvania Ave. NW (331-9404). Metro: Federal Triangle. Continuous live jazz and ethnic food. By the same people who organize the Duke Ellington Birthday Celebration.

National Frisbee Festival, early Sept., on the Washington Monument Grounds (301-645-5043). Metro: Smithsonian. The largest non-competitive frisbee festival in the U.S., with frisbee studs and disc-catching dogs. Free.

African Cultural Festival, early Sept. at Freedom Plaza, 14th St. and Pennsylvania Ave. NW. Metro: Federal Triangle. African cooking, sounds, and stuff. Noon-7pm.

D.C. Blues Festival, early Sept. at the Carter-Barron Amphitheatre near Rock Creek Park (828-3028). Blues people twang, wail, and moan. Free.

National Symphony Orchestra Labor Day Weekend Concert, Sunday at 8pm on the West Lawn of the U.S. Capitol (416-8100 or 800-444-1324). Metro: Federal Center SW. Free.

Kennedy Center Open House, mid-Sept. (467-4600). Metro: Foggy Bottom. A 1-day medley of classical, jazz, folk and ethnic music, dance, drama, and film from D.C. performers including members of the National Symphony Orchestra. Free.

Adams-Morgan Day, traditionally the first Sunday after Labor Day, unrolls along 18th St. between Columbia Rd. and Florida Ave. NW in its namesake neighborhood (332-3292). Live music on 3 stages, stuff for sale, and the wondrous kaleidoscope of ethnic food for which Adams-Morgan is justly famous. Free.

Saints Constantine and Helen Greek Orthodox Church Bazaar, third weekend in Sept. at 4115 16th St. NW (829-2910). Greek food, crafts, and dancing.

White House Fall Garden Tours, mid-Oct. (619-7222). Like the spring garden tours, but this time with military band music. Free, but fills up fast; call ahead.

Veteran's Day Ceremonies, Nov. 11, around Arlington Cemetery (703-607 8052). Metro: Arlington Cemetery. Solemn ceremony with military bands honors the nation's fallen soldiers. The president or a substitute lays a wreath at the Tomb of the Unknown Soldier. Free. Vietnam Veterans Memorial (619-7222) also holds ceremonies. Free.

Kennedy Center Holiday Celebration, throughout December (467-4600). Musical events colonize the Kennedy Center from Dec. 1 to the New Year. Free performances include classical chamber, choral, cello, and "Tubachristmas" concerts, a gospel music concert, and the hugely popular sing-along to Handel's *Messiah*.

People's Christmas Tree Lighting (224-6645), in mid-Dec. on the Capitol's West Lawn. Metro: Federal Center SW. Congress lights its own Christmas tree while the military band plays on. 5pm. Free.

National Christmas Tree Lighting/Pageant of Peace, on the Ellipse south of the White House (619-7222). Metro: McPherson Sq. The President switches on a Christmas tree and a Hanukkah Menorah in mid-Dec.; the Ellipse hosts choral music, a Nativity scene, a burning yule log, and lit-up trees from the 50 states until the New Year crashes in. Free.

Washington National Cathedral Christmas Celebration and Services (537-6247), Dec. 24-25 at the Cathedral, Massachusetts and Wisconsin Ave. NW. Christmas carols and choral music during the day, but the nighttime service is more famous. Dec. 24: pageant 4pm, service 10pm. Dec. 25: service 9am. Free.

White House Christmas Candlelight Tours (619-7222). See the President's Christmas decorations between 5 and 7pm, generally on the three days immediately following Christmas. Call for exact dates. Free.

Weights and Measures

Although the metric system has made considerable inroads into American business and science, the British system of weights and measures continues to prevail in the U.S. The following is a list of U.S. units and their metric equivalents:

1 inch (in.) = 25.4 millimeters (mm)
1 foot (ft.) = 0.30 meters (m)
1 yard (yd.) = 0.91 meters (m)
1 mile (mi.) = 1.61 kilometers (km)
1 ounce (oz.; mass) = 28.35 grams (g)
1 fluid ounce (fl. oz.; volume) = 29.59 milliliters (mL)
1 pound (lb.) = 0.45 kilograms (kg)
1 liquid quart (qt.) = 0.95 liters (L)
1 gallon (gal.) = 3.78 liters (L)

Electricity

Electrical outlets throughout the U.S., Canada, and Mexico provide current at 117 volts, 60 cycles (Hertz), and American plugs usually have two rectangular prongs; plugs for larger appliances often have a third prong for purposes of grounding. Appliances designed for the European electrical system (220 volts) will not operate without a transformer and a plug adapter (this includes electric systems for disinfecting contact lenses). Transformers are sold to convert specific wattages (e.g., 0-50 watt transformers for razors and radios, larger watt transformers for hair dryers and other appliances).

■ Time

U.S. residents tell time on the 12-hour, rather than the 24-hour, clock. Hours after noon are *post meridiem* or pm (e.g. 2pm); hours before noon are *ante meridiem* or am (e.g. 2am). Noon is sometimes referred to as 12pm and midnight as 12am; *Let's Go* uses "noon" and "midnight." The Continental U.S. is divided into four **time zones:** Eastern, Central, Mountain, and Pacific. Hawaii and Alaska claim their own time zones as well. When it's noon Eastern time, it's 11am Central, 10am Mountain, 9am Pacific, 8am Alaskan, and 7am Hawaiian-Aleutian. D.C. follows Eastern Standard Time (EST) and, like most states, advances its clocks by one hour for **daylight saving time.** In 1997, daylight saving time will begin on Sunday, April 5, at 2am. It will end on Sunday, October 25, at 2am; set your clocks back one hour to 1am then.

■ Metrorail Quick-Glance Chart

Sight	Metro Station	Sight	Metro Station
American University	RED: Tenleytown-AU	Martin Luther King, Jr. Memorial Library	GREEN/YELLOW/RED: Gallery Pl./Chinatown or ORANGE/BLUE/RED: Metro Center
Arlington Cemetery	BLUE: Arlington Cemetery	National Academy of Sciences	ORANGE/BLUE: Foggy Bottom-GWU
Botanical Gardens	ORANGE/BLUE: Federal Center SW	National Aquarium	ORANGE/BLUE: Federal Triangle
Capitol Building	ORANGE/BLUE: Capitol South	National Geographic Society	RED: Farragut North
Capital Children's Museum	RED: Union Station	National Theater	ORANGE/BLUE/RED: Metro Center
Chinatown	GREEN/YELLOW/RED: Gallery Pl./Chinatown	National Zoo	RED: Woodley Park-Zoo
Constitution Hall	ORANGE/BLUE: Farragut West	Old Post Office	ORANGE/BLUE: Federal Triangle
D.C. Armory/Starplex	ORANGE/BLUE: Stadium-Armory	Old Town Alexandria	YELLOW/BLUE: Braddock Rd.
Federal Bureau of Investigation (FBI)	ORANGE/BLUE/RED: Metro Center or ORANGE/BLUE: Federal Triangle	Pentagon	YELLOW/BLUE: Pentagon
Folger Shakespeare Library	ORANGE/BLUE: Capitol South	Phillips Gallery	RED: Dupont Circle
George Washington University	ORANGE/BLUE: Foggy Bottom-GWU	Renwick Gallery	ORANGE/BLUE: Farragut West
Hirshhorn Museum & Sculpture Garden	GREEN/YELLOW/ORANGE/BLUE: L'Enfant Plaza	RFK Stadium	ORANGE/BLUE: Stadium-Armory
Howard University	GREEN: Shaw-Howard U.	Shakespeare Theater	GREEN/YELLOW: Archives-Navy Memorial
Iwo Jima Memorial	ORANGE/BLUE: Rosslyn	Supreme Court	ORANGE/BLUE: Capitol South
Kennedy Center	ORANGE/BLUE: Foggy Bottom-GWU	Washington Monument	ORANGE/BLUE: Smithsonian
Library of Congress	ORANGE/BLUE: Capitol South	White House	ORANGE/BLUE: McPherson Sq.
Lincoln Memorial	ORANGE/BLUE: Smithsonian	Woolly Mammoth Theatre	GREEN: U St.-Cardozo or RED: Dupont Circle

■ Mileage Chart

	Atlanta	Boston	Chic.	Dallas	**D.C.**	Denver	L.A.	Miami	New O.	NYC	Phila.	Phnx.	St. L.	San F.	Seattle	Trnto.	Vanc.	Mont.
Atlanta		1108	717	783	**632**	1406	2366	653	474	886	778	1863	560	2492	2699	959	2825	1240
Boston	22hr.		996	1794	**442**	1990	3017	1533	1542	194	333	2697	1190	3111	3105	555	3242	326
Chicago	14hr.	20hr.		937	**715**	1023	2047	1237	928	807	767	1791	302	2145	2108	537	2245	537
Dallas	15hr.	35hr.	18hr.		**1326**	794	1450	1322	507	1576	1459	906	629	1740	2112	1457	2255	1763
D.C.	**12hr.**	**10hr.**	**14hr.**	**24hr.**		**1700**	**2689**	**1043**	**1085**	**2375**	**139**	**2350**	**845**	**2840**	**2788**	**526**	**3292**	**665**
Denver	27hr.	38hr.	20hr.	15hr.	**29hr.**		1026	2046	1341	1785	1759	790	860	1267	1313	1508	1458	1864
L.A.	45hr.	57hr.	39hr.	28hr.	**55hr.**	20hr.		2780	2005	2787	2723	371	1837	384	1141	2404	1285	2888
Miami	13hr.	30hr.	24hr.	26hr.	**20hr.**	39hr.	53hr.		856	1346	1214	2368	1197	3086	3368	1564	3505	1676
New O.	9hr.	31hr.	18hr.	10hr.	**21hr.**	26hr.	38hr.	17hr.		1332	1247	1535	677	2331	2639	1320	2561	1654
NYC	18hr.	4hr.	16hr.	31hr.	**5hr.**	35hr.	53hr.	26hr.	27hr.		104	2592	999	2923	2912	496	3085	386
Phila.	18hr.	6hr.	16hr.	19hr.	**3hr.**	33hr.	50hr.	23hr.	23hr.	2hr.		2511	904	2883	2872	503	3009	465
Phoenix	40hr.	49hr.	39hr.	19hr.	**43hr.**	17hr.	8hr.	47hr.	30hr.	45hr.	44hr.		1503	753	1510	2069	1654	2638
St. Louis	11hr.	23hr.	6hr.	13hr.	**15hr.**	17hr.	35hr.	23hr.	13hr.	19hr.	16hr.	32hr.		2113	2139	810	2276	1128
San Fran.	47hr.	60hr.	41hr.	47hr.	**60hr.**	33hr.	7hr.	59hr.	43hr.	56hr.	54hr.	15hr.	45hr.		807	2630	951	2985
Seattle	52hr.	59hr.	40hr.	40hr.	**54hr.**	25hr.	22hr.	65hr.	50hr.	55hr.	54hr.	28hr.	36hr.	16hr.		2623	146	2964
Toronto	21hr.	11hr.	10hr.	26hr.	**11hr.**	26hr.	48hr.	29hr.	13hr.	11hr.	13hr.	48hr.	14hr.	49hr.	48hr.		4563	655
Vancvr.	54hr.	61hr.	42hr.	43hr.	**60hr.**	27hr.	24hr.	67hr.	54hr.	57hr.	56hr.	30hr.	38hr.	18hr.	2hr.	53hr.		4861
Montreal	23hr.	6hr.	17hr.	28hr.	**12hr.**	39hr.	53hr.	32hr.	31hr.	7hr.	9hr.	53hr.	23hr.	56hr.	55hr.	7hr.	55hr.	

Index

Numerics

INDEX

★Let's Go 1997 Reader Questionnaire ★

Please fill this out and return it to **Let's Go, St. Martin's Press,** 175 5th Ave. NY, NY 10010

Name: ____________________ **What book did you use?** ______________

Address: ____

City: ______________________ **State:** ______ **Zip Code:** __________

How old are you? under 19 19-24 25-34 35-44 45-54 55 or over

Are you (circle one) in high school in college in grad school employed retired between jobs

Have you used Let's Go before? yes no

Would you use Let's Go again? yes no

How did you first hear about Let's Go? friend store clerk CNN bookstore display advertisement/promotion review other

Why did you choose Let's Go (circle up to two)? annual updating reputation budget focus price writing style other: ______________________

Which other guides have you used, if any? Frommer's $-a-day Fodor's Rough Guides Lonely Planet Berkeley Rick Steves other: ______________________

Is Let's Go the best guidebook? yes no

If not, which do you prefer? ______________________

Which part of Let's Go do you feel needs most to be improved, if any (circle up to two)? packaging/cover practical information accommodations food cultural introduction sights practical introduction ("Essentials") directions entertainment gay/lesbian information maps other: ______________________

How would you like to see these things improved?

____

____

How long was your trip? one week two weeks three weeks one month two months or more

Have you traveled extensively before? yes no

Do you buy a separate map when you visit a foreign city? yes no

Have you seen the Let's Go Map Guides? yes no

Have you used a Let's Go Map Guide? yes no

If you have, would you recommend them to others? yes no

Did you use the internet to plan your trip? yes no

Would you buy a Let's Go phrasebook adventure/trekking guide gay/lesbian guide

Which of the following destinations do you hope to visit in the next three to five years (circle one)? Australia China South America Russia other: ______________________

Where did you buy your guidebook? internet chain bookstore independent bookstore college bookstore travel store other: ______________________

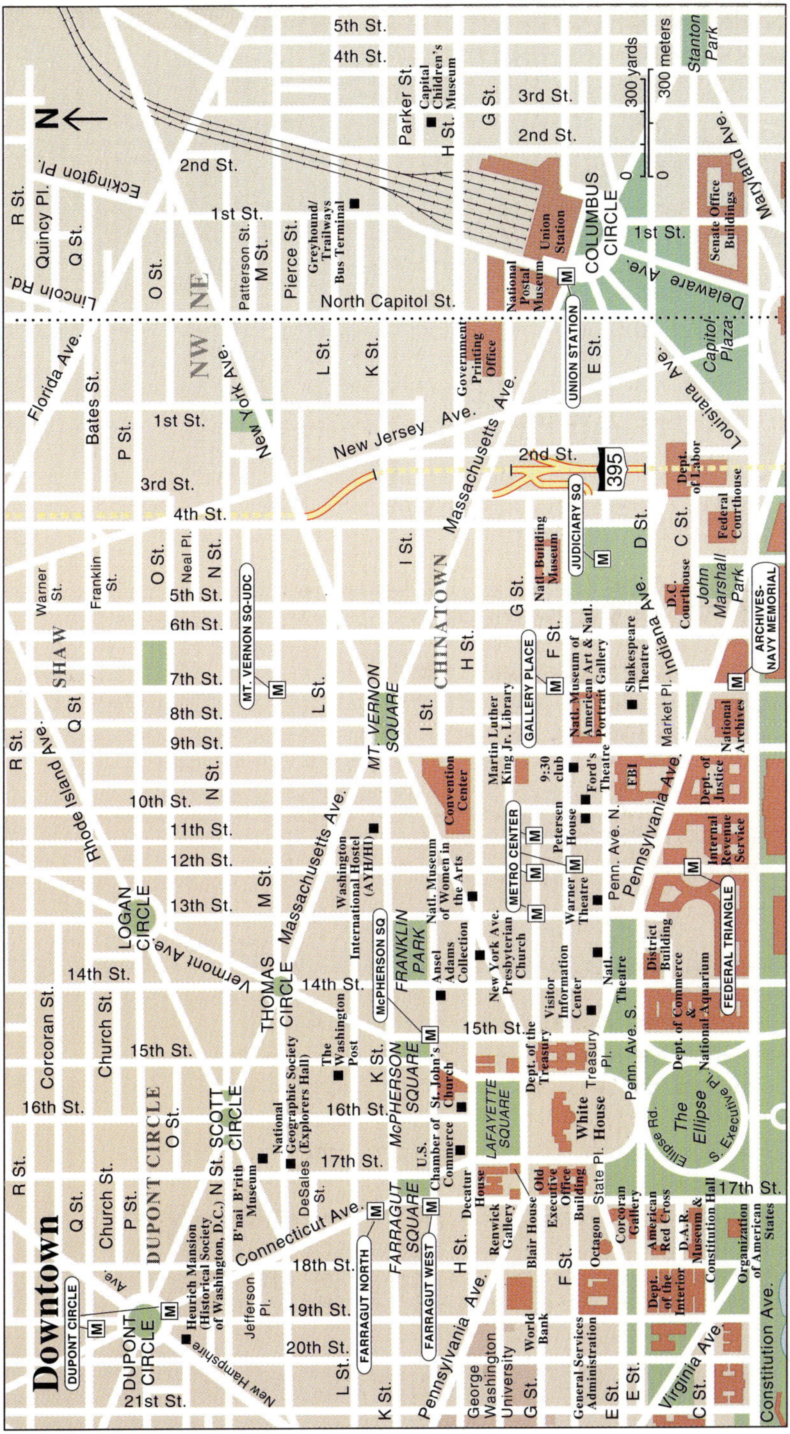
Downtown
N
300 yards
300 meters
Dupont Circle
Farragut North
Farragut West
McPherson Sq
Metro Center
Gallery Place
Mt. Vernon Sq-UDC
Judiciary Sq
Union Station
Archives-Navy Memorial
Federal Triangle
Dupont Circle
Scott Circle
Thomas Circle
Logan Circle
Shaw
NW
NE
Farragut Square
McPherson Square
Franklin Park
Mt. Vernon Square
Chinatown
Lafayette Square
Columbus Circle
Heurich Mansion (Historical Society of Washington, D.C.)
B'nai B'rith Museum
National Geographic Society (Explorers Hall)
The Washington Post
Washington International Hostel (AYH/IH)
Natl. Museum of Women in the Arts
Ansel Adams Collection
New York Ave. Presbyterian Church
Convention Center
Martin Luther King Jr. Library
Natl. Museum of American Art & Natl. Portrait Gallery
Natl. Building Museum
9:30 club
Ford's Theatre
Petersen House
Warner Theatre
Natl. Theatre
Visitor Information Center
Shakespeare Theatre
FBI
National Archives
Dept. of Justice
Internal Revenue Service
District Building
Dept. of Commerce & National Aquarium
Dept. of the Treasury
White House
The Ellipse
U.S. Chamber of Commerce
St. John's Church
Decatur House
Renwick Gallery
Blair House
Old Executive Office Building
Octagon
Corcoran Gallery
American Red Cross
D.A.R. Museum & Constitution Hall
Organization of American States
Dept. of the Interior
General Services Administration
World Bank
George Washington University
D.C. Courthouse
John Marshall Park
Federal Courthouse
Dept. of Labor
Government Printing Office
National Postal Museum
Union Station
Greyhound/Trailways Bus Terminal
Capital Children's Museum
Senate Office Buildings
Capitol Plaza
Stanton Park
395
Connecticut Ave.
Massachusetts Ave.
Rhode Island Ave.
Vermont Ave.
New Hampshire Ave.
New York Ave.
New Jersey Ave.
Pennsylvania Ave.
Indiana Ave.
Louisiana Ave.
Delaware Ave.
Maryland Ave.
Constitution Ave.
Virginia Ave.
Florida Ave.
Lincoln Rd.
Eckington Pl.
North Capitol St.
Penn. Ave. N.
Penn. Ave. S.
Ellipse Rd.
S. Executive Pl.
State Pl.
Treasury Pl.
Market Pl.
Jefferson Pl.
DeSales St.
Quincy Pl.
Patterson St.
Pierce St.
Bates St.
Warner St.
Franklin St.
Neal Pl.
Parker St.
Corcoran St.
Church St.
R St.
Q St.
P St.
O St.
N St.
M St.
L St.
K St.
I St.
H St.
G St.
F St.
E St.
D St.
C St.
1st St.
2nd St.
3rd St.
4th St.
5th St.
6th St.
7th St.
8th St.
9th St.
10th St.
11th St.
12th St.
13th St.
14th St.
15th St.
16th St.
17th St.
18th St.
19th St.
20th St.
21st St.

Central Washington, D.C.

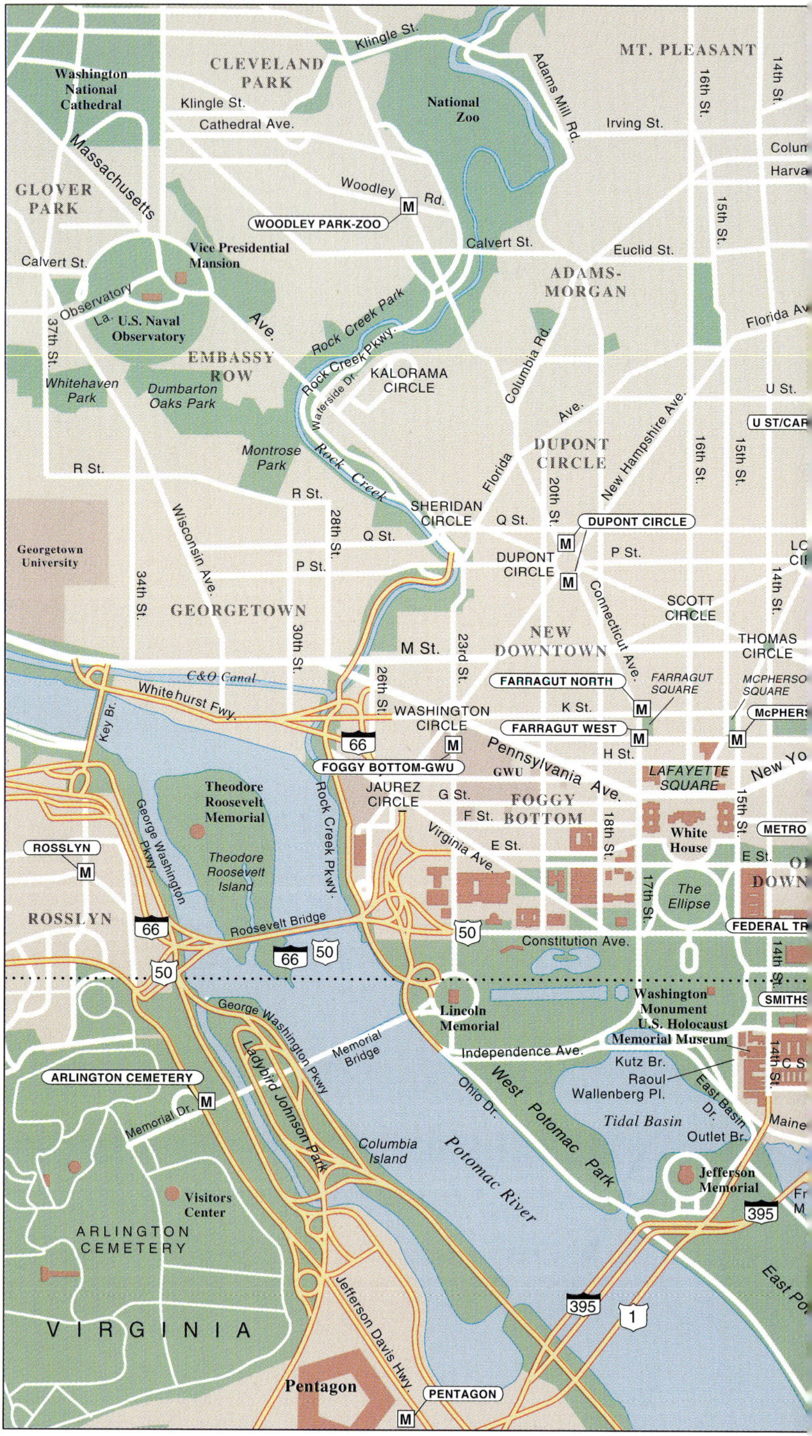

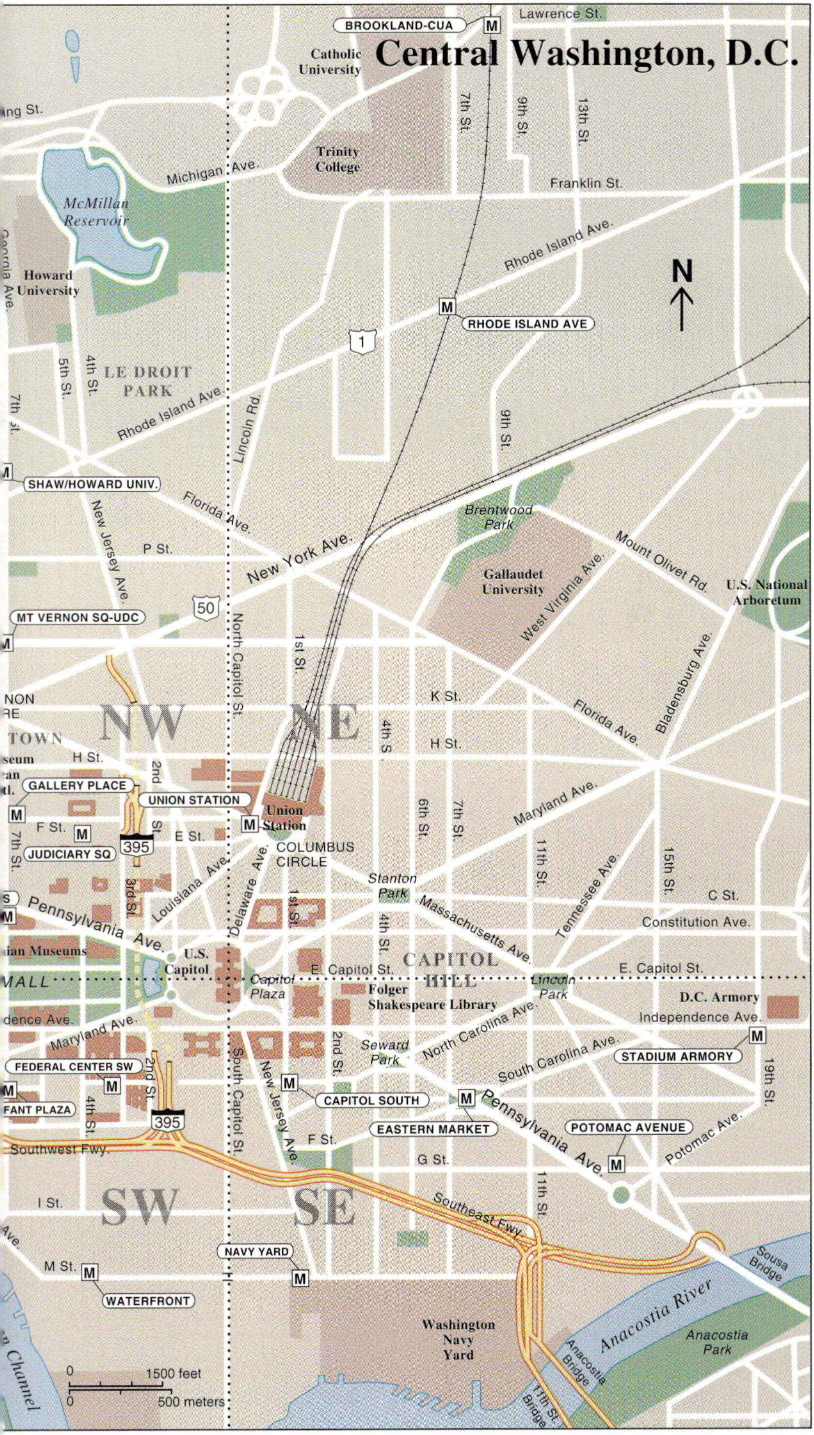
Central Washington, D.C.
BROOKLAND-CUA
Lawrence St.
Catholic University
7th St.
9th St.
13th St.
Trinity College
Michigan Ave.
Franklin St.
McMillan Reservoir
Howard University
Rhode Island Ave.
RHODE ISLAND AVE
N
1
LE DROIT PARK
5th St.
4th St.
Lincoln Rd.
9th St.
SHAW/HOWARD UNIV.
Florida Ave.
New Jersey Ave.
P St.
New York Ave.
Brentwood Park
Gallaudet University
West Virginia Ave.
Mount Olivet Rd.
U.S. National Arboretum
MT VERNON SQ-UDC
50
North Capitol St.
1st St.
K St.
Bladensburg Ave.
NW
NE
4th St.
H St.
GALLERY PLACE
2nd St.
UNION STATION
Union Station
Maryland Ave.
F St.
E St.
395
JUDICIARY SQ
COLUMBUS CIRCLE
6th St.
7th St.
11th St.
15th St.
Louisiana Ave.
Delaware Ave.
Stanton Park
Tennessee Ave.
C St.
3rd St.
Pennsylvania Ave.
Massachusetts Ave.
Constitution Ave.
U.S. Capitol
CAPITOL HILL
E. Capitol St.
MALL
Capitol Plaza
Lincoln Park
Folger Shakespeare Library
D.C. Armory
Independence Ave.
North Carolina Ave.
Maryland Ave.
Seward Park
South Carolina Ave.
STADIUM ARMORY
FEDERAL CENTER SW
2nd St.
South Capitol St.
New Jersey Ave.
CAPITOL SOUTH
19th St.
EASTERN MARKET
POTOMAC AVENUE
Potomac Ave.
F St.
G St.
Southwest Fwy.
I St.
SW
SE
Southeast Fwy.
NAVY YARD
M St.
WATERFRONT
Washington Navy Yard
Sousa Bridge
Anacostia River
Anacostia Park
Anacostia Bridge
11th St. Bridge
0 1500 feet
0 500 meters

The Mall Area, Washington, D.C.

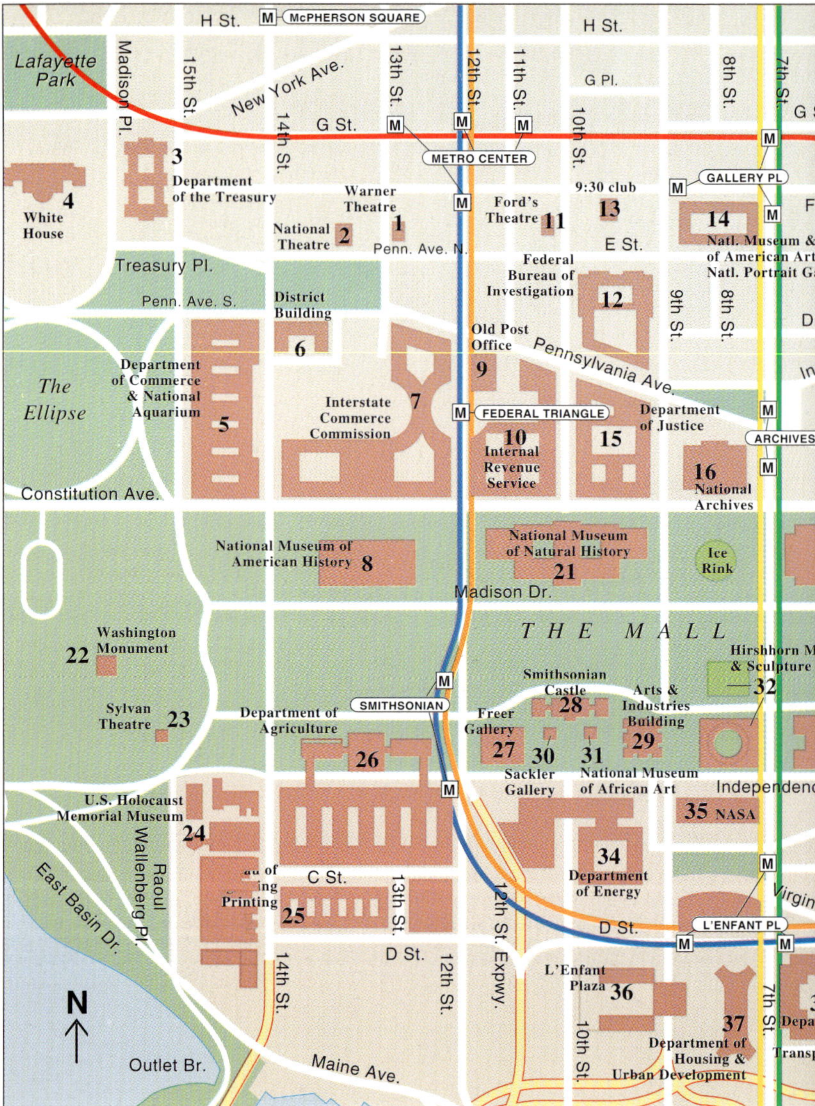

Mall Area

9:30 club, 13
Arts & Industries Building, 29
Bureau of Engraving & Printing, 25
Cannon House Office Building, 50
D.C. Courthouse, 17
Department of Agriculture, 26
Department of Commerce, 5
Department of Energy, 34
Department of Health & Human Services, 40
Department of Housing & Urban Development, 37
Department of Justice, 15
Department of Labor, 19
Department of Transportation, 38
Department of the Treasury, 3
Dirksen Senate Office Building, 46
District Building, 6
Federal Bureau of Investigation, 12
Federal Courthouse, 20
Folger Shakespeare Library, 48
Ford's Theatre, 11
Freer Gallery, 27
Hirshhorn Museum & Sculpture Garden, 32
Internal Revenue Service, 10
Interstate Commerce Commission, 7
L'Enfant Plaza, 36
Library of Congress, 49
Longwoth House Office Building, 51
National Aquarium, 5

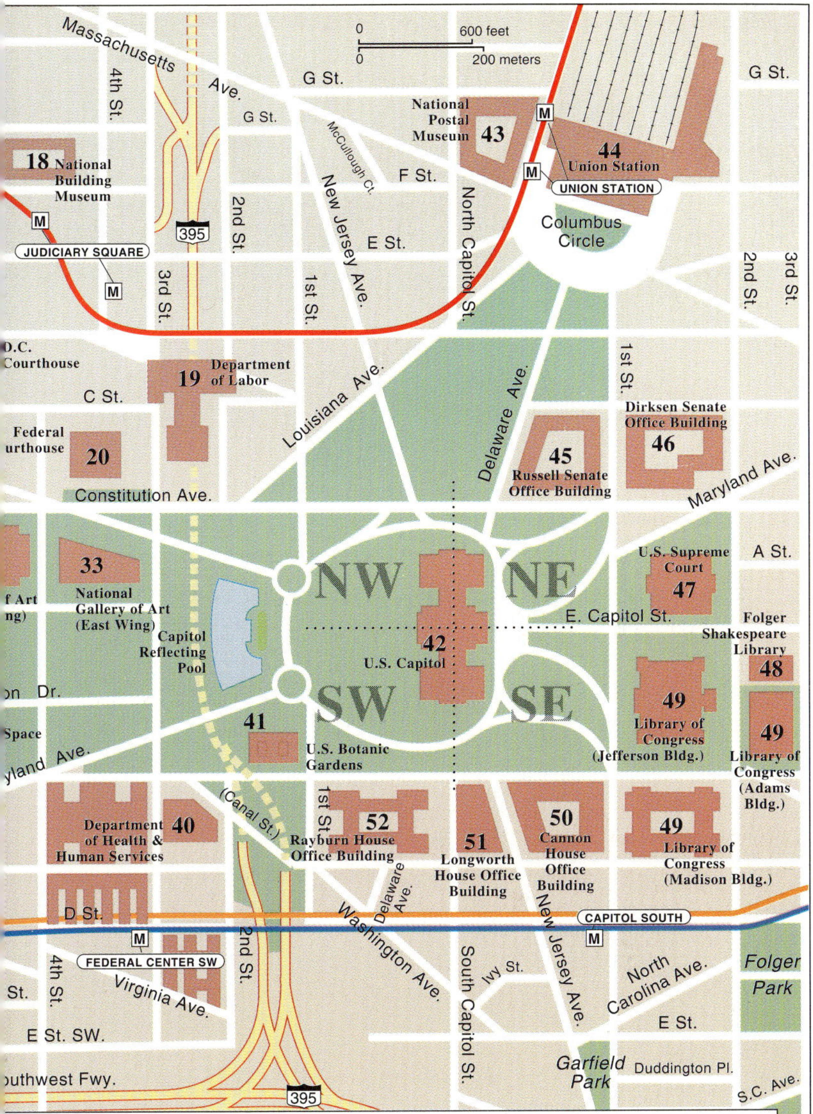

NASA, 35
National Air & Space Museum, 39
National Archives, 16
National Building Museum, 18
National Gallery of Art, 33
National Museum of African Art, 31
National Museum of American Art, 14
National Museum of American History, 8
National Museum of Natural History, 21
National Portrait Gallery, 14
National Postal Museum, 43
National Theatre, 2
Old Post Office, 9
Rayburn House Office Building, 52
Russell Senate Office Building, 45
Sackler Gallery, 30
Smithsonian Castle, 28
Sylvan Theatre, 23
Union Station, 44
U.S. Botanic Gardens, 41
U.S. Capitol, 42
U.S. Holocaust Memorial Museum, 24
U.S. Supreme Court, 47
Warner Theatre, 1
Washington Monument, 22
White House, 4

White House Area, Foggy Bottom, and Nearby Arlington

Jefferson Pl.
Connecticut Ave.
M St.
National Geographic Society
THOMAS CIRCLE
11th St.
M St.
8th St.
DeSales St.
20th St.
19th St.
18th St.
17th St.
15th St.
Vermont Ave.
Massachusetts Ave.
L St.
The Washington Post
13th St.
12th St.
FARRAGUT NORTH
K St.
MT. VERNON SQUARE
FARRAGUT SQUARE
McPHERSON SQUARE
Franklin Park
16th St.
FARRAGUT WEST
McPHERSON SQ
U.S. Chamber of Commerce
St. John's Church
National Museum of Women in the Arts
New York Ave.
I St.
Convention Center
H St.
H St.
Decatur House
LAFAYETTE SQUARE
15th St.
New York Ave. Presbyterian Church
Martin Luther King Jr. Library
G Pl.
G St.
Renwick Gallery
World Bank
Jackson Pl.
Madison Pl.
U.S. Treasury
14th St.
G St.
Blair House
Old Executive Office Building
10th St.
METRO CENTER
F St.
Visitor Information Center
Natl. Theatre
Warner Theatre
9:30 club
White House
General Services Administration
Octagon
State Pl.
Treasury Pl.
E St.
Ford's Theatre
Corcoran Gallery
Executive Ave.
E St.
11th St.
Federal Bureau of Investigation
9th St.
Pennsylvania Ave.
District Building
17th St.
Interior Department
D St.
Ellipse Rd.
Market Pl.
THE ELLIPSE
FEDERAL TRIANGLE
Old Post Office
D.A.R. Constitution Hall
Department of Commerce
Department of Justice
C St.
S. Executive Pl.
Internal Revenue Service
National Archives
Organization of American States
Constitution Ave.
Constitution Ave.
Constitution Gardens
Natl. Museum of American History
Natl. Museum of Natural History
Memorial to the Signers of the Declaration of Independence
Madison Dr.
THE MALL
Washington Monument
Arts & Industries Building
Smithsonian Castle
Freer Gallery of Art
14th St.
Reflecting Pool
SMITHSONIAN
Sylvan Theatre
Independence Ave.
D.C. War Memorial
U.S. Holocaust Memorial Museum
Natl. Museum of African Art
Department of Agriculture
C St.
Kutz Br.
Department of Energy
Japanese Lantern
East Basin Dr.
15th St.
Bureau of Engraving & Printing
13th St.
12th St. Expwy.
L'Enfant Promenade
9th St.
D St.
Paddleboats
Tidal Basin
12th St.
L'Enfant Plaza
W. Basin Dr.
Cherry Trees
Outlet Br.
Maine Ave.
West Potomac Park
Ohio Dr.
Jefferson Memorial
H St.
Francis Case Memorial Br.
Maine Ave.
Water St.
395
Washington Channel
George Mason Bridge
Natl. Park Service Visitors Welcome Center & Park Police Headquarters
Williams Memorial Bridge
395
1
East Potomac Park
White House Area, Foggy Bottom, and Nearby Arlington

Metrorail System, Washington, D.C.

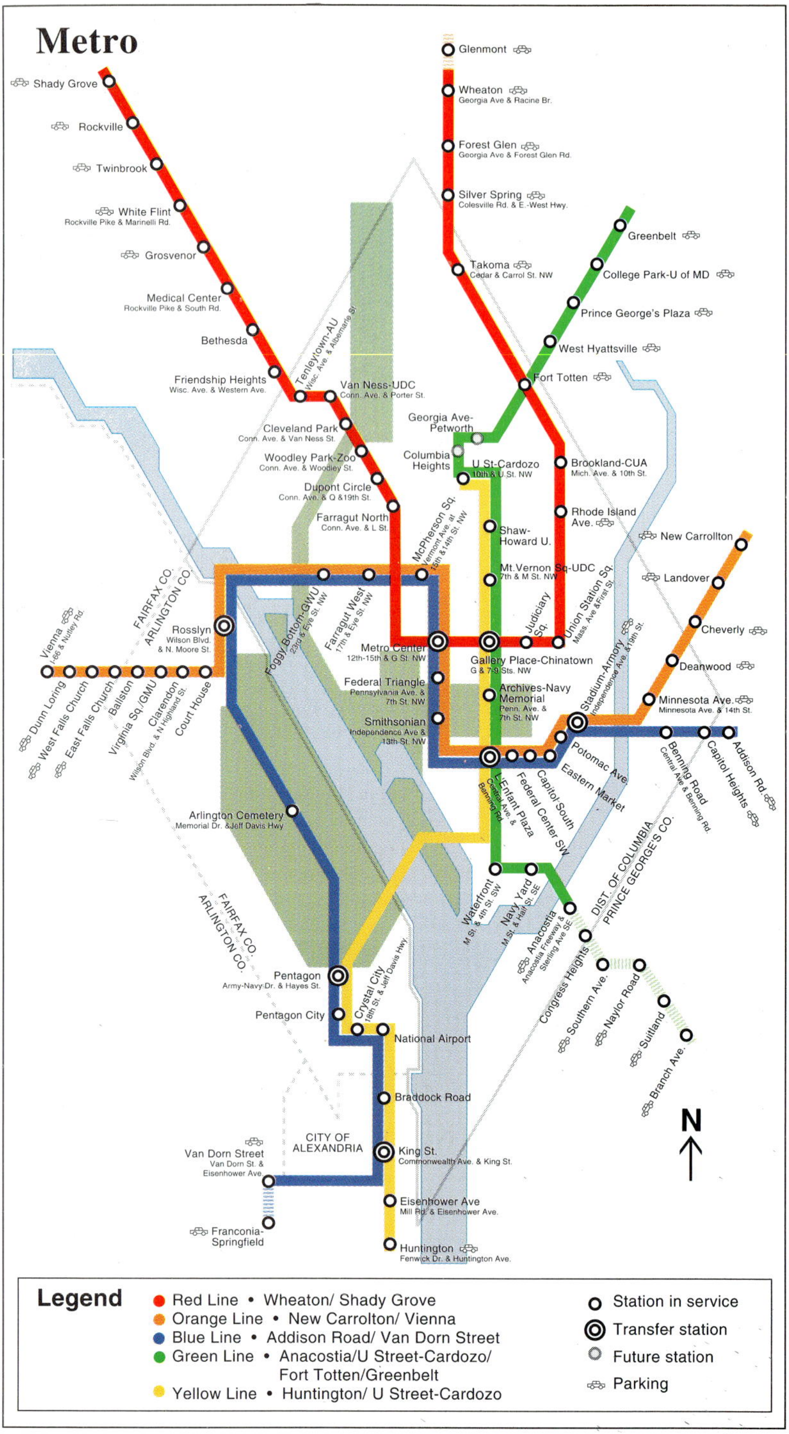